How to Use This B

This book spans a self-training period that converts a n░░░░░░░░░░░
OOP Turbo C++ programmer in 21 days. OOP (object-oriented programming) is
the new programming phenomenon that, with the help of Turbo C++, is changing
the way programmers across the country approach programming. You'll learn as early
as Day 1 why so many programmers are switching to Turbo C++ and OOP.

You'll learn that OOP is more of a philosophy than anything else. Object-oriented
programming requires a different approach to writing programs. To support that
approach, the programming language has to be revised a bit to support OOP, and C++
is the OOP language of choice. The leader in C++, Borland, has continually broken
sales records since the first release of Turbo C++.

Just in case you need some review, Appendix E highlights some of the features of the
C language. Turbo C++ was strongly based on C, and Turbo C++ supports, compiles,
and runs C programs. However, after you take this three-week, easy-to-learn course
on Turbo C++, you'll probably never write another C program. As a matter of fact,
you'll wonder how you ever finished any program without OOP and Turbo C++!

Special Features of This Book

This book contains some special features unique to the "Teach Yourself in 21 Days"
series. Syntax boxes show you how to write some of the new Turbo C++ language
features. Each syntax box provides an example and a full explanation of the syntax and
use of the language element. For example, here's a syntax box found in Chapter 4
(don't worry about the details now):

Syntax

Defining References

dataType refName & expression

dataType is any intrinsic data type such as int or float, or a user-defined data type
created with struct, union, enum, or class. *refName* is any valid variable name, and
expression is the variable or expression you want to reference.

Example

```
// Filename: REFSYN.CPP
// Illustrates a reference to a variable and an expression
#include <iostream.h>
#include <iomanip.h>
#include <conio.h>
main()
{
  clrscr();
  float value = 123.45;          // Regular floating-point
```

```
float value2 = 87.12;      // 2nd regular float
float & ref1 = value;      // Reference to value
float & ref2 = 45 * 2.123; // Reference to expression
cout << setprecision(2);
cout << setiosflags(ios::showpoint);
cout << "value is " << value << "\n";
cout << "ref1 is also " << ref1 << "\n";
cout << "ref2 is an alias to an expression: " << ref2 << "\n";
ref1 = value2;
cout << "Both value and ref1 now refer to " << value << "\n";
return 0;
}
```

Throughout the book, you'll also find numerous DO/DON'T boxes that provide lots of tips and shortcuts as well as some warnings about what to avoid.

DO	**DON'T**

DO have fun as you learn Turbo C++. This book will help!

DON'T take the material too fast. Twenty-one days is plenty of time to let the new OOP concepts sink in, but you'll want to practice along the way and write as much code as you can.

This book contains approximately 200 complete programs, with full explanations, to help you learn Turbo C++. To help you review, you'll find a Q&A section containing pertinent questions and their answers. These Q&A questions are usually "thought" questions that require detailed answers, and the book includes those detailed answers below each question.

After each Q&A section, there is also a Workshop (you'll think you're in school!) that contains lots of questions and programming exercises. You'll find the answers to the questions and exercises in Appendix D.

Conventions Used in This Book

The following typographic conventions are used in this book:

☐ Command and function names are in monospace. In addition to code lines, variable names and any text you would see on the screen are also in monospace.

☐ Placeholders (text that you'll replace with other values when you use a command) within code syntax appear in *italic monospace*.

☐ User input is shown in **bold monospace**.

☐ New terms, which can be found in the Glossary, are in *italic*.

Teach Yourself

Object-Oriented Programming with Turbo C++

in 21 Days

Teach Yourself

Object-Oriented Programming with Turbo C++ in 21 Days

Greg Perry

SAMS
PUBLISHING

A Division of Prentice Hall Computer Publishing
201 West 103rd Street, Indianapolis, Indiana 46290

I haven't seen two dear friends, Sharon Arms and Ken Whitehead, for a while, but their impact on my life still shines. Ken, thanks for the motivational encouragement that you never knew you gave me. Sharon, thanks for being a pal when I really needed it. This book is for both of you.

Copyright © 1993 by Sams Publishing

Trademarks

Overview

Contents

Acknowledgments

This book is the result of the caring editors at Sams who were patient where others wouldn't be. So many of the Sams editorial staff are becoming my friends. I want the reader to know that Sams Publishers want to produce the books you want, and they strive above and beyond the call of duty to produce these books.

I especially want to thank Stacy Hiquet for her devotion to this book and to every other book that she works on. Stacy leaves me alone while I write and supplies what I need when I request software, materials, books, or more time. I'd also like to thank editors Cheri Clark, Dean Miller, and Tad Ringo, as well as technical editors Scott Parker, Gary E. Walker, and Brad Jones.

My family is my backbone. My beautiful bride, Jayne, and my parents, Glen and Bettye Perry, encourage all that I do. I thank all three of you for being with me and for me in every way.

Greg Perry

About the Author

Greg Perry is a speaker and writer in both the programming and the applications sides of computing. He is known for bringing programming topics down to the beginner's level. Perry has been a programmer and trainer for the past 16 years. He received his first degree in computer science, and then a master's degree in corporate finance. Besides writing, he consults and lectures across the country, including at the acclaimed Software Development programming conferences. Perry is the author of more than 20 computer books, including *Absolute Beginner's Guide to Access, Absolute Beginner's Guide to C, Absolute Beginner's Guide to QBasic, Absolute Beginner's Guide to Programming, C++ Programming 101, Moving from C to C++, QBasic Programming 101*, and *Turbo C++ Programming 101*. He also has a book on rental-property management. In addition, he has published articles in several publications, such as *Software Development, PC World,* and *Data Training.*

Get ready to begin a tour of Turbo C++! This first week launches your three-week training regimen that will teach you OOP (object-oriented programming) using Turbo C++ in 21 days. If you don't have *any* idea what OOP is all about, the veil of mystery will be completely lifted in 21 days. This book was designed to offer a perfect combination of text, exercises, descriptions, review questions, and review exercises (with all answers listed in Appendix D) that work together to teach you OOP concepts and, more important, to teach you how to use Turbo C++ to write OOP programs.

Each day's lesson ends with reviews and quizzes that hone your OOP skills learned that day. At the end of each day's chapter, you should be able to answer all the questions and write working programs that fulfill the exercise requirements. (As you work through the exercises, please remember that there are several ways to write the same program. The exercise programs that you write, therefore, might not match the book's answer exactly, but that's OK.)

Welcome to the First Week

The first seven days walk you through Turbo C++'s non-OOP concepts. You bought this book to learn OOP, and this book teaches you OOP. However, there are three distinct OOP-learning divisions that fit into a course on object-oriented programming, and this book's three weekly sections fit those three divisions perfectly. The first week, you'll learn non-OOP elements of the Turbo C++ language so that you'll understand the foundation of OOP. (It turns out that the seemingly non-OOP language improvements offered by Turbo C++ were really put there to support OOP logic.)

When you first learn OOP, you'll see that Turbo C++ offers a better programming solution than its C predecessor language. If you never learn OOP, but only learn the first week's material, you would still think that C++ is better than C (and you would be right).

Note: This book assumes that you have some C background. If you want a quick refresher, read Appendix E for a review of the primary C language elements.

The creators of Turbo C++ did not set out just to make a better C. They designed the language so that the language supported OOP. As a result, C++ is better than C, but those improvements work to support OOP features as well as non-OOP programming.

In this first week, you'll learn a little about how Turbo C++ improves the way you input and output data to and from programs. You'll see why Turbo C++ programmers don't use printf() and scanf() anymore (just when you thought you had mastered them!).

The first week also shows you how to improve the way you design and write functions. Turbo C++ adds so many shortcuts and time-saving features that you'll begin using some in the first two days. From a simple change in the comment syntax to rewriting the built-in functions so that they work the way you need them to work, this first week provides a hands-on tutorial of the language's non-OOP commands and improvements over the C language that Turbo C++ was based on.

By the way, the nice thing about programming in Turbo C++ is that all your C knowledge doesn't go to waste. Turbo C++ supports almost every C feature, command, and idiom, and all the header files and functions you know and love (well, know and accept) work in Turbo C++ programs. Usually, when you learn a new language, you have to start all over again learning about data types and assignment statements, but with Turbo C++ you'll be writing long programs from the start.

After you master the first week's material, you'll be ready to use that information to dive into object-oriented programming with Turbo C++.

The C++
Phenomenon

Welcome to *Teach Yourself OOP in 21 Days*! This chapter begins whetting your appetite for C++. Today, you learn about the following topics:

☐ How C++ came to be

☐ What object-oriented programming (OOP) can do

☐ The advantages that C++ provides for the OOP programmer

Welcome to OOP's C++ World

C++ is here to stay! Although some people consider C++ to be an extension of C, C++ is much more than that—it's a stand-alone language. C++ greatly improves upon C. Nevertheless, C programmers would be fooling themselves if they didn't recognize that C is the firm foundation of the C++ language. One of the reasons so many people are moving to C++ is that so many people already know C. Whereas C blossomed in the 1980s, C++ is blossoming in the 1990s.

People make the switch from C to C++, and from other languages to C++, because of C++'s *object-oriented* features. Object-oriented programming, or *OOP* as it is affectionately known, takes the traditional programming approach a step beyond the procedural programming that got the industry to the 1980s.

Object-oriented programming provides a better programming vehicle that helps programmers reach their goals (finished and debugged applications) faster than the straight procedural approach they are used to. In a nutshell, object-oriented programming makes your data active; instead of waiting around for code to manipulate variables, the program's variables know how to take care of themselves. When it comes time to print the contents of a variable, you don't print the variable, but you tell the variable to print itself! This magical programming method is actually an extremely natural way of programming.

The History of C++

The man credited with creating C++ is Bjarne Stroustrup. He developed C++ to help program event simulations that he was modeling overseas a few years ago. Stroustrup found that regular non-OOP programming languages couldn't handle the task of simulating real-world events as well as an object-oriented language.

Stroustrup worked closely with AT&T's Bell Laboratories to develop and improve C++ over the years. The American National Standards Institute (ANSI), the group that standardizes most computer-related languages, has yet to agree on a C++

standard, although the group is working diligently on one now. It is because ANSI has not standardized C++ that a de facto standard, the AT&T standard, is considered to be the C++ language to emulate.

Borland, International, is the maker of Turbo C++ and Borland C++. All of Borland's C++ language products, beginning with version 3.0, are compatible with AT&T's 3.0 standard. Being AT&T 3.0 compatible is the benchmark that determines whether a compiler is modern enough to be used for a serious C++ compiler. If you don't use one of Borland's C++ compilers, you will probably be happy with yours as long as it follows AT&T's de facto 3.0 standard. Starting with version 8.0, Microsoft's C++ compiler closely follows AT&T except that Microsoft's compiler has yet to implement the *template* feature (described in Day 19's chapter, "Templates: Create Once, Use Forever"). Templates are considered to be vital for serious C++ programmer productivity. Although templates are important, if you ever use a compiler that does not support them but supports every other aspect of the AT&T 3.0 standard, you should be fairly happy with the compiler and most of the programs in this book barring those documented to use specific Borland features and templates. Nevertheless, Borland's C++ products are considered to be the premiere PC C++ compilers, and this book's bias for Turbo C++ resulted from the industry's respect for Borland's product.

Note: Over the years, AT&T approved many non-OOP features of C++ that made C++ better than C. So many improved features were added to C++ that the ANSI committee has borrowed several C++ elements for their approved C language. For example, function prototypes did not begin with C, although they've been part of the C language for several years now. Function prototypes first began with C++, and because they made for better programs, ANSI stuck the feature into the C language.

The Way We Program Without OOP

When you program without using OOP, you are programming procedurally. A *procedural* program is a step-by-step program that guides the application through a sequence of instructions. A procedural program executes each statement in the literal order of its commands, even if those commands cause the program to branch into all directions. C, Pascal, QBasic, and COBOL are all examples of procedural programming languages.

Today's computing world does not lend itself well to procedural programs. For instance, *graphical user interfaces* (*GUIs*) such as Windows can be programmed in procedural languages, but it makes more sense to write GUI programs with object-oriented languages.

The icons, dialog boxes, and selection boxes on a GUI's screen become active when an event such as a mouse click or a keystroke takes place. When writing GUI applications with a procedural language, you have to test continually for these events using programming constructs such as gigantic C switch statements. As mentioned in a previous section (and explained throughout the rest of this book), an object-oriented programming language allows for active data. All the GUI elements on-screen become active data items in the program.

Real-World Programming

As you progress through this book, you will see that OOP much more closely mirrors the real world than non-OOP procedural languages do. The pundits of OOP say that OOP "eliminates a layer of abstraction" from programs.

Eliminating a layer of abstraction simply means that your programs more closely act like the applications they are modeling. The closer your programs model the applications, the faster you can write the programs and the easier it will be to debug them. For instance, if you were writing a CD-ROM controller in C++ to play your favorite audio CDs on your computer's CD-ROM drive, you could create variables for the Play, Rewind, Fast Forward, and Eject buttons. When the user clicked the Play button on-screen, the play variable would actively take over for a while and start the music.

In procedural languages, variables have properties. A Sales variable might be single-precision and hold a number. A FirstName variable might be a string variable or character array that holds a person's first name. In OOP languages, variables have both properties and *behaviors*. The behaviors are the active triggers for the data. When you give a variable behavior, you teach the variable (by writing code) how to initialize itself, display itself, calculate its own values, and so forth.

When your variables take on behaviors as well as properties, the rest of your programming job becomes easier. You no longer have to write code that manipulates the variables every time you use them.

To activate variables, C++ approaches user-defined data much more thoroughly than C. When you define your own data type with struct, you are in many ways adding a new data type to the C++ language. In C, when you declare a structure, you must repeat the struct keyword when you define variables for that structure. In C++, when you declare a structure with struct, you don't have to repeat the struct keyword. Although the use of user-defined data items goes much further than saving your typing of the struct keyword, it is important to note early that your own data types are almost as important to C++ as integers and characters.

Note: Incidentally, C++ programmers use the class keyword more often than struct to define their own data types.

What's Wrong with Non-OOP Programming?

If you have programmed for a while using procedural non-OOP methods, there is nothing wrong with the way you now program. A well-written structured procedural program is always better than a poorly written OOP program. Today, companies use millions of lines of non-OOP code every day successfully. There is little reason to rewrite the code that now works well, no matter what method or language that code was written in.

Today's computing world, however, offers a few more challenges than yesterday's. Not only are people moving toward graphical user environments (which are inherently much more difficult to program and maintain), but the world is becoming a global economy, businesses must interact with all kinds of unforeseen data, the amount of data that must be processed is unthinkable, and the backlogs of data processing departments continue to grow every day.

Something has to be done to lessen the programming load in today's world. New approaches to programming must be used to overcome the programming bottlenecks that everyone faces. Not a data processing department in existence has programmers sitting around idly because all the programs that need to be written are in place and the computer is on autopilot.

Object-oriented programming is not an answer to all of today's programming problems. Nevertheless, OOP does help solve many programming bottlenecks. There are many C++ industry leaders who say that C++ will more than double programmer productivity—they say that a veteran C++ programmer can produce faster, more accurate, and better-written applications by a factor of *ten* or *twenty* times compared with a procedural programmer! Also, you can reuse the code you wrote in C++ more easily than code written in other programming languages. After you write a C++ program, that program or a section of it can easily form the basis of other programs.

Given the promised productivity increases in OOP, and given the bottlenecks of the procedural data processing industry, OOP is a natural progression and evolution for today's programmers. OOP is not a panacea that will solve the bottlenecks and produce blissful data processing managers, but proper OOP practices will help overcome the burdens of programming.

OOP is a natural way to program. There is a debate around the programming industry that goes something like this: OOP is such a better and more natural programming method that all beginning programmers should be taught to program using OOP. The opposing view is that OOP is better learned second, after a procedural programming language such as C is learned.

Both sides of the argument have good points, but the argument ignores this current problem: Whether or not OOP is best for beginners, we have an abundant supply of programmers today who don't know OOP but need to learn it. Whether they should have been taught OOP from the beginning is moot because many learned to program before OOP was ever dreamed of. The rest are well-founded in non-OOP programming today but must make the shift to OOP for tomorrow. This book helps you make that shift.

Almost everybody agrees that well-documented, well-structured programming techniques are better than unstructured techniques. Despite that agreement, how many of us find ourselves writing "quick and dirty" programs that are unstructured and undocumented, just to see what happens, just to scratch out a design, and just to get started? Too many of those quick-and-dirty programs later move straight into production. We never get around to rewriting them, and the nightmares flare when maintenance has to be done later.

OOP programmers find that it is difficult *not* to write OOP programs! One of the premiere advantages of OOP is its natural way of coding. You'll find yourself using OOP principles on even the smallest and most trivial programs. OOP is a technique that programmers practice; OOP becomes a good habit. On the other hand, as good as structured programming is, people find that it is all too easy to ignore structured principles "just for this one program."

DO	DON'T

DO approach OOP with the idea of easier, faster, and more productive programming.

DO expect to find OOP a natural way of programming.

DON'T expect results overnight; it takes a while to become acclimated to the OOP environment.

DON'T discount the learning curve to move from procedural programming to OOP. It takes time to make the mental switch.

Relax and Enjoy

All this talk about variable behaviors, properties, and OOP might seem to imply that you have a lot of learning ahead of you. You do, but the move from C to C++, or from any procedural language to an OOP language, is not as rigorous as it might first seem.

If you have read articles about C++, you might have heard terms such as *encapsulation, polymorphism,* and *inheritance.* These terms do nothing but frighten the newcomer to OOP. Any time you learn a new subject, you'll have to learn the new terms that go with that subject because there are new features and procedures that must be named something. However, the newcomer to C++ and OOP doesn't have to master these kinds of terms before learning the language. It is this author's opinion that the concepts underlying encapsulation and polymorphism are easier to learn than the terms themselves. Many times, this book will teach you new concepts before mentioning the names for those concepts.

Don't rush C++. Although OOP is a more natural way of programming, many people find that their productivity *decreases* at first when they are switching to OOP from C. The new syntax that is sometimes required and the new OOP concepts that come your way will slow you down at first. Often, you'll write new C++ programs by looking at existing C++ programs, such as the many examples from this book. It takes a while to write C++ programs from scratch, so be ready to follow examples and get ready to try a few things that won't work the way you first expect.

What Is an Object Anyway?

You now know that OOP data becomes active, and you might have guessed that this active data composes the *object* in the term *object-oriented*. Technically, an object is nothing more than the variables you are already used to using. However, an OOP language such as C++ takes the concept of data to the next higher level, giving that data behavior as discussed previously in this chapter.

In C++, the term *object* is usually reserved for user-defined data types, such as those defined with `struct` and `class`. It is inside these user-defined data types that you specify the object's behavior by adding functions to the data itself. Whereas you used to write functions to work on objects, you will now write functions so that objects know how to behave. At this point, the distinction might be hazy; that's fine because you've got 20 more daily chapters to finish before the haze lifts completely!

Are All Variables Objects?

As previously explained, an object is data with behavior, and C++ objects are usually user-defined variables such as the structures you have worked with in the past. A simple integer variable is technically an object, but OOP programmers generally reserve the actual term *object* for user-defined data types.

Any time that you have lots of occurrences of something, such as employee records, controls on the screen, and inventory items, those occurrences generally make good object candidates.

Knowing what to make as an object and what to leave as an ordinary variable sometimes takes practice and trial and error. A simple counter that keeps track of customers as they make purchases in your store might make a good candidate for an object rather than a stand-alone integer variable. You could have the counter increment itself as customers make purchases and display itself when you want a customer count. Requesting behavior from data almost always makes that data a good candidate for an object.

OOP, C++, and C

The nice thing about C++ is that it's an OOP language based on C, a language many people already know. C++ is called a *hybrid* OOP language because it is a procedural

language with hooks that turn it into an OOP language. C++ was not designed completely from scratch to be an object-oriented language because so much of C++ was based on the non-OOP C. C++ was designed to take features found in C and make them available to OOP programmers who wanted to use them.

Most of a C++ program looks just like a C program. That's the beauty of C++ and why it is only natural that C fosters C++ programmers. Listing 1.1 shows an example C++ program. The program is neither the easiest nor the hardest C++ program you'll see in this book. Don't try to figure out the program at this time; instead, study how most of the statements look just like the C programming statements you are already familiar with.

> **Note:** The only initial C++ difference worth noting at this time is that C++ comments begin with two slashes, //, instead of being enclosed in /* and */. You'll read more about C++ comments in the next chapter.

 Listing 1.1. C++ programs look a lot like C programs.

```
 1:  // Filename: FIRST.CPP
 2:  // A first look at a C++ program
 3:  #include <iostream.h>
 4:  #include <ctype.h>
 5:
 6:  class animalType
 7:  {
 8:    char breed[40];            // Array of characters
 9:  public:
10:    void getBreed(void)        // Get the animal's breed name
11:      { cout << "What is the breed? ";
12:        cin >> breed;          // User types the name
13:      }
14:    void prBreed(void)
15:      { cout << "\nThe animal's breed is " << breed;
16:      }
17:  };
18:
19:  // Actual program starts here
20:  void main(void)
21:  {
22:    animalType *animals[25];    // C++ doesn't need class keyword
23:    int num = 0;
24:    char ans;
25:
```

continues

Listing 1.1. continued

```
26:   do
27:     { animals[num] = new animalType;    // Allocate space
28:       animals[num++]->getBreed();
29:       cout << "Do you want to enter another animal? ";
30:       cin >> ans;
31:     }
32:   while (toupper(ans) != 'N');
33:
34:   // Now, print each of the breeds
35:   for (int ctr=0; ctr<num; ctr++)
36:     { animals[ctr]->prBreed(); }
37: }
```

One of the nice things about C++ is that you don't have to implement *any* of the object-oriented features to prefer C++ over C. The next six daily chapters of this book teach the non-OOP features of C++. It turns out that the designers of C++ had to add most of these features to implement object-orientation, but even if you don't use these features to their fullest OOP extent, your regular non-OOP programs will be easier to write.

The fact that C++ offers non-OOP advantages over C is another reason that C++ is a separate stand-alone language and should be considered on its own merits, not just because it is C-like.

C++ is a stronger type-checking language than C. Actually, C++ is a stronger *everything*-checking language. The C++ compiler is stricter than C. Many C programmers who want to write accurate and well-written C programs find that they can run their C programs through the Turbo C++ compiler and find bugs and potential problem areas that their C compiler could not catch. It says a lot for the C++ language that it accepts both C (albeit well-written C programs) and C++ code and compiles both equally well.

Turbo C++ and This Book

Every example in this book is written to the Turbo C++ compiler specifications. Nevertheless, if you have another C++ compiler that conforms well to the AT&T C++ standard (3.0 or later), you should have little or no trouble making these programs work as written. If a Turbo C++–specific command or function is used, the book will make it clear that the example might not work with some compilers.

This book is aimed at those who have programmed before, specifically in C, and hopefully in Turbo C. No time is taken to explain what a loop is, for instance, but if a C++ loop behaves differently from what you might expect in your previous programming work, you'll read why the difference appears.

Also, this book does not walk you through each Turbo C++ editor feature. Nevertheless, there are a few things you should know about the Turbo C++ editor that you might not have considered when using the editor for regular C programs.

> **Note:** If you have *Borland C++* (as opposed to Turbo C++), including any of Borland's C++ compilers for the Windows environment, every program in this book works with your compiler also.

Although Turbo C++ does not require it, Borland strongly suggests that you follow the industry-standard file-naming convention by using the .CPP filename extension on all your programs. Therefore, one of the things you'll do when saving your first C++ program is change the filename extension to .CPP.

As you already know, Turbo C++ comes with both a C and a C++ compiler. Turbo C++ includes a helpful option that uses the C++ compiler automatically whenever a program filename ends in .CPP, and uses the C compiler whenever a program filename ends in .C. You might think that the compiler should do so automatically without your specifying an option, but Turbo C++ is not always set to take that action. Therefore, before you go any further with this book, load your Turbo C++ compiler and follow these steps to automate the C++ compiler for .CPP programs:

1. Select **O**ptions from the menu bar.

2. Choose **C**ompiler from the pull-down menu.

3. Choose C++ options... from the pull-down submenu. Turbo C++ displays the C++ Options dialog box, shown in Figure 1.1.

4. Unless you are never going to write a regular C program again, make sure that CPP extension is selected and not **C**++ always. You are telling Turbo C++ that you want it to use the C++ compiler only if your filename ends in .CPP.

   Now, you have the responsibility to save your program using a .CPP extension before compiling the program. If you don't save your program before compiling it, Turbo C++ assigns the generic name NONAME00.C to the program. Select **F**ile S**a**ve as... to save the file under a different name. Saving the file not only ensures that the C++ compiler will be used but also safely tucks away your program on the disk in case something happens (power failure or programmer failure) to mess it up later.

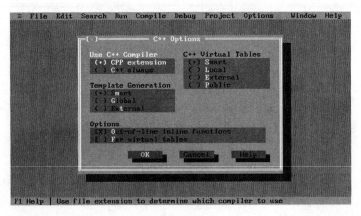

Figure 1.1. *Selecting the proper C++ compiler.*

5. Click **OK**. To make the change permanent and not just for the current editing session, select **O**ptions one more time from the menu bar, and choose **S**ave before pressing Enter. You are now ready to begin writing C++ programs using Turbo C++.

After you save your program under a C++ filename, compiling and running the program requires the same steps as a regular C program requires, as Figure 1.2 shows. Figure 1.2 shows that several source files (some of which are called *class header files*) and several object files might make up the compilation process. Day 14's chapter, "Loose Ends: *static* and Larger Programs," explains how you might use C++ to write larger systems composed of several class headers, source files, and object files.

As with regular C programs, after you've saved the program under a filename with a .CPP extension, you only have to press Ctrl+F9 (the shortcut key for **R**un **R**un) to compile, link, and run the program all in one step. Ctrl+F9 runs all the examples in this book up to Chapter 14, which explores separate compilation and linking.

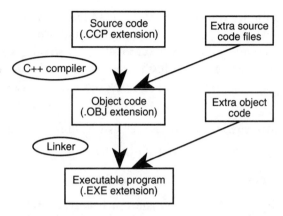

Figure 1.2. *Compile and run C++ programs just as you do C programs.*

DO note that C++ relies a lot on your knowledge of C. Many features of C++ will quickly become second nature to you, not only because C++ is a natural way of programming but also because C++ is so C-like.

DO change the Turbo C++ option so that the C++ compiler kicks in when your program's filename requires it.

DON'T attempt to compile a C++ program unless you've saved the program under the .CPP extension.

What You Should Already Know

There is no way this book could accomplish its mission, teaching you C++ in 21 days, unless a few assumptions can be made. The book assumes that you know C. "Knowing C," however, means different things to different people. Many know C but would never consider themselves masters at C. You don't have to be a master at C to learn C++. As a matter of fact, if you feel you are still learning C's finer points but are fairly comfortable in the language, it is probably time to move on to C++. Some of the things you do now in C will have to be "unlearned," so it might be a good time to change gears before you do consider yourself a master of C.

The following list describes a few C concepts and features that you should have used before or should feel that you have a basic understanding of. This list is intended only as a guide. For example, if you've never totally understood C's `malloc()` and `free()` functions, you might be fine with C++ because C++ allocates memory in a much cleaner way than those two C functions. Nevertheless, you should probably know something about most of the items on this list before tackling C++ in 21 days.

☐ The fundamental C data types such as `int`, `float`, and `char`

☐ The concept of local and global variables

☐ C arrays: how to initialize and work with array elements

☐ Programming language commands such as `if`, `switch`, and `for`

☐ `#include` and `#define`

☐ `printf()`, `scanf()`, `getch()`, `putch()`, and related I/O functions

☐ Passing and receiving arguments among functions

☐ User-defined data types with `struct`

☐ Dynamic memory allocation using `malloc()` and `free()`

Appendix E provides a quick review of introductory C concepts.

What's Ahead for You

Now that this chapter has shown you the advantages that OOP has to offer, get ready to purge all that from your mind and learn C++! C++ is a language that should slowly creep up on you. Don't expect miracles, because C++ takes time to master. Learning the language syntax and object-oriented methods is not extremely difficult, but learning when and how to best use the new OOP mechanisms takes time, patience, and practice. Read and learn each day's chapter without worrying about improving your productivity, because you'll be disappointed if you keep score.

For about the first half of this book, you'll be learning additions to C that make C++ a better language, both a better procedural language and a better object-oriented language. Sometimes, you'll read about the way you now program in C and then you'll see how to accomplish the same result, with a completely different method, in C++.

The last half of the book is not as much learning new C++ language elements as it is learning philosophies and uses of C++.

Summary

After reading this chapter, you should have more questions than answers! This chapter only whets your OOP appetite and tries to give you an overview of what to look for as well as a brief feel for objects and OOP. The rest of this book explains in great detail what OOP is and how to implement OOP using Turbo C++.

In this chapter, you saw that writing a Turbo C++ program involves the same procedures as writing a Turbo C program: creating the source code with the editor, then compiling, linking, and running the program. Borland's Ctrl+F9 shortcut keystroke converts your C++ source program into executable code in one step, assuming that there are no errors and that you first saved the program with the .CPP extension.

As long as you have a fair grasp of C, you are ready to learn OOP with Turbo C++ in 21 days. This book presents OOP in a way that you have not yet seen—you'll learn why an OOP concept is important, and you'll see how to implement that concept before getting a long definition or a new term. Too many people teach OOP from a theorist viewpoint, but that style hinders the student. C++ is better than C, and OOP is better than the procedural way you now program. To convince you of that, however, will take lots of examples and explanation, so how about getting started on Day 2's chapter?

Q&A

1. Why should I switch from C to C++?

   To use the words of Bjarne Stroustrup, "C++ is a better C." Even if you never use the object-oriented concepts of C++, you'll like C++ more than C because the language is improved over C.

   If you continue with C++ and master the OOP techniques that the language offers, you'll find your productivity increasing, your debugging time decreasing, and your programming throughput getting better and better. C++ also enables you to reuse code more easily than most other languages.

2. Do I have to learn a new compiler?

   No, the Turbo C++ compiler used for your C programs also works for C++. You only must ensure that the C++ compiler options are properly set and that your program's filename extension is .CPP, as explained in this chapter.

3. What makes an OOP program stand apart from a non-OOP program?

   OOP data, composing the *object* in *object-orientation,* becomes active. Instead of waiting around for other parts of a program to process them, OOP variables take active roles in their own behaviors. After you give behavior to an object, you don't have to worry about that object throughout the rest of the code because the object will take care of itself. It sounds magical at this point, but before 21 days are up, the mystery will be unveiled to you.

4. Why do OOP programmers tend to use OOP for all their programs?

   OOP is a natural way of programming. Although structured programming is considered better than unstructured programming, too many programmers write unstructured code because of the excuse of time. In the long run, programmers spend more time maintaining unstructured code than they would if they had structured the code in the first place.

   OOP programmers find themselves using OOP without thinking about the process. Therefore, after you master OOP, the OOP side of your brain will go into autopilot mode, and you'll be writing OOP programs each time you start Turbo C++.

5. True or False: Only expert C programmers should attempt to learn C++ programming.

   False. Knowing C helps you learn C++ much faster; however, you don't have to be an expert in C to move to C++. An average C programmer might make the best candidate for C++ for two reasons: (1) he or she is already grounded in the primary C-like language elements, and (2) he or she is not so firmly rooted in C's procedural way of programming that making the switch to OOP would be difficult.

Workshop

The Workshop offers quiz questions and exercises to hone your skills and give you feedback on today's lesson. You'll find some proposed answers in Appendix D.

Quiz

1. What does *OOP* stand for?

2. How much of a programming improvement can a skillful C++ programmer expect over that of a non-C++ programmer?

3. The ANSI committee has yet to approve a C++ standard. Does that mean there is no way to judge a good C++ compiler from a bad one? If not, why?

4. What is the term for non-OOP languages?

5. What is the keyword that C++ programmers use more often than struct when defining new object data types?

6. What filename extension should you use for C++ programs?

Exercises

1. Enter, compile, and run the program listed in Listing 1.1.

2. Change the comments in Listing 1.1 to the old-style /* and */ C comments, and rerun the program using the C++ editor. You'll see that C++ enables you to use C's style of comments as well as C++'s. Now that you've proved to yourself that the C++ compiler works with C code, turn the page to move to C++ code—you'll never go back to regular C again!

C++ Is
Superior!

Change all your C program filename extensions to .CPP right now! Even if you wait to tackle object-oriented Turbo C++, there are lots of non-OOP features of Turbo C++ that will improve your programming accuracy, power, and enjoyment. You will find that several Turbo C++ features make Turbo C++ an easy language to write procedural programs in. Later, you will find out why these important features were really added to Turbo C++; without many of them, object-orientation would be impossible.

Many of the things you do in C++ require a shift in the way you do what you already do in C. All of C's functions, as well as C's commands, are available to Turbo C++. Nevertheless, using the Turbo C++–specific commands and style almost always makes your C programs more effective. Today, you learn about the following topics:

☐ C++ program comments

☐ How Turbo C++ treats user-defined data

☐ Prototyping in Turbo C++

☐ Specifying `void` argument lists

☐ Turbo C++ data concerns: `char` sizes, variable definitions, constants, and scope

☐ Typecasting improvements

☐ A better alternative to `#define`

Commenting on Your Work

One of the first things a newcomer to Turbo C++ notices is the new kind of comment specifier. The C-style comments are simply too cumbersome to use; every time you open a comment with /*, you must remember to close the comment with */. Forgetting to close a comment is easy to do and frustrating because doing so usually costs you time for an extra compile.

Another drawback to the C style of commenting is that you cannot nest C comments. The following lines from a C program will *not* compile error-free:

```
for (i=0; i<10; i++)      /* Start of the loop */
  { printf("%d\n", i);    /* Print a number     */
    /* i = i + 1;         /* Increment i an extra time */
      if (i == 5)
        { printf("Halfway\n"); } */
  }
```

It appears that the lines `i = i + 1;` through the `printf()` are commented out. Sometimes, programmers will comment out one or more C statements by enclosing the statements within comment symbols. The problem here occurs because the first line already has a comment. When the programmer mistakenly tries to comment out the three lines, thinking that the lines would not then execute, Turbo C++ complains because you cannot nest comments. Turbo C++ thinks that the comment ends at the first `*/`. When the compiler then encounters the `printf()`'s `*/`, seemingly without an opening `/*`, an error results.

> **Note:** Turbo C++ does include an option (through **O**ption **C**ompiler **S**ource... **N**ested comments) that you can set to allow nested comments. If you turn on this option, Turbo C++ enables you to nest C-style comments. Nested comments are not approved by the ANSI committee for C, though, and ANSI will probably not approve nested C-style comments in their upcoming ANSI C++. You are best advised to stay away from nesting C-style comments and stick to the easier C++ style.

In your Turbo C++ programs, you can begin any and all comments with two forward slashes, `//`. That's it. Everything after `//` is ignored. The following two statements are equivalent in every way:

```
if (x == y)    /* Test the coordinates */
```

and

```
if (x == y)    // Test the coordinates
```

The C++ Comment: `//`

`[C++ code] // Your comment text`

C++ code is optional, as the brackets indicate. The *C++ code* is any C++ statement or group of statements, whether you write a C++ command or function call. If you don't put *C++ code* before the `//`, the entire line is a comment. Notice that there is no ending comment symbol. Everything following `//` to the end of the line is a comment.

If you want to comment out a section of code, just insert two slashes at the beginning of the code. Even if another comment appears to the right of the code you are commenting out, Turbo C++ will not complain and will consider the entire line a comment.

Example

```
// Filename: NEWCOMM.CPP
// This entire line is a comment
#include <stdio.h>
main()
{
  int age;
  printf("How old are you? ");        // Ask a question
  scanf(" %d", &age);
  // Test the age for a message
  if (age > 18)
    { printf("You are an adult.\n");  // Voting age
    }
  return 0;    // Go back to DOS
}
```

DO   DON'T

DO switch to // C++ comments. These comments are easier to type. Turbo C++ even enables you to use // comments in your regular C programs with the .C filename extension.

DON'T try to end a // comment with any symbol, and don't put executable statements anywhere to the right of // unless you want to comment out the code. The end of the line ends a comment begun with //.

Less Is More with Turbo C++

These are three keywords you have probably used in the past for defining your own data types in C:

- [ ] struct

- [ ] enum

- [ ] union

These are sometimes collectively called *aggregate data types*. The most common, struct, enables you to define exactly how your data looks in a record format called a *structure*. The enum keyword enables you to create enumerated named constants, and the union keyword enables you to create structures whose members overlap the same memory location. Before you can define structure variables, enumerated constants, or union variables, you must first declare the "look" of the data.

Everything that you learned in C still applies in Turbo C++, but Turbo C++ respects your own data types more than C. For example, after you've defined a structure, you don't have to repeat the struct keyword because Turbo C++ remembers your structure's definition.

Listing 2.1 shows a program that declares a structure, an enumerated constant, and a union. There are probably some readers who have worked very little with enum or union, and that's fine. The struct keyword (and its improved class keyword, which you'll read about in the upcoming chapters) is much more common in both C and C++.

Listing 2.1. Declaring a struct, enum, and union the Turbo C++ way.

```
1:  // Filename: USERDEFS.CPP
2:  // Demonstrates struct, enum, and union.
3:  #include <stdio.h>
4:  // First, declare the format of each aggregate data type.
5:  struct aStruct {
6:    int i;
7:    float x;
8:  };
9:  enum colors {
10:   Red, Blue, Green
11: };
12: union bitFields {
13:   int first;
14:   float second;
15:   double third;
16: };
17:
18: main()
19: {
20:   // Define variables for each aggregate data type
21:   int number1;
22:   float number2;
23:   aStruct myStructVar;
24:   colors myEnumVar;
25:   bitFields myUnionVar;
26:   // Store values in the new variables to show they are defined
27:   number1 = 10;
28:   number2 = 20;
29:   myStructVar.i = 100;
30:   myStructVar.x = 75.5;
31:   myEnumVar = Red;
32:   myUnionVar.second = 123.45;
33:   return 0;
34: }
```

This program produces no output, but study the code to see how Turbo C++ handles aggregate data types. Turbo C++ will issue a warning because the defined variables are not used for anything after you assign values to them, but that's OK. The important lines to consider here are lines 23 through 25. The `struct`, `enum`, and `union` keywords did not have to be repeated before each of the variable definitions. If this were a C program, `struct`, `enum`, and `union` would have to appear at the beginning of each line.

When you declare your own data type, Turbo C++ remembers the name (called the *tag*) and adds that name to its list of internal data types. For the rest of the program, you can treat your data type *almost* as if it were part of the Turbo C++ language.

DO	**DON'T**

DO declare your aggregate Turbo C++ data types just as you do in C.

DON'T repeat the `struct`, `enum`, or `union` keywords when you define variables for those aggregate data types.

C++ Prototypes

C *recommends* that you prototype every function in your program—C++ *requires* that you prototype every function. The word *prototype* means model, and a prototype is just a declaration or a model for a function that follows somewhere in the program. By prototyping all your functions before calling those functions, you tell the C++ compiler what the upcoming function's *signature* will look like.

The signature of a function is the look of its return value (if any) and argument list (if any). The signature of a function whose first line is

```
void myfun(int a)
```

would be a `void` return type and one integer argument. The signature of the function

```
people * getName(long int empNumber, float salesTot)
```

would be a returned pointer to `people` and two arguments, one integer and the other single-precision floating point. A prototype completely defines a function's signature.

If you haven't prototyped diligently, you might not understand the importance of prototypes, especially because C doesn't require them. A prototype tells the compiler

what to expect when you call a function. If the first line of a function is

```
void myfun(int a)
```

but you try to call the function with the statement

```
myfun(39.6543)
```

the compiler does not complain if you haven't prototyped. It quietly converts 39.6543 to the integer 39 and uses the integer, even if the converted integer produces a wrong answer later.

Prototypes end with a semicolon. Most programmers make their prototypes look just like the function's first line. The prototype for the previous statement looks like this:

```
void myfun(int a);
```

This prototype tells the compiler that you will never pass the `myfun()` any argument other than an integer. If you pass a floating point, a character, or any other kind of non-integer argument, the compiler will catch the error and complain. The prototype helps keep errors from slipping into your output. If you don't prototype in C programs, some of the resulting errors are hard to find. If you don't prototype in C++, the compiler refuses to compile the program until you do prototype. (Options that ease Turbo C++'s prototype restriction are available, but you should not use them.)

 Note: You prototype built-in functions in Turbo C++ (just like you do with any C compiler) by including the function's header file.

Put all prototypes before the `main()` function. Some programmers use `#include` to include a text file with nothing more than several lines of prototypes and header file inclusions.

DO   DON'T

DO always prototype every function in your C++ program, or Turbo C++ will complain when you compile the program.

DON'T forget to prototype the built-in functions by including their header files.

DON'T confuse the terms *function declaration* and *function definition*. A function declaration is a prototype, and the function definition begins at the actual first line of the function.

It is easy for C programmers to get lax and forget to prototype. When you make the change to C++, the compiler will teach you right away to prototype. Even if you use a built-in function such as `printf()`, Turbo C++ will refuse to compile the program until you include STDIO.H. You never have to prototype `main()` because it is known as a *self-prototyping* function. `main()` is the first function to execute, and no other function calls `main()`.

A function that is prototyped with no return value should always return an integer. As in C, no return type in the function prototype or function definition tells Turbo C++ to assume that you are returning an integer. The following prototypes are the same in Turbo C++:

```
calcAmt(float a, int c);        // Assumes an integer return
```

and

```
int calcAmt(float a, int c);  // Explicit integer return
```

The program in Listing 2.2 includes a function named `compArea()` that returns the area of a room as an integer value.

 Listing 2.2. Using prototypes.

```
1:  // Filename: AREACOMP.CPP
2:  // Program that includes a function to compute a room's area
3:  #include <stdio.h>
4:  int compArea(int length, int width);     // Prototype
5:  main()
6:  {
7:    int length, width, area;
8:    printf("What is the room's length in feet? ");
9:    scanf(" %d", &length);
10:   printf("What is the width? ");
11:   scanf(" %d", &width);
12:   // Calculate the area
13:   area = compArea(length, width);
14:   printf("\nThe room's area is %d.\n", area);
15:   return 0;
16: }
17: compArea(int length, int width)
18: {
19:   return (length * width);
20: }
```

```
What is the room's length in feet? 10
What is the width? 12

The room's area is 120.
```

> **Note:** You don't have to specify variable names when prototyping. The fourth line in Listing 2.2 could have read like this and still worked the same:
>
> ```
> int compArea(int, int)      // Prototype
> ```

Analysis The 15th line in Listing 2.2 is optional in C, and even return; without the returned integer value is OK with C. However, C++ *requires* that Listing 2.2's main() and compArea() functions both return some kind of integer value. If you left the return 0; statement out of the program, Turbo C++ would complain with a warning.

Prototypes are your contract with Turbo C++ that you will follow the prototype exactly. If you specify a certain signature (even if you use the default int return type by not specifying a return type), you should follow that signature in the function's definition.

One last prototyping point is important to know about Turbo C++: You can place void in front of main() to eliminate return 0; when you have nothing to return from main(). The true ANSI C standard will not enable you to specify a void main() function.

Empty Prototype Argument Implies *void*

If you leave argument parentheses empty in your Turbo C++ prototype, Turbo C++ assumes a void argument list. This differs from C. C assumes that you are passing an unspecified number of arguments if you don't specify any arguments in the prototype.

The following prototypes are exactly the same in Turbo C++:

```
prBanner();      // No arguments will be passed
```

and

```
prBanner(void);  // No arguments will be passed
```

Note: You can use unspecified argument lists by typing … for a prototype's argument list. Day 6's chapter, "Communicating with Functions," explains more about unspecified argument lists as well as variable argument lists.

C++ and Data

Turbo C++ treats data differently from regular C in several ways. The next few sections explain how Turbo C++ handles data differently from what you are used to.

char Consumes One Byte

All char data consumes one byte of memory. In regular Turbo C programs, char data happened to consume one byte of memory as well, but the ANSI C committee does not require that chars take one byte of memory. It makes sense that a character is a single byte when you understand that ASCII characters each consume one byte.

Even though it seems that all characters *should* take a byte, you could never count on that with a regular C compiler. The C compiler that comes with some older Borland C compilers (as opposed to Turbo C++ since version 1.0) acted as though char data took two bytes, and sizeof verifies this. Many C compilers have traditionally stored characters as integers. There are times, however, when OOP requires that characters and integers remain separate, and the designers of C++ were much more strict in their definition of character data.

Note: The other data types, such as int and double, are always open to change in future versions of Turbo C++, but the char will always consume a single byte.

The program in Listing 2.3 shows that Turbo C++ stores character data as a single byte of memory.

Listing 2.3. Looking at the size of chars.

```
1:  // Filename: CHARSIZE.CPP
2:  // Program that prints the size of character data.
```

```
3:   #include <stdio.h>
4:   void main()               // No return necessary now
5:   {
6:     // Type cast the sizeof() operator to int for printing
7:     printf("\nThe size of char is %d\n", (int) sizeof(char));
8:   }
```

The size of char is 1

2

The Location of Variable Definitions

You can define variables anywhere within a Turbo C++ program as long as you define the variables before you use them. Consider the program in Listing 2.4.

Listing 2.4. Four variables defined throughout `main()`.

```
1:   // Filename: VARDEF.CPP
2:   // Program that defines four variables in 4 different places
3:   #include <stdio.h>
4:   void main()
5:   {
6:     int n1;     // Define the first variable
7:     n1 = 20;
8:     int n2;     // Define the second variable
9:     n2 = 30;
10:    int n3;     // Define the third variable
11:    n3 = 40;
12:    int avg = (n1 + n2 + n3) / 3;  // Define the last variable
13:    printf("\nThe average is %d\n", avg);
14: }
```

The average is 30

In most block-structured languages, including C, you can define variables only at the beginning of a block. As you know, a block begins with an opening brace, {, in C, and the same holds true for C++. The program in Listing 2.4 contains variable definitions on lines 6, 8, 10, and 12 with other executable statements in-between.

C++ enables you to define variables throughout a program, but Listing 2.4 is an extreme. For such a simple program as Listing 2.4, it would probably be clearer and

33

therefore easier to maintain if you defined all four variables at the top of the block. Listing 2.4 is an extreme case to show you what is possible.

Where Oh Where?

There is disagreement among some C++ programmers as to the value of arbitrary variable definitions. Many staunchly hold the view that all variables should be defined together, at the top of every block. In this way, when you maintain the program later, you can easily go back to the variable definition section and find the data type for any variable in the block.

Other C++ programmers feel that a variable should be defined only right before its use. When maintaining a program, you don't have to search back to the beginning of a block to find a variable's data type.

(Still others argue that if you write well-structured OOP programs, with short function listings and well-documented variable names, the location of variable definitions doesn't matter because the definitions will always appear close to their use.)

Being able to define variables close to their initial use does have some OOP advantages as well as the advantage mentioned in the next few paragraphs. The important thing to remember is that there is never one *correct* way to write any program, and if you use what is most comfortable and most maintainable for you and other programmers who work with you, that way is usually the best way.

You will usually find the defining of variables right before their use most commonly in for loops (at least until you learn a few OOP concepts later). Consider the following loop:

```
for (int ctr=0; ctr++; ctr<10)
  { printf("Happy Birthday!"); }
```

The ctr variable is defined *inside* the for statement. There is no way to accomplish this in C because no executable statements can appear (or even begin as done here) until all variables in the block are defined. Almost all C++ programmers agree on this usage of variable definition because the ctr variable is a trivial variable, used for the loop's control, so there is no reason to define ctr a long way from the loop itself.

Being able to define variables anywhere before they are used introduces an interesting scope consideration, as Listing 2.5 demonstrates.

Listing 2.5. Considering the scope of free variable definition.

```
1:  // Filename: SCOPFREE.CPP
2:  // Illustrates the placement of local variable scope
3:  #include <stdio.h>
4:  main()
5:  {
6:    int i=10;
7:    printf("i is %d\n", i);
8:    // Loop with defined variable follows
9:    for (int ctr=1; ctr<=5; ctr++)
10:     { printf("ctr is currently %d\n", ctr);
11:       if (ctr != 5)    // Don't print next message if last time
12:         { printf("(and getting larger...)\n"); }
13:     }
14:    // i and ctr are still known here
15:    printf("By the way -- i is still %d, ", i);
16:    printf("and ctr is at %d.\n", ctr);
17:    return 0;
18: }
```

```
i is 10
ctr is currently 1
(and getting larger...)
ctr is currently 2
(and getting larger...)
ctr is currently 3
(and getting larger...)
ctr is currently 4
(and getting larger...)
ctr is currently 5
By the way -- i is still 10, and ctr is at 6.
```

Both variables, i and ctr, go out of scope at the end of the program, line 18, because line 18 closes the block that both variables are local to. All local variables, whether defined at the top or in the middle of a block, lose their scope at the end of the block. Some beginning C++ programmers mistakenly believe that ctr goes out of scope at line 13 because line 13 ends the for loop's block. However, ctr is defined before the for loop's block even begins, so it remains visible after the loop ends.

DO	**DON'T**

DO define for loop variables within the for loop when you don't need those same variables before the for loop for something else.

DON'T overdo the freedom of variable definition; until you decide which method is best for you, and until you learn a little more about OOP, continue defining variables at the top of code blocks (except minor loop variables) until you are comfortable with moving the placement of variable definitions.

Typecasting Isn't Just for Hollywood

C++ provides for a new typecasting syntax. The syntax for typecasting C data was rather confusing because you had to put the new data type inside parentheses before the value being typecast. In other words, to convert an int to a float, C required this:

```
x = (float)i;
```

C++ still supports that syntax, but C++ also supports a more convenient function-call syntax that makes typecasts look just like function calls. The preceding statement can be written like this in C++:

```
x = float(i);
```

You know that float is not a function name, despite the look of this statement. In Day 12's chapter, "Extending Operator Overloads," you will learn how to write your own typecasting functions using some OOP components of C++. To support writing your own typecasting, the designers of C++ had to change the syntax of typecasting to make typecasting look more like the function calls you are already used to.

The Scope Resolution Operator, ::

Just when you thought you had learned all the operators a language (C) could possibly offer, C++ walks in with several additional operators. One of them, the *scope resolution operator,* provides a way for you to resolve the scope of different variable combinations.

The scope resolution operator is made up of back-to-back colons, ::. As with most features of C++, the scope resolution operator has many OOP uses, but non-OOP programmers can use the operator also.

Usually, if you have two variables with the same name, one global and one local, the local variable takes priority over the global variable. Listing 2.6 shows what happens without the scope resolution operator.

Listing 2.6. The most local variable takes priority.

```
1:  // Filename: MOSTLOC.CPP
2:  // The most local variable has priority.
3:  #include <stdio.h>
4:  // Define a global variable
5:  int aVar = 10;
6:  main()
7:  {
8:    int aVar = 25;    // Local variable
9:    // Print aVar to see which one is used
10:   printf("aVar is %d\n", aVar);
11:   return 0;
12: }
```

```
aVar is 25
```

Line 8 defines a second aVar variable, local to main(). The global variable holds a 10 while the local variable holds a 25. Because the most local variable always takes priority over a global variable with the same name, the value of the local variable prints in line 10.

The scope resolution operator tells C++ to use the global variable whenever a local and a global variable have the same name. (There are more important OOP uses of :: that you'll read about later.) Therefore, if you want the value of a global variable to take precedence over the local variable, precede the variable with :: as done in Listing 2.7.

Listing 2.7. Using :: to override the scope.

```
1:  // Filename: GLOBSCOP.CPP
2:  // Using the scope resolution operator to override local scope
3:  #include <stdio.h>
4:  // Define a global variable
5:  int aVar = 10;
6:  main()
7:  {
```

continues

37

Listing 2.7. continued

```
8:    int aVar = 25;    // Local variable
9:    // Print aVar to see which one is used
10:   printf("aVar is %d\n", ::aVar);  // Notice before aVar!
11:   return 0;
12: }
```

aVar is 10

 You can see from the output that the global variable's value overrides that of the local variable due to the scope resolution operator before aVar's name in line 10.

 Note: Turbo C++ displays a warning when you compile the program in Listing 2.7 telling you that you've defined a variable, aVar, but never used it. Turbo C++ is referring to the *local* variable aVar, and the compiler is correct. The scope resolution operator causes the global aVar to print, and the local aVar is completely ignored after its definition on line 8.

Scoping of Global Constants

The const keyword was introduced in an early version of C++. By using const, you can define variables whose values cannot change in the program; in other words, const values can never appear on the left side of an equal sign (known as an *lvalue*) or in any other position in a program that might change (such as the object of an increment or decrement operator).

 Note: const was not originally available in C. After const's use in C++, the ANSI C committee decided to add it to C.

When you define a global const value, the const value has *internal linkage*. Internal linkage is a fancy name that means the value has *file scope*, or is known for the rest of the file in which it is defined. Consider Listing 2.8, which defines a global const value in main() and uses that same value in fun() without passing or defining the value again inside fun().

Listing 2.8. const values have file scope.

```
1:  // Filename: CONST1.CPP
2:  // Both main() and fun() share the same const value
3:  #include <stdio.h>
4:
5:  float fun(float a, float b);     // Prototype
6:
7:  const float cFact = .45;
8:  main()
9:  {
10:    float mainA = 10, mainB = 20;
11:    float factAns;
12:    // Call a function that uses global constant
13:    factAns = fun(mainA, mainB);
14:    printf("The resulting factor is %.2f.\n", factAns);
15:
16:    return 0;
17: }
18:
19: float fun(float a, float b)
20: {
21:    float temp;
22:    temp = (a + b) * cFact;
23:    return temp;
24: }
```

The resulting factor is 13.50.

Analysis Listing 2.8 might seem trivial if you understand the difference between global and local data (and you should, as Day 1's chapter, "The C++ Phenomenon," pointed out). The const value in line 7, cFact, can be used *only* in this source file, not in any other file that you link this code to. In other words, if you were to put fun() into its own file, compile the two modules separately, and then link them together, the linker would complain because fun() could not use main()'s cFact.

The reason the file scope of const is worth pointing out is that C programmers who use const are used to const values having *external linkage*, meaning that the const values can be used inside other code linked to the program without being redefined or passed. In C++, if you want to share const values among several different compile modules that you will eventually link together, you must declare each of the const values in the linked modules as external variables (with the extern keyword).

Note: By giving global const values internal linkage, Turbo C++ keeps name clashes from occurring. If you are writing a large program with a team of programmers as is often the case in data processing departments, you can safely define global const values in your code without fearing that another programmer's global const value of the same name will interfere.

Listing 2.9 shows a stand-alone function that is separately compiled and linked to other code. The value of cAmt is defined elsewhere in one of the other modules that will eventually be linked to saFun().

Listing 2.9. A function that relies on another function to initialize cAmt.

```
1:  // Filename: CONST2.CPP
2:  // A stand-alone function that uses another
3:  // function's global const value
4:  #include <stdio.h>
5:
6:  extern int cAmt;
7:  int saFun(int i, float x)
8:  {
9:     if (float(i) > x)
10:       { return cAmt; }
11:    else
12:       { return i; }
13: }
```

Note: Day 14's chapter, "Loose Ends: *static* and Larger Programs," describes how to go about compiling, linking, and running separate code modules using Turbo C++.

Throw Out *#define*

Now that you are used to using #define, forget about ever using #define again! C++ provides two much better alternatives to #define: const and *inline functions*.

const Replaces Simple #*define* Constants

The preceding section discussed const, the first replacement of the #define directive. Instead of defining constants with #define like

```
#define LIMIT 100
```

you can use const to define constants (also known as *naming constants*) like this:

```
const int LIMIT = 100;
```

If you are defining integer constants, you don't have to specify the int keyword. Therefore, this statement is equivalent to the preceding const statement:

```
const LIMIT = 100;
```

Be *const*antly Clear!

Although you don't have to specify int if your const value is an integer, go ahead and explicitly state that the constant will be an integer.

Today's better programmers know that clear code produces more readable and maintainable code. If you explicitly define a constant as int even when you do not have to, you let the next person who maintains your code know that you intended for the constant to be an integer and you didn't leave out the data type accidentally (thereby creating possible data type errors later).

You can define any kind of variable as a constant. The following statement defines a constant array that holds a string:

```
const char myName[] = "Heath Barkley";
```

Turbo C++ requires that you give the constant an initial value. After all, after the constant is created, nothing you do in the rest of the program can change it. If you didn't specify an initial value, the constant would *never* have another chance at initialization.

Unlike #define constants, the const constants have specific data types, so the C++ compiler can perform more stringent type-checking. Whereas #define directives blindly search and *replace* code, defining const variables (a seemingly contradictory statement!) creates better compile-time checking. More important, the const variables all have regular local or global scope depending on where you define them. #define values are always globally changed from the point of #define down in the source file.

Perhaps the most important reason to avoid #define is that it changes your source code after the source code leaves your editor and heads for the compiler. What you saw is *not* what the compiler sees with #define. Listing 2.10 demonstrates a potential maintenance problem with #define.

Listing 2.10. Be careful when using #define.

```
 1:  // Filename: DEFPROB1.CPP
 2:  // Demonstrates a potential problem with #define
 3:  #include <stdio.h>
 4:
 5:  main()
 6:  {
 7:     int a = 1;
 8:     #define TOT1 a + a
 9:     #define TOT2 TOT1 - TOT1
10:     printf("TOT2 is %d\n", TOT2);  // Probably not what you expect!
11:
12:     return 0;
13:  }
```

Before you're told the output of this seemingly simple program, what do you think is printed at line 10? Be careful, and look again.

It would first appear that this is printed:

```
TOT2 is 0
```

That's not the case, however. If you thought that a 0 would print for the value of TOT2, you are treating TOT2 as if it were a variable, but it is not. #define causes even the best programmers to get confused in such situations. Here is the output from the program:

```
TOT2 is 2
```

Here is what Turbo C++ sees in place of your line 10:

```
printf("TOT2 is %d\n", a + a - a + a);
```

The precedence of addition and subtraction operators is the same for each. a plus a equals 2, then a is subtracted from the 2 giving 1, then one last a is added to result in the printed value of 2.

Listing 2.11 is just like Listing 2.10 except const replaces the two #defines.

Listing 2.11. const does not lend itself to ambiguity as does #define.

```
1:  // Filename: DEFCOR1.CPP
2:  // Correcting the potential problem with const
3:  #include <stdio.h>
4:
5:  main()
6:  {
7:     int a = 1;
8:     const TOT1 = a + a;
9:     const TOT2 = TOT1 - TOT1;
10:    printf("TOT2 is %d\n", TOT2);    // That's better!
11:
12:    return 0;
13: }
```

```
TOT2 is 0
```

Listing 2.11 produces correct results because const defines two variables that behave like variables, and the compiler sees exactly what you see on line 10. No preprocessor came in behind your back and changed the source code.

const values are great to use for array subscripts when defining arrays. Consider the following code:

```
#include <stdio.h>
main()
{
  const employees = 230;
  char * empNames[employees];    // Reserve the names
  float salaries[employees];     // Reserve the salaries
// and so on...
```

Whenever the rest of the program needs to step through the array values, you can now use employees for the boundary, such as

```
for (ctr=0; ctr<employees; ctr++)
```

instead of repeating the numeric literal 230 throughout the program. If the number of employees changes, you only have to change the const statement instead of searching through the program for all references to 230.

Note: Many Turbo C++ programmers spell const variable names with all uppercase letters, just as they learned with C #define constants. The uppercase letters warn you that you cannot assign values to the const variables later.

inline Functions
Improve on *#define* Macros

The danger of #define constants can be seen even further when you use #define to define parameterized macros. Listing 2.12 shows a program with a parameterized macro that doubles whatever value is sent to the macro.

Listing 2.12. Program that uses a parameterized #define to double values.

```
1:  // Filename: DOUBI.CPP
2:  // Includes a macro to double values
3:  #include <stdio.h>
4:
5:  #define doub(x) x * 2
6:
7:  main()
8:  {
9:    for (int i=1; i<=5; i++)
10:     { printf("%d doubled is %d.\n", i, doub(i)); }
11:
12:    return 0;
13: }
```

```
1 doubled is 2.
2 doubled is 4.
3 doubled is 6.
4 doubled is 8.
5 doubled is 10.
```

The simple #define macro used in this program seems innocent enough. Whatever value is sent to doub's parameter x is doubled by the macro. These types of macros are often used to save the programming time and overhead of calling a separate function to perform a simple routine.

It is important to realize that all macros expand *inline* inside the program. In other words, the `printf()` statement does not look to the compiler the way you type it in line 10. Rather than

```
doub(i)
```

being sent to the compiler at the end of the `printf()`,

```
i * 2
```

is sent, because `#define` ensures that the occurrence of `doub()` is turned into the macro code.

Given this background, what do you think will print in the following `printf()`?

```
printf("1 + 2 doubled is %d.". doub(1 + 2));
```

Be very careful! It looks as though a 6 will print because 1 + 2 doubled is 6. Not so, according to the `doub()` macro! You must always keep in mind that a `#define`'s code expands inline, and what you type is not what the compiler sees. Here is what the compiler sees after `#define` does its macro expansion:

```
printf("1 + 2 doubled is %d.". 1 + 2 * 2);
```

And here is what would print from this statement:

```
1 + 2 doubled is 5.
```

The precedence of operators forces the multiplication to calculate before the addition. Therefore, the 2 * 2 first produces 4, then a 1 is added to produce the 5.

Note: If you have never used parameterized `#define` directives before, consider yourself lucky because you have less to unlearn!

Despite the drawbacks of parameterized macros, many programmers use them for efficiency. When a program must call a function, lots of overhead is spent setting up return values and passing arguments. Instead of writing a separate routine for simple functions, programmers can save function overhead by writing parameterized `#define` macros. The code within the macros will be expanded, as shown here, and no function will be called.

What do you do? Give up efficiency and use function calls, or live with the dangerous side effects that defined macros provide? With C++, you don't have to do either. By writing functions where you would have written parameterized macros before, and by using the `inline` keyword that tells Turbo C++ to inline the function if possible, you get efficiency and safety at the same time.

To use `inline`, insert `inline` before any function definition that you want to be expanded inline. Listing 2.13 shows an improved doubling routine specified as an inline function rather than as a macro. The inlined function offers all the advantages of macros without the side effects. The listing shows that the `inline` function works for single values as well as for expressions such as `1 + 2`.

  Listing 2.13. Using inline functions for efficiency.

```
1:  // Filename: DOUBINLN.CPP
2:  // Includes a macro to double values
3:  #include <stdio.h>
4:
5:  inline doub(int x)
6:  {
7:    return x * 2;
8:  }
9:
10: main()
11: {
12:   for (int i=1; i<=5; i++)
13:     { printf("%d doubled is %d.\n", i, doub(i)); }
14:   printf("1 + 2 doubled is %d.\n", doub(1 + 2));
15:
16:   return 0;
17: }
```

```
1 doubled is 2.
2 doubled is 4.
3 doubled is 6.
4 doubled is 8.
5 doubled is 10.
1 + 2 doubled is 6.
```

 Listing 2.13 might not look right to you if you are used to seeing the `main()` function first in a C or C++ program. `main()` is usually placed first in a program. Although `main()`'s placement is not mandatory, `main()` is always the first function that executes, and consistent programmers like to list `main()` first in programs. A program with `inline` functions, however, cannot have `main()` listed first. An `inline` function must be completely defined before it can be called.

Most Turbo C++ programmers put their `inline` functions in a header file and `#include` the header before `main()`. By including the header file, `main()` can still *look* as though it comes first in the program although the `inline` functions will actually be defined first.

Note: The placement of main() at the beginning of the program will become less and less important as you progress throughout this book. When you make data active with OOP, the data's code (yes, data can have code in Turbo C++!) is almost as important as, and many times more important than, the code in main().

Perhaps the only *disadvantage* to using inline is that inline is a request to Turbo C++ but not an order. Turbo C++ is free to ignore your inline request and treat the function as if it were a regular function with function call overhead. Therefore, if you use inline to gain efficiency (so that no real function calls take place, but the function's code is expanded inline where the function is called), Turbo C++ might ignore the request, and you will not gain the efficiency.

When Turbo C++ will ignore an inline request is difficult to determine. If your inline function is eight or more lines long, Turbo C++ usually decides to ignore the inline request. If the function has any kind of looping statement, Turbo C++ will probably refuse to inline the function. Turbo C++ never inlines recursive functions either.

If Turbo C++ did inline all of your inline requests, your code could grow to a tremendous size. All inline function calls would get expanded to the size of the entire function being called. If your Turbo C++ program calls an inline function 20 times throughout the code, Turbo C++ has to place 20 occurrences of the function throughout the code.

The *inline* Function

inline *functionName*(*optionalArguments*)

To make a function inline, you only have to precede the function's regular definition with inline. The function can still receive arguments and return values. All inline functions must appear in full before the code that calls them.

Example

```
// Here is an inline function
inline int GetProd(int n1, int n2, int n3, int n4)
{
  int tot;
  tot = n1 * n2 * n3 * n4;
  return tot;
}
```

47

DO / DON'T

DO use `const` when naming constants in your program.

DO use `const` values for array subscripts when defining arrays.

DO remember to use the equal sign after a `const` variable's definition. `#define` does not enable you to put an equal sign because no assignment is made with `#define`.

DO always specify an initial value for `const` variables. If you don't, Turbo C++ assumes an initial value of zero, and you can never change the value later (because it's a constant).

DO use inline functions when you want short functions to execute quickly and efficiently.

DON'T use `#define` because it changes your source code and too many problems can develop, especially when defining parameterized macros.

DON'T use inline functions if memory and disk space are at a premium. However, adding more memory and disk space to your PC never hurts either. Generally, you can and should use inline functions wherever you would use parameterized `#define` macros.

DON'T expect Turbo C++ to respect all of your `inline` requests; however, if Turbo C++ does not decide to inline a function or two, it generally has good reason to leave the function alone.

You might think that as long as you are aware of `#define`'s potential problems, you can take the needed steps to avoid those problems. It's true that if you were extremely careful, you could use `#define` the proper way, but why bother with `#define` when using `const` and inline functions takes care of everything? You might as well use the C++-preferred way and get used to `const` and inlines; you don't have time to waste on bugs because there are too many programs waiting to be written!

 Note: There is another advantage that inline functions offer over parameterized macros. In Day 7's chapter, "Overloaded Functions Lessen Your Load," you'll learn how to write *overloaded functions*. Overloaded functions save you programming time by enabling you to reuse function code for different types of arguments. You cannot overload parameterized `#define` macros.

Some Useful
Turbo C++ Identifiers

Turbo C++ comes supplied with several identifiers that you can often use in your programs. These predefined identifiers are sometimes called *symbolic constants*. Table 2.1 lists some of the more useful identifiers. (The identifiers are just like global variables that you can use—but not change—in your programs.)

Table 2.1. Some useful predefined Turbo C++ identifiers.

Identifier Name	Type	Description
__DATE__	String	Date when the source file is processed.
__FILE__	String	Name of the current source file (including disk name). __FILE__ changes whenever another #include runs.
__LINE__	Decimal	The number (beginning with 1) of the current source file that contains __LINE__.
__TIME__	String	Time when the preprocessor began processing this source file.

Note: There are many intrinsic date and time functions (such as getdate() and gettime()) that return the date and time that a program runs; the __DATE__ and __TIME__ identifiers, however, use only compile-time values.

Listing 2.14 uses the __TIME__ and __DATE__ identifiers to print the time and date of compilation, and functions to print the run time and run date.

Listing 2.14. Determining the date and time of compilation.

```
1:  // Filename: DATETIME.CPP
2:  // Program that uses __DATE__ and __TIME__ identifiers
3:  #include <stdio.h>      // For printf()
4:  #include <dos.h>        // For date and time functions
5:  #include <conio.h>      // For clrscr() function
6:  main()
7:  {
8:    char cDate[] = __DATE__;  // Define and initialize both the
9:    char cTime[] = __TIME__;  // date and time arrays
10:   clrscr();                 // Turbo C++ function to erase screen
11:   printf("This code was compiled at %s on %s.\n", cTime, cDate);
12:
13:   // Find the current run time and date
14:   time t; //Required to store internal date
15:   gettime(&t);  // Must pass by address to fill time structure
16:   printf("This program was run at %2d:%02d:%02d on ",
17:          t.ti_hour, t.ti_min, t.ti_sec);
18:
19:   date d;
20:   getdate(&d);  // Must pass by address to fill date structure
21:   printf("%d/%d/%d.\n", d.da_mon, d.da_day, d.da_year);
22:
23:   return 0;
24: }
```

```
This code was compiled at 16:27:38 on December 1 1992.
This program was run at 11:32:40 on 11/30/1993.
```

Notice that the __DATE__ and __TIME__ identifiers return strings that you store in arrays and that you treat just like any other string literals in your programs. This program initializes and stores the time and date in two arrays at lines 8 and 9.

The majority of the program is setting up non-C++ statements. The program demonstrates that all the usual Turbo C functions work as-is inside your Turbo C++ programs. Three header files are included in lines 3 through 5 to support the functions used in the program. (Be careful when using // C++ comments to the right of #include statements if you ever use a compiler other than Turbo C++; not all C++ preprocessors recognize C++ comments to the right of the C-like directives.)

The clrscr() function called in line 10 is a Turbo C++–specific function that is not approved by the AT&T standard and probably will not be approved by the ANSI C++ committee. Nevertheless, erasing the screen before a program's output helps keep things cleaner. Most of the programs in the rest of this book will clear the screen before generating any output.

Lines 13 through 21 do nothing that you couldn't do with Turbo C, but all the code is necessary to generate the current date and time when the program executes. As you might or might not know from previous programming, you must define special `date` and `time` structure variables before calling `getdate()` and `gettime()` that fill those structures with date and time values. Of course, thanks to C++, lines 14 and 19 don't need the `struct` keyword. The declarations for the `date` and `time` structures appear in the DOS.H header file.

Listing 2.15 uses the two identifiers `__LINE__` and `__FILE__`. Often, Turbo C++ programmers use these identifiers for debugging programs. If you are producing several lines of output all throughout a program, you might want to print the `__LINE__` value every once in a while so that you can tell from the program's output which source code lines produced the output. The `__FILE__` can help find lost source files. Although most Turbo C++ programmers give their compiled programs the same name as the source code (such as PROG.EXE and PROG.CPP), some don't. There is also the matter of dealing with several source files compiled together. While debugging large programs, you might want to print the name of each source file being processed. `__FILE__` enables you to do just that.

Type Listing 2.15. Using `__LINE__` and `__FILE__`.

```
1:  // Filename: LINEFILE.CPP
2:  // Program that uses __LINE__ and __FILE__ identifiers
3:  #include <stdio.h>      // For printf()
4:  #include <conio.h>      // For clrscr() function
5:
6:  main()
7:  {
8:    clrscr();
9:    printf("Line %d being processed...\n", __LINE__);
10:   printf("This source code is named %s.\n", __FILE__);
11:   printf("Line %d being processed...\n", __LINE__);
12:
13:
14:   return 0;
15: }
```

Output
```
Line 9 being processed...
This source code is named C:LINEFILE.CPP.
Line 11 being processed...
```

Note: You don't have to include a header file for the Turbo C++ pre-defined identifiers. The identifiers are available to all programs.

51

DO	**DON'T**

DO use __LINE__ during debugging if you want to know when certain lines are executing. (Turbo C++'s on-line debugger is better to use, but __LINE__ is especially helpful to print line numbers on printed output that goes to paper.)

DON'T use __DATE__ and __TIME__ to print the *current* date or time when the program runs. All the identifiers are set to compile-time values, not runtime values.

DON'T ever define your own variables or constants with the same names as the predefined identifiers.

Summary

This chapter gave you a taste of the differences in C++ over C. Throughout this book, as you learn OOP you will see why the designers of Turbo C++ chose to include the features discussed here. Nevertheless, even if you never learn OOP, the material in this chapter is useful and should help improve your code over regular C code.

From comments to inline functions, the goal of Turbo C++ is to make your programming easier, not harder. Whereas some of the differences between C++ and C are trivial (such as the linkage of global const values), most help you by speeding your program development.

The next chapter dives into Turbo C++'s I/O (input/output) features. Turbo C++ is a language that takes I/O to levels not achievable in C. You will find that I/O is much simpler in Turbo C++.

Q&A

1. How can regular C comments get you in trouble?

   The problem with the enclosing /* and */ is that you cannot nest them. During debugging sessions, programmers like to comment out code that they know works to help spot code with errors. They also like to comment out the code with errors to test the rest of the program for consistency. When you place C-style comments to the right of statements, you cannot

just insert an opening comment, /*, and then several lines later insert the closing comment, */, and expect Turbo C++ to work things out.

When using the C++ comment, you only have to insert // at the beginning of every line you want to comment out regardless of what else is on the line.

2. How does C++ save you time when you're writing with struct, enum, and union?

You don't have to repeat the struct, enum, or union keywords when defining variables. The data type, such as your structure, is almost a part of the Turbo C++ language after you declare what the aggregate data type looks like.

3. Are C++'s strict prototype requirements a drawback to using C++?

Not at all. Despite the extra work needed to prototype every function and include all needed header files, prototypes are for your own good. By prototyping your functions, you tell Turbo C++ exactly how you want to execute those functions later. If you break this contract by passing to a function data types that you should not, Turbo C++ will not want to compile the program.

4. Why is inline only a suggestion to Turbo C++?

If the body of an inline function does too much, Turbo C++ makes an executive order and ignores your inline request. The reason that you specify inline is to save function call overhead without letting the drawbacks of parameterized macros creep into your code. If the function is too long or complicated, that long or complicated code would have to be placed inline everywhere the function is called. Making such a replacement could make the code too large, so inline is only a hint to Turbo C++ (as is register if you are familiar with that) that you want a function inlined where it is called.

Workshop

The Workshop offers quiz questions and exercises to hone your skills and give you feedback on today's lesson. You'll find some proposed answers in Appendix D.

Quiz

1. C++ comments begin with //. What ends a C++ comment?

2. What is a function's signature?

3. True or False: The following function prototypes are equivalent:

```
float fun(int a, float b, char * c);
```

and

```
float fun(int, float, char *);
```

4. True or False: The following functions' first lines are equivalent:

```
float fun(int a, float b, char * c)
```

and

```
float fun(int, float, char *)
```

5. True or False: Turbo C++ considers the following prototypes equivalent:

```
int fun();
```

and

```
int fun(void);
```

6. What two predefined identifiers are useful for debugging?

7. If a program is compiled on Jan 1, 1994, and is run on July 7, 1994, what value would the program's __DATE__ identifier produce?

Exercises

1. Rewrite the following code with the two printf()s commented out:

```
#include <stdio.h>
main()
{
  printf("Welcome to Turbo C++.\n");  // Output
  printf("The power is yours!\n");
  return 0;
}
```

2. Rewrite the following code without using #define:

```
// Filename: NODEFINE.CPP
#include <stdio.h>
#define PI 3.14159
```

```
#define cirArea(r) PI * (r * r)

main()
{
  float radius;
  printf("What is the circle's radius in inches? ");
  scanf(" %f", &radius);
  printf("The area of the circle is %.2f inches.\n",
cirArea(radius));

  return 0;
}
```

Simple I/O

Input and output, or *I/O,* occur when you send data from the computer to an output device such as a printer, or when your computer receives data from an input device such as a keyboard or disk.

I/O is nothing new to you, but the way Turbo C++ handles I/O will be new. Turbo C++ provides one of the easiest I/O systems available in any language. What's more, after you learn more about OOP, you'll be able to extend Turbo C++'s I/O capabilities so that they behave exactly the way you want them to and work with your own data types.

Although some of Turbo C++'s I/O syntax will be new to you, after you get used to it, you'll wonder how you ever wrote a program without it. You can easily format your output using simple Turbo C++ specifiers. Today, you learn about the following topics:

- [ ] Turbo C++ stream I/O

- [ ] Outputting with `cout` `<<`

- [ ] Inputting with `cin` `>>`

- [ ] Error displaying with `cerr` `<<`

- [ ] The I/O manipulators and format flags

Output Your Data with *cout* and `<<`

Before going any further, get used to using the following header file at the top of all your Turbo C++ programs:

```
#include <iostream.h>
```

IOSTREAM.H is the header file that replaces STDIO.H in Turbo C++. If you use a function such as `gets()` (but there is almost always a better Turbo C++ method of I/O than C's old I/O functions), you'll have to include STDIO.H for those functions. However, for the C++ I/O to work the way this chapter explains, you'll want to include IOSTREAM.H in every Turbo C++ program you write (the best place to include the file is before `main()`).

You are used to using the `printf()` function for output. Instead of using a function, Turbo C++ uses an *object.* Yes, that's the same object as in *object-oriented programming,* but you don't have to understand objects to use Turbo C++'s output object. The name of Turbo C++'s output object is `cout`.

Note: For the time being, think of cout as being your screen. Actually, cout might be your screen, your printer, or anywhere else you redirect your computer's standard output through DOS. If you are unfamiliar with redirecting of output, you're not missing much—there now are better ways to route output to various devices that you'll learn about throughout this book.

Figure 3.1 simplifies the concept of cout as much as possible. If you want to send something to your screen, whether that something is a string, an integer, or a floating-point value, send that data to cout. Figure 3.1 also shows a new Turbo C++ operator not found in the C language. The << operator is called the *inserter* operator, but C++ programmers rarely call it that. (Many talk as if cout is the output operator, as in "Next, you *cout* the value.")

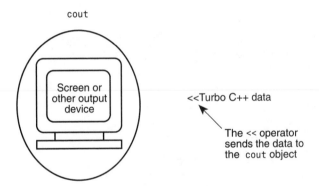

cout

Screen or other output device

<<Turbo C++ data

The << operator sends the data to the cout object

Figure 3.1. *The screen is the* cout *object.*

As long as you think of your screen as being the cout object, and as long as you know that the inserter operator, <<, is the output operator, you can send data to the screen by routing the data into the cout object using <<. You might have seen << used as the C bitwise left-shift operator; << is still the bitwise left-shift operator in Turbo C++, but << is also used for output. Turbo C++ decides the correct usage of << from the context in which you use it.

For example, the following statement prints I'm learning OOP! on-screen:

```
cout << "I'm learning OOP!";
```

Note: Can't you just picture Turbo C++ sending the message I am learning OOP! to the cout object? The cout is the screen, so the << operator sends that message directly to the screen. The format of cout and << looks just like their resulting action.

You already know that printing this same message in C is about as easy. Here is a printf() that does just that:

```
printf("I'm learning OOP!");
```

The big difference and advantage of cout comes to light when you print values other than strings. With printf() you must specify format codes such as %d and %f. You don't need to specify formats when outputting with cout. Consider the program in Listing 3.1.

Type   Listing 3.1. Output with cout.

```
1:  // Filename: COUT1ST.CPP
2:  // Demonstrates cout
3:  #include <iostream.h>
4:  #include <conio.h>
5:  main()
6:  {
7:    int i = 65;
8:    float f = 1.234567;
9:    double d = -9485.675544;
10:   clrscr();        // Erase the screen
11:   cout << "Here is i: ";
12:   cout << i;
13:   cout << "\n";
14:   cout << "Here is f: ";
15:   cout << f;
16:   cout << "\n";
17:   cout << "Here is d: ";
18:   cout << d;
19:   cout << "\n";
20:   return 0;
21: }
```

```
Here is i: 65
Here is f: 1.234567
Here is d: -9485.675544
```

The \n works in Turbo C++ just as it does in C and sends the cursor to the next line.

The nice thing about cout is that you don't have to specify %d and %f when printing numeric values. More important, you can combine the output of more than one value on a single line. Listing 3.2 illustrates how you can group the cout in Listing 3.1 into a more compact form.

 Listing 3.2. Combining the output.

```
1:  // Filename: COUT2ND.CPP
2:  // Demonstrates grouped cout
3:  #include <iostream.h>
4:  #include <conio.h>
5:  main()
6:  {
7:    int i = 65;
8:    float f = 1.234567;
9:    double d = -9485.675544;
10:   clrscr();    // Erase the screen
11:   cout << "Here is i: " << i << "\n";
12:   cout << "Here is f: " << f << "\n";
13:   cout << "Here is d: " << d << "\n";
14:   return 0;
15: }
```

Output

```
Here is i: 65
Here is f: 1.234567
Here is d: -9485.675544
```

 Not only does this syntax take fewer lines of code, but it is easier to understand. You can group as many output values as you like into the cout object.

Later sections in this chapter will show you how to control the output format such as the number of decimal places printed. cout defaults to outputting six decimal places but drops trailing zeros unless you want them retained, as you'll learn later.

Control Characters

Feel free to use \n, \a, \t, and all the other control characters you used in C printf() functions to display newlines, ring the terminal's bell, print leading tab characters, and so on. Put the control characters in the string or character being output with cout.

The following cout rings the PC bell three times:

```
cout << "\a\a\a";   // Sound the alarm
```

There are Turbo C++ replacements for some of the format characters such as \n that you will read about later in this chapter.

DO	**DON'T**

DO include IOSTREAM.H in all your Turbo C++ programs that take advantage of C++ input/output.

DO use cout and the inserter operator, <<, for all your Turbo C++ output.

DON'T use format specifiers such as %f with cout. There are ways to control formatted output, but cout usually guesses correctly as to how you want your data to look.

Input Is Just As Easy with *cin* and >>

Toss away scanf()! Although most seasoned C programmers stop using scanf() when they collect better input routines from bulletin boards, from friends, and when they write their own, C programmers still throw in a scanf() here and there. Turbo C++ rises above the rigors of scanf() and finally makes input as easy as output with the cin object and the *extractor* operator, >>.

Just as you can picture cout as being the screen, cin is your keyboard. More accurately, cin is the standard input device usually routed to your keyboard unless you change that routing through DOS (which we rarely do anymore). Figure 3.2 illustrates cin and >>. Notice the data-flow direction indicated by the >>—data is going from the keyboard into variables.

Suppose that you needed to ask the user for an inventory quantity. Here is how you can do that:

```
int quant;
cout << "How many items are in the inventory? ";
cin >> quant;
```

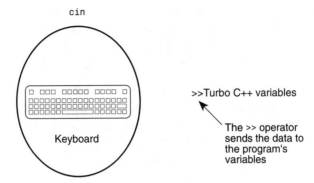

cin

Keyboard

>>Turbo C++ variables

The >> operator
sends the data to
the program's
variables

Figure 3.2. *The keyboard is the* cin *object.*

The third line takes the keyboard input (the cin object) and sends the keyboard's data
to the quant variable. If the variable is floating-point, there is no difference. Consider
this:

```
float price;
cout << "How much does the item cost? ";
cin >> price;
```

Turbo C++ stores whatever the user enters for the price in price. You can group
together more than one input variable using a single cin, as Listing 3.3 shows.

Listing 3.3. Input with cin.

```
1:  // Filename: MULTICIN.CPP
2:  #include <iostream.h>
3:  #include <conio.h>
4:  main()
5:  {
6:     int quant;
7:     float price;
8:     clrscr();      // Erase the screen
9:     cout << "What is the number and price? ";
10:    cin >> quant >> price;   // Combine the input with caution!
11:    cout << "\n\nNumber: " << quant << "\nPrice: " << price << "\n";
12:    return 0;
13: }
```

```
What is the number and price? 3 4.56

Number: 3
Price: 4.56
```

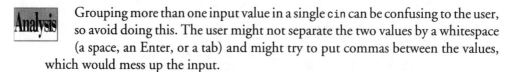

Analysis Grouping more than one input value in a single cin can be confusing to the user, so avoid doing this. The user might not separate the two values by a whitespace (a space, an Enter, or a tab) and might try to put commas between the values, which would mess up the input.

cin is not capable of inputting strings of more than one word. Although a string ends with a null-terminating zero, cin only accepts strings up to the first space. The space tells cin (arguably incorrectly) that the current string ends, and then Turbo C++ saves the rest of the string in the input buffer until the next cin executes. There are ways to input strings that contain spaces; you'll see how later in this chapter.

DO	**DON'T**
DO use cin and the extractor operator, >>, for your Turbo C++ input.	
DON'T group more than one input value together. If you want to ask the user for three values, use three separate cin statements.	
DON'T use cin to input strings that might have spaces in them (most do).	

How to Display Error Messages

In a perfect world, with perfect programmers, perfect programs, and perfect users, you could skip this section. Nevertheless, you are well aware of the importance of good error checking and helpful, clear, and concise error messages when appropriate.

Most computer applications in use today consist of error checking and error message handling code. Some estimate that 35 percent of the lines in all programs used today are error checks and handling when things go wrong at the user's end. Throughout this book, you'll see why OOP is so advantageous to programmers. Petty details of programming are lifted off your programming back so that you can concentrate on the application and not as much on error checking and other details.

You still have to check for errors, but you can teach your data to check itself through OOP practices you'll learn a little later. You'll find that the main() function and all the functions that main() calls shrink dramatically in size when you move to object-oriented programming because your data takes over a lot of tedious tasks and your code is not as burdened with mundane tasks such as user-input checking.

Nevertheless, *somewhere* in your programs, you'll have to display warnings and errors to your users. When you write the code for your active data objects, you'll have to write the output statements that display the errors. OOP, however, enables you to write this kind of code once, and your data will automatically trigger that code when needed.

Rather than cout, most Turbo C++ programmers route their error messages to the cerr object. cerr, which is the screen, works just like cout. (cerr is always unbuffered, in case you are interested. Being unbuffered means that your user sees the error as soon as it's generated, not later when it might be too late as with buffered output.)

Suppose that you wanted to calculate an average price for the user, but the user's input wouldn't enable you to (you cannot divide by zero). The following code checks the user's input value and prints an error message accordingly:

```
cout << "What was the total dollar amount of last month's sales? ";
cin >> sales;
cout << "How many units did you sell? ";
cin >> num;
if (num == 0)
  { cerr << "The average cannot be computed.\n"; }
else
  { avgSales = sales / num;
    cout << "The average selling price per unit was ";
    cout << avgSales << "\n";
  }
```

Of course, the program could have sent the error to cout. However, under the small chance that the user routed the standard output to another device, cerr always prints to the screen so that the user can see the message immediately. cerr is equivalent in every way to C's stderr.

Note: A fourth I/O object named clog is sometimes used for error messages. clog, however, is buffered, and it's possible that error messages might not display if a serious error occurs. The error itself might involve the output device or put the computer in an infinite loop, and the buffered clog error message might never get displayed. Always use cerr and you won't have the problem.

DO use the unbuffered cerr for displaying error messages.

DON'T use clog because the buffering can keep error messages from displaying.

Using the I/O Objects: *cout, cin,* and *cerr*

Syntax

```
cout << dataValue [<< formatSpecifiers] [<< dataValue...];
cin >> variable [<< formatSpecifiers] [>> variable...];
cerr << errorMessage [<< formatSpecifiers] [<< errorMessage];
```

You can follow the << or >> with multiple values to group output and input into single statements, but it is generally agreed that you should group only output and not more than one input value together.

You do not have to use any format specifiers. You can control the way the data is output or input by inserting data-manipulating objects and format control before the data being input or output. If you do not specify any formatting, Turbo C++ displays the data in its native format, and often no format control is necessary.

Example

```
// Filename: IOTHREE.CPP
// Demonstrates the I/O objects and operators
#include <iostream.h>
#include <stdlib.h>
#include <conio.h>
// stdlib.h has prototype for exit()
main()
{
  int age;
  clrscr();
  cout << "How old are you? ";        // Ask a question
  cin >> age;
  if ((age < 0) || (age > 150))       // Check for extremes
    { cerr << "You can't be that age!\n";
      exit(1);   // Stop program
    }
  if (age < 21)
    {cout << "Have some ice cream.\n"; }
  else
    { cout << "Have some wine.\n"; }
  return 0;
}
```

What's Down the Road?

The most important reason to switch to Turbo C++'s I/O is not its ease of use but the extensibility of the I/O objects and operators. You can set up the operators, using the object-oriented capabilities that you'll learn throughout this book, so that they work on your own data types and behave exactly as you want them to behave.

What if you want to send the contents of a huge structure to the screen? Suppose you wanted to print the contents of this structure:

```
struct Person {
  char    last[15];
  char    first[15];
  int     age;
  double  salary;
  int     dependents;
  char    address[25];
  char    city[15];
  char    state[3];
  char    zip[6];
  long    yearBegan;
  int     extension;
  int     officeNumber;
} employee[1000];   // Defines 1,000 employee records
```

Normally, you would call a function to display each member in the structure variable being printed. In Turbo C++, however, you have to do only this:

```
cin >> employee[i];   // Get the next employee's data
```

That single `cin` prompts the user for each member and retrieves the user's input. It can even check for input errors and display error messages if needed!

Obviously, Turbo C++ cannot read your mind; you have to set up `cin` and `>>` so that they behave the way you want them to. On Days 11 and 12 you'll learn how to extend the way Turbo C++ operators work and make them work seamlessly with your own data types, such as the structure shown here. You still have to write the code that Turbo C++ needs so that Turbo C++ knows what to do when you want to fill a structure variable. However, after you teach Turbo C++ how to retrieve such data in the format you want, you only have to use the single-line `cin` just shown to get data into any variable derived from this structure.

All the mysteries of such input will be solved as you progress through this book. This section is not trying to tease you with material you're not ready for; in fact, this section is attempting to explain a supportable, concrete, and extremely helpful reason for learning the I/O techniques in this chapter.

By the way, you can make the cout and << work on your own data as well. If you want, you can instruct Turbo C++ to display the full-screen display shown in Figure 3.3 when the following simple statement executes:

```
cout << employee[2];   // Outputs the structure variable's members
```

*** Employee Entry Screen ***

- - - - - - - - - - - - - - - - -

Last name: Johnson	First: Fred	Age: 34

Address: 1013 S. Illinois Ave.

City: St. Louis	State: MO	ZIP: 63043

Salary: $54,245.10	Dependents: 2

Year began: 1985	Phone ext: 421	Office: 52

Figure 3.3. *A simple* cout *can produce this output screen.*

Note: You have already read several times in this book that Turbo C++ helps speed your program development. After you set up the I/O to work with your data types, isn't it easier to write cout every time you want to display an output screen or cin every time you want to get the user's input than to remember function names or place the I/O code everywhere you want it executed?

Manipulating the Output

Turbo C++ includes many helpful *manipulators* that manipulate your output so that the data looks the way you want it to look. As you saw earlier in this chapter, you don't have to format Turbo C++ output, but there will be times when you want exactly two decimal places or when you want to specify a certain output justification that a cout by itself will not provide.

Table 3.1 lists all the I/O manipulators, and Table 3.2 lists some support values, called *format flags*, that go with some of the manipulators. The data that you input or output is called a *stream,* and these manipulators are formally called *stream manipulators.* You embed the manipulators inside cout as shown next. (On Day 12, you'll learn how to write your own I/O manipulators and use them just as though they were built into Turbo C++.)

 Note: Include IOMANIP.H when you use any of these manipulators.

3

Table 3.1. The I/O stream manipulators.

Manipulator	Description
dec	Sets decimal conversion base.
hex	Sets hexadecimal conversion base.
oct	Sets octal conversion base.
endl	Inserts newline and flush stream.
ends	Inserts null zero in string.
flush	Flushes an output stream.
setbase(int *n*)	Sets conversion base to base *n* (0 for decimal default, 8 for octal, 10 for decimal, and 16 for hexadecimal).
resetiosflags(long *f*)	Clears the format specified by *f*. *f* is a format flag from Table 3.2.
setiosflags(long *f*)	Sets the format specified by *f*. *f* is a format flag from Table 3.2.
setfill(int *c*)	Sets the fill character to *c*.
setprecision(int *n*)	Sets the floating-point precision to *n*.
setw(int *n*)	Sets the field width to *n*.

Note: All the manipulators with parentheses accept arguments and are called *parameterized manipulators.*

Table 3.2. Format flag values for `resetiosflags()` and `setiosflags()`.

Format Flag Name	Description
`ios::left`	Left-justifies output within the `setw()` width.
`ios::right`	Right-justifies output within the `setw()` width.
`ios::scientific`	Formats output in scientific notation.
`ios::fixed`	Formats numbers in decimal format (rather than scientific notation).
`ios::dec`	Formats numbers in base 10.
`ios::hex`	Formats numbers in base 16.
`ios::oct`	Formats numbers in base 8.
`ios::uppercase`	Formats all hexadecimal and scientific notation value characters in uppercase (such as `1.32E+03` rather than `1.32e+03`).
`ios::showbase`	Prints a leading numeric base prefix (either `0x` for hexadecimal or `0` for octal).
`ios::showpos`	Outputs a plus sign, `+`, when printing positive numbers. (The plus sign is suppressed otherwise.)
`ios::showpoint`	Displays trailing zeroes when needed for precision.

Note: The format flags look strange with the embedded scope resolution operator in them. These values are just constants (as `#define` produced named constants in C) that trigger a certain action depending on their values. The format flags work in the two functions `resetiosflags()` and `setiosflags()`.

The program in Listing 3.4 shows how the base-conversion manipulators dec, hex, and oct output the same number in different bases.

 Listing 3.4. Using each of the base-conversion manipulators.

```
1:  // Filename: BASES.CPP
2:  // Prints numbers in three bases
3:  #include <iostream.h>
4:  #include <iomanip.h>
5:  #include <conio.h>
6:  main()
7:  {
8:    int num = 211;
9:    clrscr();        // Erase the screen
10:   cout << "The decimal num: " << num << "\n";   // Base 10
11:   cout << "The hexadecimal num: " << hex << num << "\n";   // Base 16
12:   cout << "The octal num: " << oct << num << "\n";   // Base 8
13:   return 0;
14: }
```

```
The decimal num: 211
The hexadecimal num: d3
The octal num: 323
```

 The decimal number 211 is equivalent to the hexadecimal number d3 and the octal number 323 (octal is rarely used anymore). Turbo C++ remembers each of the base-conversion manipulators until the program ends or until you supply a different value. Therefore, if you want all of your integer values to print in hexadecimal format, specify hex in the first cout and all subsequent cout statements will also output in hexadecimal.

 Note: You don't have to specify dec, because Turbo C++ defaults to base 10 output. However, if you print in a different base and then want to change back to base 10, use dec.

Instead of using the three manipulators dec, hex, and oct, you can use the setbase() parameterized manipulator to specify the base you want to use for output. Listing 3.5 produces the same output as Listing 3.4 but uses setbase() rather than the individual base-conversion manipulators. The choice of base manipulators is up to you.

Listing 3.5. Using the setbase() manipulator.

```
1:  // Filename: BASES2.CPP
2:  // Prints numbers in three bases using setbase()
3:  #include <iostream.h>
4:  #include <iomanip.h>
5:  #include <conio.h>
6:  main()
7:  {
8:    int num = 211;
9:    clrscr();        // Erase the screen
10:   cout << "The decimal num: " << setbase(10) << num << "\n";
  ➡// Base 10
11:   cout << "The hexadecimal num: " << setbase(16) << num << "\n";
  ➡// Base 16
12:   cout << "The octal num: " << setbase(8) << num << "\n";  // Base 8
13:   return 0;
14: }
```

```
The decimal num: 211
The hexadecimal num: d3
The octal num: 323
```

Table 3.1 contains some end-of-output manipulators that you might use every once in a while. You often see the `endl`, `ends`, or `flush` manipulators used at the end of data being output. `endl` does the same thing as the newline character `'\n'` followed by `flush`, by sending a newline and flushing the output buffer. These statements all do the same thing:

```
cout << "Hello there\n" << flush;
cout << "Hello there" << '\n' << flush;
cout << "Hello there" << endl;
```

Note: If you are writing to the screen, you rarely need these manipulators.

The `ends` manipulator outputs a null zero at the end of a string of characters. You might need to terminate a string of individual characters with the terminating zero if you print the characters to a disk file or modem. Although the following statement appears to print individual characters, it actually prints a string because a string is always a group of characters terminated by a null zero.

```
cout << 'a' << 'b' << 'c' << ends;
```

The `ends` manipulator produces an extra blank when you output it to the screen.

Sticky Manipulation

All the I/O manipulators in Table 3.1 except for setw() are sometimes called *sticky manipulators.* All but setw() remain in effect for the rest of the program unless you override them by specifying new manipulators.

The setw() manipulator works only for the cout in which it appears.

The setw() manipulator specifies exactly how wide of a field to use for output data. Often when printing tables of data, you want the data to print uniformly within the same number of spaces so that your columns align with each other. Specify setw() on every cout line for which you want a width set. Turbo C++ always defaults to variable-width output in cout lines that don't contain setw().

 Note: All values are right-justified within the setw() field width unless you use format flags from Table 3.2 as shown later in this section. If the data is wider than the argument in setw(), Turbo C++ ignores the setw() width and prints the entire value.

The program in Listing 3.6 prints various data values within different field widths so that you can see how the width specifier controls the placement of the data within their printed fields.

 Listing 3.6. Printing within different field widths.

```
1:  // Filename: WIDTHS.CPP
2:  // Prints data using different field widths
3:  #include <iostream.h>
4:  #include <iomanip.h>
5:  #include <conio.h>
6:  main()
7:  {
8:    clrscr();        // Erase the screen
9:    cout << "Without a field width set:\n";
10:   cout << "abcdefg" << "\n";
11:   cout << 12345 << "\n";
12:   cout << 123.45 << "\n";
13:   cout << "With a 10-character field width set:\n";
14:   cout << setw(10) << "abcdefg" << "\n";
15:   cout << setw(10) << 12345 << "\n";
```

continues

Listing 3.6. continued

```
16:   cout << setw(10) << 123.45 << "\n";
17:   return 0;
18: }
```

Without a field width set:
abcdefg
12345
123.45
With a 10-character field width set:
    abcdefg
      12345
     123.45

As you can see, the fill character that Turbo C++ uses to pad justified fields is a blank. The `setfill()` manipulator enables you to change the fill character. By placing the statement

```
cout << setfill('x');
```

before the `cout` statements in Listing 3.6, you force the program to produce this output:

```
Without a field width set:
abcdefg
12345
123.45
With a 10-character field width set:
xxxabcdefg
xxxxx12345
xxxx123.45
```

`setfill('*')` would be useful for printing payroll check amounts so that the numbers cannot be altered.

After learning `setw()`, you're ready to learn about `setiosflags()` and `resetiosflags()` (and you'll also wonder why the designers of C++ wrote names that long!). If you want to left-justify data within the width, use `setiosflags()` with the `ios::left` format flag. Using the `ios::right` parameter with `ios::setiosflags` resets the justification to the right. Listing 3.7 prints the Listing 3.6 values left-justified rather than right-justified as is the default.

Note: If you left-justify output, the fill character will fill from the right rather than from the left.

Listing 3.7. Printing left-justified within different field widths.

```
1:  // Filename: WIDTHLFT.CPP
2:  // Prints data using different field widths
3:  #include <iostream.h>
4:  #include <iomanip.h>
5:  #include <conio.h>
6:  main()
7:  {
8:    clrscr();        // Erase the screen
9:    cout << "Without a field width set:\n";
10:   cout << "abcdefg" << "abcdefg" << "\n";
11:   cout << 12345 << 12345 << "\n";
12:   cout << 123.45 << 123.45 << "\n";
13:   cout << "With the default right-justified 10-character ";
14:   cout << "field width set:\n";
15:   cout << setw(10) << "abcdefg" << setw(10) << "abcdefg" << "\n";
16:   cout << setw(10) << 12345 << setw(10) << 12345 << "\n";
17:   cout << setw(10) << 123.45 << setw(10) << 123.45 << "\n";
18:   // Force left-justification
19:   cout << setiosflags(ios::left);
20:   cout << "With a left-justified 10-character field width set:\n";
21:   cout << setw(10) << "abcdefg" << setw(10) << "abcdefg" << "\n";
22:   cout << setw(10) << 12345 << setw(10) << 12345 << "\n";
23:   cout << setw(10) << 123.45 << setw(10) << 123.45 << "\n";
24:   return 0;
25: }
```

Output

```
Without a field width set:
abcdefgabcdefg
1234512345
123.45123.45
With the default right-justified 10-character field width set:
   abcdefg   abcdefg
     12345     12345
    123.45    123.45
With a left-justified 10-character field width set:
abcdefg   abcdefg
12345     12345
123.45    123.45
```

Unlike several of the previous program listings, Listing 3.7 prints two columns of data using three different methods: no width set, a right-justified width set, and a left-justified width set. This listing enables you to see the effects of setw() and setiosflags().

The ios::dec, ios::hex, and ios::oct flags enable you to use setiosflags() to set the numeric base rather than the other base-conversion manipulators described earlier. For example, the following statement prints the 37 in base 16 as 2c:

```
cout << setiosflags(ios::hex) << 44; // Outputs 2c
```

The setiosflags() accepts more than one argument if you separate the arguments with a bitwise OR operator, ¦. Suppose that you wanted a hexadecimal value printed left-justified in a width of 10. The following statement does just that:

```
cout << setw(10)<<setiosflags(ios::hex¦ios::left)<<44<<45<<endl;
```

Here is the output from this cout:

```
2c        2d
```

The ios::uppercase ensures that all alphabetic hexadecimal values print in upper-case. The following statement prints 2C because of the ios::uppercase inside the setiosflags() along with the ios::hex parameter:

```
cout << setiosflags(ios::hex ¦ ios::uppercase) << 44;
```

The resetiosflags() resets any or all of the parameters in effect. For example, if you used the preceding cout to print 44 in an uppercase hexadecimal format, the following statement would reset (turn off) the ios::uppercase format, but keep the ios::hex in effect:

```
cout << resetiosflags(ios::uppercase) << 45;
```

Of course, not all hexadecimal numbers have alphabetic characters in them. Therefore, you can request that Turbo C++ output the hexadecimal or octal base prefix characters, 0x and 0, so that the user knows what base to use for interpreting the numbers. Listing 3.8 prints the number 10 in three different bases with their appropriate base prefix.

Listing 3.8. **Printing with base prefix characters.**

```
1:  // Filename: BASESHOW.CPP
2:  // Prints different bases with base prefix characters
3:  #include <iostream.h>
4:  #include <iomanip.h>
5:  #include <conio.h>
```

```
6:   main()
7:   {
8:     clrscr();        // Erase the screen
9:     cout << setiosflags(ios::showbase);
10:    cout << 10 << endl;                        // Base 10
11:    cout << setiosflags(ios::hex) << 10 << endl;  // Base 16
12:    cout << setiosflags(ios::oct) << 10 << endl;  // Base 8
13:    return 0;
14:  }
```

```
10
0xa
012
```

To print a number in scientific notation, use the `ios::scientific` parameter in `setiosflags()`. The lines

```
cout << 12345.678 << endl;
cout << setiosflags(ios::scientific) << 12345.678 << endl;
```

produce this output:

```
12345.67
1.234567e+04
```

The `ios::fixed` format flags returns the output to a decimal non-scientific notation format.

If you want to see a plus sign before a positive number, use the `ios::showpos` flag as Listing 3.9 illustrates.

Listing 3.9. Printing the plus sign.

```
1:   // Filename: SHOWPOS.CPP
2:   // Prints plus signs before positive numbers
3:   #include <iostream.h>
4:   #include <iomanip.h>
5:   #include <conio.h>
6:   main()
7:   {
8:     clrscr();        // Erase the screen
9:     int i = 7, j = -8;
10:    cout << "i is " << i << " and j is " << j << endl;
11:    cout << setiosflags(ios::showpos);  // Turn on plus sign
12:    cout << "i is " << i << " and j is " << j << endl;
13:    return 0;
14:  }
```

```
i is 7 and j is -8
i is +7 and j is -8
```

One of the most important formatting requirements for numbers is the capability to limit decimal places. Use setprecision() to set the precision of your output. Listing 3.10 prints the number 1.2345678 using nine different precision settings.

Listing 3.10. Printing precisions.

```
 1:  // Filename: PRECNINE.CPP
 2:  // Prints nine different precisions of same number
 3:  #include <iostream.h>
 4:  #include <iomanip.h>
 5:  #include <conio.h>
 6:  main()
 7:  {
 8:    clrscr();        // Erase the screen
 9:    cout << "The original number is " << 1.2345678 << endl;
10:    for (int i=0; i<8; i++)
11:      { cout << setprecision(i) << 1.2345678 << endl; }
12:    return 0;
13: }
```

```
The original number is 1.234568
1.234568
1.2
1.23
1.235
1.2346
1.23457
1.234568
1.2345678
```

Notice that setprecision(0) doesn't seem to affect the precision. Turbo C++'s default precision is six decimal places, and setprecision(0) always restores the precision to that default. If you don't want the right side of the decimal point to print, typecast your number to an integer before printing it.

When printing values such as dollars and cents, you *always* want two decimal places printed. setprecision(2), however, doesn't always print two places; rather, setprecision(2) prints *at most* two places. Therefore, the following cout will not print the trailing zero that is needed for the change:

```
cout << setprecision(2) << "Your change is " << 3.40;
```

To ensure that Turbo C++ always prints two decimal places (or however many decimal places you desire), you must use the ios::showpoint along with setprecision().

The following statement does print the change correctly as `3.40`:

```
cout << setprecision(2);
cout << setiosflags(ios::showpoint) << "Your change is " << 3.40;
```

3

DO / DON'T

DO	DON'T

DO include IOMANIP.H when using the I/O manipulators.

DO combine several format flags inside a single `setiosflags()` or `resetiosflags()` by separating them with a bitwise OR operator, `|`.

DO combine `setprecision()` and `setiosflags(ios::showpoint)` if you want a fixed number of decimal places printed with trailing zeros when appropriate.

DON'T specify `dec` for base 10 numbers unless in the same program you set the output to a different base. Decimal output is the default.

DON'T use `ios::uppercase` for text data. `ios::uppercase` prints only hexadecimal and scientific notation letter values in uppercase rather than their lowercase default.

Looking at Input

The discussions in the preceding section were concerned with output. User input is just as important. C was never known for extremely accurate user input control. Turbo C++'s `cin` accepts user input, and you can basically control the way the user enters that input. Still, Turbo C++ provides only a limited framework for input, and you'll have to write a lot of input routines or use one written by someone else (the computer magazines and bulletin boards are full of C++ I/O libraries that you can order).

Using `cin` and `>>`, Turbo C++ reads the next character into the character variable after `>>`, or the next value (string or number) into the non-character variable after `>>`. Either way, Turbo C++ skips whitespace characters such as newlines, tabs, and spaces to get the input.

The program in Listing 3.11 shows how Turbo C++ treats single-character input. Remember that `cin >>` skips all whitespace, unlike regular C.

Listing 3.11. Inputting single characters.

```
1:  // Filename: INPUTSIN.CPP
2:  // Gets five single characters
3:  #include <iostream.h>
4:  #include <iomanip.h>
5:  #include <conio.h>
6:  main()
7:  {
8:    char  c;
9:    for (int i=0; i<5; i++)
10:     { cout << "What is the next character? ";
11:        cin >> c;
12:        cout << "You typed " << c << endl;
13:  }
14:
15:    return 0;
16: }
```

```
What is the next character? a
You typed a
What is the next character? b
You typed b
What is the next character? c
You typed c
What is the next character? d
You typed d
What is the next character? e
You typed e
```

This program seems trivial unless you are used to getting single-character input with regular C's scanf() or getchar() functions. When the user enters a single character, such as a, the user must press Enter to end the data-entry of the a. Therefore, it appears that a\n goes to the input buffer, and it does. (In C, you would have to add another cin that accepted the \n and discarded the \n just to get the \n out of the way for the next character's input.) The next time this program inputs a character, however, cin skips the preceding character's \n because that's what cin does.

If you want to get whitespace characters into the character variable, you must use the get() function. The get() function's syntax doesn't look like anything you are used to, but by the time you finish learning Turbo C++, you'll understand why the syntax looks the way it does. In the meantime, here is how you can get a single character into a character variable *without* skipping the whitespace:

```
cin.get(myInit);   // Waits for user to type a letter
```

The Enter key ends user input. Therefore, pressing a single key (other than Enter) is not enough to store that key's character into the myInit variable. When using cin.get(), you must add a second cin.get() to discard the Enter's newline character. The following code does store the user's entered character in myInit:

```
cin.get(myInit);   // Get's user's first letter
cin.get(nl);       // The variable nl will hold '\n'
```

The bottom line is this: If you want to get individual characters and skip whitespace characters, use cin >>, and if you want to read all characters typed, even those that are whitespace characters, use cin.get().

get() is actually a multiple-purpose function. You can get characters and strings depending how you use it. get() is known as an *overloaded function,* meaning that you can pass it a different number and type of arguments and it behaves differently. You'll learn how to write your own overloaded functions in Day 6's chapter, "Communicating with Functions."

get() is useful for getting strings of data. Unlike simple cin >>, get() does not stop at the first whitespace. Therefore, you can get the user's strings with embedded spaces with get(). Here are the arguments for get() when used to get string input:

```
get(char * cp, int len [, char terminator])
```

The terminator's default is \n, but you can change it by passing the third parameter to get(). The *terminator* tells Turbo C++ which character to input up to and stop.

The program in Listing 3.12 asks for the user's entire name and then prints it.

 Listing 3.12. **Getting strings with get().**

```
1:  // Filename: STGET.CPP
2:  // String-input program
3:  #include <iostream.h>
4:  #include <iomanip.h>
5:  #include <conio.h>
6:  main()
7:  {
8:    char name[80];  // Will hold user's full name
9:    clrscr();       // Erase the screen
10:   cout << "What is your full name? ";
11:   cin.get(name, 80);  // The function uses at most 79 characters of
12:                       // input and leaves the rest on input buffer
13:   cout << "Your name is " << name << endl;
14:   return 0;
15: }
```

What is your full name? **William Harper Littlejohn**
Your name is William Harper Littlejohn

If you used cin >> to get the name, Turbo C++ would receive only the first name, William, and the rest would be left in the input buffer. Also, if the user were to enter a string longer than 79 characters (80 with the terminator), Turbo C++ would store only the first 79 characters in the name array and would leave any remaining characters on the input buffer for the next input. The second argument protects your arrays so that the user does not overwrite the array.

The getline() function works like get(), except getline() discards the terminating newline keystroke whereas get() leaves the newline on the input buffer. The program in Listing 3.13 demonstrates the problems that can occur when you use get() followed by a second get().

**Listing 3.13. Having two get()
functions in a row causes problems.**

```
1:  // Filename: GETBAD.CPP
2:  // String-input program with a bad get()
3:  #include <iostream.h>
4:  #include <iomanip.h>
5:  #include <conio.h>
6:  main()
7:  {
8:    char name[80];  // Will hold user's full name
9:    char city[25];  // Supposed to hold user's city name
10:   clrscr();        // Erase the screen
11:   cout << "What is your full name? ";
12:   cin.get(name, 80);  // The function uses at most 79 characters of
13:                       // input and leaves the rest on input buffer
14:   cout << "Your name is " << name << endl;
15:   cout << "What is your city? ";    // Will NOT wait for user!
16:   cin.get(city, 80);
17:   cout << "Your city is " << city << endl;  // Nothing prints!
18:   return 0;
19: }
```

What is your full name? **Theodore Marley Brooks**
Your name is Theodore Marley Brooks
What is your city? Your city is

Notice that the second get() does not wait for the user to type anything. That's because the first get() left a \n on the input stream and get() does not skip whitespace characters, so the second get() malfunctions. Changing the get() functions to getline()s fixes everything, as Listing 3.14 shows.

 Listing 3.14. Two getline() functions in a row work fine.

```
1:  // Filename: GETLINE.CPP
2:  // String-input program with getline()s
3:  #include <iostream.h>
4:  #include <iomanip.h>
5:  #include <conio.h>
6:  main()
7:  {
8:    char name[80];  // Will hold user's full name
9:    char city[25];  // Will hold user's city name
10:   clrscr();       // Erase the screen
11:   cout << "What is your full name? ";
12:   cin.getline(name, 80);  // The function uses at most 79 characters
13:              // of input and leaves the rest on input buffer
14:   cout << "Your name is " << name << endl;
15:   cout << "What is your city? ";
16:   cin.getline(city, 80);
17:   cout << "Your city is " << city << endl;  // The city prints
18:   return 0;
19: }
```

```
What is your full name? Theodore Marley Brooks
Your name is Theodore Marley Brooks
What is your city? New York
Your city is New York
```

When getting numbers, you can specify which base you want to accept for numeric input. In other words, if you expect the user to enter a hexadecimal or octal number, you can use a base manipulator directly inside the cin >> line to accept that base. If you don't specify a base manipulator, Turbo C++ defaults to decimal input. The following statement expects the user to type a decimal value:

```
cin >> num;
```

The following statement expects the user to type an octal value:

```
cin >> oct >> num;
```

If the user does not type an octal number (for example, f8 is not an octal number), num retains the same value it had before the cin. The following statement expects the user to type a hexadecimal value:

```
cin >> hex >> num;
```

If the user enters anything but a hexadecimal number, num does not change. In all numeric input, if the first part of the value is valid but the last is not, Turbo C++ stops reading until the invalid value. For example, if the user entered **12v** in response to the following `cin >>`

```
cin >> num;
```

the 12 would go into `num` and the `v\n` would be left on the input stream.

DO	**DON'T**

DO use `cin >>` if you want Turbo C++ to ignore whitespace.

DO use `get()` if you want Turbo C++ to read whitespace characters into character variables.

DON'T use `cin >>` to get string input that contains spaces. `cin >>` can get only one word at a time.

DON'T let the user overwrite character array boundaries; use `getline()` to keep input strings within their target array limits.

Summary

Turbo C++ programmers rarely use `printf()`, `scanf()`, or the family of the `getchar()` functions because `cin` and `cout` are so much easier and faster to code. Outputting data with `cout` and inputting data with `cin` makes a lot of sense when you picture the `cout` object as being your screen and `cin` as being the keyboard.

The overloaded `<<` and `>>` operators send data to and from your screen and keyboard in conjunction with the `cout` and `cin` objects. All the regular C I/O functions are available for your Turbo C++ programs, but you rarely need them.

Always include IOSTREAM.H when using `cout` and `cin`, and also include IOMANIP.H when formatting with the manipulators and format flags.

Q&A

1. Why does thinking about `cout` and `cin` as screen and keyboard objects make sense?

   The look of output statements using `cout`, as in `cout << "Turbo C++";`, actually makes you think that `Turbo C++` is being pushed into the `cout` screen device and `cin >> myName;` shows, through the >> direction indicator, that data is coming from the keyboard and being pushed into the variable `myName`.

Technically, `cout` and `cin` are your standard output and standard input device, which can be rerouted to devices other than your screen and keyboard. However, Turbo C++ programmers rarely redirect their output from these devices.

2. What is wrong with this statement:

```
cout >> age;
```

The direction of << is wrong. If you picture `cout` as being the screen, you can see that the screen cannot send data to variables, but variables *can* go to the screen. Although the `cin` and `cout` inserter and extractor operators, << and >>, point in different directions, their directions are easy to remember if you remember that `cout` represents the screen and `cin` represents the keyboard.

3. Why would I write to `cerr` when the screen is `cout`?

In your programs, send all error messages to the `cerr` error device. `cerr` will always be your screen. Under the slim chance that the user has redirected `cout` output somewhere else, `cerr` will still be pointing to the screen, and your error messages will be read.

4. Can I specify more than one format flag with `setiosflags()` and `resetiosflags()`?

Yes, you can, by separating the format flags with the bitwise OR, ¦, operator. For example, if you wanted to print a number in octal format, left-justified within a field width of 8 with the base prefix showing, you could do so in a single `setiosflags()` manipulator like this:

```
cout << setw(8) << setiosflags(ios::left¦ios::octal¦ios::
➥showbase) << i;
```

5. Why would you ever use `getline()` over `cin >>` when inputting strings?

`cin >>` gets only a word at a time, stopping at the first whitespace character including a blank. `cin >>` leaves all input to the right of blanks on the input stream.

Often, you'll want to input strings of data that contain blanks. You can by using `getline()`. `getline()` keeps reading a string until the user presses the terminator character (usually the \n unless you've specified the optional third parameter of `getline()`) or types the maximum number of characters allowed by the `getline()`.

Workshop

The Workshop offers quiz questions and exercises to hone your skills and give you feedback on today's lesson. You'll find some proposed answers in Appendix D.

Quiz

1. What is the header file you must include to use cout, cin, and cerr?

2. What is the header file you must include to use the I/O manipulators?

3. How does setw() behave differently from all the other manipulators?

4. When you specify a width with setw(), will the subsequent numeric value print left-justified or right-justified within the width?

5. True or false: The following statements print three numbers right-justified within a column of eight characters:

   ```
   cout << setw(8) << setiosflags(ios::right) << 25 << endl;
   cout << 26 << endl;
   cout << 27 << endl;
   ```

6. How does endl differ from ends and flush?

7. When would you use cin >> over get()?

8. True or false: Using getline(), you can keep the user from overwriting character array boundaries.

Exercises

1. Convert the following three cout statements into a single cout statement.

   ```
   cout << "Hi!";
   cout << "\n";
   cout << setprecision(2) << setiosflags(ios::showpoint) << amt;
   ```

2. Write the cin statement that reads the data 234A and stores the 234 in an integer variable and the A in a character variable.

3. Write a Turbo C++ program that uses cin and cout to ask the user for three prices. Print the dollar total of those prices on-screen. Print the total within a field of 20 spaces and left-fill the leftover spaces with asterisks. Also, be sure that the total prints to two decimal places as dollars and cents should print.

Powerful
Pointers

Pointers separate the *real* programmers from all the rest. Actually, some people view pointers as difficult to master, but if you've used them at all, you've probably found them to be powerful and straightforward.

The true power of pointers comes to light when you use pointers to pass arguments between functions and allocate memory dynamically on the heap. Today, you'll learn about Turbo C++ pointer manipulation, especially honing in on the differences between Turbo C++'s pointer and that of C. Most of what you already know about C pointers holds true in Turbo C++ programs with little exception.

This chapter will concentrate on pointer issues that affect object-oriented programming the most. Today, you learn about the following topics:

☐ How Turbo C++ handles void pointers

☐ What reference variables are

☐ The differences between pointer constants and pointers to constants

☐ How to declare a read-only alias to a variable

☐ The advantage of const definitions

Working with *void* Pointers

A void pointer is a pointer variable that can point to *any* data type. Some mistakenly think that a void pointer points to null zero, but a *null pointer* points to null zero. (To keep people really confused, C and C++ programmers also call the null zero *ASCII zero, binary zero,* and *terminating zero.*) Figure 4.1 helps clarify the distinction between void pointers and null pointers.

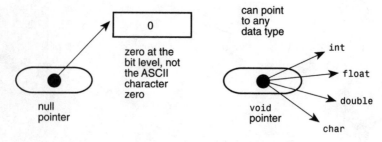

Figure 4.1. *Don't confuse* void *pointers with null pointers.*

 Note: void pointers are sometimes called *generic pointers.*

You have probably used void pointers in your C programming, but void pointers are even more important in Turbo C++ than in C. Turbo C++ is a stronger data type-checking language than C, and sometimes you'll need the freedom that void pointers allow.

You can assign any pointer variables—*other than* const or volatile pointers (volatile data is usually changeable from a source outside the program as in embedded electrical systems)—to void pointers. Turbo C++ even enables you to assign function pointers to void pointers as well, although not all C++ compilers enable you to do so.

As you know, to define a pointer, you must use the dereferencing operator to let the compiler know that you are defining a pointer and not a regular variable. For example, the following statement defines an integer:

```
int i;
```

The following statement, however, defines a *pointer* to an integer (loosely called an *integer pointer*):

```
int * ptrI;
```

As with every other kind of variable, pointers are not initialized with valid data until you store something in them. In the preceding statements, you don't know what value i or ptrI holds. To store a value in i, assign it a value, and to store a value in ptrI, assign it an address because pointers can hold only addresses of other values. The following statements store 10 in i and the address of i in ptrI:

```
i = 10;
ptrI = &i;     // & is the "address of" operator
```

The reason you have walked through this review is that defining a void pointer takes no more effort than defining a pointer of any other data type, except you use the keyword void rather than data types. The following statement defines a void pointer named vPtr:

```
void * vPtr;   // Defines a void pointer
```

Integer pointers can point *only* to integers, floating-point pointers can point *only* to floating points, and character pointers can point *only* to characters. void pointers can point to *any* data type; they don't even have to typecast to a specific data type.

Listing 4.1 defines two void pointers, an integer pointer, and a floating-point pointer. Even experienced C pointer users might have to think twice about some of the statements, especially the last two couts.

4

89

Listing 4.1. Working with several kinds of pointers.

```
1:  // Filename: LOTSPTRS.CPP
2:  // Defines several pointers and assigns them values
3:  #include <iostream.h>
4:  #include <iomanip.h>
5:  #include <conio.h>
6:  main()
7:  {
8:      clrscr();
9:      void  * vPtr1;      // Defines two void pointers
10:     void  * vPtr2;
11:     int i = 15;         // Defines a regular integer variable
12:     int   * iPtr;       // Defines an integer pointer
13:     float f = 4.68;     // Defines a regular floating-point variable
14:     float * fPtr;       // Defines a floating-point pointer
15:
16:     // Assign the pointers in several ways
17:     iPtr = &i;          // iPtr points to i
18:     fPtr = &f;          // fPtr points to f
19:     vPtr1 = &i;         // A void pointer points to an integer
20:     vPtr2 = &f;         // A void pointer points to a float
21:     vPtr1 = fPtr;       // Directly assigns a float pointer to a void
22:     vPtr1 = iPtr;       // Assign to that same void pointer an integer
23:
24:     // Print values using typecast void pointers
25:     cout << "vPtr1 points to " << *((int *)vPtr1) << "\n";
26:     cout << "vPtr2 points to " << *((float *)vPtr2) << "\n";
27:
28:     return 0;
29: }
```

```
vPtr1 points to 15
vPtr2 points to 4.68
```

Lines 17–22 show you ways to assign values to pointer variables. iPtr and fPtr are assigned the address of regular variables in lines 17 and 18. The two void pointers are assigned the address of the two regular variables in lines 19 and 20, showing that a void pointer can point to any address no matter what kind of data is stored in that address. Lines 21 and 22 also show that you can directly assign the values of pointers to void pointers.

The strange syntax (and luckily, the syntax that programmers don't use a lot!) appears in lines 25 and 26. You can assign any type of pointer to a void pointer, but when it's

time to do something with the data stored in the void pointer, you usually have to typecast that void pointer to the proper data type. It would be nice if you could print the value pointed to by vPtr1 and vPtr2 by a simple dereference like this:

```
cout << "vPtr1 points to " << *vPtr1 << "\n";
cout << "vPtr2 points to " << *vPtr2 << "\n";
```

You cannot, however, print the dereferenced simple void pointer, because Turbo C++ cannot magically read your mind and know what type of data the void pointers point to. Turbo C++ does not know how to print void pointer data. Technically, if a void pointer is pointing to an integer, Turbo C++ would have to print the two bytes pointed to by the void pointer, and if a void pointer is pointing to a floating-point value, Turbo C++ would have to print the four bytes pointed to by the void pointer. The couts cannot determine exactly how much memory to dereference by the dereference symbol alone; you must typecast the void pointer to the proper pointer data type before dereferencing. Figure 4.2 helps illustrate how the typecast works.

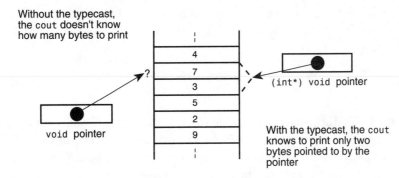

Figure 4.2. *The pointer typecast tells Turbo C++ how much memory to dereference.*

As with most convoluted expressions in Turbo C++, read the expression `*((int *)vPtr1)` from right to left and you'll understand it. The void pointer vPtr1 is typecast to an integer pointer with `(int *)`. (Without the *, you would be typecasting the pointer to a regular integer, which wouldn't work.) By typecasting, you tell Turbo C++ how much memory to dereference. After you've properly typecast the pointer, the dereference operator, *, knows to grab the integer (two bytes) at vPtr's address. Line 26 then typecasts the floating-point pointer before dereferencing it.

Don't Assign Void to Non-Void

Not only must you typecast void pointers before dereferencing them, but you must also typecast void pointers before assigning them to pointers of other data types. The following statement is invalid:

```
iPtr = vPtr1;   // Not allowed
```

As long as you typecast iPtr, you can make the assignment. This statement is OK:

```
iPtr = (int *)vPtr1;   // Allowed
```

You can, as you saw in Listing 4.1, assign regular pointer variables to void pointers. This statement is fine:

```
vPtr1 = iPtr;   // Allowed
```

When typecasting pointers, you must include the asterisk in the typecast and use the C style of typecasting. This statement is a bad typecast and is not allowed:

```
iPtr = int *(vPtr1);   // Bad typecast syntax
```

All of this discussion dealing with the assignment of void pointers to regular pointers and vice versa pertains to passing arguments between functions as well. You cannot pass a void pointer to a non-void pointer unless you typecast the void pointer to the target pointer's data type first. You can, however, pass non-void pointers to void pointers.

Note: C allows implicit conversion from a non-void to a void pointer so that malloc()'s syntax was eased a bit and you didn't *have* to typecast the return value of malloc(). You can assign a non-void pointer to a void pointer without a typecast, and C attempts to resolve the pointers. However, Turbo C++ requires that you explicitly typecast the assignment as shown in this section when assigning a non-void pointer to a void pointer. By the way, after Day 5, you'll never use malloc() again, so requiring explicit void typecasting won't present problems anyway.

DO	**DON'T**

DO use void pointers when you want to store several kinds of pointers in a single pointer throughout the program.

DO typecast void pointers before assigning them to non-void pointers or dereferencing them in any way.

DON'T typecast regular pointers before assigning them to void pointers.

DON'T confuse void pointers with null pointers. A void pointer can point to any data type, whereas a null pointer points to zero (a terminating zero).

DON'T attempt to assign a const or volatile pointer to a void pointer.

References Refer to Data

References are new to C++ and don't appear in C. It is easy to confuse pointers and references, so right off the bat, here is the best definition of a reference that you'll see: A reference is a pointer that is automatically dereferenced for you. That definition almost seems circular, but as you learn more about references, you'll see that the definition fits the term perfectly.

References are basically pointer variables. You use them like pointer variables, but references are easier to work with. Being *automatically dereferenced* means, on one level, that you don't have to use the dereference operator, *, to get to a reference's value. References also enable you to create *aliases* for other variables. The true power of references, however, appears when you pass and return references between functions.

Before going too far, you should know how to define reference variables. The following statements define a regular integer variable, a pointer to an integer variable, and a reference to an integer:

```
int i=19;            // Regular integer variable
int * iPtr = &i;     // Pointer to the integer
int & rPtr = i;      // Reference to the integer
```

Notice that you use the *address of* operator, &, to define references. The address of operator appears in the definition line just to differentiate the reference definition from other kinds of variables. In other words, the & lets the compiler know that you are defining a reference, but the & is not part of the variable name just as the * is not part of iPtr's name.

Never define a reference without initializing it. The initialization links the reference to its associated value. rPtr is now an *alias* for i, and anything you do to rPtr will be done to i (and vice versa), until you change rPtr to reference a different variable.

> **Note:** Some Turbo C++ programmers prefer to remove the spaces from between the * and & and the variable names. These two statements do the same thing as the last two statements in the preceding code:
>
> ```
> int *iPtr = &i;    // Pointer to the integer
> int &rPtr = i;     // Reference to the integer
> ```
>
> The following statements contain no spaces between the data type and the operator, which is legal as well:
>
> ```
> int* iPtr = &i;    // Pointer to the integer
> int& rPtr = i;     // Reference to the integer
> ```
>
> Use whichever style you prefer, because Turbo C++ doesn't care.

If you want to use the value of i through the iPtr pointer variable, you must dereference the pointer variable with *. If you want to use the value of i through the rPtr reference variable, you don't have to do anything special because rPtr is already dereferenced. The program in Listing 4.2 shows what happens when you change a variable and the reference to that variable.

Listing 4.2. If you change a reference, the reference's aliased variable changes also.

```
1:  // Filename: REFINTRO.CPP
2:  // Introduces references
3:  #include <iostream.h>
4:  #include <conio.h>
5:  main()
6:  {
7:    clrscr();
8:    int i=19;
9:    int *iPtr = &i;  // Pointer to the integer
10:   int &rPtr = i;   // Pointer to the reference
11:   iPtr = &i;
12:   rPtr = i;
13:   cout << "i is " << i << endl;
14:   cout << "*iPtr is " << *iPtr << endl;
15:   cout << "rPtr is " << rPtr << endl;    // rPtr is alias to i
16:   i = 25;
```

```
17:    cout << "After changing i to 25:\n";
18:    cout << "i is " << i << endl;
19:    cout << "*iPtr is " << *iPtr << endl;
20:    cout << "rPtr is " << rPtr << endl;
21:    rPtr = 100;    // Store 100 in i as well!
22:    cout << "After changing rPtr to 100:\n";
23:    cout << "i is " << i << endl;
24:    cout << "*iPtr is " << *iPtr << endl;
25:    cout << "rPtr is " << rPtr << endl;
26:    return 0;
27: }
```

Output

```
i is 19
*iPtr is 19
rPtr is 19
After changing i to 25:
i is 25
*iPtr is 25
rPtr is 25
After changing rPtr to 100:
i is 100
*iPtr is 100
rPtr is 100
```

Analysis

This output shows how a reference acts like an alias to a variable. The variable i can be changed and used in three ways: by working directly with i, by dereferencing the iPtr pointer, and by changing the reference rPtr. The reference is a pointer to i in every sense of the word except that you don't have to dereference the reference as you would a pointer. Figure 4.3 shows the computer's memory right before Listing 4.2 finishes. As Figure 4.3 shows, rPtr is more than a pointer; rPtr is an alias to i.

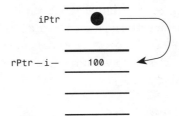

Figure 4.3. *A reference is an alias and is always attached to its variable.*

References lighten your coding burden because you don't have to include the dereferencing symbol, *, every time you use the reference's value.

A reference is always attached to a single variable. For example, if the program in Listing 4.2 contained an integer variable named j and you assigned the reference to j like

```
rPtr = j;   // Assigns the referenced i the value of j
```

you have not made rPtr a reference to j but have simply changed the value of i. As Figure 4.3 showed, the reference is an attached alias to the variable it refers to, and that attachment lasts for the entire scope of the reference variable.

You can define references to literal values and expressions, not just variables. The following reference named ref refers to the expression 8 * 7:

```
int & ref = 8 * 7;   // A reference to an expression
```

In normal expressions, Turbo C++ would discard the result of 8 * 7 as soon as its answer was used, but when you create a reference to an expression, Turbo C++ has to keep the expression around as long as the reference variable is in scope. Every time you refer to ref later, the compiler must give you the value of 8 * 7. In effect, you have a pointer to an expression.

When you reference an expression as done with ref here, Turbo C++ issues the following warning message:

```
Temporary used to initialize 'ref'
```

The warning is informational letting you know that Turbo C++ had to evaluate the expression and then attach the reference to the result. The result had to be placed in a temporary memory location that will go away when the reference goes out of scope. There is no way to change the value of 8 * 7, even if you assign ref a new value. When you change ref, you'll be changing the temporary value.

The temporary value used to initialize references plays an important role when defining a reference of one data type and then associating that reference to a different data type. Turbo C++ has to convert the value being referenced to the same data type of the reference. To clarify how Turbo C++ creates temporary values for some references, study Listing 4.3.

Listing 4.3. Turbo C++ sometimes has to create temporary values.

```
1:  // Filename: REFTYPES.CPP
2:  // Defining an integer reference for a double variable
3:  #include <iostream.h>
4:  #include <conio.h>
5:  main()
```

```
6:  {
7:     clrscr();
8:     double sales = 5123.43;  // A regular double variable
9:     int & iref = sales;         // Temporary result generated
10:    cout << "sales is " << sales << "\n";
11:    cout << "iref is " << iref << "\n";
12:    iref = 26;                  // sales does not change!
13:    cout << "After the assignment to iref:\n";
14:    cout << "sales is " << sales << "\n";
15:    cout << "iref is " << iref << "\n";
16:    return 0;
17: }
```

```
sales is 5123.43
iref is 5123
After the assignment to iref:
sales is 5123.43
iref is 26
```

Line 9 produces the warning message saying that Turbo C++ had to create a temporary value for initializing `iref`. The temporary value comes from the typecast value of `sales`. `sales` is `double`, so `iref` could not be a reference to `sales`. Turbo C++ created an integer from `sales` and stored that integer in an integer location (the *temporary* location). Line 9 simply produces a reference to a value, `sales`.

In effect, `iref` is no longer a true reference. `iref` refers *not* to `sales`, but to the temporary integer created from `sales`. That integer will be around as long as `iref` is in scope, but as shown in line 14, changing `iref` will not change `sales`.

Now that you understand references, you might be asking yourself why you need them. After all, pointers still work as usual in Turbo C++. And pointers seem to have the advantage over references in that you can make pointers point to different memory locations whereas references are always fixed to their original referenced location. The advantage that references provide is that you can use them as pointers without dereferencing them *when passing and returning parameters* from one function to another. Day 6's chapter, "Communicating with Functions," will show you how to streamline Turbo C++ functions using references.

Defining References

dataType refName & expression

dataType is any intrinsic data type such as `int` or `float`, or a user-defined data type created with `struct`, `union`, `enum`, or `class`. *refName* is any valid variable name, and *expression* is the variable or expression you want to reference.

Example

```
// Filename: REFSYN.CPP
// Illustrates a reference to a variable and expression
#include <iostream.h>
#include <iomanip.h>
#include <conio.h>
main()
{
  clrscr();
  float value = 123.45;      // Regular floating-point
  float value2 = 87.12;      // 2nd regular float
  float & ref1 = value;      // Reference to value
  float & ref2 = 45 * 2.123; // Reference to expression
  cout << setprecision(2);
  cout << setiosflags(ios::showpoint);
  cout << "value is " << value << "\n";
  cout << "ref1 is also " << ref1 << "\n";
  cout << "ref2 is an alias to an expression: " << ref2 << "\n";
  ref1 = value2;
  cout << "Both value and ref1 now refer to " << value << "\n";
  return 0;
}
```

DO   DON'T

DO define a reference using the & operator.

DO use a reference as an automatically dereferenced pointer.

DO use references for pointers to pointers in order to ease the complicated double-dereferencing syntax needed when pointing to pointers or arrays.

DON'T define a reference without initializing it at the same time.

DON'T ever dereference a reference variable with *. References are automatically dereferenced, and Turbo C++ generates an error if you attempt to dereference a reference variable.

DON'T use references just for aliasing variables. Although a reference in effect gives you a second name to the same variable, calling the same variable two different names can create interesting debugging sessions. The true advantage of references appears when you use references for passing and returning parameters shown in Day 6's chapter.

Constants Stay *const*

A constant defined with const remains constant, and Turbo C++ makes sure of it. Turbo C++ protects the programmer better than C did. Look at the program in Listing 4.4 that attempts to change a const value through a pointer.

Listing 4.4. There's no way to change a const value through a pointer.

```
1:  // Filename: CONSTPTR.CPP
2:  // Turbo C++ doesn't let you change constants
3:  #include <iostream.h>
4:  #include <conio.h>
5:  main()
6:  {
7:    clrscr();
8:    const int minAge = 18;   // A constant integer
9:    int * agePtr;            // An integer pointer
10:   agePtr = & minAge;       // Error happens here
11:   return 0;
12: }
```

If you attempt to compile Listing 4.4's program, Turbo C++ displays the following error message:

```
Cannot convert 'const int _ss *' to 'int *'
```

This fancy error message is Turbo C++'s attempt at trying to associate a regular pointer to a constant value. Only pointers to const can point to const values.

Note: Turbo C++ will enable you to typecast away a const, but be careful if you do so and question yourself three times before doing such a thing. If you find yourself typecasting away a const, perhaps the value should not have been const to begin with.

Why do you think Turbo C++ does now allow line 10? Such code would allow for sneaky manipulation of a const value. For example, you already know not to change minAge because it is a const value. You could never attempt this:

```
minAge = 16;    // Cannot change a const
```

Turbo C++ knows that if you could make a pointer variable point to a const value, you could change the const through the pointer. If line 10 in Listing 4.4 were allowed, you could change the const like this:

```
*agePtr = 16;    // Thankfully, Turbo C++ guards against this!
```

To help clarify pointers and constants further, the next section describes everything you ever wanted to know about pointers and constants—but were afraid to code.

Don't Forget Constant Arrays

If you define an array and want to keep the rest of the program (or another programmer who might maintain the program) from changing the array, use const when you define the array. The following statement defines a constant array of integers:

```
const int monthDays[] = {31, 28, 31, 30, 31, 30, 31, 31,
   30, 31, 30, 31};
```

Throughout the rest of the program, you can use the array, but you can never change the array with statements such as this:

```
monthDays[2] = 31;    // Not allowed
```

Turbo C++ will not even compile the program if you attempt to change one of the array elements.

---

const Used with Pointers and References

You will find that Turbo C++ programmers use const more faithfully than C programmers do. Turbo C++ programmers are more accustomed to C++'s strictness; using const for values that don't change clarifies code and makes the intent of the constants better known. As mentioned in Day 2's chapter, "C++ Is Superior!" Turbo C++ programmers use const rather than #define, so const is seen more by Turbo C++ programmers, and they are more accustomed to using it than many C programmers are.

Nevertheless, using the const keyword can add confusion for programmers just beginning to use it. When mixing pointers, constants, and references, newcomers to Turbo C++ programming can get confused enough to eliminate the const keyword

from their programs when the compiler starts complaining too much. Removing const is not a good solution to compiler errors and warnings. Learning how to use const with pointers is easy and a better approach.

There are three combinations of pointers and const value:

☐ Pointers to constants

☐ Constant pointers

☐ Constant pointers to constants

All of these items are different to Turbo C++, but they sometimes seem to run together for people using them. The following sections explain them one at a time.

Pointers to Constants

A *pointer to constant* is just that: a pointer variable points to a const value. In the section called "Constants Stay const," you learned that you cannot directly assign a pointer variable to a const, but you can use the const keyword to do so. Using const tells the compiler that you are aware of the const but still want to point to the const with the pointer. The compiler will enable you to point to a constant as long as you specify const when defining the pointer like this:

```
const minAge = 18;              // Regular constant
const int * aPtrAge = minAge;   // Pointer to a constant
```

Always read variable definitions from right to left starting at the equal sign. This definition of aPtrAge tells Turbo C++ this:

> *"Define a variable named* aPtrAge *that points to an integer constant.*
> *Initialize* aPtrAge *by making it point to* minAge."

Without const, Turbo C++ would not enable you to define aPtrAge because the compiler fears that you might try something like this:

```
*aPtrAge = 16;   // Not allowed
```

With const, however, you are making a commitment to Turbo C++ that you will never change the constant that the pointer points to, and if you try to, the compiler complains and does not allow it.

Figure 4.4 shows the computer's memory being defined by aPtrAge. The bold box around minAge indicates that minAge is a constant and cannot be changed.

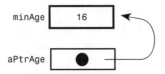

Figure 4.4. *aPtrAge can change but minAge cannot, even through the pointer.*

You *can* change the value of aPtrAge! aPtrAge is a regular pointer variable, but it just happens that aPtrAge points to a constant. aPtrAge is a pointer *to* a constant, not a *constant pointer.* This statement is allowed in the program:

```
aPtrAge = & newAge;    // Changes aPtrAge
```

However, you can never change that value pointed to by aPtrAge using aPtrAge.

Note: You can use pointers to constants as lvalues, but you cannot use *dereferenced* pointers to constants as lvalues. An lvalue is a variable that cannot be changed.

Technically, aPtrAge does not have to point to a constant, but Turbo C++ acts as though any value pointed to by aPtrAge is a constant. Listing 4.5 shows a regular integer pointed to by a pointer to a constant.

Listing 4.5. **You can change the integer, but not with the pointer.**

```
1:  // Filename: REGCONST.CPP
2:  // A regular integer that acts like a constant when pointed to
3:  #include <iostream.h>
4:  #include <conio.h>
5:  main()
6:  {
7:    clrscr();
8:    int i = 7;
9:    const int * pi = &i;
10:   cout << "*pi is " << *pi << "\n";
11:   // Now change the integer but not with the pointer.
12:   // You could NEVER do this:
13:   // *pi = 18;
14:   i = 18;
15:   cout << "*pi is now " << *pi << "\n";
16:   return 0;
17: }
```

```
*pi is 7
*pi is now 18
```

Although line 9 defines a pointer to an integer constant, the integer i is not really an integer constant. Nevertheless, Turbo C++ learns in line 9 that you'll never attempt to change i through pi (as shown in lines 11–13). You can change i as done in line 14, however, because i is a regular integer variable.

Constant Pointers

Just as the name implies, a *constant pointer* never changes—but the value that it points to can change. As with all constants, you have to initialize a constant pointer when you define it, or you'll never have another chance because constants can never change.

Here is the definition of a constant pointer:

```
int age = 20;              // Regular integer
int * const pAge = &age;   // Pointer constant
```

Notice that the keyword const appears on the right side of the * whereas it appeared on the left when defining pointers to constants. Reading from right to left before the equal sign, the second statement tells Turbo C++ that you want this:

> *"Define a variable named* pAge *that is a constant pointer to an integer. Initialize the pointer constant with the address of* age.*"*

age can change because age is not a constant. However, you can do nothing to change pAge, or Turbo C++ will complain. By creating a constant pointer, you have created a fixed pointer that can never move even though the data it points to might change. Figure 4.5 shows memory after the previous definitions are in place.

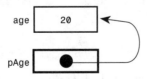

Figure 4.5. age *can change but* pAge *cannot.*

Sometimes, *embedded* Turbo C++ programmers use constant pointers to change external events. Embedded programs often control non-computer devices. For instance, the computer inside your car is controlled by a program. The program is burned into the computer's ROM (*read-only memory*), and the program controls external devices attached to the car's computer. The devices throughout the car, such as the transmission sensor, are attached to actual memory locations in the computer chip's memory. The sensor wire's location leading from the transmission never changes, but its signal can change. The program would contain a constant pointer to that sensor's location. Through the pointer, the program could read and set the sensor wire's signal, but the pointer's address would never change because the location of the sensor wire would never change.

Note: An array name is a constant pointer. You cannot use an array name as an lvalue, but you can change the contents of an array. An array name is just a constant pointer that points to the first element in an array. If you want to reserve heap memory (as shown in tomorrow's chapter) and use that heap memory as if it were an array, point to the heap with a constant pointer.

Constant Pointers to Constants

The epitome of constants (and confusion) appears when you define constant pointers to constant values. There is nothing inherently difficult in the concept of constant pointers to constants; they simply form a combination of the previous two subjects: pointers to constants and constant pointers.

A constant pointer to a constant is a pointer that cannot change pointing to a value that cannot change. To define a constant pointer to a constant, you must first define the constant and then define the constant pointer. The following statements define an integer constant named ic and a constant pointer to that integer constant named pc:

```
const int ic = 10;              // A constant
const int const * pc = & ic;   // Constant pointer to a constant
```

The second statement tells Turbo C++ this:

"Define a variable named pc *that is a constant pointer to an integer constant. Initialize the pointer constant with the address of* ic*."*

Figure 4.6 shows how Turbo C++ defines ic and pc.

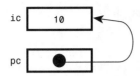

Figure 4.6. *Defining a constant pointer to a constant.*

As with the previous figures, Figure 4.6's dark boxes indicate memory that cannot change. Nothing you do in code can change the value of pc; you cannot make pc point to any other address in memory, which means that pc can never be an lvalue. Neither can you change the integer constant ic.

Actually, ic doesn't have to be defined as a constant. In the definition

```
int ic = 10;                      // A regular integer
const int const * pc = & ic;  // Constant pointer to a constant
```

ic is a regular variable. However, the second statement tells the compiler that you will never attempt to change pc and that you will never attempt to change ic through the pointer named pc.

DO	DON'T

DO use const for safety to protect those values that should not change.

DON'T ever attempt to change a const value through a pointer.

DON'T ever attempt to change a const pointer after it is defined.

DON'T ever attempt to change a const pointer *or* the const it points to if you define a constant pointer to a constant.

Read-Only Aliases

Closely related to constant pointers are *read-only aliases.* A read-only alias is a reference to a constant value. Earlier in this chapter, you learned how to create references to variables and use either the reference or the variable name to change the value in the variable. When you create a read-only reference, you can change the variable but not with the reference.

The following statements define one integer variable named iv and a read-only alias reference to that variable named rv:

```
int iv = 25;          // Regular integer variable
const int & rv = iv;  // Read-only alias
```

Turbo C++ enables you to change iv as long as you use the variable's actual name. However, the reference is a reference to a constant. Even though iv is not really a constant, the second statement tells this to Turbo C++:

> *"Define a reference named rv to the constant named iv. I will never use the reference to change iv because I am defining a reference to a constant (a read-only reference)."*

The following statement stores 89 in iv:

```
iv = 89;
```

If you want to print the value of iv, you can use either the variable or its reference. Both of the following statements print 89:

```
cout << iv << "\n";
cout << rv << "\n";
```

You cannot change iv through the reference, however, as you would be able to do if rv were a regular integer reference. Turbo C++ will not enable you to do this:

```
rv = 45;   // You cannot use rv as an lvalue!
```

Advantageous Constants

const values are always constant...unless you override their "constantness" with typecasting. Programmers often create constants to protect the program's variables from themselves as much as other programmers who might come along later and maintain the program.

Defining a value as constant creates a contract between you and Turbo C++. Without using tricky typecasts, you cannot break your end of the contract, and Turbo C++ will never enable you to change a constant value.

If somebody wants to come along later and remove const from your data's definition, the programmer then has the freedom to change the value as much as he or she wants to. Therefore, you can do nothing to ensure that your const data remain constant, but const is a very strong suggestion.

When you explicitly define a value as constant, you put the burden of constant-checking onto Turbo C++'s back—where it belongs. Being able to catch errors at compile time is much more productive than trying to find errors that show up at runtime. Runtime errors produce incorrect results that you must trace, but the errors generated at compile time are much easier to fix. When you enter into a contract with Turbo C++ and define a variable as constant, and then you break that contract by trying to change the constant, Turbo C++ catches the error before your program finishes compiling.

Summary

Today's chapter has been a data-oriented chapter with an emphasis on references and constants. If you pick up virtually any C++ book or magazine, you'll see references defined and used all the time. A reference is an automatically dereferenced pointer. Unlike with pointers, you never have to dereference a reference variable.

A reference is an alias to another variable. You can use either the name of the variable or the name of the reference, and you'll be printing or changing the same value. Most Turbo C++ programmers don't define references for aliases; instead, Turbo C++ programmers define references to help clarify their pointer usage and the passing and returning of parameters between functions, as you'll see in future daily lessons.

As you saw on a previous day, #define is used much less frequently in C++ than in C. Many Turbo C++ programmers have eliminated all #define preprocessor directives from their programs. The replacement, const, is often misunderstood when used with pointers and references.

When you want to point to a constant but not change the constant through the pointer, create a pointer to the constant. When you want a pointer to point to the same place in memory at all times, define a constant pointer. When you want both—a constant pointer that never changes pointing to data that cannot change—define a constant pointer to a constant.

There is a special kind of reference you can create that generates read-only aliases. When you define a reference to a constant, you define a read-only alias. You can read the value being aliased with the alias name, but you cannot change the value via the alias name. You can always change the variable using its original name as long as the variable is not defined with const.

4

Q&A

1. What is a `void` pointer?

   A `void` pointer is a pointer that can point to *any* data type. Non-`void` pointers such as `int` pointers and `float` pointers can point only to `ints` and `floats`, respectively. `void` pointers are generic; you can assign a `void` pointer the address of any data type.

2. What is a reference?

   Simply stated, a reference is a pointer that is always dereferenced. A reference closely resembles a pointer, and you can use a reference anywhere you would use a dereferenced pointer. A reference acts like an alias, a second name for a variable.

   Aliases aren't the primary reason for using references. References simplify programming because they eliminate the need for the dereferencing operator, `*`, and they simplify the passing and returning of parameters between functions, as you'll see in Day 6's chapter, "Communicating with Functions."

3. How do I define a reference?

   Use the address of operator, `&`, to define a reference. Because a reference closely resembles a pointer, you usually create a reference that points to a value of the same data type. In other words, you could create an `int` reference to a `float`, but Turbo C++ does not generate a true reference when you do. (Turbo C++ creates a reference to an integer temporarily created from the `float`.)

   To define a reference to a `char` variable named `c`, you would use this statement:

   ```
   char & rc = c;    // rf is a reference to c
   ```

   You must initialize a reference when you define it. Turbo C++ will not enable you to use this statement:

   ```
   char & rc;        // Not allowed
   ```

4. What is the difference between a constant pointer and a pointer to a constant?

   A constant pointer cannot be changed. Therefore, you cannot redirect a constant pointer to a different memory location from its original value when you defined it. A pointer to a constant is just that—a pointer variable that points to a value that cannot change. You can redirect the pointer to any other memory location that you want, but you cannot change the memory location through the pointer.

Combining a constant pointer with a pointer to a constant creates the most solid of all data ties possible in Turbo C++; a constant pointer to a constant is a pointer that cannot change pointing to a value that cannot change.

5. What is a read-only alias?

   In Turbo C++, an alias is a reference. A read-only alias is a reference to a constant. More accurately, a read-only alias is a reference defined as if it were pointing to a constant, but in reality, the value being referenced was not defined with const. You can use the reference name to retrieve the reference's value, but you must use the variable's original name to change the value stored in the variable.

6. How does the use of const clarify my code?

   By specifying const for every variable in your program that will not change (including arguments when you receive them), you protect yourself from inadvertently changing those variables. You also help ensure that other programmers who might later maintain your program doesn't inadvertently change values that shouldn't change.

   When you violate the contract of const values by trying to change a const, Turbo C++ issues an error when you compile the program. Fixing compile-time errors is much easier than debugging program errors at runtime.

Workshop

The Workshop offers quiz questions and exercises to hone your skills and give you feedback on today's lesson. You'll find some proposed answers in Appendix D.

Quiz

1. True or false: The following statement defines a pointer variable and a reference variable:

```
char * pPtr;
char & rPtr;
```

2. How would you change the value of i through a reference variable named `ri`?

3. Each of the following v variable definitions fits into one of the following categories:

    1. Regular integer variable

    2. Constant integer variable

    3. Reference to an integer

    4. Pointer to an integer

    5. Pointer to an integer constant

    6. Constant pointer to an integer

    7. Constant pointer to a constant integer

    8. Read-only alias

Which of these descriptions best fits the following definitions?

    A. `const int v = 9;`

    B. `const int * v = &anotherInt;`

    C. `int * const v = &anotherInt;`

    D. `const int const * v = &anotherInt;`

    E. `int v = anotherInt;`

    F. `int & v = anotherInt;`

    G. `const int & v = anotherInt;`

    H. `int * i = &anotherInt;`

4. True or false: The following statement initializes a `void` pointer:

```
ptr = 0;
```

Exercises

1. Write a program that initializes a regular integer array with the days in each of the 12 months in each element. (Ignore leap years.) After defining and initializing the array, create a constant pointer that points to the first element of the array. Write a loop that prints the elements of the array by using the constant pointer, not by using the array name.

2. Write a program that defines, initializes, and prints the value of each of these:

☐ Integer constant variable

☐ Reference to an integer

☐ Read-only alias

☐ Pointer to an integer

☐ Pointer to an integer constant

☐ Constant pointer to an integer

☐ Constant pointer to a integer constant

4

Memory Allocation: There When You Need It

Dynamic memory allocation enables you to use as much or as little memory as you need. Not only that, but you can get the memory or release it whenever your program is ready for it.

If you have done much C programming, you are accustomed to using the `malloc()` and `free()` functions to allocate and deallocate memory. `malloc()` (as with all its related functions such as `calloc()` and `realloc()`) requires practice and is prone to programmer errors because of its cryptic nature.

Turbo C++ programmers don't use `malloc()` and `free()` because Turbo C++ includes two new operators, `new` and `delete`, that take the place of `malloc()` and `free()`, respectively. `new` and `delete` are extremely easy to use and do much more behind-the-scenes work than their corresponding functions.

If you never learn the OOP parts of Turbo C++, you will probably still switch to Turbo C++ when you see how easy and powerful `new` and `delete` are. When you master OOP, however, you'll see how to use `new` and `delete` to work with objects, and you will even learn to write your own memory-allocation operators using `new` and `delete`. Today, you learn about the following topics:

- ☐ How to allocate memory with `new`

- ☐ How to deallocate memory with `delete`

- ☐ How to allocate arrays and matrixes on the heap

- ☐ How to write event-driven programs that automatically check for allocation errors using Turbo C++'s exception handling routine

Note: Although the words `new` and `delete` do not look like regular operators such as + and *, they are operators in the same way that `sizeof()` is an operator even though `sizeof()` often looks and acts like a built-in function.

new to Allocate, *delete* to Eliminate

As with most of the C functions, Turbo C++ supports the `malloc()` and `free()` functions if you want to use them, but there is little reason for either function in Turbo C++ programs. `malloc()` and `free()` are cumbersome and require detailed syntax. To use `malloc()` properly, you must include the STDLIB.H header file and always typecast the return pointer from `malloc()` to a data type pointer that you are working with.

`malloc()` returns a `void` pointer, and as you learned from the preceding day's chapter, you must typecast all `void` pointers before doing much with them—`malloc()`'s return value is no exception.

`malloc()` becomes especially difficult when you have to allocate an array of structures on the heap. Here is a `malloc()` function call that allocates 75 structure variables named `players` on the heap:

```
players = (struct players *)malloc(75 * sizeof(struct players));
```

Turbo C++ does not require the repetition of the `struct` keyword that is shown here, which offers a slight improvement over C's `malloc()`, but that improvement by itself doesn't justify changing to `new`. The other drawbacks of `malloc()` discussed in this chapter justify using `new` rather than `malloc()` because `new` and Turbo C++ take much of the work off your back.

How Important Is Allocation, Really?

Every day, computer memory and disk space are getting cheaper and more abundant. Whereas 256K was considered plenty of room a short time ago, 4 *megabytes* of memory is considered squeezing things today.

Many PC computer systems come equipped with 8 to 16 megabytes of RAM and hundreds of megabytes of disk space. With disk-doubling technologies and with the prices of RAM decreasing as fast as the density of RAM increases, you might tend to think that memory allocation problems would go away; after all, when you've got *tons* of memory and you use only a fraction of it, why bother with allocating memory for variables? Why not just use local variables and not worry about freeing the memory later in the program?

Experts agree that more memory in your systems requires even *more* reason to allocate memory when and only when you need it. With more powerful computer systems, people use more powerful programs, especially networked, windowing, multitasking, and multi-user computers and programs. As soon as your program begins sharing the same resource space (especially memory) with another task, memory becomes a premium, and both tasks

5

need all they can get to maintain speed and functionality. If your program needs a large amount of memory for a short time, your program should use memory only during that time and free that memory for other tasks which might need the memory next.

Given that memory allocation is more important than ever, a good case can be made for learning Turbo C++'s easy memory allocation operators, new and delete.

To summarize Turbo C++'s memory allocation operators, keep the following two points in mind as you read the rest of this chapter:

new is Turbo C++'s heap allocation operator replacement for the malloc() function.

delete is Turbo C++'s heap deallocation operator replacement for the free() function.

The Concept of Memory Allocation

It might be prudent to review the process of dynamic memory allocation briefly so that all readers will be on common ground. The heap is a large chunk of unused memory in your PC (see Figure 5.1). The size of the heap changes when you (or another task running such as MS-DOS or Windows) allocate variables and deallocate variables.

Note: The word *dynamic* means changing, so *dynamic memory allocation* refers to the changing heap size as you allocate and deallocate memory.

Some people mistakenly believe that using local variables eliminates the need for dynamic memory allocation. After all, the variables go into scope when needed, and when they are no longer needed (when their block ends), they go out of scope and are no longer available.

Local variables are no longer visible when they go out of scope, but they still consume memory for the life of the program. When you run a Turbo C++ program, the program loader makes room for all global *and* local variables needed in the program. The

local variables are reserved on the *stack* (an area of memory that changes somewhat like the heap but on a smaller scale), and the global variable space is already attached to your executable program. (Turbo C++ actually appends global variable space to your executable program, which is one reason why programs with global variables take more disk space than the same program with fewer or no global variables.)

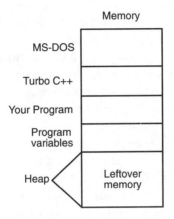

Figure 5.1. *The heap is memory left over after DOS, Turbo C++, and your program take all they need.*

Given this background, you'll understand why learning about dynamic memory allocation is so critical. Although you should use local variables as much as possible, they do not improve your use of memory during runtime.

You would never want to allocate *every* variable on the heap. And in reality, you couldn't allocate every variable on the heap because you have to define nonheap pointers that point to heap data to get to the heap's data. Most arrays are perfect candidates for heap allocation because you rarely use every element in every array throughout an entire program. Using dynamic memory allocation, you can grab more array elements from the heap when you need them and put them back when you are through with them.

Note: Some fixed arrays, such as day-of-the-week names, are better left as local arrays (and arguably global arrays, but only if you use them throughout many functions). Dynamic memory allocation is fairly efficient, but it is still less efficient than allocating local and global arrays. Small arrays that don't change in size are best left as regular arrays.

Memory Allocation: There When You Need It

Memory that you allocate is available to your program just like variables are, except that you can only point to allocated memory, not assign names to heap memory as you do with regular variables. As a matter of fact, dynamic memory allocation is perhaps the most important reason for learning about pointers in the first place; you can't access the heap without pointers.

It helps to think of the heap as a pile of memory, not a sequential listing of memory as it is in reality. When you deallocate memory, your program releases the data from the reserved heap and puts that memory back to the heap so that another process (either your program or another such as the operating system) can get to that memory when needed. The reason it helps to view the heap as a big pile of memory is that when you deallocate memory, you must assume that you no longer know where that memory is. In other words, if you deallocate memory (with `delete` or `free()`), for a few microseconds and maybe longer that memory will probably still be at the same place on the heap with the values you left in it. However, you must assume that the memory is no longer where you first allocated it because another task could have taken the memory as soon as you released it. That's the entire idea of deallocating anyway— the memory is thrown back to the free heap (sometimes called the *free store*) so that the resource is given back to other tasks that might need it.

Figure 5.2 shows three kinds of data allocated on the heap. A character array, an integer, and a floating-point value are all allocated. Notice that pointers (through dereferencing) are the only means for getting to the heap values.

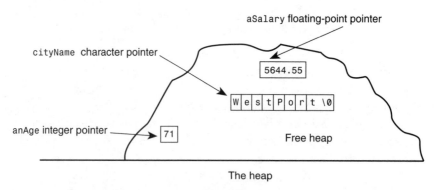

Figure 5.2. *After allocating three kinds of data.*

When you deallocate heap memory, your pointers are, in effect, disconnected from the heap, and the heap manager knows to give up the freed portion of the heap if another process wants it.

Note: Don't ever mix new and `free()`, or `malloc()` and `delete`. Although some combinations seem to work, the results are unpredictable and could wreak havoc in large programs. If you allocate with `malloc()`, use `free()` to deallocate; if you allocate with new, use `delete` to deallocate.

Specifying *new* for a Heap of Memory

When you allocate with new, you don't have to typecast the return pointer. Turbo C++ is smart enough to determine the right kind of pointer you need.

Suppose that you want to allocate a new integer on the heap. First, you must define an integer pointer such as this:

```
int * anAge;    // Define an integer pointer
```

Then you must allocate the heap memory. To tell Turbo C++ that you want a new integer from the heap and you want anAge to point to that integer, you can use this statement:

```
anAge = new int;    // Allocates a new integer
```

Notice why you don't need a typecast: The int keyword tells Turbo C++ exactly what kind of heap data you want. You can combine the pointer definition with the heap allocation in one statement if you want memory allocated close to the pointer's definition like this:

```
int * anAge = new int;    // Defines pointer and allocates heap
```

Because you can define variables anywhere in a Turbo C++ program (as long as you define them before using them), you don't have to allocate a heap pointer way ahead of the time you want it.

To define a floating-point pointer and allocate a `float` value on the heap, you can use this statement:

```
float * aSalary = new float;  // Define and allocate pointer
```

Of course, allocating single variables isn't that beneficial; the pointers to the data take almost as much space as the integers and floating-point values themselves do. However, when allocating arrays, you can allocate as many elements as you like and still point to the elements with a regular pointer like this:

```
char * cityName = new char[9];   // Allocate a character array
```

To allocate an array, simply put the number of array elements (including room for the null zero if you allocate a character array that will hold a string) in brackets after the data type. Turbo C++ will reserve that many elements (if the free heap has a large enough space for the array at the time of the new).

After the preceding three definitions are completed, you'll have the heap reserved like the one you saw in Figure 5.2. The following three statements initialize the heap memory to Figure 5.2's values:

```
*anAge = 17;         // Use dereferencing to initialize
*aSalary = 5644.55;  // the values on the heap
strcpy(cityName, "Westport");
```

Note: The heap is not automatically initialized for you, so be sure to initialize the heap with data yourself.

The program in Listing 5.1 allocates strings for as long as the user wants to enter new names. The program does not free the allocated memory, but it should. The program relies on DOS to take care of putting memory back to normal when the program ends. When you learn the details of delete a little later in the chapter, you'll see how to properly deallocate memory. (In other words, this program is to illustrate new, but it stinks when it comes to cleaning up after itself. As a master Turbo C++ programmer, you'll *always* deallocate heap memory when you finish with it, even if the last line in the program contains a delete.)

 Listing 5.1. Allocating strings for the user's input.

```
1:  // Filename: NAMENEW.CPP
2:  // Allocates strings on the heap
3:  #include <iostream.h>
4:  #include <string.h>
5:  #include <conio.h>
6:  main()
7:  {
8:    clrscr();
9:    const int MAX = 50;    // We'll hold up to 50 names on heap
10:   char inputName[80];    // A place to hold name entered
11:   // Each of the names[] pointers will point to a different name
12:   char * names[MAX];
13:   cout << "** Name Entering Program **\n";
14:   for (int num=0; num<MAX; num++)
```

```
15:   { cout << "Please enter a name (End quits) --> ";
16:     cin.getline(inputName, 80); // Get a string up to 80 characters
17:     if (!stricmp(inputName,"END"))   // Continue only if not END
18:       { break; }
19:     // The following statement does a lot of work. It allocates
20:     // just enough characters to hold the name entered by the user
21:     // along with a null zero at the end of the string.
22:     names[num] = new char[strlen(inputName)+1];
23:     // Copy the entered name to the heap
24:     strcpy(names[num], inputName);
25:   }
26:   cout << "\nHere are the names you entered:\n";
27:   for (int j=0; j<num; j++)
28:    { cout << names[j] << "\n"; }
29:   return 0;
30: }
```

```
** Name Entering Program **
Please enter a name (End quits) --> Sam Spade
Please enter a name (End quits) --> Doc Savage
Please enter a name (End quits) --> Steve Austin
Please enter a name (End quits) --> Heath Barkley
Please enter a name (End quits) --> end

Here are the names you entered:
Sam Spade
Doc Savage
Steve Austin
Heath Barkley
```

This program asks for up to 50 names. (You can easily increase the maximum number of names by changing the MAX constant in line 9 to a different value.) One character array is defined in line 10 to hold the user's input of each name. After the user enters a name, strlen() determines the length of the name. The result is then sent to the new operation on line 22 to allocate enough heap memory for that string plus one for the string terminator. When the user types end (in either uppercase or lowercase because stricmp() is not case-sensitive), the program stops asking for user input and allocates the strings on the heap.

Figure 5.3 shows what the strings look like when the program allocates them given the output just shown. Each element in the character pointer array called names points to a different string on the heap. As Figure 5.3 shows, the strings don't necessarily appear on the heap in the order in which they were allocated.

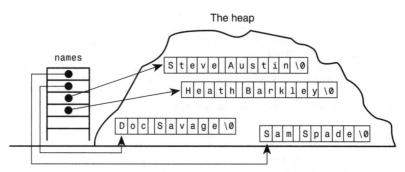

Figure 5.3. *The look of the heap after allocating the user's strings.*

 Note: Notice on line 28 that you don't dereference character pointers when printing them with cout. All strings are passed as pointers to the operators, and Turbo C++ knows to dereference the pointer for you.

Initializing While Allocating

If you want to specify an initial value for your allocated data, Turbo C++ supports a special syntax that enables you to. You can initialize the allocated heap memory with a value only when you allocate the memory.

To initialize heap memory at the time you allocate it, enclose the initial value inside parentheses at the right of the statement with new. For example, to initialize an integer value you are allocating on the heap, you can use this statement:

```
int * myVal = new int (0);  // Allocates and initializes
```

Turbo C++ puts a zero in the myVal on the heap. Initializing with the parenthetical value is similar to using calloc(), except that calloc() always initializes with zero and you can initialize with any value you want when using new.

 Note: The initialization syntax looks strange, but it works efficiently and is better than using an assignment later to initialize the value on the heap.

You cannot automatically initialize array values on the heap. Later in the book, you'll see how to write your own array initialization new operator. (Yes, in Turbo C++, you can change the way operators work with your data!)

The program in Listing 5.2 shows several kinds of values being allocated on the heap, and all are initialized at the time of their allocation. As with the program in Listing 5.1, the allocated memory is not freed as it should be (putting the burden on DOS's back). But the next section will demonstrate how to free heap memory properly with Turbo C++.

 Listing 5.2. **Allocating and initializing heap data.**

```
1:  // Filename: ALLINIT.CPP
2:  // Allocates and initializes several values on the heap
3:  #include <iostream.h>
4:  #include <conio.h>
5:  main()
6:  {
7:    clrscr();
8:    // Allocate single data values
9:    char * cPtr = new char ('X');
10:   int * iPtr = new int (0);
11:   float * fPtr = new float(1.1);
12:   double * dVal = new double (12345.678);
13:   // Print the values to show the initialization
14:   cout << "cPtr is " << cPtr <<
   ➥"\n"; // Don't dereference char pointers
15:   cout << "iPtr is " << *iPtr << "\n";
16:   cout << "fPtr is " << *fPtr << "\n";
17:   cout << "dVal is " << *dVal << "\n";
18:   return 0;
19: }
```

```
cPtr is X
iPtr is 0
fPtr is 1.1
dVal is 12345.678
```

 As you can see in lines 9 through 12, you can initialize any kind of heap data with any value you want at the time of the allocation.

Syntax

Using *new*

```
pointerVar = new datatype [ [numElements] ] [ (initialVal) ]
```

The brackets within brackets indicate that the number of elements is optional if you want to allocate an array on the heap. If you do allocate an array, you must specify the initial number of elements in the array, and you must enclose the number of elements within brackets. You must enclose the initial value in parentheses, and you cannot specify an initial value if you allocate an array on the heap.

Example

```
// Examples of using the new operator
main()
{
  // Allocate single data values
  char * cPtr1 = new char;  // Allocate without initialization
  int * iPtr1 = new int;
  float * fPtr1 = new float;
  // Allocate with initialization
  char * cPtr2 = new char('a');
  int * iPtr2 = new int(40);
  float * fPtr2 = new float(-5.7);
  // Allocate arrays of any data type
  char * cAra = new char [100];
  int * iAra = new int [60];
  float * fAra = new float [35];
  // Be sure to deallocate when you are done with the data
  // Rest of program would follow
```

Deallocating with *delete*

The delete operator deallocates memory allocated with new just as the free() function deallocates memory allocated with malloc(). To free memory, simply list the pointer's name of the allocated memory after delete. For example, the following statement deallocates a section of the heap pointed to by aPtr:

```
delete aPtr;  // Give the memory back to the heap
```

When you delete heap memory, the size of the free heap expands by the amount of the deleted memory (along with a little extra for overhead). When you delete memory, you release that memory back to the heap so that other tasks running will have access to the heap.

The Heap Is Efficient—But Not Perfect

As you allocate and deallocate, fragmented holes can begin to appear in your heap and slow down tasks that use the heap. Turbo C++ does not defrag-ment the heap (by collecting all the unused holes of memory into a contiguous chunk at the end of the heap), because doing so would slow down a running program greatly during the heap's clean-up process.

Heap fragmentation occurs if you allocate and deallocate lots of small chunks of heap memory. Although you'll rarely notice that heap fragmenta-tion is occurring, you could reach a point at which you have heap memory left but cannot allocate any more because there is not one single block of free heap left as large as you want to allocate. Figure 5.4 shows how the heap can become cluttered with small chunks of free memory that used to be allocated.

Through the years, C and C++ programmers have offered solutions to heap fragmentation. If you plan to allocate and deallocate hundreds of small blocks from the heap, consider allocating one big chunk and using an array of your own pointers within that heap memory to simulate allocation for the rest of the program. Doing so is not a trivial programming task, but the speed improvement might be worth it to you.

As computers get faster and faster, Borland might consider offering a heap defragmentation routine or Turbo C++ might defragment automatically. At this time, however, programmers are happier having the efficiency of speed at the trade-off of fragmentation.

The program in Listing 5.3 properly deallocates the memory first allocated in List-ing 5.2.

Listing 5.3. Freeing heap memory when done.

```
1:  // Filename: ALLINIT2.CPP
2:  // Allocates and deallocates several values on the heap
3:  #include <iostream.h>
4:  #include <conio.h>
5:  main()
6:  {
7:    clrscr();
8:    // Allocate single data values
9:    char * cPtr = new char ('X');
```

continues

125

Listing 5.3. continued

```
10:    int * iPtr = new int (0);
11:    float * fPtr = new float(1.1);
12:    double * dVal = new double (12345.678);
13:    // Print the values to show the initialization
14:    cout << "cPtr is " << cPtr <<
       ➡"\n"; // Don't dereference char pointers
15:    cout << "iPtr is " << *iPtr << "\n";
16:    cout << "fPtr is " << *fPtr << "\n";
17:    cout << "dVal is " << *dVal << "\n";
18:    delete cPtr;    // Free memory for other tasks
19:    delete iPtr;
20:    delete fPtr;
21:    return 0;
22: }
```

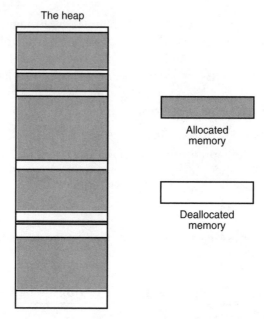

Figure 5.4. *The heap can become full of unused memory holes too small to be used for later allocations.*

When deallocating memory reserved for arrays, you must use a special syntax for delete. Insert a pair of brackets between delete and the pointer to the heap's array.

The following statement deallocates an array of memory allocated with `new`:

```
delete [] myName;    // Deallocates an array from the heap
```

Note: Older versions of C++ (those before AT&T version 2.1) required a number inside `delete`'s brackets telling C++ how many elements to delete. Turbo C++, as with most modern C++ compilers, keeps track of the allocated elements for you so that you type only the empty brackets and Turbo C++ knows how many elements to deallocate based on how many elements you allocated previously.

The brackets tell Turbo C++ that you want to deallocate an array of values and not just a single pointer's value from the heap. For example, suppose you allocated an array of 16 characters on the heap and assigned the heap array a value like this:

```
char * lotsOfText;
lotsOfText = new char [16];  // Allocate 16 characters
strcpy(lotsOfText, "Dan's Bake Sale");
```

If you attempted to deallocate the array like

```
delete lotsOfText;    // Only a partial deallocation
```

then only the first of the 16 allocated characters will be deallocated. However, if you properly deallocated the array like

```
delete [] lotsOfText;    // Full deallocation
```

then all 16 characters would properly be returned to the free heap. Figure 5.5 shows the difference between the two deallocations.

Not deallocating all the memory defeats the purpose of dynamic memory allocation. Being able to release all your memory back to the rest of the system is the primary reason to use `new` and `delete`.

The program in Listing 5.4 demonstrates dynamic memory allocation and deallocation with `new` and `delete` for television-show data. A structure is declared, and an array holds pointers to the initialized allocated structure variables as the user enters data. A menu controls whether the user wants to add data or see the data. Before the program ends, all the memory is freed from the heap.

5

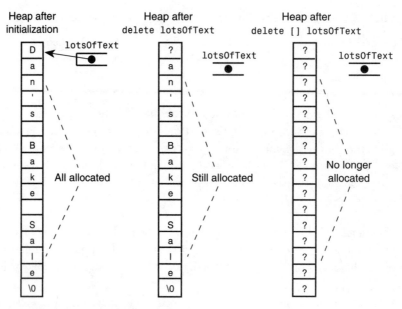

Figure 5.5. *Be sure to deallocate everything!*

Listing 5.4. A television-show program demonstrating allocation and deallocation.

```
1:  // Filename: TVSHOWS.CPP
2:  // Uses the heap for allocating and deallocating structures
3:  #include <iostream.h>
4:  #include <conio.h>
5:  #include <string.h>
6:  struct show {
7:    char * showName;
8:    int dayNum;      // 0-Sun, 1-Mon, ..., 6-Saturday
9:    int length;      // In minutes
10: };
11: // Program prototypes follow
12: void dispMenu(void);
13: void addShows(show * shows[], int * showCnt);
14: void prShows(show * shows[], int showCnt);
15: void errPrint(void);
16: void delAll(show * shows[], int showCnt);
17:
18: main()
19: {
20:   char ans, cr;
21:   const int MaxShows = 100;
22:   show * shows[MaxShows];   // All TV shows are stored on heap
23:   int showCnt = 0;      // Count of the number of shows on heap
```

```
24:    do
25:    {  dispMenu();
26:       cin >> ans;
27:       cin.get(cr);          // Discard the Enter keystroke
28:       switch (ans)
29:       {  case '1' : addShows(shows, &showCnt);
30:                     break;
31:          case '2' : prShows(shows, showCnt);
32:                     break;
33:          case '3' : break;
34:          default  : errPrint();
35:                     break;
36:       }
37:    } while (ans != '3');
38:    delAll(shows, showCnt);  // Must free both names and structures
39:    return 0;
40: }
41: ///////////////////////////////////////////////////////////////////
42: // Function to display a menu
43: void dispMenu(void)
44: {
45:    clrscr();
46:    cout << "** Television Show Program **\n";
47:    cout << "\n\nDo you want to:\n";
48:    cout << "1. Add a television show to the list\n";
49:    cout << "2. Print the current list of shows\n";
50:    cout << "3. Exit the program\n";
51:    return;
52: }
53: ///////////////////////////////////////////////////////////////////
54: // Function to add shows to the heap
55: void addShows(show * shows[], int * showCnt)
56: {
57:    char inLine[80];               // Need a temporary place to hold
58:                                   // the user's entered data
59:    cout << "\nWhat is the next show's name? ";
60:    cin.getline(inLine, 80);
61:    shows[*showCnt] = new show;  // Allocate the structure
62:    // The structure holds a character pointer to the show's
63:    // name so allocate data for the show name as well
64:    shows[*showCnt]->showName = new char[strlen(inLine) + 1];
65:    strcpy(shows[*showCnt]->showName, inLine);
66:    cout << "What day is the show on?\n";
67:    cout << "(0=Sunday, 1=Monday, 2=Tuesday, ..., 6=Saturday) ";
68:    cin >> shows[*showCnt]->dayNum;
69:    cout << "How long is the show (in minutes)? ";
70:    cin >> shows[*showCnt]->length;
71:    (*showCnt)++;
72:    return;
73: }
```

continues

Listing 5.4. continued

```
74: /////////////////////////////////////////////////////////////
75: // Function to print the shows from the heap
76: void prShows(show * shows[], int showCnt)
77: {
78:    char * weekDay[] = {"Sunday", "Monday", "Tuesday", "Wednesday",
79:                        "Thursday", "Friday", "Saturday"};
80:    char cr;    // Key Enter keystroke
81:    if (showCnt == 0)
82:    {
83:      cout << "\n** There are no shows entered yet...\n";
84:    }
85:    else
86:    {  for (int cnt=0; cnt<showCnt; cnt++)
87:       { cout << "\nShow name: " << shows[cnt]->showName << "\n";
88:         cout << "Day of show: " << weekDay[shows[cnt]->dayNum];
89:         cout << "\nShow length: " << shows[cnt]->length << "\n";
90:       }
91:    }
92:    cout << "\nPress Enter to continue...";
93:    cin.get(cr);  // Let user press Enter to resume program
94:    return;
95: }
96: /////////////////////////////////////////////////////////////
97: // Function to print an error if the user enters a bad menu choice
98: void errPrint(void)
99: {
100:    char * enterPress = 0;    // Just to discard the newline
101:    cout << "\n\n*** You did not enter a correct menu option...\n";
102:    cout << "Press Enter to return to the menu and try again.\n";
103:    cin.getline(enterPress, 2);
104:    return;
105: }
106: /////////////////////////////////////////////////////////////
107: // Function to deallocate all the heap data
108: void delAll(show * shows[], int showCnt)
109: {
110:    for (int cnt=0; cnt<showCnt; cnt++)
111:    {
112:      // First delete the name pointed to by
113:      // the structure's first member
114:      delete [] shows[cnt]->showName;
115:      // Now delete the memory of the rest of the structure
116:      delete [] shows[cnt];
117:    }
118:    // Now only the array of pointers is left
119:    return;
120: }
```

```
** Television Show Menu **

Do you want to:
1. Add a television show to the list
2. Print the current list of shows
3. Exit the program
What is your choice? 1

What is the next show's name? The C Programmer's Comedy Club
What day is the show on?
(0=Sunday, 1=Monday, 2=Tuesday, ..., 6=Saturday) 2
How long is the show (in minutes)? 30

** Television Show Menu **

Do you want to:
1. Add a television show to the list
2. Print the current list of shows
3. Exit the program
What is your choice? 1

What is the next show's name? The Computerist's Kitchen
What day is the show on?
(0=Sunday, 1=Monday, 2=Tuesday, ..., 6=Saturday) 5
How long is the show (in minutes)? 120

** Television Show Menu **

Do you want to:
1. Add a television show to the list
2. Print the current list of shows
3. Exit the program
What is your choice? 2

Show name: The C Programmer's Comedy Club
Day of show: Tuesday
Show length: 30

Show name: The Computerist's Kitchen
Day of show: Friday
Show length: 120

Press Enter to continue...

** Television Show Menu **

Do you want to:
1. Add a television show to the list
2. Print the current list of shows
3. Exit the program
What is your choice? 3
```

Analysis   This program is the most extensive so far in the book, but like most programs, its look is worse than its *byte* (sorry about the pun). As Figure 5.6 shows, not only are the structure variables allocated but data within each allocated structure points to other allocated memory. Notice that within each allocated structure is a pointer to showName that also points to allocated memory. The only memory taken by the program for its entire run (other than a few working variables) is the array of 100 pointers. The structure data that each pointer points to is not allocated until the user is ready to enter a new show.

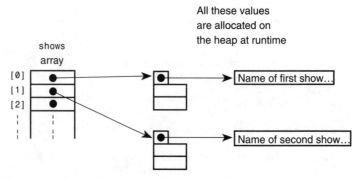

Figure 5.6. *Each allocated structure points to an allocated name.*

Although the days of the week could have been put on the heap as well, there was not a good reason for taking the coding and execution time to do so. The days of the week never change, and there are always seven of them. The heap is best left for changing data such as new values being entered by the user over time as the program runs.

> **Note:** You will also note that showCnt had to be passed by address to the addShows() function. Tomorrow's chapter will show you a much better way of passing data than by address when you have a function that must change a value passed to it.

Using *delete*

```
delete [ [] ] pointerVar;
```

The brackets within brackets indicate that brackets are optional. You specify the brackets only when you want to deallocate array memory on the heap. Turbo C++ always deallocates the proper amount of memory. For example, if *pointerVar* is a

pointer to `double`, `delete` deallocates enough memory for the `double` value being pointed to.

Example

```
// Examples of using the delete operator
main()
{
  // First allocate data values
  char * cPtr1 = new char;
  int * iPtr1 = new int (8);
  float * fPtr1 = new float;
  char * cPtr2 = new char[100];
  // Deallocate the data
  delete cPtr1;    // Deallocates a single character
  delete iPtr1;    // Deallocates a single integer
  delete fPtr1;    // Deallocates a single floating-point
  delete [] cPtr2; // Deallocates all 100 characters
```

Multidimensional Arrays

Although arrays with more than one or two dimensions seem rare, there might be times when you must keep track of data that fits best within a *matrix* (a matrix is an array with more than one dimension, also called a *table*).

The most important part of allocating matrixes with new is to define the array properly. After you define the array, allocating the space for the array with new is trivial.

The general format of defining a matrix variable is

dataType (*matrixName)[numEls]...

in which *dataType* is any data type, such as `int`, `double`, or a user-defined data type such as a structure. The *matrixName* is a variable name you want to give the matrix. Following the *matrixName*, list one or more sets of subscripts enclosed in brackets. Each subscript should be the maximum possible dimension size. *Don't specify the first subscript, however.* List only the remaining subscripts after the first one.

Note: The matrix variable definition does not yet reserve space for the matrix, but only the pointer to the matrix. You'll use new for allocating the entire matrix in a moment. The matrix variable definition simply tells Turbo C++ that the pointer will eventually point to a matrix of more than one dimension.

The following statement defines a two-dimensional matrix of floating-point values. The first dimension is unspecified, and the second holds six elements for each of the first dimension's elements.

```
float (*table)[6];  // Define the matrix name
```

After you define the matrix, you can allocate the matrix with new like this:

```
table = new float[5][6]; // Allocate 30 floating-point values
```

Only when you allocate the memory on the heap do you specify the first dimension.

You can combine the two statements like this:

```
float (*table)[6] = new float[5][6]; // Define and allocate
```

Figure 5.7 shows what the resulting heap's matrix looks like.

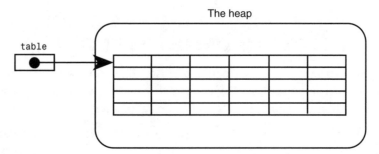

Figure 5.7. *The matrix allocated on the heap.*

As with arrays, you need only to specify a single bracket when deallocating a matrix, and Turbo C++ takes care of deallocating the entire matrix. The following statement deallocates the table matrix defined earlier:

```
delete [] table;  // Frees all 30 floating-point values
```

The program in Listing 5.5 allocates three regions' sales. Each region contains five salespeople, and the table holds 12 months worth of data for the five salespeople. The program simply allocates the three-dimensional matrix, fills the matrix with random values, and then deallocates the matrix.

Note: Rarely, if ever, will you need more than two dimensions. If your programming up to this point required only single-dimensioned arrays, you'll probably not have much need for them in the future. A lot of scientific and mathematical programs require multidimensional tables.

Type

Listing 5.5. Allocating and deallocating a three-dimensional matrix.

```
1:  // Filename: SALESMAT.CPP
2:  // Allocates, initializes, and deallocates a three-dimensional table
3:  #include <iostream.h>
4:  #include <stdlib.h>
5:  main()
6:  {
7:    float (*sales)[5][12];
8:    sales = new float [3][5][12];   // Allocates 180 heap elements
9:    for (int region=0; region<=3; region++)
10:   {
11:     for (int people=0; people<5; people++)
12:     {
13:       for (int months=0; months<12; months++)
14:       {
15:         // Store a random number in each element
16:         sales[region][people][months] = float(rand());
17:       }
18:     }
19:   }
20:   // Now, deallocate the data with a single statement
21:   delete [] sales;    // Deallocates all 180 elements
22:   return 0;
23: }
```

Analysis

Here is what line 7 actually says:

"Define a pointer to floating-point values. The pointer will eventually point to a matrix with a second dimension of 5 elements and a third dimension of 12 elements."

5

DO	**DON'T**

DO use `new` and `delete` rather than `malloc()` and `free()`.

DO initialize heap values with the parenthetical syntax if you want the same initial value stored in the element you are allocating.

DO free heap arrays using the bracket syntax.

DO be careful to define the matrix pointer properly before allocating the matrix from the heap.

DON'T assume that Turbo C++ initialized or zeroed heap memory for you; you must initialize your heap data yourself.

DON'T ever mix `new` with `free()` or `malloc()` with `delete`. The results are unpredictable and even disastrous in Turbo C++.

If the Heap Has a Problem

There is a physical limit to the size of your heap no matter how much memory your computer holds. Instead of blindly allocating memory hoping that there will be enough when you need it, you should always make sure that new did its job. One way to determine whether the heap allocation was successful is to see whether new's pointer points to NULL (the same as 0 in Turbo C++, but this does not always hold true for all C++ compilers) after the new statement.

Suppose that you requested 500 floating-point elements from the heap but Turbo C++ cannot find 500 continuous floating-point heap values. The following code would print a warning message and terminate the program if the heap space was not available:

```
float * values = new float[500];  // Attempt allocation
if (values == NULL)
{
  cerr << "Cannot allocate the requested memory.\n";
  exit (1);  // Terminate the program
}
// The rest of the program would continue if the
// heap allocation was successful.
```

new never produces a NULL pointer value unless the allocation failed. Many factors affect allocation, and you should *always* check that the allocation attempt worked (by comparing the pointer to NULL) every time you use new.

There is a problem with checking new's success, however. The problem is that you are busy writing an application that deserves your attention, and every time you allocate memory, you have to check for the success or failure of that allocation.

Luckily, Turbo C++ makes your programming life easier by providing an *automatic* method for checking new's success. As you learn more and more of Turbo C++, you'll see how Turbo C++ takes the tedium out of programming and takes care of a lot of the petty details that you would have to handle yourself in other programming languages such as C.

Turbo C++ offers a new *exception handler*. An exception handler is simply a function that you write which contains code you want executed when and if an allocation fails. The function can be as long or short as you like. Many Turbo C++ programmers just print an error message and terminate the program such as in the previous code you saw. After you set up the failed allocation function, you never have to check for allocation success again; Turbo C++ automatically calls the function when and if an allocation fails.

Here is the previous allocation-failure code turned into a function:

```
void newError(void)
{
  cerr << "Cannot allocate the requested memory.\n";
  exit (1);  // Terminate the program
}
```

You must now tell your Turbo C++ program that this function, newError(), is to execute when and if an allocation fails. Turbo C++ includes a special allocation-failure testing routine prototyped in NEW.H called set_new_handler(). This routine takes as its only argument the name of your error-handling function. For example, the following statement sets up the link between Turbo C++'s internal handler and your function named newError():

```
set_new_handler(newError);  // Sets up your error function
```

That's it on your part, and now Turbo C++ does the rest behind your program's back during execution of the program. If a new ever fails, Turbo C++ immediately calls your newError() function, but your function never executes if all the program's new statements work.

Listing 5.6 shows how to install the exception-handler function in a program that allocates more memory than can be gotten from the heap to show the resulting error message.

5

Listing 5.6. Forcing the allocation-failure function's execution.

```
1:  // Filename: ALLFAIL.CPP
2:  // Attempts a bad heap allocation
3:  #include <iostream.h>
4:  #include <stdlib.h>
5:  #include <new.h>
6:  void newError(void);
7:
8:  // Regular program appears next
9:  main()
10: {
11:    set_new_handler(newError);
12:    // Now, attempt to allocate memory
13:    char * c1 = new char[2];
14:    cout << "First allocation worked properly.\n";
15:    // Now, attempt a bad allocation
16:    char * c2 = new char[64000U];
17:    cout << "Second allocation worked properly.\n";
18:    delete [] c1;  // Deallocate if previous ones worked
19:    delete [] c2;
20:    return 0;
21: }
22: /////////////////////////////////////////////////////////////////
23: // The following function executes only if new fails
24: void newError(void)
25: {
26:   cerr << "Cannot allocate the requested memory.\n";
27:   exit (1);  // Terminate the program
28: }
```

```
First allocation worked properly.
Cannot allocate the requested memory.
```

The first allocation works, but the second fails because too many heap characters are being allocated. The second line of output was produced from line 26 because Turbo C++ automatically called the newError() function when it realized that the new request could not be filled successfully.

Summary

You now have the tools to allocate and deallocate memory using Turbo C++'s new and delete functions. There are many advantages to new and delete over the older malloc() and free() functions. new and delete are easier to type, use, and understand than their function counterparts.

Because new and delete are operators, you don't have to specify the sizeof() operator as with malloc(). You can easily reserve arrays and matrixes on the heap by inserting the maximum subscript in brackets after new. If you like, you can initialize allocated non-array values by enclosing the initial value in parentheses at the end of the new.

One of the most useful and time-saving features of new and delete is Turbo C++'s automatic execution of your allocation-failure function. It is this exception handler that enables you to concentrate more on the problem you are programming and less on the tedious coding for details such as error-checking.

Q&A

1. Why is dynamic memory allocation becoming even more important as time goes by?

   More and more people are using multitasking and networked multi-user PCs. Your running program should use only those resources it needs so that other tasks and users can have all the free resources they might need.

2. Why is new better than malloc()?

   new's syntax is cleaner than malloc()'s. malloc() is a function and not an operator, so malloc() cannot automatically recognize storage requirements of heap values. You have to specify your own sizeof() operator when using malloc(), whereas new can figure out the size of your data for you.

   With new, you can also specify your own error-handling function that Turbo C++ executes if the allocation fails.

3. Why is delete better than free()?

   Given that new is better than malloc(), delete is the corresponding deallocation operator to new. You cannot properly free() memory allocated with new, so when using new, you should always use delete to deallocate the memory.

   Later in this book, you'll learn how to change the behavior of new and delete so that they work exactly the way you want them to, a claim that cannot be made about malloc() and free().

4. What is an exception handler?

   The term *exception handler* is a general term applied to functions that automatically execute when an error (the *exception*) occurs. Turbo C++'s exception-handler function, set_new_handler(), executes automatically when a new allocation fails.

5

Workshop

The Workshop offers quiz questions and exercises to hone your skills and give you feedback on today's lesson. You'll find some proposed answers in Appendix D.

Quiz

1. What are the Turbo C++ equivalents of `malloc()` and `free()`?

2. What is wrong with the following code's outline?

```
// First part of program here
int * i = new int;
// Middle of program
free(i);
// Last part of program
```

3. True or false: The following statement both allocates and initializes an integer on the heap to zero:

```
int * myVal = new int (0);
```

4. True or false: The following statement both allocates and initializes an integer array on the heap to zero:

```
int * myArray = new int[40] (0);
```

5. How many table values are reserved with the following definition?

```
float (*table)[6];   // Define the matrix name
```

    A. 6

    B. 30

    C. Cannot be determined

6. What is the name of new's exception handler?

7. Why won't the following `delete` operation delete an array with 50 values from the heap?

```
delete [50] heapPtr;
```

Exercises

1. Write a program that asks the user for his or her age (for a maximum of 100). Allocate a string for each year in the user's age that contains the words `Make every year a good one!`. Print the strings on-screen, then deallocate them before the program ends.

2. Write an exception-handler function that rings the computer's bell, displays `Memory Problem!`, and terminates the program when a memory allocation fails. (Hint: The bell character is `\a`, for *alarm*.) Show how the function is hooked to the `main()` function using it.

5

Communicating
with Functions

Turbo C++ promotes the building-block approach to programming by supporting function calls and parameter passing better than its predecessor, C. Some of the Turbo C++ features you learned in earlier days' chapters prepared you for today's chapter. Today's chapter goes hand-in-hand with tomorrow's as well. Turbo C++ supports so many features related to functions that it takes two days to cover them all.

Turbo C++ eases the syntax needed when passing and returning values from one function to another by enabling you to pass *by reference*. Whereas C enables you to pass parameters by address and by value, Turbo C++ adds the third method of passing by reference that provides the same capabilities of passing by address but cuts down on the messy syntax involved.

When writing multipurpose functions, you will sometimes need to work with *command-line arguments* (values typed at the DOS prompt and passed to your program) and variable-length argument lists using unspecified argument lists. Turbo C++ implements some of these features in a manner similar to C, but there are some differences related to the following topics worth noting:

- ☐ Passing reference values

- ☐ Returning reference values

- ☐ Using default arguments when receiving parameters

- ☐ Turbo C++ and command-line arguments

- ☐ Unspecified arguments and variable-length argument lists

Passing by Reference

In the past, the terms *passing by address* and *passing by reference* were synonymous. Although some of the predecessors to C, such as Algol, offered three ways to pass parameters (by address, by value, and by reference), C offered only two, and somehow, passing by address was referred to by some C programmers as passing by reference. Anyway, all that has changed because Turbo C++ supports the third, separate, and distinct parameter-passing version called *passing by reference*.

When you pass by value (also called *by copy*), you pass a copy of a non-array variable's value. When you pass by address, you pass an array or a pointer to a function. To pass by reference, you only need to pass a reference variable. Adding the third method does not add a great deal of confusion, as you'll soon see. As a matter of fact, there is little reason to pass by address after you learn how to pass by reference, so you are still left with two primary means of communicating between functions in Turbo C++: passing by value and passing by reference.

A quick background won't hurt. The sole reason you pass values has to do with the nature of local variables. Global variables cause too many problems due to name clashes that can occur when two or more programmers write routines for the same program. Local variables are preferred over global variables because they offer safety. Local variables are visible only within the block they are defined. A function that does not have access to a variable cannot change it. Therefore, if you want two or more functions to work with the same variable, you must somehow pass that variable from one function to the next.

The difference between the two older methods of passing parameters (by value and by address) lies in the way the receiving function changes or does not change the parameters sent. You might recall the following rules:

☐ If the receiving function is to change parameters sent to it, and if those parameters are to be known in the calling function, pass by address.

☐ If the calling function's parameters are to remain unchanged by the receiving function, pass by value.

Listing 6.1 demonstrates the difference between the two methods.

Type

Listing 6.1. Passing by address and by value to the same function.

```
 1:  // Filename: VALADD.CPP
 2:  // Passes and receives parameters by value and by address
 3:  #include <iostream.h>
 4:  #include <conio.h>
 5:  void passVals(int * canChange, int cannotChange);
 6:  main()
 7:  {
 8:    clrscr();
 9:    int canChange = 10;
10:    int cannotChange = 50;
11:   cout << "Before calling passVals:\n";
12:   cout << "canChange is " << canChange << "\n";
13:   cout << "cannotChange is " << cannotChange << "\n";
14:   passVals(&canChange, cannotChange);
15:   cout << "After calling passVals:\n";
16:   cout << "canChange is " << canChange << "\n";
17:   cout << "cannotChange is " << cannotChange << "\n";
18:   return 0;
19: }
20: ///////////////////////////////////////////////////////////////
21: // Receive two parameters using two different passing values
22: void passVals(int * canChange, int cannotChange)
23: {
```

continues

6

Listing 6.1. continued

```
24:    *canChange = 99;      // Must use * everywhere it appears
25:    cannotChange = 99;
26:    cout << "Inside passVals:\n";
27:    cout << "canChange is " << (* canChange) << "\n";
28:    cout << "cannotChange is " << cannotChange << "\n";
29:    return;
30: }
```

```
Before calling passVals:
canChange is 10
cannotChange is 50
Inside passVals:
canChange is 99
cannotChange is 99
After calling passVals:
canChange is 99
cannotChange is 50
```

In this program, canChange and cannotChange are two integers local to main().
It is because the variables are local that they must be passed to passVals() before
passVals() can work with them. On line 14, canChange is passed by address.
(More specifically, the address of canChange is passed.) Because canChange is passed
by address, if passVals() changes the variable, it will also be changed back in main().
It is because cannotChange is passed *by value* that passVals() cannot affect the value
when main() resumes.

When you receive a parameter that is passed by address, you must dereference the
parameter everywhere you use it in the receiving function. Therefore, if passVals()
were 30 lines long, and 20 of those lines used the variable canChange, you would have
to dereference canChange by putting the dereferencing operator, *, before the variable
name in each of those lines.

Note: If you do not dereference variables passed by address, the receiving
function will work with the *addresses* and not the values stored in those
addresses. (This discussion holds true for non-array variables passed by
address. You'll learn about passing arrays in a moment.)

Figure 6.1 helps demonstrate the results of passing by each method. The arrow heads
show you that passing values by address is a two-way pass because the changed values
are known in both functions.

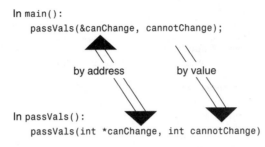

In main():
```
    passVals(&canChange, cannotChange);
```

by address   by value

In passVals():
```
    passVals(int *canChange, int cannotChange)
```

Figure 6.1. *When you pass variables by value, the original contents are left unchanged.*

When you pass variables by value, you pass them more safely than when passing them by address because there is no way the receiving function can modify the calling function's variables.

Not Just Easier, but Safer Too!

This book is not intended to be a rehash of your C learning, but this background is crucial to understanding some of the upcoming OOP issues. In these first few chapters, you have been reading how Turbo C++ takes a lot of tedious details out of your hands and frees you to concentrate on the more important tasks related to your application.

Turbo C++ brings an additional improvement over its language predecessors. Turbo C++ adds a layer of safety to your programs. When following proper coding techniques, you will not overwrite unintended variables as easily as in C.

Make sure that you understand local variables and the issues related to passing them before moving into the second week of this book, which begins the deeper OOP concepts.

All arrays are automatically passed by address, and you cannot pass arrays by value. Remember that an array name is a pointer and a pointer always contains the address of data. As long as you receive arrays with their array brackets or a dereferencing operator in the receiving parameter list, you can change passed arrays in the receiving function and those arrays will also be changed in the calling function, as Listing 6.2 shows.

Listing 6.2. Arrays are always passed by address.

```
1:  // Filename: ARRADD.CPP
2:  // Passes and receives an array by address
3:  #include <iostream.h>
4:  #include <string.h>
5:  #include <conio.h>
6:  void addFun(char compName[]);
7:  main()
8:  {
9:    clrscr();
10:   char compName[] = "C Compiler";
11:   cout << "Before calling addFun():\n";
12:   cout << "compName[] holds: " << compName << "\n";
13:   addFun(compName);   // Pass the array by address
14:   cout << "After calling addFun():\n";
15:   cout << "compName[] holds: " << compName << "\n";
16:   return 0;
17: }
18: ////////////////////////////////////////////////////////////
19: // Receive the array and change it both here and in main()
20: void addFun(char newArrayName[])
21: {
22:   strcpy(newArrayName, "Turbo C++");
23:   return;
24: }
```

```
Before calling addFun():
compName[] holds: C Compiler
After calling addFun():
compName[] holds: Turbo C++
```

The array's value after calling addFun() is different from its original value before calling addFun(). Turbo C++ passes the array by address, so main()'s array is changed when the array changes in the called function. Notice that it doesn't matter whether you change the array name in the receiving parameter list (line 20). The contents of the array change because the address is passed.

When you're passing by address, arrays have a definite advantage over non-array variables. You don't have to dereference an array every time you use it. (Technically, using array subscripts dereferences the array for you.) The syntax of passing non-array variables by address is cumbersome. That is, it *was* cumbersome until Turbo C++ came along!

Pass by Address Cleanly by Passing Reference Variables

Turbo C++ enables you to pass non-array values from one function to another as if by address and without the mess of dereferencing each variable. You might have already guessed that if you pass a reference variable, Turbo C++ automatically dereferences the reference pointer for you. Automatic dereferencing is the primary purpose for using reference variables, as you learned in Day 4's chapter, "Powerful Pointers."

Any non-array variable can be passed by reference. The variable does not have to be a reference variable to begin with. Indicate that a variable is passed by reference by inserting an ampersand, &, in the receiving parameter list.

> **Note:** Actually, you don't *pass* by reference as much as you actually *receive* by reference. You can pass either reference variables or non-reference variables, but as long as the receiving parameter list contains the ampersand, the variables will be received by reference.

There is little or no reason for passing by address again, except for the natural by-address method used for passing arrays and pointers. The main() function in Listing 6.3 passes the same variable by reference that was passed in Listing 6.1 by address. Notice that you don't have to dereference canChange everyplace it appears in the receiving function.

 Listing 6.3. Passing by reference is cleaner than passing by address.

```
1:  // Filename: ADDREF.CPP
2:  // Passes and receives parameters by address and by reference
3:  #include <iostream.h>
4:  #include <conio.h>
5:  void passVals(int * canChange1, int & canChange2);
6:  main()
7:  {
8:    clrscr();
9:    int canChange1 = 10;
10:   int canChange2 = 50;
11:   cout << "Before calling passVals:\n";
12:   cout << "canChange1 is " << canChange1 << "\n";
```

continues

149

Listing 6.3. continued

```
13:    cout << "canChange2 is " << canChange2 << "\n";
14:    // Nothing special needed for reference
15:    passVals(& canChange1, canChange2);  // & before address parameter
16:    cout << "After calling passVals:\n";
17:    cout << "canChange1 is " << canChange1 << "\n";
18:    cout << "canChange2 is " << canChange2 << "\n";
19:    return 0;
20: }
11: ////////////////////////////////////////////////////////////////
12: // Receive two parameters using two different passing values
13: void passVals(int * canChange1, int & canChange2)
14: {
15:    * canChange1 = 99;
16:    canChange2 = 99;    // No need for the * here, but result is same!
17:    cout << "Inside passVals:\n";
18:    cout << "canChange1 is " << (* canChange1) << "\n";
19:    cout << "canChange2 is " << canChange2 << "\n";
20:    return;
21: }
```

```
Before calling passVals:
canChange1 is 10
canChange2 is 50
Inside passVals:
canChange1 is 99
canChange2 is 99
After calling passVals:
canChange1 is 99
canChange2 is 99
```

Both versions—the pass-by-address variable, canChange1, and the pass-by-reference variable, canChange2—are changed by the passVals() function. To indicate that canChange2 is being passed by reference, only an ampersand was needed on line 13.

Note: Although passing by reference produces the same result as passing by address, the syntax is cleaner because you don't have to keep the dereferencing operator, *, in front of the receiving function's variable everywhere the variable appears.

Efficiency and Safety with Reference Passing

You can precede received reference parameters with const to keep the function from inadvertently changing reference parameters.

At first, you might wonder why you would want to pass parameters by reference if you didn't want the receiving function to change the calling function's values. It might seem that passing the parameters by value would be easier and would ensure that the receiving function couldn't touch the sending function's values.

Passing parameters by value adds some inefficiency to your programs. When passing variables by value, especially large structure variables, Turbo C++ has to take some needed runtime to make a local copy of the variable. (That's why the term *by value* is often called *by copy*.)

However, when you pass variables by address or by reference, a pointer is passed to the data rather than the data itself. (The pointer is automatically dereferenced when you are passing by reference.) Therefore, if efficiency is important—and it is a lot of times—you'll want to pass by reference but precede the receiving value with the const modifier if the receiving function is not supposed to change the parameters.

Syntax

Receiving Reference Parameters

`functionName(& parameter [, & parameter])`

Precede each parameter being received by reference with an ampersand symbol. In the rest of the function, don't carry the ampersand or dereferencing operator in front of the variable because Turbo C++ automatically dereferences the variable for you. Also, the parameters being sent don't have to be reference variables in the calling function. If the receiving function changes a reference parameter, the parameter will still be changed when the calling function regains control.

Example

```
// Filename: REFSYNT.CPP
// Examples of passing by reference
void doubIt(int & i);
#include <iostream.h>
main()
{
  int i = 20;
```

```
  doubIt(i);    // Double i in the function
  cout << "i is now " << i << "\n";  // Prints a 40
  return 0;
}
void doubIt(int & i)
{
  i *= 2;  // Multiply i by 2
}
```

Returning a Reference

Another advantage to learning about reference variables appears when you see how to return a reference value from a function. As with most programming languages, you can return a maximum of one value from a function. (If a function is to change more than one value, you have to pass those parameters by address or by reference so that they will be changed when the calling function regains control.)

Here is the prototype of a function that accepts three reference parameters and returns a reference to a character:

```
char & refFun(int & i, char & c, float & f);
```

Most programmers are used to using functions as *rvalues* and not *lvalues* (loosely speaking, values that can appear on the left side of an assignment). That is, you are used to something like

```
ans = refFun(num, initial, amt);  // Assign the return value
```

but you have not put a function call on the *left* side of an equal sign like this:

```
refFun(num, initial, amt) = hisInitial;
```

In this statement, the function is used as an lvalue. The reason you can use the refFun() function as an lvalue is that it returns a reference to a variable. A reference is always a dereferenced pointer. In other words, the return variable from the function is assigned the value in the assignment statement.

When you first see a function used as an lvalue, you can easily become confused by the syntax, but the program in Listing 6.4 will help clarify what takes place. The program zeroes the minimum and maximum of two values returned from functions.

    Listing 6.4. Returning references to functions.

```
1:  // Filename: MINMAX.CPP
2:  // Returns references to functions and changes those return values
3:  #include <iostream.h>
```

```
4:   #include <conio.h>
5:   int & max(int & num1, int & num2);
6:   int & min(int & num1, int & num2);
7:   main()
8:   {
9:       int num1, num2;
10:      clrscr();
11:      cout << "Enter the first number: ";
12:      cin >> num1;
13:      cout << "Enter the second number: ";
14:      cin >> num2;
15:      max(num1, num2) = 0;     // Zero-out the maximum number
16:      cout << "\nAfter putting zero in the largest, the numbers are";
17:      cout << "\n" << num1 << " and " << num2 << "\n";
18:      cout << "\nNow, please enter two more numbers.\n";
19:      cout << "Enter the first number: ";
20:      cin >> num1;
21:      cout << "Enter the second number: ";
22:      cin >> num2;
23:      min(num1, num2) = 0;   // Zero-out the minimum number
24:      cout << "\nAfter putting zero in the smallest, the numbers are";
25:      cout << "\n" << num1 << " and " << num2 << "\n";
26:      return 0;
27: }
28: ////////////////////////////////////////////////////////////////
29: // Find and return the greatest number
30: int & max(int & num1, int & num2)
31: {
32:    return (num1 > num2) ? num1: num2;   // Return the greatest
33: }
34: ////////////////////////////////////////////////////////////////
35: // Find and return the smallest number
36: int & min(int & num1, int & num2)
37: {
38:    return (num1 < num2) ? num1: num2;   // Return the smallest
39: }
```

6

```
Enter the first number: 27
Enter the second number: 98

After putting zero in the largest, the numbers are
27 and 0

Now, please enter two more numbers.
Enter the first number: 34
Enter the second number: 85

After putting zero in the smallest, the numbers are
0 and 85
```

Without the advantage of returning by reference, you would have to expand lines 15 and 23 into a multiple-line if-else statement. For example, you would have to find the maximum number and assign zero to that number, then do the same for the minimum. Returning reference values becomes especially critical on Days 11 and 12 when you learn how to change the way operators work on your user-defined data types.

Please realize that lines 32 and 38 *do not* return integer values! Lines 32 and 38 return references to integer values so that you can change the return value's contents of the function calls themselves.

DO	**DON'T**

DO pass by reference rather than by address because the syntax is easier to use and less error-prone.

DO insert ampersands (&) in front of parameters when receiving them by reference.

DO return a reference value when the calling function needs to change the return value directly.

DO use the const modifier when receiving values by reference that you don't want changed.

DON'T pass by value when efficiency is important. When passing by value, Turbo C++ must make a copy of each parameter, and that takes runtime away from the program.

Default Arguments Speed Program Development

Have you ever written functions that almost always receive the same value? For instance, suppose you write a function that computes sales tax for your store's point-of-sale computer. A large majority of the time, you'll be calling the function to compute sales tax for your city. Every once in a while, however, the mail-order portion of the program will call the function, and the sales tax routine will have to compute tax for an out-of-town purchase.

Many times, you can simplify the *calling* of functions by specifying *default argument lists*. A default argument list is a function's argument list that does not have to be sent values; if you call the function without passing values, the default values are accepted. If, however, you call the function and pass values, the values you pass override the default values.

Default argument lists are always specified in the receiving function. Here is the prototype for the sales tax function just described:

```
sTax(float taxRate = .07); // Use 7% unless another value is passed
```

Note: Specify the default argument list in the prototype, not in the function's actual first line. The prototype is sometimes called the *function declaration,* and the function's first line is sometimes called the *function definition.*

You've probably never seen an assignment in a parameter list before this one. The assignment to `taxRate` tells Turbo C++ to use `.07` for the value of `taxRate` in the function *if another value is not passed to override it.* If `main()` or another function calls `sTax()` like

```
sTax();   // Call the sales tax function with default tax rate
```

then Turbo C++ executes the `sTax()` function as though you had passed it `.07` for the tax rate. If, however, you call `sTax()` like

```
sTax(.12); // Call the sales tax function with a nondefault rate
```

Turbo C++ executes the `sTax()` function and passes the value of `.12` to the `taxRate` parameter.

6

Does This Really Save Me Work?

Default argument lists *do indeed* save you work. You do not have to type the parameter if you want the default value passed. As you will soon see, specifying more than one default value in functions that accept multiple parameters enables you to call the same functions in several different ways without having a different function for each combination of parameters.

Default argument lists are just another entry in the long list of advantages and shortcuts that Turbo C++ provides to help lessen the details of writing programs.

Listing 6.5 includes a complete program that calculates a sales tax computation based on either the default sales value or one that is passed.

Listing 6.5. Calling the sales tax function two different ways.

```
 1: // Filename: STAXDEF.CPP
 2: // Calls a sales tax function using a default argument value
 3: #include <iostream.h>
 4: #include <iomanip.h>
 5: #include <conio.h>
 6: float sTax(float taxRate=.07);
 7: main()
 8: {
 9:   float salesTotal;
10:   clrscr();
11:   salesTotal = sTax();    // Uses the default .07 value
12:   cout << setprecision(2) << setiosflags(ios::fixed); // Proper cents
13:   cout << "Your first total is " << salesTotal << "\n\n";
14:   // Now call the function using a passed value for the tax rate
15:   salesTotal = sTax(.11); // Uses .11 for the passed value
16:   cout << "The second total is " << salesTotal << "\n";
17:   return 0;
18: }
19: ////////////////////////////////////////////////////////////////
20: // Function that uses either default argument value or passed one
21: float sTax(float taxRate)
22: {
23:   float sales;
24:   cout << "What is the total sales? ";
25:   cin >> sales;
26:   return (sales + (sales * taxRate));  // Send the total sales back
27: }
```

```
What is the total sales? 1.00
Your first total is 1.07

What is the total sales? 1.00
The second total is 1.11
```

Notice that the *sane function*, sTax(), produces a different result even though the same sales value in Line 25 is entered (1.00) both times the function is called.

Using Multiple Default Arguments

Turbo C++ does not limit you to one default argument. You can specify as many default argument values as you require. Not all of your parameters to any given function have to be default or otherwise; you are free to mix default arguments and regular arguments.

Note: Technically, you *pass arguments* and *receive parameters*. The calling function passes a value (the argument), and the receiving function receives that value (the parameter when it is received) by value, by reference, or by address. Among friends (and we are friends), the distinction between an argument and a parameter is rather trivial. The value inside a function's parentheses can be called either name without too much confusion. When the distinction is important so that you can clarify the difference between a calling function's list of values inside the parentheses and that of a receiving function, this book uses the terms *calling function* or *receiving function* in addition to *parameter* or *argument* so that you'll know which is being discussed.

Although you can mix default and regular arguments, you must mix them in a required order. Turbo C++ requires that all default arguments go at the end of the argument list.

Figure 6.2 shows a function prototype with four arguments, two of which are regular arguments and two of which are default arguments.

6

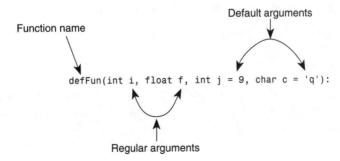

Figure 6.2. *Mixing regular arguments with default arguments.*

Notice that you can specify any type of argument, including character arguments, to be default arguments. Here are three different ways to call this function:

```
defFun(2, 30.2, 17, 'A'); // Pass all four values
defFun(2, 30.2, 17);  // Pass three values
defFun(2, 30.2);   // Pass two values
```

If you pass all four arguments, the default values are not used. If you pass three arguments, Turbo C++ uses the default value of 'q' for the fourth argument. If you pass only two arguments, Turbo C++ uses the default values for both j and c. In regular C, you would have to write three different functions to accomplish the same thing, calling one of the three depending on the values you have to pass at the time. More functions mean more remembering on your part. You don't need lots of details getting in the way of a running program—you need fewer petty details slowing you down.

You are not allowed to list default values anywhere but at the end of an argument list. The following function prototype is invalid because one of the default arguments (j) doesn't appear at the end of the prototype:

```
defFun(int i, int j=9, float f, char c='q'); // Cannot do this!
```

There is just no way to specify values for the first and third regular arguments when calling defFun(). The following statement could not correctly call defFun() if the preceding prototype were allowed. This is because Turbo C++ would not know whether it should use 67 for j or skip the j because it has a default value and propagate the 67 to a 67.0 and pass the 67.0 to the floating-point argument f.

```
defFun(1, 67);  // Where does 67 go?
```

Note: As with all prototypes, you don't have to list variable names after the default argument data types. Here is a perfectly good prototype for the defFun() being described in this section:

```
defFun(int, float, int=9, char='q');
```

Most Turbo C++ programmers include variable names in prototypes because they copy and paste the function's first line to the prototype section of the program before compiling. The variable names are required in a function's first line (the function's definition), but the default values are not allowed in the function definition.

The function shown in Listing 6.6 calculates payroll for hourly employees and those salespeople who get commission. If the function is passed a commission value, that commission is added to the total pay. If, however, the commission is not passed to the function, the function's default commission value of 0 is used, and no commission is added into the pay.

Listing 6.6. A function that contains two
regular arguments and a default argument.

```
1:  // Function that returns a total pay and optionally uses a
2:  // commission in the calculation if one is passed.
3:  float computePay(int hours, float rate, float commission=0.0)
4:  {
5:    float totalPay;
6:    totalPay = (hours * rate) + commission;
7:    return totalPay;
8:  }
```

Analysis If you were to embed Listing 6.6's function inside another program, computePay()'s prototype should list the default values rather than the function's definition line. If this function is called with a statement such as

```
payAmt = computePay(40, 10.00);   // Compute hourly payroll
```

then the payAmt variable will receive 400.00 because no commission is added into the calculation (the commission is assumed to be zero). If, however, the function were called like

```
payAmt = computePay(40, 10.00, 50.00);   // Compute sales payroll
```

then the payAmt variable will receive 450.00 because Turbo C++ uses the commission passed in the function call.

6

A Built-In Function That Uses Default Arguments

Back in Day 3's chapter, "Simple I/O," you learned about the getline() function that accepts a line of keyboard input. Although the syntax for getline() is strange to a newcomer of Turbo C++, the function is easy enough to use. The following statement receives up to 25 characters of input from the user and stores that input in the character array named city:

```
cin.getline(city, 25);
```

The getline() function contains *three* arguments, but usually, you'll use just the two shown here. The third argument to getline() is a default argument that specifies the character that ends the input. Most of the time, the new-line character produced by the Enter keystroke is used to signal that the user is done with data entry. However, if you were to call the getline() function like

```
cin.getline(city, 25, '#');
```

the Enter keystroke is still required to end the data entry, but Turbo C++ stops storing the input in city as soon as a # is reached. If the user types Joplin, the entire city name is stored in city, but if the user types Jop#lin, only Jop is stored in city and the remaining input characters remain on the buffer to be read at the next input statement.

Rarely will you specify a non-newline terminating character when getting user input. A lot of times, a different terminating character is used to read data from disk files whose records might not be delimited with newline characters.

Syntax

Specifying Default Arguments

functionName(type arg [= defaultVal] [, type arg [= defaultVal]]);

The function prototype always contains the default values. When you specify a default argument, that argument must appear at the end of the prototype. Therefore, if you mix several default and nondefault arguments, you must place the default arguments at the end of the argument list.

Example

```
myFun1(int i=10);   // A single default argument

myFun2(int i, int j=20);   // A regular and default argument
myFun2(int i, float x=9.1, char x='*'); // 1 regular, 2 default
```

DO   **DON'T**

DO use default arguments instead of writing more than one function that differs only in numbers of arguments passed.

DO put all default arguments at the *end* of their prototypes. You cannot insert default arguments in the middle of a prototype and place nondefault arguments at the end.

DO pass the `getline()` function a third argument (a character argument) if you want `getline()` to stop reading input when it reaches a character other than newline.

DON'T include the default values in the function's definition line (the actual first line of the function), but rather specify the default values in the function's prototype.

Turbo C++ and Command-Line Arguments

Sometimes, you'll write a Turbo C++ program that needs to get values from outside its domain, DOS to be exact. Perhaps a batch file or a Turbo C++ program executes your program, and values from the batch file or program must be sent to your program's variables. Maybe you wrote a program that compresses a file and the filename comes from the user at the DOS prompt.

Values sent to a program on its start-up are called *command-line arguments*. As you are aware, even the `main()` function has argument parentheses. `main()`, however, is the first function that executes in any Turbo C++ program, so how can you send `main()` arguments? You can send `main()` command-line arguments from the DOS prompt.

Note: If you run your program from within Turbo C++'s environment, you'll see in a moment how to use the Turbo C++ menu system to send command-line arguments to `main()`. Many Turbo C++ programmers test their programs within the IDE editor before distributing their programs as .EXE files.

When you type one or more command-line arguments, they are described to your program by two variables: an integer that holds the number of arguments you typed and an array of character pointers that holds the arguments, one argument pointed to by each array element.

For example, suppose you compiled your program and called it MYPROG.EXE. If you wanted to pass three arguments to MYPROG.EXE when you started the program, you could do so by typing this at the DOS prompt:

```
C:\> MYPROG.EXE 17.8 George 15
```

Separate command-line arguments by at least one space. The three arguments, 17.8, George, and 15, are sent to main(), which must be set up to receive the arguments. Here is the way to code main() to receive such command-line arguments:

```
main(int argc, char *argv[])
```

> **Note:** The *argv[] is an array of pointers. An array name is really just a constant pointer, so argv is actually a pointer to other pointers. You'll sometimes see Turbo C++ programs written to receive the arguments like this:
>
> ```
> main(int argc, char ** argv)
> ```
>
> The double-dereference operator seems to add confusion. If you stay with an array of pointers, you'll find that your code is slightly easier to write and maintain.

As you know, when a function receives an array of any kind, you don't have to specify the number of elements in that array. Therefore, the empty brackets let Turbo C++ know that main() is receiving arguments and that they will be stored in the array of pointers by the program loader, but you don't know ahead of time how many command-line values are passed to main(). The first argument, argc, contains the number of arguments actually passed plus one extra for the DOS path and program name.

By the way, the names argc and argv are industry-standard names, but you can call the command-line arguments anything you like. Sticking to the industry-accepted standard, though, makes your program more maintainable to those who might have to change it later.

Figure 6.3 shows the contents of main()'s two arguments after typing the DOS line shown previously. Although you'll rarely care about the first argument (the DOS command needed to start the program), it sometimes comes in handy, especially when you need to inform the user of a program error during the development of several programs chained together in a batch file.

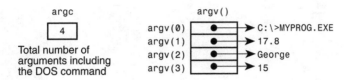

Figure 6.3. *After passing command-line arguments to* main().

The program in Listing 6.7 echoes the user's command-line arguments to the screen.

 Listing 6.7. Printing the command-line arguments.

```
1:  // Filename: CMDARGS.CPP
2:  // Accepts command-line arguments and prints them back to the user
3:  #include <iostream.h>
4:  main(int argc, char * argv[])
5:  {
6:    cout << "\nYou typed these words to begin this program:\n";
7:    for (int i=0; i < argc; i++)
8:      { cout << argv[i] << "\n";}     // Prints one per line
9:    return 0;
10: }
```

```
C:\>CMDARGS 17.8 George 15 ─────────────── User typed
You typed these words to begin this program:   this line from
C:\>CMDARGS.EXE                                 the DOS
17.8                                            prompt
George
15
```

Note: Although you don't have to type the .EXE extension when running this program, the first command-line argument always points to a string containing the path and full filename of the executable program.

If you want to supply command-line arguments from within Turbo C++'s IDE editor, select **R**un **A**rguments... from the pull-down menus, and type the command-line arguments in the Program Arguments dialog box like the one shown in Figure 6.4.

It often helps to add an error-checking routine to the command-line arguments in case the user does not supply enough arguments. For example, the program in Listing 6.8 attempts to print the average of the three command-line argument values. If the user types fewer than three numbers, the program displays an error message and shows the user what he or she should have typed.

Communicating with Functions

```
≡  File  Edit  Search  Run  Compile  Debug  Project  Options     Window   Help
┌─[■]─────────────────── D:\WINWORD\TEACHCPP\CMDCHK.CPP ──────────────2═[↕]─┐
│ // Filename: CMDCHK.CPP                                                    │
│ // Displays error if the user doesn't enter a                             │
│ // correct number of command-line arguments.                             │
│ #include <iostream.h>                                                     │
│ #include <iomanip.h>                                                      │
│ #include <stdlib.h>                                                       │
│ main(int ar┌─[ ]═══════════════ Program Arguments ═══════════════┐        │
│ {           │                                                    │        │
│    float avg│  ┌Arguments                                        │        │
│    if (argc │  │ 17.8 George 15                               ↓│ │        │
│     { cerr  │  └──────────────────────────────────────────────┘│      "; │
│       cerr  │                                                    │        │
│       cerr  │        ┌────────┐   ┌────────┐   ┌────────┐        │        │
│     }       │        │   OK   │   │ Cancel │   │  Help  │        │        │
│    else     │        └────────┘   └────────┘   └────────┘        │        │
│     { avg = └────────────────────────────────────────────────────┘ 3;    │
│                                                                           │
│       cout << setprecision(2);                                           │
│       cout << "The average of your three numbers is " << avg << "\n";    │
│     }                                                                     │
│    return 0;                                                              │
│─── 13:33 ═══◄┤                                                        ├─▲ │
└ F1 Help │ Enter command-line arguments to be passed to your program ─────┘
```

Figure 6.4. *Specifying command-line arguments inside the IDE editor.*

**Listing 6.8. Making sure the user
types the right number of arguments.**

```
1:  // Filename: CMDCHK.CPP
2:  // Displays error if the user doesn't enter a
3:  // correct number of command-line arguments.
4:  #include <iostream.h>
5:  #include <iomanip.h>
6:  #include <stdlib.h>
7:  main(int argc, char * argv[])
8:  {
9:    float avg;
10:   if (argc != 4)    // User MUST enter 3 values after program name
11:     { cerr << "\n** You did not start this program correctly!\n";
12:       cerr << "Type three numbers after the program name like
        ➥this:\n";
13:       cerr << "C:\>CMDCHK 32 45 21\n";
14:     }
15:   else
16:     { avg = (atoi(argv[1]) + atoi(argv[2]) + atoi(argv[3])) / 3;
17:
18:       cout << setprecision(2);
19:       cout << "The average of your three numbers is " << avg
        ➥<< "\n";
20:     }
21:   return 0;
22: }
```

```
C:>CMDCHK 10 20 30 40
** You did not start this program correctly!
Type three numbers after the program name like this:
     C:>CMDCHK 32 45 21
C:>CMDCHK 10 20 30
The average of your three numbers is 20
```

User typed
these lines
from the
DOS prompt

 Notice that the built-in `atoi()` function is used on lines 16 and 17 to convert the command-line argument strings to their numeric integer equivalents. All the `ato...()` functions are useful for converting strings to various types of numbers. (The name `atoi()` stands for *alpha-to-integer*.) The `ato...()` functions are prototyped in the STDLIB.H header file.

Using Variable-Length Argument Lists

Programmers don't program variable-length argument lists too often because of their cryptic nature, but you might at some time want to offer an open-ended function that can take as many parameters as the calling program wants to send. The old `printf()` and `scanf()` functions are variable-length argument functions because you can pass one or more arguments to them.

Note: Because of the cryptic nature of variable-length argument lists, consider passing an array of character pointers to a function instead of using variable-length argument lists.

When passing a variable number of arguments, you must somehow signal to Turbo C++ that it has come to the end of the list of values. For example, if -99 will never be a value that you pass to the function, use -99 for the end-of-argument signal. The next program explains how to use this signal value.

Turbo C++ includes the same set of variable-length argument macros as C does. You must prototype the argument lists with an ellipsis, a series of three periods (...). Always include the STDARG.H or VARARGS.H header files when working with variable-length argument lists so that Turbo C++ will recognize the macros that you use. Although you, as a programmer, should use `inline` functions in place of `#define` macros, as Day 2's chapter pointed out, the variable-length argument macros are supplied by Borland and work fine if you want to use them.

Table 6.1 lists the macros you need and their descriptions to help you pick off each argument passed and use the argument in a function. You must pass at least one fixed argument (that is, at least one regular argument must precede the ellipsis in the variable-length argument list).

Table 6.1. The variable-length argument macros.

Macro Name	Parameters	Description
va_list	*ap*	Defines a special variable that holds the variable-length argument list, called *ap* in this table.
va_arg()	va_list *ap*, *type*	Picks off the next parameter from the argument list and converts it to the *type* specified. (The *type* cannot be char, unsigned char, or float.)
va_end()	va_list *ap*	Cleans up the variable-length argument work and is required bookkeeping when you are through grabbing all the arguments from the list.
va_start()	va_list *ap*, *lastfix*	Initializes the ap variable defined with va_list and requires that you send the last-named argument as well so that va_list() knows when to begin. In other words, if there were three fixed arguments specified before the ellipses, you must pass the last of those three arguments to va_start() so that va_start() can find the first variable-length argument that comes next.

Suppose you wanted to write a function that returned the largest value from a list of arguments passed to it. The function is to be called from several places throughout a

program, and the number of arguments sent to the function changes depending on
what part of the program calls it. Listing 6.9 contains such a function.

 Listing 6.9. Finding the maximum argument in a list.

```cpp
1:  // Filename: VARARGS.CPP
2:  // Program that contains a variable argument list.
3:  // The end of list is signaled by the -99 at the end
4:  // of the function calls.
5:  #include <iostream.h>
6:  #include <stdarg.h>
7:  #include <conio.h>
8:  void totNums(int numPassed, ...);
9:  main()
10: {
11:    clrscr();
12:    // -99 is used to trigger the end of the variable arguments
13:    totNums(23, 43, 1, 3, 45, 66, 8, 5, 5, 23, 55, 77, -99);
14:    totNums(1, 2, -99);
15:    totNums(4, 5, 77, 32, 4, 77, 87, 13, -99);
16:    totNums(1, -99);
17:    return 0;
18: }
19: ///////////////////////////////////////////////////////////////
20: // Variable-length argument function
21: void totNums(int numPassed, ...)
22: {
23:    int total;
24:    int num;
25:    va_list ap;    // Points to the list of arguments
26:    va_start(ap, numPassed); // Tells Turbo C++ where to begin
27:    total = numPassed;       // Store the first argument to total
28:    while ((num = va_arg(ap, int)) != -99)
29:    {
30:      total += num;    // Add next value to grand total
31:    }
32:    va_end(ap);        // Cleanup that is always needed
33:    cout << "The total of this list is " << total << "\n";
34: }
```

```
The total of this list is 354
The total of this list is 3
The total of this list is 299
The total of this list is 1
```

 Line 28 is the most difficult line in the program. The va_arg() macro picks off
the next integer from the list. That value is stored in num and then compared to
-99 to control the termination of the while loop.

Note: The prototype on line 8 indicates that totNums() contains an *unspecified number of arguments*. In regular C, you can get by with using empty argument lists in the prototype to indicate an unspecified number of arguments, but as you learned in Day 2's chapter, "C++ Is Superior!" Turbo C++ interprets an empty argument list as if you specified void.

You can sometimes send the total number of arguments when calling the variable-length argument function. Listing 6.10 shows the same program as in Listing 6.9, but the number of arguments passed at each function call is specified by the first argument.

Listing 6.10. Another way to find the maximum argument in a list.

```
1:  // Filename: VARARG2.CPP
2:  // Program that contains a variable argument list
3:  // with an argument that tells how many arguments follow
4:  #include <iostream.h>
5:  #include <stdarg.h>
6:  #include <conio.h>
7:  void totNums(int numPassed, ...);
8:  main()
9:  {
10:   clrscr();
11:   totNums(12, 23, 43, 1, 3, 45, 66, 8, 5, 5, 23, 55, 77);
12:   totNums(2, 1, 2);
13:   totNums(8, 4, 5, 77, 32, 4, 77, 87, 13);
14:   totNums(1, 1);
15:   return 0;
16: }
17: ////////////////////////////////////////////////////////////////
18: // Variable-length argument function
19: void totNums(int numPassed, ...)
20: {
21:    int total=0;
22:    int num;
23:    va_list ap;    // Points to the list of arguments
24:    va_start(ap, numPassed); // Tells Turbo C++ where to begin
25:    for (int i=0; i<numPassed; i++)
26:    {
27:      num = va_arg(ap, int);   // Get next integer
28:      total += num;   // Add next value to grand total
29:    }
30:    va_end(ap);        // Cleanup that is always needed
31:    cout << "The total of this list is " << total << "\n";
32: }
```

 Analysis The output of Listing 6.10 is identical to the output of Listing 6.9. The only difference between the two programs is that Listing 6.10 picks off arguments from the list as determined by the first value, which tells the function how many arguments follow.

> **Note:** You might wonder how the `printf()` function knows how to end. When you call `printf()`, you don't have to specify a trailing value, and you don't have to tell `printf()` how many values are in the list. Actually, the first argument in `printf()`, the format argument, indirectly tells the `printf()` code how many arguments follow. The `printf()` function scans the format to determine how many arguments are supposed to follow. The code inside `printf()` knows to stop calling `va_arg()` when all the arguments are read that satisfy the format.

Summary

Today's chapter is the first of two that prepare you for Turbo C++'s use of function calls and parameter passing. You learned in this chapter how to pass and return reference values. Actually, you receive parameters by reference instead of passing them by reference, despite what the description, *pass by reference*, would lead you to believe.

When passing by reference, you get all the benefit of passing by address without the extra dereferencing operator preceding your variables throughout the function. If you want the efficiency of passing by reference but you want the safety of passing by value, pass references and receive with the const modifier so that the receiving function cannot change the reference arguments.

By returning reference values, you can save a step or two while programming. Suppose that you want to assign the return value of a function a specific value. Returning a reference returns an actual dereferenced variable so that you can assign a function call a value (when that function call returns a reference). The return value, stored in a reference variable, will be assigned the new value.

Default argument lists save you time when you're programming. If you often write functions that receive the same values *most* of the time, consider making those values default arguments. Specify default arguments in the function prototype. If you choose to call the function but not pass a value to an argument, the default will be used for that argument.

Command-line arguments become important when you pass to a compiled program values from a DOS batch file or from another program that calls yours. `main()` can receive arguments just like any other function can. `main()` receives those arguments in an array of pointers that you have to convert to the proper data type. For extra safety, you can check to ensure that the user passed the correct number of arguments and print an error message if needed.

Today's chapter ended with an explanation on variable-length argument lists. As with the `printf()` function, you might need to pass a function a different number of arguments every time you call that function. The syntax for the variable-length argument macros is a little strange, and many programmers stay away from variable-length argument lists. Using variable-length arguments is not difficult, but you are perhaps better off passing an array of pointers when sending varying amounts of data to a function.

Q&A

1. How do I pass by reference?

   Actually, you receive by reference by preceding all parameters with an ampersand, `&`, like this:

   ```
   recFun(int &i, char &c)
   ```

2. What is the advantage of learning yet another way to pass parameters in addition to *by address* and *by value*?

   Although passing by address is sometimes dangerous (because a function might inadvertently change a sending function's value that it should not change), passing by address is more efficient than passing by value. It's more efficient because a copy of the data is not passed, only the address is passed. Nevertheless, when you pass by address, you must use a dereferencing operator before all non-array variables. The dereferencing operator is syntactically messy and sometimes error prone.

   When you pass by reference, you don't have to repeat the dereference operator in front of all the parameters in the receiving function, but you still receive the same efficiency gains offered by address passing.

   One of the nice side effects of reference variables is in the *returning* of reference variables from functions. When you return a reference variable, you can actually assign the function call a new value (use a function call as an *lvalue*). When the function call finishes, its return variable will be assigned the new value.

3. Why can I not put default arguments at the beginning of an argument list when I also have nondefault arguments in the list?

   There would be no way for Turbo C++ to know which defaults to use. For example, study this function prototype (an incorrectly written one):

   ```
   fun(char i=8, int j, int k=10);  // Not allowed
   ```

   How could you pass the middle variable, j, a value? If you called the function like

   ```
   fun(10);
   ```

   then Turbo C++ could not tell whether the 10 was to replace the default for i or whether j was supposed to receive the value. Turbo C++ does not support the use of extra commas such as this:

   ```
   fun(, 10);  // Not allowed
   ```

4. What are command-line arguments, and why would I need them?

   Command-line arguments are passed to your program (via main()) from DOS or another program. Sometimes, a program must use values gotten from outside its code.

   When you receive command-line arguments, Turbo C++ passes the number of command-line arguments as an integer followed by an array of character pointers to the individual arguments. Your program can then search the array and convert each of the arguments to a different data type if needed.

5. What is the difference between command-line arguments and variable-length arguments?

   In one sense, command-line arguments are variable-length arguments because a program cannot tell in advance how many command-line arguments will be passed to it. Nevertheless, command-line arguments are supplied by the program loader at runtime, and command-line arguments are slightly easier to use than variable-length arguments.

   When writing functions that use variable-length arguments, you must prototype the functions with ellipses (called an *unspecified argument list*) rather than argument descriptions. You must use the variable-length argument macros supplied in the STDARG.H header file to set up and retrieve variable-length arguments in the function that receives them.

6

Workshop

The Workshop offers quiz questions and exercises to hone your skills and give you feedback on today's lesson. You'll find some proposed answers in Appendix D.

Quiz

1. Which is more efficient: passing by value or passing by reference?

2. Is this a function declaration or definition?

   ```
   void fun(int i);
   ```

3. Is this a function declaration or definition?

   ```
   void fun(int i)
   ```

4. True or false: You can pass arguments to main().

5. When you are passing by reference, if the receiving function changes a parameter, does that same value change in the sending function?

6. What do ellipses signify in a function prototype?

7. What is the *first* argument passed to main() when it is receiving command-line arguments?

8. How can you protect reference parameters so that they cannot be changed by the receiving function?

Exercises

1. Write a program with one function that accepts two arguments: a character and an integer. The function prints a line of characters as many times as specified by the integer. If a pound sign and 40 are passed to the function, the function is to print 40 pound signs on a line. If no character is passed, the function is to print an asterisk. If no integer is passed either, the function is to print a line of 10 asterisks (the default). In main(), pass several combinations of values to the function to see the results.

2. Write a program that prints the product (the multiplied total) of all the values that are passed to it from the command line. (Hint: You must convert the arguments to integers after you retrieve them and store the result in a long int in case the answer is large.)

3. Write a function that accepts variable-length arguments and prints the average of those arguments. (Hint: Assume that the first argument passed holds the number of values that follows.)

6

Overloaded Functions Lessen Your Load

Today's chapter concludes yesterday's chapter, which discussed Turbo C++–specific function mechanisms. Today's chapter teaches you a new concept which has become one of the most important OOP concepts that exists in Turbo C++.

Turbo C++ enables you to write more than one function with the same name. Although this sounds a little strange, and possibly even error prone, today's chapter shows you why *overloading functions* helps take more of the tedious details out of your programming job while enabling you to concentrate on the application you are programming.

As you will see, being able to overload functions requires that Turbo C++ perform a little trick behind your back. In doing so, Turbo C++ makes it a little harder for you to use the C functions you have written for other programs that you might want to port to Turbo C++. However, when you inform Turbo C++ that you want to use a C function, using the notation explained in today's chapter, Turbo C++ bypasses its usual C++ mechanism for your C functions and enables you to integrate old C and new C++ within the same Turbo C++ program.

One of the most important reasons to learn about overloaded functions is so that you can write your own *overloaded operators.* An overloaded operator is one that works on your own data types in the way *you* describe, not the way the compiler-writers describe. Although the true power of overloaded operators will not become apparent until Days 11 and 12, you'll get an introduction here, involving the following topics:

- ☐ Overloading functions of the same name
- ☐ Using C functions in Turbo C++ programs
- ☐ Simple operator overloading

Overloading Functions

Turbo C++ extends your control of functions by offering *overloaded functions.* Overloaded functions are functions you write that have the same name but contain different code. At first, the idea of overloaded functions in the same program seems at worst dangerous and at best confusing for the programmer. After all, if you call a function whose name appears on several function definitions in the same program, how would Turbo C++ know which function to execute?

You are already used to overloading functions because you did something similar in your past C programs! For example, what does the * do in this statement?

```
a = 8 * 3;
```

Of course, the * means multiply. What does the * do here?

```
f = *ptr;
```

In this statement, the * is used for dereferencing a pointer's value. Although you used the same operator, neither you nor Turbo C++ got confused because the *context* of the operator's use clearly showed which version, multiply or dereference, you wanted to use at the time.

In the same manner, you can give similar functions the same name. Here's the only rule to remember:

> *"Overloaded functions of the same name must differ in their argument lists by number of arguments, type of arguments, or both."*

The argument list is how Turbo C++ knows which version of the function to call. A function's name and argument list is called the function's *signature*. As long as you change the argument list, Turbo C++ recognizes that specific function's signature and calls the proper function. When you write prototypes for programs with overloaded functions, you must supply the prototype for each function. Each of the prototypes will have the same function name, but their argument lists will differ somehow.

Note: Notice that changing the return data type has no impact when you want to overload two or more functions. In other words, something in the parameter lists and *not* return values must differ between functions before Turbo C++ knows which function call to resolve and execute.

Overloaded functions are the primary reason that Turbo C++ considers a char data type to be different from an int although regular C compilers convert chars to ints and store them the same way. When two overloaded functions differ by only a single argument, one being char and the other int, Turbo C++ must be able to distinguish between the two data types and make a correct decision as to which version of the function to call.

The program in Listing 7.1 returns to the maximum/minimum problem similar to one you saw in yesterday's lesson (Listing 6.4). The main() function initializes three arrays, all with different types of values in them, and calls maxFind() and minFind(). Turbo C++ calls the appropriate function based on the data type of the arrays being passed.

Listing 7.1. A function that contains
two regular arguments and a default argument.

```
1:  // Filename: MAXMINAR.CPP
2:  // Finds the maximum and minimum values in
3:  // arrays based on their data type.
4:  #include <iostream.h>
5:  #include <iomanip.h>
6:  #include <conio.h>
7:  int maxAra(int iAra[]);  // Only two function names in
8:  float maxAra(float fAra[]);    // these six functions
9:  double maxAra(double dAra[]);
10: int minAra(int iAra[]);
11: float minAra(float fAra[]);
12: double minAra(double dAra[]);
13: main()
14: {
15:   int  iAra[10] = {5, 8, 4, 2, 1, 10, 9, 3, 5, 7};
16:   float fAra[10] = {45.5, 2.3, 63.2, 19.3, 70.1,
17:                 35.4, 51.2, 53.7, 39.4, 59.2};
18:   double dAra[10] = {45.54323, 2.46763, 63.29876, 19.67863,
19:       80.34541, 35.44009, 51.20392, 53.40967, 39.80604, 59.11112};
20:   clrscr();
21:   cout << setprecision(5);  // 5 digits maximum precision in output
22:   cout << "Largest value in the iAra is " << (maxAra(iAra)) << "\n";
23:   cout << "Largest value in the fAra is " << (maxAra(fAra)) << "\n";
24:   cout << "Largest value in the dAra is " << (maxAra(dAra)) << "\n";
25:   cout << "Smallest value in the iAra is " << (minAra(iAra)) << "\n";
26:   cout << "Smallest value in the fAra is " << minAra(fAra) << "\n";
27:   cout << "Smallest value in the dAra is " << minAra(dAra) << "\n";
28:   return 0;
29: }
30: ////////////////////////////////////////////////////////////////
31: // Overloaded functions follow
32: int maxAra(int iAra[])
33: {
34:   int max=0;  // Trigger value for first element in the array
35:   for (int i=0; i<10; i++)
36:   { if (iAra[i] > max)
37:       { max= iAra[i]; }
38:   }
39:   return max;
40: }
41: float maxAra(float fAra[])
42: {
43:   float max=0.0;  // Trigger value for first element in the array
44:   for (int i=0; i<10; i++)
45:   { if (fAra[i] > max)
46:       { max= fAra[i]; }
47:   }
48:   return max;
```

```
49: }
50: double maxAra(double dAra[])
51: {
52:   double max=0.0;  // Trigger value for first element in the array
53:   for (int i=0; i<10; i++)
54:   { if (dAra[i] > max)
55:     { max= dAra[i]; }
56:   }
57:   return max;
58: }
59: int minAra(int iAra[])
60: {
61:   int min=9999;  // Trigger value for first element in the array
62:   for (int i=0; i<10; i++)
63:   { if (iAra[i] < min)
64:     { min= iAra[i]; }
65:   }
66:   return min;
67: }
68: float minAra(float fAra[])
69: {
70:   float min=9999.9;  // Trigger value for first element in the array
71:   for (int i=0; i<10; i++)
72:   { if (fAra[i] < min)
73:     { min= fAra[i]; }
74:   }
75:   return min;
76: }
77: double minAra(double dAra[])
78: {
79:   double min=99999.9;  // Trigger value for first item in the array
80:   for (int i=0; i<10; i++)
81:   { if (dAra[i] < min)
82:     { min= dAra[i]; }
83:   }
84:   return min;
85: }
```

```
Largest value in the iAra is 10
Largest value in the fAra is 70.1
Largest value in the dAra is 80.34541
Smallest value in the iAra is 1
Smallest value in the fAra is 2.3
Smallest value in the dAra is 2.46763
```

In these minimum and maximum functions, a standard algorithm is used to find the largest and smallest values in the arrays. Before the program looks for the largest value in the maximum functions, a zero is stored in the max variables (lines 34, 43, 52) so that the first array element is always larger than max and the rest of the function compares the remaining elements to that first element. Before the program looks for the smallest value in the minimum functions, an extremely large value is stored in the min variables (lines 61, 70, 79) so that the first array element is always smaller than max and the rest of the function compares the remaining elements to that first element.

At this time, the most important point to note about this program is that its last six functions share two names, maxAra() and minAra(). Turbo C++ knows which function to call by looking at the argument you pass. The argument's data type determines which function executes. When you have similar functions, you don't have to give each function a slightly different name as you do in C because Turbo C++ steps in and does a little extra compile-time work for you to figure out which function to call.

Wrangle with Name-Mangling

Turbo C++ uses an interesting method for differentiating overloaded functions at compile time. Turbo C++ *name-mangles* your function signatures. *Name-mangling* is fancy computer lingo for changing the function names after the compiler sees them.

To mangle the names, Turbo C++ combines the overloaded functions' original names with their argument data types and creates new names for the functions. Everywhere in the program one of these functions is prototyped, called, and defined, Turbo C++ refers to the function by its mangled name.

For example, if you used two functions prototyped like

```
int myAns(float x, int j);
int myAns(int i, char c);
```

and if you called them with statements such as

```
ans1 = myAns(14.2, 25);
ans2 = myAns(62, 'x');
```

then Turbo C++ might change the names, after the source code leaves your hands but before the code is compiled to these:

```
int myAnsFLTINT(float x, int j);
int myAnsINTCHA(int i, char c);
```

Turbo C++ would also change the places these functions are called, such as these:

```
ans1 = myAnsFLTINT(14.2, 25);
ans2 = myAnsINTCHA(62, 'x');
```

Given these new names (Turbo C++ uses a slightly more extensive naming algorithm, but you get the idea), Turbo C++ has no problem calling myAnsFLTINT() when it's requested and myAnsINTCHA() when it's requested. After your program is compiled, the names are back the way you left them. Turbo C++ mangles the names only so that it can distinguish between them when you overload functions.

Note: Turbo C++ mangles *all* C++ function names, even those that are not overloaded. Therefore, if you want to link to Turbo C++ program functions that you wrote and compiled using a C compiler, you'll have to request that the compiler not mangle the C function names when the C++ program calls them. Otherwise, Turbo C++ will never find the C functions, because they were compiled without a name-mangling compiler. The next section in this chapter explains how to combine C and C++ code in one Turbo C++ program so that name-mangling affects only the C++ functions.

DO   DON'T

DO overload functions that are similar but require a different type or number of arguments. You'll have fewer function names to remember.

DO prototype all your overloaded functions.

DON'T change only the return value of two overloaded functions, or Turbo C++ will balk at the name clash that results. The parameter list is all that differentiates one overloaded function from another.

7

Calling Your C Functions

There is little need to rewrite your libraries of C code just because you move to Turbo C++. As you have seen so far, Turbo C++ supports just about everything in the C language. However, you might have written or purchased some routines that are compiled and thoroughly tested, such as some fancy input/output functions, that you want to call from your Turbo C++ programs.

As you read in the preceding section, Turbo C++ calls functions with names that are different (mangled) from the names you wrote. You give a function a name, and Turbo C++ mangles that name into something completely different, using the parameters, so that overloaded versions of the functions can be distinguished from each other.

Note: Day 14's chapter, "Loose Ends: *static* and Larger Programs," delves more fully into multiple-module programs and separate compilation and linking. You'll learn how to use Turbo C++ to handle multiple code modules.

If you want to keep Turbo C++ from mangling C function calls, you must include a statement at the top of your Turbo C++ program (somewhere before main() is best, or perhaps in a header file) telling Turbo C++ to keep a list of function calls nonmangled.

If you want to call a C function named cFun() from a Turbo C++ program, include the following extern statement:

```
extern "C" void cFun(int i, float x);
```

If you had two or more C functions to call, you could declare them individually like this:

```
extern "C" void cFun1(int i, float x);
extern "C" float cFun2(float x, float y);
extern "C" double cFun3(char c);
```

Or you could group them into a single extern statement with a pair of braces like this:

```
extern "C" {
   void cFun1(int i, float x);
   float cFun2(float x, float y);
   double cFun3(char c);
}
```

The main() function shown in Listing 7.2 calls these three functions. The extern statement tells Turbo C++ not to mangle the function calls because the C functions will eventually be linked to the current source code, and the names must be left intact.

 Listing 7.2. A main() function that calls three C functions.

```
 1:  // Filename: CALLC.CPP
 2:  // main() function that calls three C functions already
 3:  // compiled and waiting to be linked to this program.
 4:  #include <iostream.h>
 5:  extern "C" {
 6:      void cFun1(int i, float x);
 7:      float cFun2(float x, float y);
 8:      double cFun3(char c);
 9:  }
10:  main()
11:  {
12:      float ans1;
13:      double ans2;
14:      cFun1(10, 20.5);           // Call first C function
15:      ans1 = cFun2(43.2, 905.3); // Call second C function
16:      ans2 = cFun3('x');         // Call third C function
17:      cout << "ans1 and ans2 are " << ans1 << " and " << ans2;
18:      return 0;
19:  }
```

 This program compiles with no errors if you select **C**ompile from the **C**ompile pull-down menu (Alt+F9 is the shortcut key). The **C**ompile **C**ompile menu option compiles the program without automatically linking the program as **R**un **R**un (Ctrl+F9) does. This program will not successfully link unless you link the three compiled C functions to them. (The three C functions are not listed here because their contents are trivial to understanding the problem at hand, name-mangling.)

Note: The reason Turbo C++ successfully compiles Listing 7.2's source code, even though the code is missing three function listings, is that the extern statement tells Turbo C++ that the three functions reside outside the current source file. The extern statement also informs Turbo C++ that the functions are C functions so that their function calls in lines 15, 16, and 17 will not be mangled.

Calling C Functions

```
extern "C" {
  prototypeForCfunction;
    ;
}
```

This `extern` statement is needed when you want to call C functions from your Turbo C++ code. The C functions are assumed to be already compiled and will be linked to the current Turbo C++ program. Otherwise, if you insert the C code directly into your Turbo C++ program source code, there is no need to use the `extern` because Turbo C++ mangles both the function calls and the function definitions; Turbo C++ cannot mangle a definition for functions already compiled.

Example

```
extern "C" {
  void compAmt(float sales, float tax);
  int skyIt(int t);
}
```

Simple Operator Overloading

It's time to introduce a concept that you'll read about in more depth on Days 11 and 12. Starting tomorrow, you'll begin to explore the true OOP capabilities of Turbo C++. This section is going to whet your appetite a bit and hint at what's ahead.

Operators such as plus (+) and less-than (<) operate on data. (It's a good thing they're called *operators,* isn't it?) Even function-call parentheses, type casts, and `sizeof` are operators. You can overload almost all the operators, making them work on your data the way you define.

Note: The most notable operator that you cannot overload is the conditional operator (`?:`). The *ternary arguments* (fancy computer lingo meaning that the operator requires three values to work, whereas most require only two) make overloading the conditional operator impossible. You also cannot overload the scope resolution operator (`::`), the dereference operator (`*`), and the member dot operator (`.`).

Appendix C lists all the Turbo C++ operators and their precedence. You cannot change the precedence of the Turbo C++ operators. (Just because you can change the

way the operators work doesn't mean you can change their precedence.) Also, you cannot change the way operators work on the built-in data types such as int and char. You can only change the way the operators work with your user-defined data types such as struct variables.

> **You Use Overloaded Operators All the Time**
>
> Although the term *overloaded operator* might be new to you, you have used overloaded operators when writing C programs. You know that * is the multiplication operator *and* the dereferencing operator. Turbo C++ uses a few additional overloaded operators, such as the << for output when << is also used for bitwise left-shifting.
>
> Turbo C++ knows when * means multiplication by the *context* in which you use the *. When you write your own overloaded operators, Turbo C++ knows to use your overloaded operator routine in place of the one that is built-in because of the context of the data types you use. Turbo C++ looks for your overloaded operator when you apply an operator to your own data types, and it uses its built-in operator code when you apply operators to built-in data types.

The most important reason to overload operators is to perform seemingly built-in operations on your own data types. Suppose you defined your own data type called People and defined two People variables like this:

```
struct People {
  int age;
  char name[25];
  int numKids;
  float salary;
} emp1, emp2;
```

Suppose you want to add these two structure variables, emp1 and emp2, together. How about the following statement?

```
total = emp1 + emp2;   // I don't think so!
```

What's wrong with the addition of the two variables? The answer is that the two variables are not built-in data types but are user-defined data types. Turbo C++ knows how to add two integers and even knows how to add a float to a double, but Turbo C++ does not have any idea what you want done when you attempt to add two People variables. Turbo C++ complains with this error message:

```
Illegal structure operation
```

185

Think for a moment what could be accomplished if you *could* add two People variables together. You could get a total of their salaries if you wanted. Salary totals are used all the time for payroll budgeting and reporting. You would probably not have a use for adding the ages, unless you wanted to compute an average employee age. Therefore, when you want to add two People variables, you really don't want to add one entire structure variable to another, you just want to add a piece of each one.

Of course, you can use the addition operator along with the dot operator to add two salaries like this:

```
total = emp1.salary + emp2.salary;   // Add the two salaries
```

Adding two specific People variables has always required extra work. Until operator overloading, you would probably write a function to add these two kinds of variables together. The function might look something like this:

```
double addPeople(struct People p1, struct People p2)
{
  double temp;
  temp = p1.salary + p2.salary;
  return temp;   // Return the combined salaries
}
```

When using Turbo C++, you don't have to use the struct keyword as long as the People structure is already defined in the program as shown a little earlier. Also, for efficiency and safety, you might want to pass const reference values to addPeople(). Here is a better version of the same function:

```
double addPeople(const People & p1, const People & p2)
{
  double temp;
  temp = p1.salary + p2.salary;
  return temp;   // Return the combined salaries
}
```

The function enables you to define what is meant by "add two People variables together." By definition, when you want to add two People variables, you really just want their salaries added together. To add two People salaries, you can now do this:

```
total = addPeople(emp1, emp2);   // Add the salaries
```

In ordinary programming languages, the dilemma is solved because you can now "add" two People variables using the function. However, Turbo C++ is no ordinary programming language. Turbo C++ acts as if you've just slowed yourself down by writing that function, and in a way you have. You now have two different ways to perform a similar operation. When you want to add two built-in data types, you must remember to use the plus sign, and when you want to add two People variables, you

must remember the function name. The problem becomes even worse when you write an addition function for all your structure variables because you have to remember a different name for each user-defined data type.

Improving the Situation with Overloading

Red flags might be waving in your head because you are thinking that function overloading would help. After all, you can name each of the adding functions the same name, and your different `struct` data types will distinguish which one gets called when the compiler sees something like this:

```
total = addPeople(emp1, emp2);  // Add the salaries
```

The designers of Turbo C++ did not stop at function overloading. The designers of Turbo C++ actually thought you should be able to make operators work the way you want them to. Why should you have to remember *any* function name when you want to add something? You already know the + operator, so that's what you should be able to use for both your own and the compiler's built-in data types. By extending function overloading to *operator overloading,* you can add practically anything you need with built-in operators.

The *operator...()* Functions

Turbo C++ provides an interesting mechanism for overloading operators. You must write functions named `operator` followed by the operator that you want to overload. Therefore, to overload the plus sign, you would write a function named `operator+()`. All the other overloaded operators would be named in a similar manner, as Figure 7.1 suggests.

These functions…	Perform these operations
operator+()	Addition
operator-()	Subtraction
operator*()	Multiplication
operator/()	Division
operator<()	Less than
…and so on	

Figure 7.1. *It's easy to see which operator triggers the operator functions.*

Whenever Turbo C++ encounters a function named operator...() (replace the ellipses with the operator of your choice), Turbo C++ looks at the data types passed to the function. If Turbo C++ ever sees those data types on either side of the operator, *your function* will execute, not the built-in operator's regular routine.

Renaming the preceding addition function produces this:

```
double operator+(const People & p1, const People & p2)
{
  double temp;
  temp = p1.salary + p2.salary;
  return temp;   // Return the combined salaries
}
```

The two parameters inside the parentheses determine when Turbo C++ calls this function. Whenever a plus sign appears between two People data types, Turbo C++ calls this operator+() function. Therefore, rather than

```
total = operator+(emp1, emp2);   // Adds 2 structures
```

you can do this:

```
total = emp1 + emp2;   // Adds 2 structures
```

Figure 7.2 shows how Turbo C++ decides when to call operator+(). When a People variable appears on each side of a +, Turbo C++ automatically calls operator+().

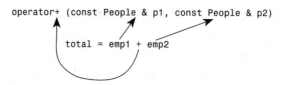

Figure 7.2. operator+() *is called when you add two People variables.*

Isn't that much better? The program in Listing 7.3 uses the People structure and operator+() function to add two salaries.

Type   Listing 7.3. Using operator+().

```
1:  // Filename: ADDEMP.CPP
2:  // Overloading the plus operator
3:  #include <iostream.h>
4:  #include <iomanip.h>
5:  #include <conio.h>
6:  struct People {
7:    int age;
8:    char name[25];
9:    int numKids;
```

```
10:   float salary;
11: };
12: double operator+(const People & p1, const People & p2);
13: main()
14: {
15:    // Define and initialize two structure variables
16:    People emp1 = {26, "Robert Nickles", 2, 20933.50};
17:    People emp2 = {41, "Don Dole", 4, 30102.32};
18:    float totalSal;
19:    clrscr();
20:    totalSal = emp1 + emp2;
21:    cout << setprecision(2) << setiosflags(ios::fixed);
22:    cout << "The total salary is " << totalSal << "\n";
23:    return 0;
24: }
25: //////////////////////////////////////////////////////////////////
26: // Overloaded plus operator function appears next
27: double operator+(const People & p1, const People & p2)
28: {
29:    // Parameters were renamed from emp1 and emp2 just to show you
30:    // that the names used don't matter. When you pass by reference,
31:    // you work with the same data no matter what you call it in
32:    // both the calling and the receiving functions.
33:    double temp;
34:    temp = p1.salary + p2.salary;
35:    return temp;
36: }
```

The total salary is 51035.82

Notice that the People structure had to be declared (lines 6–11) before the operator+() function could be prototyped because operator+() referred to the People structure.

Expanding the Power of Operator Overloading

If you want to take operator overloading to an extreme, you might consider changing the operator+() function slightly to look like this:

```
People operator+(const People & p1, const People & p2)
{
  People tempEmp;
  tempEmp.salary = p1.salary + p2.salary;
  return tempEmp;    // Return the combined salaries
}
```

The return value in this function differs from the one in the preceding function. Rather than a `double` being returned, a `People` structure variable is returned. The only member in the returned structure variable that is initialized is `salary`, but you can now stack several additions together like this:

```
People totalEmps;   // Define a structure variable
totalEmps = emp1 + emp2 + emp3 + emp4;
```

You can perform operator overloading on any of the operators (except for the handful mentioned earlier) in a similar manner. You can even write an overloaded operator function that works with both your own data type and a built-in data type. Consider the following function:

```
People operator+(const People & p1, int i)
{
  People temp;
  temp.age = p1.age + i;
  return temp;
}
```

Note: Notice that the first parameter is a `People` parameter. This function determines what you mean when you add an integer to a `People` variable. The following statement causes this `operator+()` to execute:

```
olderEmp = emp1 + factor;
```

However, the statement

```
olderEmp = factor + emp1;   // Not yet coded
```

would not execute the previous function because the arguments are reversed.

If you want to define the combination that adds a `People` variable to an integer, write another function reversing the two arguments. If you want to overload the function using reversed arguments, Turbo C++ will know which one to call when you add a `People` and an integer value using either order.

In this function, it is `age`, not `salary`, that Turbo C++ uses for the primary `operator+()` goal. The idea is that you can make `operator+()` do anything you want with your own data types. You can even force some kind of subtraction to take place if you coded `operator+()` to subtract (although you should stick to the spirit of the operator's original meaning).

If you included this `operator+()` with `People` and `int` arguments in the same program as the preceding `operator+()`, Turbo C++ would call the appropriate one when the time came because the functions' signatures differ. Combining your data types with built-in data types could be useful for adding or multiplying a single value on every element of an array with a single + or * operation.

Your overloaded operator functions do what you define them to do. Just to drive the point home a little more clearly, this function appears to be a modulus (%) operator function, but it actually prints a message:

```
People operator %(const People & p1, const People & p2)
{
  cout << "\n\n** Just doing a modulus **\n\n";
  return p1;
}
```

If Turbo C++ were to reach a statement such as

```
total = emp1 % emp2;
```

this is what would print:

```
** Just doing a modulus **
```

Some Final Warnings

If you want to learn more about operator overloading, you'll get more than you bargain for on Days 11 and 12. For now, today's chapter is an attempt to show you what Turbo C++ can really do. Before expanding on operator overloading any further, you should get some OOP concepts behind you. After you learn OOP, you'll overload your program's operators a little differently from the way they are described in this chapter because you'll be able to take advantage of some of the OOP mechanisms that improve upon operator overloading.

Don't violate the spirit of the original operator. Don't make a * perform division. You also will not have to overload every operator for all your own data types. Not only would that be a waste of your time, but you'll soon learn how Turbo C++ and OOP make it easy for you to extend your programs later if you need additional operators.

Listing 7.4 gives you a feel for some additional ways to overload operators. Look through the program to get some ideas of other operator overloadings you can try. If you've ever explicitly called a function to perform a standard operation on your own data types, you'll appreciate this bonus feature (operator overloading) that Turbo C++ provides to make your code cleaner; you'll now have to do less work and remember fewer function names.

Listing 7.4. Overloading several operators.

```cpp
1:  // Filename: OVRLOTS.CPP
2:  // Demonstrates overloading of several operators
3:  #include <iostream.h>
4:  #include <iomanip.h>
5:  #include <conio.h>
6:  struct People {
7:    int age;
8:    char name[25];
9:    int numKids;
10:   float salary;
11: };
12: double operator+(const People & p1, const People & p2);
13: int operator-(const People & p1, const People & p2);
14: int operator>(const People & p1, const People & p2);
15: main()
16: {
17:   // Define and initialize two structure variables
18:   People emp1 = {26, "Robert Nickles", 2, 20933.50};
19:   People emp2 = {41, "Don Dole", 4, 30102.32};
20:   double totalSal;
21:   int ageDiff;
22:   clrscr();
23:   if (emp1 > emp2)
24:     { cout << "The first employee makes more than the second.\n"; }
25:   else
26:     { cout << "The second employee makes more than the first.\n"; }
27:   totalSal = emp1 + emp2;
28:   ageDiff = emp2 - emp1;
29:   cout << setprecision(2) << setiosflags(ios::fixed);
30:   cout << "The total of the salaries is " << totalSal << ".\n";
31:   cout << "The age difference is " << ageDiff << ".\n";
32:   return 0;
33: }
34: /////////////////////////////////////////////////////////////////////
35: // Overloaded function to add two People variables
36: double operator+(const People & p1, const People & p2)
37: {                      // You cannot stack these
38:   return (p1.salary + p2.salary);
39: }
40: /////////////////////////////////////////////////////////////////////
41: // Overloaded function to subtract two People variables
42: int operator-(const People & p1, const People & p2)
43: {                      // You cannot stack these
44:   return (p1.age - p2.age);
45: }
```

```
46: /////////////////////////////////////////////////////////////
47: // Overloaded function to compare two People variables
48: int operator>(const People & p1, const People & p2)
49: {                          // You cannot stack these
50:   if (p1.salary > p2.salary)
51:     { return 1; }
52:   else
53:     { return 0; }
54: }
```

Output

```
The second employee makes more than the first.
The total of the salaries is 51035.82.
The age difference is 15.
```

Analysis

Isn't it a lot clearer to compare two `People` variables with a simple > operator (line 23) than to write a function or do the memberwise comparison in the `main()` function? Of course, you still have to write the code that tests the individual members (lines 48–54), but after you've written the overloaded `operator>()` function, the rest of the program only has to use a simple comparison operator to compare two `People` variables.

The `operator>()` function must return an integer result because the > operator returns an integer 1 or 0 for true or false. When you overload operator functions, try to mirror their regular operator counterparts as closely as possible.

DO   DON'T

DO overload operators when you want to perform a built-in operation on your own data types.

DO return the proper kind of object if you want to string together operators such as multiply three or more of your data types in a single statement.

DO think about future maintenance of your programs. If you overload -, you might also consider overloading the -=.

DON'T overload a plus operator to perform subtraction. Stay with the original spirit of the operators when you write your own.

DON'T overload every operator unless your program actually needs that many operators defined.

7

Summary

After you learn to overload functions, you are on your way to simplifying your programs. Instead of remembering a bunch of names for functions that behave the same but work on different data types, you can now use the *same* function names. You then eliminate extra memory work on your part because Turbo C++ takes over for you and calls the appropriate functions. As long as the function arguments differ, you can overload two or more functions.

To achieve operator overloading, Turbo C++ combines a function name with its arguments and mangles the name. Every function prototype, function call, and function definition in Turbo C++ is mangled right before the program is compiled so that the compiler can properly execute overloaded functions.

The name-mangling can cause problems if you attempt to link C functions you wrote and call those C functions from your Turbo C++ program. To keep Turbo C++ from mangling a function name, include an `extern` statement that lists all the C functions called by your program, and Turbo C++ then leaves those functions alone.

When you define an overloaded operator function, you are defining operations for your own data types. You cannot rewrite the way an operator works on built-in data, and you cannot change the natural order of precedence from that of Appendix C's Turbo C++ operator precedence table.

In your overloaded operator function, you can make the function do anything you want. The function is *your* definition of what that operator means when applied to your data types. You do not even have to code a math operation. For instance, you can print a message when two specific kinds of variables are added, subtracted, multiplied, or whatever.

One of the biggest advantages of overloaded operators appears in Day 12's chapter, "Extending Operator Overloads," when you see how to overload >> and << to make the input and output of your structure variables as simple as getting and printing integers.

Please remember that overloading an operator in one program doesn't overload it in all the rest. The program that contains the overloaded operator function is the program that works the operator on those data types. The foundation laid here will be greatly expanded on in later chapters, starting tomorrow, when you'll tackle some OOP concepts.

Q&A

1. What is the advantage of overloaded functions?

   You often run across the need for writing several functions that differ only in their argument lists. Some programmers have to write lots of functions that perform the same math calculation on all the different data types. Before Turbo C++ came along, all those functions had to have different names. Now, if you want to perform the cubed root on an integer, floating-point, and double, you only have to call cube() (if that's the name you gave the three overloaded functions) rather than something like cubeInt(), cubeFlt(), and cubeDoub().

   Even more important, overloaded functions give you the ability to overload operators as well. Operator overloading is the epitome of Turbo C++'s elimination of petty details from your programs. Instead of writing functions that apply common operations on your built-in data types, you can overload operator functions—named operator...() in which ... is one of the built-in operators—and apply the regular operators to your own data. The operators will behave the way you defined them in the overloaded operator functions.

2. I've never seen a function name mangled. When does it happen?

   When you send your program to be compiled, Turbo C++ then mangles the function prototypes, function calls, and function definitions. After the name-mangling, all the overloaded functions have different names (the compiler made sure of it), so Turbo C++ can then properly resolve the function calls.

   After your program is compiled and you again look at the source code, the function names are back the way you left them. Turbo C++ name-mangles in the same way that the old #define constants were changed—the change is made after the source code leaves your editor to be compiled, and everything is restored before you see it again. The idea of name-mangling is that you have to mess with only *one* function name and then you let Turbo C++ figure out how to differentiate the functions.

3. I wrote a program that overloaded the division operator, but each time I try to use that division operator in other programs, I get an Illegal structure operation error. What am I doing wrong?

An overloaded operator function remains in effect for only the program in which it appears. Therefore, you have to include the overloaded operator function in each program that needs it.

4. How can I mix C and C++ functions, and why would I need to?

You might never need to mix C and C++ functions within the same Turbo C++ program. However, most programmers migrate to C++ from C, and those programmers have written many libraries of functions over the years. They don't want to recompile the functions using C++ code because it would take too much time and would not be worth the effort.

To seamlessly link those C functions to your C++ programs, you must tell the C++ code, via an `extern "C"` declaration, the names of all the C code used in the program. When Turbo C++ compiles the source program that calls the external C function, Turbo C++ will not mangle the function calls. (The C compiler did not mangle the function names when you compiled the functions, so Turbo C++ would not be able to match the function calls with the functions if you didn't stop Turbo C++ from mangling the C function calls.)

5. What is the difference between overloaded functions and default argument lists?

Often, you can use either default arguments or overloaded functions to do the same job. However, as you progress into OOP, each has a better purpose than the other at different times. You'll see as you go along where each is best used.

To see their sometimes-confusing similarities, consider these function calls:

```
fun();
fun(10);
fun(20, 'c');
```

Are these function calls calling one function with default arguments prototyped like this:

```
void fun(int = 50, char = 'x');
```

Or are these function calls calling one of these three overloaded functions:

```
void fun(void);
void fun(int);
void fun(int, char);
```

The answer is that you cannot tell from the information given. This shows you how the distinction and use of overloaded functions and default argument lists are not always easy to determine.

Workshop

The Workshop offers quiz questions and exercises to hone your skills and give you feedback on today's lesson. You'll find some proposed answers in Appendix D.

Quiz

1. How does Turbo C++ differentiate one overloaded function from another?

2. True or false: All the following statements properly overload the same function:

```
int  fun(int, char, float);
void fun(int, int, int, float);
int  fun(float);
```

3. True or false: All the following statements properly overload the same function:

```
int  fun(int, char, float);
void fun(int, int, int, float);
int  fun(int, char, float);
```

4. If you wanted to overload the operators &&, ¦¦, and *=, what is the name of the functions you would have to write?

5. What do you have to do to change the + to work differently for integer data types?

6. What do you have to do to stack several overloaded operators together (that is, add three or more structure variables together in a single statement)?

7. Why would you need an extern "C" statement in some of your Turbo C++ programs?

8. Here is a short program with two overloaded functions. There is a problem with the code. See whether you can spot it.

```
void prFun(int i);        // Prototypes
void prFun(float f);
```

```
#include <iostream.h>
main()
{
  prFun(7);
  prFun(7.35);
  return 0;
}
void prFun(int i=0)          // First overloaded function
{
  cout << "i is now " << i << "\n";
}
void prFun(float f=999.9) // Second overloaded function
{
  cout << "f is now " << f << "\n";
}
```

9. Rewrite the following C function call declarations as a single `extern` statement:

```
extern "C" char * getName(void);
extern "C" float amtDoub(float x);
```

Exercises

1. Write a program with two functions that have the same name. The first function is to return the average of an integer array passed to it, and the second function is to return the average of a floating-point array.

2. Add two overloaded operator functions to Listing 7.4's program. Overload both the `+=` and the `-=` operators to add compound addition and subtraction.

Now that you've finished the first week, you might like to see a long program that brings together much of the material from the first seven days. The program in Listing WR1.1 illustrates several Turbo C++ features you now understand.

Type **Listing WR1.1. Week one review listing.**

```
1:  // Filename: TRVAGNCY.CPP
2:  // Program that reviews the first week's
    ➡ lessons. This program
3:  // defines an array of client structures for
    ➡ a travel agency. After
4:  // the user enters data for the array, the
    ➡ program prints the data
5:  // and performs some calculations based on
    ➡ overloaded operator
6:  // functions.
7:  #include <iostream.h>
8:  #include <iomanip.h>
9:  #include <conio.h>
10: #include <ctype.h>
```

continues

Listing WR1.1. continued

```
11: #include <string.h>
12: const int TOTCUST = 25;
13: struct Client {
14:    char * name;
15:    int trips;         // Number of trips booked so far
16:    float balance;     // Total balance owed, if any
17:    double totHist;    // Total spent with agency to date
18: };
19: void prTitles(void);
20: void fillAra(Client clients[], int & numCur);
21: void getData(char cName[]);
22: void getData(int & trips);
23: void getData(float & balance);
24: void getData(double & totHist);
25: int compAvgTrips(const Client clients[], const int & numCur);
26: float compAvgBal(const Client clients[], const int & numCur);
27: double compToDateTot(const Client clients[], const int & numCur);
28: void delAllNames(Client client[], const int numCur);
29: void operator+=(double & temp, const Client & client);
30: void operator+=(float & temp, const Client & client);
31: void operator+=(int & temp, const Client & client);
32: main()
33: {
34:    int numCur = 0;              // Holds current number of clients
35:    int avgTrips;
36:    float avgBal = 0;
37:    double totalToDate = 0.0;
38:    Client clients[TOTCUST];    // Define enough places for clients
39:    clrscr();
40:    prTitles();     // Print some opening titles
41:    fillAra(clients, numCur);   // Fill the arrays
42:    avgTrips = compAvgTrips(clients, numCur);
43:    avgBal = compAvgBal(clients, numCur);
44:    totalToDate = compToDateTot(clients, numCur);
45:    cout << setprecision(2);
46:    cout << "\nThe average number of trips taken per customer is ";
47:    cout << avgTrips << "\n";
48:    cout << "The average balance owed per customer is $";
49:    cout << avgBal << "\n";
50:    cout << "The total income to date is $" << totalToDate << "\n";
51:    delAllNames(clients, numCur);   // Deallocate the name heap
52:    return 0;
53: }
54: //////////////////////////////////////////////////////////////////
55: // Function that prints an opening title
56: void prTitles(void)
```

```
57: {
58:   cout << "** Travel Agency Computation System **\n\n";
59:   cout << "This program will ask for some travel agency data
      ➡ and\n";
60:   cout << "compute some statistics for you.\n\n";
61:   cout << "Buon Viaggio! Andiamo Italia!\n\n";
62: }
63: /////////////////////////////////////////////////////////////////
64: // Function that controls the input of data
65: void fillAra(Client clients[], int & numCur)
66: {
67:   char ans, cr;
68:   do {
69:     getData(clients[numCur].name);   // Overloaded input routines
70:     getData(clients[numCur].trips);
71:     getData(clients[numCur].balance);
72:     getData(clients[numCur].totHist);
73:     numCur++;
74:     cout << "Are there more clients? (Y/N) ";
75:     cin.get(cr);   // Discard the newline from previous input
76:     cin.get(ans);
77:     cin.get(cr);   // Discard the newline
78:   } while (toupper(ans) == 'Y');
79: }
80: /////////////////////////////////////////////////////////////////
81: // Each of the following overloaded functions gets a different
82: // client structure member, and the data type dictates which
83: // version of the function Turbo C++ calls.
84: // This program does not do anything with the client names, but
85: // routines could be added later that do.
86: void getData(char * cName)
87: {
88:   // Get the client's name by allocating enough spaces
89:   char buffer[80];   // Local holding place for input
90:   cout << "What is the client's name? ";
91:   cin.getline(buffer, 80);
92:   cName = new char[strlen(buffer) + 1];
93:   strcpy(cName, buffer);   // Copy entered name
94: }
95: /////////////////////////////////////////////////////////////////
96: void getData(int & trips)
97: {
98:   // Get the client's number of trips taken so far
99:   cout << "How many trips has the client taken from this
      ➡agency?";
100:   cin >> trips;
101: }
102: /////////////////////////////////////////////////////////////////
103: void getData(float & balance)
```

continues

Listing WR1.1. continued

```
104: {
105:    // Get the client's balance owed if any
106:    cout << "How much does the client owe from previous trips? ";
107:    cin >> balance;
108: }
109: ///////////////////////////////////////////////////////////////////
110: void getData(double & totHist)
111: {
112:    // Get the client's balance owed if any
113:    cout << "How much has the client spent on all trips to date? ";
114:    cin >> totHist;
115: }
116: ///////////////////////////////////////////////////////////////////
117: // Overloaded operator so the program can average
118: // the number of trips per client
119: int compAvgTrips(const Client clients[], const int & numCur)
120: {
121:    float avg = 0;
122:    for (int i=0; i<numCur; i++)
123:    {  avg += clients[i]; } // Call overloaded operator function
124:    avg /= numCur;
125:    return int(avg);   // Discard partial trip in the average
126: }
127: ///////////////////////////////////////////////////////////////////
128: void operator+=(int & temp, const Client & client)
129: {
130:    temp += client.trips;
131: }
132: ///////////////////////////////////////////////////////////////////
133: // Overloaded operator so the program can average
134: // the outstanding balances
135: float compAvgBal(const Client clients[], const int & numCur)
136: {
137:    float avg = 0.0;
138:    for (int i=0; i<numCur; i++)
139:    {  avg += clients[i]; } // Call overloaded operator function
140:    avg /= numCur;
141:    return avg;
142: }
143: ///////////////////////////////////////////////////////////////////
144: void operator+=(float & temp, const Client & client)
145: {
146:    temp += client.balance;
147: }
148: ///////////////////////////////////////////////////////////////////
149: // Function to add each client's total history
150: double compToDateTot(const Client clients[], const int & numCur)
151: {
```

```
152:    double temp = 0.0;
153:    for (int i=0; i<numCur; i++)
154:    { temp += clients[i]; }  // Call overloaded operator function
155:    return temp;
156: }
157: //////////////////////////////////////////////////////////////////
158: void operator+=(double & temp, const Client & client)
159: {
160:   temp += client.totHist;
161: }
162: //////////////////////////////////////////////////////////////////
163: // Function to deallocate each client's name from the heap
164: void delAllNames(Client client[], const int numCur)
165: {
166:   for (int i=0; i<numCur; i++)
167:   { delete client[i].name; }
168: }
```

The program computes simple statistics for a travel agency using many of the concepts you learned in your first week with this book. Comments explain a lot of this program, and all the comments use the Turbo C++ // style rather than the older /* */ style.

Lines 11–30 declare the client structure and prototype the functions in the program. This section of code would probably be better put in a header file and included in this code. Include this kind of declaration section in your programs when possible to keep the "real" program from getting too cluttered.

Line 11 uses const to define a constant and not #define as C programmers would do. Turbo C++ programmers avoid using #define.

Although the program does nothing with the client names except ask for them and store them, you'll notice in lines 85–93 that the new operator is used to reserve heap memory for each client's name. The program then deallocates those names in lines 163–167 right before the program ends.

The most important thing to note about the code is its extensive use of overloaded functions. Notice that getData() is called in lines 68–71. Because each member of the client's structure is a different data type, and each member is passed to getData() every time getData() is called, a different getData() executes due to the differences in the argument data types.

You'll also notice toward the end of the program that there are several over-loaded operator+=() functions. To allow this, each set of arguments to the operator+=() functions is different.

When an argument is left unchanged in a receiving function, the receiving function receives that argument as a constant (such as in line 149). Also, when a variable such as numCur is changed by the receiving function, that variable is passed by reference (as in line 64), so the calling function's value changes along with it. There is little reason to pass such values by address now that you know how to pass by reference.

Now that you've got a good foundation in some of Turbo C++'s advantages and language features, sit down, because as they say, "You ain't seen nothin' yet!"

The seven chapters contained in the second week's section will change the way you view programming for a long time, maybe even for the rest of your programming career. Instead of writing the same old code that works on data, you'll learn in the next chapter how to activate your data so that the data determines how to initialize, print, or erase itself from the heap. As you study and learn each day's chapter, your main() code and the functions that follow main() will diminish in size. You'll write programs whose main() function is rather trivial because all the work will be done by the data itself, not by program code that manipulates the data.

In a nutshell, you're about to learn what the *object* in *object-oriented programming* really means.

The Second Week's Objectives Are Objects

The next seven days will provide you with a newcomer's introduction to OOP concepts without talking down to you. Tomorrow's Day 8 chapter explains how to write Turbo C++ structures in the way that Turbo C++ likes best: using the `class` keyword rather than `struct` to provide data protection unlike data protection you've ever seen before.

At the end of the second week, you will be an expert at overloading every Turbo C++ operator, and you'll learn how to take advantage of C++ mechanisms to write better overloaded operator functions than you were able to write last week.

After six heavy OOP chapters (heavy, challenging, but extremely fun), Day 14's chapter will wrap up some loose ends and give you a slight breather from the bombardment of OOP concepts. You'll learn more about combining multiple program functions into one program, and you'll see a little about how Turbo C++'s online debugger and profiler work.

Note: If you've tried to tackle OOP before but failed (it happens to all of us the first time, it seems), you'll be pleasantly surprised at the approach taken by this book. There is nothing unusual about the methodology of the teaching, but you'll see that many examples and topics are explained as fully as possible before you are moved to the next topic. OOP topics build on themselves; you have to know the early concepts fully before moving to the more advanced ones. If you learn the basics well, the "harder" material never seems hard.

Add
Some *class*
to Your Data

Today's chapter begins your exploration of object-oriented programming. The groundwork laid today forms the basis of all your future programming in Turbo C++. This chapter is the first to show you what a Turbo C++ *object* really is.

Technically, an object is any variable at all, but today, you'll learn how to create objects called *class variables*. A class variable is what most Turbo C++ programmers think of when they hear the word *object*.

After you're done with this chapter, you'll rarely or never use struct again. A class variable takes the place of structure variables in most Turbo C++ programs.

Perhaps the most important reason to learn about OOP and class variables is that class variables provide better data protection than anything you've ever seen in programming. Local variables are *far* more visible than many class variables. If a certain section of code shouldn't have access to a variable, Turbo C++ ensures that no access is given.

Before getting too far ahead, this chapter slows down and shows you lots of overlapping examples. When learning C++, many people jump in too fast, but this chapter won't let you. You're here for the entire day, and it will be a full day.

Today, you learn about the following topics:

☐ Abstract data types

☐ The class keyword

☐ True data hiding and protection provided with class

☐ Access specifiers private and protected

Abstract Data Types

An abstract data type is a data type that you create. An abstract data type is not one of the built-in data types, although you combine built-in data types to create your own abstract data types.

The following data types aren't abstract because they are all built into the Turbo C++ language:

```
int     long     float     double
```

Abstract data types exist in both the C and the C++ languages. You have used the struct keyword to create abstract data types in the past. When you build abstract data types, you combine the built-in data types to form a new "look."

Building an Abstract Data Type

Suppose that you have to keep track of an employee's weekly salary and you have to determine the best way to hold that salary in a program. Although you could create an abstract data type (a `struct`) to hold the salary, you probably shouldn't. After all, one of the built-in data types works fine, as shown here:

```
float wkSal;    // Holds the weekly salary
```

Suppose that you had to store 100 employees' weekly salaries. You could define an array of floating-point salaries as done here:

```
float wkSal[100];    // Holds 100 weekly salaries
```

You could also define a pointer and let the heap hold the 100 salaries like this:

```
float * wkSal = new float[100];   // Holds 100 weekly salaries
```

All the previous definitions had one thing in common: there was no need to define an abstract data type to hold the salaries because the built-in data types worked just fine. Defining structures would have been redundant and less memory-efficient and would have causesd the program to run slower, so there was no need to bother with structures for the salaries.

There is another point worth making here that most programmers take for granted. You never have to tell Turbo C++ (or C for that matter) what a `float` is. It's built in. It's there, you can use it—why even worry about it?

To move into the OOP-like way of thinking, consider for a moment what you would have to do if you were required to tell Turbo C++ what a `float` is before defining a `float` variable. You would have to decide how much memory each `float` could take. You wouldn't want to use too much memory or memory would be wasted, and you wouldn't want to use too little memory for each `float` or the program couldn't store very large `float` values. You would have to tell the compiler that floating-point values have decimal points (they are *real numbers*) and that the fraction is always carried in addition to the whole portion of the number.

Aren't you glad you don't have to tell Turbo C++ what a `float` is before using one? If so, you might be surprised to learn that some OOP languages such as Smalltalk do not even know what a `float` is. If you write in those languages, you must define *all* data types, including integer and floating-point data types, before you can define your first variable. These languages are called *pure object-oriented languages* because every data type is an abstract data type and every data type builds on data types already defined in the program.

Turbo C++ is known as a *hybrid object-oriented programming language,* although the additional term *hybrid* is usually dropped. Being a hybrid OOP language does not imply that Turbo C++ is inferior to the pure OOP languages (although some pure OOP proponents make good arguments that the hybrid languages are inferior to the pure ones).

One reason so much emphasis is placed on the term *abstract data type* in Turbo C++, whereas it was not emphasized as much in C, is that the abstract data types in Turbo C++ become extremely important when you are writing OOP programs.

They're Less Abstract in Turbo C++!

Unlike in C, the term *abstract* is a little misleading in C++. This is because when you define a new data type using a `struct` (and `class`, as you'll see later today), you basically add that data type to Turbo C++'s built-in list of data types.

Do you remember all the way back in Day 2's chapter, "C++ Is Superior!" when you learned that you don't have to repeat the keyword `struct` every time you refer to a structure data type? Only when you first declare a structure do you have to use `struct`. When you've declared a structure, Turbo C++ recognizes that structure and doesn't require the redundant `struct` keyword.

In a way, Turbo C++ is the best of both the hybrid and the pure OOP world. With Turbo C++, you get a lot of common built-in data types. You therefore don't have to mess with defining them when you almost always will need some or all of them in every program. You can also define your own data types and use those new data types almost as though they were built in. Through the next two weeks, you'll learn ways to teach Turbo C++ how to recognize and work with your abstract data types more and more. The more that Turbo C++ recognizes and reacts to your abstract data types as though they were built in, the less abstract those data types become and the more fine-tuned the resulting program is when working with your data.

Going back to the weekly salary example introduced earlier in the chapter, suppose that you want to keep track of each employee's salary and employee code. You could keep track of two separate arrays, one with floating points and one with a character-pointer array to the employee codes, but a structure makes a more natural holding vehicle for this kind of data. Here is a structure declaration:

```
struct empData {
  char empCode[8];
  float wkSalary;
};
```

The structure named `empData` is an abstract data type. By declaring the structure, you told Turbo C++ exactly what an `empData` value looks like. You've now told Turbo C++ that all `empData` values have an eight-character array followed by a floating-point value. Turbo C++ now recognizes `empData` as easily as `int`s and `float`s.

Before, you saw a floating-point variable defined like this:

```
float wkSal;   // Holds the weekly salary
```

An `empData` variable is defined like this:

```
empData emp1;   // Holds employee data
```

Look at the similarities in the two variable-definition statements. They each have a data type, `float` and `empData`, and a variable that is to take on that data type's characteristics. You don't have to tell Turbo C++ what `empData` means because you told it earlier in the structure declaration. You don't have to tell Turbo C++ what a `float` is because Turbo C++ already knows that.

Listing 8.1 creates, initializes, and displays a few `empData` values and offers a structure variable refresher before taking structures to their next logical OOP level.

Listing 8.1. Using a structure variable and pointer to a structure.

```
1:  // Filename: STREVIEW.CPP
2:  // Simple program that demonstrates abstract data type structures
3:  #include <iostream.h>
4:  #include <string.h>
5:  #include <iomanip.h>
6:  #include <conio.h>
7:  struct empData {
8:    char empCode[8];
9:    float wkSalary;
10: };
11: main()
12: {
13:   empData emp1;    // Regular structure variable
14:   empData * emp2;  // Pointer to a structure
15:   clrscr();
16:   // Initialize the structure variable with the dot operator
17:   strcpy(emp1.empCode, "ACT08");
18:   emp1.wkSalary = 1092.43;
```

continues

Listing 8.1. continued

```
19:    // Allocate and initialize a structure on the heap
20:    emp2 = new empData;
21:    strcpy(emp2->empCode, "MKT21");  // Use structure-pointer operator
22:    emp2->wkSalary = 1932.23;
23:    // Print the data
24:    // Without setiosflags(ios::fixed), Turbo C++ tends to print
25:    // floating-point data in scientific notation
26:    cout << setprecision(2) << setiosflags(ios::fixed);
27:    cout << "Employee 1:\n";
28:    cout << "Code:\t" << emp1.empCode << "\n";
29:    cout << "Salary:\t" << emp1.wkSalary << "\n\n";
30:    cout << "Employee 2:\n";
31:    cout << "Code:\t" << emp2->empCode << "\n";
32:    cout << "Salary:\t" << emp2->wkSalary << "\n\n";
33:    delete empData;
34:    return 0;
35: }
```

```
Employee 1:
Code:   ACT08
Salary: 1092.43

Employee 2:
Code:   MKT21
Salary: 1932.23
```

This program is fairly basic. As a review, remember to use the dot operator, ., to access structure variable members, and the structure pointer operator, ->, to access structure members when the structure is pointed to (as in lines 31 and 32). Otherwise, you have to dereference the structure pointer and use the dot operator.

From the Abstract to the Abstract

There's one more subject to review before reaching the point of no return (that is, before ending your use of struct forever!). Defining a structure that contains another structure is perhaps the most obvious example showing that when you define a structure, you have added a new data type to Turbo C++.

Suppose that a company wants to track more than the employee's salary and code. The company wants to track the employee name, age, and number of years of service. At the same time, the company needs to track the employee code and weekly salary separately for some of its functions. The company needs to keep the employee structure but then include that structure *within* another structure.

Note: Structures within structures are called *nested abstract data types* or *nested structures*. When you define a structure, you can then use that structure as a member of another as if that structure were a built-in data type.

The program in Listing 8.2 defines this structure within a structure and assigns data to it. Pay attention to the fact that a structure becomes just another data type after you define it.

 Listing 8.2. Using a structure to define another one.

```
1:  // Filename: STRINSTR.CPP
2:  // When defined, a structure is available to be used inside others
3:  #include <iostream.h>
4:  #include <string.h>
5:  #include <iomanip.h>
6:  #include <conio.h>
7:  struct empData {
8:     char empCode[8];
9:     float wkSalary;
10: };
11: // Now, define a second structure using the previous one as a member
12: struct employee {
13:    char name[25];
14:    int age;
15:    int yrsServ;
16:    empData workData;
17: };
18: main()
19: {
20:    employee empl1;   // Regular structure variable
21:    employee * empl2; // Pointer to a structure
22:    clrscr();
23:    // Initialize the structure variable with the dot operator
24:    strcpy(empl1.name, "George Wilbur");
25:    empl1.age = 42;
26:    empl1.yrsServ = 3;
27:    strcpy(empl1.workData.empCode, "ENG11");
28:    empl1.workData.wkSalary = 1439.08;
29:    // Allocate and initialize a structure on the heap
30:    empl2 = new employee;
31:    strcpy(empl2->name, "Julie Meyers");
32:    empl2->age = 29;
33:    empl2->yrsServ = 6;
34:    strcpy(empl2->workData.empCode, "SEC50");
```

continues

Listing 8.2. continued

```
35:     empl2->workData.wkSalary = 2711.57;
36:     // Print the data
37:     // Without setiosflags(ios::fixed), Turbo C++ tends to print
38:     // floating-point data in scientific notation
39:     cout << setprecision(2) << setiosflags(ios::fixed);
40:     cout << "Employee 1:\n";
41:     cout << "Name:\t" << empl1.name << "\n";
42:     cout << "Age:\t" << empl1.age << "\n";
43:     cout << "Years:\t" << empl1.yrsServ << "\n";
44:     cout << "Code:\t" << empl1.workData.empCode << "\n";
45:     cout << "Salary:\t" << empl1.workData.wkSalary << "\n\n";
46:     cout << "Employee 2:\n";
47:     cout << "Name:\t" << empl2->name << "\n";
48:     cout << "Age:\t" << empl2->age << "\n";
49:     cout << "Years:\t" << empl2->yrsServ << "\n";
50:     cout << "Code:\t" << empl2->workData.empCode << "\n";
51:     cout << "Salary:\t" << empl2->workData.wkSalary << "\n\n";
52:     delete empl2;
53:     return 0;
54: }
```

```
Employee 1:
Name:    George Wilbur
Age:     42
Years:   3
Code:    ENG11
Salary: 1439.08

Employee 2:
Name:    Julie Meyers
Age:     29
Years:   6
Code:    SEC50
Salary: 2711.57
```

Figure 8.1 shows what the employee structure looks like. The fourth member of employee (line 14) is separately defined earlier in the program (lines 7–10). Please keep in mind that the employee structure has only four members: a character array, two integers, and an empData structure. The members within empData don't count in the employee member list. If you want to access data in a member in the embedded structure, you have to use two dot operators, as done in line 44, or combine the dot operator and structure pointer operator, as done in line 50.

Nothing proves that a defined structure is a new data type better than a nested structure. After you define a structure, you can use it along with other built-in data types to "build" a new structure.

```
                              struct employee {
                                char name[25];
                                int age;
                                int yrsServ;
struct empData {                empData workData;
  char empCode[B];            };
  float wkSalary;
};
```

Figure 8.1. *A defined structure becomes a new abstract data type that you can use inside other structures.*

Out with *struct*—In with *class*

You might be asking, "So why spend all that time reviewing structures?" That's a good question, especially when you learn that the rest of this book tells you to eliminate the use of struct from your programming toolkit!

Actually, you don't have to eliminate struct, but the more modern Turbo C++ replacement offers better safety than struct. Turbo C++ programmers almost exclusively use class in place of struct.

Here's an example of using a class. This statement declares a class that looks like the empData structure declared earlier:

```
class empData {
  char empCode[8];
  float wkSalary;
};
```

Note: As with structure declarations, most Turbo C++ programmers declare their classes globally and their class variables locally. Over time you'll write many class declarations. If you put the class declarations in header files (grouping the ones that go together in the same header files) and include those headers when needed (with #include), you'll be able to keep your programs cleaner. If your class declarations change, you'll only have to change one header file and recompile instead of changing every source program in which the same class declaration appears.

There's not a lot of deep-level thinking needed at this time to understand the `class` keyword. You can define variables of the `empData` type now because `class`, just as `struct`, declares new data types. The following statement defines a variable named `employ`:

```
empData employ;
```

As with `struct`, you can carry the `class` keyword down on the variable definition line if you prefer, such as this:

```
class empData employ;    // class is redundant
```

There is little need to do so, however. `class` adds a new data type to Turbo C++, just as `struct` did as was explained throughout the first part of today's chapter.

If you were to look in memory at the description of the `employ` variable, you would see a new variable that looks *exactly* like a `struct` variable of the same configuration. In fact, other than an extremely minor difference (minor, but not trivial) `class` does everything that `struct` does by declaring new aggregate data types—or more accurately for this discussion, `class` declares abstract data types and declares them to Turbo C++ so that the compiler can recognize data in the format you require.

As with structures, after you declare a new class abstract data type, you can then use that class data type as a member of a new class like this:

```
class empData {
  char empCode[8];
  float wkSalary;
};
// Now, define a second class using the previous one as a member
class employee {
  char name[25];
  int age;
  int yrsServ;
  empData workData;
};
```

Figure 8.1's structure-within-a-structure looks just like the class-within-a-class created here. In memory, both the structure and the class look the same, and you can point to a class or define a class variable on the heap exactly like you do with structures.

Note: As with structures, always add a trailing semicolon at the end of a `class` declaration's closing brace. The semicolon is always required, whether you declare just the `class`, as just done, or define variables along with the `class` like this:

```
class empData {
  char empCode[8];
  float wkSalary;
} emp1, emp2;
```

Getting into Objects—Finally!

Guess what? You can now define an object! Actually, if you take the technical definition of *object* literally, all variables are objects. However, Turbo C++ programmers like to reserve the term *object* for their class variables. Define class variables just as you do structures. Listing 8.3 contains a simple program that defines object variables from the employee class described earlier.

 Listing 8.3. Defining objects from a class.

```
1:  // Filename: CLASSOBJ.CPP
2:  // Define objects from a class and an embedded class definition
3:  #include <iostream.h>
4:  #include <string.h>
5:  #include <iomanip.h>
6:  #include <conio.h>
7:  class empData {
8:    char empCode[8];
9:    float wkSalary;
10: };
11: // Now, define a second class using the previous one as a member
12: class employee {
13:   char name[25];
14:   int age;
15:   int yrsServ;
16:   empData workData;
17: };
18: main()
19: {
20:   empData employed;    // First class variable
21:   employee fullEmp;    // Nested class variable
22:   return 0;
23: }
```

 When you compile this program, Turbo C++ issues two warnings that let you know you are creating variables (in lines 20 and 21) that aren't used for anything. Ignore the warnings for now. The important thing to notice is that creating class variables is the same as creating structure variables. Those variables (employed and fullEmp) are objects.

After you declare the class, that class becomes a new abstract data type to Turbo C++. There was no data type that looked like an eight-character array followed by a float until lines 7–10 added one to the compiler's repertoire. (The abstract data type, however, only stays around for the scope of this program, whereas the built-in data types are permanent.)

Have a Little Faith

The advantage of using class to create objects is not yet known to you. The advantage will be known soon enough. For now, get used to class and realize that class and struct do *basically* the same things and that their minor difference (which you'll learn about in a moment) makes class the preferred choice for Turbo C++ programmers.

Later sections of the book will refer to parts of this in-depth discussion, and you'll see that your time was well spent here.

Figure 8.2 helps further clarify the difference between a class and a class's *object*. The class is the declaration that describes a new abstract data type to Turbo C++, and the object is the creation of an *instance* of that class.

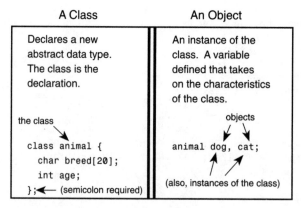

Figure 8.2. *A* class *declares what eventually becomes the object variable.*

> **Note:** Many Turbo C++ programmers use the term *instance;* this book
> will be no exception. Objects are the definition of variables from classes,
> but a specific object is often called an instance of the `class`. Turbo C++
> programmers further expand their vocabulary (and confuse others more)
> by saying that *a class is instantiated,* meaning that you've defined an
> instance of the class—or in simpler terms, you've just defined a new
> variable for the `class`.

DO   DON'T

DO use classes in place of structures. With classes, you can create the objects
that most Turbo C++ programmers refer to when they use the term *object-
oriented programming.*

DON'T forget the semicolon that must go at the end of all `class` declarations whether or not you define variables along with the `class`.

DON'T let new terms throw you. An *instance* of a `class` is just a variable
that you define from that `class`. An *object* is the same thing as an instance or
`class` variable as well. All three terms, *object, instance,* and `class` *variable,*
will be used throughout this book as is done in the C++ community.

The Only Difference
Between *class* and *struct*

There is only a tiny difference between a `class` declaration and a `struct` declaration.
Suppose that you define some `class` variables like this:

```
class abc {
  int i;
  float x;
  char c;
};
main()
{
    abc var1, var2, var3;
// Rest of program would follow
```

Add Some *class* to Your Data

main() cannot use the variable. main() cannot initialize the class variable, main() cannot print the class variable, main() cannot use the class variable in a calculation. More specifically, main() cannot access *any* of the members of the class variable! (Are any warning sirens going off in your head yet?)

It's true that class variables are not usable in main() because class members are *private* by default. struct variables are *public* by default. The public/private difference is the only thing that differentiates a class instance of a variable from a struct instance of a variable.

You are familiar with two kinds of visibility: local and global (the technical name for local visibility is *block scope,* and the technical name for global visibility is *file scope*). There are also other kinds of scope that some C programmers are aware of, such as *prototype scope,* but the two most important ones for most programs are local and global scopes. A local variable is visible only within the block in which it's defined. In Listing 8.4, the variable i cannot be printed by the cout at the bottom of the program because i is local to main()'s inner block and i is not visible when its block ends at its terminating brace.

Type **Listing 8.4. Incorrect use of a local variable.**

```
1:  // Filename: LOCGLB.CPP
2:  // Define a global and local object
3:  #include <iostream.h>
4:  #include <conio.h>
5:  int g = 7;    // Global variable
6:  main()
7:  {
8:    cout << "g is " << g << "\n";
9:    // Open a new block to limit i's scope
10:   {
11:     int i = 10;
12:     cout << "Inside the inner block, i is " << i;
13:     cout << " and g is still " << g << "\n";
14:   }  // When the block ends, i goes away completely
15:   cout << "After the inner block, i is " << i;  // Error!
16:   cout << " and g is " << g << "\n";
17:   return 0;
18: }
```

 Analysis If you were to compile this code, Turbo C++ would generate this error message:

```
Undefined symbol 'i'
```

The problem occurs at line 15. The program attempts to print i, but because i is no longer in scope, the variable cannot be printed. There is no problem with printing g because g is visible for the entire file. Because g is global, it could be printed on line 16 if you removed line 15 so that the program could compile properly.

Turbo C++ introduces a new kind of scope to your repertoire called *class scope*. When a variable has class scope, that variable can be used only *within the class*. Look again at this section of code while reading the discussion that follows.

```
1:   class abc {
2:      int i;
3:      float x;
4:      char c;
5:   };
6:   main()
7:   {
8:      abc var1, var2, var3;
9:   // Rest of program would follow
```

As mentioned earlier, you are extremely limited as to what you can do with the class variables. You can define them by reserving their storage on the heap, you can define an array or a table of the class variables, you can pass the variables between functions, and you can deallocate their storage, but you cannot use the members of the class because of class scope. Notice where the members are declared: inside the class section of the program. As with structures, you declare class members inside the class, but when you do, those members can be used only within the class because all class members have class scope. Even though main() "owns" the class variables, and even though the class variables are local to main(), main() can only define, pass, and deallocate the variables, but main() has no access to the members within the class variables.

Do you see how Turbo C++ protects your data? As reviewed earlier, local variables are well protected within their block (Listing 8.4), but class variables are even more protected. class variables are so protected, because they have class scope, that their members aren't available to functions even though the class variables are local to those functions.

Note: Many Turbo C++ programmers prefer to capitalize the first letter of class names. Throughout the rest of this book, the standard will be followed. All variable names, however, whether they are class variables or non-class variables, will not have capitalized first letters.

Listings 8.5 and 8.6 differ in only a single keyword. Listing 8.5 uses struct and Listing 8.6 uses class. As expected, Listing 8.5's main() can access the structure members, but Listing 8.6's main() cannot.

Listing 8.5. A program with a struct works OK.

```
1:  // Filename: STRUCT.CPP
2:  // Program that uses a structure and its members
3:  #include <iostream.h>
4:  struct Time {
5:    int hours;
6:    int minutes;
7:    int seconds;
8:  };
9:  main()
10: {
11:   Time clock;
12:   Time * watch;
13:   clock.hours = 10;
14:   clock.minutes = 23;
15:   clock.seconds = 47;
16:   watch = new Time;
17:   watch->hours = 11;
18:   watch->minutes = 41;
19:   watch->seconds = 19;
20:   cout << "The clock says " << clock.hours << ":" << clock.minutes;
21:   cout << ":" << clock.seconds << "\n";
22:   cout << "The watch says " << watch->hours << ":" << watch->minutes;
23:   cout << ":" << watch->seconds << "\n";
24:   delete watch;
25:   return 0;
26: }
```

```
The clock says 10:23:47
The watch says 4:1:19
The clock says 10:23:47
The watch says 11:41:19
```

Listing 8.6. The same program with a class seems useless because it doesn't work.

```
1:  // Filename: CLASS.CPP
2:  // Program that attempts to use a class and its members
3:  #include <iostream.h>
4:  class Time {
5:    int hours;
6:    int minutes;
7:    int seconds;
8:  };
9:  main()
10: {
```

```
11:    Time clock;
12:    Time * watch;
13:    clock.hours = 10;
14:    clock.minutes = 23;
15:    clock.seconds = 47;
16:    watch = new Time;
17:    watch->hours = 11;
18:    watch->minutes = 41;
19:    watch->seconds = 19;
20:    cout << "The clock says " << clock.hours << ":" << clock.minutes;
21:    cout << ":" << clock.seconds << "\n";
22:    cout << "The watch says " << watch->hours << ":" << watch->minutes;
23:    cout << ":" << watch->seconds << "\n";
24:    delete watch;
25:    return 0;
26: }
```

 When you compile this program, you'll get several error messages such as these:

```
Error C:\TURBOC\CLASS.CPP 13: 'Time::hours' is not accessible
Error C:\TURBOC\CLASS.CPP 14: 'Time::minutes' is not accessible
Error C:\TURBOC\CLASS.CPP 15: 'Time::seconds' is not accessible
```

The error messages are Turbo C++'s way of letting you know that the class Time's members cannot be accessed by main(). Turbo C++ doesn't display undefined variable error messages because the Time variables are visible to main(). It's just that main() cannot use any members of variables defined from the Time class.

Here's the Bottom Line

The members of a structure are public by default; the members of a class are private by default. Although class variables are local to whatever block defines them, the members of those variables are protected with their private access.

The public and private access defaults are the only difference between variables defined with class and variables defined with struct.

Luckily, you can change these defaults if and when you need to.

Overriding Public and Private Access

Turbo C++ introduces two new keywords, public and private, that change the default status of class and struct members. The public and private keywords must appear before the members that you want to have public or private access. Structures don't need the public keyword because their members are public by default. Classes don't need the private keyword because their members are private by default.

Here is a class declaration whose members are all public:

```
class Time {
public:                   // All members are now available
  int hours;
  int minutes;
  int seconds;
};
```

Note: Notice that public: must end with a colon, :. If you use private, terminate it too with a colon.

public tells Turbo C++ to make *every* member that follows the public keyword available to all blocks in the program that use the class variable. If private appears later in the list of members, all members following private then have private access. Although you can intersperse several occurrences of public and private within the same class declaration, good coding practices dictate that you keep all private members together and all public members together in the same class declaration.

Listing 8.7 contains a fixed version of the Time class program shown earlier. A single insertion of the public keyword at the top of the class lets main() access all the members.

Listing 8.7. Finally, Time class variables that main() can use.

```
1:  // Filename: CLASSPUB.CPP
2:  // Program that fixes access to the class members
3:  #include <iostream.h>
4:  class Time {
5   public:        // Make the members available
6:    int hours;
7:    int minutes;
8:    int seconds;
```

```
 9:  };
10:  main()
11:  {
12:    Time clock;
13:    Time * watch;
14:    clock.hours = 10;
15:    clock.minutes = 23;
16:    clock.seconds = 47;
17:    watch = new Time;
18:    watch->hours = 11;
19:    watch->minutes = 41;
20:    watch->seconds = 19;
21:    cout << "The clock says " << clock.hours << ":" << clock.minutes;
22:    cout << ":" << clock.seconds << "\n";
23:    cout << "The watch says " << watch->hours << ":" << watch->minutes;
24:    cout << ":" << watch->seconds << "\n";
25:    delete watch;
26:    return 0;
27:  }
```

```
The clock says 10:23:47
The watch says 11:41:19
```

The output shows that main() now has access to the members of Time object variables. The public keyword on line 5 lets *any* function with access to Time variables access the members as well.

Although this might now seem trivial, Listing 8.8 shows the same program as Listing 8.7, except that a struct is used with the private access keyword inserted before the structure's first member.

Listing 8.8. A private struct is protected just like a class.

```
 1:  // Filename: STRPRIV.CPP
 2:  // Program that keeps main() away from structure access
 3:  #include <iostream.h>
 4:  struct Time {
 5:  private:            // Make the members unavailable
 6:    int hours;
 7:    int minutes;
 8:    int seconds;
 9:  };
10:  main()
11:  {
12:    Time clock;
13:    Time * watch;
```

continues

Listing 8.8. continued

```
14:    clock.hours = 10;
15:    clock.minutes = 23;
16:    clock.seconds = 47;
17:    watch = new Time;
18:    watch->hours = 11;
19:    watch->minutes = 41;
20:    watch->seconds = 19;
11:    cout << "The clock says " << clock.hours << ":" << clock.minutes;
12:    cout << ":" << clock.seconds << "\n";
13:    cout << "The watch says " << watch->hours << ":" << watch->minutes;
14:    cout << ":" << watch->seconds << "\n";
15:    delete watch;
16:    return 0;
17: }
```

 If you compile this program, you'll get "not accessible" error messages because the `private` keyword keeps `main()` from accessing members of the structure.

 Note: The `private` and `protected` keywords are called *access specifiers*. Although the term is new, it makes sense because `private` and `public` determine whether you can access members of structures and classes. There is a third access specifier called `protected` that you'll read about in future chapters.

Mix and Match Access Specifiers

Figure 8.3 illustrates two sets of structure and class declarations that are equivalent. Depending on the default access and the access specifier that you specify, classes act like structures and structures act like classes.

```
struct abc{                    class abc {
 int i;                         public:
 float x;      <equivalent>      int i;                Both allow
};                               float x;             open access
                                };
```

```
struct abc{                    class abc {
 private:                        int i;
 int i;        <equivalent>      float x;              Neither allows
 float x;                       };                    open access
};
```

Figure 8.3. *A* class *can mirror a* struct *when you use the appropriate access specifiers.*

If They're the Same, Why Use *class*?

That's a good question for which there is a reasonable answer. Turbo C++ programmers prefer class over struct because of the default safety that classes provide.

It might seem as though the class default (private) is too limiting because the program cannot access the members. However, along with the lack of access comes true data protection.

Private members are as protected from access as possible in the Turbo C++ programming language. Through some function mechanisms that you'll learn in tomorrow's chapter, you can get to private members, but only through strictly controlled methods (and, it just so happens, the technical term for those access ways are indeed named *methods*).

To take advantage of the OOP philosophy, you've got to be able to achieve this powerful data protection. You don't have to specify private explicitly when using class declarations, and it is because the default is private that programmers prefer class over struct declarations.

Here's an additional note to ponder: Even though class defaults to private, and that's the most important reason to use class, many Turbo C++ programmers *still* insert private before their class members just to show their intent to make the class members private.

Although you can specify more than one `private` or `public` access specifier in the same class, your code will be clearer if you group all the public and private members together, preferably putting the private ones at the top of the class (their usual location) and the public members at the bottom. Here is a sample class that includes a mixture of `private` and `public` access specifiers:

```
class MixedBad {
public:
  float x;
private:
  char name[25];
public:
  int * atom;
private:
  int age;
public:
  double * amount;
private:
  char initial;
};
```

Obviously, the following declaration is preferred even though it does the same thing as the preceding class:

```
class MixedBetter {
private:
  char name[25];
  int age;
  char initial;
public:
  float x;
  int * atom;
  double * amount;
};
```

Note: Get in the habit of listing the private member group at the top of the class and leave the public members at the bottom. If you forget to specify `private`, you'll still have the default private class protection.

Figure 8.4 shows a diagram of the `MixedBetter` class and illustrates how the program has access only to the last three members.

```
class MixedBetter {
private:
     char name[25];          These data members cannot be
     int age;                used outside this class.
     char initial;
public:
     floatx;                 The rest of the program
     int*atom;               can access these members.
     double*amount;
};
```

Figure 8.4. *The program can access only members designated as* `public`.

Note: Turbo C++ programmers often use the term *data hiding* to refer to the `private` mechanism available in classes (and structures if you use them with `private` specified). The data hiding capabilities provided with classes go far beyond those of regular local variables.

Listing 8.9 includes a program that defines two `class` object variables with both public and private members.

Type **Listing 8.9. Using the public members in a class.**

```
 1: // Filename: CARSCLSS.CPP
 2: // Program that declares private and public members of a class
 3: // that describes an automobile inventory. Until access mechanisms
 4: // to private members are learned, all access to the class variables
 5: // (called objects) can be for only the public members, not the
 6: // private ones.
 7: #include <iostream.h>
 8: #include <iomanip.h>
 9: #include <string.h>
10: #include <conio.h>
11: // Class declaration next
12: class Car {
13: private:
14:    float wholesalePrice;
15:    int maxMPH;
16: public:
17:    char make[10];
18:    char model[25];
19:    int year;
20:    float retailPrice;
21: };
22: main()
23: {
```

continues

Listing 8.9. continued

```
24:    Car sedan, roadster;
25:    // Initialize the public members
26:    strcpy(sedan.make, "Chord");
27:    strcpy(sedan.model, "RushMobile");
28:    sedan.year = 1994;
29:    sedan.retailPrice = 28675.99;
30:    strcpy(roadster.make, "Gee 'Em");
31:    strcpy(roadster.model, "Sprinter");
32:    roadster.year = 1967;   // Really used car!
33:    roadster.retailPrice = 24344.01;
34:    // Print the data
35:    clrscr();
36:    cout << setprecision(2) << setiosflags(ios::fixed);
37:    cout << "Cars:\n";
38:    cout << "Make:\t" << sedan.make << "\n";
39:    cout << "Model:\t" << sedan.model << "\n";
40:    cout << "Year:\t" << sedan.year << "\n";
41:    cout << "Price:\t$" << sedan.retailPrice << "\n\n";
42:    cout << "Make:\t" << roadster.make << "\n";
43:    cout << "Model:\t" << roadster.model << "\n";
44:    cout << "Year:\t" << roadster.year << "\n";
45:    cout << "Price:\t$" << roadster.retailPrice << "\n\n";
46:    return 0;
47: }
```

```
Cars:
Make:    Chord
Model:   RushMobile
Year:    1994
Price:   $28675.99

Make:    Gee 'Em
Model:   Sprinter
Year:    1967
Price:   $24344.01
```

Analysis If you run this program, Turbo C++ issues neither errors nor warnings even though you declare members but never use them (wholesalePrice and maxMPH). Turbo C++ knows that you cannot use these two members in the normal sense of the word as you do with regular members.

DO — DON'T

DO use class in place of struct to protect your data as much as possible. The two can offer the same protection if you specify the appropriate access specifiers, but the default private access of classes provides safer protection and you don't risk forgetting to specify private as you would have to do to protect struct private members.

DO insert the `public` keyword in front of those members that must be accessed directly in `main()` and the rest of the program. Leave the rest specified as `private`. You'll learn how to get at those private members in tomorrow's chapter.

DO explicitly specify `private` for private class members even though they default to private because doing so shows your intent and helps document the code. However, leaving off `private` at the top of a `class` does no harm (whereas forgetting `private` when working with structures could expose members that shouldn't be exposed).

DON'T mix lots of private and public members throughout a class. Keep all your private members in one place (at the top of the class is best) and all the public members in another place.

Summary

If you think that a lot of this discussion is elementary, you're right—it is. But remember one thing: *all* of Turbo C++ is elementary. Learning Turbo C++ doesn't take an advanced degree in computer science!

Note: If you learn the basics well (these next few days), you'll have no problem tackling some of the more advanced OOP topics. If, however, you skim through the basics as a lot of newcomers to OOP concepts do, you'll lack the deeper understanding needed to master OOP concepts.

This chapter began with a review that was intended to drive home the point that structures create abstract data types. In Turbo C++, unlike its C predecessors, the `struct` keyword (and also the `class` keyword) doesn't have to precede the variable being defined.

In reality, the term *abstract data type* is a little misleading, because to Turbo C++, there is very little about your declared data types that is abstract. As you learn more about OOP, you'll learn more ways to make your abstract data types mimic the built-in data types even more. Perhaps the most obvious application which shows that an abstract data type becomes like a built-in data type is when you nest structures and classes. After you've defined a class, you can use that class as a member of another class.

The last part of today's chapter explained the access specifiers that enable you to use the `class` keyword to create very well-protected data—so well, in fact, that `main()` cannot have access to that data.

All data protection is done at the member level by the access specifiers `private` and `public`. In other words, you cannot protect an entire class variable, just its members. The ordinary rules for local and global variables apply to class variables.

Q&A

1. What is an *abstract data type?*

   An abstract data type is a data type that you define and add to your program. You are probably used to adding structure variables to a program. Before creating structure variables, you have to tell C and Turbo C++ what the format of your structure looks like. You don't, however, have to tell C or Turbo C++ what an `int` looks like because, unlike abstract data types, built-in data types are already understood by the compiler.

   After you add an abstract data type to a program, the rest of that program treats the abstract data type *almost* as if it were a supplied built-in data type.

2. What is the difference between `struct` and `class`?

   Despite all the articles and books written about classes, there is one and only one difference: class members are private by default, whereas structure members are public by default. In every other way, `struct` and `class` do the very same thing.

   The class was introduced in C++ to handle special data-hiding protection needed when programming with objects. The designers of C++ added to the capabilities of structures (tomorrow's chapter will explain the new capabilities) and gave those same capabilities to classes. Structures can now do more than hold members of data, as can classes. However, Turbo C++ programmers prefer to use class variables because they add an extra layer of data-protection by default.

3. Can I keep using the familiar `struct` keyword because I am most used to it? (I'll keep everything `private` that should be.)

   You can keep using `struct`, as long as you place the `public` and `private` keywords properly. If, however, you leave off `private` when data hiding is critical, a structure offers no protection, whereas a class does.

   It's best to begin using `class` and eliminate `struct` from your programming vocabulary because you'll rarely see an OOP-like C++ program that uses structures but not classes.

4. Can I define an abstract data type with a `class`?

   Of course you can because a class is no different from a structure except for the default access provided. After you declare a class, you don't have to use the `class` keyword to define variables for that class. Assuming that you've declared a class named `Child`, both of the following statements define variables for that class:

   ```
   Child girl;
   ```

   and

   ```
   Child boy;
   ```

5. If I cannot get to private members, why define them?

   Beginning in tomorrow's chapter, you'll learn why most Turbo C++ programmers specify *all* `class` members as `private`. Although putting members out of reach of the program seems absurd, the data protection afforded by the hiding of members will eventually provide you with less debugging time when writing programs.

   There are some well-defined ways to get at those private members, but beginning in tomorrow's chapter, you'll have to learn a brand-new OOP concept called *member functions*.

   (In Turbo C++, a `class`—and `struct` because they are the same thing—can have *both* data *and* functions, as you'll see tomorrow.)

Workshop

The Workshop offers quiz questions and exercises to hone your skills and give you feedback on today's lesson. You'll find some proposed answers in Appendix D.

Quiz

1. What is an object?

2. Questions A through E refer to this class and defined variables at the bottom of the class:

```
class computer {
    int RAM;
    int ROM;
public:
    float price;
    char * name;
    int yrBuilt;
} PC, Mac;
```

   A. How many members are private?

   B. What is the name of the class?

   C. How many objects are defined?

   D. If you were to add the `private` specifier without changing the meaning of the class now, where would `private` go?

   E. If the keyword `class` were replaced with `struct`, how many private members would then be defined?

3. True or false: Access to a member is determined by the access to the class or structure variable itself; if `main()` has access to a class variable, `main()` also has access to the private members within that class.

4. True or false: These are equivalent in every way:

```
struct abs {
    int i;
public:
    float x;
};
```

   and

```
class abs {
private:
    int i;
public:
    float x;
};
```

5. True or false: These are equivalent in every way:

```
struct abs {
  int i;
public:
  float x;
};
```

and

```
class abs {
public:
  int i;
public:
  float x;
};
```

Exercise

1. Rewrite the structure program from Listing 8.1 using class in place of
   struct on line 7. You don't need to modify the program very much to
   make it produce the same output using a class rather than a structure.

Member Functions Activate *class* Variables

Today's chapter shows you how to use the private, hidden data inside your classes. Through *member functions,* you can access all of your program's private data.

Turbo C++ doesn't keep you from getting to the private members totally; if it did, the private section would be worthless. After yesterday's chapter, you know how to protect data by making it private, and after today's, you'll appreciate how Turbo C++ keeps private data protected while still offering access to that data. The access to private data is achieved through a well-defined *controlled* access you can supply.

When you learn how to get to private data through the controlled access offered by member functions, you'll begin to shift the way you think about data. You'll begin to see how Turbo C++ data is *active* data that "knows" how to manipulate itself. When you want a variable printed, you won't print the variable, but the variable will print itself! This magical data activity is all performed through an object's member functions.

Today, you learn about the following topics:

- ☐ How to specify member functions

- ☐ How to call member functions

- ☐ The way to activate objects

- ☐ Using the scope resolution operator to code member functions outside a `class`

- ☐ Member function argument lists

- ☐ How member functions work inside the class scope

- ☐ That *encapsulation* is little more than a long word

- ☐ What the `*this` pointer is all about

Note: A member function is sometimes called a *method* because it provides a strict method that dictates how to access private data. This book sticks to the more obvious term *member function.* You'll see why the term *member function* is clearer when you see how to place member functions inside a class.

Member Functions Combined with Data Members

You are already well-aware of what data members are. The following class has three of them:

```
class Abc {
  char a;       // A character data member
  int b;        // An integer data member
  float c;      // A floating-point data member
};
```

You could say that this class has *characteristics*. The characteristics describe the format of the class. The characteristics include a character member, an integer member, and a floating-point member. All of these members compose the characteristics of the Abc class.

OK, hang on to your hats because here comes the single most important concept that differentiates Turbo C++ from other non-OOP languages:

> *You can insert functions directly inside a* class *(or* struct*) declaration!*

Here is a function located inside the Abc class:

```
class Abc {
  char a;       // A character data member
  int b;        // An integer data member
  float c;      // A floating-point data member
  void pr(void)
  {
    cout << "a is " << a << "\n";
    cout << "b is " << b << "\n";
    cout << "c is " << c << "\n";
  }
};
```

Isn't that the strangest thing you've ever seen? The Abc class now has *four* members, three data members and one member function. The data items inside the class declaration are called data members. If there are functions inside class declarations, they are called *member functions* (the name makes sense because functions are members of the class).

All four members are private because the default protection offered by classes is private, unless you override that protection with a public access specifier. It is said that the Abc class still has the same characteristics described earlier: three data members. The Abc class now has *behavior* as well. It is that behavior that really distinguishes Turbo C++ OOP objects. In its practical definition, an object variable has both characteristics and behaviors.

239

Note: Structures won't be mentioned much for the remainder of this book, but as yesterday's chapter taught, a `struct` is *exactly* the same as a `class` in Turbo C++, and you can add functions to structures just as you can to classes. The only difference is the default public access provided by structures versus the private access provided by classes. (Structures could not contain member functions in C.)

When your member functions are private, the rest of the program cannot access them. Therefore, you usually see member functions in the `public` section of classes. (There are some member functions best left in the `private` section, and this chapter explains when that is appropriate.)

DO   **DON'T**

DO insert member functions directly inside a `class` definition to add behaviors to the class.

DON'T put needed member functions in the `private` section of a class if the nonclass portion of the program is going to use them.

Using Public Member Functions

Although the `Abc` class is simple, there are some modifications that make the class usable by the program that contains the `Abc` class. For starters, it would be smart to keep all the data members in the `private` section and put some member functions in a `public` section.

What are some of the things programmers do with class data? Defining an `Abc` class variable is simple because `main()`, and any other function, can define `Abc` variables as long as the class declaration remains global (but the data members won't be available). There must be a way to initialize the data by putting values in the members. Also, the data members must be printable to see what they contain.

Listing 9.1 contains a program that includes the `Abc` class with two public member functions. One function initializes the data and the other prints the data. The `main()`

function executes the member functions and the Analysis section after the program explains how the member functions are triggered.

Listing 9.1. Looking at a class with data members and member functions.

```
1:  // Filename: CLSFUN.CPP
2:  // First program with data members and a member
3:  // function in the same class.
4:  #include <iostream.h>
5:  #include <conio.h>
6:  class Abc {
7:  private:         // Not needed but recommended
8:    char a;
9:    int b;
10:   float c;
11: public:          // main() can "see" the rest of the class
12:   void init(void)
13:    { a = 'x';      // Assign the data members some values
14:       b = 100;
15:       c = 12.345;
16:    }
17:   void prAbc(void)
18:    { cout << "a is " << a << "\n";
19:       cout << "b is " << b << "\n";
20:       cout << "c is " << c << "\n";
21:    }
22: };
23: main()
24: {
25:    clrscr();
26:    Abc aVar;       // Defines an Abc variable
27:    aVar.init();    // Initialize the variables
28:    aVar.prAbc();   // Print the data
29:    return 0;
30: }
```

```
a is x
b is 100
c is 12.345
```

Although the program initializes and prints data, main() is extremely small. One of the characteristics of object-oriented Turbo C++ programs is that main() and the rest of the nonclass portion of the program shrink in size from a comparable non-OOP program. The entire program's size is about the same as that of a non-OOP program, but much of the code moves up into the class section.

The only members of the class that `main()` can access are the two public member functions. If there were public data members, `main()` could access those. Lines 27 and 28 trigger the execution of each of the public member functions. Notice that the dot operator executes the member functions; you use the dot operator to access data members of class variables and to execute member functions of class variables as well.

Before getting too far ahead (and the questions in your head are probably flying, but they'll be answered shortly), take a look at a variation on this program that assigns random values to the data members rather than constants. Rather than one class variable, the program in Listing 9.2 defines two variables, each having different data due to the random values assigned to each.

 Listing 9.2. Defining two class variables.

```
1:  // Filename: CLSFUN2.CPP
2:  // Program with two class variables
3:  #include <iostream.h>
4:  #include <conio.h>
5:  #include <stdlib.h>
6:  class Abc {
7:  private:        // Not needed but recommended
8:     char a;
9:     int b;
10:    float c;
11: public:         // main() can "see" the rest of the class
12:    void init(void)
13:      { a = (rand() % 27) + 65;   // Random ASCII from 'A' to 'Z'
14:        b = rand() % 100;
15:        c = float(rand() * .25);
16:      }
17:    void prAbc(void)
18:      { cout << "a is " << a << "\n";
19:        cout << "b is " << b << "\n";
20:        cout << "c is " << c << "\n";
21:      }
22: };
23: main()
24: {
25:    clrscr();
26:    Abc aVar1, aVar2;  // Defines two Abc variables
27:    aVar1.init();      // Initialize the first variable
28:    aVar1.prAbc();     // Print the first variable
29:    aVar2.init();      // Initialize the second variable
30:    aVar2.prAbc();     // Print the second variable
31:    return 0;
32: }
```

```
a is W
b is 30
c is 2745.5
a is K
b is 56
c is 1779.25
```

Lines 27 through 30 show that the member functions apply to the object variables that trigger those functions. In other words, init() is applied to the aVar1 or aVar2 objects depending on which variable appears in front of the dot operator.

It is important to note that there is not really a separate copy of the member functions in each object, although there are separate copies of the data members. Figure 9.1 shows that the object variables share the same member functions (through some internal pointers) but have their own copies of data members to make good use of memory.

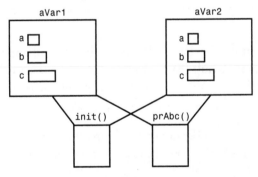

Figure 9.1. *Turbo C++ acts as if each object variable contains its own data and member functions.*

Note: For all practical purposes, consider that the objects have their own copies of the member functions even though they don't. As the next section points out, thinking of the objects as containers of both data and functions helps objects mirror the real world they represent.

If you defined pointers to classes rather than class variables, you can use the structure pointer operator to trigger the execution of member functions. For example, suppose you created a pointer to the Abc class like this:

```
Abc * avarPtr;
```

And then you allocated the class data space on the heap like this:

```
avarPtr = new Abc;
```

You could then initialize the heap with the init() function, and then print the heap space with the prAbc() function like this:

```
avarPtr->init();    // Initialize the heap object
avarPtr->prAbc();   // Print the heap data
```

That's What Objects Are All About

You might be wondering what was gained by adding member functions to objects. Certainly, the length of the program was not reduced, just the length of main(). (In longer programs, you will see some shortening of the code, but brevity does not always occur and is not the OOP goal by any means—readability and maintainability are the goals of OOP.)

By adding member functions to the objects, you have just added behaviors to the data. You have a smart variable that is active and not passive as non-OOP variables are. For example, consider what you are requesting when you type this:

```
aVar1.init();
```

Although the syntax of the dot operator preceding a function call is new to you, the actual execution of the init() function is not really that big of a deal, and you can figure out what is going on. You are doing more than just telling Turbo C++ to execute a function, however—you are telling a *variable* to execute that function. You are telling the aVar1 variable, "Go initialize yourself."

After your data contains behaviors as well as characteristics, your data can manipulate itself. You still have to write the code that tells the data what it can do. The member function, in effect, teaches the data how to behave.

As mentioned briefly in yesterday's chapter, a member function is sometimes called a *method*. The method is what the variable uses to fulfill your request. Perhaps this other common term for the execution of the member function is even more appropriate: *passing a message to an object.*

Use your imagination and picture the statements

```
aVar1.init();
aVar1.prAbc();
```

as instructing the aVar1 object variable to go initialize and print itself. In effect, you are whispering a message to the objects directing them to go off on their own and do something.

After your objects "know" how to behave, they become active parts of your program. You have to train them by writing their code, code that would usually appear in the body of the program, but after you write the code for those behaviors, the rest of your program becomes simply a director that directs when objects are to do their thing.

An object-oriented programmer does not so much write code as write directions for objects. The code that describes the behaviors of the objects, the member functions, could conceivably take more source-code real estate than the entire rest of the program. This could happen because all the details are contained in the class so that the objects know what to do. Most of the program's details rise to the class level. You are left with a handful of directions that are *much* more manageable than if the details were left in the main body of the code.

Again consider the program back in Listing 9.2. The main() function, the primary body of the program, is much shorter than the class itself. The size of main() shrank considerably. Also, the simpleness of main() increased.

In other words, when you take the details out of main(), you write programs at an abstraction level *above* that of regular structured programming techniques. All the details are taken out of your primary program's hands and put into the class's hands.

Assembly-Line Programming

For years, the backlogs in programming departments kept programmers working frantically to produce the programs demanded. Although manufacturing of almost every product has been automated into a smooth assembly-line process, programming remains too personal and detail-prone to automate to the level where production gains can be made that equal those of other industries.

Finally, OOP brings that assembly-line automation to programming. It is because of the efficiency improvements offered by OOP that the programming backlogs might tend to level off eventually and cost efficiencies in programming can finally be achieved. (Some estimate that OOP improves programmer productivity by factors of 10 or more.)

When a plant builds an automobile, the employees take prefabricated parts and put those parts into place. The car makers don't have to make the windshield glass, attach the rubber to the wiper blades, and tread the tires because all those details are left up to the experts who make those items. The car experts do what they do best: assemble the cars.

Some day, you'll be able to buy classes that contain all the details (member functions for the behaviors and data members for the storage) for specific applications, such as accounting classes, payroll classes, and inventory classes. Your program will only have to direct the objects and order their creation and manipulation without having to understand all the petty details inside the classes. The car builder doesn't know or care how the windshield was made; the OOP programmer does not have to know about all the petty details inside a class to use a store-bought class. Programmers will be able to pick and choose classes to build their programs just as an assembly-line picks and chooses parts that go into the production of a product.

In addition, businesses are already popping up that write classes you can buy and use in your own programs. Someday, you might write classes for others to use.

You Now Have Controlled Access

The private data and public member functions compose a fully protected data class. The data within the class is protected, much more than with regular non-OOP local variables, because *nothing* in the rest of the program can change the data members. The data members can be changed only through the member functions.

The primary purpose of member functions is to control access to data for the rest of the program. When you want data initialized, you don't directly initialize the data, you initialize the data through member functions. When you want to see values in variables, you have to call displaying member functions that show the values.

Figure 9.2 shows that all access to and from the data members is to be handled by the member functions. The member functions, sometimes called *access functions* for obvious reasons, access the data for the rest of the program. The access to all data will now be controlled access. If data is not to be changed, don't provide a member

function which changes that data. If data is to be used for calculations but never printed, don't provide a printing member function for the data but provide only a function that returns the value of the data so that the data can be used in other calculations.

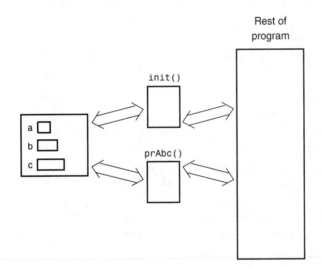

Figure 9.2. *The member functions provide all access to objects throughout the rest of the program.*

The next section shows you how to use the member functions to pass values to objects from the rest of the program. The member functions provide the vehicle that the rest of the program uses to change class data. The advantage with OOP programming, as you'll see, is that bad values *never* end up in your variables whereas there is no way to control such occurrences in regular non-OOP programming without a lot of bulky and cumbersome error-checking routines after each assignment statement.

Less Abstraction

Here's another OOP difference to keep a lookout for: Notice that the program doesn't really need to know what a class's member function code looks like. Someday when you buy off-the-shelf classes, you'll be provided with a `class` header that shows the private data members and the public member function *prototypes*, but you won't be privy to the code inside the member functions (you'll see how to set up such a class later in today's chapter). There is no reason why the programmer who uses a member access function has to know the contents of that function. The programmer needs to know only what kind of access (initialization, displaying, or allocating) the function provides. When you use a microwave oven, you don't have to know what wires are behind the button panel in order to use the High setting; when you use a class, you don't have to know the code underneath the access functions to use the access functions and manipulate the class data.

Our object data values are becoming more like the real-world objects they represent. There is less abstraction between your program objects, such as an employee object, and real-world counterparts. An employee clocks in, works so many hours, gets paid, and so forth. Your employee objects can now take on those kinds of behaviors too because OOP objects have behaviors provided by member functions. You can tell an employee object to go home (by passing a message such as emp.goHome()), and the goHome() function executes on that employee's data and stops the hour totaling for that employee.

The more you learn about Turbo C++ and OOP, the more you'll see your programming reflect the real-world behaviors and the easier your programs will be to write and maintain.

main() Can Pass
Data to an Object

If an initialization member function always assigned the same value to an object, or if a member function always assigned random values to an object (as today's earlier listings did), the whole OOP concept would be worthless. Luckily, however, there is nothing that says a member function cannot initialize an object with user input or through data passed from main().

The program in Listing 9.3 shows the Abc class program with two different initialization member functions. The first one, getVals(), asks the user for the three values from within the member function and assigns the data members those values. The

second initialization member function named init() assigns values passed from main() to the data members for whatever object gets the message to initialize. The program shows how member functions act to transfer values from main() to your data members.

Listing 9.3. Passing values to member functions.

```
1:  // Filename: INIT2.CPP
2:  // A class that initializes itself from outside sources.
3:  #include <iostream.h>
4:  #include <iomanip.h>
5:  #include <conio.h>
6:  // Class declaration next
7:  class Abc {
8:  private:
9:    char a;
10:   int b;
11:   float c;
12: public:
13:   void getVals(void)
14:   { cout << "What is the value of a? ";
15:     cin >> a;
16:     cout << "What is b? ";
17:     cin >> b;
18:     cout << "What is c? ";
19:     cin >> c;
20:   }
21:   void init(char mainA, int mainB, float mainC)
22:   { a = mainA;   // Assign the data members whatever
23:     b = mainB;   // values are passed from main().
24:     c = mainC;
25:   }
26:   void prAbc(void)
27:   { cout << "here are the values:\n";
28:     cout << "a is " << a << "\n";
29:     cout << "b is " << b << "\n";
30:     cout << "c is " << c << "\n";
31:   }
32: };
33: main()
34: {
35:   Abc aVar1, aVar2;
36:   clrscr();
37:   aVar1.getVals();   // User will initialize these members
38:   aVar2.init('x', 12, 56.65);  // main() initializes these
39:   cout << setprecision(2);
40:   cout << "\nFor aVar1, ";
41:   aVar1.prAbc();
42:   cout << "\nFor aVar2, ";
43:   aVar2.prAbc();
```

continues   249

Listing 9.3. continued

```
44:    return 0;
45: }
```

```
What is the value of a? q
What is b? 12
What is c? 3.4
```

```
For aVar1, here are the values:
a is q
b is 12
c is 3.4

For aVar2, here are the values:
a is x
b is 12
c is 56.65
```

Line 37 calls a member function that first asks the user for three values and then assigns those values to the data members. Turbo C++ knows which object variable, aVar1, to initialize because in main()'s line 37, aVar1 was sent the message to initialize using the getVals() member function. Line 38 passes values directly from main() to the member function, and the member function assigns those three values to the data members of the class variable. main() could not directly assign values to the three data members, so the access function initializes the data for main().

Again, notice that main() is becoming little more than an outline of a program. main() is just a high-level set of instructions that directs the objects and tells them what to do by passing them messages (via member functions).

Note: Notice that there is no need to prototype the member functions because they are seen by the compiler before main() triggers their execution. In regular C programs, main() usually physically appears in the program before the first function that it calls, so you have to prototype non-OOP functions called by main(). (Member functions are sometimes called *self-prototyping functions* because their definition appears before they are called, even though they are not called in the usual way.) There are exceptions, however, and you'll see a little later in today's chapter why you should prototype some member functions.

It's interesting to see the way some Turbo C++ programmers would program the arguments for the `init()` function. Consider this rewritten version of `init()`:

```
void init(char A, int B, float C)
{ a = A;  // Assign the data members whatever
  b = B;  // values are passed from main().
  c = C;
}
```

The only difference between this version and the one on lines 21–25 is that the parameter names differ. Notice that uppercase versions of the data member names are used. The case of variable names is critical to Turbo C++ just as it is to C. An uppercase variable named A is different from a lowercase variable named a. The parameters are named with the same names, with the case differences, as the data members they initialize. You'll find that such parameter names are common throughout the C++ community.

Many Turbo C++ programmers take full advantage of default argument lists. If you put default values in member function argument lists (in the class header), the data members will be initialized to those default values unless `main()` or another user of the initialization function passes values to override those defaults. As with all Turbo C++ functions, you can overload member functions as well. Throughout this book, you'll read all about overloaded member functions and default argument lists in them.

Don't Attempt to Initialize Class Definitions!

There is no way to initialize class data members like this:

```
class Abc {
private:
  char a = 'q';      // Can't do because there are no
  int b = 33;        // class variables defined yet!!
  float c = 98.76;
public:
  // Rest of class goes here
};
```

You can store data only after defining variables. The `class` is being defined here, but no storage is reserved that can hold data until later when you define variables with statements such as these:

```
Abc aVar1, aVar2;    // Defines 2 class variables
```

Although most programmers know not to initialize structure members inside the structure definition, it helps for you to be reminded that classes work the same way.

DO   DON'T

DO add arguments to your member functions if you want the rest of the program to be able to pass values to the member functions.

DON'T prototype member functions such as the ones you have seen. Later in today's chapter, you'll see how to move member function code from the class to an area outside the class, and you'll have to prototype the functions when you do that.

DON'T attempt to initialize class members inside the `class` definition. The `class` definition defines the format of the class; you can store data only after you define variables for that class.

Returning from Member Functions

Member functions are not just one-way data tunnels to your objects. A member function can return a value to main() very easily as long as you set up a return values from the member function.

The program in Listing 9.4 is the same as the one in Listing 9.3 with one exception. main() needs to total the object variables' floating-point values. Therefore, main() must be given the capability to read the contents of the data members.

Note: Lots of times, you'll write a member function that does nothing more than return the value of one of the data members. Again, main() cannot directly read the data members, so a public access function has to be written to return the value to main(). These kinds of member functions are read-only member functions; they return values but do no initialization of data members.

Listing 9.4. A member function might need to return member values to the rest of the program.

```cpp
1:  // Filename: INITRET.CPP
2:  // A class that initializes itself from outside sources
3:  // and returns a value to main().
4:  #include <iostream.h>
5:  #include <iomanip.h>
6:  #include <conio.h>
7:  // Class declaration next
8:  class Abc {
9:  private:
10:   char a;
11:   int b;
12:   float c;
13: public:
14:   void getVals(void)
15:   { cout << "What is the value of a? ";
16:     cin >> a;
17:     cout << "What is b? ";
18:     cin >> b;
19:     cout << "What is c? ";
20:     cin >> c;
21:   }
22:   void init(char mainA, int mainB, float mainC)
23:   { a = mainA;  // Assign the data members whatever
24:     b = mainB;  // values are passed from main().
25:     c = mainC;
26:   }
27:   void prAbc(void)
28:   { cout << "here are the values:\n";
29:     cout << "a is " << a << "\n";
30:     cout << "b is " << b << "\n";
31:     cout << "c is " << c << "\n";
32:   }
33:   float getC(void)    // Does nothing more than return a data member
34:   { return c; }
35: };
36: main()
37: {
38:   Abc aVar1, aVar2;
39:   float total;
40:   clrscr();
41:   aVar1.getVals();    // User will initialize these members
42:   aVar2.init('x', 12, 56.65);  // main() initializes these
43:   cout << setprecision(2);
44:   cout << "\nFor aVar1, ";
45:   aVar1.prAbc();
46:   cout << "\nFor aVar2, ";
```

continues

Listing 9.4. continued

```
47:    aVar2.prAbc();
48:    // Now, get the total of the floats
49:    total = aVar1.getC() + aVar2.getC();   // Adds the return values
50:    cout << "\nThe total of the c's is " << total << ".\n";
51:    return 0;
52: }
```

What is the value of a? **u**
What is b? **6**
What is c? **76.5**

For aVar1, here are the values:
a is u
b is 6
c is 76.5

For aVar2, here are the values:
a is x
b is 12
c is 56.65

The total of the c's is 133.15.

Although main() cannot directly access the data members of aVar1 and aVar2, the getC() access function hands main() the values of the appropriate floating-point values so that main() can use them.

Note: Some programmers automatically add a read-only member function, such as the one shown in Listing 9.4's lines 33 and 34, for every data member. Although having read-only access for every member is sometimes overkill, you'll find yourself writing lots of them. Letting main() (and the rest of the program) read public values directly does not offer as much control (and safety) as providing access functions that return values when appropriate.

Cleaning Up the Class

The Abc class is getting quite large. Pretty soon, the class will be as big as an entire equivalent non-OOP program! Actually, you are doing little more than moving details out of the main() program and into the class. Although the amount of coding

is not less, the way you are beginning to look at programs is extremely different. Fairly soon, you'll hardly remember putting details of a class's manipulation down into the primary part of the program because the class member functions will seem so natural. After all, it is the objects that should do all the work, even though non-OOP procedural programming has made the roles of variables passive. A small shift in thinking can activate variables, putting that activity where it belongs.

There is a common way to clean up a `class` definition a little using the scope resolution operator, `::`, that you read about back in Day 2's chapter, "C++ Is Superior!" You can prototype your member functions in the class, leaving only a *class header* (an outline of the class with data members and member function prototypes) and put the body of the member functions following the class (but before `main()` as is usually done).

Listing 9.5 contains the same program as Listing 9.4 except that the class is cleaned up greatly because only the class header is left in the class definition. The body of the member functions follows the `Abc` class. Notice the definition lines of each member function; you'll see the `::` operator used on each line. The analysis section after the program explains how the scope resolution operator helps the `Abc` class find its member functions.

Type

Listing 9.5. Cleaning up the class and leaving only a class header.

```
1:  // Filename: CLSSHEAD.CPP
2:  // After cleaning up the class.
3:  #include <iostream.h>
4:  #include <iomanip.h>
5:  #include <conio.h>
6:  // Class declaration next
7:  class Abc {
8:  private:
9:     char a;
10:    int b;
11:    float c;
12: public:
13:    void getVals(void);
14:    void init(char mainA, int mainB, float mainC);
15:    void prAbc(void);
16:    float getC(void);
17: };
18: void Abc::getVals(void)
19:    { cout << "What is the value of a? ";
20:      cin >> a;
```

continues

Listing 9.5. continued

```
21:      cout << "What is b? ";
22:      cin >> b;
23:      cout << "What is c? ";
24:      cin >> c;
25:    }
26: void Abc::init(char mainA, int mainB, float mainC)
27:    { a = mainA;  // Assign the data members whatever
28:      b = mainB;  // values are passed from main().
29:      c = mainC;
30:    }
31: void Abc::prAbc(void)
32:    { cout << "here are the values:\n";
33:      cout << "a is " << a << "\n";
34:      cout << "b is " << b << "\n";
35:      cout << "c is " << c << "\n";
36:    }
37: float Abc::getC(void) // Does nothing more than return a data member
38:    { return c; }
49: //////////////////////// Class ends here /////////////////////////////
40: main()
41: {
42:    Abc aVar1, aVar2;
43:    float total;
44:    clrscr();
45:    aVar1.getVals();   // User will initialize these members
46:    aVar2.init('x', 12, 56.65);  // main() initializes these
47:    cout << setprecision(2);
48:    cout << "\nFor aVar1, ";
49:    aVar1.prAbc();
50:    cout << "\nFor aVar2, ";
51:    aVar2.prAbc();
52:    // Now, get the total of the floats
53:    total = aVar1.getC() + aVar2.getC();  // Adds the return values
54:    cout << "\nThe total of the c's is " << total << ".\n";
55:    return 0;
56: }
```

Analysis

The scope resolution operators seem strange at first. After all, without the Abc::
in front of the getVals() function on line 18, wouldn't Turbo C++ still be able
to find getVals()? It turns out that *class scope,* introduced in yesterday's chapter,
plays a role here that requires the use of the class name followed by :: in front of every
function you define outside a class.

Every member of a class has class scope. If you wanted, you could define many more
classes in Listing 9.5's program, *all with the same member function names.* The function

names can be the same because each name is scoped to the class in which it is prototyped or defined.

It is because more than one function could have a function named getVals() that you must resolve the scope of the getVals() function along with every other function defined after the class. The fact that there is only a single class in this program has no bearing on the need to resolve the class scope of getVals(). If you define the body of a member function directly inside the class header, there is no need to resolve its scope, but if you place the body of the member function outside the class, you must resolve its scope as shown in lines 18, 26, 31, and 37.

Most Turbo C++ programmers leave their member function definitions outside their class headers. When a class header is left without member function code, the class is cleaner and easier to maintain.

Many Turbo C++ programmers prefer to type their class headers in their source code, but they include (with the #include directive) the member function definitions. These programmers' class header (or headers if more than one class is used by the program, as is frequently done) is then available for them to peruse while programming, and the details are left in the included files for compilation.

Perhaps the most important reason for separating class headers from their member function code is for class distribution. It is possible to compile (but not link) class member function code by itself and store that compiled object code as a stand-alone file. Whenever you write programs which use that class, the programs need only a copy of the class header (which is usually included with #include), and the member functions are then linked to the compiled program which uses that class.

Separate compilation of classes lets class vendors (people who write classes for a living) sell their class code without distributing source code to their classes. When you purchase math or I/O classes to use with your own programs, the class vendor usually supplies you with the following three items:

1. A class header amply commented.

2. A compiled object file with the class's member function definitions.

3. Documentation that tells how to use the class and what the class provides.

The class header (and sample documentation) is all you need in order to write programs with other people's classes. As mentioned earlier in this chapter, you need not know the details of a class to use the class just as you need not know the inside components of your monitor to plug it in and use it. Classes are going to be available, if predictions are correct, for all kinds of professions and computing needs. When you want to write OOP programs, you won't *write* them as much as you'll *build* them with parts (other people's classes as well as classes you have written).

This building-block approach is why the programming industry is so gung-ho about OOP. Perhaps there really might be an end to the programming backlog that plagues data processing departments across the country.

DO	**DON'T**

DO write access member functions that do nothing more than return member values when main() or another part of the program needs to use one of the members.

DO write clean class headers by placing the member function definitions beneath the class. An even better practice would be to place all class definitions in a header file and include the class code with an #include directive. The best practice of all is to supply the class header but compile the class member functions and link the compiled code to your programs which use that class.

DON'T forget to resolve the scope of all member function definitions you place outside the class. You must precede *every* member function with its class name and scope resolution operator before Turbo C++ can match the function to the class in which it belongs.

Use *inline* for Efficiency

There is one simple addition you can make to your classes that improves their efficiency. Add the inline keyword to your class member functions. You learned in day 2's chapter that inline suggests to the compiler (Turbo C++ can ignore the suggestion) that it expand the function call into the function code itself.

When Turbo C++ is able to inline your member function code successfully, your class member function executions become more efficient. Inlining class member functions requires nothing more than adding the inline keyword before the member function names, as shown in Listing 9.6. Listing 9.6 does the same thing as Listing 9.5. The only differences are the inline keywords on lines 18, 26, 31, and 37.

Listing 9.6. Improving your program's efficiency with `inline`.

```cpp
 1: // Filename: CLSSINL.CPP
 2: // Adding inline to improve efficiency.
 3: #include <iostream.h>
 4: #include <iomanip.h>
 5: #include <conio.h>
 6: // Class declaration next
 7: class Abc {
 8: private:
 9:    char a;
10:    int b;
11:    float c;
12: public:
13:    void getVals(void);
14:    void init(char mainA, int mainB, float mainC);
15:    void prAbc(void);
16:    float getC(void);
17: };
18: inline void Abc::getVals(void)     // First inlined function
19:    { cout << "What is the value of a? ";
20:       cin >> a;
21:       cout << "What is b? ";
22:       cin >> b;
23:       cout << "What is c? ";
24:       cin >> c;
25:    }
26: inline void Abc::init(char mainA, int mainB, float mainC)
27:    { a = mainA;   // Assign the data members whatever
28:       b = mainB;   // values are passed from main().
29:       c = mainC;
30:    }
31: inline void Abc::prAbc(void)
32:    { cout << "here are the values:\n";
33:       cout << "a is " << a << "\n";
34:       cout << "b is " << b << "\n";
35:       cout << "c is " << c << "\n";
36:    }
37: inline float Abc::getC(void)
38:    { return c; }
39: ///////////////////////// Class ends here /////////////////////////
40: main()
41: {
42:    Abc aVar1, aVar2;
43:    float total;
44:    clrscr();
45:    aVar1.getVals();   // User will initialize these members
46:    aVar2.init('x', 12, 56.65);  // main() initializes these
47:    cout << setprecision(2);
48:    cout << "\nFor aVar1, ";
```

continues

Listing 9.6. continued

```
49:    aVar1.prAbc();
50:    cout << "\nFor aVar2, ";
51:    aVar2.prAbc();
52:    // Now, get the total of the floats
53:    total = aVar1.getC() + aVar2.getC();  // Adds the return values
54:    cout << "\nThe total of the c's is " << total << ".\n";
55:    return 0;
56: }
```

 Note: You don't have to specify `inline` if you list member function code directly inside the class. Turbo C++ automatically inlines those functions.

Make Classes Self-Protecting

Although the `Abc` class has been useful for illustrating class fundamentals, there has been very little advantage to creating the private `Abc` `class` data and making all the class data public. After all, `main()` could initialize the `class` members with any value at all, in effect, through the access member functions, giving `main()` full write-access to the class data.

Most of the time, member functions ensure that *proper* data gets sent to the `class` members. If any values could be assigned, through member functions, the member function does little more than add overhead to programs.

The program in Listing 9.7 provides a little more class functionality to `Abc` data by showing you how the member functions can act as data protectors to the `class`. The member functions ensure that only lowercase letters of the alphabet are passed to the a data member, that only the values from 1 to `10` are passed to the b data member, and that only positive values below `100.0` are passed to c. Notice how `main()` doesn't change in length even though you've added all this checking—the objects themselves now "know" how to initialize with good values and reject bad ones.

 Listing 9.7. Adding error checking to member functions.

```
1:    // Filename: CLSSCHK.CPP
2:    // Access member functions should check to make sure that
3:    // data members never get out-of-range values.
```

```
4:   #include <iostream.h>
5:   #include <iomanip.h>
6:   #include <stdlib.h>
7:   #include <conio.h>
8:   // Class declaration next
9:   class Abc {
10:  private:
11:    char a;
12:    int b;
13:    float c;
14:  public:
15:    void init(char mainA, int mainB, float mainC);
16:    void prAbc(void);
17:  };
18:  inline void Abc::init(char mainA, int mainB, float mainC)
19:    { if (mainA >= 'a' && mainA <= 'z')
20:       {  a = mainA;  } // Assign the data members only correct values
21:      else
22:       { cerr << "a cannot be initialized with " << mainA << ".\n";
23:         exit(1);
24:       }
25:      if (mainB >= 1 && mainB <= 10)
26:       { b = mainB; }
27:      else
28:       { cerr << "b cannot be initialized with " << mainB << ".\n";
29:         exit(1);
30:       }
31:      if (mainC >= 0.0 && mainC < 100.00)
32:       { c = mainC; }
33:      else
34:       { cerr << "c cannot be initialized with " << mainC << ".\n";
35:         exit(1);
36:       }
37:  }
38:  inline void Abc::prAbc(void)
39:    { cout << "here are the values:\n";
40:      cout << "a is " << a << "\n";
41:      cout << "b is " << b << "\n";
42:      cout << "c is " << c << "\n";
43:    }
44:  ///////////////////////// Class ends here /////////////////////////////
45:  main()
46:  {
47:    Abc aVar1, aVar2;
48:    clrscr();
49:    aVar1.init('x', 3, 56.65);
50:    cout << setprecision(2);
51:    cout << "\nFor aVar1, ";
52:    aVar1.prAbc();
53:    // aVar2 will get a bad value
54:    aVar2.init('a', 12, 33.0);  // 12 will trigger the error
```

continues

Listing 9.7. continued

```
55:    cout << "\nFor aVar2, ";
56:    aVar2.prAbc();
57:    return 0;
58: }
```

```
For aVar1, here are the values:
a is x
b is 3
c is 56.65
b cannot be initialized with 12.
```

The error checking done in lines 19–36 make sure that the data members get only the values that fall within their range. When a bad value, the 12, is sent to the data members in line 54 (via the init() member function call), the error-checking member function keeps the bad data from getting to the class variable by stopping the program instead of letting the values get through.

It's worth noting that another member function could have been called just to do the checking. The more you break down your class into separate member functions with their own unique tasks, the easier it will be to spot bugs and the more general-purpose your classes become. For instance, consider this class (the entire program is not listed here, just the class), which lets another member function handle the error correction:

```
class Abc {
private:
  char a;
  int b;
  float c;
public:
  void init(char mainA, int mainB, float mainC);
  void prAbc(void);
  void checkData(char mainA, int mainB, float mainC);
};
inline void Abc::init(char mainA, int mainB, float mainC)
  { checkData(mainA, mainB, mainC);
    // Code gets here only if checkData() didn't terminate
    a = mainA;
    b = mainB;
    c = mainC;
  }
inline void Abc::checkData(char mainA. int mainB, float mainC)
  { if (mainA < 'a' || mainA > 'z')
    { cerr << "a cannot be initialized with " << mainA << ".\n";
      exit(1);
    }
    if (mainB < 1 || mainB > 10)
```

```
    { cerr << "b cannot be initialized with " << mainB << ".\n";
      exit(1);
    }
  if (mainC < 0.0 || mainC >= 100.00)
    { cerr << "c cannot be initialized with " << mainC << ".\n";
      exit(1);
    }
  }
inline void Abc::prAbc(void)
  { cout << "here are the values:\n";
    cout << "a is " << a << "\n";
    cout << "b is " << b << "\n";
    cout << "c is " << c << "\n";
  }
```

The checkData() member function exists only for internal use within the class. init()
calls checkData(), and as long as checkData() finds no data out of bounds, init()
regains control and initializes the data members. However, if checkData() finds a bad
data value, init() will never regain control, and the program will terminate via an
exit() call.

Can you see any reason why checkData() should remain in the public section of the
class? There is no reason why it should. Another member in the class calls checkData(),
not main(). If a function outside the class has no need for access to a class member,
make that member private. Therefore, the better way of arranging the previous class
would be like this:

```
class Abc {
private:
  char a;
  int b;
  float c;
  void checkData(char mainA, int mainB, float mainC);
public:
  void init(char mainA, int mainB, float mainC);
  void prAbc(void);
};
inline void Abc::init(char mainA, int mainB, float mainC)
  { checkData(mainA, mainB, mainC);
    // Code gets here only if checkData() didn't terminate
    a = mainA;
    b = mainB;
    c = mainC;
  }
inline void Abc::checkData(char mainA. int mainB, float mainC)
  { if (mainA < 'a' || mainA > 'z')
    { cerr << "a cannot be initialized with " << mainA << ".\n";
      exit(1);
    }
```

```
    if (mainB < 1 || mainB > 10)
      { cerr << "b cannot be initialized with " << mainB << ".\n";
        exit(1);
      }
    if (mainC < 0.0 || mainC >= 100.00)
      { cerr << "c cannot be initialized with " << mainC << ".\n";
        exit(1);
      }
  }
inline void Abc::prAbc(void)
  { cout << "here are the values:\n";
    cout << "a is " << a << "\n";
    cout << "b is " << b << "\n";
    cout << "c is " << c << "\n";
  }
```

The sixth line is the first time you've seen a member function in the private section of a class, but it makes sense to keep the member function there. Only another member function calls checkData(), so checkData() should remain hidden from the rest of the program that has no need to use it.

To Correct, or Not to Correct...

When an error occurs in a class member function, such as main() attempting to initialize with out-of-range values, should the member function terminate the program as done in the previous program, or should it assign a good value that falls in the range and continue?

Your specific application's needs must dictate the answer to that. Most of the time, you will probably want to terminate the application with appropriate error messages if a bad value is sent to a data member. However, you might have a situation in which the member function can fix values. For instance, if the smallest value that is to go in a data member is zero, and the initialization member function gets a negative initial value, the function might assign a zero and continue as though nothing bad had happened.

Only you know whether a function should change a bad initial value to one that is correct because you know the consequences of such data when you write your programs. Handling an error or correcting the problem is secondary to the overall charge of controlled access member functions; such functions should provide the access to the private data members and be the gateway through which other parts of the program access the data.

DO	**DON'T**

DO use `inline` on your shorter member functions so that Turbo C++ will eliminate the function call overhead when possible.

DO provide data protection through your member functions so that `class` data is not sent incorrect values. The more protection you add to a class, the less work you have to do when *using* that class. That's one reason why you'll become a much faster programmer as you create classes that you can reuse; the classes will contain their own error checking, and you can concentrate on the more important details of the application without putting error checks throughout your programs.

DON'T forget to write two-way access classes. `main()` (and the rest of the program) must have a way to look at and change data members. A read-only access function simply returns the value of a data member so that `main()` can work with the value.

DON'T use `inline` on functions you completely define inside a class header. Turbo C++ inlines those functions automatically.

A More Useful Example

The program in Listing 9.8 contains a class that keeps track of lemonade sales for a kid's neighborhood lemonade stand (if the kid needs a computer to track lemonade sales, it must be good lemonade!). There are two kinds of lemonade sold: sweetened for 50 cents a glass and unsweetened for 45 cents a glass.

The `Lemon` class contains a data member that keeps track of the total dollar amount of lemonade sold and the number of glasses left to sell (beginning with 100 at the start of the day). The amount of sugar teaspoons left (each sweetened lemonade consumes two) is tracked as well. The member function `showTot()` prints the grand total sold.

As customers come to buy lemonade, the member function `buySweet()` adds 50 cents to the total income, and `buyUnSweet()` adds 45 cents. Either way, the number of glasses remaining is decreased automatically.

One `switch` statement and menu controls the program. Notice how `main()` is extremely simple now that the class does all the work. `main()` acts only as a guide ordering the events and directing the objects just as a movie director would direct actors who know how to act.

Listing 9.8. An OOP class program that tracks lemonade sales.

```
1:  // Filename: LEMONS.CPP
2:  // Child's lemonade-sale tracking program
3:  #include <iostream.h>
4:  #include <iomanip.h>
5:  #include <stdlib.h>
6:  #include <conio.h>
7:  // Lemonade class declaration next
8:  class Lemon {
9:  private:
10:    int totalLeft;        // Will start at 100
11:    int sugarTeasp;       // Starts at 80
12:    float total;          // Income for day
13: public:
14:    void init(void);      // Initialize members upon program start-up
15:    void showTot(void);   // Print the day's total income
16:    void buySweet(void);  // Executes when customer buys sweetened
17:    void buyUnSweet(void); // Executes when customer buys unsweetened
18: };
19: void Lemon::init(void)
20: {  totalLeft = 100;
21:    sugarTeasp = 80;
22:    total = 0.0;
23: }
24: void Lemon::showTot(void)
25: { cout << setprecision(2) << setiosflags(ios::fixed);
26:    cout << setiosflags(ios::showpoint); // Ensure that decimal prints
27:    cout << "\nTotal so far today is $" << total << "\n\n";
28: }
29: void Lemon::buySweet(void)
30: {
31:    if (totalLeft == 0)
32:      { cerr << "Sorry, no more lemonade is left.\n\n";}
33:    else
34:      if (sugarTeasp == 0)
35:        { cerr << "No more sugar is left. Sorry.\n\n"; }
36:      else
37:        { cout << "Enjoy your drink!\n\n";
38:          totalLeft--;        // One less glass left
39:          sugarTeasp -= 2;    // Each glass takes 2 teaspoons
40:          total += .50;
41:        }
42: }
43: void Lemon:: buyUnSweet(void)
44: {
45:    if (totalLeft == 0)
46:      { cerr << "Sorry, no more lemonade is left.\n\n";}
47:    else
```

```
48:      { cout << "Enjoy your drink!\n\n";
49:        totalLeft--;        // One less glass left
50:        total += .45;
51:      }
52: }
53: ////////////////////// Class ends here ////////////////////////////
54: main()
55: {
56:   Lemon drink;
57:   int ans;
58:   clrscr();
59:   drink.init();  // Initialize data members to start of day
60:   do {
61:     cout << "What's happening?\n";
62:     cout << "  1. Sell a sweetened.\n";
63:     cout << "  2. Sell an unsweetened.\n";
64:     cout << "  3. Show total sales so far.\n";
65:     cout << "  4. Quit the program.\n";
66:     cout << "What do you want to do? ";
67:     cin >> ans;
68:     switch (ans)
69:      { case 1 : drink.buySweet();
70:                 break;
71:        case 2 : drink.buyUnSweet();
72:                 break;
73:        case 3 : drink.showTot();
74:                 break;
75:        case 4 : drink.showTot();  // Print total one last time
76:                 exit(1);
77:      }
78:   } while (ans >=1 && ans <= 4);
79:   return 0;
80: }
```

```
What's happening?
   1. Sell a sweetened.
   2. Sell an unsweetened.
   3. Show total sales so far.
   4. Quit the program.
What do you want to do? 3

Total so far today is $0.00

What's happening?
   1. Sell a sweetened.
   2. Sell an unsweetened.
   3. Show total sales so far.
   4. Quit the program.
What do you want to do? 1
Enjoy your drink!
```

```
What's happening?
   1. Sell a sweetened.
   2. Sell an unsweetened.
   3. Show total sales so far.
   4. Quit the program.
What do you want to do? 3

Total so far today is $0.50

What's happening?
   1. Sell a sweetened.
   2. Sell an unsweetened.
   3. Show total sales so far.
   4. Quit the program.
What do you want to do? 2
Enjoy your drink!

What's happening?
   1. Sell a sweetened.
   2. Sell an unsweetened.
   3. Show total sales so far.
   4. Quit the program.
What do you want to do? 1
Enjoy your drink!

What's happening?
   1. Sell a sweetened.
   2. Sell an unsweetened.
   3. Show total sales so far.
   4. Quit the program.
What do you want to do? 3

Total so far today is $1.45

What's happening?
   1. Sell a sweetened.
   2. Sell an unsweetened.
   3. Show total sales so far.
   4. Quit the program.
What do you want to do? 4

Total so far today is $1.45
```

Analysis   The program tracks sales of lemonade through a lemonade class that is fairly smart. Although main() cannot directly access any data member, all the member functions of the class take care of initialization, updating, and printing when needed. main() simply guides the drink object and tells it what to do based on user response to the menu.

If more than 40 glasses of sweetened lemonade are sold, the user sees the message

```
No more sugar is left. Sorry.
```

and the total sales is not updated. When all 100 glasses of the lemonade are sold, the message from line 32 or 46 prints depending on the type of lemonade someone is trying to buy.

Here's a Tongue-Twister: Encapsulation

A capsule is an enclosed shell that usually contains several items. A space capsule contains people and equipment. A cold capsule contains granules of cold medicine.

Do you see how a class can be thought of as a capsule? The data members and the member functions are all stored in this capsule called an object.

As you peruse object-oriented programming magazines and reference manuals, you'll run across the term *encapsulation* often. It seems that computer people never use an easy word when a difficult one will do nicely and confuse more people. Nevertheless, the term *encapsulation* will not throw you now because it is obvious to you what encapsulation means: encapsulation is the binding together of data members and member functions in classes (and also structures) so that smart objects that contain both characteristics and behaviors can be created.

The Lemon class in Listing 9.8 is said to be encapsulated with code and data. You'll not be thrown by that word if you read it again!

The Hidden *this* Pointer

If you are the curious kind, you've probably wondered how Turbo C++ matches up the correct objects to data members. (If you haven't wondered why, you'll still be intrigued at the answer.) In other words, when a main() function in the Turbo C++ class Abc program initializes a variable like

```
aVar1.init('x', 3, 56.65);
```

you should understand how Turbo C++ applies the init() function to aVar1 and not to other variables in the program. Turbo C++ pulls some sleight-of-hand during compilation. The reason that you should know about the method is that at times you will need to use this knowledge to make a program behave in a way that you otherwise could not.

Turbo C++ converts the preceding `init()` function call to this:

```
init(&aVar1, 'x', 3, 56.65);
```

In other words, Turbo C++ passes the object variable to the function (by address). The `init()` function's prototype, however, doesn't have a place for the extra variable. The prototype looks like this:

```
void init(char mainA, int mainB, float mainC);
```

Although that's the prototype you entered, Turbo C++ changes it to this during the compilation of your program:

```
void init(Abc * this, char mainA, int mainB, float mainC);
```

The pointer variable, called the *this pointer,* lets the function modify the object in question because pass-by-address lets a called function modify its calling function's values. You never have to remember that this extra argument is being sent. Try to think of statements such as

```
aVar1.init('x', 3, 56.65);
```

as messages being sent to objects. In this case, the statement says, "Hey, aVar1, go initialize yourself with the data values x, 3, and 56.65." The hidden *this pointer ensures that aVar1 keeps any changes made to it by the `init()` member function call.

Note: If you ever need to return an object from a function (and you do need to at times), return the *this value with the following statement:

```
return (*this);
```

Returning the *this pointer ensures that whatever object triggered this function is returned. You don't know ahead of time whether the function will act on aVar1 or aVar2 (keeping the same variable names used in this chapter's examples), but *whatever* object variable triggers the function will be returned by the return statement shown here.

One more thing: Never modify the *this pointer in a member function. Although the data members can change, consider the *this pointer a constant, and you'll always be safe in explicitly referring to it inside a member function if the need arises.

Summary

Today's chapter taught you a lot, and you're probably ready for a break. If so, take a siesta because you have just cleared a major hurdle in the object-oriented programming learning curve.

Member functions are functions that you place directly inside a class (or structure). It is the member function that gives a class its behavior and activates that class by making objects operate on their own.

You don't have to define the entire function inside the class. Most Turbo C++ programmers declare a class header with member function prototypes and then code the function definitions later in the code or include (or link) the member function's code.

Although data members are almost always private to maintain the data protection that Turbo C++ is known for, most of your member functions will be public to allow controlled access to your private data. Instead of the rest of the program accessing data directly, the program will be able to call public member functions when a data value has to be changed or printed.

You'll end up with several member functions in each class. Often, the member functions will grow your classes so that they are larger than the rest of the program that contains them. The more member functions you write, the more kinds of access the rest of the program has to your private data.

When you add argument lists to member functions, the rest of the program can pass values directly to private data via the member functions. When the rest of the program needs to use one of the private data values, you can supply an access function that returns a private value, all the while protecting the value from modification outside the class.

Turbo C++ programmers have coined a word for the canning together of both data and functions into class objects: *encapsulation.* Encapsulation describes the process of binding together the functions and data into capsule-like forms and giving objects their active role in OOP programs.

In today's chapter, you also learned how a hidden *this pointer works behind the scenes to properly give access to objects and their member functions. Every time you pass a message to a member function by triggering one of its member functions, a pointer to that object is secretly passed to the member function so that Turbo C++ will have the object inside the function to work with. Most of the time, you can ignore the hidden `*this` pointer and act as if you know nothing about it.

Q&A

1. Why are objects said to be active rather than passive?

   Objects are said to be active because, compared to non-OOP programs, objects do seemingly take on behaviors and intelligence by initializing themselves, printing themselves, and even allocating themselves. This activity is accomplished by appropriate member functions inside the class.

   When you write member functions instead of putting those functions throughout the rest of the program, you bind the member functions to the objects defined. The rest of the program (from `main()` down) then becomes a director directing objects that take care of themselves instead of manipulating the variables as in non-OOP programs.

   After the class is written, the resulting program's details are reduced considerably. Over time, as you write more and more classes that provide for active data, you'll reuse those classes and build programs much more quickly than before because you'll leave error checking and other tedious details for the class's member functions to handle.

2. Is there an advantage to separating my member function code from my class headers?

   By separating your member function code from the class, leaving just a class header that contains prototypes to those functions, you not only clean up the class but also allow for separate compilation of member function code.

   Separate compilation is how class vendors supply their classes. Suppose you want to write programs that produce 3-D graphics and you find an advertisement that sells a top-notch 3-D graphics class library you can use in your own programs. When you order the class, you'll get the source code for the class header, documentation for using the class, and an object file (the compiled class member functions) that you can link your program to.

3. How can public access member functions protect my private data?

   If your program uses public access functions to access private class data members, those public access functions can check to ensure that data passed

to the public functions are inside the boundary limits required by the class. For example, if you need to initialize an age data member, the access function can keep negative ages from being stored in the member by printing an appropriate error message when needed (ages cannot be negative).

Often, as shown in today's chapter, an access function calls a private member function to do the data checking.

4. How is a *layer of abstraction* removed when I program with objects?

   Objects mirror the real world they represent better than regular non-OOP variables in other kinds of programs. If you were writing a Turbo C++ program that simulated a stoplight, you would write a class that contains a data member, lightColor, and member functions such as turnOnGreen(), turnOnYellow(), and turnOnRed(). The object variable, perhaps aptly named stopLight, would actually seem to change colors on its own when you told it to do so with statements such as this one:

   ```
   stopLight.turnOnRed();   // Tell the light to go red
   ```

   An equivalent non-OOP program would have to set up codes or enumerated data types that set appropriate color codes to the stoplight variable, and functions would have to be called with the light passed to them before the light could change color. In other words, there would be more abstraction between the real-world counterpart and the program.

   The closer your program mirrors the real world that it represents, the faster you will be able to code because your programs will more accurately reflect their real-life counterparts.

5. What exactly is a *this pointer?

   The *this pointer, which is secretly passed to all member functions, is a pointer that points to the object triggering the member function call.

   By passing the *this pointer, Turbo C++ gives member functions access to whatever object variable is triggering the member function at the time. In some instances you will have to work directly with the *this pointer, but most of the time you can ignore the pointer completely.

Workshop

The Workshop offers quiz questions and exercises to hone your skills and give you feedback on today's lesson. You'll find some proposed answers in Appendix D.

Quiz

1. Describe two ways to call member functions.

2. Why must you use a scope resolution operator when coding member function bodies outside class headers?

3. What is meant by the phrase *sending messages to objects?*

4. True or false: You can use default argument lists but not overloaded functions in member functions.

5. How does main() access private data members when data has to be printed?

6. True or false: You can change the *this pointer's data members through a member function, but not the *this pointer itself.

Exercises

1. Write the beginnings of a grading program for a teacher. Create a class named LetterGrades that contains a single character data member named grade. Write two public member functions, one that passes a letter grade to the class variable from main() and one that prints the letter grade. Make sure the first function contains a default argument of 'A' so that the program doesn't have to pass an 'A', just other grades. Define several variables (representing different student scores), and initialize and print them.

2. Add a private member function to the LetterGrades class which ensures that the letter grade falls in the range from A to F (convert lowercase letters a through f to uppercase if needed). Call the member function from the public initialization function before initializing the grade with a value.

3. Add another private function to the lemonade program in Listing 9.8 so that the program prints a warning message when fewer than five glasses are left. Call the function from both sales functions so that a message prints when either the sugar or the lemonade runs low. Optionally, add a fifth menu option that enables the user to supply another 80 spoons of sugar and another 100 glasses of lemonade when needed (the answer to the optional portion is not included in the Appendix D answers).

friends When You Need Them

WEEK 2

10

DAY

Yesterday's chapter was the most important chapter in the book. All knowledge of Turbo C++ and OOP that you gain from this point will be based on the foundation you learned yesterday.

If you understood everything in yesterday's chapter, it is all downhill from here. If you are still a little unsure about the material, please give it some review before continuing. Newcomers to OOP will give up about here if they haven't mastered yesterday's material because everything else in the language is based on member function access to private data. Nothing else will seem difficult if you understand member functions.

To give you some breathing room and time for review, today's chapter lightens things a bit. Today, you'll learn about friend functions and classes, specified by the `friend` keyword. Today's chapter is a little shorter than yesterday's; you need the extra time to review yesterday's chapter. You'll find that friend functions and friend classes are, well, *friendly* and fairly easy to learn.

Friend functions give you a back door to private data that you would otherwise not have access to except through member functions. Although you shouldn't rely on friend functions to bypass normal private access, you'll see some uses for friend functions as this book progresses, especially on Days 11 and 12 (starting tomorrow) when you learn how to overload operators using OOP member functions.

Today, you learn about the following topics:

- ☐ When and how to use friend functions
- ☐ When and how to use friend classes

Why Use Friends?

Suppose that you create a class properly by putting the data members in a private section and member functions in a public section only to find that you need to give data access to certain functions in the program that aren't in the class. There are basically three ways to get around the private specification.

You can insert the `public` keyword at the top of the class, but that defeats the whole purpose of proper data hiding, and you might as well return to non-OOP programming for good if you find yourself eliminating the privatization of data. You can write access functions for the data that return, change, or display the values that the other function needs. Access functions are an important part of OOP programs, as you saw in yesterday's chapter and as you'll see throughout this book.

However, there are some non-member functions and secondary classes which must have intimate access to data that should remain private to other parts of the program. Sometimes, a function needs to have access to data that no other part of the program, outside the class, needs. *Friend functions* and *friend classes* provide access to certain functions and classes without giving up the safety of privatization of the data in general.

 Note: As you progress through this book, especially during Days 11 and 12, you'll see when friend functions are needed most. Some Turbo C+ programmers shy away from using friend functions as much as possible because they believe, and rightfully so, that declaring a function as a `friend` defeats the class mechanism that protects data so well. For now, learn how to specify and use friend functions and friend classes. This book points out when their use is appropriate and when it's inappropriate. Limit your use of the `friend` keyword to those cases described by this book. Unless otherwise needed, reserve all other uses of friends for your social get-togethers.

Friend Functions

A function specified as a `friend` has access to class members but doesn't have to be a part of that class. For example, in the following set of classes, each class has its own printing and initialization member functions:

```
class girlsSoftball {
  char name[25];
  int age;
  float batAvg;
public:
  void prData(void);
  void init(void);
};

class boysSoftball {
  char name[25];
  int age;
  float batAvg;
public:
  void prData(void);
  void init(void);
};
```

There's nothing incorrect about using the same function name in both classes because member functions have class scope and there's no discrepancy in the use of the same name twice. (The same class, however, cannot have two members with the same name.)

Suppose that the person who manages both softball teams was computerizing the two teams' records. Sometimes the manager wants to print the girls' roster and sometimes the manager wants to print the boys' roster. Sometimes, however, the manager wants to print a combined list of both rosters. That's where you encounter the problem that you cannot solve with your current bag of OOP knowledge (without incorrectly inserting public at the top of the classes).

It is possible to set up a friend function that accesses both classes at the same time while still keeping the classes private to all other parts of the program. Before getting into the specifics of adding a friend to both classes, the next section shows you how to write a friend for a single class.

Use *friend* to Specify Friend Functions

Here is a smaller version of the girlsSoftball class shown earlier. The prData() member function is left out. Given the class as it now stands, there is no way for the program to print the contents of the class data because the data is in the private section of the class.

```
class girlsSoftball {
  char name[25];
  int age;
  float batAvg;
public:
  void init(void);
};
```

If you want to add a function to print the data members, that function has to be either a member of the class or a friend function. Remember that a friend function is *not* a member of the class, but is a function completely outside the class scope.

To specify a friend function, insert the function prototype inside the class just as if the function were a member function. Precede the prototype with the friend keyword like this:

```
class girlsSoftball {
  char name[25];
  int age;
  float batAvg;
public:
```

```
    void init(void);
    friend void prData(girlsSoftball p1);   // Friend function
};
```

The `prData()` is now the *only* function besides the member function `init()` that can access the class's private data. If you noticed that `prData()` no longer contains a `void` argument list (it did when `prData()` was a member function), you'll learn why the argument list had to be passed in a moment.

The Class Decides the Friendship

The class itself must offer the friendship. In other words, without the `friend` keyword in front of the function's prototype in the class, no function can be a friend of the class.

Although friend functions slightly bend the data-protection rules, it is the class that contains the `friend` declaration, and therefore it is the class that dictates who is its friend and who is not. Functions cannot gain access to a class's private members unless the class contains the `friend` declaration.

Therefore, the rules are bent. Although a function outside the class can gain private access, the friend is limited to those functions specifically listed as a friend, and a function cannot on its own gain access to a class unless the class contains the `friend` keyword.

The friend function declaration can appear in either the private or the public sections of a class. The location does not matter because the friend function is not a member function. The friend function is just a function outside the class (neither public nor private) that can access the data within the class. The best place to put friend function declarations is along with the rest of your member functions. Many Turbo C++ programmers put friend function declarations at the end of the public section because the function is not really part of the class, and the end placement helps distinguish the function from the member functions that come before it.

Listing 10.1 contains a working program with the girls' softball class and the friend function described earlier. Notice that `prData()`'s function definition appears after `main()` and `main()` calls the function. Unlike most non-member functions called by `main()`, you don't have to prototype `prData()` because it is already prototyped in the class at the `friend` declaration.

Listing 10.1. The friend function accesses private data.

```cpp
1: // Filename: FRND1.CPP
2: // First program that uses a friend function to access a class's
3: // private data members.
4: #include <iostream.h>
5: #include <iomanip.h>
6: #include <string.h>
7: #include <conio.h>
8: class girlsSoftball {
9:    char name[25];
10:    int age;
11:    float batAvg;
12: public:
13:    void init(char N[], int A, float B);
14:    friend void prData(const girlsSoftball pl);
15: };
16: void girlsSoftball::init(char N[], int A, float B)
17: {
18:    strcpy(name, N);
19:    age = A;
20:    batAvg = B;
21: }
22: ///////////////////Primary Program Code Follows///////////////////////
23: main()
24: {
25:    clrscr();
26:    girlsSoftball player1, player2, player3;
27:    player1.init("Stacy", 12, .344);
28:    player2.init("Judith", 13, .326);
29:    player3.init("Leah", 12, .468);
30:    prData(player1);  // Call friend function
31:    prData(player2);
32:    prData(player3);
33:    return 0;
34: }
35: // Friend function's code appears next
36: void prData(const girlsSoftball pl)   // Friend function
37: {
38:    cout << setprecision(3);
39:    cout << "Player name:     " << pl.name << "\n";
40:    cout << "Player age:      " << pl.age << "\n";
41:    cout << "Player average: " << pl.batAvg << "\n\n";
42: }
```

```
Player name:     Stacy
Player age:      12
Player average:  0.344

Player name:     Judith
Player age:      13
Player average:  0.326

Player name:     Leah
Player age:      12
Player average:  0.468
```

The first place to start the analysis is on line 14, the declaration of the friend function named prData(). The friend function requires an argument list so that prData() knows which object variable to print. The following rule holds true for all friend functions, and it is critical that you understand it:

> *Because friend functions are not member functions, they don't get a copy of the* *this *pointer whereas regular member functions do.*

Because prData() doesn't get a copy of a *this pointer to the object, you have to pass the object to prData() just as you would any other non-member function. A friend function is not a member function in any sense of the word; a friend function has access to a class's data, but that's its only advantage over non-friend functions. Friend functions always contain some kind of argument list because you have to get object data to them that they can work with.

Never attempt to execute a non-member function with the dot operator like

```
player1.prData();
```

or Turbo C++ will issue this compiler error message:

```
'prData' is not a member of 'girlsSoftball'
```

Only member functions can execute by the dot operator; all other functions must be called explicitly and passed any data they have to work with.

A Friend of Two Classes

As mentioned earlier, friend functions are often used to access data from more than one class. Suppose that the softball manager wanted to print a list of players' names from *both* teams, the girls' and boys'. A stand-alone prData() function could do so, but only if it were a friend of both classes. Listing 10.2 shows a program in which such is the case.

Listing 10.2. A friend of two classes.

```
1:  // Filename: FRND2.CPP
2:  // First program that uses a friend function to access
3:  // two different class's private data members.
4:  #include <iostream.h>
5:  #include <iomanip.h>
6:  #include <string.h>
7:  #include <conio.h>
8:  class boysSoftball;  // Forward reference (prototype)
9:
10: class girlsSoftball {
11:   char name[25];
12:   int age;
13:   float batAvg;
14: public:
15:   void init(char N[], int A, float B);
16:   friend void prData(const girlsSoftball plG,
        ➥const boysSoftball plB);
17: };
18: void girlsSoftball::init(char N[], int A, float B)
19: {
20:   strcpy(name, N);
21:   age = A;
22:   batAvg = B;
23: }
24: class boysSoftball {
25:   char name[25];
26:   int age;
27:   float batAvg;
28: public:
29:   void init(char N[], int A, float B);
30:   friend void prData(const girlsSoftball plG,
        ➥const boysSoftball plB);
31: };
32: void boysSoftball::init(char N[], int A, float B)
33: {
34:   strcpy(name, N);
35:   age = A;
36:   batAvg = B;
37: }
38:
39: /////////////////Primary Program Code Follows/////////////////////
40: main()
41: {
42:   girlsSoftball Gplayer1, Gplayer2, Gplayer3;
43:   boysSoftball Bplayer1, Bplayer2, Bplayer3;
44:   clrscr();
45:   Gplayer1.init("Stacy", 12, .344);
46:   Gplayer2.init("Judith", 13, .326);
47:   Gplayer3.init("Leah", 12, .468);
```

```
48:    Bplayer1.init("Jim", 11, .231);
49:    Bplayer2.init("Michael", 13, .543);
50:    Bplayer3.init("Larry", 12, .345);
51:    prData(Gplayer1, Bplayer1);   // Call friend function
52:    prData(Gplayer2, Bplayer2);
53:    prData(Gplayer3, Bplayer3);
54:    return 0;
55: }
56: // Friend function's code appears next
57: void prData(const girlsSoftball plG, const boysSoftball plB)
58: {
59:    cout << setprecision(3);
60:    cout << "Player name:    " << plG.name << "\n";
61:    cout << "Player age:     " << plG.age << "\n";
62:    cout << "Player average: " << plG.batAvg << "\n\n";
63:    cout << "Player name:    " << plB.name << "\n";
64:    cout << "Player age:     " << plB.age << "\n";
65:    cout << "Player average: " << plB.batAvg << "\n\n";
66: }
```

```
Player name:    Stacy
Player age:     12
Player average: 0.344

Player name:    Jim
Player age:     11
Player average: 0.231

Player name:    Judith
Player age:     13
Player average: 0.326

Player name:    Michael
Player age:     13
Player average: 0.543

Player name:    Leah
Player age:     12
Player average: 0.468

Player name:    Larry
Player age:     12
Player average: 0.345
```

In general, if you understood the program in Listing 10.1, there is not much more to look at here. The friend function now receives two arguments, one for each object it works with. If the friend function were to work with three classes at the same time (there are only two in this program), then all three class variables would have to be passed to the friend function.

Perhaps the most important part of Listing 10.2 is the simple-looking but strangely placed statement on line 8. Line 8 looks as if the boysSoftball class is about to be defined, but as you can see, the statement doesn't define anything. Line 24 begins the definition of the boysSoftball class.

Line 8 is required because of line 16. The friend function requires two different class variables, and one of those variables is a boysSoftball class object; the boysSoftball class, however, is not defined until later in the program. To eliminate a compile-time error, you often have to give a *forward reference* telling Turbo C++ that a class will be defined later. Between the forward reference and the class definition, you can use the class to declare arguments and so forth without getting an error on line 16.

In a way, the forward reference is a prototype for a class. Rearranging the boysSoftball class with the girlsSoftball class will not help because the boysSoftball prData() prototype would then contain a forward reference to the girlsSoftball class before it is defined.

Note: On Day 19, you'll learn how to create *template* classes that speed class writing when two classes are as closely matched as Listing 10.2's are.

Keep in mind that prData() is a regular stand-alone function in the program, callable from main() or from any other function in the program. The friend keyword gives the function access to the private data, but that's the only thing special about the function.

Figure 10.1 shows a diagram of the relationship prData() has with the two classes. Although prData() lies outside both classes, it has access to the data members.

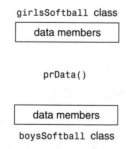

Figure 10.1. *The prData() function is a friend of both classes but not a member of either.*

Listing 10.3 adds three more friend functions to the softball program. Each class has its own individual friend function that computes the batting average of each class. And each class shares two friend functions, one that prints the average of both class averages and the prData() friend function shown previously.

Type Listing 10.3. Adding more friend functions.

```
1:  // Filename: FRND3.CPP
2:  // Adding more friend functions.
3:  #include <iostream.h>
4:  #include <iomanip.h>
5:  #include <string.h>
6:  #include <conio.h>
7:  class boysSoftball;  // Forward reference (prototype)
8:
9:  class girlsSoftball {
10:    char name[25];
11:    int age;
12:    float batAvg;
13: public:
14:    void init(char N[], int A, float B);
15:    friend void gAvg(const girlsSoftball plG[]);
16:    friend void combAvg(const girlsSoftball plG[],
        const boysSoftball plB[]);
17:    friend void prData(const girlsSoftball plG,
        const boysSoftball plB);
18: };
19: void girlsSoftball::init(char N[], int A, float B)
20: {
21:    strcpy(name, N);
22:    age = A;
23:    batAvg = B;
24: }
25: class boysSoftball {
26:    char name[25];
27:    int age;
28:    float batAvg;
29: public:
30:    void init(char N[], int A, float B);
31:    friend void bAvg(const boysSoftball plB[]);
32:    friend void combAvg(const girlsSoftball plG[],
        const boysSoftball plB[]);
33:    friend void prData(const girlsSoftball plG,
        const boysSoftball plB);
34: };
35: void boysSoftball::init(char N[], int A, float B)
36: {
37:    strcpy(name, N);
38:    age = A;
39:    batAvg = B;
```

Listing 10.3. continued

```
40: }
41: /////////////////Primary Program Code Follows//////////////////////////
42: main()
43: {
44:    girlsSoftball Gplayers[3];
45:    boysSoftball Bplayers[3];
46:    clrscr();
47:    Gplayers[0].init("Stacy", 12, .344);
48:    Gplayers[1].init("Judith", 13, .326);
49:    Gplayers[2].init("Leah", 12, .468);
50:    Bplayers[0].init("Jim", 11, .231);
51:    Bplayers[1].init("Michael", 13, .543);
52:    Bplayers[2].init("Larry", 12, .645); // New value to raise average
53:    // Call the friend functions
54:    gAvg(Gplayers);
55:    bAvg(Bplayers);
56:    combAvg(Gplayers, Bplayers);
57:    for (int i=0; i<3; i++)
58:       { prData(Gplayers[i], Bplayers[i]); }
59:    return 0;
60: }
61: //////////////////////////////////////////////////////////////////////
62: // Friend functions are listed next
63: void gAvg(const girlsSoftball plG[])
64: {
65:    float gAvg = 0.0;
66:    for (int i=0; i<3; i++)
67:       { gAvg += plG[i].batAvg; }
68:    gAvg /= 3.0;
69:    cout << setprecision(3);
70:    cout << "The girls' average is " << gAvg << "\n";
71: }
72: //////////////////////////////////////////////////////////////////////
73: void bAvg(const boysSoftball plB[])
74: {
75:    float bAvg = 0.0;
76:    for (int i=0; i<3; i++)
77:       { bAvg += plB[i].batAvg; }
78:    bAvg /= 3.0;
79:    cout << "The boys' average is " << bAvg << "\n";
80: }
81: //////////////////////////////////////////////////////////////////////
82: void combAvg(const girlsSoftball plG[], const boysSoftball plB[])
83: {
84:    float totalAv = 0.0;
85:    for (int i=0; i<3; i++)
86:       { totalAv += (plG[i].batAvg + plB[i].batAvg); }
87:    totalAv /= 6.0;
88:    cout << "The total average of all six players is " << totalAv
        ➥<< "\n\n";
```

```
89: }
90: /////////////////////////////////////////////////////////////
91: void prData(const girlsSoftball plG, const boysSoftball plB)
92: {
93:    cout << "Player name:     " << plG.name << "\n";
94:    cout << "Player age:      " << plG.age << "\n";
95:    cout << "Player average: " << plG.batAvg << "\n\n";
96:    cout << "Player name:     " << plB.name << "\n";
97:    cout << "Player age:      " << plB.age << "\n";
98:    cout << "Player average: " << plB.batAvg << "\n\n";
99: }
```

Output

```
The girls' average is 0.379
The boys' average is 0.473
The total average of all six players is 0.426

Player name:     Stacy
Player age:      12
Player average: 0.344

Player name:     Jim
Player age:      11
Player average: 0.231

Player name:     Judith
Player age:      13
Player average: 0.326

Player name:     Michael
Player age:      13
Player average: 0.543

Player name:     Leah
Player age:      12
Player average: 0.468

Player name:     Larry
Player age:      12
Player average: 0.645
```

Figure 10.2 shows the relationship of the friend functions and classes in Listing 10.3.

DO   **DON'T**

DO use friend functions when a non-member function must work with private data from one or more classes.

DO place the `friend` keyword in the class that is offering the friendship.

DON'T repeat the `friend` keyword before the function's definition itself.

DON'T forget that a friend function cannot be passed a `*this` pointer. Therefore, you must pass object variables to friend functions.

DON'T overdo friend functions, because they are not intended to bypass the safety mechanisms of `private` class declarations.

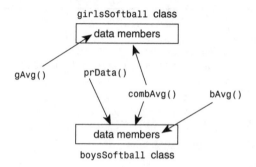

Figure 10.2. *The relationship of Listing 10.3's friend functions.*

Friend Classes

In rare instances, you might want to make one class a friend of another class. Doing so gives all the friend class members access to the other class at once. Specifying a friend class requires trickier logic and doesn't lend itself to extremely readable code. Limit your use of friend classes to those classes that need full access to another class.

Good Design Might Be at Risk

Don't overdo the use of friend functions and classes. If you find that one class needs access to all of another class's members, study your class design to make sure that you can't combine the two classes into one.

The `friend` keyword breaks down the private barriers set up by the `class` designation. Friends are needed in some programs, especially when certain operators are being overloaded, as you'll see in tomorrow's chapter. Also, friends help you write functions that work with more than one class.

Nevertheless, if you write enough access functions that return private values from within classes, you can write functions that work with data from more than one class while still maintaining the class barriers.

Some Turbo C++ programmers cringe at the use of friends, but they realize that friends do fill a need sometimes (we all get lonely...). Therefore, they write friend functions, but they use access functions to get private data even though they could access the private data directly. About the only generally accepted use of friend functions is for operator overloading, as you'll see in tomorrow's chapter. There is widespread agreement that one rarely if ever needs to define friend classes.

Listing 10.4 shows a program that contains a class named regClass and one named frndClass. The frndClass is a friend of the other class and therefore has total access to all the members. Notice that the frndClass prData() member function is able to print anything it wants from the other class and can also call a private function from the other class.

Type **Listing 10.4. A friend class has full access to everything.**

```
1:  // Filename: FRNDCLS.CPP
2:  // Working with a friend class
3:  #include <iostream.h>
4:  #include <iomanip.h>
5:  #include <string.h>
6:  #include <conio.h>
7:  // First regular class follows
8:  class regClass {
9:    int num;
10:   void trip(void);
11:   // Notice there are NO public members!
12:   void init(int i);
13:   friend class frndClass;
14: };
15:
16: void regClass::trip(void)     // Member function definitions
17: {
18:   cout << "Before the triple, num is " << num << "\n";
19:   num = num * 3;
20:   cout << "num is now " << num << " after tripling.\n";
21: }
22: void regClass::init(int i)
23: {
```

continues

Listing 10.4. continued

```
24:    num = i;
25: }
26: // Friend class follows
27: class frndClass {
28:    regClass classVar;    // A member is another class!
29: public:
30:    void prData(int mainI);
31: };
32:
33: void frndClass::prData(int mainI)   // Member function definitions
34: {
35:    classVar.init(mainI); // Calls the regular class's private function
36:    classVar.trip();
37: }
38: /////////////////////////////////////////////////////////////////////
39: // main() isn't much now because the classes do all the work
40: main()
41: {
42:    clrscr();
43:    frndClass item;
44:    item.prData(25);
45:    return 0;
46: }
```

```
Before the triple, num is 25
num is now 75 after tripling.
```

There are all sorts of tricky things going on here, and trickiness is often a part of embedding friend classes. As you know, your goal should be readable code, not tricky code, but if you find yourself writing lots of friend functions to get around private walls, perhaps a friend class with its own functions could maintain the privatization from the rest of the program while getting to the private members it needs.

In main(), a frndClass object named item is defined on line 43, and that object is used to call the prData() routine on line 44. prData() does little in itself. It takes the value passed from main() and on line 35 calls a private function named init() from the other class. prData() acts like a buffer class between main() and regClass. main() cannot initialize regClass data because there are no public functions in the regClass class. prData() collects main()'s value and passes that value onto the private functions in regClass.

In a way, the frndClass is the go-between between main() and a class whose members are all private. Would it have been better to add some public member functions to regClass? Probably so, but if there were other reasons to keep a class fully private, a friend class could get into that class for other parts of the program and still maintain some kind of controlled integrity to the private class.

 Note: The frndClass did not have to be a friend to declare a class member on line 28, but frndClass couldn't get to the private parts of regClass if it weren't a friend.

Friend classes are one-way paths. In other words, regClass is *not* a friend of frndClass even though frndClass is a friend of regClass. If two classes are to be friends of each other, both have to include a friend declaration for the other class. Doing so often creates the need to declare the second class (as done on line 8 of Listing 10.2) before its definition.

DO	DON'T

DO declare friend classes when one class needs access to several or all of the private data members and private member functions of another class.

DON'T forget that the friend declaration generates tricky code, and if you find yourself using friend classes a lot, you might need to combine two classes together into one.

Summary

Today's chapter introduced friend functions and friend classes. The chapter is short to give you a breather from yesterday's chapter, but also there is little to friend functions and classes.

Friend functions are useful when a function is to access more than one class. A regular member function can access only the class in which it is defined. However, a friend function of two or more classes can work with the data in all those classes.

A friend function is a function that has full access to a class's private and public members. The friend designation is always described with the `friend` keyword in the class giving the friendship. A friend function is an ordinary function in all respects except for its access to members that it would otherwise not have access to. Therefore, Turbo C++ never passes the `*this` pointer to friend functions; if you want a friend function to work with an object (and you usually do), you'll have to pass that object to the friend function.

A friend class is a class used as a member of another class. If the class that contains the embedded class wants access to the private members (and it usually does), the embedded class must offer its friendship to the class.

The most important reason for limiting `friend` declarations is this: Friend declarations can produce tricky code and create hard-to-follow programs. There are times when overloading operators (explained in tomorrow's chapter) require the use of friends, and you'll learn for certain in those cases when to use friends and when not to. However, for other times, friends generally offer little more than logic problems except when you *must* write functions that use members from more than one class.

Q&A

1. What is a friend function?

   A friend function is a function that has access to another class's private members but is not a member function. Friend functions are designated by the `friend` keyword in the class giving its friendship. A function or class cannot be a friend to another class unless that class clearly defines the friend relationship.

   Friend functions are most useful when they must access members from more than one class.

2. Why do I have to pass objects to friend functions but I don't have to pass objects to member functions?

   Friend functions are *not* member functions. If they were, there would be no need to specify them as a `friend` because they already have access to the private members of the class.

   Turbo C++ does not automatically pass a `*this` pointer to friend functions, so you'll have to pass all data to a friend that it needs to work with. Keep in mind that friend functions are regular non-member functions, often called by `main()`. Friend functions cannot be triggered by using the dot operator or structure pointer operator as member functions can.

3. What is the difference between a friend function and a friend class?

   As the name implies, a friend function is a function that has access to a class's private and public members. That friend function can access, change, and print any data from within the class. A friend class is a separate class that can access all the members of another class.

   A friend class contains a member whose type matches that of the original class providing the friendship. If the friend class were not a friend, the friend class could include members of the other class but not access the private members of that other class.

Workshop

The Workshop offers quiz questions and exercises to hone your skills and give you feedback on today's lesson. You'll find some proposed answers in Appendix D.

Quiz

1. If you were writing a program and a function needed to have access to private data members of a class, would you put the `friend` keyword before the function declaration, before the function definition, or inside the class itself?

2. True or false: A friend function can have access to a class's public members but not the private members.

3. Why do you sometimes need to declare a class in advance?

4. Where must a friend function or friend class declaration go: in the private or public section of a class?

5. True or false: Friends often improve the readability of a program.

6. Assuming that `doInit()` is a friend function of a class, why could you not execute `doInit()` like this:

   ```
   aClassVar.doInit();
   ```

Exercise

1. Rewrite Listing 10.2 so that main() defines an array of three pointers to each class. Allocate the players on the heap instead of defining individual object variables. Optionally, allocate a linked list with private pointers that point to the next item so that you can eliminate the array of three pointers. Doing so improves your memory usage and enables you to easily add to the program functions and add extra players when needed. (The answer to the optional portion is not trivial and is also not included in the Appendix D answers because of its advanced nature; the linked-list algorithm is outside the scope of this book's goals.)

Introduction to Overloading Operators

Way back on Day 7, you learned about overloaded functions and got a glimpse of overloaded operators. Perhaps you were amazed that you could make Turbo C++'s operators behave the way you want them to behave. Operator overloading is one of the primary reasons why programmers move to Turbo C++.

Nevertheless, when overloaded operators were introduced on Day 7, you did not know anything about classes, the *this pointer, member functions, and all the parts of Turbo C++ that form the basis for OOP. Without OOP, you can overload operators as you read on Day 7, but with OOP, you can really get down to business!

You'll learn starting today (there are so many operators that it takes two days to cover them all) how to overload Turbo C++ operators the OOP way. After you understand member functions and friend functions, you'll be able to use overloaded operators that are easier to write than before your introduction to OOP concepts. Virtually every useful Turbo C++ program that takes advantage of OOP uses operator overloading because of its power, but more important, because of the ease with which you manipulate class data after you overload operators.

When you increase the capability of Turbo C++—and that is exactly what you are doing when you teach the language how to operate on data types that you write—you are *extending* the language. The term *extensibility* is one of those long buzzwords that Turbo C++ programmers use a lot. It simply means that you aren't limited to the base language but you can extend the language's behavior.

Today, you learn about the following topics:

- [ ] How to overload math operators using member functions
- [ ] How the *this pointer affects operator overloading
- [ ] How to overload compound operators that update their first operand
- [ ] How to overload the relational and logical operators
- [ ] How to overload increment and decrement operators
- [ ] How to distinguish between increment and decrement operator postfix and prefix functions

Note: You cannot overload the conditional operator, ?:, the scope resolution operator, ::, the dereference operator, *, or the member dot operator, ..

A Quick Review

Recall that Turbo C++ enables you to overload operators by writing overloaded functions whose names begin with operator and end with the actual operator. For example, the overloaded operator function for addition is operator+(), and the overloaded operator for modulus is operator%().

You cannot change the way Turbo C++ operators work on built-in data types. You cannot make the plus sign do anything to two integers except add the integers together. Unless you write overloaded operator functions, Turbo C++ does not have the capability to operate on your class (or structure) data. You cannot add two class variables together by inserting the plus sign between them because Turbo C++ wouldn't understand what it means to add two data types that you created.

Note: It might help to think of the built-in operators as having their own operator...() functions. For instance, think of Turbo C++ as having an internal operator+(int, int) function, an internal operator/(float, float) function, and so on. When you write operator functions that contain your own class data types as arguments, you simply overload those functions already built into the compiler. It is through the overloading capability that Turbo C++ knows what to do when it sees a plus sign between two integers and a plus sign between two class variables.

However, after you write overloaded operator functions for your classes, then Turbo C++ *does* know how to add two class variables or perform any other operation on your class variables because you teach Turbo C++ what to do when you write overloaded operator functions.

Listing 11.1 contains a simple class and overloaded operator+() function that lets one class variable be added to another. The operator+() function is set up to add the integer members together and ignore the floating-point members. Again, an overloaded operator does *whatever* you program it to do. You don't even have to add when overloading the plus sign, but obviously, your programs are more maintainable if you keep the spirit of the original operator intact.

Note: The class members were all kept public for this example. The next section explains how to write overloaded operator functions using safer private members.

Introduction to Overloading Operators

Listing 11.1. A simple overloaded operator program.

```
 1:  // Filename: OVCLSMP.CPP
 2:  // Simple overloading of a class.
 3:  #include <iostream.h>
 4:  #include <conio.h>
 5:  class aClass {
 6:  public:        // All members are public
 7:     float x;
 8:     int i;
 9:     char c;
10:     void init(float X, int I, char C)
11:     { x = X;
12:        i = I;
13:        c = C;
14:     }
15:  };
16:  int operator+(const aClass & v1, const aClass & v2);
17:  /////////////////////////////////////////////////////////////////
18:  main()
19:  {
20:     aClass aVar1, aVar2;
21:     int total1, total2;
22:     clrscr();
23:     aVar1.init(12.34, 10, 'a');  // Put data in both class variables
24:     aVar2.init(56.78, 20, 'b');
25:     total1 = operator+(aVar1, aVar2);  // Add them one way
26:     cout << "total1 is " << total1 << "\n";
27:     total2 = aVar1 + aVar2;      // Add the better way
28:     cout << "total2 is " << total2 << "\n";
29:     return 0;
30:  }
31:  /////////////////////////////////////////////////////////////////
32:  // Overloaded plus operator function follows
33:  int operator+(const aClass & v1, const aClass & v2)
34:  {
35:     return v1.i + v2.i;
36:  }
```

```
total1 is 30
total2 is 30
```

Notice that the class variables are added using two different styles in lines 25 and 27. Obviously, it makes more sense to add the class variables using the simple plus sign (line 27) because Turbo C++ calls operator+( ) for you when it sees two class variables between the plus sign.

The arguments are passed to operator+() by reference for efficiency and as constants because operator+() does not modify the variables.

> **Note:** Although it doesn't promote extremely good coding habits, many of the member functions in this book don't receive const arguments, and many don't receive their arguments by reference when it might seem prudent to do so. Lines can get extremely long when argument lists contain the const and & qualifiers. Those lengthy lines, especially those so long they must be wrapped to the next line, would detract from your understanding more than they would help. When writing your own functions, use const for any arguments left unmodified by their receiving functions, and pass by reference whenever you can to improve efficiency.

OOPing the Operator Overloads

operator...() functions generally are *not* listed outside a class as shown in Listing 11.1. It makes sense to specify overloaded operator functions as members of a class because specific operator functions work on individual class data.

Remember that the primary difference between a member function and a regular non-member function is that the member function is automatically passed the *this pointer. When you first read about the *this pointer on Day 9, you probably didn't think it would keep cropping up as much as it has in today's and yesterday's chapters. Nevertheless, although you don't directly use the *this pointer much, it is vital that you remember it is there passing object data to member functions. The member function call

```
cVar.prData();
```

actually looks like this when the compiler analyzes it:

```
prData(&cVar);
```

And the implementation of the prData() member function that you typed like

```
void prData(void)
{
```

```
   cout << "The first data item is " << a << "\n";
   cout << "The last data item is " << b << "\n";
}
```

looks like this when the compiler analyzes it:

```
void prData(myClass *this)
{
   cout << "The first data item is " << this->a << "\n";
   cout << "The last data item is " << this->b << "\n";
}
```

Without the *this pointer, Turbo C++ would not know which object's a and b to print. Luckily, Turbo C++ adds the *this pointer behind your back. This way, you can code generic member functions that work on data members by the member names and let the compiler send the appropriate object when compiling the program.

The way that Turbo C++ calls overloaded operator functions becomes critical if you really want to master overloaded operators and know them well enough to code them without remembering a bunch of rules. The operator+() prototype

```
int operator+(aClass v1, aClass v2);
```

declares what happens when two aClass variables appear on each side of the plus sign (the const and reference operator are left out to keep the prototype simpler). As Listing 11.1 pointed out, when you add two aClass variables together like

```
total = aVar1 + aVar2;
```

Turbo C++ actually calls the operator+() function like this:

```
total = operator+(aVar1, aVar2);
```

The variable on the left of the plus sign (or whatever operator is being overloaded) is sent as the first argument to operator+(), and the variable on the right of the plus sign is sent as the second argument to operator+().

> **Note:** You'll want to make operator...() functions member functions when possible (sometimes, as explained later, the operator...() functions cannot be member functions) because the operator...() functions often work with private data members.

When an operator...() function becomes a member function, the look of the function changes slightly, even though the same method is used to accomplish the overloading. Consider the following class, which contains operator+() as a member function:

```
class aClass {
  float x;  // Private members
  int i;
  char c;
public:
  void init(float X, int I, char C);  // Defined later in code
  int operator+(aClass v2)   // No more first argument!!!
  {
     return i + v2.i;   // this pointer helps out
  }
};
```

Look at the i variable sitting by itself in the operator+() member function. How does Turbo C++ know *which* object's i to add to v2's i? The answer is easy if you recall the *this pointer. The Turbo C++ compiler acts as though you typed the following class:

```
class aClass {
  float x;  // Private members
  int i;
  char c;
public:
  void init(float X, int I, char C);  // Defined later in code
  int operator+(aClass * this, aClass v2)   // No more first argument!!!
  {
     return this->i + v2.i;   // this pointer helps out
  }
};
```

Never specify the first argument when writing overloaded operator member functions because the first argument of *all* member functions is the *this pointer. (If you were to code the first argument, Turbo C++ would see *three* arguments because the *this pointer is always passed to member functions no matter what else you pass to the member functions.) All occurrences of i by itself are preceded with the hidden (and dereferenced) *this pointer, and all occurrences of v2.i are left alone because the v2 overrides the insertion of the *this pointer.

Now, when you code something like

```
total = var1 + var2;    // Assume var1 and var2 are aClass objects
```

to trigger the execution of the function, Turbo C++ converts your statement into the following function call:

```
total = var1.operator+(var2);
```

This function call is actually the following when you rearrange the function call as the compiler will do:

```
total = operator+(&var1, var2);
```

Figure 11.1 illustrates this behind-the-scenes behavior more fully.

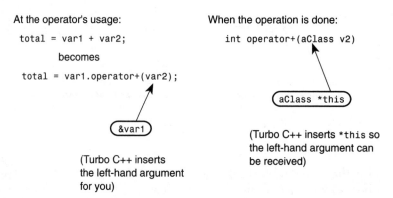

At the operator's usage:

```
total = var1 + var2;
```

becomes

```
total = var1.operator+(var2);
```

&var1

(Turbo C++ inserts
the left-hand argument
for you)

When the operation is done:

```
int operator+(aClass v2)
```

aClass *this

(Turbo C++ inserts *this so
the left-hand argument can
be received)

Figure 11.1. *The hidden* *this *pointer provides the lefthand argument for the operator.*

Keep Going!

It helps to look at and write a few simple overloaded operator functions before you can fully appreciate the *this pointer background on operator member functions. Use this chapter's overloaded operator...() functions as patterns for your own.

After you write a few overloaded operator member functions, reread the preceding few paragraphs, and you'll perhaps better understand how Turbo C++ uses the *this pointer and eliminates your specific receiving of the class variable at the left of the operator's argument list.

Listing 11.2 contains a rewritten version of Listing 11.1 with the operator+() function as a member function inside the class. The class data members can now be private because the operator+() has full access to the class's private data now that operator+() is a member of the class.

 Listing 11.2. Using an overloaded member operator+().

```
1:   // Filename: OVCLMEM.CPP
2:   // Using a member function to overload the plus sign.
3:   #include <iostream.h>
4:   #include <conio.h>
5:   class aClass {
6:     float x;   // Private data
7:     int i;
```

```
8:    char c;
9:  public:
10:    void init(float X, int I, char C);
11:    int operator+(const aClass & rightArg)
12:    {
13:      return (i + rightArg.i);
14:    }
15:    // The operator+() definition could also be listed outside
16:    // the class using the scope resolution operator as init() is.
17: };
18: void aClass::init(float X, int I, char C)
19:    {  x = X;
20:       i = I;
21:       c = C;
22:    }
23: ///////////////////////////////////////////////////////////////
24: main()
25: {
26:    aClass aVar1, aVar2;
27:    int total;
28:    clrscr();
29:    aVar1.init(12.34, 10, 'a');   // Put data in both class variables
30:    aVar2.init(56.78, 20, 'b');
31:    total = aVar1 + aVar2;        // Add using member function
32:    cout << "total is " << total << "\n";
33:    return 0;
34: }
```

 Output

```
total is 30
```

Analysis

The most important part of the program for you to focus on at this time is in lines 10–14. The righthand side of the plus sign in line 31 is passed to operator+() as the *this pointer, so you only have to tell the function that the second argument is coming. Every time you reference the i member of the first argument, just use i because there will be a hidden this-> placed in front of the i. You have to specifically tell the member function on line 13 to use the righthand argument when referring to its i inside the function.

Don't Forget to Allow Stacking

You might recall that Day 7's chapter taught you how to write overloaded operator functions that you stack together several times.

For instance, in Listing 11.2's `operator+()` function, the function returns an integer, so you can use the overloaded plus sign only when an integer result is needed. However, what if you had several objects and wanted to add them all together like this:

```
totalCl = aVar1 + aVar2 + aVar3;
```

To stack several operations together, you must return a class variable, not a built-in data type. The preceding stacked assignment becomes a nested `operator+()` function call that gets changed by the compiler to look like this:

```
totalCl = operator+(aVar1, operator+(aVar2, aVar3));
```

If the innermost `operator+()` returned an `int`, Turbo C++ would fail trying to find a prototype for this:

```
operator+(class aClass, int);
```

Therefore, the `operator+()` has to return a class variable so that the outside `operator+()` works. The big problem *then* is that you cannot assign the stacked values to an integer, but you have to assign them to another class variable (called `totalCl` here) unless you have overloaded another member `operator+()` function whose righthand operand argument is an integer.

Listing 11.3 begins to show the real power of overloaded operators. The `nClass` contains three integer data members and four floating-point data members. Five class object variables are defined and then added together using stacked plus signs. The program defines the plus sign so that an `nClass` total variable contains the total of all seven members from the five objects, as illustrated in Figure 11.2.

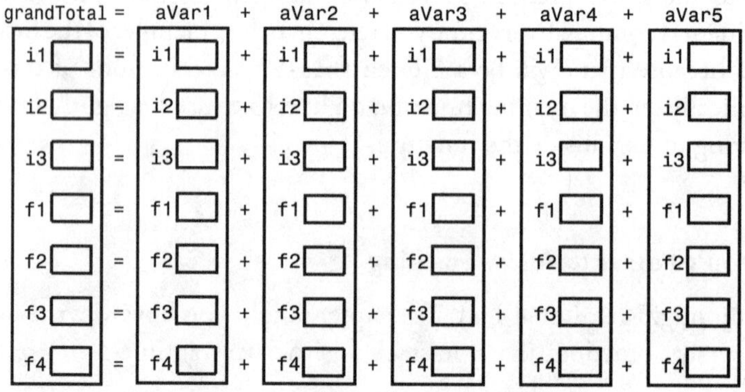

Figure 11.2. *The meaning of adding together* `nClass` *object variables.*

Listing 11.3. Overloading the addition operator and stacking additions together.

```
1:  // Filename: OVFULL.CPP
2:  // Overloading (with stacking capability) the plus operator.
3:  #include <iostream.h>
4:  #include <iomanip.h>
5:  #include <conio.h>
6:  class nClass {
7:    int i1, i2, i3;
8:    float f1, f2, f3, f4;
9:  public:
10:   inline void init(int I1, int I2, int I3, float F1, float F2,
      ➡float F3, float F4);
11:   inline nClass operator+(const nClass & rightArg);
12:   int getI1(void) { return i1; }   // Must have read-access member
13:   int getI2(void) { return i2; }   // functions to print the members
14:   int getI3(void) { return i3; }   // of the total object variable.
15:   float getF1(void) { return f1; }
16:   float getF2(void) { return f2; }
17:   float getF3(void) { return f3; }
18:   float getF4(void) { return f4; }
19: };
20: void nClass::init(int I1, int I2, int I3, float F1, float F2,
    ➡float F3, float F4)
21: {
22:   i1 = I1; i2 = I2; i3 = I3;
23:   f1 = F1; f2 = F2; f3 = F3; f4 = F4;
24: }
25: nClass nClass::operator+(const nClass & rArg)
26: {
27:   nClass gTotal;
28:   gTotal.i1 = i1 + rArg.i1;
29:   gTotal.i2 = i2 + rArg.i2;
30:   gTotal.i3 = i3 + rArg.i3;
31:   gTotal.f1 = f1 + rArg.f1;
32:   gTotal.f2 = f2 + rArg.f2;
33:   gTotal.f3 = f3 + rArg.f3;
34:   gTotal.f4 = f4 + rArg.f4;
35:   return gTotal;
36: }
37: /////////////////////////////////////////////////////////////////
38: main()
39: {
40:   nClass aVar1, aVar2, aVar3, aVar4, aVar5;
41:   nClass grandTotal;   // Class variable that will hold the total
42:   clrscr();
43:   // Put data in the object variables
44:   aVar1.init(4, 2, 5, 12.34, 10.4, 7.6, 5.3);
45:   aVar2.init(2, 5, 9, 2.47, 7.52, 5.06, 6.2);
46:   aVar3.init(8, 3, 8, 2.03, 11.67, 4.4, 3.9);
```

continues

Listing 11.3. continued

```
47:    aVar4.init(3, 6, 7, 5.3, 4.30, 7.5, 2.1);
48:    aVar5.init(1, 3, 1, 2.8, 5.23, 4.2, 7.7);
49:    // Add using operator member function
50:    grandTotal = aVar1 + aVar2 + aVar3 + aVar4 + aVar5;
51:    cout << setprecision(2) << setiosflags(ios::fixed);
52:    cout << "After adding the objects together, here are";
53:    cout << "\nthe contents of the total variable's members:\n";
54:    cout << "i1: " << grandTotal.getI1() << "\n";
55:    cout << "i2: " << grandTotal.getI2() << "\n";
56:    cout << "i3: " << grandTotal.getI3() << "\n";
57:    cout << "f1: " << grandTotal.getF1() << "\n";
58:    cout << "f2: " << grandTotal.getF2() << "\n";
59:    cout << "f3: " << grandTotal.getF3() << "\n";
60:    cout << "f4: " << grandTotal.getF4() << "\n";
61:    return 0;
62: }
```

```
After adding the objects together, here are
the contents of the total variable's members:
i1: 18
i2: 19
i3: 30
f1: 24.94
f2: 39.12
f3: 28.76
f4: 25.2
```

At first glance, this program might seem intimidating, but the concepts in it are simple. Most of the code is contained in four repetitive sections: the read-access member functions in lines 12–18 (coded inline because they are so short), the adding together of matching members in lines 28–34, the initialization of data in lines 44–48, and the printing of the total object's members in lines 54–60.

The operator+() function in lines 25–36 adds the plus sign's right argument to the *this pointer's variable, which produces the grandTotal value in line 50. Notice how easy it is to add nClass variables.

The local class variable defined on line 27 is needed to hold and return a class value so that operators can be stacked together. After you've learned how to write special functions called *constructors* in Day 13's chapter, "Constructing and Destructing," you'll learn a cleaner way to return class values from overloaded operator functions.

Remember that Turbo C++ knows to call the operator+() function whenever an nClass object appears on each side of the plus sign. Later in today's chapter (in the section "Mixing Class and Built-In Data Types"), you'll learn how to write overloaded

operator functions that execute when Turbo C++ encounters an operator surrounded by your data type and also a built-in data type.

> **Note:** The overloaded operators offer just one additional proof that Turbo C++ improves your coding productivity and eliminates the tedious details. Sure, you still have to write the `operator...()` functions and "define" what you want done when you perform an operation on one of your data types. After you've written an overloaded operator function, however, the rest of the program can use the familiar operator when you want an operation performed rather than your having to remember a bunch of different function names.

11

DO — DON'T

DO use overloaded operator functions when you want to perform operations on your own data types that are similar to the built-in operations on built-in data types.

DO overload as many `operator...()` functions as you need to in order to perform that operation on all the combinations of data that will appear on each side of the operator.

DON'T pass too many arguments when overloading operator member functions. Turbo C++ takes care of sending and receiving the `*this` pointer as it does with all member functions.

DON'T swerve too far from an operator's original meaning when you overload an `operator...()` function.

The Remaining Simple Math Operators

There is very little more that can be said about overloading the regular math operators, `-`, `*`, `/`, and `%`. They overload in a manner similar to the `operator+()` described in the preceding section. Again, the `operator+()` function does *whatever* you define it to do, and so do all the other overloaded operator functions.

Just so you can see an example of each overloaded operator, Listing 11.4 expands the preceding listing to include overloaded functions for all five standard math operators (+, -, *, /, and %). The program performs the arithmetic on each member in the class. For example, when you subtract one nClass variable from another, Turbo C++ subtracts all the members of one class from the other and stores the resulting values in the class variable being assigned to the answer inside main(). Other than the additional overloaded operator functions, Listing 11.4 includes an extra printing member function to eliminate the class's need for a lot of get...() member functions that simply return single values.

Note: It is because the modulus operator, %, is defined just for integers that the operator%() function works only with integers and returns zeros for the floating-point members in the object answer.

Listing 11.4. Overloading +, -, *, /, and %

```
1:  // Filename: OVFALL.CPP
2:  // Overloading (with stacking capability) the math operators.
3:  #include <iostream.h>
4:  #include <iomanip.h>
5:  #include <conio.h>
6:  class nClass {
7:     int i1, i2, i3;
8:     float f1, f2, f3, f4;
9:  public:
10:    inline void init(int I1, int I2, int I3, float F1, float F2,
       ➥float F3, float F4);
11:    inline void prData(void);
12:    inline nClass operator+(const nClass & rightArg);
13:    inline nClass operator-(const nClass & rightArg);
14:    inline nClass operator*(const nClass & rightArg);
15:    inline nClass operator/(const nClass & rightArg);
16:    inline nClass operator%(const nClass & rightArg);
17:  };
18:  void nClass::init(int I1, int I2, int I3, float F1, float F2,
     ➥float F3, float F4)
19:  {
20:    i1 = I1; i2 = I2; i3 = I3;
21:    f1 = F1; f2 = F2; f3 = F3; f4 = F4;
22:  }
23:  void nClass::prData(void)
24:  {
25:    cout << setprecision(2) << setiosflags(ios::fixed);
26:    cout << "i1: " << i1 << "\n";
```

```
27:    cout << "i2: " << i2 << "\n";
28:    cout << "i3: " << i3 << "\n";
29:    cout << "f1: " << f1 << "\n";
30:    cout << "f2: " << f2 << "\n";
31:    cout << "f3: " << f3 << "\n";
32:    cout << "f4: " << f4 << "\n";
33: }
34: nClass nClass::operator+(const nClass & rArg)
35: {
36:    nClass gTotal;
37:    gTotal.i1 = i1 + rArg.i1;
38:    gTotal.i2 = i2 + rArg.i2;
39:    gTotal.i3 = i3 + rArg.i3;
40:    gTotal.f1 = f1 + rArg.f1;
41:    gTotal.f2 = f2 + rArg.f2;
42:    gTotal.f3 = f3 + rArg.f3;
43:    gTotal.f4 = f4 + rArg.f4;
44:    return gTotal;
45: }
46: nClass nClass::operator-(const nClass & rArg)
47: {
48:    nClass gTotal;
49:    gTotal.i1 = i1 - rArg.i1;
50:    gTotal.i2 = i2 - rArg.i2;
51:    gTotal.i3 = i3 - rArg.i3;
52:    gTotal.f1 = f1 - rArg.f1;
53:    gTotal.f2 = f2 - rArg.f2;
54:    gTotal.f3 = f3 - rArg.f3;
55:    gTotal.f4 = f4 - rArg.f4;
56:    return gTotal;
57: }
58: nClass nClass::operator*(const nClass & rArg)
59: {
60:    nClass gTotal;
61:    gTotal.i1 = i1 * rArg.i1;
62:    gTotal.i2 = i2 * rArg.i2;
63:    gTotal.i3 = i3 * rArg.i3;
64:    gTotal.f1 = f1 * rArg.f1;
65:    gTotal.f2 = f2 * rArg.f2;
66:    gTotal.f3 = f3 * rArg.f3;
67:    gTotal.f4 = f4 * rArg.f4;
68:    return gTotal;
69: }
70: nClass nClass::operator/(const nClass & rArg)
71: {
72:    nClass gTotal;
73:    gTotal.i1 = i1 / rArg.i1;
74:    gTotal.i2 = i2 / rArg.i2;
75:    gTotal.i3 = i3 / rArg.i3;
76:    gTotal.f1 = f1 / rArg.f1;
77:    gTotal.f2 = f2 / rArg.f2;
```

continues

Listing 11.4. continued

```
78:    gTotal.f3 = f3 / rArg.f3;
79:    gTotal.f4 = f4 / rArg.f4;
80:    return gTotal;
81: }
82: nClass nClass::operator%(const nClass & rArg)
83: {
84:    nClass gTotal;
85:    gTotal.i1 = i1 % rArg.i1;
86:    gTotal.i2 = i2 % rArg.i2;
87:    gTotal.i3 = i3 % rArg.i3;
88:    gTotal.f1 = 0.0;
89:    gTotal.f2 = 0.0;
90:    gTotal.f3 = 0.0;
91:    gTotal.f4 = 0.0;
92:    return gTotal;
93: }
94:
95: /////////////////////////////////////////////////////////////////////
96: main()
97: {
98:    nClass aVar1, aVar2, aVar3, aVar4, aVar5;
99:    nClass grandTotal;   // Class variable that will hold the total
100:   clrscr();
101:   // Put data in the object variables
102:   aVar1.init(4, 2, 5, 12.34, 10.4, 7.6, 5.3);
103:   aVar2.init(2, 5, 9, 2.47, 7.52, 5.06, 6.2);
104:   aVar3.init(8, 3, 8, 2.03, 11.67, 4.4, 3.9);
105:   aVar4.init(3, 6, 7, 5.3, 4.30, 7.5, 2.1);
106:   aVar5.init(1, 3, 1, 2.8, 5.23, 4.2, 7.7);
107:   // Add using operator member function
108:   grandTotal = aVar1 + aVar2 + aVar3 + aVar4 + aVar5;
109:   cout << "After adding the objects together, here are";
110:   cout << "\nthe contents of the total variable's members:\n";
111:   grandTotal.prData();
112:   grandTotal = aVar3 - aVar5;
113:   cout << "After subtracting the fifth object from the third, here";
114:   cout << "\nare the contents of the total variable's members:\n";
115:   grandTotal.prData();
116:   grandTotal = aVar1 * aVar2 * aVar3;
117:   cout << "After multiplying the first three objects, here are";
118:   cout << "\nthe contents of the total variable's members:\n";
119:   grandTotal.prData();
120:   grandTotal = aVar4 / aVar2;
121:   cout << "After dividing the 2nd object from the 4th objects, ";
122:   cout << "\nhere are the total variable's members:\n";
123:   cout << "(the integers were divided using integer division)\n";
124:   grandTotal.prData();
125:   grandTotal = aVar3 % aVar4;
126:   cout << "After performing modulus on the 3rd and 4th objects, ";
```

```
127:    cout << "\nhere are the total variable's members:\n";
128:    grandTotal.prData();
129:    return 0;
130: }
```

After adding the objects together, here are
the contents of the total variable's members:
i1: 18
i2: 19
i3: 30
f1: 24.94
f2: 39.12
f3: 28.76
f4: 25.2
After subtracting the fifth object from the third, here
are the contents of the total variable's members:
i1: 7
i2: 0
i3: 7
f1: -0.77
f2: 6.44
f3: 0.2
f4: -3.8
After multiplying the first three objects, here are
the contents of the total variable's members:
i1: 64
i2: 30
i3: 360
f1: 61.87
f2: 912.69
f3: 169.21
f4: 128.15
After dividing the 2nd object from the 4th objects,
here are the total variable's members:
(the integers were divided using integer division)
i1: 1
i2: 1
i3: 0
f1: 2.15
f2: 0.57
f3: 1.48
f4: 0.34
After performing modulus on the 3rd and 4th objects,
here are the total variable's members:
i1: 2
i2: 3
i3: 1
f1: 0
f2: 0
f3: 0
f4: 0

The `operator...()` member functions coded in lines 34–93 are fairly routine. You'll write lots of them using the same format that you see here. Remember to return the object's data type if you want to stack operators. When you stack them, you'll have to collect the answer in a designated total object (as in line 112) and print what you want from that total variable. Of course, the code body of your own `operator...()` functions for the common math operators will differ from that in Listing 11.4 depending on your application's specific needs.

It's interesting to note that Turbo C++ doesn't even care if you put the *same* variable name on each side of an overloaded operator. If you were to code

```
grandTotal = aVar3 - aVar3;
```

then Turbo C++ would put zeros in all of `grandTotal`'s members. You can even zero an object's contents like this:

```
aVar3 = aVar3 - aVar3;   // Subtract from itself
```

The only requirement of Listing 11.4's `operator...()` functions is that you collect the answer to the operation in a class variable, or stack the operations together with other class variables.

In Listing 11.4, you could never attempt

```
grandTotal = aVar3 - 5;
```

or

```
grandTotal = 3 + aVar3;
```

because there are no overloaded operator member functions that accept both a class variable and an integer. (You'll see how to code such functions in a moment, but it's worth pointing out that friend functions are required to combine built-in data types with your own.)

Overloading Relational and Logical Operators

The relational and logical testing operators return a 1 or 0 indicating whether the test was true or false. Table 11.1 reviews the relational and logical operators. These comparison operators are often used to test to see whether two class variables are equal, greater than, or less than another. Depending on the format of your class, when a comparison is made, you might want to base the true-false result on only an individual data member out of several other members.

Table 11.1. The relational and logical operators.

Operator	Name
>	Greater than
<	Less than
==	Equal to
!=	Not equal to
>=	Greater than or equal to
<=	Less than or equal to
&&	AND (logical)
¦¦	OR (logical)

You'll find that you won't overload the logical operators much because they usually fall between two relationals that already return 1 or 0. In other words, the following statement's logical && operator combines two overloaded relational operators:

```
if ((costOfFruit < costOfMeat) && (moneyInPocket <= 10.00))
```

If you properly overload these relational < and <= operators, they return 1 or 0 integers. The built-in && is already designed to work with 1s and 0s without your overloading an operator&&() function.

After you overload the relational operators, you use the built-in operators to perform comparisons on your own data types. For instance, you might want to compare payroll objects to see whether one employee makes more than another. Although an employee class variable might have 100 members, the comparison could be made on only a single salary member.

Note: Although the bitwise operators aren't included in Table 11.1, you overload them in the same way as shown here for their counterparts. You'll manipulate your own data types using the bitwise operators according to the meaning you want to apply to the overloaded bitwise operators.

If you want to stack several relational and logical operators together, you don't have to do anything different from overloading them for single uses. As shown earlier in this chapter, the regular math operators are often overloaded to return different data types depending on your using them stacked together or individually. A comparison operator in Turbo C++ (as in C) always returns an integer result of 1 or 0, and if you stack several, a 1 or 0 return value always works just as it does when you use one of the comparison operators by itself.

The biggest decision you have to make when writing comparison operators is which members are to be included in whatever comparison is being made at the time.

There is one efficiency loss that occurs when you overload logical && and ¦¦ operators. When Turbo C++ sees the if statement

```
if (2 == 2) ¦¦ (a < b)    // Rest of 'if' would follow
```

Turbo C++ will *not* evaluate the a < b test because it will compute a True result with the equality comparison of the 2s, and True OR anything else is still True. Short-circuiting logical tests can also occur with the && like this:

```
if ((2 < 2) && (a < b))    // Rest of 'if' would follow
```

In this statement, the 2 < 2 is False, and False AND any other value is False. Turbo C++ ignores the a < b and saves a microsecond or two of execution time by bypassing the expression.

No short-circuiting is done when class data appears on either side of the logical operators. Therefore, if stuff1 and stuff2 in the statement

```
if (stuff1 ¦¦ stuff2)    // Rest of 'if' would follow
```

are class variables, Turbo C++ will always evaluate both sides of the ¦¦, even if it determines that the left side is True.

The program in Listing 11.5 defines a few payroll objects and then uses overloaded conditional operators to compare the payroll objects to each other. Notice how clean main() can become when the comparisons begin. In C or any programming language that includes record data types such as classes and structures, you would have to call functions to compare aggregate data types or individually compare members every time you compared.

 Listing 11.5. Overloading the relational operators.

```
1:  // Filename: PAYCOMP.CPP
2:  // Overload comparison relational operators.
3:  #include <iostream.h>
4:  #include <string.h>
5:  #include <conio.h>
6:  class payClass {
```

```
 7:    char name[25];
 8:    float salary;
 9:  public:
10:    inline void init(char N[], float S);
11:    inline char * getName(void);
12:    inline int operator<(const payClass & emp);   // Relational
13:    inline int operator>(const payClass & emp);   // operators
14:    inline int operator==(const payClass & emp);
15:    inline int operator!=(const payClass & emp);
16:    inline int operator>=(const payClass & emp);
17:    inline int operator<=(const payClass & emp);
18: };
19: void payClass::init(char N[], float S)
20: {
21:    strcpy(name, N);
22:    salary = S;
23: }
24: char * payClass::getName(void)
25: {
26:    return name;    // Return pointer to the name
27: }
28: // All the comparison operators will compare the salary members
29: int payClass::operator<(const payClass & emp)
30: {
31:    // For review: This function is called like this:
32:    //   if (emp1 < emp2) ...
33:    // The emp1 is passed and dereferenced automatically (as this)
34:    // so its salary member is directly referred to, but emp2's has to
35:    // be received and specified like emp.salary
36:    if (salary < emp.salary)
37:      return 1;        // True
38:    else
39:      return 0;        // False
40: }
41: int payClass::operator>(const payClass & emp)
42: {
43:    if (salary > emp.salary)
44:      return 1;        // True
45:    else
46:      return 0;        // False
47: }
48: int payClass::operator==(const payClass & emp)
49: {
50:    if (salary == emp.salary)
51:      return 1;        // True
52:    else
53:      return 0;        // False
54: }
55: int payClass::operator!=(const payClass & emp)
56: {
```

continues

Listing 11.5. continued

```
57:    if (salary != emp.salary)
58:      return 1;        // True
59:    else
60:      return 0;        // False
61: }
62: int payClass::operator<=(const payClass & emp)
63: {
64:    if (salary <= emp.salary)
65:      return 1;        // True
66:    else
67:      return 0;        // False
68: }
69: int payClass::operator>=(const payClass & emp)
70: {
71:    if (salary >= emp.salary)
72:      return 1;        // True
73:    else
74:      return 0;        // False
75: }
76: ////////////////////////////////////////////////////////////////
77: main()
78: {
79:    payClass emp1, emp2, emp3, emp4;
80:    clrscr();
81:    // Put data in the object variables
82:    emp1.init("Stacy Miller", 4323.45);
83:    emp2.init("Dean Hiquet", 6534.56);
84:    emp3.init("Richard Short",9345.67);
85:    emp4.init("Lloyd Swadley", 2932.41);
86:    // Perform comparisons
87:    if (emp1 < emp3)
88:      { cout << emp3.getName() << " makes less than "
         ➥<< emp1.getName();
89:        cout << "\n";
90:      }
91:    if (emp2 != emp4)
92:      { cout << emp2.getName() << " and " << emp4.getName()
         ➥<< " don't make ";
93:        cout << "the same salary.\n";
94:      }
95:    if (emp3 > emp4)
96:      { cout << emp3.getName() << " makes more than "
         ➥<< emp4.getName();
97:        cout << "\n";
98:      }
99:    if (emp1 >= emp3)
100:     { cout << emp1.getName() << " makes at least as much as ";
101:       cout << emp3.getName() << "\n";
102:     }
```

```
103:    // Didn't have to overload && to use it between two comparisons
104:    if ((emp3 > emp2) && (emp4 < emp2))
105:      { cout << emp3.getName() << " makes more than "
        ➥<< emp2.getName();
106:        cout << " and so does " << emp4.getName() << "\n";
107:      }
108:
109:    return 0;
110: }
```

Richard Short makes less than Stacy Miller
Dean Hiquet and Lloyd Swadley don't make the same salary.
Richard Short makes more than Lloyd Swadley
Richard Short makes more than Dean Hiquet and so does Lloyd Swadley

Although all the relational operators are overloaded in this program, `main()` doesn't happen to use them all (such as `<=`). However, you can see how the relational operators (and the logical operators if you had data that needed to be compared with them) are overloaded.

`main()` is just a controller for the comparisons now. It is as easy to compare class objects as it is to compare two integers, demonstrated by lines 87, 91, 95, 99, and 104. All the overloaded relational operator functions return integers to mimic the built-in relational operators as much as possible.

11

Be Careful When Comparing *float*s

As in any programming language, comparing floating-point values for equality is tricky and usually error prone. The `operator==()` and `operator!=()` functions coded in Listing 11.5 are kept short and consistent with the surrounding overloaded operator functions to help you learn overloading operators.

However, when comparing floating-point values in "real life," compare a range of values instead of comparing for exact equalities or inequalities. For example, the following comparison would catch any internal rounding differences and compare two floating-point values as being "about equal," which is about all you can do. (The smaller the range of the comparison, the more accurate the equality test will be.)

```
int payClass::operator==(const payClass & emp)
{
    // Make sure salaries are approximately equal
```

```
// due to the natural internal rounding of
// real numbers inside the computer.
if ( ((salary - .001) < emp.salary)
        && ((salary + .001) > emp.salary))
    return 1;      // True
else
    return 0;      // False
}
```

Now, the Compound Operators Are a Snap!

The compound math operators, listed in Table 11.2, are just as easy to overload as the other math operators. When writing overloaded operator functions, think about what is happening with the operators. Although the following statements use different operators, they are equivalent:

```
c = c + 24;
```

and

```
c += 24;
```

(If you add other expressions and variables to the expression, however, the + differs from += because of their different placements in the operator hierarchy.) When you code two values on either side of a compound operator, you want the math operation to be performed and the result to be placed inside the variable on the left. (The left operand to any of the compound operators must be an lvalue.)

Table 11.2. The compound math operators.

Operator	Name
+=	Compound addition
-=	Compound subtraction
*=	Compound multiplication
/=	Compound division
%=	Compound modulus

 Note: The compound bitwise operators aren't discussed in this text, but their overloading is just as straightforward.

The program in Listing 11.6 again shows a class (defined earlier in Listing 11.4) with several integer and floating-point members. Compound operators are overloaded to achieve the same effect as that shown in Figure 11.2. You might want to overload the compound operators so that updating object values is easier to code. Also, if you overload the standard math operators, consider overloading their compound operator equivalents for completeness, although the regular overloaded operators aren't included in Listing 11.6 for the sake of brevity.

There is one difference to look for in this program that didn't appear in any previous overloaded operator. The overloaded compound operator functions require that you specifically return a dereferenced *this pointer.

 Listing 11.6. Overloading the compound operators.

```
1:   // Filename: COMPOV.CPP
2:   // Overloading the compound math operators.
3:   #include <iostream.h>
4:   #include <iomanip.h>
5:   #include <conio.h>
6:   class nClass {
7:     int i1, i2, i3;
8:     float f1, f2, f3, f4;
9:   public:
10: inline void init(int I1, int I2, int I3, float F1, float F2,
    ➡float F3, float F4);
11:    inline void prData(void);
12:    inline nClass operator+=(const nClass & rightArg);
13:    inline nClass operator-=(const nClass & rightArg);
14:    inline nClass operator*=(const nClass & rightArg);
15:    inline nClass operator/=(const nClass & rightArg);
16:    inline nClass operator%=(const nClass & rightArg);
17:  };
18:  void nClass::init(int I1, int I2, int I3, float F1, float F2,
    ➡float F3, float F4)
19:  {
20:    i1 = I1; i2 = I2; i3 = I3;
21:    f1 = F1; f2 = F2; f3 = F3; f4 = F4;
22:  }
23:  void nClass::prData(void)
24:  {
25:    cout << setprecision(2) << setiosflags(ios::fixed);
26:    cout << "i1: " << i1 << "\n";
```

continues

Listing 11.6. continued

```
27:    cout << "i2: " << i2 << "\n";
28:    cout << "i3: " << i3 << "\n";
29:    cout << "f1: " << f1 << "\n";
30:    cout << "f2: " << f2 << "\n";
31:    cout << "f3: " << f3 << "\n";
32:    cout << "f4: " << f4 << "\n";
33: }
34: nClass nClass::operator+=(const nClass & rArg)
35: {
36:    i1 += rArg.i1;    // Compound adding to the this pointer's data
37:    i2 += rArg.i2;
38:    i3 += rArg.i3;
39:    f1 += rArg.f1;
40:    f2 += rArg.f2;
41:    f3 += rArg.f3;
42:    f4 += rArg.f4;
43:    return *this;
44: }
45: nClass nClass::operator-=(const nClass & rArg)
46: {
47:    i1 -= rArg.i1;    // Compound subtracting from the this pointer
48:    i2 -= rArg.i2;
49:    i3 -= rArg.i3;
50:    f1 -= rArg.f1;
51:    f2 -= rArg.f2;
52:    f3 -= rArg.f3;
53:    f4 -= rArg.f4;
54:    return *this;
55: }
56: nClass nClass::operator*=(const nClass & rArg)
57: {
58:    i1 *= rArg.i1;    // Compound multiplying to the this pointer
59:    i2 *= rArg.i2;
60:    i3 *= rArg.i3;
61:    f1 *= rArg.f1;
62:    f2 *= rArg.f2;
63:    f3 *= rArg.f3;
64:    f4 *= rArg.f4;
65:    return *this;
66: }
67: nClass nClass::operator/=(const nClass & rArg)
68: {
69:    i1 /= rArg.i1;    // Compound dividing to the this pointer's data
70:    i2 /= rArg.i2;
71:    i3 /= rArg.i3;
72:    f1 /= rArg.f1;
73:    f2 /= rArg.f2;
74:    f3 /= rArg.f3;
75:    f4 /= rArg.f4;
```

```
76:    return *this;
77: }
78: nClass nClass::operator%=(const nClass & rArg)
79: {
80:    i1 %= rArg.i1;    // Compound modulus on the this pointer's data
81:    i2 %= rArg.i2;
82:    i3 %= rArg.i3;
84:    f1 = 0.0;
85:    f2 = 0.0;
86:    f3 = 0.0;
87:    f4 = 0.0;
88:    return *this;
89: }
90: //////////////////////////////////////////////////////////////////
91: main()
92: {
93:    nClass aVar1, aVar2, aVar3, aVar4, aVar5;
94:    clrscr();
95:    // Put data in the object variables
96:    aVar1.init(4, 2, 5, 12.34, 10.4, 7.6, 5.3);
97:    aVar2.init(2, 5, 9, 2.47, 7.52, 5.06, 6.2);
98:    aVar3.init(8, 3, 8, 2.03, 11.67, 4.4, 3.9);
99:    aVar4.init(3, 6, 7, 5.3, 4.30, 7.5, 2.1);
100:   aVar5.init(1, 3, 1, 2.8, 5.23, 4.2, 7.7);
101:   // Use the overloaded operator member functions
102:   aVar1 += aVar2;
103:   cout << "After updating aVar1 with aVar2's values (using +=),";
104:   cout << "\nhere are the contents of aVar1's members:\n";
105:   aVar1.prData();
106:   // Put aVar1 back the way it was
107:   aVar1 -= aVar2;
108:   cout << "\nAfter updating aVar1 with aVar2's values (using -=),";
109:   cout << "\nhere are the contents of aVar1's members:\n";
110:   aVar1.prData();
111:   // Update aVar2 by multiplying
112:   aVar2 *= aVar3;
113:   cout << "\nAfter updating aVar2 with aVar3's values (using *=),";
114:   cout << "\nhere are the contents of aVar2's members:\n";
115:   aVar2.prData();
116:   // Put them back by dividing
117:   aVar2 /= aVar3;
118:   cout << "\nAfter updating aVar2 with aVar3's values (using /=),";
119:   cout << "\nhere are the contents of aVar2's members:\n";
120:   aVar2.prData();
121:   // Perform a modulus update on the integer members of aVar4
122:   aVar4 %= aVar1;
123:   cout << "\nAfter updating aVar4's members with aVar1's values ";
124:   cout << "(using %=), \nhere are aVar2's members:\n";
125:    aVar4.prData();
126:   return 0;
127:}
```

```
After updating aVar1 with aVar2's values (using +=),
here are the contents of aVar1's members:
i1: 6
i2: 7
i3: 14
f1: 14.81
f2: 17.92
f3: 12.66
f4: 11.5

After updating aVar1 with aVar2's values (using -=),
here are the contents of aVar1's members:
i1: 4
i2: 2
i3: 5
f1: 12.34
f2: 10.4
f3: 7.6
f4: 5.3

After updating aVar2 with aVar3's values (using *=),
here are the contents of aVar2's members:
i1: 16
i2: 15
i3: 72
f1: 5.01
f2: 87.76
f3: 22.26
f4: 24.18

After updating aVar2 with aVar3's values (using /=),
here are the contents of aVar2's members:
i1: 2
i2: 5
i3: 9
f1: 2.47
f2: 7.52
f3: 5.06
f4: 6.2

After updating aVar4's members with aVar1's values (using %=),
here are aVar2's members:
i1: 3
i2: 0
i3: 2
f1: 0
f2: 0
f3: 0
f4: 0
```

 Every overloaded compound operator function shown here returns a dereferenced `this` value (lines 43, 54, 65, 76, and 88). Think about what's going on, and you'll understand the need to return the object (via `*this`). By their definitions, compound operators assign values to their left operands. When Turbo C++ executes the statement

```
a += b;
```

Turbo C++ takes the left operand, the `a`, and then adds the right operand, `b`, to `a`. The left operand is always changed (and, therefore, always must be an lvalue). Although the member functions you saw previously could access the left operand's members, they didn't need to return a modified left operand.

Also, don't be concerned that member functions sometimes use `*this` but never define the `*this` pointer explicitly. Turbo C++ passes the `*this` pointer, receives it, and properly defines it for you. Usually, the `*this` pointer stays behind the curtains from the cover of your source, but you sometimes have to use the `*this` pointer directly as shown here.

Where's the Assignment Operator, =?

You'll not find an overloaded equal sign in this chapter. There are many times, however, when you want to assign objects to other objects in ways that aren't defined by the memberwise default assignment performed by Turbo C++. You can overload the equal sign, but there are extra considerations when doing so that you're not quite ready for. You'll learn how to overload the equal sign on Day 13.

Although overloading the equal sign is fairly straightforward, it is too close in nature to two other Turbo C++ topics, regular constructors and copy constructors, to discuss here. You'll learn about all these topics together where they logically belong, in the "Constructing and Destructing" chapter.

DO   DON'T

DO overload compound operators if you overload their regular equivalent operators. In other words, if you overload multiplication, `*`, also overload compound multiplication, `*=`. Doing so is not a requirement, but you'll improve the richness of the class.

DO return a dereferenced `*this` pointer when overloading compound operators. Compound operators must return a modified copy of their lefthand operand.

DON'T expect perfect results when comparing floating-point (or double floating-point) values. It is difficult representing real numbers at the computer's binary level. Compare against a small range of values so that you'll test for "approximate equality" rather than exact equality.

DON'T overload the logical operators and then expect the short-circuiting efficiency feature that occurs when surrounding `&&` or `||` with built-in operators. Turbo C++ must evaluate both sides of overloaded logical operators, even though it doesn't have to for regular built-in data types using the same operators.

DON'T attempt to overload the assignment operator, `=`, just yet. That comes on Day 13.

Mixing Class and Built-In Data Types

Although you cannot change the way operators work on built-in data types, you *can* change the way operators work on combinations of your data types and the built-in data types. Consider for a moment that you have customer objects defined in a program and that each customer is assigned a special discount based on his or her buying history and economic conditions. The customer class might look something like this:

```
class Cust {
  char name[25];
  char custCode[5];
  float outBalance;
  int timesPurchased;
  float discPercent;      // We're interested in this now
public:
  // The public member functions would go here
};
```

You could create an array of customer objects like this:

```
Cust customers[100];
```

Assuming that you were having an exceptional year, you decide to increase each customer's discount by 10 percent over current levels. To increase a value by 10 percent, you multiply it by 1.10. For example, 25 times 1.10 is 27.5. The following loop would increase each customer's discount by 10 percent, assuming that you overloaded the * operator to handle the discount increase:

```
for (int c=0; c<100; c++)
  { customers[c] = customers[c] * 1.10; }
```

(Of course, a compound *= operator would be cleaner, but we're keeping this extra simple just to demonstrate the current topic.)

Here is another way to accomplish the same discount increase:

```
for (int c=0; c<100; c++)
  { customers[c] = 1.10 * customers[c]; }
```

The only difference between the two routines is the location of the 1.10 constant. In the first routine, the 1.10 appears after the * operator, and in the second routine, the 1.10 appears before the *.

What kind of overloaded operator*() member function is needed? You'll have to define an operator*() function to receive a Cust and a float value for the first routine. That's easy. When Turbo C++ sees customers[c] * 1.10, it calls the function operator*(&customers[c], 1.10) and looks for a corresponding operator*(*this, float) function. (When you wrote the function, you didn't specify *this, but you knew that the compiler would add it for you.) Here's an overloaded * operator member function that might handle the first routine:

```
Cust operator*(float f)
{
  Cust tempCust;
  tempCust.discPercent = discPercent * f;
  return tempCust;   // (You could have used *this also)
}
```

By now, it should come as no surprise to you that Turbo C++ changes this member function into this during compilation:

```
Cust operator*(Cust *this, float f)
{
  Cust tempCust;
  tempCust.discPercent = this->discPercent * f;
  return tempCust;   // (You could have used *this also)
}
```

It turns out that to write an overloaded operator function for the second routine takes a completely different kind of overloaded operator function! To overload the second operator, with a float as the first argument and a Cust class as the second, you must use a friend function and not a member function.

The following member function is just a mirror-image of the preceding one, but it will not work for multiplying a float times a Cust:

```
Cust operator*(float f, Cust c)      // INVALID!
{
  Cust tempCust;
  tempCust.discPercent = c.discPercent * f;
  return tempCust;    // (You could have used *this also)
}
```

Think for a moment why this function won't work. Here's a hint: It's a *member* function. Turbo C++ sticks the *this pointer in *every* member function, even when you don't want the *this pointer there! Turbo C++ would convert the preceding function, if it were a member function, to this:

```
Cust operator*(Cust *this, float f, Cust c)      // INVALID!
{
  Cust tempCust;
  tempCust.discPercent = c.discPercent * f;
  return tempCust;    // (You could have used *this also)
}
```

After the *this pointer is added, there is no way that Turbo C++, through function overloading, will match this operator*() with the expression 1.10 * customers[c]. Therefore, you need a function that is *not* passed the *this pointer but one that still has access to private members of the class. Friend functions fill that need nicely.

Remember that friend functions have full access to private class members, but they never get passed a *this pointer. Although this means you must specifically receive both arguments in the friend function whereas most operator member functions need only one argument from you, the friend function always enables you to combine a built-in data type with a derived data type when the built-in data type appears to the left of the operator.

Here is the class and friend function that enables you to multiply 1.10 times a Cust object:

```
class Cust {
  char name[25];
  char custCode[5];
  float outBalance;
  int timesPurchased;
  float discPercent;       // We're interested in this now
public:
  friend Cust operator+(float f, Cust c);
  // The public member functions would go here
};
```

```
// The following function is NOT part of the class
friend Cust operator+(float f, Cust c)
{
  Cust tempCust;
  tempCust.discPercent = f * c.discPercent;
  return tempCust;   // (You could have used *this also)
}
```

The bottom line is this: If you ever need a built-in data type on the left side of an operator and your own data type on the right, you'll have to overload a friend operator function so that the *this pointer doesn't get in your way.

Overloading ++ and --

The increment and decrement unary operators are easy to overload. The most important consideration to give them is that they require only one operand (only a single lvalue is incremented or decremented by the ++ and -- operators), and that operand is always a dereferenced *this pointer. You therefore never explicitly pass arguments to operator++() and operator--() functions unless you write them as friend functions.

However, there are two sets of increment and decrement operators: postfix and prefix. Turbo C++ (beginning back in version 2.0) enables you to distinguish between overloaded increment and decrement operators by inserting the int keyword in the overloaded increment and decrement member functions' argument lists. The int is there only to distinguish between postfix and prefix. Therefore, most Turbo C++ programs that include overloaded increment and decrement operator member functions include four of them, prototyped here:

```
className operator++(void);     // Prefix ++

className operator++(int);      // Postfix ++

className operator--(void);     // Prefix --

className operator--(int);      // Postfix --
```

You can code each set the same or differently depending on whether you want a different routine to execute when the user uses postfix or prefix. Again, the int is there just for the determination of postfix and prefix. You'll *never* pass an integer to these functions. Therefore, if you increment an nClass variable named aVar1 like

```
aVar1++;        // Postfix
```

then Turbo C++ calls the member function prototyped like this:

```
className operator++(int);      // Postfix ++
```

But if you increment aVar1 like

```
++aVar1;        // Prefix
```

then Turbo C++ calls the member function prototyped like this:

```
className operator++(void);     // Prefix ++
```

The program in Listing 11.7 includes a set of increment and a set of decrement operator member functions for the nClass class used in some previous listings. The increment and decrement are applied to all integer members within the class. The overloaded member functions could have been written to increment the floating-point members as well, but the next section of the chapter explains more about applying these overloaded operators to floats.

Just to show you that the compiler distinguishes between prefix and postfix, a message is printed to let you know which is called, even though the same operation code appears in both increment functions and both decrement functions.

Note: As with the compound operators, both ++ and -- operate on an lvalue (they change the operand that triggers their execution). Therefore, overloaded increment and decrement member functions always return *this.

Listing 11.7. Overloading increments and decrements.

```
1:  // Filename: INCDECOV.CPP
2:  // Overloading increments and decrements
3:  #include <iostream.h>
4:  #include <iomanip.h>
5:  #include <conio.h>
6:  class nClass {
7:     int i1, i2, i3;
8:     float f1, f2, f3, f4;
9:  public:
10:    inline void init(int I1, int I2, int I3, float F1, float F2,
    ➡float F3, float F4);
11:    inline void prData(void);
12:    inline nClass operator++(); // No argument needed for prefix
13:    inline nClass operator-();
14:    inline nClass operator++(int); // int argument needed for postfix
15:    inline nClass operator-(int);
16:    };
17:  void nClass::init(int I1, int I2, int I3, float F1, float F2,
    ➡float F3, float F4)
```

```
18:  {
19:    i1 = I1;  i2 = I2;  i3 = I3;
20:    f1 = F1;  f2 = F2;  f3 = F3;  f4 = F4;
21:  }
22: void nClass::prData(void)
23:  {
24:    cout << setprecision(2) << setiosflags(ios::showpoint);
25:    cout << "\ni1: " << i1 << "\t\t" << "i2: " << i2 << "\t\t";
26:    cout << "i3: " << i3;
27:    cout << "\nf1: " << f1 << "\t" << "f2: " << f2 << "\t";
28:    cout << "f3: " << f3 << "\n";
29:    cout << "f4: " << f4 << "\n";
30:  }
31: nClass nClass::operator++()      // No argument needed for prefix
32:  {
33:    cout << "(prefix ++ being done...)\n";
34:    i1++;
35:    i2++;
36:    i3++;     // Leave all float members alone
37:    return *this;
38:  };
39: nClass nClass::operator--()      // No argument needed for prefix
40:  {
41:    cout << "(prefix -- being done...)\n";
42:    i1--;
43:    i2--;
44:    i3--;     // Leave all float members alone
45:    return *this;
46:  };
47: nClass nClass::operator++(int)    // Ignore the postfix int argument
48:  {
49:    cout << "(postfix ++ being done...)\n";
50:    i1++;
51:    i2++;
52:    i3++;     // Leave all float members alone
53:    return *this;
54:  };
55: nClass nClass::operator--(int)    // Ignore the postfix int argument
56:  {
57:    cout << "(postfix -- being done...)\n";
58:    i1--;
59:    i2--;
60:    i3--;     // Leave all float members alone
61:    return *this;
62:  };
63: /////////////////////////////////////////////////////////////////
64: main()
65:  {
66:    nClass aVar1, aVar2, aVar3, aVar4;
67:    clrscr();
```

continues

Listing 11.7. continued

```
68:    // Put data in the object variables
69:    aVar1.init(4, 2, 5, 12.34, 10.4, 7.6, 5.3);
70:    aVar2.init(2, 5, 9, 2.47, 7.52, 5.06, 6.2);
71:    aVar3.init(8, 3, 8, 2.03, 11.67, 4.4, 3.9);
72:    aVar4.init(3, 6, 7, 5.3, 4.30, 7.5, 2.1);
73:    aVar1++;
74:    ++aVar2;
75:    aVar3--;
76:    --aVar4;
77:    // Show that overloaded functions worked
78:    aVar1.prData();
79:    aVar2.prData();
80:    aVar3.prData();
81:    aVar4.prData();
82:    return 0;
83: }
```

```
(postfix ++ being done...)
(prefix ++ being done...)
(postfix -- being done...)
(prefix -- being done...)

i1: 5          i2: 3          i3: 6
f1: 12.34      f2: 10.40      f3: 7.60
f4: 5.30

i1: 3          i2: 6          i3: 10
f1: 2.47       f2: 7.52       f3: 5.06
f4: 6.20

i1: 7          i2: 2          i3: 7
f1: 2.03       f2: 11.67      f3: 4.40
f4: 3.90

i1: 2          i2: 5          i3: 6
f1: 5.30       f2: 4.30       f3: 7.50
f4: 2.10
```

Look in the initialization lines 69–72 to find the original values for the i1 through i3 variables. The increment and decrement operators were not overloaded here to do anything with the floating-point values. You can see from the four printed messages at the top of the output that each postfix and prefix version of the increment and decrement operators were called.

The overloaded postfix operator functions don't use the int argument because it is there just to let Turbo C++ know that the function is postfix. If you were to follow

the general guidelines of argument lists, you would put a variable name after int such as this:

```
nClass nClass::operator++(int notUsed)
```

Putting an argument there forces Turbo C++ to issue the warning

```
Warning C:\TC\INCDECOV.CPP 54: Parameter 'notUsed' is never used
```

during compilation because the argument notUsed is defined but never used in the function. If you leave off an argument name after the int, you still let Turbo C++ know about the postfix designation, but you eliminate the compiler warning as well.

More Hints of Extensibility

Have you ever wished you could apply the increment and decrement operators to floating-point and double floating-point variables? You can by creating specialized classes that contain the data type (float or whatever) for which you want to apply a customized operator. After you see some of the ways that Turbo C++ customizes how operators work with your data, you'll understand why the entire data processing industry seems to be migrating to C++.

The program in Listing 11.8 contains two classes: Float (the first letter is capitalized to distinguish it from the built-in float) and charAlph. You can apply increment and decrement to any variable defined as a Float because a set of overloaded operators (prefix only to retain some brevity here) is included to handle the incremented and decremented floating-point values. Also, charAlph objects show how incrementing and decrementing *character* data is possible. When a charAlph object is incremented or decremented, the next highest or lowest alphabetic character is stored in the object. If an attempt is made to decrement before A or increment after Z, the appropriate overloaded operator wraps around to the last or first of the alphabet (A decrements to Z, and Z increments to A).

Listing 11.8. Extending the normal operation of floats and chars.

```
1:  // Filename: FLTCHAR.CPP
2:  // Overload a float-like class and a special alphabetic-only class
3:  #include <iostream.h>
4:  #include <iomanip.h>
5:  #include <conio.h>
6:  class Float {     // Will simulate a special floating-point
7:    float f;
```

continues

Listing 11.8. continued

```
 8:  public:
 9:    void init(float F) {f = F;}   // Inline because it is short
10:    inline Float operator++(void);
11:     inline Float operator--(void);
12:     float getFloat(void) { return f; };
13:   };
14:  Float Float::operator++(void)    // Adds 1 to the float
15:  {
16:     f += 1.0;
17:     return *this;
18:  }
19:  Float Float::operator--(void)    // Subtracts 1 from the float
20:  {
21:     f -= 1.0;
22:     return *this;
23:  };
24:  // Second class next
25:  class charAlph {
26:     char c;
27:  public:
28:     void init(char C) {c = C;}  // Inline because it is short
29:     inline charAlph operator++(void);
30:     inline charAlph operator--(void);
31:     char getAlph(void) { return c; }
32:  };
33:  charAlph charAlph::operator++(void)
34:  {
35:     if (c == 'Z')
36:       c = 'A';
37:     else
38:       c++;     // Turbo C++ will add an ASCII 1 to the character
39:     return *this;
40:  }
41:  charAlph charAlph::operator--(void)
42:  {
43:     if (c == 'A')
44:       c = 'Z';
45:     else
46:       c--; // Turbo C++ will subtract an ASCII 1 from the character
47:     return *this;
48:  }
49:  ///////////////////////////////////////////////////////////////////
50:  main()
51:  {
52:     Float fVal;
53:     charAlph initial;
54:     clrscr();
55:     fVal.init(34.5);
56:     cout << "Before increment, fVal is " << fVal.getFloat() << "\n";
57:     ++fVal;
```

```
58:    cout << "After increment, fVal is " << fVal.getFloat() << "\n";
59:    --fVal;
60:    cout << "After decrement, fVal is " << fVal.getFloat() << "\n\n";
61:    initial.init('Y');
62:    cout << "Before increment, initial is " << initial.getAlph()
     ➥<< "\n";
63:    ++initial;
64:    cout << "After increment, initial is " << initial.getAlph()
     ➥<< "\n";
65:    ++initial;
66:    cout << "Incrementing initial again produces "
     ➥<< initial.getAlph() << "\n";
67:    --initial;
68:    cout << "After decrementing, initial is " << initial.getAlph()
     ➥<< "\n";
69:    return 0;
70: }
```

```
Before increment, fVal is 34.5
After increment, fVal is 35.5
After decrement, fVal is 34.5

Before increment, initial is Y
After increment, initial is Z
Incrementing initial again produces A
After decrementing, initial is Z
```

Perhaps little more has to be said about this program except that it gives you some insight in writing your own *type-safe* data types. That is, you now have the power to create data classes that protect themselves and act the way you want them to.

In a couple of days, you'll learn how to write completely self-governing classes, such as charAlph here, that never accept values other than those that fall within the ranges you specify. For example, you could write your own integer class that prints an error message if any value is assigned that is outside the normal range of int data. You will also be able to write true alpha-like data types that accept and work only with alphabetic characters, just as Listing 11.8 begins to do with the increment and decrement operator member functions.

 DO   **DON'T**

DO feel free to overload operators so that they work with a built-in data type and your own data type. Many Turbo C++ programs contain three sets of overloaded operator functions: one set handles two class variables of the same type, one set handles a built-in data type used as the left operand, and the third set handles a built-in data type used as the right operand.

DO write friend functions when the left operand is a built-in data type. You cannot use a member function to overload such operations because the `*this` pointer gets in the way.

DON'T overload the prefix increment and decrement functions without overloading postfix as well, unless you're sure that both kinds won't be used.

DON'T use an argument name after `int` in postfix increment and decrement functions or you'll receive a compiler warning from Turbo C++.

Summary

You've mastered the primary discussion about overloaded operators. About 75 percent of all the operators you ever overload will use code that mirrors the examples from this chapter. Although there is more to learn about operator overloading (and the remaining operator overloading material will be saved for tomorrow's chapter), you now have a good part of operator overloading behind you.

In today's chapter, you learned how to overload all the primary math operators, using them as member functions. When using member functions, don't pass the first operand because of the `*this` pointer that's passed for you by Turbo C++. As long as you want to use operators that work with your data types, or a combination of your data type and a built-in data type, Turbo C++ enables you to overload functions to handle the job.

It makes sense to use member functions for overloaded operator functions as much as possible because the functions must have access to private data members.

Overloading the relational and logical operators simply requires that you return an integer True or False (1 or 0) value. The comparison operator functions actually compare internal members from the class variables on either side. Remember, though, that the short-circuiting feature of the built-in logical operators won't apply to expressions you've overloaded.

Although this chapter didn't show a specific example, you can overload an operator to operate on variables from two different classes. Simply make sure that the argument in the overloaded operator function contains the second class's data type.

Finally, overloading increment and decrement operations is easy. You don't even have to specify an argument because these operators are unary operators and `*this` is passed

automatically. By inserting the `int` keyword inside the argument list (with no argument name after `int`), you indicate that the function is postfix rather than the default prefix.

Q&A

1. **What's the difference between overloading using regular functions as learned on Day 7, and overloading using member functions?**

   Member functions never need to be passed the first operand. Turbo C++ always passes the first operand as the hidden `*this` pointer, so you specify only the right operand (if you aren't overloading the unary increment and decrement operators that take only one operand) in the overloaded operator function's argument list.

   There are times when you'll still use non-member functions to overload operators (when using friend functions). However, the increment and decrement operators, as well as operators that work solely on two of your own data types, should always be member functions; you won't have to worry about passing the left operand as an argument.

2. **Why do some overloaded operator member functions return `*this`?**

   You must always remember that some operators, such as the compound operators and the increment and decrement operators, change their left operand. The statement

   ```
   aVar += aVarNew;
   ```

   changes `aVar`. It is said that the compound operators (and the increment and decrement as well) *update* one of their operands. The `*this` pointer always holds a pointer to the first operand. After updating the first operand, you must return that operand with its new value so that the compiler will retain the newly updated value in the program's variable.

3. **When would I ever use a friend function for an overloaded operator function?**

   Remember that the `*this` pointer is never passed to friend functions because friend functions are stand-alone non-member functions. The only difference between a friend function and any other function that appears after `main()` is that a friend function has access to a class's private members.

When you want to overload an operator to work on a built-in data type as the left operand and one of your own data types, you have to specify that the function be a friend function or else the *this pointer that is always passed as a first argument will get in the way.

4. How does Turbo C++ distinguish between postfix and prefix increment and decrement overloaded operator functions?

If you want to overload an increment or decrement operator using a member function, insert int inside the parentheses of the function like this:

```
aClass operator++(int)     // Postfix
{
  member1++;
  member2++;
  member3 += 1.0;
  return *this;
}
```

The int lets Turbo C++ know that it should call this increment when a postfix operator is applied to an aClass object like this:

```
aVar++;     // Add 1 with a postfix operator function
```

Workshop

The Workshop offers quiz questions and exercises to hone your skills and give you feedback on today's lesson. You'll find some proposed answers in Appendix D.

Quiz

1. How many arguments do most overloaded operator member functions take (not counting increment and decrement member functions)?

2. How does Turbo C++ know which operator function to call if you've coded more than one?

3. What are the names of the prefix increment overloaded function and the postfix increment overloaded function?

4. Explain why overloaded logical operators don't always perform as efficiently as regular built-in logical operators.

5. What data type should overloaded relational and logical operators have to return?

6. Would the following prototype be used for prefix or postfix decrement?

```
aClass operator--(int);
```

7. What is usually the return data type of overloaded operators that you want to stack together like this:

```
aClassVar = aClassVar1 + aClassVar2 + aClassVar3 + aClassVar4;
```

8. What does the return statement usually look like for overloaded compound operator and overloaded increment/decrement functions?

9. How does *this sometimes get in your way?

10. Why shouldn't you put an argument name after int when overloading postfix operators?

Exercises

1. Rewrite the program in Listing 11.8 so that lowercase letters will be "safe" as well (the a would wrap around to z, and z would wrap around to a).

2. Write a program with a class that has two private integer values. Overload the logical operators, && and ¦¦, so that True or False results if both integers of objects on both sides of the logical operators have non-zero values.

Extending Operator Overloads

Today's chapter explains how to overload the remaining operators, including I/O operators such as <<, >>, and the I/O manipulators. You'll also see some additional ways you can use overloading to make Turbo C++ do exactly what you want it to do.

The primary reason for overloading operators is to make your programming life easier. When you overload operators, you can concentrate on the application details of your program (the program's goals) instead of worrying about lots of details.

Isn't it easier to use + than remember `addEmps()`, `addCusts()`, `addVendors()`, `addInventory()`, and so on? Of course, you have to initially write the code that performs the overloading details on the class data, but after you do, the rest of the program is much more straightforward, and you'll find yourself reusing the same code from certain overloaded operator functions among several programs.

Today, you learn about the following topics:

☐ How to overload << to output your own class data

☐ How to overload >> to input your own class data

☐ How to write your own I/O manipulators

☐ How to overload subscripts

Note: Some of the concepts in today's chapter will be improved on after you learn the material in tomorrow's chapter, "Constructing and Destructing." Many of the details found so far in the book, such as long initialization routines in the primary part of the program, will be eliminated after tomorrow's chapter.

Overloading Input and Output Operators

Overloading I/O forms the epitome of operator overloading. After you learn how to overload << and >>, you'll be inputting and outputting entire class variables in single statements such as

```
cin >> employee;  // This cin could possibly ask for 50 members
```

and

```
cout >> employee;
```

In one sense, << and >> are already overloaded. Consider this statement:

```
i = u << 3;    // Bitwise left-shift
```

The << used in this statement is a bitwise left-shift operator. You might have never used the bitwise operators in your programming career. Many C and C++ programmers program for years and never need them. Nevertheless, the statement shown here works at the internal bit level of memory. The internal bit representation of u is shifted to the left three places (zeros fill in from the right), and the result is stored in the variable i (u is left unchanged).

Now, consider how this next statement differs from the preceding bitwise statement:

```
cout << i << u << 3;
```

You now know that the cout object is the standard output device, normally the screen. Therefore, the << insertion operator tells Turbo C++ to send the values of i, u, and then 3 to the screen. (There won't be any spacing between the output values.)

How does Turbo C++ know that the first use of << meant bitwise left-shift and the second use of << meant output? Turbo C++ contains its own built-in overloaded operator functions. Although you cannot access the code, internally Turbo C++ contains these overloaded operator function prototypes:

```
friend int operator<<(int, int);
```

and

```
ostream & operator<<(int);
```

12

Note: These prototypes are intentionally left simpler than the true internal prototypes really appear.

You can guess that the bitwise << is a friend function (unless you write an overloaded << that takes a class for an operand), because an integer appears as the left operand. You learned in yesterday's chapter that a friend function is needed any time an operator's left operand is a non-class variable.

The second prototype implies that a simple output statement such as

```
cout << 10;
```

actually becomes this overloaded operator function:

```
cout.operator<<(10);
```

(The compiler would then insert the cout object into the argument list and receives it as a *this pointer as usual.)

Way back in Day 3's chapter, "Simple I/O," you learned that cout and cin are *objects,* but you were told not to concern yourself with that term yet because you had yet to be exposed to class variables and objects. Now, however, the term *object* should make perfect sense. Somewhere inside the compiler, there are classes for cout and cin (and other I/O objects). When you apply the << or >> operators to them, Turbo C++ calls overloaded operator<<() and operator>>() functions that use those I/O objects.

Object or Class?

If the cout and cin objects are really objects, they must be instantiated (be created) from some I/O class within Turbo C++, and they are. The cout object is from the output class called ostream, and cin is from the input class named istream. That's why the overloaded << function prototype in the file IOSTREAM.H always returns a reference ostream object. Because a reference to an object is returned, you can stack cout with multiple <<'s.

If you fail to include the file IOSTREAM.H at the top of your Turbo C++ programs, you'll get a message similar to this one if you attempt to use cout:

```
Undefined symbol 'cout'.
```

Before looking at the specific details of I/O overloading, consider how Turbo C++ handles these kinds of statements:

```
cout << i << u << 3;
```

Turbo C++ first notices that cout is a member of the ostream class. Finding the overloaded operator<<() function that accesses an ostream object as its first argument, Turbo C++ first changes the statement to look something like this:

```
cout.operator<<(i) << u << 3;
```

As shown a moment ago, operator<<() returns a reference to an ostream object, which is just a fancy (and more accurate) way of saying that cout is returned from operator<<(). When Turbo C++ interprets the second << in this cout, the compiler then changes the statement to this:

```
cout.operator<<(cout.operator<<(i), u) << 3;
```

Using the same logic, Turbo C++ then changes the statement to this to handle the third <<:

```
cout.operator<<(cout.operator<<(cout.operator<<(i), u), 3);
```

Right before the program is compiled, Turbo C++ converts this nested overloaded function call to the *this pointer notation, moving cout inside the function parentheses as the first argument. Figure 12.1 shows an additional way of interpreting the actions of Turbo C++ when the previous cout executes.

Left-to-right associativity of <<:
```
            cout << i << u << 3;
                 \  /
                cout << u << 3
                     \  /
                    cout << 3;
```

Figure 12.1. *Each pair of operands surrounding* << *must return a* cout *object (more accurately, a reference to one) to successfully stack together output values.*

Note: By the way, this discussion has attempted to offer a background on how the overloading of >> and << works, but if you aren't sure you fully understand the ostream and istream classes, they will become more obvious to you the more you overload << and >>. Today's chapter now has the theory out of the way and can concentrate on the coding necessary to get the job done.

12

The Details of Overloading << for Output

Here's output overloading in a nutshell: Almost every overloaded >> output function you write will have the format

```
ostream & operator<<(ostream & out, yourClass & object)
{
  // Body of function goes here
  return out;
}
```

This overloaded function must be a friend function. If you could create it as a member function, you wouldn't have to specify the first argument (the one that receives cout) because Turbo C++ would send a pointer to cout as *this. However, you must specify overloaded I/O operator functions as friend functions because they have to work with the IOSTREAM.H header file in a way that requires the friend availability. The nice thing also about making them friend functions is that you can output like

```
cout << myObject << 2;
```

and like

```
cout << 2 << myObject;
```

Limiting overloaded << outputs to those whose left operands are class objects, as you would have to do with member functions, would be too constraining.

The body of the operator<<() function contains *whatever* code you want executed when the rest of the program (often called the *user of the class*) uses the overloaded operator with cout. Listing 12.1 contains a class with six members. The program initializes an object of the class and then outputs all six members with appropriate titles using a single cout output statement.

Listing 12.1. Overloading a class for easy output of objects.

```
1: // Filename: SIXOUT.CPP
2: // Outputs an object using overloading
3: #include <iostream.h>
4: #include <string.h>
5: class aClass {
6:   char c;
7:   char s[25];
8:   int i;
9:   long l;
10:   float x;
11:   double d;
12: public:
13:   inline void init(char, char [], int, long, float, double);
14:   friend ostream & operator<< (ostream &, aClass);
15: };
16: void aClass::init(char C, char S[], int I, long L, float X,
      double D)
17:   { c = C; strcpy(s, S); i = I; l = L; x = X; d = D; }
18: // Overloaded output function next
19: ostream & operator<<(ostream & out, aClass obj)
20: {
21:   out << "Here's the object:\n";
22:   out << "c is " << obj.c << "\n";
```

```
23:    out << "s is " << obj.s << "\n";
24:    out << "i is " << obj.i << "\n";
25:    out << "l is " << obj.l << "\n";
26:    out << "x is " << obj.x << "\n";
27:    out << "d is " << obj.d << "\n";
28:    return out;    // Allows stacking
29: }
30: ///////////////////////////////////////////////////////////////////
31: main()
32: {
33:    aClass anObject;
34:    anObject.init('Q', "Turbo C++", 14, 54234L, 6.75, 456.5432);
35:    cout << anObject;    // ALL output done here!
36:    return 0;
37: }
```

```
Here's the object:
c is Q
s is Turbo C++
i is 14
l is 54234
x is 6.75
d is 456.5432
```

The entire output of the aClass object is done using a single, simple cout on line 35. Why do you think the operator<<() class contains out << and not cout << (lines 21–27)? The reason is that the class must send its output to the local object named out, the data being output. That local object is the same thing as main()'s cout. Remember that when Turbo C++ sees

```
cout << anObject;
```

in main(), Turbo C++ changes it to this after rearranging the object as the first argument:

```
operator<<(cout, anObject);
```

The function operator<<() contains a local ostream object variable named out that receives by reference main()'s cout object when operator<<() is called.

The out object is returned on line 28 so that stacking of the << operator could occur. If main() defined two object variables and printed them like

```
main()
{
  aClass anObject1, anObject2;
  anObject1.init('Q', "Turbo C++", 14, 54234L, 6.75, 456.5432);
  anObject2.init('W', "OOP's easy!", 25, 98455L, 8.01, 90210.90210);
  cout << anObject1 << anObject2;    // ALL output done here!
```

12

```
    return 0;
}
```

you would then see this output:

```
Here's the object:
c is Q
s is Turbo C++
i is 14
l is 54234
x is 6.75
d is 456.5432
Here's the object:
c is W
s is OOP's easy!
i is 25
l is 98455
x is 8.01
d is 90210.9021
```

Note: Do you see how main() collapses down to virtually nothing? The lines of output consume more programming statements than all of main(). Again, overloading the << operator is just one way to rid the primary sections of your programs of typical tedious details. After you overload the I/O, you use standard >> and << to input and output complete class data.

The program in Listing 12.2 takes the output of the aClass's six member functions to the extreme. Using ASCII line-drawing characters available on the PC, the output of the class object outputs using fancy boxes. Figure 12.2 shows what the output from the program looks like. Despite the advanced control of the screen, all the output is accomplished, just as it was back in Listing 12.1, with this simple statement:

```
cout << anObject;
```

You ought to be imagining how easy it will be to write programs after the output of complicated class data becomes as easy as outputting an integer. Sure, you still have to write the output code. But you separate it from the primary part of the program, and you're then able to see the application's direction without lots of messy details getting in the way. As you write your programs, you'll be coding simple statements for major output instead of keeping track of lots of function names that do the work. Object-oriented programming promotes a much more natural way of getting your job done.

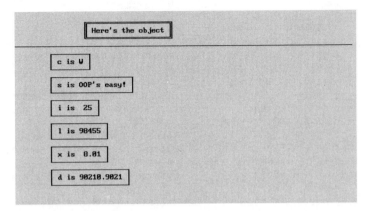

Figure 12.2. *No matter how fancy your output, overload << to handle it easily.*

Listing 12.2. Drawing boxes around output.

```
1: // Filename: FANCYOUT.CPP
2: // Outputs an object using overloading
3: #include <iostream.h>
4: #include <iomanip.h>
5: #include <string.h>
6: #include <conio.h>
7: class aClass {
8:    char c;
9:    char s[25];
10:   int i;
11:    long l;
12:    float x;
13:    double d;
14:  public:
15:    inline void init(char, char [], int, long, float, double);
16:    friend ostream & operator<< (ostream &, aClass);
17:  };
18:  void aClass::init(char C, char S[], int I, long L, float X,
    ➡double D)
19:    { c = C; strcpy(s, S); i = I; l = L; x = X; d = D; }
20: // Overloaded output function next
21: ostream & operator<<(ostream & out, aClass obj)
22: {
23:   clrscr();
24:   out << "\n\t\t" << '\xC9';      // Title's corner
25:   for (int i=0; i<19; i++) // Double-lined top of box
26:     { out << '\xCD'; }
27:   out << "\xBB\n";
28:   out << "\t\t\xBA Here's the object \xBA\n";
29:   out << "\t\t" << '\xC8'; // Double-lined corner
```

continues

Listing 12.2. continued

```
30:    for (i=0; i<19; i++)
31:      { out << '\xCD'; }        // Double-line bottom of box
32:    out << "\xBC\n";
33:    for (i=0; i<79; i++)
34:      { out << '\xC4'; }        // Straight line across the screen
35:    out << "\n\t\xDA";          // c's output (upper-right corner)
36:    for (i=0; i<8; i++)
37:      { out << '\xC4'; }        // Top of straight-lined box
38:    out << "\xBF\n";            // Upper-right corner of c's box
39:    out << "\t\xB3 c is " << obj.c << " \xB3\n";
40:    out << "\t\xC0";            // Left-bottom corner of c's box
41:    for (i=0; i<8; i++)
42:      { out << '\xC4'; }        // Bottom line of c's box
43:    out << "\xD9";              // Right-bottom corner of c's box
44:    out << "\n\t\xDA";          // s's output (upper-right corner)
45:    for (i=0; i<(7+strlen(obj.s)); i++)
46:      { out << '\xC4'; }        // Top of straight-lined box
47:    out << "\xBF\n";            // Upper-right corner of s's box
48:    out << "\t\xB3 s is " << obj.s << " \xB3\n";
49:    out << "\t\xC0";            // Left-bottom corner of s's box
50:    for (i=0; i<(7+strlen(obj.s)); i++)
51:      { out << '\xC4'; }        // Bottom line of s's box
52:    out << "\xD9";              // Right-bottom corner of s's box
53:    out << "\n\t\xDA";          // i's output (upper-right corner)
54:    for (i=0; i<10; i++)
55:      { out << '\xC4'; }        // Top of straight-lined box
56:    out << "\xBF\n";            // Upper-right corner of i's box
57:    out << "\t\xB3 i is " << setw(3) << obj.i << " \xB3\n";
58:    out << "\t\xC0";            // Left-bottom corner of i's box
59:    for (i=0; i<10; i++)
60:      { out << '\xC4'; }        // Bottom line of i's box
61:    out << "\xD9";              // Right-bottom corner of i's box
62:    out << "\n\t\xDA";          // l's output (upper-right corner)
63:    for (i=0; i<12; i++)
64:      { out << '\xC4'; }        // Top of straight-lined box
65:    out << "\xBF\n";            // Upper-right corner of l's box
66:    out << "\t\xB3 l is " << setw(5) << obj.l << " \xB3\n";
67:    out << "\t\xC0";            // Left-bottom corner of l's box
68:    for (i=0; i<12; i++)
69:      { out << '\xC4'; }        // Bottom line of l's box
70:    out << "\xD9";              // Right-bottom corner of l's box
71:    out << "\n\t\xDA";          // x's output (upper-right corner)
72:    for (i=0; i<12; i++)
73:      { out << '\xC4'; }        // Top of straight-lined box
74:    out << "\xBF\n";            // Upper-right corner of x's box
75:    out << "\t\xB3 x is " << setw(5) << obj.x << " \xB3\n";
76:    out << "\t\xC0";            // Left-bottom corner of x's box
77:    for (i=0; i<12; i++)
78:      { out << '\xC4'; }        // Bottom line of x's box
```

```
79:    out << "\xD9";              // Right-bottom corner of x's box
80:    out << "\n\t\xDA";          // d's output (upper-right corner)
81:    for (i=0; i<17; i++)
82:       { out << '\xC4'; }       // Top of straight-lined box
83:    out << "\xBF\n";            // Upper-right corner of d's box
84:    out << "\t\xB3 d is " << setw(10) << obj.d << " \xB3\n";
85:    out << "\t\xC0";            // Left-bottom corner of d's box
86:    for (i=0; i<17; i++)
87:       { out << '\xC4'; }       // Bottom line of d's box
88:    out << "\xD9";              // Right-bottom corner of d's box
89:    return out;                 // Allows stacking
90: }
91: ////////////////////////////////////////////////////////////////////////
92: main()
93: {
94:    aClass anObject;
95:    anObject.init('W', "OOP's easy!", 25, 98455L, 8.01, 90210.90210);
96:    cout << anObject;    // ALL output done here!
97:    return 0;
98: }
```

The output was shown in Figure 12.2.

Lines 24–88 seem extremely confusing, but their primary purpose is to draw the box around the member data. The PC's ASCII table contains single-line and double-line box-drawing characters (corners and straight lines), and these are all printed to the screen by sending their hex representations to the out object. There is not much going on here; the ASCII hex values of appropriate box-drawing characters are printed to surround the member data values.

Notice that, other than different initial data, main() didn't change at all from the main() in Listing 12.1, yet the outputs from the two programs differ greatly. The beauty of Turbo C++ is its maintainability and extensibility. If you want to change the look of your program's output, you no longer have to sift through all the code looking for function names and change how they are called. *You only have to change the class that outputs the data using overloaded functions.*

Overloading << to Streamline Class Output

```
ostream & operator<<(ostream & out, yourClass & object)
{
   // Body of function goes here
   return out;
}
```

out is the received argument name for the output object cout, and *object* is the function's local name for the class variable being output. Always return the out object if you want to stack several couts together in succession.

Example

```
ostream & operator<<(ostream & out, Date & d)
{
  out << "\n";
  out << "The day is " << d.day << "\n";
  out << "The month is " << d.month << "\n";
  out << "The year is " << d.year << "\n";
  return out;
}
```

The Details of Overloading >> for Input

Overloading the >> character for input requires a mirror-image overloaded function from the output's operator<<() function. The whole purpose of overloading operators is to make your data types (declared with classes) behave like the built-in ones do. Suppose you want to ask the user for the six member values from the aClass shown in the previous listings. You could have separate member functions that request each member, but main() would have to call them individually or would have to call a public member function, which in turn would print the data.

Why not overload >> so that a simple statement such as

```
cin >> anObject;
```

produces all the prompting and input needed to fill the members with data?

To overload >>, you'll have to write an operator>>() function that looks something like this:

```
istream & operator>>(istream & in, yourClass & object)
{
  // Body of function goes here
  return in;
}
```

 Note: Whereas the reference symbol, &, before the second argument was optional when overloading output, it is required for *both* arguments in operator>>().

You'll need to return a reference to the istream input object, just as you did with the output object before, so that you can stack several inputs together like this:

```
cin >> anObject1 >> anObject2;
```

As with the operator<<() function, your operator>>() functions must be friend functions so that they interact with the IOSTREAM.H file properly.

Listing 12.3 contains a version of Listing 12.1 that does not initialize the object directly, but instead asks the user for the initialization inside an overloaded operator>>() function. (Listing 12.2's box-drawing commands were left out of this operator<<()'s code for brevity.)

Listing 12.3. Overloading a class for easy input of objects.

```
1: // Filename: SIXIN.CPP
2: // Both inputs and outputs an object using overloading
3: #include <iostream.h>
4: #include <iomanip.h>
5: #include <conio.h>
6: #include <string.h>
7: class aClass {
8:    char c;
9:    char s[25];
10:   int i;
11:    long l;
12:    float x;
13:    double d;
14:  public:
15:    friend ostream & operator<< (ostream &, aClass);
16:    friend istream & operator>> (istream &, aClass &);
17: };
18: // Overloaded output function next
19: ostream & operator<<(ostream & out, aClass obj)
20: {
21:   out << "\nHere's the object:\n";
22:   out << "c is " << obj.c << "\n";
23:   out << "s is " << obj.s << "\n";
24:   out << "i is " << obj.i << "\n";
25:   out << "l is " << obj.l << "\n";
26:   out << "x is " << obj.x << "\n";
27:   out << "d is " << obj.d << "\n";
28:   return out;    // Allows stacking
29: }
30: istream & operator>>(istream & in, aClass & obj)
31: {
32: // This function does a lot of work
33:   clrscr();
```

continues

Listing 12.3. continued

```
34:    cout << "I need some data for the class.\n";
35:    cout << "What is the value of c? ";
36:    in >> obj.c;
37:    cout << "What is s? ";
38:    in.ignore();
39:    in.get(obj.s, 25);
40:    cout << "What is i? ";
41:    in >> obj.i;
42:    cout << "What is l? ";
43:    in >> obj.l;
44:    cout << "What is x? ";
45:    in >> obj.x;
46:    cout << "What is d? ";
47:    in >> obj.d;
48:    return in;    // Allows stacking
49: }
50: ////////////////////////////////////////////////////////////////////
51: main()
52: {
53:    aClass anObject;
54:    cin >> anObject;    // Easy, right?
55:    cout << anObject;
56:    return 0;
57: }
```

```
I need some data for the class.
What is the value of c? r
What is s? Turbo C++
What is i? 3
What is l? 4
What is x? 5.6
What is d? 7.8

Here's the object:
c is r
s is Turbo C++
i is 3
l is 4
x is 5.6
d is 7.8
```

This program introduces the use of the ignore() input member function included in Turbo C++. ignore (on line 38) gets rid of the newline character that is left on the input stream (istream) buffer after the single character is input. The in object is used rather than cin because in is receiving all the input in this function. As you can see, the cin's member function named get() works for in and enables the user to enter a full string with embedded spaces (up to 25 characters in length) on line 39 rather than only a single word.

Now that you've mastered I/O overloading, check out Listing 12.4. It asks the user for the time inside an overloaded operator>>() function, performing input error checking. You now can write classes that prevent the user from entering bad values!

  Listing 12.4. **Creating a time class that checks itself.**

```
1: // Filename: TIMECHK.CPP
2: // Requires that the user enter correct time values
3: #include <iostream.h>
4: #include <conio.h>
5: class Time {
6:    int hour;
7:    int minute;
8:    int second;
9: public:
10:    friend ostream & operator<< (ostream &, Time);
11:     friend istream & operator>> (istream &, Time &);
12: };
13: // Overloaded output function next
14: ostream & operator<<(ostream & out, Time t)
15: {
16:    out << "\nHere's the time:\n";
17:    out << t.hour << ":" << t.minute << ":" << t.second << "\n";
18:    return out;    // Allows stacking
19: }
20: istream & operator>>(istream & in, Time & t)
21: {
22:    clrscr();
23:    cout << "Please enter the time as follows:\n";
24:    do {
25:       cout << "What is the hour (0-23)? ";
26:       in >> t.hour;
27:    } while ((t.hour < 0) ¦¦ (t.hour > 23));
28:    do {
29:       cout << "What is the minute (0-59)? ";
30:       in >> t.minute;
31:    } while (t.minute < 0 ¦¦ t.minute > 59);
32:    do {
33:       cout << "What is the second (0-59)? ";
34:       in >> t.second;
35:    } while (t.second < 0 ¦¦ t.second > 59);
36:    return in;    // Allows stacking
37: }
38: //////////////////////////////////////////////////////////////////
39: main()
40: {
41:    Time now;
42:    cin >> now;            // Get the time
43:    cout << now;           // Print it
44:    return 0;
45: }
```

```
Please enter the time as follows:
What is the hour (0-23)? 34
What is the hour (0-23)? 332
What is the hour (0-23)? 5454
What is the hour (0-23)? 565
What is the hour (0-23)? 21
What is the minute (0-59)? 50
What is the second (0-59)? 31

Here's the time:
21:50:31
```

——— It took the user
five times to enter
a correct hour

This program's `Time` class is a smart class that doesn't enable the user to enter values that are out of range. Throughout this book, you'll see other ways that objects can be made smart like this. Eventually, you'll be able to write classes that never, through assignment or user input, allow bad data to get into the class, thus creating fully safe and protected classes.

Through a series of `do-while` loops (such as the one in lines 24–27), the program ensures that the user enters correct values into the 24-hour `Time` members. `main()` is about as simple as it can be.

Overloading >> to Streamline Class Input

```
istream & operator>>(istream & in, yourClass & object)
{
  // Body of function goes here
  return in;
}
```

`in` is the received argument name for the output object `cin`, and *object* is the function's local name for the class variable being input. Always return the `in` object if you want to stack several `cin`s together in succession. You *must* receive *object* by reference—operator>>() will not work properly if you don't.

Example

```
istream & operator>> (istream & in, Date & d)
{
  cout << "\n";
  cout << "What is the month (1-12)? ";
  in >> d.month;
  cout << "What is the day (1-31)? ";
  in >> d.day;
  cout << "What is the year (1980-2100)? ";
  in >> d.year;
  return in;
}
```

DO specify your overloaded I/O operator functions as friend functions.

DO use all the I/O manipulator and input functions that you want when overloading input with `operator>>()`. Just be sure to use the `istream` object's name and not cout inside the function. `ignore()`, `getline()`, and `get()` all work inside overloaded `operator>>()` functions.

DO return a reference to the input or output object if you want to stack several cins or couts together in sequence.

DON'T forget to add error-checking routines to your overloaded input operations. Your data becomes self-policing, and therefore the main part of the program has to do much less at each input.

Creating Your Own I/O Manipulators

Although you might not have a daily need to do so, you can overload the I/O manipulators so that they modify your output the way you want it modified. You might find it easier to overload a manipulator (which usually means writing your own manipulator and naming it yourself).

To create your own manipulators, all you have to do is write a friend function that takes an `ostream` object as its only operator. Although doing this does not qualify the function as an overloaded operator function, the use of `ostream` fits in neatly with the first part of this chapter that introduced `ostream`. `ostream` is just the output stream. (You can also define manipulators for the input stream, `istream`, although these are rarer.)

Suppose that you wanted to create an I/O manipulator named `ring` that rang the PC's speaker whenever it appeared in an output stream. In other words, when you typed

```
cout << ring;
```

the speaker would beep. You would also want the capability to embed the `ring` manipulator inside stacked outputs such as this:

```
cout << oldMessage << ring << newMessage << ring << "\n";
```

12

The following function named `ring` would create the manipulator:

```
ostream & ring(ostream & out)
{
  out << '\x07';   // 7 is ASCII bell-ring character
  return out;
}
```

ASCII 7 beeps your computer's speaker whenever it is printed. Because the ASCII value of 7 is difficult to remember and you don't always have an ASCII chart handy, creating this manipulator makes programming easier. You could insert this code together with other manipulators you write and place them in a header file that you include at the top of your programs.

Note: Code your manipulator functions as friend functions so that all classes can use them.

Listing 12.5 includes the `ring` manipulator as well as three tabbing manipulators, called `tab5`, `tab10`, and `tab15`. Each of the `tab...` manipulators tabs a different number of spaces when you embed them in an output stream.

Type **Listing 12.5. Defining new manipulators.**

```
 1:  // Filename: MANIP.CPP
 2:  // Includes several user-defined output manipulators
 3:  #include <iostream.h>
 4:  #include <conio.h>
 5:  ostream & ring(ostream & out);
 6:  ostream & tab5(ostream & out);
 7:  ostream & tab10(ostream & out);
 8:  ostream & tab15(ostream & out);
 9:  main()
10:  {
11:    cout << "Hi. Here's a bell." << ring << "\n";
12:    cout << "tab..." << tab5 << "5 spaces later." << "\n";
13:    cout << "tab..." << tab10 << "10 spaces later." << "\n";
14:    cout << "tab..." << tab15 << "15 spaces later." << "\n";
15:    return 0;
16:  }
17:  /////////////////////////////////////////////////////////////////
18:  ostream & ring(ostream & out)
19:  {
20:    out << '\x07';   // 7 is ASCII bell-ring character
21:    return out;
22:  }
```

```
23: ostream & tab5(ostream & out)
24: {
25:    out << "      ";
26:    return out;
27: }
28: ostream & tab10(ostream & out)
29: {
30:    out << "           ";
31:    return out;
32: }
33: ostream & tab15(ostream & out)
34: {
35:    out << "                ";
36:    return out;
37: }
```

Output

```
Hi. Here's a bell.
tab...      5 spaces later.
tab...          10 spaces later.
tab...              15 spaces later.
```

Analysis

The program in Listing 12.5 doesn't happen to have classes, but if there were classes in the program, as well as overloaded operator>>() and operator<<() functions, any of them could use the manipulators coded there. (The classes, of course, would have to list the manipulator functions as friends if the manipulator needed access to any of the class's private members.)

Lines 5–8 include function prototypes because main() calls, albeit indirectly, the manipulator functions, and all functions called by main() must be prototyped.

Syntax

Creating I/O Manipulators

```
ostream & manipName(ostream & out)
{
  // Output manipulator code goes here
  return out;
}
```

and

```
istream & manipName(istream & in)
{
  // Input manipulator code goes here
  return in;
}
```

out and in receive the output or input of the manipulation code that you write.

12

Example

```
ostream & line20(ostream & out)
{
  for (int i=0; i<19; i++)    // Outputs 20 hyphens
    { out << " "; }
  return out;
}
```

Subscript Overloading

If you want to, you can overload the subscript operator to work the way you need with your own data types. Consider this class named `Sales`:

```
class Sales {
  char compName[25];
  float divisionTotals[5];    // 5 divisions
public:
  // Public members go here
};
```

The company is divided into five divisions, and the sales totals of each of the divisions are stored in the object's floating-point array.

The most important members of the class are stored in the division total values. In using the class, you'll be initializing, printing, and calculating with the five division totals. Instead of writing some kind of access function for each of the five divisions, you can overload the subscript operator to ease your programming considerably.

Note: You'll often overload subscript operators so that they return members, or individual array elements of members, from inside your class.

For example, you could overload the subscript operator so that using it with a `Sales` object returns that subscript from the `divisionTotals` array. Listing 12.6 does just that.

Type   **Listing 12.6. Overloading subscripts.**

```
1:  // Filename: SUBOV.CPP
2:  // Overload subscript operators so that accessing a class object
3:  // via a subscript returns one of the members.
4:  #include <iostream.h>
5:  #include <iomanip.h>
6:  #include <string.h>
```

```
 7:   #include <conio.h>
 8:   class Sales {
 9:     char compName[25];
10:     float divisionTotals[5];
11:   public:
12:     inline void init(char [], float []);
13:     inline float & operator[](const int);
14:     char * getName(void) { return compName; };
15:   };
16:   void Sales::init(char CN[], float DT[])
17:   {
18:     strcpy(compName, CN);
19:     for (int i=0; i<5; i++)
20:       { divisionTotals[i] = DT[i]; }
21:   }
22:   float & Sales::operator[](const int sub)
23:   {
24:     return divisionTotals[sub];
25:   }
26:   //////////////////////////////////////////////////////////////////
27:   main()
28:   {
29:     float totalSales=0.0, avgSales;
30:     float divs[5] = {3234.54, 7534.45, 6543.23, 5665.32, 1232.45};
31:     Sales company;
32:     clrscr();
33:     company.init("Swiss Cheese", divs);
34:     cout << setprecision(2) << setiosflags(ios::showpoint);
35:     cout << setiosflags(ios::fixed);
36:     cout << "Here are the sales for " << company.getName();
37:     cout << "'s divisions:\n";
38:     for (int i=0; i<5; i++)
39:       { cout << company[i] << "\n"; }   // Overloaded subscript
40:     // Add the sales for the divisions
41:     for (i=0; i<5; i++)
42:       { totalSales += company[i]; }
43:     cout << "The total sales are $" << totalSales << "\n";
44:     // Compute average sales
45:     avgSales = totalSales / 5.0;
46:     cout << "The average sales are $" << avgSales << "\n";
47:     return 0;
48:   }
```

Output

```
Here are the sales for Swiss Cheese's divisions:
3234.54
7534.45
6543.23
5665.32
1232.45
The total sales are $24209.99
The average sales are $4842.00
```

Accessing the company object with a subscript would normally make no sense in this program because there is no array of company objects. Nevertheless, the subscript is overloaded here to work in a special way when applied to the company object. The subscript will always return the division's total that matches the subscript number.

The reason it's important to return a reference to a floating-point value is that you might want to *assign* a value to one of the division totals from within main(). The overloaded subscript operator is one way of doing that. Therefore, instead of using the init() function, main() can directly assign divisionSales[] values even though the divisionSales[] array is private. Here is just one example of how main() can initialize the divisionSales[] array:

```
company[0] = 1234,56;
company[1] = 4234.09;
company[2] = 9248.63;
company[3] = 5434.94;
company[4] = 9242.45;
```

You know by now that main() probably isn't the best place in a program to be assigning values to private values. What if main() were to do something like this:

```
company[64] = 4009.81;  // Not possible!
```

If main() attempted to assign a value to the element numbered 64, the operator[]() function would insert the value in the 64th element of divisionSales[]—of which there is none. We're back to letting main() damage values that it shouldn't be able to damage in spite of their private access. However, it's extremely easy to modify the operator[]() function so that it does not allow bad subscripts! Doing so provides a self-protected class that still allows limited modifying access from within main().

Listing 12.7 shows a modified version of the previous program. This time, the overloaded subscript operator includes code that checks for array boundary problems.

Listing 12.7. Overloading smarter subscripts.

```
1:  // Filename: SUBOV2.CPP
2:  // Overload subscript operators so that accessing a class object
3:  // via a subscript returns one of the members.
4:  #include <iostream.h>
5:  #include <iomanip.h>
6:  #include <string.h>
7:  #include <conio.h>
8:  #include <stdlib.h>
9:  class Sales {
10:   char compName[25];
11:   float divisionTotals[5];
12: public:
```

```
13:    inline void init(char []);   // No longer needed float array
14:    inline float & operator[](const int);
15:    char * getName(void) { return compName; };
16: };
17: void Sales::init(char CN[])
18: {
19:    strcpy(compName, CN);
20: }
21: float & Sales::operator[](const int sub)
22: {
23:    if (sub < 0 || sub > 4)    // Subscript checking routine
24:      { cerr << "Bad subscript! " << sub << " is not allowed.\n";
25:        exit(1); }
26:    return divisionTotals[sub];
27: }
28: ////////////////////////////////////////////////////////////////////
29: main()
30: {
31:    float totalSales=0.0, avgSales;
32:    Sales company;
33:    clrscr();
34:    company.init("Swiss Cheese");
35:    company[0] = 3245.76;    // Assign values to individual
36:    company[1] = 2900.93;    // and private members.
37:    company[2] = 9455.32;
38:    company[3] = 3447.11;
39:    company[4] = 7533.01;
40:    cout << setprecision(2) << setiosflags(ios::showpoint);
41:    cout << setiosflags(ios::fixed);
42:    cout << "Here are the sales for " << company.getName();
43:    cout << "'s divisions:\n";
44:    for (int i=0; i<5; i++)
45:      { cout << company[i] << "\n"; }  // Overloaded subscript
46:    // Add the sales for the divisions
47:    for (i=0; i<5; i++)
48:      { totalSales += company[i]; }
49:    cout << "The total sales are $" << totalSales << "\n";
50:    // Compute average sales
51:    avgSales = totalSales / 5.0;
52:    cout << "The average sales are $" << avgSales << "\n";
53:    return 0;
54: }
```

Output

```
Here are the sales for Swiss Cheese's divisions:
3245.76
2900.93
9455.32
3447.11
7533.01
The total sales are $26582.13
The average sales are $5316.43
```

The `operator[]()` function no longer allows bad values to be sent to the `company` object, but `main()` can assign values to the division totals (as in lines 35–39). If, however, `main()` were to *incorrectly* assign a value using a bad subscript like

```
company[64] = 4009.81;  // Not possible!
```

then the program would produce this error message:

```
Bad subscript! 64 is not allowed.
```

 Note: Turbo C++ does not include array bounds checking. Neither C nor C++ checks for array subscripts boundary problems because doing so would slow down the execution and reduce efficiency. Now that you know how to overload the subscript operator, you should consider putting all your arrays in their own classes and adding array bounds-checking code such as that shown in Listing 12.7. The third exercise at the end of the chapter helps illustrate this point further.

Summary

Today's chapter concludes the direct discussion of overloading operators. In tomorrow's chapter, you'll see how to overload the assignment operator because the assignment operator's overloading relates to the material presented there. Other than the assignment operator, you've now seen how to overload virtually any operator you'll ever need to overload to make that operator work on your class data.

Being able to overload the insertion, <<, and extraction, >>, operators means that you can, in yet another way, get rid of tedious details from `main()` and leave the details to your classes. By coding a simple overloaded `operator<<()` function, you can display a fancy boxed screen with a class's complete list of members and titles with a simple `cout`. Conversely, you can get the contents of a complete class from the user with a single `cin`.

While reading about the ins and outs (should we say, *cins and couts?*) of operator overloading, you learned that the `istream` and `ostream` objects are connected to the input and output data streams. Being able to access those streams enables you to write your own I/O manipulators.

The subscript operator is an operator you can overload that lets the rest of the program access individual members or a member's array elements. Using the subscript operators, you can create safe arrays that check for their own array boundary problems.

Q&A

1. How can overloaded I/O operators save me time?

   By overloading the << and >> operators, you can input or output complete classes with simple cout and cin objects just as you input or output built-in data types such as integers and floating-point values.

   The overloaded I/O operator functions provide one more reason for needing reference operators. When overloaded I/O operator functions return the I/O streams by reference, they then enable you to stack several inputs and outputs in succession while still ensuring that your I/O code executes to produce the I/O.

2. How can overloading a subscript operator help me?

   Overloading subscript operators let main() (and the rest of the program) access individual object array elements or individual object members with subscripts. Even if your classes don't contain arrays, you can write an overloaded subscript operator function that returns any of the members based on the array subscript used.

   Not only will overloading subscript operators give your programs more controlled access to private object members, but it also will give you the ability to define safe arrays.

3. What is meant by the term *safe array*?

   A safe array is one that checks for its own array boundary limitations, or rather the overloaded subscript function checks for array boundary subscripts problems. When main() or another part of the program uses a good array subscript, the operator[]() function uses the subscript to return an appropriate value from the class.

Workshop

The Workshop offers quiz questions and exercises to hone your skills and give you feedback on today's lesson. You'll find some proposed answers in Appendix D.

Quiz

1. What are the names of the overloaded operator functions that overload input and output?

2. Why should overloaded operator functions be friend functions?

3. True or false: When you write an I/O manipulating function, you must use function parentheses after the manipulator's name in the I/O stream that uses the manipulator.

4. What is the name of the function that overloads the subscript operator?

5. True or false: The second argument of `operator>>()` should always be received with a reference operator, `&`.

6. How can you ensure that overloaded I/O operations can be stacked together?

7. Why does Turbo C++ not provide for array bounds checking automatically?

8. True or false: If you overload the subscript operator for a class, that class must contain an array as one of its members.

Exercises

1. Write a simple date class that asks the user for a date and prints the correct date. Ask the user for the date in the format *dd*, *mm*, and *yy*, in which *dd* represents the day number (1–31), *mm* represents the month number (1–12), and *yy* represents a year (1980–2100). Add error checking to the overloaded input routine. Print the date with a full month name inside the overloaded output operator.

2. Write a simple overloaded operator function that overloads the comma operator so that it can take the place of `<<` in integer output statements. Rather than

   ```
   cout << 12 << "\t" << 'c' << amount << "\n";
   ```

   you can do this:

   ```
   cout . 12 , "\t" , 'c' , amount , "\n";
   ```

3. Write a class that holds the total number of days in each of the 12 months. Add an initialization function that assigns the values of the days in each month (such as 28, 30, 31) automatically. Define a `year` object. Overload the subscript operator so that the rest of the program can access any month's number of days using the subscripts 1–12 (rather than the usual 0–11 found in Turbo C++ arrays). In other words, when `main()` prints `year[1]`, you'll make sure that the number of days in January prints.

Constructing
and
Destructing

Most of the programs you've seen so far that contained class data included initialization member functions that assigned initial values to the class objects. The initialization functions were needed because main() could not directly access and initialize private data members, and the public initialization function allowed main() just enough access to get initial data into the objects.

Turbo C++ offers a much better way for initializing objects. With *constructors,* you can both define and initialize an object's data members at the same time.

Constructors are member functions, just as any other initialization function is. However, when you specify a function as a constructor function, Turbo C++ recognizes the function as being different from the others. You'll find that you can use constructors to initialize data in ways that other member functions cannot easily provide.

When you are done with object data, you can provide *destructors* that get rid of the data in the way that you specify. A destructor is a special member function you write that "cleans up" your program's data.

Throughout this second week's chapters, you've not seen object data that contained members initialized on the heap. Of course, you'll often want to use the heap with objects, but constructors and destructors are the perfect vehicle functions for allocating and deallocating your objects. Although public member functions can allocate and deallocate, you'll learn in today's chapter how constructors and destructors do more automatically for you than other functions can do.

After you learn how constructors and destructors work, you'll understand a few remaining Turbo C++ function overloading advantages, including the overloading of the assignment operator and how to write your own typecasting functions.

Today, you learn about the following topics:

- [ ] How to code and use constructor functions
- [ ] How to code and use destructor functions
- [ ] How to specify overloaded constructors
- [ ] How to overload the assignment operator
- [ ] How to write your own typecast operators
- [ ] How to write copy constructors

 Note: Throughout this chapter, remember that constructors and destructors are nothing more than member functions that create, initialize, and get rid of object data. You can overload constructor functions, so there might be more than one for a class because some classes might need to be constructed in one of several ways. (You cannot overload destructor functions, however, but you won't ever need to.)

Defining Constructors

Constructors and destructors are best learned by seeing them in use. Therefore, instead of reading a lot of theory in advance, you need to learn how to specify constructor and destructor functions. That's where today's chapter begins.

A constructor function is a member function that has the same name as the class itself. Therefore, if a class is named `aClass`, the constructor function will be named `aClass()`. If the class is named `Customer`, the class constructor will be named `Customer()`.

Constructors never have return values, and you cannot specify a return type, not even `void` (this is true for destructors as well). When you overload functions, only the argument lists differentiate, in number of arguments or data types, one overloaded function from another.

Here is a class header that includes three constructor functions:

```
class Children {
  char name[25];
  int age;
  float weight;
public:
  void prData(void);
  char * getName(void);
  int getAge(void);
  float getWeight(void);
  Children(void);                // Three constructors begin here
  Children(int, float);
  Children(char *, int, float);
};                               // No destructor specified
```

 Note: Constructors can have default arguments if needed.

You'll see later that you rarely call constructors explicitly. Turbo C++ calls them for you when you define an object.

Defining Destructors

A destructor function is a member function that has the same name as the class itself preceded by a tilde character, ~. Therefore, if a class is named aClass, the constructor function will be named ~aClass(). If the class is named Customer, the class constructor will be named ~Customer().

A class can contain at most one destructor function. Destructor functions are member functions that have no return data type *and no arguments* (not even void). It is because destructors are not allowed argument lists that you cannot overload destructors.

Here is the Children class you saw earlier with a destructor function added:

```
class Children {
  char name[25];
  int age;
  float weight;
public:
  void prData(void);
  char * getName(void);
  int getAge(void);
  float getWeight(void);
  Children(void);                 // Three constructors begin here
  Children(int, float);
  Children(char *, int, float);
  ~Children();                    // Here's the destructor
};
```

If you supply a constructor function that allocates memory for data members, you'll always want to supply a destructor that deallocates the memory. You then won't have to worry about the heap in the main part of your program.

Why Constructors and Destructors Are Needed

Turbo C++ already contains several built-in constructor functions. There is a constructor function that "knows" how to create an integer variable. When you use the statement

```
int abc;
```

the constructor function finds an empty place in memory, reserves storage the size of an integer, and names that storage location abc. Whatever values happened to be in that variable's location before the constructor began are left there after construction. Therefore, uninitialized variables have garbage in them when you define them.

Why Didn't They Do More?

The designers of Turbo C++'s predecessor C language could have chosen to initialize variables with a value, but they didn't do so for two reasons: The more the compiler does for you, the more that efficiency is lost. Also, how could the designers of C know what initial values you would want in all your variables? They could not. You don't always want your variables zeroed out when you first use them.

Even if Turbo C++ were to initialize your variables with zeros for you, good coding practices dictate that you explicitly initialize data yourself. By doing so, you make your intentions known and you eliminate uncertainties during program maintenance (such as, "Did I really intend to use this variable's initial value, or did I just forget to initialize it with another value?").

Constructors enable you to write your own initializer routines so that you can create initialized data with whatever values you want the data to have.

When you use the statement

```
int abc=25;
```

the constructor function not only reserves and names an integer location, but the constructor also inserts a 25 there, as Figure 13.1 shows.

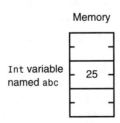

Figure 13.1. *The internal integer constructor function created and initialized* abc *for you.*

All the constructors for `float`, `int`, and the other built-in data types are invisible to you. The variables' values remain reserved and available in memory as long as they remain in scope. When a variable goes out of scope, Turbo C++ calls a built-in destructor function which returns that memory space to the available pool of memory.

> **Note:** All local variables are reserved on the stack. The stack is an accordion-like area in memory whose data space grows and shrinks as programs work with data. The stack is different (although similar in concept as far as the compiler and DOS are concerned) from the heap in that you cannot specifically allocate and deallocate the stack unless you call internal assembly-language code. All global variables are reserved in the name space of your executable program.

As you learn how to write your own constructors and destructors, keep in mind that these tasks are nothing new to the compiler, but they're new to you. You've probably never thought much about how Turbo C++ creates variables when you've defined variables. When moving to OOP, you must be made more aware of data creation because you will not always like the way Turbo C++ creates objects for you; many times you'll want to replace Turbo C++'s default constructors with your own.

Although this information might surprise you, Turbo C++ even contains a built-in constructor function for your own class data as the preceding paragraph implied. For example, when you create a class variable like

```
main()
{
  Children kid;
  // Rest of program follows
```

Turbo C++ calls its internal *default constructor function* and creates a class variable for you by reserving the space in free memory and assigning the name `kid` to that space. As with built-in constructors for the built-in data types, Turbo C++ cannot and does not make any guesses about initial values. Whatever happened to be located in `kid`'s memory space before you defined the variable is still there after `kid` is defined.

When `main()`'s block ends, `kid` goes out of scope. "Going out of scope" is a fancy way of saying that a variable's default destructor is called. The destructor function releases the `kid` from memory and returns the space to the free pool of memory. If `kid` were a variable local to an internal block of code inside `main()`, `kid` would go out of scope, meaning the destructor function would be called, as soon as the block ends.

The reason you are learning how to code constructors and destructors is that Turbo C++ sometimes has to guess how you want class data reserved, and sometimes Turbo C++ doesn't guess well! Many times, you'll want Turbo C++ to construct a class variable in a special way, and if so, you'll probably need to destruct that variable in a special way as well. When you write your own constructor and destructor functions for class data (you cannot write constructors and destructors for built-in data types), your constructor functions will override the default constructor functions, and your destructor functions will override the default destructor functions.

The Bottom Line

Turbo C++ already contains *default constructor functions* and *default destructor functions*. When you define a variable, whether that variable is a class variable or a variable of a built-in type, a default constructor is called to reserve the variable's space and to assign the variable name to the variable.

When a variable goes out of scope, the default destructor function is called that releases that memory back to the free memory pool.

You'll learn in the rest of this chapter how to *override* the default constructor and destructor functions. When you specify your own constructor, Turbo C++ executes it and not the default constructor. When you specify your own destructor, Turbo C++ executes it and not the default destructor.

When are default constructors called? When a variable is *first* defined. When are default destructors called? As soon as a variable goes out of scope. When you replace default constructors and destructors with your own specific versions, Turbo C++ calls your constructors when the variables are first defined, and Turbo C++ calls your destructors when the variables go out of scope. You don't explicitly call constructors or destructors because Turbo C++ automatically calls them as soon as data goes in and out of scope.

13

DO   DON'T

DO give constructors the same name as the class they reside in.

DO give destructors the same name as the class they reside in, but precede their name with a tilde (~).

DON'T specify a return type, even void, for constructors and destructors.

> DON'T attempt to write constructors and destructors for the built-in data types. Turbo C++ has to use its own default constructors and destructors for its built-in data types.

Timing Is the Key

The timing of constructor member functions takes place automatically. Turbo C++ calls them for you when you define variables. Turbo C++ calls destructor member functions when variables go out of scope.

Constructor and destructor functions can do anything any other functions can do. They can initialize, print, loop, read and write to disk, and so forth. Usually, though, constructor functions initialize data members and possibly allocate member data on the heap when dynamic memory allocation is required. Destructors then deallocate heap memory when required.

Note: Even if dynamic memory allocation isn't being used, always define a destructor if your program has a constructor function. You're more likely to use the destructor if you change to memory allocation, and in the advanced OOP that you'll read about in next week's chapters, destructors are sometimes required.

Constructors and destructors should be made public member functions. Even though they are called by Turbo C++ when it creates your objects, Turbo C++ knows that main() (or whatever other function defines the class variable) triggered the constructor's execution, and therefore, the constructor must have public access. In a way, you *do* call constructors, but you do so indirectly by defining new object variables. (You'll see later today some cases in which you will actually call constructor functions by name just as you would a regular member function—another reason to keep them public.)

The program in Listing 13.1 demonstrates the timing of constructor and destructor calls. The constructor doesn't really construct anything, but instead, it prints a message letting you know that it has been called. The destructor function also prints a message. In main(), a class object variable had to be defined to trigger the execution of the constructor.

Listing 13.1. Printing messages to show constructor and destructor timing.

```
1:  // Filename: CONSMESG.CPP
2:  // Demonstrates the timing of constructors and destructor
3:  // functions by printing messages when each is called.
4:  #include <iostream.h>
5:  #include <conio.h>
6:  class aClass {
7:    int i;     // Nothing's done with i
8:  public:
9:    aClass(void);   // Constructor
10:   ~aClass(void);  // Destructor
11:  };
12:  aClass::aClass(void)    // Constructor's implementation code
13:  {
14:    cout << "The constructor is being called...\n";
15:  }
16:  aClass::~aClass(void)   // Destructor's implementation code
17:  {
18:    cout << "The destructor is being called...\n";
19:  }
20:  /////////////////////////////////////////////////////////////////
21:  main()
22:  {
23:    clrscr();
24:    aClass var;             // Automatically calls constructor
25:    return 0;
26:  }
```

Note: Constructor and destructor function bodies can be coded inside the class if they are short, but most Turbo C++ programmers opt to keep their class header files clear of code except for data members and member function prototypes.

```
The constructor is being called...
The destructor is being called...
```

If the constructor and destructor functions had not been included with the aClass class, Turbo C++ would have executed its default constructor and destructor. The var variable would still be created and would still go out of scope, but no messages would print.

Constructing and Destructing

Line 24 forces the execution of the aClass constructor because an aClass class object variable is being defined. The constructor and destructor messages prove that those member functions are executing even though main() does very little except define a variable and return to the operating system.

Note: As this program demonstrates, if you start at main() and trace through the program line by line, OOP programs don't follow the normal sequential progression that other programs do. It seems as if events are triggered on their own accord—and they are! That's the nice thing about OOP; objects initialize themselves so that you don't have to in the main part of the program.

The constructor function is typically used to initialize data, and that's just what the program in Listing 13.2 does. The constructor function assigns the i data member a value. In previous chapters, main() called an initialization member function, but the constructor is a better place for initialization because main() doesn't have to do anything special to initialize data when it defines variables. (Therefore, you don't have to remember to initialize data either! Using constructors for data initialization is safer than relying on main() or other functions to execute member functions.)

 Listing 13.2. Initializing data in the constructor.

```
 1:  // Filename:  CONSINIT.CPP
 2:  // Uses a constructor to initialize a data member
 3:  // and the destructor then zeroes out the member when done.
 4:  #include <iostream.h>
 5:  #include <conio.h>
 6:  class aClass {
 7:    int i;     // i will be initialized by the constructor
 8:  public:
 9:    void prClass(void);
10:    aClass(void);   // Constructor
11:    ~aClass(void);  // Destructor
12:  };
13:  void aClass::prClass(void)
14:  {
15:    cout << "The value of i inside the class is " << i << "\n";
16:  }
17:  aClass::aClass(void)      // Constructor's implementation code
18:  {
19:    cout << "The constructor is being called...\n";
20:    i = 25;    // Initialize the data member
21:  }
```

```
22: aClass::~aClass(void)    // Destructor's implementation code
23: {
24:   cout << "The destructor is being called...\n";
25:   i = 0;      // Zero out the 25
26: }
27: //////////////////////////////////////////////////////////////
28: main()
29: {
30:   clrscr();
31:   aClass var;             // Automatically calls constructor
32:   var.prClass();          // Print the initialized data member
33:   return 0;
34: }
```

```
The constructor is being called...
The value of i inside the class is 25
The destructor is being called...
```

The first question you might ask is why the destructor function assigns a zero to the object's data member, overwriting the original 25 assigned in the constructor, even though the variable is about to go out of scope never to be used again.

The destructor assigns the zero on line 25 just to show you that a destructor could be used for anything you want it to be used for. Instead of zeroing-out data, destructors are often used to close files, close windows, deallocate heap memory, and so forth. Having a destructor assign zeros to data members right before their object goes out of scope is not an efficient use of execution time, but we're more concerned here with your understanding the timing of destructors than the overall timing efficiency of the program.

One more iteration will really improve this program, and that's a version that uses the heap for storage. The program in Listing 13.3 includes the class shown earlier, but the i data member is now a pointer to an array on the heap rather than a stand-alone integer variable. (Notice that main() did absolutely nothing to allocate the data on the heap!) The output messages are removed from Listing 13.3 because you now understand when constructors and destructors are called.

 Listing 13.3. Allocating within the constructor.

```
1: // Filename: CONSHEAP.CPP
2: // Uses a constructor to allocate and initialize data members on
3: // the heap and the destructor then deallocates the heap memory.
4: #include <iostream.h>
5: #include <conio.h>
6: class aClass {
7:   int * i;     // i is pointer to heap
```

continues

Listing 13.3. continued

```
 8: public:
 9:   void prClass(void);
10:   aClass(void);    // Constructor
11:    ~aClass(void);   // Destructor
12:  };
13:  void aClass::prClass(void)
14:  {
15:    cout << "Here's the memory at i:\n";
16:    for (int ctr=0; ctr<25; ctr++)
17:      { cout << i[ctr] << " "; }
18:  }
19:  aClass::aClass(void)    // Constructor's implementation code
20: {
21:   i = new int[25];      // Allocate the data member
22:   for (int ctr=0; ctr<25; ctr++)
23:     { i[ctr] = ctr; }   // Initialize heap with 0-24
24: }
25: aClass::~aClass(void)    // Destructor's implementation code
26: {
27:    delete [] i;          // Deallocate all the heap
28: }
29: ////////////////////////////////////////////////////////////////
30: main()
31: {
32:   clrscr();
33:   aClass var;           // Automatically calls constructor
34:   var.prClass();        // Print the initialized data member
35:   return 0;
36: }
```

Here's the memory at i:
0 1 2 3 4 5 6 7 8 9 10 11 12 13 14 15 16 17 18 19 20 21 22 23 24

Does object-oriented programming really make your programming life easier? You bet it does. Think for a moment about the implications of Listing 13.3. If you decide to store the class data on disk and read the initial values into the class array, or if you decide to ask the user for the initial values, or whatever you want to do to change the way the array in aClass is stored and initialized, main() *never* changes! Only the constructor changes. main() goes about its merry way not knowing or caring how the data got to the array.

Even in the best well-structured non-OOP programs, data storage techniques are combined with the code that accesses the data. There is no separation of the data storage (lines 19–24) from the non-class part of the program that uses the class (lines 32–35). Often, a few changes in a non-OOP data structure can wreak havoc in a program because the data structure is referenced throughout the entire program.

DO   DON'T

DO all class cleanup, such as deallocation, in the destructor function.

DO let the constructor initialize your data so that main() doesn't have to.

DON'T forget to deallocate with a destructor if you allocate with a constructor.

Constructing with Arguments

By passing data to constructors, and by allowing for default argument lists, you can write constructor functions that interact better with the surrounding program than the three programs shown so far.

You might want to perform some calculations with user input in main() (or another function called by main()) and then construct an object using results from those calculations. You learned in Day 2's chapter, "C++ Is Superior!" that Turbo C++, unlike regular C, enables you to define variables anywhere in a program that you need the variables, not just at the top of a block.

The only trouble with adding argument lists to constructor functions is that there must be some way for you to pass the arguments to the constructor but you never explicitly called constructor functions. The way you pass data to a constructor function is to put those parameters after the object's name when you define the object. Turbo C++ then constructs the object and passes the parameters.

Without arguments, you would call the Group class constructor like this:

```
Group people;  // Define only
```

With four constructor arguments (an int, a char, a float, and another int for example), you could call Group's constructor like this:

```
Group people(14, 'A', 21.44, 100);  // Define and initialize
```

When you want to define and initialize class data at the same time, use a constructor with an argument list. Turbo C++ constructs the object and passes the arguments to the constructor function.

Listing 13.4 contains a program that defines and initializes four automobile objects by sending initial values to the constructor function. Note also that the << is overloaded to print the four cars. main() is almost as optimized and about as high-level now as it can be despite the fact that there's lots going on behind the scenes in the class.

Listing 13.4. Constructing with arguments.

```
1:  // Filename: CONSARG.CPP
2:  // Constructor arguments that are passed from main().
3:  #include <iostream.h>
4:  #include <iomanip.h>
5:  #include <string.h>
6:  #include <conio.h>
7:  class Auto {
8:    char name[25];
9:    float price;
10:   char styleCode;
11:    int miles;
12:  public:
13:    friend ostream & operator<<(ostream & out, Auto & car);
14:    Auto(char [], float, char, int);   // Constructor with arguments
15:    ~Auto(void);  // Destructor
16:  };
17:  Auto::Auto(char N[], float P, char S, int M)
18:  {
19:    strcpy(name, N);
20:    price = P;
21:    styleCode = S;
22:    miles = M;
23:  }
24:  Auto::~Auto(void)   // Destructor's implementation code
25:  {
26:    // Nothing to deallocate, but future maintenance
27:    // could be easier with a destructor.
28:  }
29:  ostream & operator<<(ostream & out, Auto & car)
30:  {
31:    out << setprecision(2) << setiosflags(ios::fixed);
32:    out << "Here's a car's statistics:\n";
33:    out << "Name:\t" << car.name << "\n";
34:    out << "Price:\t" << setw(8) << car.price << "\t";
35:    out << "Style:\t" << car.styleCode << "\t";
36:    out << "Miles:\t" << car.miles << "\n\n";
37:    return out;
38:  }
39:  /////////////////////////////////////////////////////////////////
40:  main()
41:  {
42:    clrscr();
43:    Auto car1("PowerHorse", 18334.32, 'D', 2592);
```

```
44:     Auto car2("Go Get'um", 7334.32, 'S', 30901);
45:     Auto car3("Mover", 19123.45, 'A', 93);
46:     Auto car4("ZoomZoom", 23112.32, 'I', 627);
47:     // Print the objects using overloaded operator
48:     cout << car1 << car2 << car3 << car4;
49:     return 0;
50: }
```

```
Here's a car's statistics:
Name:    PowerHorse
Price:   18334.32       Style:  D      Miles:  2592

Here's a car's statistics:
Name:    Go Get'um
Price:   7334.32        Style:  S      Miles:  30901

Here's a car's statistics:
Name:    Mover
Price:   19123.45       Style:  A      Miles:  93

Here's a car's statistics:
Name:    ZoomZoom
Price:   23112.32       Style:  I      Miles:  627
```

 On lines 43–46, the program defines four Auto objects and initializes them at the same time. You're used to defining and initializing regular variables at the same time like this:

```
char Company[] = "XYZ Industries";
```

Now you can do the same for object variables. Each of the four arguments is passed from main() to the public constructor function.

13

 Note: The car's name was not initialized on the heap, but it could have been, and the destructor could then deallocate the heap's name. The destructor on lines 24–28 had nothing to do, but the shell was left there in case the constructor is changed later and needs cleanup by the destructor.

You won't always know the values of each member when you construct an object variable. Sometimes, you might know all the values, and if you do, you can use arguments such as the ones in the preceding program. If you know *some* of the arguments, you can use a constructor default argument list such as the ones used in Listing 13.5. The constructor shown in this program contains default values for each member. In main(), none, one, two, three, or all four initial values are sent to the constructor when the five objects are defined.

 Listing 13.5. **Constructing with default arguments.**

```
1:  // Filename: CONSARG2.CPP
2:  // Constructor default arguments
3:  #include <iostream.h>
4:  #include <iomanip.h>
5:  #include <string.h>
6:  #include <conio.h>
7:  class Auto {
8:    char name[25];
9:    float price;
10:   char styleCode;
11:    int miles;
12:  public:
13:    friend ostream & operator<<(ostream & out, Auto & car);
14:    Auto(char []="Standard Stock", float=20000.0,
15:        char='X', int=0);   // 4 default arguments
16:    ~Auto(void);  // Destructor
17:  };
18:  Auto::Auto(char N[], float P, char S, int M)
19:  {
20:    strcpy(name, N);
21:    price = P;
22:    styleCode = S;
23:    miles = M;
24:  }
25:  Auto::~Auto(void)    // Destructor's implementation code
26:  {
27:    // Nothing to deallocate, but future maintenance
28:    // could be easier with a destructor.
29:  }
30:  ostream & operator<<(ostream & out, Auto & car)
31:  {
32:    out << setprecision(2) << setiosflags(ios::fixed);
33:    out << setiosflags(ios::showpoint);  // Always show decimal point
34:    out << "Here's a car's statistics:\n";
35:    out << "Name:\t" << car.name << "\n";
36:    out << "Price:\t" << setw(8) << car.price << "\t";
37:    out << "Style:\t" << car.styleCode << "\t";
38:    out << "Miles:\t" << car.miles << "\n\n";
39:    return out;
40:  }
41:  ////////////////////////////////////////////////////////////////
42:  main()
43:  {
44:    clrscr();
45:    Auto car1;                  // Use all defaults
46:    Auto car2("Go Get'um");    // Override 1 default
```

```
47:    Auto car3("Mover", 19123.45);    // Override 2 defaults
48:    Auto car4("ZoomZoom", 23112.32, 'W');    // Override 3 defaults
49:    Auto car5("Fireball", 17528.41, 'F', 823);  // All overridden
50:    // Print the objects using overloaded operator
51:    cout << car1 << car2 << car3 << car4 << car5;
52:    return 0;
53: }
```

```
Here's a car's statistics:
Name:    Standard Stock
Price:   20000.00         Style:  X      Miles:  0

Here's a car's statistics:
Name:    Go Get'um
Price:   20000.00         Style:  X      Miles:  0

Here's a car's statistics:
Name:    Mover
Price:   19123.45         Style:  X      Miles:  0

Here's a car's statistics:
Name:    ZoomZoom
Price:   23112.32         Style:  W      Miles:  0

Here's a car's statistics:
Name:    Fireball
Price:   17528.41         Style:  F      Miles:  823
```

 This program defines five Auto object variables in lines 45–49. Each one of the objects uses a different combination of default arguments. The car1 object is constructed using all four default arguments, and car5 is constructed using four values that override the default arguments.

As with all default argument lists, the constructor's prototype on lines 14 and 15 contains the default values that are used when and if needed. Using constructor default arguments is useful because you sometimes know initial values and other times you want to accept defaults, such as zeros or some other helpful initial value.

 Note: Do you see that the program in Listing 13.5 could *not* contain a constructor prototyped as Auto(void);? If there were a prototype with a void argument list, Turbo C++ could not know which one to call, it or the prototype with all four default arguments, when you defined an object like this:

```
Auto car1;     // Take the default or void?
```

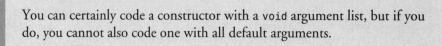

You can certainly code a constructor with a void argument list, but if you do, you cannot also code one with all default arguments.

Nowhere in `main()` could the statement

```
Auto car();    // Not allowed
```

appear because Turbo C++ would look for a matching constructor function with void as an argument list, and it would find none. Remember that in C++, an empty argument means the same as void. When defining an object without initializing that object at the same time, leave the parentheses off the object unless you do code a constructor that defines void as its argument list.

You Can Now Overload Typecasts!

You now have all the tools you need in order to overload the typecast operator! Although you might not have thought about it, you'll need to typecast data from built-in data types to your class data, and you'll also need to typecast your class data to the built-in data types.

Actually, writing typecasts to convert built-in data types to your class data is the easiest to do. Using the Auto class with default constructor lists shown in Listing 13.5, what happens when Turbo C++ sees this?

```
Auto car2("Go Get'um");
```

As you know from the previous program, Turbo C++ creates a car2 object with the string as the name, and the default arguments fill the rest of the data members. This statement is a typecast, although you probably didn't think of it in that way. The statement typecasts a string to an Auto class variable!

Remember that in Turbo C++, these statements are both the same:

```
i = int(5.42);  // New style
```

and

```
i = (int)5.42;  // Old style
```

The new style is easier to read, but even more important, the new style lends itself to overloading typecasts yourself. When the compiler sees the statement

```
Auto car2("Go Get'um");
```

Turbo C++ knows that it must take the string Go Get'um and convert that string to an Auto object.

What if you wanted to overload the int typecast operator so that an integer can be converted to an Auto variable? You'll only have to write a constructor function that takes a single integer as its argument like this:

```
Auto(int M)
{
    miles = M;                  // Here's the argument
    strcpy(name, "Stock");  // Place initial values
    price = 20000.00;
    styleCode = 'A';
}
```

When you typecast an integer to an Auto variable like

```
cout << Auto(32);
```

Turbo C++ calls the overloaded constructor function, uses the integer for the miles data member, and initializes the remaining members as dictated by the function.

Note: If you like the old style of typecasts, you can accomplish the same conversion from integer to Auto by coding the typecast like this:

```
cout << (Auto)32;    // Not as clear, but more familiar
```

It's only slightly more difficult to typecast from a class data type to a built-in data type. The first thing you must do is write the operator typecast function. An operator typecast function for built-in data types takes the name of the data type. However, because data types use words and not operators, you have to separate the operator from the data type before the function parentheses. For example, here are the three overloaded operator function prototypes that convert to int, float, and char:

```
int & operator int(void);       // Note the space
float & operator float(void);   // after operator and
char & operator char(void);     // before ()
```

Note: Don't overload an int data type and call the operator function operatorint() because Turbo C++ will never realize (without the space before the int keyword) that you want to overload the int typecast operator.

You must then decide what you want done when the typecasting occurs in the program. For example, if a program typecasts an `Auto` object to a `float`, that programmer might want to return the floating-point member named `price` from the typecast. Here's the short function that accomplishes the `Auto` to `float` overloading:

```
float operator float(void)
{
  return price;    // The  "converted" value
}
```

When to Call Constructors Explicitly

There are times when you might directly call a constructor by its name. One of those times appears when you want to return an object from a function, such as an overloaded operator function. Any time a function returns a class value, you can save a step if you use a constructor (assuming that you've defined one with arguments) instead of defining a stand-alone local class variable.

For example, in Day 11's chapter, "Introduction to Overloading Operators," you saw the following `operator*()` function:

```
Cust operator*(float f)
{
  Cust tempCust;
  tempCust.discPercent = discPercent * f;
  return tempCust;    // (You could have used *this also)
}
```

The function handles operations such as

```
newCustomer = oldCustomer * 1.23;
```

in which a class `Cust` object is multiplied by a floating-point constant. The local variable `tempCust` is unneeded. Take a look at this rewritten version of the `operator*()` function that does the same thing in a more elegant way:

```
Cust operator*(float f)
{
  float tempDiscount;
  tempDiscount = discPercent * f;
  return Cust(tempDiscount);
}
```

To make this function work, there has to be a Cust constructor that takes one floating-point value as its argument. This constructor is called explicitly in the return statement. In other words, an object is created and initialized with the computed floating-point value, and return's newly created object (one that is nameless) exists just long enough for the multiplication to complete in the statement that triggered operator*(). The newly created Cust object then goes away when operator*()'s closing brace appears.

It is slightly more efficient, especially if your class has many members, to create local variables for the needed calculations (as done with tempDiscount) and construct a nameless object using those local variables in the return, as shown here.

The constructor is also useful to call directly when you want to define and initialize heap data in the same statement. For example, the following statement initializes a new Auto (from Listing 13.5) on the heap and also initializes that heap space with the values in the parentheses:

```
Auto *car = new Auto("Roadster", 42123.43, 'A', 12);
```

If the Auto constructor has all default arguments, those defaults will be sent to the heap if you don't override them with other values.

DO / DON'T

DO specify default argument values for your constructors if you don't want to initialize all arguments every time you call the constructor.

DO call the constructor by name only when returning temporary objects or allocating heap data.

DO use constructors to convert from a built-in data type to a class data type.

DON'T forget the space when overloading a typecast operator that converts from a class value to a built-in data type.

DON'T use parentheses after an object when you define it unless you are passing parameter values to the object's constructor.

DON'T define both a constructor that takes no arguments and one that includes all default arguments, or Turbo C++ won't know which one to call when you define an object without initializing it.

13

Default Constructor Function Considerations

You read earlier in this chapter that Turbo C++ uses a built-in constructor if you don't supply one. If you specify any constructor with arguments, you *must* construct using those arguments unless all of them are default arguments. In other words, after you define a constructor that receives arguments, you can no longer define a class variable like this:

```
Auto car1;  // Invalid if at least one argument is required
```

Even though Turbo C++ uses its internal constructor if you don't supply one, if you *do* supply one, Turbo C++ uses only yours. The next section of the book expands on this a bit. The bottom line is that if you write your own constructor or set of overloaded constructors, your object definition must be such that one of your constructors can be used to initialize the object. If you supply no constructor, Turbo C++ creates the object for you, but you lose the advantage of automatic heap allocation and other important constructor advantages that you'll read about later.

As long as you supply a constructor with *all* default arguments or one with *no* arguments specified, you can define a variable without initial values as just shown.

> **Note:** Any time Turbo C++ can create an object without your supplying an initial value of any kind, Turbo C++ is using a *default constructor.* A default constructor is one with void in the argument list or with all arguments in the argument list given default values.

Constructing Arrays of Objects

All the constructor examples so far have constructed only a single object at a time. What if the programmer of the Auto class wanted to allocate an array of 50 cars? The constructor function would be applied to each object in the array. It is this array mechanism that assures you that every element of every object array is initialized when you use constructors (and the reverse happens with destructors).

 Note: If you supply no constructor, the array of objects will still be defined by Turbo C++'s internal default constructor, but each object's members will hold garbage until you assign them something. Supplying your own default constructor with default values enables you to initialize every element in the object array at the time that you define the array.

The program in Listing 13.6 expands on the Auto class program a bit by defining an array of five cars. The default arguments in the constructor are assigned to each of the five array elements when they are defined. The program could then change the data in each of the array elements, but it's not done here for brevity. Notice that the name member is now allocated on the heap (by the constructor), so the destructor has to deallocate each car's name. The destructor is called when main() deallocates the array with delete.

 Note: The program in Listing 13.6 demonstrates one of the most important reasons to use constructors and destructors rather than malloc() and free() (besides the obvious notational advantages). Turbo C++ automatically calls constructors and initializes data for you as soon as the data is defined or as soon as you allocate new occurrences of that data on the heap. Turbo C++ automatically calls destructors for you when an object goes out of scope or when you deallocate an object. malloc() and free() are never called automatically.

 Listing 13.6. Constructing and destructing an array of objects.

```
1:  // Filename: CONSDEST.CPP
2:  // Constructor and destructor program using the heap.
3:  #include <iostream.h>
4:  #include <iomanip.h>
5:  #include <string.h>
6:  #include <conio.h>
7:  class Auto {
8:    char * name;     // Now must be allocated by constructor
9:    float price;
10:   char styleCode;
11:    int miles;
12:  public:
```

continues

Listing 13.6. continued

```
13:    friend ostream & operator<<(ostream & out, Auto & car);
14:    Auto(char []="Standard Stock", float=20000.0,
15:        char='X', int=0);   // 4 default arguments
16:    ~Auto(void);  // Destructor
17:  };
18:  Auto::Auto(char N[], float P, char S, int M)
19:  {
20:   name = new char[25];  // Allocate name space
21:   strcpy(name, N);
22:   price = P;
23:   styleCode = S;
24:   miles = M;
25:  }
26:  Auto::~Auto(void)    // Destructor's implementation code
27:  {
28:   // Must deallocate what main() allocated
29:   delete [] name;   // Brackets required
30:  }
31:  ostream & operator<<(ostream & out, Auto & car)
32:  {
33:   out << setprecision(2) << setiosflags(ios::fixed);
34:   out << setiosflags(ios::showpoint);  // Always show decimal point
35:   out << "Here's a car's statistics:\n";
36:   out << "Name:\t" << car.name << "\n";
37:   out << "Price:\t" << setw(8) << car.price << "\t";
38:   out << "Style:\t" << car.styleCode << "\t";
39:   out << "Miles:\t" << car.miles << "\n\n";
40:   return out;
41:  }
42:  ///////////////////////////////////////////////////////////////////
43:  main()
44:  {
45:   clrscr();
46:   Auto * cars = new Auto[5];   // Allocates 5 cars on the heap
47:   // Print the objects using overloaded operator
48:   cout << cars[0] << cars[1] << cars[2] << cars[3] << cars[4];
49:   delete [] cars;
50:   return 0;
51:  }
```

The output consists of five repetitions of

```
Here's a car's statistics:
Name:   Standard Stock
Price:  20000.00        Style:  X        Miles:  0
```

because all five cars are initialized with the same default arguments.

 Figure 13.2 shows the data structure of the Auto data after the constructor finishes its job. main() allocates the five car objects, and then each object's individual constructor allocates the name space for the car's name. Both main() and the constructor's delete (in lines 49 and 29) have to delete arrays. The constructor must delete the name array, and main() must delete the cars array of objects.

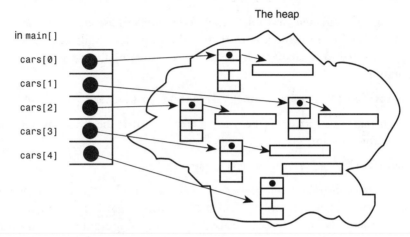

Figure 13.2. *Showing how the objects and heap relate.*

You might wonder why main() has to deallocate the cars array. main() allocated the object array, just not the individual names within each object. Therefore, good programming practices dictate that main() deallocate what it allocated.

 Note: main()'s delete could not deallocate the name member heap space because main() didn't allocate the name space.

 13

operator=() and the Copy Constructor

A special kind of constructor, called the *copy constructor*, defines exactly what happens when you define an object from another object. It is easy to confuse the copy constructor with regular constructors and with the assignment operator, but all three are different. Often, programs contain both a copy constructor and an overloaded

Constructing and Destructing

assignment. The `operator=()` was saved for this section of the book because it makes the most sense to discuss it and the copy constructor at the same time.

All three of the following statements are different:

```
Auto car1;         // Use the default constructor
Auto car2 = car1;  // Use the copy constructor
car3 = car2;       // Use the overloaded assignment statement
```

In the first statement, a regular default constructor is used to create `car1`. If the `Auto` class contains no defined constructor, the compiler's built-in default constructor will be used to create `car1`. If the `Auto` class contains a constructor with all default arguments such as

```
Auto(char []="Standard Stock", float=20000.0, char='X', int=0);
```

then that constructor will be used to create `car1`. If the `Auto` class contains a constructor with no arguments specified such as

```
Auto(void);  // Simple constructor
```

then that constructor will be used to create `car1`. Both of these constructors, the one with four default arguments and the one with a `void` argument list, are default constructors because they can be used without passing arguments to the constructor.

The second statement, `Auto car2 = car1;` is different from the first statement because a new object is being created from the old. By definition, Turbo C++ uses the copy constructor to create `car2`. The copy constructor is different from the default constructor and is used whenever one object is created from another. The `operator=()` is not used here because a new object is being created.

If you don't write a copy constructor, Turbo C++ copies all the members from `car1` to `car2`. This *memberwise copy* occurs by default by the compiler if you don't supply a copy constructor. If you supply a copy constructor, your copy constructor will be called when you create a new object from an existing object. A copy constructor always has this format:

```
className(className &);
```

Therefore, the prototype of the copy constructor for the `Auto` class always looks like this:

```
Auto(Auto &);  // Copy constructor
```

This special syntax of the copy constructor, with a reference to the class as the argument, tells the compiler to use this copy constructor whenever one `Auto` object is created from another. As with all constructors, never code a return value for copy constructors.

 Note: Although it's easy to forget, the copy constructor is also called when objects are passed by value or returned by value. Your copy constructor determines how the copy of the value is made, either through memberwise copy or via your copy constructor if you code one.

Many times, the default copy constructor works fine, but if your class contains pointers, the memberwise copy of the default copy constructor won't produce correct results. For example, if car1 contains a name member that points to its name on the heap, and a memberwise copy is performed to create car2, both cars will have the same name. That's OK, because when you create one object from another like

```
Auto car1 = car2;
```

you expect both objects to have the same data. The problem occurs later when you deallocate car1 (by car1 going out of scope or if you explicitly change the data located at car1's name pointer). When that name changes, so does car2's. But when you created car2 from car1, you wanted them to have the same data values but different occurrences of those values. Therefore, a copy constructor usually contains a straight memberwise copy of all the non-pointer members and the creation of separate pointers for members that are pointers. The following rule holds true when copying objects that contain pointer members:

> *When you are copying objects using memberwise copy, the pointers get copied, but not the data getting pointed to.*

When you create one object from another but the second object does not point to a copy of the first one's data, you'll have problems because when you change one object's pointed-to data, the other object's data changes as well. The next example program demonstrates a copy constructor's body.

The operator=() is a third kind of function you can write. When your compiler runs across a statement such as

```
car3 = car2;
```

an assignment is being performed. car2 must already be constructed, so neither a default constructor nor a copy constructor is used here. Turbo C++ uses a default operator=() function unless you supply your own. As with the default copy constructor, the default operator=() function performs a memberwise copy of the data, which is fine in many cases, but not when pointers are involved. Most programmers code their own operator=() function in case they ever add pointers as members later when they expand the class.

The `operator=()` function takes on the following format except in extremely rare cases:

```
className & operator=(const className &)
```

☐ Destructor code for the target object. When you assign car2 to car1 with car1 = car2;, car1 is the *target* object and car2 is the *source*. Before destructing the target object, check to make sure that the target and the source objects aren't the same thing.

☐ The copy constructor code.

☐ A return of `*this` (to allow stacked assignments).

The destruction ensures that the target is properly deallocated if needed. Usually pointers are involved, or you wouldn't be worrying about `operator=()` because the regular memberwise copy works fine on non-pointer data. However, because pointers are involved, you often have to clean up the target pointer on the heap before assigning new data to the target pointer.

Right before you destruct, however, you'll want to check to make sure that the user code hasn't called `operator=()` like this:

```
car1 = car1;    // OK to do, but watch out for it in operator=()
```

You will want to check to make sure the target is not the same as the source. If you don't, you'll destruct the source and, therefore, destruct the target at the same time.

The program in Listing 13.7 contains all three kinds of functions described in this section: a default constructor, a copy constructor, and an overloaded `operator=()` function. Almost all your programs that contain pointers as members will contain these functions as does Listing 13.7.

No C++ book would be complete without a version of a `String` class program. Listing 13.7 contains a simple but workable implementation of a string class to show you what true power you have with Turbo C++. There is no string data type in Turbo C++ and its predecessor C, although there is in just about every other programming language. You must use functions to copy strings when simple assignment statements are all that's needed in other programming languages. Now, by using this `String` class, you can have a string class that operates almost exactly like strings in other languages. You can overload = to assign one string to another, and you can overload operators such as + to concatenate strings without resorting to `strcpy()` and `strcat()`. All string data is stored on the heap in the program.

Listing 13.7. A String class that overcomes string deficiencies in Turbo C++.

```cpp
 1:  // Filename: STRCLASS.CPP
 2:  // Program that contains a string class and a main() that
 3:  // uses the class. The highlights of this program are
 4:  //    1. A safe string class is provided for string initialization,
 5:  //       assignment, and concatenation.
 6:  //    2. A copy constructor is provided to show the format of such
 7:  //       constructors.
 8:  //    3. An operator=() is provided to show how destruction should
 9:  //       first take place before assignment of objects that contain
10:  //       pointers for members.
11:  #include <iostream.h>
12:  #include <string.h>
13:  #include <conio.h>
14:  class String {
15:    char *st;            // Points to the heap
16:  public:
17:    String & operator=(const String &);  // Overloaded assignment
18:    friend String operator+(const String &, const String &);
19:    friend ostream & operator<<(ostream &, const String &); // Output
20:    String();                  // Default constructor
21:    String(const char *);      // Initializer constructor
22:    String(const String &);    // Copy constructor
23:    ~String();                 // Destructor
24:  };
25:  String & String::operator=(const String & s) // Overloaded assignment
26:  {
27:    // The overloaded assignment makes sure that a copy of data is
28:    // made, not just a copy of pointers as would otherwise be
29:    // the case.
30:    if (this == &s)     // Make sure you don't destroy target
31:      { return *this; }  // No need for operator=() after all
32:    delete [] st;       // Deallocate target string to clean it up
33:    // The next two lines are just like the copy constructor
34:    st = new char[strlen(s.st)+1];  // Allocate target based on length
35:                        // of source string plus string terminator
36:    strcpy(st, s.st);  // Now that room is made, copy the source string
37:    return *this;       // Always allow for stacked assignments
38:  }
39:  String::String()    // Default constructor
40:  {
41:    st = '\0';   // Creates a null string
42:  }
43:  String::String(const char * s)
44:  {
45:    // Allocate heap space and copy initialization string
46:    st = new char[strlen(s) + 1];
```

continues

393

Listing 13.7. continued

```
47:    strcpy(st, s);
48: }
49: String::String(const String & s)    // Copy constructor
50: {
51:   st = new char[strlen(s.st) + 1];
52:   strcpy(st, s.st);
53: }
54: String::~String()       // Destructor
55: {
56:   delete [] st;    // Deallocate memory used by string
57: }
58: String operator+(const String & source, const String & tar)
59: {
60:   // Concatenate two strings
61:   // First, see if concatenation is really necessary
62:   if (!strlen(source.st))      // If there's nothing to append to,
63:      return tar;               // don't do concatenation
64:   else if (!strlen(source.st))  // If there's nothing to append,
65:     return source;                  // don't do concatenation
66:   String temp;     // Uses default constructor
67:   // Reserve room for both strings and the null
68:   temp.st = new char[strlen(source.st) + strlen(tar.st) + 1];
69:   strcpy(temp.st, source.st);    // Copy source first
70:   strcat(temp.st, tar.st);    // Append target onto source
71:   return temp;
72: }
73: ostream & operator<<(ostream & out, const String & s) // Output
74: {
75:   out << s.st << "\n";
76:   return out;
77: }
78: ////////////////////////////////////////////////////////////////
79: main()
80: {
81:   String myName;       // Use default constructor
82:   String yourName("Sandy");   // Use initializer constructor
83:   String hisName = yourName;  // Use copy constructor
84:
85:   clrscr();
86:
87:   myName = "Terry";   // Use operator=()
88:   // By the way, isn't it nice to assign directly to strings?
89:   cout << "My name is " << myName;
90:   cout << "Your name is " << yourName;
91:   cout << "His name is " << hisName;
92:   hisName = "Jim";
93:   cout << "Oops! I mean his name is " << hisName;
94:   // Now combine them all
95:   String ourName;
96:   ourName = myName + yourName + hisName;
```

```
97:    cout << "Our names are " << ourName;
98:    return 0;
99: }
```

```
My name is Terry
Your name is Sandy
His name is Sandy
Oops! I mean his name is Jim
Our names are TerrySandyJim
```

Although main() is kept simple, that's the beauty of the program! Look how easy it is for main() to assign, change, and concatenate strings!

The program contains lots of comments to walk you through the code. Basically, the default constructor enables you to safely create empty strings, and the heap allocation is done for you (lines 39–42). The copy constructor enables you to create one string from another (lines 49–53) and ensures that the second string contains not only a new pointer, but a new copy of the data as well (all on the heap). The assignment operator (lines 25–38) enables you to assign strings to one another after those strings are created as done on lines 87 and 92.

Actually, line 96 uses *both* the overloaded plus sign for concatenation and the overloaded assignment operator for the assignment of the concatenated strings.

Note: By the way, the strings could have been assigned embedded spaces, but the example happened not to use any spaces in the names.

13

DO   DON'T

DO write constructors and destructors when you define arrays of objects. Turbo C++ applies the constructor to every element of the object array when the array is created, and the destructor cleans up all the objects when they go out of scope or when you delete them.

DO write overloaded assignment and copy constructor functions when you create objects that contain pointers as members.

DON'T write an overloaded assignment operator without first checking to see that the two operands are different.

DON'T forget to destruct the first operand in `operator=()` before performing the assignment.

Summary

Today's chapter strengthened your OOP skills by teaching you constructors and destructors. The constructor takes all the work out of your hands when you define new objects. Whether you define single objects or arrays of objects, the constructor automatically executes for you when those objects go into scope. When objects go out of scope, whether their block ends or you deallocate them, the destructor is called.

Constructors and destructors are nothing more than member functions. Constructors always have the same name as the class. So do destructors, except you must precede destructors with the tilde ~.

If you do not write constructors and destructors, Turbo C++ uses built-in default constructors and destructors. Usually, however, if you want allocation or initialization performed automatically, you should code your own constructors and destructors for the cleanup.

There is a special type of constructor known as the copy constructor. The copy constructor takes as its argument a reference to a class variable. The copy constructor is called when you initialize one object from another or when you pass and return objects by reference. Again, if you don't define a copy constructor, Turbo C++ uses its own, but if your class has pointer members, you should probably write your own copy constructor.

This chapter ended with a program demonstrating a string class. With the string class, you can create, initialize, copy, and concatenate strings as if they were built-in data types. The program demonstrated how to overload the assignment operator so that string data, not just pointers to the data, gets copied.

Q&A

1. Why do I need constructors and destructors?

   You don't really *have* to have constructors and destructors if you're willing to do all the work in `main()` and in functions that `main()` calls. Constructors set up or create object data in the way you want automatically when the data

goes into scope, and destructors destroy data automatically when the data goes out of scope.

With constructors and destructors, you'll have to worry about all the details of creating and initializing your objects. The beauty of classes is that after you write them, all your programs that use those classes become much more simple and easier to write (consider the string class program's main() function in Listing 13.7). The more you let Turbo C++ do in the class, the less you'll ever have to do again.

2. What is a default constructor?

A default constructor takes no arguments and tells the compiler exactly what to do when you define an object without initialization.

Turbo C++ includes its own default constructors and destructors. That's why you were able to define objects before this chapter. However, when you write your own constructors and destructors, Turbo C++ uses your functions rather than its own, and you understand your data needs much better than Turbo C++.

3. What if I want to construct an entire array of objects?

The nice thing about Turbo C++ constructors is that if you want to construct an array of objects, you don't have to do anything special. Turbo C++ applies the constructor on every element in the array!

4. What is the copy constructor?

The copy constructor describes what happens when you define a class variable and assigns that variable a value at the time of definition. The copy constructor is used whenever one object is created from another. For example, if you have created a Book class object called title, you can construct a new title from the current one with this statement:

```
Book newTitle = title;  // Use copy constructor
```

operator=() is not called here. The newTitle is created from title using the copy constructor. When a new object is created from an existing one, all members from the existing object are copied to the new object. The copy is performed either the way you've defined with an explicit copy constructor or member-by-member (the compiler's default). A copy constructor always follows the same syntax, and as with all constructors, copy constructors never return values.

5. What's the difference between the copy constructor and the assignment operator?

Both perform memberwise copies of data unless you provide your own versions of them. You learned in today's chapter that memberwise assignment becomes troublesome when pointers are involved. If you change one object's pointed-to data, the other's changes as well. Therefore, you'll often write your own copy constructor and `operator=()` functions to create new copies of pointed-to data whenever a copy or assignment is made.

The `operator=()` usually contains a destruction of the argument being assigned to, followed by the copy constructor's code, followed by a return of `*this` so that stacked assignments can be made.

Workshop

The Workshop offers quiz questions and exercises to hone your skills and give you feedback on today's lesson. You'll find some proposed answers in Appendix D.

Quiz

1. True or false: A class can contain more than one constructor function.

2. What is the maximum number of destructors a class can contain?

3. When are default constructors called?

4. When are your class constructors called?

5. When are destructors called?

6. True or false: When using constructors and destructors, `main()` never has to allocate and deallocate again.

7. What is called when the following statement executes: a copy constructor, a default constructor, or an `operator=()`?

   ```
   classVar2 = classVar1;
   ```

8. What is called when the following statement executes: a copy constructor, a default constructor, or an `operator=()`?

   ```
   class CV ClassVar2;
   ```

9. What is called when the following statement executes: a copy constructor, a default constructor, or an `operator=()`?

   ```
   class CV classVar3 = classVar2;
   ```

10. When should you code a copy constructor and `operator=()`?

Exercises

1. Add two member functions that return the lefthand or righthand portion of a string created with the `String` class. The function should receive a value that determines how many characters must be returned.

2. Write a program for a beverage company that contains a class called `Drinks`. Include a member for the individual drink name, wholesale price, and retail price. Create a default constructor and copy constructor, and overload the assignment so that `main()` can create and manipulate drink objects with ease. Keep all string data on the heap. Also, overload the `<<` and `>>` operators so that input and output are easy. Have `main()` initialize, assign, and print several objects to the screen. Be sure that the destructors properly clean up the objects before the program finishes.

Loose Ends: *static* and Larger Programs

Object-oriented programs don't execute in the sequential-like fashion of non-OOP programs. Even if a non-OOP program contains loops and branches, you can generally follow the code and trace the path of the execution line by line.

You can do the same with Turbo C++ OOP programs, but the act gets trickier because so many things, such as constructors and destructors, occur automatically. That's the *nice* thing about OOP, however. As you've seen, your objects take on more active roles and do things on their own, and sometimes, as is the case with constructors, they do so behind your back.

Learning OOP is not always an easy task because there are so many pieces of the OOP puzzle, and it's difficult to learn them sequentially. Today's chapter tries to wrap up this week's material by tying up some loose ends. Today, you'll learn about static objects and functions, and you'll also see how to work with multipart programs that require separate compilation and linking.

Many of the concepts presented here are not covered in other books because it is assumed that you already know them or that you'll learn them elsewhere. The problem is that not everybody knows how to compile multipart programs and there isn't always another resource that tells you why you would want to work with several source programs scattered over more than one file.

There might be some topics in this chapter that you've already learned. If so, feel free to skip those topics. Today's chapter is an attempt to give you some rest from the grueling overloaded operators and constructor chapters of the past few days. Although the static objects and functions are OOP-like, much of this chapter gives you a better feel for Turbo C++'s capabilities as a compiler and perhaps introduces you to some parts of the compiler you weren't aware of before.

Today, you learn about the following topics:

- [ ] How static affects local and global variables
- [ ] How static affects non-member functions
- [ ] How to define and use static data members
- [ ] The need for static member functions
- [ ] The advantages of Turbo C++'s project manager when working with multipart programs

All About *static*

You have probably used the static keyword before in your C programs. The static keyword ensures that local variables aren't destroyed when their blocks end. static goes before int, float, or any of the other data types, and you can put static before your own data types as well. Later sections in today's chapter will talk about static and class data more fully.

For built-in data, Turbo C++ handles the static keyword in the same way as C. Here's a quick review of static to get you in the static thinking mode before introducing new static topics a little later today.

static Maintains Values

static is sometimes called *duration* because being static affects how long (the duration) a variable retains its value. The opposite of static duration is auto duration. You've probably never seen auto in a C program because auto is the default. The following three variables are all automatic variables:

```
int i=25;
float f = 76.543;
char c = 'Q';
```

The following three variable definitions are exactly the same as the former three definitions because the former ones were auto by default and these are explicitly specified auto:

```
auto int i=25;
auto float f = 76.543;
auto char c = 'Q';
```

 Note: The placement of auto and static before the data type is a standard but not a requirement. auto and static can go after the data type if it makes more sense to you to place them there.

Some people confuse static and auto with local and global. static and auto dictate how durable a variable is, meaning that they determine how long a variable retains its value. local and global determine how visible variables are from other parts of the program. If a variable is auto, that variable loses its value when its block ends. If a variable is static, it retains its value when its block ends.

Consider the program in Listing 14.1. The program contains a static variable named st and an auto variable named a. Variables declared as static are initialized *only* the first time their block begins. That means that the line which assigns 25 to st occurs only the first time main() calls the function named seeVars().

Listing 14.1. static variables retain their values; auto variables are always reinitialized.

```
1:  // Filename: STAUTO.CPP
2:  #include <iostream.h>
3:  #include <conio.h>
4:  void seeVars(void);
5:  main()
6:  {
7:   clrscr();
8:   seeVars();
9:   seeVars();
10:  seeVars();
11:  seeVars();
12:  return 0;
13:}
14:  //////////////////////////////////////////////////////////////////
15:  void seeVars(void)
16:  {
17:  static int st = 25;
18:  int a = 10;   // auto by default. a is always assigned the 10
19:  cout << "st is " << st << "\n";
20:  cout << "a is " << a << "\n\n";
21:  // Change both variables
22:  st += 25;
23:  a += 20;
24:  }
```

```
st is 25
a is 10

st is 50
a is 10

st is 75
a is 10

st is 100
a is 10
```

Analysis

main() calls seeVars() four times. Inside seeVars() the st and a integer variables are printed and then updated with new values in lines 22 and 23. If you trace the output, you'll see that a's updated value is not carried through to the next

seeVars() function call, but st's new value is. In other words, even though 10 is added to a each time seeVars() executes, the value doesn't remain in a because a is automatic. The duration of a's value is much shorter than that of st because a is defined as auto and st is defined as static.

To see why you shouldn't confuse static and auto with local and global, consider the visibility of the two variables in seeVars(). Both variables are local, and main() could not print seeVar()'s local variables because both are local to seeVars().

To drive the point home further, the program in Listing 14.2 contains a global variable. Although defining global variables between two functions is not the best thing you can do (the global variable definitions are too difficult to find when looking through the program), you'll see that the global variable named g must be static, and it is. All global variables are static, and a global variable can never be defined as auto.

 Listing 14.2. The global variable named g is static.

```
 1:  // Filename: GLOBST.CPP
 2:  #include <iostream.h>
 3:  #include <conio.h>
 4:  void doSomething(void);
 5:  main()
 6:  {
 7:   clrscr();
 8:   doSomething();
 9:   doSomething();
10:   doSomething();
11:   doSomething();
12:   doSomething();
13:   return 0;
14:  }
15:  //////////////////////////////////////////////////////////////////
16:  //    *** Look at the next line for a global variable ***
17:  int g = 100;
18:  //    *** g is static because all globals are static
19:  //////////////////////////////////////////////////////////////////
20: void doSomething(void)
21: {
22:   cout << "g is " << g << "\n\n";
23:   // Change global variable
24:   g += 100;
25: }
```

14

g is 100

g is 200

g is 300

g is 400

g is 500

If the global variable g were not `static`, it would not retain its value every time `doSomething()` is called. However, the global variable is `static`. Global variables cannot be defined with `auto` because they are initialized at compile time, not at runtime.

Think about the placement of the variable on line 17. No part of the program actually executes line 17; the program executes *around* line 17 because functions surround the variable. Turbo C++ could not initialize g at runtime because no execution of line 17 really takes place. Therefore, g is defined at compile time, and when g changes during runtime, its value is retained.

Note: g is global but not visible to `main()` because all global variables are defined from their point of definition *down* in the source file.

Here's the bottom-line rule for distinguishing between `local` and `global`:

All global variables are `static` by default and cannot be defined as `auto`. All local variables are `auto` by default, but you can define local variables with `static`. Whether `static` or `auto`, local variables are always local to the block in which they are defined, but local `static` variables retain their values when their blocks end.

There's One Slight Variation with *static* Globals

As you read in the last section, all global variables have static duration, and there's nothing you can do to make global variables `auto`. However, the following global variable definitions do not quite do the same thing:

```
int gSta = 5;
```

and

```
static int gSta = 5;
```

If `gSta` were a local variable, these would be two different statements indeed because local variables are automatic unless you override their duration with `static`.

When you explicitly define a global variable with the `static` keyword, you are telling Turbo C++ to give that global variable single file scope. In other words, if you link another set of functions to the program with the `static` global variable (as will be explained later in today's chapter), those other functions will not be able to use your file's global variable. An explicit `static` definition tells the compiler not to let other files have access even when linked to the current source file.

If you do not give a global variable `static` duration, all other files linked to yours can access the global variable as long as they contain the `extern` keyword like this:

```
extern int gSta;    // Use another file's global variable
```

Functions Can Be *static* Too!

As with global variables, you can limit a function's visibility from other source files that might be linked to yours by preceding the function's definition with `static`. Listing 14.3 shows a program that contains both a `static` global and a `static` function. If another program is linked to this one that uses the same names, there will not be a name clash.

Listing 14.3. static before a function name limits the use to the current source file.

```
1:  // Filename: STATFN.CPP
2:  // Includes a static function and global variable
3:  #include <iostream.h>
4:  #include <conio.h>
5:  // Global variable comes next
6:  static char gc = 'Q';
7:  // Static function's prototype appears next
8:  static void doFun(void);
9:  main()
10: {
11:    clrscr();
12:    cout << "In main(), gc is " << gc << "\n";
13:    doFun();   // Never pass global variables because they don't
14:               // have to be passed.
15:    return 0;
16: }
17: //////////////////////////////////////////////////////////////////
18: // Static function is next and can be called only in this file
19: void doFun(void)
20: {
```

continues

Listing 14.3. continued

```
21:   cout << "Welcome to doFun() where gc is still " << gc << "\n";
22: }
```

In main(), gc is Q
Welcome to doFun() where gc is still Q

If other functions written in separately compiled source files are to be linked and called from this one, they could never access gc or doFun(), even if an extern statement were included in their listings. When all the code is linked together, the functions from the other files that call doFun() or that use the gc variable will get an error because of this file's static keywords on lines 6 and 8. Notice that the static keyword doesn't have to be listed again in front of the function definition (line 19) as long as it appears in the function's prototype.

By the way, if you want a source file to be able to call another file's non-static function after you link them together, you must prototype the function in all files that call your file's function with the function's prototype preceded by extern like this:

```
extern void prData(int, char *);  // Call another file's function
```

Using Another File's Globals and Functions

Using multiple source files and determining which global variables and functions can be shared and which ones must be limited with static becomes an important topic in programming departments in which several programmers might work on different parts of the same program.

You just cannot arbitrarily name variables and functions when your code will be linked to someone else's producing single executable modules. There must be communication between all programmers, and a central repository of variable and function names (sometimes called the *data dictionary*) must be kept so that the programmers don't use duplicate names that clash when all the separate files are linked together.

If you want to create a variable or function that will never clash with those of another programmer who might link files with yours, add static before the global variables and file names. In this way you'll ensure that those names are available only from within your source file. (You must, however, be sure to compile your source file separately before linking to the other files.)

It is said that non-static functions and non-static global variables have *external linkage*. That is, other source code external to the current source file can use the non-static definitions. static data and functions have *internal linkage* because only internal routines to the current source file can use them.

Objects Are No Exception

Just because you're now putting data into class objects doesn't mean that the rules of local, global, auto, and static change. You can create static object variables that have internal linkage and static local object variables that retain their values when their block is reentered.

Listing 14.4 contains a program that defines a local object variable in a second function called by main(). Every time the function is called, its object variable's previous value is still known.

 Listing 14.4. You can define objects to be static too.

```
1:  // Filename: STATOBJ.CPP
2:  // Objects can be static too
3:  #include <iostream.h>
4:  #include <conio.h>
5:  static void doFun(void);
6:  class aClass {
7:    int i;
8:    float f;
9:  public:
10:   aClass(int I, float F) {i = I; f = F;}
11:   ~aClass() {};        // Nothing needed in destructor
12:   void setI(int I) { i = I; }
13:   void setF(float F) {f = F; }
14:   int getI(void) { return i; }     // Access functions
15:   float getF(void) { return f; }
16:  };
17:  main()
18:  {
19:    clrscr();
20:    for (int i=0; i<5; i++)
21:    { doFun(); }
22:    return 0;
23:  }
24:  ///////////////////////////////////////////////////////////////////
25:  // The next function contains a static object
26:  void doFun(void)
27:  {
28:    static aClass aVar(10, 65.0);
```

continues

Listing 14.4. continued

```
29:    // Print the object
30:    cout << "aVar contains the member values of " << aVar.getI();
31:    cout << " and " << aVar.getF() << "\n";
32:    // Change the value of the data
33:    aVar.setI(aVar.getI()*3);   // Multiply member by 3
34:    aVar.setF(aVar.getF()*2.5);  // Multiply member by 2.5
35: }
```

```
aVar contains the member values of 10 and 65
aVar contains the member values of 30 and 162.5
aVar contains the member values of 90 and 406.25
aVar contains the member values of 270 and 1015.625
aVar contains the member values of 810 and 2539.0625
```

There was not enough of a program here to overload an output operator, so some access member functions were added to get the member data for printing. From the output, you'll see that the class variable retained its former value and was never reinitialized when doFun() was called again. static kept the constructor on line 28 from constructing the object each time through the function.

You might wonder about the embedded function calls on lines 33 and 34. doFun() has no read or write access to the two data members of aVar. The inside function on lines 33 and 34 get the member's value, and the outside function stores that value after multiplying the value by another number.

If you were simply to remove static from the constructor on line 28, this would be the output of the program:

```
aVar contains the member values of 10 and 65
aVar contains the member values of 10 and 65
aVar contains the member values of 10 and 65
aVar contains the member values of 10 and 65
aVar contains the member values of 10 and 65
```

Without static, aVar is reconstructed (and, therefore, reinitialized) each of the five times main() calls doFun().

When you are defining global static objects (not that you'll do that a lot), Turbo C++ defines the objects just like all other global variables. If you ever define global object variables, you should probably define them before main() and not sneak them in between two other functions.

Defining global objects brings up an interesting sidelight: There is no guaranteed preset order in which Turbo C++ creates objects for programs. Therefore, cin and cout might not be created before your global objects are created, so all constructors must use the old printf() and scanf() (and other built-in functions) if they perform any I/O.

The program in Listing 14.5 creates a global static object with a constructor that prints a message (with printf()). Throughout this book, you've read how Turbo C++ takes the details out of main() and moves those details into the class. Here's a program that takes that to the extreme: main() has no code except a return even though the program produces output! See whether you can tell why.

Listing 14.5. Global static object can take over the program (see main()).

```
1:  // Filename: GLOSTAOB.CPP
2:  // Interesting program with no main() but with output
3:  #include <iostream.h>
4:  #include <stdio.h>
5:  #include <conio.h>
6:  class aClass {
7:     int i;
8:  public:
9:     aClass();      // Place all the program's output in constructor
10:    ~aClass() {}; // Nothing needed in destructor
11: };
12: // Constructor produces the output
13: aClass::aClass()
14: {
15:    i = 25;
16:    clrscr();
17:    printf("Here's the program output.\n");
18:    printf("Let's generate some stuff...\n");
19:    for (int ctr=0; ctr<10; ctr++)
20:      { printf("Counting at %d\n", ctr); }
21: }
22: /////////////////////////////////////////////////////////////////
23: // Global object next!
24: aClass anObject;
25: /////////////////////////////////////////////////////////////////
26: main()
27: {
28:    return 0;
29: }
```

```
Here's the program output.
Let's generate some stuff...
Counting at 0
Counting at 1
Counting at 2
```

```
Counting at 3
Counting at 4
Counting at 5
Counting at 6
Counting at 7
Counting at 8
Counting at 9
```

 When is constructor code called? You know that constructor code is called at the time an object is defined. When is the anObject object defined? In line 24 before main(). Therefore, anObject's constructor is called before main() because all global variables that reside before main() must be created before main() begins. The constructor in lines 13–21 produces a lot of output that's unrelated to the object being created, but the point of all this is to study global objects.

You'd do best to stay away from global variables completely. As you see in Listing 14.5, global objects cause your program to behave a little differently than you might expect (including the suggested use of printf()... ugh!). Global objects also can cause name clashes later if you're not careful about using static. However, global variables are sometimes useful, especially when virtually every function in a program needs access to the same variable. In that case, you would be foolish to pass the same local variable between every function.

DO   DON'T

DO define local variables with the static keyword if you want them to retain their values every time execution of the program reenters their block of code.

DO use static if you want to limit a global variable's access to the current file only.

DO put static before all functions if you don't want those functions to be called from other routines eventually linked to yours.

DON'T try to define global variables (or functions for that matter) with auto, or you'll get an error message. Global variables are always static by default.

DON'T use cout and cin in constructors for global static objects because the cout and cin objects might not yet be constructed.

Special Use of *static* Inside Classes

Perhaps some of the previous material was review for you, but putting static inside class headers will be new. By putting static in front of data members in your class header, you instruct Turbo C++ to create just one instance of that member, even though there will be multiple instances of all the other data members.

Consider the following two sets of classes, the second differing from the first by a single static keyword:

```
class aClass {
  int i;
  float x;
  char c;
public:
  aClass(int, float, char);  // Constructor
  ~aClass();                 // Destructor
};
```

and

```
class aClass {
  int i;
  static float x;   // Here's the difference!
  char c;
public:
  aClass(int, float, char);  // Constructor
  ~aClass();                 // Destructor
};
```

In the second class, the x member is static. The static keyword before a member name has a different (but slightly related) use from using static in front of variable definitions. A static class member appears only once no matter how many object variables are created for the class.

If you define four class objects like

```
aClass var1, var2, var3, var4
```

Turbo C++ creates four sets of three of the members for the class without the static, but there's only *one* occurrence of the member x, as Figure 14.1 illustrates. Although x is private, you can declare public data members static as well.

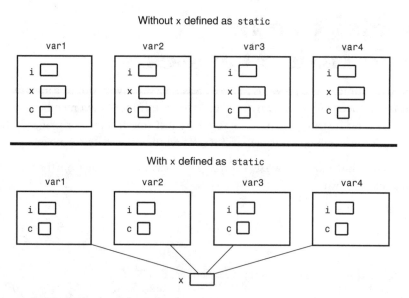

Figure 14.1. *There is only one instance of a* static *member no matter how many objects there are.*

Note: Although you can treat member functions as if a copy of each one appears in each object, Turbo C++ creates only one member function for each class. Each object instantiated from the class then contains function pointers to its member functions.

static data members are often used to keep track of the number of objects defined. For example, a constructor could add one to the static member each time it is called. In the object's destructor function, you could subtract one from the count. At any time during program execution, the static member would hold the total count of how many objects have been constructed. (Other statistical values could also be calculated and stored in static members.)

There is no single object associated with static members. It is said that static members belong to the class, not to an object. Therefore, when referencing static members, you must precede the static member name with the class name and use the scope resolution operator (::) to resolve the member instead of using an object's name. The program in Listing 14.6 makes this point clear. It uses a public static member so that main() can more easily access the number of objects created at any one time.

Listing 14.6. Using **static** to track
the number of objects created.

```
1:  // Filename: STATMEM.CPP
2:  // Members can be static too
3:  #include <iostream.h>
4:  #include <ctype.h>
5:  #include <conio.h>
6:  class aClass {
7:    int i;
8:    float f;
9:  public:
10:   static int total;    // One per class, not per object
11:   aClass(int I, float F);
12:   ~aClass();
13:  };
14:  // Modify total in constructor and destructor
15:  aClass::aClass(int I, float F)
16:  {
17:    i = I;
18:    f = F;
19:    aClass::total++;   // Another object has been created
20:  }
21:  aClass::~aClass()
22:  {
23:    aClass::total--;   // Another object has been destroyed
24:  }
25:  //////////////////////////////////////////////////////////////////
26:  // First, initialize the static total to zero
27:  int aClass::total = 0;
28:  //////////////////////////////////////////////////////////////////
29:  main()
30:  {
31:    clrscr();
32:    aClass var1(1, 2.2);
33:    aClass var2(1, 2.2);
34:    aClass var3(1, 2.2);
35:    cout << aClass::total << " objects created so far. ";
36:    cout << "\nConstructing another inside a new block...\n";
37:    {  // Ensures that a really local object is created temporarily
38:      aClass var4(1, 2.2);
39:      cout << aClass::total << " objects created so far.\n";
40:    }  // The last object will now go away
41:    cout << "... Now there are only " << aClass::total << " left.\n";
42:    return 0; // All the others will go away now also
43:  }
```

```
3 objects created so far.
Constructing another inside a new block...
4 objects created so far.
... Now there are only 3 left.
```

14

The first place to begin studying Listing 14.6 is line 27. You'll be surprised by the placement of the initialization of total. At first glance, it looks as though total is a global variable, but it's not—it's a class member, and the scope resolution operator indicates so.

static members cannot be initialized inside the class because no memory is reserved in the class header. However, there might not be object variables defined in main() for a long time, and a programmer might need access to a static value long before the first object is defined.

Therefore, static data member values are initialized in never-never land before main() begins but after the class is declared. You have to repeat the data type of the static member (int in Listing 14.6's line 27), and you have to issue an initial value.

Note: If the static member had been private in Listing 14.6, main() could access the static member only through the use of static member functions.

If you use *private* static data members, you'll need to use static member functions to manipulate those static data members. Turbo C++ always passes the *this pointer to regular member functions, but no single object variable is associated with static data members because static members belong to the class, not to objects.

Another reason to define static member functions to access static data members is that you might want to work with the static value before you define any objects in a program. Listing 14.6 could have printed the total number of objects defined, zero, before any objects were actually defined. (Of course, Listing 14.6 contained a public static data member, so no access function was needed.)

Listing 14.7 shows the same program as Listing 14.6 with a static member function that accesses the now-private static data member. You can see that a little more work is needed to use private static data members, but as always, it is usually best to keep all data, even static data, private and away from other routines except through member functions.

Listing 14.7. static member functions access static members.

```
1: // Filename: STATPRI.CPP
2: // Use static member functions when your static data is private
3: #include <iostream.h>
```

```
4:  #include <ctype.h>
5:  #include <conio.h>
6:  class aClass {
7:    int i;
8:    float f;
9:    static int total;     // One per class, not per object and private
10: public:
11:    static int getTotal(void);    // The static function defined below
12:    aClass(int I, float F);
13:    ~aClass();
14:  };
15:   int aClass::getTotal(void)
16:   {
17:     // Returns the total member so main() can print it
18:     return aClass::total;
19:   }
20: // Modify total in constructor and destructor
21: aClass::aClass(int I, float F)
22: {
23:   i = I;
24:   f = F;
25:   aClass::total++;   // Another object has been created
26: }
27: aClass::~aClass()
28: {
29:   aClass::total--;   // Another object has been destroyed
30: }
31: ///////////////////////////////////////////////////////////////////
32: // First, initialize the static total to zero
33: int aClass::total = 0;
34: ///////////////////////////////////////////////////////////////////
35: main()
36: {
37:   clrscr();
38:   aClass var1(1, 2.2);
39:   aClass var2(1, 2.2);
40:   aClass var3(1, 2.2);
41:   cout << aClass::getTotal() << " objects created so far. ";
42:   cout << "\nConstructing another inside a new block...\n";
43:   {  // Ensures that a really local object is created temporarily
44:     aClass var4(1, 2.2);
45:     cout << aClass::getTotal() << " objects created so far.\n";
46:   }  // The last object will now go away
47:   cout << "... Now there are only " << aClass::getTotal()
       ➡<< " left.\n";
48:   return 0; // All the others will go away now also
49: }
```

14

Output

```
3 objects created so far.
Constructing another inside a new block...
4 objects created so far.
... Now there are only 3 left.
```

Analysis

Notice that when calling `static` member functions, you must resolve the scope of such functions with the scope resolution operator just as you have to do when accessing `static` data members. On line 15, where the `static` function is defined, you don't repeat the `static` keyword; `static` appears before function names only in the class header.

Note: `static` members replace variables that used to be global before OOP came along. A global variable can be used to keep track of data as the data is allocated. However, if another programmer also works on your code and tries to define the same global variable—or even more surprising and harder to debug, if another programmer's code is linked to yours and both of you use the same global variable—a name clash will occur. The `static` member offers a much safer way of keeping count of data. The `static` member is more appropriate because it relates directly to the class. If you increment and decrement `static` members in constructors and destructors, the rest of the program never has to worry about taking care of the counts.

DO   DON'T

DO use the scope resolution operator, `::`, to access `static` data members and function members. No object is associated with `static` members, so you must use the class to call a `static` function or access a `static` member.

DO use `static` member functions to manipulate private `static` data members.

DO initialize a `static` data member before `main()` begins. You must repeat the data type of the `static` data member before its name when defining it.

DO use `static` data members to track statistics about a class, such as totals and averages.

DON'T repeat the `static` keyword before the function definition. `static` goes before the function name only in the class header.

Multifile Processing

Turbo C++ programmers almost always work with multiple source files when creating a large program. If breaking your programs into separate functions is good (and it is), breaking large programs into separate source files is good too. There are several logical places to break source files when they grow too large to manage individually.

This section of the book is not so much about OOP as it is about programming in Turbo C++ in general. Nevertheless, OOP does add extra reasons for breaking programs into separate files, especially class header files and class implementation code.

> **Note:** To review, a class header is a class with data member declarations and member function prototypes. The implementation is the definition of all the member functions (the actual code in the functions). Figure 14.2 shows the difference.

As you've seen, classes provide building-block mechanisms for programmers. When you write a class, the program that uses the class neither knows nor cares how data is stored, initialized, and retrieved. As long as you write enough access member functions, the rest of the program uses the class data members any time it needs to. The member functions, however, provide the control and safety to ensure that the user program doesn't change the data when it shouldn't be able to do so.

There are companies now that sell only class libraries that you can incorporate into your own programs. You can purchase a class library to handle database-like file access, one to handle extended precision mathematics, and one that creates and works with text windows on the screen. Also, Turbo C++ comes with class libraries to work in the Microsoft Windows environment.

The class vendors do not offer source code when they sell their programs, because they don't want to give away their coding secrets and there is just not a good reason to do so. The vendor sells a compiled class implementation file (called an *object* file). A well-written class is usable by programs. That means that enough access functions were provided and the class was designed in such as way as to make the internal class code secondary to the objects you create with the class. You'll open and close colorful windows on your screen, for instance, without regard for how those windows were constructed. Your program just issues orders to the windows to display themselves, and they do it via the class code.

When a class vendor sells a class, that vendor provides source code for the class header and also probably documentation on how to use the class to build and manipulate objects derived from the class. Instead of typing the class header yourself, you'll just merge it into your source code with an #include directive and then link the compiled class implementation to your file.

There are other reasons for breaking programs into separate files. Often, you'll find that you have a series of programs that basically do the same thing except for a few functions that differ. Instead of compiling each program separately, you can compile the code that is alike in each program, then compile the different functions separately, and link each into its own executable file. If you later have to change one of the functions, you can recompile and link it without taking the time to recompile the entire source program.

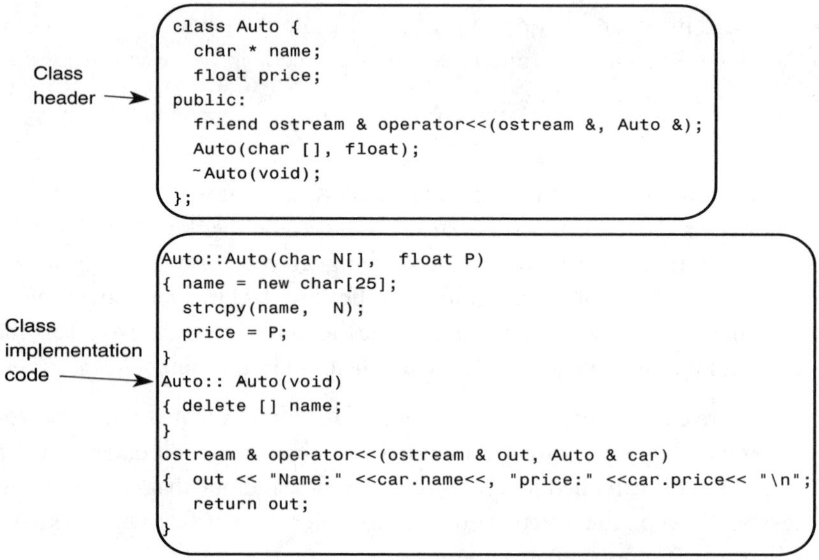

```
                      class Auto {
                          char * name;
    Class                 float price;
    header  ──►       public:
                          friend ostream & operator<<(ostream &, Auto &);
                          Auto(char [], float);
                          ~Auto(void);
                      };
```

```
                      Auto::Auto(char N[],  float P)
                      { name = new char[25];
                          strcpy(name,  N);
    Class                 price = P;
    implementation    }
    code    ──►       Auto:: Auto(void)
                      { delete [] name;
                      }
                      ostream & operator<<(ostream & out, Auto & car)
                      {   out << "Name:" <<car.name<<, "price:" <<car.price<< "\n";
                          return out;
                      }
```

Figure 14.2. *The difference between a class header and the class implementation.*

 Note: In a multifile source code that will eventually be linked into a single executable, there can be only one main() function because main() can exist only once in any executable program.

A Compile/Link Review Might Help

This book has often used terms such as *source code, object code, compilation, linking,* and *executable file* without lots of explanation because if you picked up this book and got past Day 1's chapter, you've probably worked with these terms before. You've certainly used all of them whether or not you knew the names of the terms. As a quick review to jog your memory, Table 14.1 explains the terms you need to know to continue in this chapter.

Table 14.1. A review of some multifile and compile-time terms.

Term	Description
Compile	Convert source code to object code. Often, this term is used to convert source code directly to executable (as happens when you select Alt+**R**un from Turbo C++'s menus), but you must keep in mind that an in-between linking step is being performed.
Executable	The format of a program after all compiling and linking has taken place. An executable program is one that can be run, whereas source code and object code cannot be run until you convert them to an executable program.
Link	The linking step prepares the file for execution. As your program is compiled, Turbo C++ transforms it into object code. If several parts of one program are scattered over several files on the disk, such as main() and a few functions in one source file, and other functions that main() calls in another source file, you must compile each separately into several object files. Each object file can then be linked to a single executable file, which can then run.

continues

Table 14.1. continued

Term	Description
Object	The internal binary representation of your source program. In a way, the object file is your program in the format your PC understands, and your source code is in the format that you can read. Several object files can be linked together to form a single executable program that can be run.

Note: You've probably seen the terms *compile* and *link* on the Turbo C++ pull-down menus.

Figure 14.3 helps illustrate the process of compiling and linking.

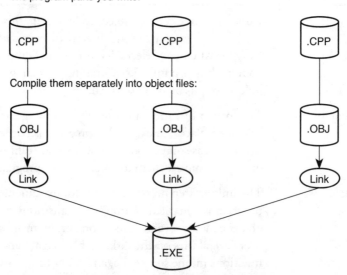

Figure 14.3. *All separate source and object files must be linked into a single executable before you can run a program.*

The nice thing about an environment such as Turbo C++ is that you don't have to know anything about source and object files to write and execute programs. The **R**un **R**un (Ctrl+F9) menu option converts your source file into an object file and then links the file into an executable file and *then* runs the file (assuming there are no errors) all in one step. If you select, however, from the **C**ompile pull-down menu, you'll find options that enable you to compile (without linking) and link already-compiled programs.

> **Note:** If you ever get linker errors when you select **R**un from the **R**un pull-down menu, you have probably misspelled a keyword, function, or variable name. Or you might have called a function from your program that doesn't exist and you failed to link another program to it that has the proper function—or you forgot to code the function altogether. The more you learn (with initial help from this chapter!) about compilation and linking, the better you'll understand error messages and the faster you'll program.

Turbo C++ follows the standard file-naming rules when compiling your program. Source programs end with the filename extension .CPP. After Turbo C++ compiles a program into object code, the object file ends with .OBJ. Linking the .OBJ file produces an executable with the extension .EXE. (The first part of the filenames before .OBJ and .EXE will be the same as the source file unless you're combining several source files, in which case you'll have to specify the first names as described a little later.)

> **Clean Up Your Act!**
>
> Over time, you'll unknowingly build up a lot of .OBJ files on the disk if you compile using **R**un **R**un. Turbo C++ keeps the in-between object files on disk in case you want to use them later.
>
> When you write stand-alone programs that aren't part of multifile pro-grams, you can delete these .OBJ files from your program directory (usually TURBOC/BIN or TC/BIN) to free up space.

You'll also find a lot of .EXE program files. If you are finished with a program and you don't need it anymore, back it up onto a floppy disk or tape (just in case!) and then delete its executable and source file from your disk to free as much space as possible.

By the way, you can execute any Turbo C++ .EXE directly from the DOS prompt by typing its filename. For instance, if you compile a program into an executable called MYPROG.EXE and exit Turbo C++ and go to the DOS prompt, you can run the program by typing its filename like this:

```
C:\>MYPROG
```

(The .EXE program has to reside in the current directory from which you're executing it from DOS, or the directory must appear in your AUTOEXEC.BAT pathname.)

Figure 14.4 shows how a larger multifile Turbo C++ program might come together to form a single executable file. Such a system of files is called a *project*. Turbo C++ contains special handling for projects that is explained in the next section. At any one time, the pieces of a project require different kinds of attention. For example, header files must be included, source files must be compiled, and object files must be linked.

Programming departments aren't the only users of multifile source programs. Even when writing fairly small programs, you might want to separate the class header, the class implementation, the source program, and additional functions you have written in the past. When you write a general-purpose function that you'll want to use again, compile that function into its own .OBJ object file, and store it in a subdirectory you designate for such a library of functions. When you write a program that needs one or more of the functions you've compiled into objects, you can link those object files to the program that calls them instead of including the source files and compiling the same functions over and over. You'll save time and finish your work faster if you compile the general-purpose functions once and link the already-compiled functions to the programs that need them.

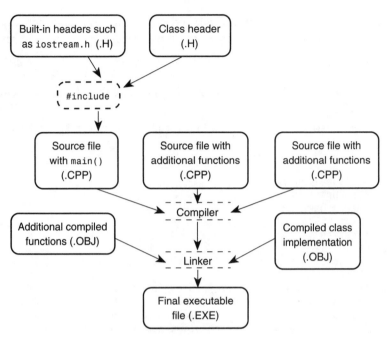

Figure 14.4. *Large projects often have several files in different stages of compilation.*

Project Files Make Multifiles a Snap

As mentioned at the end of the preceding section, a collection of multiple files that you'll eventually combine into single executable files are called projects. Instead of having to find each file to link when you need it, you can set up a *project file* in Turbo C++ that does the necessary including, compiling, and linking for you. You only then have to worry about the source code, and Turbo C++ will take care of putting needed files together.

This section of the book walks you through building and using a project file. At the end of yesterday's chapter, exercise number 2 described a beverage program to construct and print beverage data. The answer for the program appears in Appendix D. The answer, however, appears as all one file as most of the programs in this book will appear because of space limitations. However, that program is easy to separate into separate files. This section explains how to use the Turbo C++ project commands to work with the separate files.

To start with, Listing 14.8 contains the program code shown as all one long program (*long* is relative here because as usual "real world" programs go, the beverage program is short). Because the program is simple and you'll have no problem with the code itself at this point, concentrate instead on the multipart program created from this long listing.

 Listing 14.8. The beverage program as a single long file.

```
 1: // Filename: BEV.CPP
 2: // Program to track, initialize, copy, and print beverage products.
 3: #include <iostream.h>
 4: #include <iomanip.h>
 5: #include <string.h>
 6: #include <conio.h>
 7: class Drinks {
 8:   char * name;
 9:   float whole;
10:   float retail;
11: public:
12:   Drinks(char * = "Noname", float=0.0, float=0.0);
13:   ~Drinks();    // Destructor
14:   Drinks(const Drinks &);  // Copy constructor
15:   Drinks & operator=(const Drinks &);  // Assignment overload
16:   friend ostream & operator<< (ostream &, const Drinks &);
17:   friend istream & operator>> (istream &, Drinks &);
18: };
19: Drinks::Drinks(char * N, float W, float R)
20: {
21:   name = new char[strlen(N) + 1];
22:   strcpy(name, N);
23:   whole = W;
24:   retail = R;
25: }
26: Drinks::~Drinks()
27: {
28:    delete [] name;
29: }
30: Drinks::Drinks(const Drinks & d)     // Copy constructor
31: {
32:    int newLen = strlen(d.name) + 1;
33:    name = new char[newLen];
34:    strcpy(name, d.name);
35:    whole = d.whole;
36:    retail = d.retail;
37: }
38: Drinks & Drinks::operator=(const Drinks & d)  // Assignment overload
39: {
40:    if (this == &d)
41:      { return *this; }
42:    delete [] name;  // Deallocate old string
43:    name = new char[strlen(d.name) + 1];
```

```
44:    strcpy(name, d.name);   // Copy string member
45:    whole = d.whole;        // Copy float members
46:    retail = d.retail;
47:    return *this;
48: }
49: ostream & operator<< (ostream & out, const Drinks & d)
50: {
51:    out << setprecision(2) << setiosflags(ios::showpoint);
52:    out << setiosflags(ios::fixed);
53:    out << "Name: " << d.name << "\n";
54:    out << "Wholesale price: " << d.whole << "\tRetail price: ";
55:    out << d.retail << "\n\n";
56:    return out;
57: }
58: istream & operator>> (istream & in, Drinks & d)
59: {
60:    cout << "Please add to our line of beverage products.\n";
61:    cout << "What is the name of the next product? (one word
       ➥please)";
62:    char tempInput[80];     // Need to temporarily
63:    in >> tempInput;                   // store user input
64:    d.name = new char[strlen(tempInput) + 1];    // onto the heap.
65:    strcpy(d.name, tempInput);
66:    in.ignore();   // Remove carriage return
67:    cout << "What is the retail price of " << d.name << "? ";
68:    in >> d.whole;
69:    cout << "What is the wholesale price of " << d.name << "? ";
70:    in >> d.retail;
71:    return in;
72: }
73: //////////////////////////////////////////////////////////////////
74: main()
75: {
76:    clrscr();
77:    Drinks * bevs = new Drinks[5];  // Array of 5 drinks on the heap
78:    for (int i=0; i<5; i++)
79:      { cin >> bevs[i]; };    // Ask the user for the beverages
80:    cout << "\n\nHere's what you entered:\n";
81:    for (i=0; i<5; i++)
82:      { cout << bevs[i]; };       // Show the user for the beverages
83:    bevs[3] = bevs[4];          // Test the overloaded assignment
84:    Drinks newBev = bevs[1];    // Test the copy constructor
85:    Drinks another("Diet Peach Flavored", .23, .67);
86:    cout << "After some changes:\n";
87:    cout << bevs[3] << newBev << another << "\n";  // Print new values
88:    cout << "Mmmm... Made from the best stuff on earth!";
89:    delete [] bevs;
90:    return 0;
91: }
```

14

427

> **Note:** Actually, the program in Listing 14.8 is *already* a multipart file because it includes several header files in lines 3–6.

The first place to begin breaking this program into separate files begins with the class header. Here is the class header, which could be stored on the disk as BEV.H:

```
1: // Filename: BEV.H
2: class Drinks {
3:    char * name;
4:    float whole;
5:    float retail;
6: public:
7:    Drinks(char * = "Noname", float=0.0, float=0.0);
8:    ~Drinks();    // Destructor
9:    Drinks(const Drinks &);  // Copy constructor
10:    Drinks & operator=(const Drinks &);   // Assignment overload
11:    friend ostream & operator<< (ostream &, const Drinks &);
12:    friend istream & operator>> (istream &, Drinks &);
13: };
```

You might want to give your class header files a different extension from the typical header files. Some Turbo C++ programs name them with an .HPP extension, others with an .HCL extension. It doesn't matter what the filename extension is as long as you include the full filename in the source program that uses the class.

The class implementation could also be separated and turned into a stand-alone file. Here is the implementation file saved as BEVCLIMP.CPP:

```
1: // Filename: BEVCLIMP.CPP
2: #include <iostream.h>
3: #include <iomanip.h>
4: #include <string.h>
5: #include <conio.h>
6: #include <bev.h>
7: Drinks::Drinks(char * N, float W, float R)
8: {
9:    name = new char[strlen(N) + 1];
10:    strcpy(name, N);
11:    whole = W;
12:    retail = R;
13: }
14: Drinks::~Drinks()
15: {
16:    delete [] name;
17: }
18: Drinks::Drinks(const Drinks & d)     // Copy constructor
19: {
```

```
20:     int newLen = strlen(d.name) + 1;
21:     name = new char[newLen];
22:     strcpy(name, d.name);
23:     whole = d.whole;
24:     retail = d.retail;
25: }
26: Drinks & Drinks::operator=(const Drinks & d)   // Assignment overload
27: {
28:     if (this == &d)
29:       { return *this; }
30:     delete [] name;  // Deallocate old string
31:     name = new char[strlen(d.name) + 1];
32:     strcpy(name, d.name);  // Copy string member
33:     whole = d.whole;        // Copy float members
34:     retail = d.retail;
35:     return *this;
36: }
37: ostream & operator<< (ostream & out, const Drinks & d)
38: {
39:     out << setprecision(2) << setiosflags(ios::showpoint);
40:     out << setiosflags(ios::fixed);
41:     out << "Name: " << d.name << "\n";
42:     out << "Wholesale price: " << d.whole << "\tRetail price: ";
43:     out << d.retail << "\n\n";
44:     return out;
45: }
46: istream & operator>> (istream & in, Drinks & d)
47: {
48:     cout << "Please add to our line of beverage products.\n";
49:     cout << "What is the name of the next product? (one word
       ➥please)";
50:     char tempInput[80];    // Need to temporarily
51:     in >> tempInput;                   // store user input
52:     d.name = new char[strlen(tempInput) + 1];   // onto the heap.
53:     strcpy(d.name, tempInput);
54:     in.ignore();  // Remove carriage return
55:     cout << "What is the retail price of " << d.name << "? ";
56:     in >> d.whole;
57:     cout << "What is the wholesale price of " << d.name << "? ";
58:     in >> d.retail;
59:     return in;
60: }
```

Notice that the implementation file must include all the header files it needs to do its job. Built-in string functions and I/O stream routines are used, so the file must include all the support files required to prototype the built-in routines used. Also, on line 6, the BEV.H class header file had to be included because that file contains the prototypes for all the class functions and the data members for the class implementation to work with.

The class implementation file is ready for compilation. You cannot link it, however, because there is no program code with main() here that uses the class, and all executable Turbo C++ programs must have a main() function. Class implementations are usually compiled as explained earlier because the user program of the class and the programmer using the implementation code don't need to see the details of the implementation unless the programmer needs to change the implementation and has the source code to do so.

Compile BEVCLIMP.CPP by selecting **C**ompile **C**ompile (Alt+F9) from the Turbo C++ menu after entering the class implementation source code. Turbo C++ compiles the program and adds the BEVCLIMP.OBJ object file to your disk (assuming there were no typing errors).

Note: If you get an error message such as Unable to open include file, you should insert the full pathname of the BEV.H file before its name in the #include directive or change the **O**ptions **D**irectory **I**nclude pathname to the location of BEV.H on the disk.

If you wanted to delete BEVCLIMP.CPP, now you could because a compiled object version is all you need to use the class. However, leave the implementation source file intact now for possible modifications in the future.

The only thing left to do is to put the rest of the program in its own file. The rest of the program is just a main() function, but because this function begins the execution and controls the class, it's vital that you use it along with the others. Here is the main() function saved as the file named BEVREST.CPP:

```
1:    // Filename: BEVREST.CPP
2:    #include <iostream.h>
3:    #include <conio.h>
4:    #include <bev.h>
5:    // Again, you may have to insert BEV.H's pathname before bev.h above
6:    main()
7:    {
8:      clrscr();
9:      Drinks * bevs = new Drinks[5];   // Array of 5 drinks on the heap
10:     for (int i=0; i<5; i++)
11:       { cin >> bevs[i]; };   // Ask the user for the beverages
12:     cout << "\n\nHere's what you entered:\n";
13:     for (i=0; i<5; i++)
14:       { cout << bevs[i]; };    // Show the user for the beverages
15:     bevs[3] = bevs[4];         // Test the overloaded assignment
16:     Drinks newBev = bevs[1];   // Test the copy constructor
```

```
17:    Drinks another("Diet Peach Flavored", .23, .67);
18:    cout << "After some changes:\n";
19:    cout << bevs[3] << newBev << another << "\n";  // Print new values
20:    cout << "Mmmm... Made from the best stuff on earth!";
21:    delete [] bevs;
22:    return 0;
23: }
```

You now have the following files that compose your project:

☐ The BEV.H class header source file

☐ The BEVCLIMP.OBJ object class implementation file

☐ The BEVREST.CPP source code that uses the class

You're now ready to compile the BEVREST.CPP source code and link the resulting object file with the BEVCLIP.OBJ file into a single executable file by using the project feature of Turbo C++.

Close all windows in Turbo C++ and select **P**roject **O**pen. The **P**roject menu option controls all the project-building and editing commands in Turbo C++. Type the name **BEV.PRJ** (projects should have the .PRJ extension), preceding the name with the pathname of your beverage files if needed. When you press enter or click O**K**, you'll see the project window, shown in Figure 14.5.

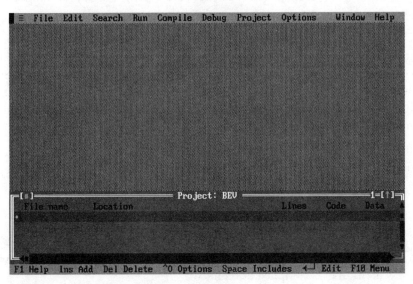

Figure 14.5. *The newly opened project window.*

All you now have to do is inform the project system of the two files needed, BEVREST.CPP and BEVCLIMP.OBJ. You don't specify the BEV.H class header file because #include in the source file takes care of the class header. To build your project, follow these steps:

1. Press the Insert key to add the first project item to the BEV.PRJ project. Turbo C++ displays another dialog box from which you can select or type a file.

2. Type **BEVREST.CPP** with a pathname specified to the location where you stored BEVREST.CPP earlier. (Optionally, you can select it from the dialog box's list.) You can type filenames in either uppercase or lowercase letters. Press Enter or click **A**dd.

   Turbo C++ adds the file to the project window's first line.

3. Type **BEVCLIMP.OBJ** with the pathname, and press Enter or click **A**dd.

4. Select **D**one to quit entering project lines.

You can now *build the project* (which means compile and link all necessary files as determined by the project's contents). If you select **C**ompile **M**ake, Turbo C++ builds the final executable file but does not run the file. If you select **R**un **R**un (with the project window still open at the bottom of the screen), Turbo C++ builds the project and runs the program.

Here's the great thing about projects: If you change the BEVREST.CPP source file, the project manager recompiles the program. If, however, you don't change the source code and want to run the program again, the project manager knows not to recompile and runs the executable file. If you *forgot* whether you changed the program, don't fret—the project manager recompiles only if needed to include the latest changes you make to the file.

If you change the BEVCLIMP.OBJ object file, again, the project manager takes care of relinking the two object files, but it won't recompile BEVREST.CPP except when you modify it.

Note: The project manager keeps accurate track of the project entries' date and time stamps and compares against its records to determine what needs to be recompiled or relinked.

You can close the project file with **P**roject **C**lose.

DO	**DON'T**

DO break your programs into separate files, especially class header and class implantation files, to speed development and keep the user program of the class cleaner.

DO use the project manager to build your projects automatically.

DON'T include any of the built-in or class header files in the project listing because the individual source code files include header files automatically when they are compiled.

Summary

Today's chapter started with a review of static basics. The OOP-specific static declarations are similar to those of non-OOP programming. static variables, as opposed to auto variables, do not lose their values when their blocks end. Although a local static variable remains local to its block, it does not get reinitialized if execution enters the block a second time.

static in front of global variables or function names forces internal linkage of those variables and functions, meaning that secondary source files cannot execute the static functions or use the static global variables even if extern is attempted in the secondary source files. Global variables cannot be declared with the auto keyword.

static data members exist *once* across all objects. In other words, the value of a static data member isn't affected by the number of other objects defined or even block scope (notice the similarity between static data members and static local variables).

You must define static variables before main() begins, and you can use those variables before class objects are defined. The static members are defined for the class, not for individual objects as are regular data members. Therefore, you must use the class name and the scope resolution operator to access static members.

After wrapping up static, today's chapter explored multifile processing. Often, you'll find it advantageous to break your programs into separate files, especially the class headers and class implementation code. You read a review of source files, object files, and executable files, and then you saw how Turbo C++'s project manager makes the building of multifile projects easy.

Although it takes a little effort (not much with the interactive help of Turbo C++) to set up a project, after you set one up, you'll never have to worry about compiling and linking the right files again. All your multifile projects will build faster because the project manager only recompiles and relinks those files needed to keep the executable file up-to-date.

Q&A

1. Why should some local variables be static and some left as automatic?

   Normally, local variables are automatic local variables (you can optionally put auto in front of their definitions). Local automatic values disappear when the block in which they're defined ends. If execution reenters the same block, the local variables are reinitialized again. If you do nothing special, these local variables remain automatic.

   If you precede local variables with the static keyword, their values will not go away when the block ends. The variable is still local, but its value remains in the variable. If, therefore, the block is executed again, the previous value of the static variable remains. static local variables are great for keeping track of totals; the total doesn't get wiped out when the block ends.

2. What is a static function?

   If you write only stand-alone programs, static functions won't add any advantage to your programming. However, many people write multipart programs, and there are lots of programs written by teams of programmers. When working with multifile programs, you'll often want to ensure that a function name you place in one file doesn't clash with another's.

   When you precede a function with static, the compiler limits that function to *internal linkage,* which means that other source files that are eventually linked to the current one can contain the same function names, and those function names won't conflict with yours.

3. What is a static data member?

   A static data member belongs to the class, not to an individual object. Turbo C++ ensures that a static data member exists only once no matter how many class objects are defined.

   Turbo C++ programmers often use static data members to keep track of the number of objects currently defined as well as other statistics such as totals and averages of object data as a whole.

4. When would I need a `static` member function?

   `static` member functions manipulate `static` data members. You cannot call regular member functions until there is at least one object defined to associate with that member function. You might want to use a `static` data member before defining a `static` object. If so, write a public `static` member function, and call that function using the class name followed by a scope resolution operator.

5. Why should I use Turbo C++'s project manager?

   The project manager manages your multifile projects. When writing programs that require several parts, or when programming in a programming department, you'll often work on pieces of a program inside stand-alone files rather than one large single source program.

   When working with lots of files, both source and object files, the project manager eases your workload by streamlining the compilation and linking of files that need compiling and linking. The project manager searches the date and time of the project's pieces and rebuilds a project in a minimum amount of time.

Workshop

The Workshop offers quiz questions and exercises to hone your skills and give you feedback on today's lesson. You'll find some proposed answers in Appendix D.

Quiz

1. True or false: Local variables are `auto` by default.

2. True or false: `static` and `auto` are synonyms for local and global variables.

3. An object called `thing` is defined from a class named `ClassStuff`. The class contains a public `static` member named `factor`. Which of the following lines properly references the `static` member?

   A. `ClassStuff::factor`

   B. `ClassStuff.factor`

   C. `thing.factor`

4. What is *internal linkage*?

5. What is *external linkage*?

6. Should `static` data members remain public or private?

7. What is a project?

8. How does a project file speed your program development?

Exercises

1. Write a program for a teacher that defines a class for students' names and grades. Add a `static` data member to the class to keep track of the class average. Define an array of five objects for the teacher's five students. Initialize the array through constructors that ask the user for the students' names and grade averages. After all the students' data is entered, print the average from the `static` data member variable.

2. Practice using the project manager by writing a stand-alone function to the beverage project described in this chapter that increases the wholesale and retail price of a beverage passed to it by 10 percent when a price increase occurs. Keep the function separate, and add it to the top of the BEV.PRJ project list. Rebuild the project and test the program. Make a change to the function and rebuild again. Now, make a change to BEVREST.CPP by adding a centered title at the top of the screen before it prints anything. Rebuild the project. Notice that the project manager recompiles only those files you change, not the files you don't change.

2

Now that you've finished the second week, you're ready for a program that brings together much of the material from the first two weeks. The program in Listing WR2.1 illustrates several Turbo C++ features you now understand, such as constructors, destructors, overloaded operators, and a static member. The program defines several house objects for a real-estate investor. The program doesn't do a lot with the data so that you can better study its details. Many elements found in the first weeks of the book are included in this program.

Type

Listing WR2.1. Week one and two review listing.

```
1:  // Filename: RENTAL.CPP
2:  // Tracks, initializes, copies, and prints
    ➡ properties.
3:  #include <iostream.h>
4:  #include <iomanip.h>
5:  #include <string.h>
6:  #include <stdlib.h>
7:  #include <conio.h>
```

continues

Listing WR2.1. continued

```
 8:   #include <new.h>
 9:   class Prop {    // Property Class
10:     char propCode[7];    // 6 characters plus null zero
11:     char * address;
12:     float askingPrice;
13:     int sqrFeet;
14:     int numRooms;
15:   public:
16:     static int number;    // Running total of Prop objects
17:     float getPrice(void) {return askingPrice; } // For average
18:     Prop();    // Default constructor
19:     Prop(const char [], const char *, const float &, const int &,
         ➡const int &);
20:     ~Prop();    // Destructor
21:     Prop(const Prop &);   // Copy constructor
22:     Prop operator=(const Prop &);   // Assignment overload
23:     // An overloaded addition so an average can be calculated
24:     Prop operator+(const Prop &);
25:     friend ostream & operator<< (ostream &, const Prop &);
26:     friend istream & operator>> (istream &, Prop &);
27:   };
28:   Prop::Prop()
29:   {
30:     Prop::number++;
31:     askingPrice = 0.0;        // Zeros mean no data yet
32:     sqrFeet = 0;
33:     numRooms = 0;
34:   }
35:   Prop::Prop(const char PC[], const char *A, const float & AP,
36:             const int & SQ, const int & NR)
37:   {
38:     Prop::number++;    // Increase static value
39:     strcpy(propCode, PC);
40:     address = new char[strlen(A) + 1];
41:     strcpy(address, A);
42:     askingPrice = AP;
43:     sqrFeet = SQ;
44:     numRooms = NR;
45:   }
46:   Prop::~Prop()
47:   {
48:     Prop::number--;    // Decrease static value
49:   // delete [] address;
50:   }
51:   Prop::Prop(const Prop & p)    // Copy constructor
52:   {
53:     Prop::number++;    // Increase static value
54:     int newLen = strlen(p.address) + 1;
```

```
55:    address = new char[newLen];
56:    strcpy(address, p.address);
57:    strcpy(propCode, p.propCode);
58:    askingPrice = p.askingPrice;
59:    sqrFeet = p.sqrFeet;
60:    numRooms = p.numRooms;
61: }
62: Prop Prop::operator=(const Prop & p)  // Assignment overload
63: {
64:    if (this == &p)
65:       { return *this; }
66:    delete [] address;  // Deallocate old string
67:    int newLen = strlen(p.address) + 1;
68:    address = new char[newLen];
69:    strcpy(address, p.address);
70:    strcpy(propCode, p.propCode);
71:    askingPrice = p.askingPrice;
72:    sqrFeet = p.sqrFeet;
73:    numRooms = p.numRooms;
74:    return *this;
75: }
76: Prop Prop::operator+(const Prop & p)
77: {
78:    // This function returns an object with asking price
79    // plus the 2nd operand's asking price
80:    // and all the other constructed arguments are null
81:    Prop sum;
82:    sum.askingPrice = askingPrice + p.askingPrice;
83:    return sum;
84: }
85: ostream & operator<< (ostream & out, const Prop & p)
86: {
87:    out << setprecision(2) << setiosflags(ios::showpoint);
88:    out << setiosflags(ios::fixed);
89:    out << "Code: " << p.propCode << "\t";
90:    out << "Address: " << p.address << "\n";
91:    out << "Asking price: $" << setw(9) << p.askingPrice << "\t";
92:    out << "Square feet: " << p.sqrFeet << "\t";
93:    out << "No. of rooms: " << setw(2) << p.numRooms;
94:    out << "\n\n";
95:    return out;
96: }
97: istream & operator>> (istream & in, Prop & p)
98: {
99:    cout << "Property Input:\n";
100:   char tempInput[80];    // Need to temporarily hold input
101:   do {
102:      cout << "What is the property code (6 character please)? ";
103:      in >> tempInput;     // store user input
```

continues

Listing WR2.1. continued

```
104:      if (strlen(tempInput) != 6)
105:        { cout << "\n*** The code can be only 6 characters
          ➥***\n\n"; }
106:    } while (strlen(tempInput) != 6);
107:    strcpy(p.propCode, tempInput);
108:    in.ignore();    // Ignore carriage return
109:    cout << "What is the address? ";
110:    in.getline(tempInput, 80);
111:    p.address = new char[strlen(tempInput) + 1];
112:    strcpy(p.address, tempInput);
113:    cout << "What is the asking price? ";
114:    in >> p.askingPrice;
115:    cout << "What is the square feet? ";
116:    in >> p.sqrFeet;
117:    cout << "What is the number of rooms? ";
118:    in >> p.numRooms;
119:    return in;
120: }
121: void newProblem()
122: {
123:    cerr << "\nMemory problem\n";
124:    exit(1);
125: }
126: int Prop::number = 0;
127: ////////////////////////////////////////////////////////////
128: main()
129: {
130:   set_new_handler(newProblem);
131:   clrscr();
132:   // First, construct a house with values already known
133:   Prop house1("HOUSE1", "220 E. Richmond", 9500.0, 800, 6);
134:   cout << house1;
135:   // Construct a house using copy constructor
136:   Prop house2 = house1;
137:   cout << house2;
138:   // Construct a house using default constructor
139:   Prop house3;
140:   cin >> house3;  // Ask user for values
141:   // Construct using default constructor,
142:   // then use operator=() to initialize
143:   cout << "\nYou entered this house:\n";
144:   cout << house3;
145:   Prop house4;
146:   house4 = house3;   // operator=() called
147:   cout << house4;
148:   // Use the static member to show total number of houses
149:   // constructed so far (even though it's obvious there are 4)
150:   cout << "\nThere are " << Prop::number << "\n";
```

```
151:    Prop total;
152:    Prop::number--;   // Don't include total variable in static
        ➥count
153:    total = house1 + house2 + house3 + house4;
154:    cout << "The average asking price is ";
155:    float avg = total.getPrice() / Prop::number;
156:    cout << avg;
157:    return 0;
158: }
```

main() first sets up the new handler. The newProblem() function automatically takes over if a memory allocation fails. The newProblem() code appears on lines 121–125, and if a problem occurs, the program quits via the exit() call on line 124.

The program then creates the house1 object with some data in it. The creation of house1 occurs through the constructor function that begins on line 35. The arguments passed to the constructor are assigned to the house1 variable inside the constructor. The overloaded << (lines 85–96) prints all the program's Prop objects to the screen.

Line 136 uses the copy constructor starting on line 51 to create a new object, house2, from house1. The copy constructor, and not the overloaded assignment, is called because house2 is constructed and didn't exist before line 136.

The default constructor is used on line 139 to create house3. The default constructor that starts on line 28 simply assigns zeros to the numeric data members. An overloaded >> function (lines 97–120) asks the user for the values of house3 before house3 is printed on line 144.

house4 is constructed on line 145 by the default constructor, and the overloaded = function then assigns all of house3's members to house4 before house4 is printed on line 147.

Despite the fact that there are four houses explicitly constructed (five if you count total on line 151), a static member named number initialized to 0 on line 126 keeps track of the object count. The default constructor (starting on line 28), the constructor with arguments (line 35), and the copy constructor (starting on line 51) all increment the static number variable so that an accurate count can be made for the average calculation on line 155. Of course, the average could have been explicitly divided by four because it's obvious that only four objects are defined. Using the static member, however, helps demonstrate the use of static. The destructor starting on line 46 must decrement the count so that number always holds the total number of objects created at any one time.

If you were to break this program into pieces, you would put the class header (lines 9–27) in a file, you would compile the class implementation (lines 28–120) and store it as an object file, and you would be left with a short and clean main() function that manipulates the Prop class objects.

3

You're now two-thirds of the way through teaching yourself OOP with Turbo C++! The foundation you have now will make the next week seem easy. Despite all the OOP hype that you read about, there isn't that much to object-oriented programming—as long as you learn it carefully through a structured approach that explains each step fully without first throwing in a bunch of buzzwords.

There are just a few new concepts left for you to learn. Most of them, inheritance, virtual functions, containers, and file I/O, build on your current OOP knowledge of overloaded functions, overloaded operators, constructors, and public/private member access data and functions.

Reuse Speeds Programming

As its name implies, inheritance enables you to create new objects from existing objects and new classes from existing classes. Rather than following the usual copy-and-paste methods to reuse code, inheritance forms a safer and more structured approach to the reuse of program sections. You'll find that when you need a class that's almost like another class you've already written, you can inherit that class and let Turbo C++ do all the work of reusing the class without your having to copy code from one place to another.

This reuse of code is actually the cornerstone of the third week of this book. Templates and containers provide mechanisms that enable you to use class outlines and Turbo C++–supplied classes in your own programs without having to worry about writing data structures to hold class data.

Note: As with most OOP concepts that are new to you, the terms *inheritance, virtual functions, templates,* and *containers* probably sound like difficult subjects. They sound that way because the terms are new to you. As you learned with the terms *class, object, instantiation, constructor functions,* and *destructor functions,* the language of OOP isn't as difficult as it sounds. The programming community doesn't often use a short easy word when a long one will do just as nicely and confuse more people! Relax. You'll understand inheritance, virtual functions, and the many other new topics in this third and last week because the OOP way of programming is the most natural way, and these terms describe extensions to programming that make a lot of sense.

The last chapter in the book explains Turbo C++ file I/O. In a way, this chapter is a breather from the new OOP subjects that have taken you through the second and third weeks of material. The file I/O routines available in Turbo C++ are class related. As with cin and cout, you'll use built-in objects and classes as well as your own to write data to and read it from disk files. You'll find that file I/O in Turbo C++ is easier than in regular C (and most other programming languages) because the file I/O is just an extension of the I/O routines you already know.

It's Hereditary: Inheriting Data

It's Hereditary: Inheriting Data

People learn things faster when new concepts are compared to ones they already know. For instance, when learning a foreign language, you see translations into the language you already know. When you're given directions, it helps when the new location is oriented with a site you already know. When you're learning OOP, it helps to relate new topics to the non-OOP ones you already know.

In data processing departments throughout the world, new programs are being designed and written all the time. When writing new programs, programmers often use code from existing programs. Although the cut-and-paste process is error prone, using parts of existing program source code is faster than rewriting all that code from scratch.

Companies merge and spin off all the time. Data processing departments are often swamped with programming projects that appear as the result of a corporate change. The new programs are rarely new systems to be put in place, but rather are modifications of existing business activities that take into account the new corporate form.

Through *inheritance,* object-oriented programming helps individuals and companies produce faster code by taking away many of the details of code reuse from the programmer while still allowing parts of one program to be used in another. More often than not, a single program contains related code because the program works with similar but different data. For example, a personnel program might track salaried and hourly employees. These two kinds of employees have similar information (names, addresses, phone numbers, ages, and so on) with some differences such as their pay determination. Those employees also share characteristics with the people variables already coded for customers in another program.

Data structures aren't the only kind of programming element from which you can inherit. You can inherit windows, screens, graphics, on-screen push-button controls, and a lot more. You can inherit anything that you can represent as an object.

Today's chapter begins a four-part tour into inheritance issues with Turbo C++. Inheritance relieves you from the burden of cutting-and-pasting code from one part of a program to another when you want to share pieces of programs. Also, inheritance keeps your code clear of duplicate data and code definitions, leaving you with a cleaner program and one you can manipulate more easily than you otherwise could.

Today, you learn about the following topics:

- ☐ The structure of inheritance
- ☐ The terminology of inheritance

☐ Setting up a base class properly with the `protected` access specifier

☐ How to derive new classes from existing ones

☐ How to specify receiving access specifiers so that an inherited class contains the kind of members it needs in order to operate

☐ How to instantiate objects from both the original class and a derived class

Note: One of the reasons Turbo C++ classes are called *classes* is because of the similar hierarchy that inherited class objects share with the classification found in the scientific community, such as mammal classifications, chemical classifications, medical classifications, and so forth.

The Structure of Inheritance

Although you cannot inherit from functions and regular variables, you can inherit from classes. (You can also inherit from structures in Turbo C++ if you want to use structures.) As you know, you can include data and function members inside classes, so classes are really all you need to use for inheritance—if any kind of computer element appears inside a class, you can inherit the class, in effect inheriting the element itself.

When inheriting, you can reuse existing classes or add functionality to existing classes and thereby create more powerful classes. To ease the inheritance learning curve as much as possible, you need to learn some common terms used throughout Turbo C++ inheritance.

The process of inheriting one class from another is called *derivation*. Derivation is the process of inheritance; that is, when you inherit one class from another, you *derive* the new class from the original class.

For example, the `Person` class

```
class Person {
  char * name;
  char * address;
  int areaCode;
  long int phone;
public:
  // Public member data and functions would follow
};
```

It's Hereditary: Inheriting Data

might be the original class from which you derive this `Customer` class:

```
class Customer {
  char * name;
  char * address;
  int areaCode;
  long int phone;
  char * custCode;       // Three new members not found
  double balanceOwed;    // in the original class
  int daysPastDue;
public:
  // Public member data and functions would follow
};
```

 Note: For now, concentrate on getting the inheritance terms down. You'll learn the C++ inheritance specifics later in today's chapter.

In inheritance terminology, the `People` class is called the *base* class, and the `Customer` class is called the *derived* class. Figure 15.1 helps illustrate the difference between the terms.

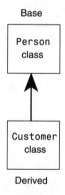

Figure 15.1. *The derived class reuses and adds functionality to the base class.*

Notice when looking at inheritance diagrams that the base class is usually listed at the top and all derived classes fall beneath the base class. The arrow showing the inheritance direction always points to the derived class (or classes).

More than one class can be inherited from another. Figure 15.2 shows three inherited classes derived from a single base class. As the figure's callouts show, the base class is sometimes called the *parent* class, and the derived classes are called *child* classes.

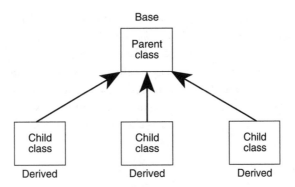

Figure 15.2. *Three child classes are derived from a parent class.*

Keeping It Simple Helps

You cannot easily take away functionality through inheritance. There-fore, the more generic the primary class from which you'll inherit is, the more fully you can use that class in later classes that you create through inheritance.

You might recall that languages such as Smalltalk (as Day 8's chapter explained) don't come supplied with any built-in data types. You have to start with a generic object and build your own data types from that.

Inheritance is the mechanism you use in such languages to create data types. Think for a moment about numeric data. You could create an integer class. Then you could inherit long integers from the integer because long integers have all the characteristics of regular integers plus some additional charac-teristics. You then could inherit floating point from the long integer class, adding characteristics such as a decimal portion to the data. Double floating point is then trivial.

Requiring that you add functionality along the inheritance path isn't ex-tremely limiting as long as you make sure your base class is generic enough to be inherited from. You'll learn some inheritance design tips in this week's chapters, but experience will be your best teacher.

The entire collection of derived classes, from the base class through all of its derived classes, is called the *inheritance hierarchy.* As with family traits, Turbo C++ inheritance hierarchies might contain several layers. For instance, a parent class named Person might produce three child classes called Employee, Customer, and Vendor. The Employee class might in itself be used to derive two more classes, Salaried and Hourly. The Hourly class might also be used to derive two more classes named PartTime and FullTime. This entire class hierarchy is shown in Figure 15.3.

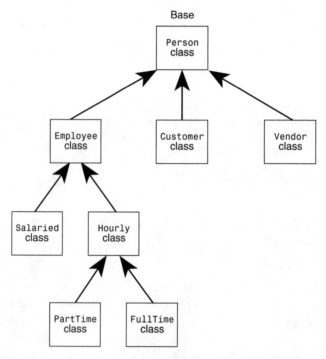

Figure 15.3. *A class hierarchy might contain many derivations.*

Note: Although the Person class is the inheritance hierarchy's base class, the sublevel hierarchies falling beneath the Person class are minihierarchies in themselves. Hourly is the parent class or base class to the derived PartTime and FullTime classes.

The inheritance hierarchies described so far have all consisted of *single inheritance.* In single inheritance hierarchies, a derived class has one and only one parent. As you learn

and read more about OOP, you'll run across the term *multiple inheritance*. A class hierarchy with multiple inheritance contains one or more derived classes with more than one parent class.

Turbo C++ supports multiple inheritance, but you'll not find multiple inheritance taught in this or in some other Turbo C++ books. The OOP industry wages endless debates on the merits or drawbacks of multiple inheritance. Many Turbo C++ programmers say that any program and any class hierarchy can be written using only single inheritance. The multiple inheritance proponents argue that multiple inheritance streamlines some classes.

Programming with multiple inheritance adds lots of confusion and complexity to your code. Get comfortable with single inheritance before attempting to learn multiple inheritance. You will probably find that you never need to learn multiple inheritance, and you'll decrease the chance of long debugging sessions if you never use multiple inheritance.

The Smalltalk pure-OOP language does not support multiple inheritance, and Smalltalk programmers do not understand why a programmer would ever need multiple inheritance. If your base classes and derived classes are designed properly, you can write any program using solely single inheritance.

Figure 15.4 shows an example of multiple inheritance. The `PartnerClient` might be both a customer and a vendor. The biggest problem with multiple inheritance is that it is conceptually easy to understand, and therefore frighteningly easy to attempt to use in programs that don't need it. This author believes that a foundation in single inheritance will guide the OOP newcomer to become a solid Turbo C++ programmer. Single inheritance gives you the power you need to write powerful OOP programs. The difficulties that come with multiple inheritance probably aren't worth your time at this point in your OOP career.

You Have Already Used Multiple Inheritance!

The IOSTREAM.H header file contains an input/output multiple inheritance hierarchy. Input and output stream classes combine to form new kinds of classes through a complicated use of multiple inheritance.

Could the IOSTREAM.H class hierarchy be written using single inheritance? Yes it could, but the fact remains that Turbo C++, and probably every other C++ compiler, contains the same multiple inheritance IOSTREAM.H header file class.

The IOSTREAM.H header file is a well-written (as well-written as multiple inheritance can be) multiple inheritance hierarchy, and it is safe to use. As with all well-written class libraries, you don't have to know that the class contains multiple inheritance to use the class effectively.

Some day, you might want to scan the IOSTREAM.H header file (don't change it!) and see how its multiple inheritance hierarchy works. Until then, keep it a secret that a class you use in every Turbo C++ program contains multiple inheritance, and maybe nobody else will realize you use multiple inheritance!

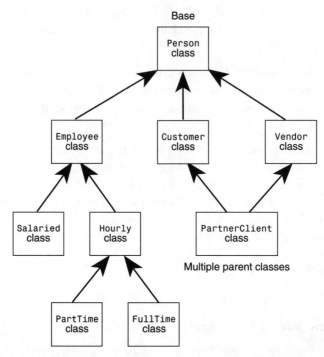

Figure 15.4. *Some customers might also be vendors, which would produce this multiple inheritance relationship.*

Inheritance terms are easy to understand. Although this book shies away from introducing new terms before explaining the code beneath the terms, inheritance mirrors the way you classify real-life elements. OOP inheritance is not just a shortcut

for programming; inheritance enables you to group like data into related units. When you use existing knowledge to learn new knowledge, you don't have to "reinvent the wheel."

Another reason for inheritance is the ease of change that inheritance provides. If you change a base class, all derived classes automatically change as well. If you were to use the old cut-and-paste approach to data processing, a change in the original class would mean a manual search and change of every other place where you use that code.

As you write object-oriented programs that require inheritance, you'll start with a basic framework class and derive new classes from that common class. With the common data and functions in the base class, you can then concentrate on programming only the changes that appear in all the derived classes that follow.

DO	**DON'T**

DO learn the terminology of inheritance. You'll learn inheritance specifics faster when common terms can be used.

DO use inheritance to speed your program development. It's easier and faster to inherit from a parent class than to rewrite a similar class from scratch.

DON'T use multiple inheritance for a while, if ever. Most Turbo C++ programmers don't use multiple inheritance because it is thought that every inheritance hierarchy can be achieved through single inheritance. Multiple inheritance adds complexity that you don't need right now.

Diving into Turbo C++ Inheritance

Some of the early inheritance examples that you study in today's chapter will use classes that contain all public members. The reason that public data members and member functions are shown is that inheritance of private members does *not* occur; in other words, a derived class can never inherit the private members of a base class.

Note: After you see a few inheritance examples that contain all public classes, you'll see ways to maintain the data protection that the `private` keyword provides without giving up inheritance limitations of private members.

Returning to the `Person` class introduced earlier in the chapter, the `Person` class was the base class and described a generic person used throughout the rest of the company's class hierarchy. Here is the `Person` class that contains all public members:

```
class Person {
public:
  char * name;
  char * address;
  int areaCode;
  long int phone;
  Person();           // Public member functions follow
  ~Person();
  Person inputPerson(void);
  prPerson(void);
};
```

Of course, a person's address contains a city, state, and ZIP code, but this class is being kept as simple as possible to focus on the inheritance specifics described here. Also, you might want to override operators and constructors so that there could be several occurrences of them.

It is common for programmers never to instantiate a base class object variable. That is, sometimes a base class exists just to provide a format for all the more specific classes derived from the base class.

Deriving a child class from a parent class requires only that you specify the parent class to inherit from and the new members you want added to the derived class. When you declare a derived class, separate the name of the derived class from the base class with a colon. The following `Employee` class derives from the `Person` class shown earlier:

```
class Employee : Person {
public:        // Keeps things simpler for now
  int dependents;
  int yrsWorked;
  int testYears(void);   // Indicates True if employed
};                       // more than 10 years
```

Figure 15.5 shows the resulting `Employee` class. It first appears that `Employee` has only three members, but the `Person` after the `Employee` name in the class's first line tells Turbo C+ to inherit all public members from `Person` and bring them down into an `Employee` class.

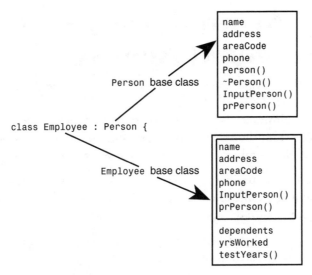

Figure 15.5. *Inheriting the Person class.*

You'll see from Figure 15.5 that constructors and destructors are not inherited. Each class must include its own constructor and destructor because the constructor and destructor functions must be so aligned with the class in which they appear. Tomorrow's chapter will explain how to create and call constructor and destructor functions when inheritance is involved.

All the public members, both data and member functions, drop down to the Employee class. No data is reserved yet because no objects are defined. But if the main() function in the program using these classes were to create a Person object, that object would contain all the members of the Person class, and any Employee object would contain all the members of the Person class (except the constructor and destructor) as well as the three new members.

DO   DON'T

DO use a colon, :, to separate a new class name from the inherited class name.

DON'T design a base class with lots of private members unless the base class is to forbid inheritance of those private members. No derived class ever inherits a private member.

DON'T attempt to inherit constructors or destructors because neither of them can be inherited from a base class to a derived class.

Getting Around *private* with *protected* Access

Don't throw the private access specifier away just because derived classes cannot inherit private members. The data protection provided by private members is too critical to lose. However, if you write generic base classes and never plan to create objects directly from those base classes (just from derived classes), feel free to use private for all the members if you want to. However, there is a better alternative.

There is a third access specifier you haven't read about so far because you never needed it before inheritance came into the picture. The protected access specifier provides the best of both worlds: data protection and inheritability.

Here is a class with all three (there are only three) access specifiers: private (the default of a class until overridden), protected, and public:

```
class BaseCl {
  int a;             // Private by default
  int b;
protected:           // Available ONLY to inherited classes
  int c;
  int d;
public:              // Available to ALL elements that access a member
  int e;
  int f;
};
```

As you can see, the protected keyword appears in the class at the location before the first protected member. All other members below protected remain protected until another access specifier changes the access. Figure 15.6 shows how the BaseCl makes the three groups of members available.

Often, a base class contains only protected and public members because inheritance needs access to all the members. Here is the Person class rewritten using protected access for the members that need it:

```
class Person {
protected:
  char * name;
  char * address;
  int areaCode;
  long int phone;
public:            // Public member functions follow
  Person();
  ~Person();
  Person inputPerson(void);
  prPerson(void);
};
```

Now, if the Employee class attempted to inherit from Person, the derived Employee class would receive all the members of Person (except, as usual, the constructor and destructor) as if they were all public. However, no other underived part of the program could access the protected members because they are protected from access by all except derived classes.

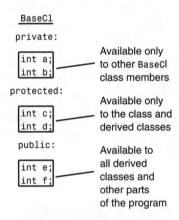

Figure 15.6. public *is available to all,* protected *is available to the class and derived classes, and* private *is available to the class only.*

 Note: You cannot apply private, protected, and public to unions. Union members are always public, and you can neither derive them nor derive from them. (Unions, however, can contain constructors.)

To summarize this section, the Person class with protected members still contains members not available to any function *outside* the inheritance hierarchy. In other words, all derived classes can inherit the protected members, but neither main() nor any other non-member function can access the protected members. As always, all program elements (main(), functions called by main(), and derived classes) have access to the public members.

DO   DON'T

DO specify protected when you want to limit member access to the class and any derived classes.

DON'T forget that a derived class can never change the access of a parent class's member. If the parent class contains a private member, there is nothing the derived class can do to access that member.

DON'T expect all your base classes to be object classes. In other words, you might create a generic base class that will be used only to derive other classes. The base class offers a uniform foundation for all the derived classes. If you put the data members that are most likely to change in a parent class, if the change does occur, you won't have to change any of the derived classes as long as the parent class's access keyword was protected or public on the members that might change.

DON'T apply the access specifiers to unions because unions cannot be used in an inherited hierarchy.

How Derived Classes View Inherited Members

At first glance, it might seem that when a derived class inherits `protected` members, those members remain protected, and when a derived class inherits public members, those members remain public. That's not always the case, however. Throughout this section, you'll learn how the derived class changes the access of members when it inherits them.

Note: Throughout the rest of the book, keep in mind that a derived class can change *nothing* about the base class. No matter what a derived class contains, the base class private members are always private, the base class protected members are always protected, and the base class public members are always public. This section shows how to receive such access so that it appears different in the derived class after inheritance takes place.

If you need to, you can add an access specifier, `private`, `protected`, or `public`, in front of the base class name when inheriting. Here are the first lines of three derived class definitions that do just that:

```
class DerivedCl1 : private BaseCl {
```

```
class DerivedCl2 : protected BaseCl {

class DerivedCl3 : public BaseCl {
```

This means that not only do you put the access specifiers in front of the base class members you want specified, but you also put the access specifiers in front of the base class name when deriving from the base class. When an access specifier appears in front of a derived class's base class name, it determines the method Turbo C++ uses to merge the base class into the derived class.

The default method of *receiving* inherited members is private. This does *not* mean that all inherited members are private. It simply means that both of the following statements are exactly the same because the receiving access of a derived class is automatically private by default:

```
class DerivedCl1 : private BaseCl {
```

and

```
class DerivedCl1 : BaseCl {          // private not needed
```

Three possible access specifiers are available for base class members, and three are available for receiving base class members in derived classes, making a total of nine combinations possible. Luckily, most Turbo C++ programmers either keep the default private derivation or specify public. The protected keyword is rarely used to receive derivations.

About the only way to tackle these access specifier combinations is to look at an example and explain each combination in turn. Listing 15.1 provides a class listing of the Person hierarchy, the top level of the one described earlier in Figure 15.3. The analysis section explains each of the derived class's receiving access specifiers. (There is no output because no main() appears in the listing.)

 Listing 15.1. Looking at the derived class specifiers.

```
1: // Filename: ACCESS.CPP
2: class Person {
3:   long int interCode;  // Internal code is only private member
4: protected:
5:   char * name;          // Four protected members
6:   char * address;
7:   int areaCode;
8:   long int phone;
9: public:               // Public member functions follow
10:   Person();
11:   ~Person();
12:   Person inputPerson(void);
```

continues

Listing 15.1. continued

```
13:    prPerson(void);
14:  };
15:  class Employee : private Person {   // Private receipt is default
16:    int dependents;
17:  protected:
18:    int yrsWorked;
19:  public:
20:    int testYears(void);  // True if employed more than 10 years
21:  };
22: class Customer : protected Person {
23:    char * custNum;
24: protected:
25:    float custBalance;
26: public:
27:    int prCust(void);
28: };
29: class Vendor : public Person {
30:    char * vendNum;
31: protected:
32:    float vendOwed;
33: public:
34:    prVend(void);
35: };
```

Notice that the base class, Person, contains members that use all three access specifiers, private, protected, and public (lines 3–13). It is the access specifiers in the base class, Person, that determine how the rest of the program can see its members.

Note: The class hierarchy is more complicated than it would probably be in a regular program. Programmers don't generally write derived classes that receive using the protected or private keywords; most derived classes receive using public. This example is good, however, in that it shows you all the possibilities of sending and receiving derived classes throughout the hierarchy.

Neither main() nor any derived classes can access the interCode member in Person. interCode is private to the class; only the rest of the Person class can access it. When another class inherits Person, no matter what the other class's receiving access specifier is, interCode will never be accessible to another class.

The members name, address, areaCode, and phone are protected. They can never be accessed by main(), but all derived classes will receive those four members (unlike interCode). No matter how a derived class inherits from Person, the derived class will contain these four members of Person.

The members Person(), ~Person(), inputPerson(), and prPerson() are all public and therefore can be used from any other part of the program. main() can access these members. Also, all derived classes that derive from Person will contain those four public members as well.

Note: The fact that the four public members are member functions has nothing to do with their access. If two were data members and two were functions, all four still would be public and would be available to all parts of the program due to their public keyword.

All the access specifiers that appear in the base class dictate how other classes see the base class members. It's time to look at how each derived class *receives* the members available in the Person base class. Here is a review list:

1. When a derived class inherits with the private keyword in front of the base class name, or when no access specifier appears before the base class name (private is the default), all inherited protected *and* public members appear in the derived class as private members.

2. When a derived class inherits with the protected keyword in front of the base class name, all inherited protected *and* public members of the base class appear in the derived class as protected members.

3. When a derived class inherits with the public keyword in front of the base class name, the inherited protected members remain protected when they get to the derived class, and all inherited public members remain public when they get to the derived class. The public keyword is the most commonly used access specifier in receiving inheritance hierarchies.

Figure 15.7 shows the derived Employee class after the inheritance takes place. The incoming members from Person are all received as private members, and the members explicitly listed in Employee (dependents, yrsWorked, and testYears()) retain their stated access.

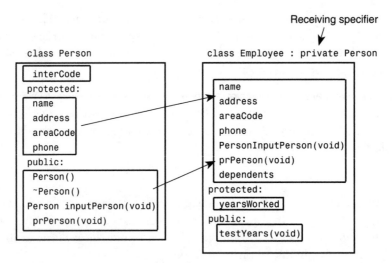

Figure 15.7. *All inherited members from* Person *appear in* Employee *as private members.*

main() has no access to any of the seven resulting private members of the Employee class. All six inherited members and the one explicitly stated member (dependents) are private to Employee. Only members of the Employee class have the capability to access the seven private members. If you were to derive another class from Employee, none of those seven members would be inherited.

 The reason that seven members are inherited from Employee is that constructors and destructors are never inherited.

Because the yrsWorked member is protected, the Employee class and any derived class have access to yrsWorked, but main() does not. The public member testYears() can be both inherited and used by main().

Figure 15.8 shows the derived Customer class after the inheritance takes place. The incoming protected and public members from Person are all received as protected members, and the members explicitly listed in Customer (custNum, custBalance, and prCust()) retain their stated access.

main() has no access to the private member of Customer (custNum) or to the seven protected members, but main() can access the public member prCust(). If you derive

a new class from Customer, the derived class could have access to the seven protected members and to the public member prCust().

Figure 15.9 shows the derived Vendor class after the inheritance takes place. The incoming members from Person are received as either protected or public depending on their access in the Person class. The four protected Person members remain protected and the two public Person members remain public when they get to Vendor.

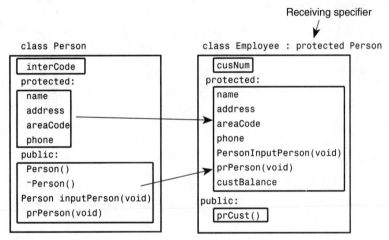

Figure 15.8. *All inherited members from* Person *appear in* Customer *as protected members.*

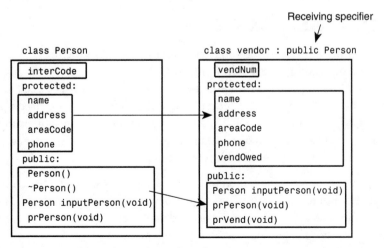

Figure 15.9. *Public inherited members from* Person *appear in* Vendor *as public, and protected inherited members from* Person *appear as protected.*

Note: Technically, private base class members are inherited but are not accessible in derived classes. The result is that private base class members don't appear to pass to their descendants.

DO	DON'T

DO give members private access if you want to keep all code outside the class, including derived classes, from using the member.

DO specify a receiving access specifier if you want to override the default private access provided automatically when inheriting. Generally, programmers inherit using the public access specifier before the inherited base class name. In this way, all base class protected members remain protected in the derived class, and all base class public members remain public in the derived class.

DON'T use the protected access specifier unless you want both protected and public inherited members to remain protected in the derived class.

Overriding the Receiving Access

Turbo C++ provides a way for you to receive inherited class members as specified in the preceding section, and override individual member access when needed. For example, in Listing 15.1, all inherited members of the Employee class are private because the members were inherited using the default private access specifier. However, what if all members are to be kept private except one? For example, what if name is to be classified as a public data member when it gets to Employee, whereas all the other inherited members are received as private?

By using the scope resolution operator, you can explicitly state which members are to be classified differently than the rest when they reach the derived class. Listing 15.2 contains the Person base class and a derived Employee class. Instead of coming into Employee as private, name comes in as a public member.

 Listing 15.2. Overriding the access receipt.

```
1:  // Filename: OVERIDE.CPP
2:  class Person {
3:    long int interCode;    // Internal code is only private member
4:  protected:
5:    char * name;           // Four protected members
6:    char * address;
7:    int areaCode;
8:    long int phone;
9:  public:            // Public member functions follow
10:    Person();
11:    ~Person();
12:    Person inputPerson(void);
13:    prPerson(void);
14:  };
15:  class Employee : private Person {   // Private receipt is default
16:    int dependents;
17:  protected:
18:    int yrsWorked;
19:  public:
20:    Person::name;        // Name would have come as private without this
21:    int testYears(void);  // True if employed more than 10 years
22:  };
```

 Figure 15.10 shows the resulting derived Employee class. Notice that name is in the public section, even though it was originally in the Person class's private section and even though all the other members inherited as private members. Line 20 told Turbo C++ to make the name public when it inherits from Person. Using the scope resolution operator and the base class in this way enables you to override the default inheritance. You could override more than one member if desired. The location of the override (in Line 20's case, the overridden classification becomes public because of its location in the public section) determines how the inherited member is received.

 Note: Even when you override inherited access, a derived class never has access to a base class's private members.

Sometimes the overridden inherited member is called a *qualified-name*. The name member is qualified in the inherited Employee class.

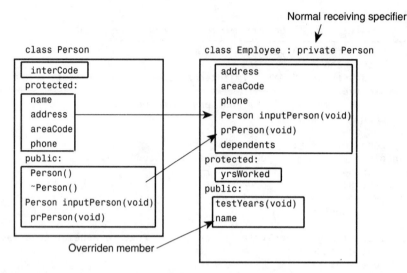

Figure 15.10. *Because all are inherited, they become private except for* name, *which is public.*

Where You're Headed

Despite all the theory today's chapter taught, you've seen very little code. The reason is that constructing derived and base class objects takes some extra constructor review. Tomorrow's chapter will explore how to construct derived and base class objects and will explain how to destruct such objects as well.

For now, realize that a derived class, after all the inheritance has taken place, is just like any other class in that it has members (some are unseen in the code because they are inherited) that take on any of the three private, protected, or public access specifiers. You can instantiate objects from derived classes or from base classes.

Given the previous Person hierarchy, you can define a Person base class object like this:

```
main()
{
  Person human;
  // Rest of program would follow
```

The human object would include four private members and four public members (see Listing 15.2 for the member names). The Person() constructor would be used to construct the human object.

If you want to define an `Employee` object, you can do that as well. The following code defines three `Employee` objects:

```
main()
{
  Employee emp1, emp2, emp3;
  // Rest of program would follow
```

You don't have to define a base class object before defining a derived class object. In fact, you don't ever have to define base class objects if the base class is set up to be a common skeleton class for all the related and derived classes that derive from the base.

It is worth noting that the built-in *default constructor* is used to create the three employee objects. No constructor exists in the `Employee` class, so none can be used. Remember that neither constructors nor destructors are inherited.

The instantiated objects behave as expected. If you want to execute the `testYears()` member function on one of the employee objects, you can do so like this:

```
emp1.testYears();
```

If you defined a `human` base class object, you can execute its `prPerson()` member function like this:

```
human.prPerson();
```

Remember, though, that you can also execute the `prPerson()` member function on the derived class objects because `prPerson()` is a public member function in the base class and so it always gets inherited. If you want an `Employee` object to execute the `prPerson()` member function, you can do so like this:

```
emp3.prPerson();
```

DO   DON'T

DO override individual derived class members when you want them to be received in the derived class differently than they would normally be received.

DO instantiate both derived and base class objects just as you do non-inherited objects.

DON'T write constructors or destructors for derived classes until you've mastered tomorrow's material. You need to read some extra cautions and learn some other procedures before writing full-blown Turbo C++ programs that contain inheritance.

Summary

Today's chapter introduced inheritance and provided lots of insight on why you need inheritance. Inheritance gives Turbo C++ a great capability to reuse class data. As you inherit from existing classes, you can add data and functionality to the inherited classes.

Terminology is important in discussions of inheritance. The class from which you inherit is called the base class or the parent class. The class produced by the inheritance is called the derived class or the child class. After deriving a child class, you can derive additional child classes from it.

This chapter introduced single inheritance. In single inheritance, every derived class has, at most, one parent class. Turbo C++ does support multiple inheritance, but deriving classes with multiple parents is tricky, error prone, and especially difficult when you're setting up constructors and destructors. Most of the programs you ever write will work faster if you stay with the simpler single inheritance. After you are comfortable with single inheritance, you can study classes that successfully use multiple inheritance.

When inheriting, the private members in the base class always remain private. There is nothing you can do to inherit private members, whether they are data members or member functions. (Of course, friend functions have access to private members, but they are a special case.)

The third (and last) access specifier, named `protected`, is needed when inheriting. When a base class contains protected members, those members remain private to everything outside the class except other derived classes (and friend functions, of course).

Not only do you have to worry about the access offered by a base class, but you also must concern yourself with the receiving access in the derived class. Depending on which of the three access specifiers you supply when inheriting, the incoming members appear in the private, protected, or public section of the derived class.

Although the inheritance rules are fairly rigid (several figures in today's chapter walked you through the different inheritance scenarios), you always can override an incoming member so that its derived access differs from what it otherwise would be.

Q&A

1. Why would I want to inherit?

   Inheritance enables you to reuse classes that you've already written. Inheritance forms the perfect vehicle for extending programs but providing data protection. If you purchase class libraries from other sources, you can inherit your own classes from those supplied even if you don't have source code to the supplied class implementations. When you need a new window that behaves differently from the one your class creates, inherit a new window class that behaves slightly differently.

   The nice thing about inheritance is that it enables you to write new code based on code you already know and understand. New classes are easily derived from existing classes that you've already written and debugged. Reusing code and data through inheritance is safer and faster than the old cut-and-paste methods used in non-OOP programming.

2. What is the `protected` access specifier used for?

   The `protected` access specifier had to be added to Turbo C++ to allow inheritance while maintaining data protection. No derived class can use a base class's private member.

   Making a base class member protected guards that member from use by outside procedures and classes but does allow derived classes access to the data. Protected data is still hidden from the rest of the program but is available to all derived classes.

   Without the protected access specifier, there would be no way to keep data private while still allowing derived access.

3. What can I change in a derived class from the base class?

   You can add data members and functionality in derived classes. In a way, a child class always outperforms its parent class because a child class contains all the members and functions of the parent class and also adds some of its own.

4. Why is single inheritance better than multiple inheritance?

   Single inheritance is many times easier to code than multiple inheritance. The benefits of multiple inheritance just don't seem to be worth the effort involved in writing code with multiple inheritance. When faced with a programming situation that requires multiple inheritance, try to rework your class to work with single inheritance so that your programming is more productive and less error prone.

5. Why must I supply an access specifier when deriving classes?

You don't *have* to supply an access specifier when receiving inherited classes because Turbo C++ defaults to private inheritance. However, in private inheritance, all inherited members, both protected and public members, become private in the derived class. Most of the time, inheriting with private access is too limiting.

When you inherit with protected access, both incoming protected and public members become protected in the derived class.

When you inherit with public access (the most common way), incoming protected members remain protected, and incoming public members remain public.

Workshop

The Workshop offers quiz questions and exercises to hone your skills and give you feedback on today's lesson. You'll find some proposed answers in Appendix D.

Quiz

1. Which of the following classes is the base class, A or B?

```
class A {
  int i;
public:
  void getI();
};
class B : A {
  int j;
public:
  void getJ();
};
```

2. Which of the classes in question 1, A or B, is the derived class?

3. In the class hierarchy of question 1, is there any way that B can access A's member named i? If so, how?

4. Given the inheritance hierarchy

```
class baseCl {
  int i;
```

```
protected:
  int j;
public:
  int k;
};
class derivedCl : public baseCl {
  float x;
public:
  prDerived();
};
```

answer the following questions:

    A. How many of baseCl's members can derivedCl work with?

    B. Is j public, protected, or private when it gets to derivedCl?

    C. Is k public, protected, or private when it gets to derivedCl?

5. Where is the one safe place to use multiple inheritance?

6. True or false: The derivedCl member c did not have to be overridden in the following code:

```
class baseCl {
  int a;
protected:
  int b;
  int c;
};
class derivedCl : public baseCl {
  int d;
protected:
  int e;
  baseCl::c;     // Override ?
public:
  int f;
};
```

Exercise

1. Add to Listing 15.1 so that it contains inheritance of all of Figure 15.3's classes.

Inherited Limits and Extensions

Today's chapter shows you complete programs that use inheritance hierarchies. Before writing programs that use inheritance, you've got to learn how constructors and destructors work in an inheritance environment. Constructor and destructor functions cannot be inherited. Simply adding a constructor and destructor to a base class does not ensure that Turbo C++ will properly construct and destruct that class until you learn how to write inheritance-related constructors and destructors correctly.

The constructors used in inheritance hierarchies look slightly different from the simple ones you've seen so far. Actually, derived class constructors are just as simple as those for stand-alone classes, but the syntax used differs when inheritance is used.

The new syntax for inheritance-related constructors includes *constructor initialization lists*. Initialization lists provide constructor values outside the body of the constructor, as you'll learn about here. You can use constructor initialization lists for all your constructors, not just for those classes you inherit. Therefore, for consistency and also to maintain the habit, many Turbo C++ programmers use constructor initialization lists for all their constructors, even for those classes that do not contain inheritance.

Although inherited class destructor functions don't differ in syntax from their stand-alone class equivalents, you've got to learn the timing of destructors when using inheritance. Today's chapter focuses on the timing of both constructors and destructors when you're working with base and derived classes.

Today, you learn about the following topics:

- [ ] The syntax of constructor initialization lists

- [ ] Constructing parent class objects from derived classes

- [ ] The order of constructing within an inheritance hierarchy

- [ ] The order of destructing within an inheritance hierarchy

- [ ] Some coding and maintenance advantages of inheritance

The Need for Initialization Lists

All the constructor functions you've seen so far have assigned initial values to members. There is a problem with a constructor doing this, however, and at first the problem seems trivial. Constructors should not assign data; assigning data is best left to overloaded assignment operator functions. (Copy constructors fall between the cracks, designed to be both a constructor and an assignor.)

Constructors should construct. The data constructed should be new objects with initial values in them at their creation. It is easy to come up with an example class that cannot be constructed with an assignment constructor like the constructors you've seen so far. The class in Listing 16.1 contains a const member. You might never have seen a const member in a class or structure before, but it is perfectly acceptable and is needed for safety in many cases.

Listing 16.1. Individual members can be constants.

```
1:  // Filename: CONSTCLS.CPP
2:  // A class with a constant member
3:  class Inventory {
4:    char name[25];
5:    int quantity;
6:    float price;
7:    const int initialQuantity;  // Original order's quantity
8:  public:
9:    // Public members go here
10: };
```

Although the body of this class is not complete, you can attempt to compile it as can all stand-alone class header files. When you try to compile the class header, Turbo C++ produces this error message:

```
Error CONSTCLS.CPP 10: Constant member 'Inventory::initialQuantity'
➥class without constructors
```

Turbo C++ notices the constant member on line 10 and informs you that you need a constructor when a constant member appears in a class. The built-in default constructor is not enough to handle constant members.

> **Note:** Remember that a built-in default constructor (as opposed to a default constructor that you supply) initializes its members with garbage values. Turbo C++ knows that if it uses its own default constructor to create an object of the Inventory class, a garbage value remains fixed in the constant member for all objects constructed. Turbo C++ wants you to supply your own constructor so that you can control the initial value placed in the initialQuantity member.

Listing 16.2 shows the Inventory class with a constructor added.

Listing 16.2. Attempting to add a constructor.

```
1:  // Filename: CONSTCL2.CPP
2:  // A class with a constant member and attempted constructor
3:  #include <string.h>
4:  class Inventory {
5:    char name[25];
6:    int quantity;
7:    float price;
8:    const int initialQuantity;  // Original order's quantity
9:  public:
10:   Inventory(char N[], int Q, float P, int I)
11:     {
12:       strcpy(name, N);       // Assign each of the passed values
13:       quantity = Q;
14:       price = P;
15:       initialQuantity = I;  // Oops, this is suspicious!
16:     }
17:   // Rest of public members go here
18: };
```

Lines 12–15 form the familiar constructor pattern that you've seen in some of the past few chapters. Of course, this constructor could have been placed outside the body of the class header, but for this short example, it was left inside the class.

The constructor is not a default constructor. The constructor is written assuming that main() will create an Inventory object and at the same time provide the initial values in a statement such as this:

```
Inventory item1("Red High stool", 16, 25.65, 10);
```

There's still a major problem with this nondefault constructor. If you attempt to compile the class header in Listing 16.2, Turbo C++ gives you both the warning and the error message shown here:

```
Warning CONSTCL2.CPP 11: Constant member 'initialQuantity' is not
➥initialized
Error CONSTCL2.CPP 15: Cannot modify a const object
```

Perhaps these compiler messages seem incorrect because initialQuantity is assigned an initial value in the constructor, and other than the constructor, the class header doesn't assign the constant initialQuantity any values. However, Turbo C++ cannot handle the statement on line 15 because this is the internal order of all constructors:

1. Construct the object by reserving memory, and attach the object name to the reserved memory location.

2. Execute the body of the constructor code after the object is reserved in memory.

It is because the body of the constructor consists of assignment statements that Turbo C++ refuses to compile the class header. At line 15, the object is already constructed, or at least memory is already reserved with the object's name attached. (Technically, *at runtime,* if this constructor were to execute, the memory would already be reserved before line 15.) The assignment statement is attempting to assign a value to a constant that is already in memory, and constants cannot be changed after they are in memory.

By using constructor initialization lists, your constructors more accurately *construct and initialize* rather than *construct and assign.* This doesn't mean that constructors should not and cannot contain assignment statements and other code, but they rarely do contain code unless dynamic memory allocation is involved.

> **Note:** Besides constructing objects with constant members, you'll reap additional side benefits of constructors after you learn how to use initialization lists rather than constructor code. Your constructors will be cleaner, and constructor initialization lists construct derived classes. Also, if a member is a reference variable, you'll face the same initialization-versus-assignment problem that you face with constants because references must be initialized at the time they are defined, just as constants must be.

When you use a constructor initialization list, Turbo C++ will truly construct and initialize at the time an object is created. Not only can your constant members therefore be initialized, but so can your other members as well.

Constructor Initialization Style

Most of the time, a constructor initialization list contains a value for every assignment statement the constructor would otherwise have. A constructor initialization list actually looks as if it is constructing individual members, and in a way it is. Here is a constructor that uses a construction initialization list to construct the Inventory class shown earlier:

```
Inventory(char N[], int Q, float P, int I) : quantity(Q), price(P),
➥ initialQuantity(I)
{
  strcpy(N, name);   // Couldn't work in initialization list
}
```

Notice that constructor initialization lists follow the constructor's closing argument list parenthesis and a colon, :. All non-array members can be initialized. In this constructor, the three members in the initialization list are *initialized*, not assigned in the sense that they would be assigned in the constructor's body. The initialization list gives the compiler the go-ahead to create the constant member `initialQuantity` with an initial value. The `const` locks that value into the member for good. (This all happens at runtime when an object variable is instantiated from the class.)

It might look strange to include constructor-like syntax for members of built-in data types, but the syntax assures initialization rather than assignment.

Notice that the character array member must be assigned in the function body. Member character arrays and pointers are usually reserved on the heap, so they require the usual assignment syntax in the body of the constructor.

Just for review, here is a simple class that contains three members and a constructor that properly constructs the members when an object is created:

```
class C {
  int i;
  char c;
  float f;
public:
  C(int I, char C, float F) : i(I), c(C) , f(F) {};
};
```

This class contains no array or pointer members to keep its initialization simple. Figure 16.1 shows how the initialization lists work like assignments, but they are assignments that occur *as* the object is being constructed.

```
                                  i=I;          f=F;
                                   ↑             ↑
        C(int I, char C, float F) :i(I), c(C), f(F) {
                                          ↓
                                        c=C;
```

Figure 16.1. *Initialization works like an assignment but occurs during construction.*

The preceding class does exactly the same thing as the next one except that C's members are initialized in the preceding code and are created and then assigned in this code:

```
class C {
  int i;
  char c;
  float f;
```

```
public:
  C(int I, char C, float F)
  { i = I;        // Assigns all the members
    c = C;
    f = F;
  }
};
```

With no arrays, constant members, or references to members, either of these two sets of code works fine. However, the first class with the initialization list is shorter and easier to code and maintains the spirit of constructors (initialization, not assignment). Most of the constructors in the rest of this book will use constructor initialization lists to initialize the members instead of doing the assignment in the body of the function. The only exception will occur when an array or the heap (or both) is involved.

Note: The definition lines of constructors with constructor initialization lists often get to be lengthy. Often, Turbo C++ programmers move the initialization list down to the line following the constructor's first line like this:

```
C(int I, char C, float F) :
  i(I), c(C) , f(F) {};
```

The extra spacing doesn't help or hurt a free-form language such as Turbo C++, but it sure helps the Turbo C++ *programmer* keep a better focus on the code.

If the implementation of your constructor appears outside the class header, there is no change in the syntax for the constructor initialization list. Listing 16.3 contains a rewritten version of the Inventory class with the constructor implementation put below the class header.

 Listing 16.3. Moving the body of the constructor.

```
1:  // Filename: CONSTCL3.CPP
2:  // A class with a constant member and constructor initialization
3:  #include <string.h>
4:  class Inventory {
5:    char name[25];
6:    int quantity;
7:    float price;
8:    const int initialQuantity;  // Original order's quantity
```

continues

Listing 16.3. continued

```
 9:   public:
10:     Inventory(char N[], int Q, float P, int I);
11:       // Rest of public members go here
12:   };
13:   // Notice that the initialization list must go with the
14:   // constructor's implementation, not the prototype above
15:   Inventory::Inventory(char N[], int Q, float P, int I)
16:                 : quantity(Q), price(P), initialQuantity(I)
17:   {
18:     strcpy(name, N);        // Array requires assignment
19:   }
```

DO   **DON'T**

DO familiarize yourself with constructor initialization lists and use them for all member initialization when your classes contain non-array members.

DO use assignment statements inside constructors, even those constructors that contain initialization lists, if you want to store data members on the heap, in arrays, or both.

DON'T use assignment statements in constructors to initialize constant or reference members.

Construct Base Classes First

A child class must take care of its parent class. That is, when you construct a child (a derived) class object, the child constructor must call the parent's (the base's) class constructor. The interrelationships of hierarchical inheritance is critical to proper construction of your derived objects.

It's easy to construct a base class object. No matter how many classes are derived from a base class, if you want to create a base class object variable, you can use the standard constructors or constructor initialization lists described until now in the book. Listing 16.4 shows a parent class named Parent and two child classes named Son and Daughter. main() then ignores the two derived classes and creates a base class object with a constructor from the base class.

Note: Base class destructors are just as straightforward as base class constructors. All the constructor/destructor material you've read to this point in the book works for base classes no matter how many classes are then derived from the base class.

Listing 16.4. Construct and destruct base class objects as usual.

```
1:  // Filename: PARENTCH.CPP
2:  // Constructs and destructs base class objects
3:  #include <iostream.h>
4:  #include <string.h>
5:  class Parent {
6:  protected:              // To allow inheritance
7:    char name[25];
8:    int age;
9:  public:
10:   Parent(char [], int);
11:   ~Parent() {};   // No body necessary because no heap work done
12:   void dispParent(void);
13:   // No overloaded output to keep program short
14: };
15: Parent::Parent(char N[], int A) : age(A) {
16:   strcpy(name, N);
17: }
18: void Parent::dispParent(void)
19: {
20:   cout << "Parent's name is " << name << "\n";
21:   cout << "Parent's age is " << age << "\n";
22: }
23: class Son : Parent {
24:   int yrInSchool;
25: public:
26:   void dispSon(void);
27: };
28: void Son::dispSon(void)
29: {
30:   cout << "Son's name is " << name << "\n";
31:   cout << "Son's age is " << age << "\n";
32: };
33: class Daughter : Parent {
34:   int yrInSchool;
35: public:
36:   void dispDaughter(void);
37: };
38: void Daughter::dispDaughter(void)
```

continues

Listing 16.4. continued

```
39: {
40:   cout << "Daughter's name is " << name << "\n";
41:   cout << "Daughter's age is " << age << "\n";
42: };
43: ///////////////////////////////////////////////////////////////////////
44: main()
45: {
46:   Parent mom("Bettye", 58); // Construct 2 parent class objects
47:   Parent dad("Glen", 57);
48:   // Print them to show they were properly constructed
49:   mom.dispParent();
50:   dad.dispParent();
51:   return 0;
52: }
```

```
Parent's name is Bettye
Parent's age is 58
Parent's name is Glen
Parent's age is 57
```

There's not much in this first rendition of the Parent hierarchy except for the normal constructor of the Parent on lines 15–17. The Parent constructor uses a constructor initialization list for the non-array member age and uses strcpy() to assign the initial name to the name member. The two Parent objects are constructed on lines 46 and 47 in the usual manner.

The next step would be the construction of Son and Daughter objects. Notice that each of these derived objects contains an extra member named yrInSchool that will have to be dealt with via a constructor. Remembering that constructors are never inherited, you'll have to define a constructor for the derived objects.

Things are not always as they might seem. Listing 16.5 contains code that appears to construct a Son object properly. The extra member, yrInSchool, is passed to the Son constructor function, and the constructor initializes the new yrInSchool member and the two inherited members.

Listing 16.5. Attempting to construct a derived class.

```
1: // Filename: PARENTSO.CPP
2: // Attempts to construct derived class objects
3: #include <iostream.h>
4: #include <string.h>
5: class Parent {
6: protected:                // To allow inheritance
```

```
7:     char name[25];
8:     int age;
9:  public:
10:    Parent(char [], int);
11:    ~Parent() {};    // No body necessary because no heap work done
12:    void dispParent(void);
13:    // No overloaded output to keep program short
14: };
15: Parent::Parent(char N[], int A) : age(A) {
16:    strcpy(name, N);
17: }
18: void Parent::dispParent(void)
19: {
20:    cout << "Parent's name is " << name << "\n";
21:    cout << "Parent's age is " << age << "\n";
22: }
23: class Son : Parent {
24:    int yrInSchool;
25: public:
26:    void dispSon(void);
27:    Son(char [], int, int);
28: };
29: Son::Son(char N[], int A, int Y)
30: {
31:    age = A;
32:    strcpy(name, N);
33:    yrInSchool = Y;
34: }
35: void Son::dispSon(void)
36: {
37:    cout << "Son's name is " << name << "\n";
38:    cout << "Son's age is " << age << "\n";
39:    cout << "Son's year in school is " << yrInSchool << "\n";
40: }
41:
42: class Daughter : Parent {
43:    int yrInSchool;
44: public:
45:    void dispDaughter(void);
46: };
47: void Daughter::dispDaughter(void)
48: {
49:    cout << "Daughter's name is " << name << "\n";
50:    cout << "Daughter's age is " << age << "\n";
51: };
52: //////////////////////////////////////////////////////////////////
53: main()
54: {
55:    Parent mom("Bettye", 58); // Construct 2 parent class objects
56:    Parent dad("Glen", 57);
```

continues

Listing 16.5. continued

```
57:    // Print them to show they were properly constructed
58:    mom.dispParent();
59:    dad.dispParent();
60:    Son boy("Luke", 17, 11);
61:    return 0;
62: }
```

The program in Listing 16.5 will not work. As a matter of fact, the program will not even compile. It looks as if line 60 properly constructs a Son object using the constructor on lines 29–34. The constructor is not accurate, however, because derived class constructors require extra considerations that base class constructors don't require.

When you attempt to compile this program, Turbo C++ displays the following message:

```
Error PARENTSO.CPP 30: Cannot find default constructor to initialize
➥base class 'Parent'
```

A derived class constructor cannot construct a derived object *until the parent is constructed*. A child class *must* construct the parent class.

> **Note:** It's easy to remember the parent-construction rule: in real life, a child cannot exist if the parent doesn't, and Turbo C++ wants to imitate real life!

Requiring the base class construction makes sense technically. After all, a child object inherits members and member functions from a parent, and that parent *has* to exist before there is anything to bring into the derived object. This does *not* mean that you have to construct a stand-alone base class object before constructing a derived class object. Although two Parent objects are constructed in Listing 16.5's lines 55 and 56 (or they *would* be constructed if the program compiled), no stand-alone Parent *object* has to exist before a Son object is constructed. However, a derived class constructor must first call the base class constructor to avoid the error message shown earlier.

Note: If a derived class is itself derived from another derived class (as in Figure 16.2), each derived class has to worry only about constructing its immediate parent. That parent, in turn, is responsible for constructing *its* parent, and so on.

16

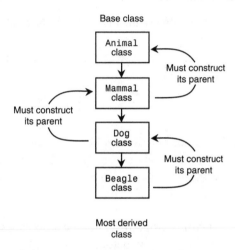

Figure 16.2. *A derived class must construct its immediate parent class.*

A derived class constructor must use constructor initialization lists to construct its parent class, or a default constructor must be supplied for the parent class. As is so often the case, a default constructor rarely works well because you want to initialize the members of the parent object that will appear in the derived object. Therefore, in most cases, a derived class will contain an initializer list item that is nothing more than a call to the parent class's constructor.

The Son constructor cannot directly assign values to the Parent class members as it is doing in Listing 16.5. Instead of trying to, like

```
Son::Son(char N[], int A, int Y)
{
  age = A;
  strcpy(name, N);
  yrInSchool = Y;
}
```

the Son constructor needs only to initialize a Parent class object like this:

```
Son::Son(char N[], int A, int Y) : Parent(N, A)
{
  yrInSchool = Y;
}
```

List the order of the base class constructor arguments in the same order as the base class constructor function arguments. If you rearrange them, the base class constructor arguments will receive incorrect values.

The Son's yrInSchool member is not an array, so it too could be added to the initializer list like this:

```
Son::Son(char N[], int A, int Y) : Parent(N, A), yrInSchool(Y)
{ // No body is necessary
}
```

Note: If the Son class contained additional members that were arrays or pointers to heap memory, the constructor body would contain additional code to set up those arrays and pointers.

After the Son constructor is properly set up, the following statement constructs a Son object because the base class constructor is now called during the Son's initialization:

```
Son boy("Luke", 17, 11);    // Construct a Son object
```

Adding a Daughter constructor is now trivial because it looks just like the Son class constructor. Listing 16.6 contains the proper base class initialization list for both the Son and the Daughter classes. The program also adds a character array member to the Daughter class to add code body to the Daughter's constructor.

 Listing 16.6. The derived classes properly construct the base class.

```
 1:  // Filename: PARENTFX.CPP
 2:  // Constructs base class objects properly
 3:  #include <iostream.h>
 4:  #include <string.h>
 5:  #include <conio.h>
 6:  class Parent {
 7:  protected:              // To allow inheritance
 8:     char name[25];
 9:     int age;
10:  public:
11:     Parent(char [], int);
12:     ~Parent() {};   // No body necessary because no heap work done
13:     void dispParent(void);
```

```
14:    // No overloaded output to keep program short
15: };
16: Parent::Parent(char N[], int A) : age(A) {
17:    strcpy(name, N);
18: }
19: void Parent::dispParent(void)
20: {
21:    cout << "Parent's name is " << name << "\n";
22:    cout << "Parent's age is " << age << "\n";
23: }
24: class Son : Parent {
25:    int yrInSchool;
26: public:
27:    void dispSon(void);
28:    Son(char [], int, int);
29: };
30: Son::Son(char N[], int A, int Y) : Parent(N, A), yrInSchool(Y)
31: {
32: }
33: void Son::dispSon(void)
34: {
35:    cout << "Son's name is " << name << "\n";
36:    cout << "Son's age is " << age << "\n";
37:    cout << "Son's year in school is " << yrInSchool << "\n";
38: }
39:
40: class Daughter : Parent {
41:    int yrInSchool;
42:    char friendsName[25];
43: public:
44:    Daughter(char [], int, int, char []);
45:    void dispDaughter(void);
46: };
47: Daughter::Daughter(char N[], int A, int Y, char F[]) :
48:                    Parent(N, A), yrInSchool(Y)
49: {
50:    strcpy(friendsName, F);
51: }
52: void Daughter::dispDaughter(void)
53: {
54:    cout << "Daughter's name is " << name << "\n";
55:    cout << "Daughter's age is " << age << "\n";
56:    cout << "Daughter's year in school is " << yrInSchool << "\n";
57:    cout << "Daughter's friend is " << friendsName << "\n";
58: };
59: //////////////////////////////////////////////////////////////////
60: main()
61: {
62:    Parent mom("Bettye", 58); // Construct 2 parent class objects
63:    Parent dad("Glen", 57);
64:    // Print them to show they were properly constructed
```

continues

Listing 16.6. continued

```
65:    clrscr();
66:    mom.dispParent();
67:    dad.dispParent();
68:    Son boy("Luke", 17, 11);
69:    boy.dispSon();
70:    Daughter girl("Jayne", 16, 10, "Melissa");
71:    girl.dispDaughter();
72:    return 0;
73: }
```

```
Parent's name is Bettye
Parent's age is 58
Parent's name is Glen
Parent's age is 57
Son's name is Luke
Son's age is 17
Son's year in school is 11
Daughter's name is Jayne
Daughter's age is 16
Daughter's year in school is 10
Daughter's friend is Melissa
```

From the output you can see that both Parent objects are properly constructed, and so are the Son and Daughter objects. The only way the two derived class objects could be constructed is for them to construct their parent class, and that's what they do. The Son constructs a Parent on line 30, and the Daughter constructs a Parent on line 48.

Notice how clean the two derived class listings are. Again, with inheritance, you don't have to repeat any of the members that appear in both classes as long as you properly construct the classes and make sure that a child class constructs a parent class.

Listing 16.7 contains an additional derived class named GrandChild. The GrandChild class derives from Girl. As you'll see in the GrandChild constructor, the GrandChild class has to worry only about properly constructing the Daughter class because the Daughter class is already set up to construct the Parent class properly.

Listing 16.7. Deriving a second class in the inheritance hierarchy.

```
1:   // Filename: GRANCHLD.CPP
2:   // Deriving classes from other derived classes
3:   #include <iostream.h>
4:   #include <iomanip.h>
5:   #include <string.h>
```

```
6:   #include <conio.h>
7:   class Parent {
8:   protected:              // To allow inheritance
9:     char name[25];
10:    int age;
11:  public:
12:    Parent(char [], int);
13:    ~Parent() {};    // No body necessary because no heap work done
14:    void dispParent(void);
15:    // No overloaded output to keep program short
16:  };
17:  Parent::Parent(char N[], int A) : age(A) {
18:    strcpy(name, N);
19:  }
20:  void Parent::dispParent(void)
21:  {
22:    cout << "Parent's name is " << name << "\n";
23:    cout << "Parent's age is " << age << "\n";
24:  }
25:  class Son : public Parent {
26:    int yrInSchool;
27:  public:
28:    void dispSon(void);
29:    Son(char [], int, int);
30:  };
31:  Son::Son(char N[], int A, int Y) : Parent(N, A), yrInSchool(Y)
32:  {
33:  }
34:  void Son::dispSon(void)
35:  {
36:    cout << "Son's name is " << name << "\n";
37:    cout << "Son's age is " << age << "\n";
38:    cout << "Son's year in school is " << yrInSchool << "\n";
39:  }
40:
41:  class Daughter : public Parent {
42:  // 'protected' was removed
43:    int yrInSchool;
44:    char friendsName[25];
45:  public:
46:    Daughter(char [], int, int, char []);
47:    Daughter(char [], int);
48:    void dispDaughter(void);
49:  };
50:  Daughter::Daughter(char N[], int A, int Y, char F[]) :
51:                   Parent(N, A), yrInSchool(Y)
52:  {
53:    strcpy(friendsName, F);
54:  }
55:  Daughter::Daughter(char N[], int A) : Parent(N, A)
56:  {  // No function body needed; the initialization list does it all
```

continues

Listing 16.7. continued

```
57: }
58: void Daughter::dispDaughter(void)
59: {
60:   cout << "Daughter's name is " << name << "\n";
61:   cout << "Daughter's age is " << age << "\n";
62:   cout << "Daughter's year in school is " << yrInSchool << "\n";
63:   cout << "Daughter's friend is " << friendsName << "\n";
64: };
65: class GrandChild : Daughter {
66:   float weightAtBirth;
67: public:
68:   GrandChild(char [], int, float);
69:   void dispGrand(void);
70: };
71: GrandChild::GrandChild(char N[], int A, float W) :
72:                       Daughter(N, A), weightAtBirth(W)
73: {  // Initialization list does it all
74: }
75: void GrandChild::dispGrand(void)
76: {
77:   cout << setprecision(1) << setiosflags(ios::fixed);
78:   cout << "Grandchild's name is " << name << "\n";
79:   cout << "Grandchild's age is " << age << "\n";
80:   cout << "Grandchild's weight at birth was " << weightAtBirth
        ➥<< "\n";
81: }
82: //////////////////////////////////////////////////////////////
83: main()
84: {
85:   clrscr();
86:   Daughter girl("Barbara", 22, 16, "Elizabeth");
87:   girl.dispDaughter();
88:   GrandChild baby("Suzie", 1, 7.5);
89:   baby.dispGrand();
90:   return 0;
91: }
```

```
Daughter's name is Barbara
Daughter's age is 22
Daughter's year in school is 16
Daughter's friend is Elizabeth
Grandchild's name is Suzie
Grandchild's age is 1
Grandchild's weight at birth was 7.5
```

A few changes had to be made to the `Daughter` class to allow the inheritance to the `GrandChild` class. The `public` receiving the access specifier was included when the `Daughter` inherited from the `Parent` in line 41 because the `GrandChild`

had to have access to the Parent's members too. (The public receiving access specifier was added to the Son class as well on line 25, but no other class derives from Son. However, if derived classes are ever added to the Son class, a public or protected keyword will be needed as the receiving access specifier.)

Back in Listing 16.6, there was no need to change the Daughter's receiving access from the private default because all of Daughter's inherited members could remain private; no other class would need the members. After the GrandChild class was added that needed access to the Daughter's members, however, the public keyword ensured that all protected and public inherited members from Parent would remain protected and public respectively when they get to Daughter. The Daughter can then pass on those members (perhaps *traits* would be a more appropriate term) to the GrandChild.

> **Note:** Figure 16.3 shows the contents of the GrandChild class and explains where each member comes from.

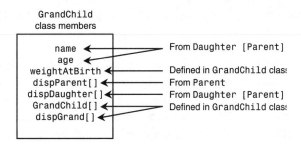

Figure 16.3. *The origin of the GrandChild class members.*

Figure 16.3 does raise a few questions that are easily answered. For example, all of Parent and Daughter's public member functions are inherited along with the data members. You would never want to apply the dispParent() or dispDaughter() function to a GrandChild object, but the inheritance makes these functions available anyway.

There is a simple solution to this situation. Give all the display functions, in each class, the *same name.* If all the functions were named display(), the following four statements would each produce different results:

```
mom.display();    // Call Parent class's display()
boy.display();    // Call Son class's display()
girl.display();   // Call Daughter class's display()
baby.display();   // Call GrandChild class's display()
```

The `display()` function in each derived class would replace the one that would otherwise be inherited if the display function names were all different, as they are in Listing 16.7. By using the same member function names for similar functions, you decrease the amount of function names you have to deal with and thus simplify your programming. Turbo C++ calls the correct function based on the object that triggers the call.

In a way, giving derived function names the same names as a parent's function names limits the inheritance. The derived class function replaces the one that would otherwise come from the parent. You can also limit the inheritance of data members by giving them the same name in a derived class. If you override their receiving access (as explained in the section of yesterday's chapter entitled "Overriding the Receiving Access"), you can change the access of a derived data member or member function as well. (Sometimes, changing or limiting the derived members is called *disabling the inheritance*.)

Note: The common function names would not clash because all members of a class have class scope, not block, function, or file scope.

Doesn't the `main()` function in Listing 16.7 provide a very high-level view of the program? It's almost as if `main()` were written in a non-C-like language because of its style. After the screen clears, a `Daughter` object is created and displays, then a `GrandChild` object is created and displays. Besides making it easy to understand what each argument means (for instance, the second `Daughter` argument is the age, the third is the number of years in school), `main()` is such that a nonprogrammer can *almost* look at it and describe what the program is doing. More important, a programmer can look at `main()` and quickly and reliably interpret what the program is doing. The real value does not lie in apparent understanding by nonprogrammers, but in real understanding by actual programmers.

When you add functionality through inheritance to your classes, you can improve your programming productivity tremendously. All the petty details are gone. A huge benefit of inheritance appears during program maintenance. If the `Parent` class changes, the change ripples through the rest of the inheritance hierarchy. For example, if you decide to store the `Parent`'s name member on the heap, you only have to change the `Parent` constructor and recompile the program. No derived class changes because Turbo C++ keeps classes encapsulated and inherits whatever needs to be inherited automatically.

What About Destructors?

The example built throughout today's chapter doesn't concentrate on destructors for these two reasons:

☐ No destructor code was really needed because nothing was allocated on the heap.

☐ Turbo C++ handles destructing the inheritance hierarchy for you, unlike constructors, which you must specifically construct in a sequential manner (up the hierarchy) as shown in today's chapter.

If you don't supply a destructor for any or all classes in a hierarchy, Turbo C++ uses a default destructor to get rid of the objects when they go out of scope. If the heap is not involved in the program, the default destructor works fine. If you supply a destructor, however, for any or all objects, Turbo C++ calls the one you supply.

As Figure 16.4 illustrates, Turbo C++ automatically destructs the child before its parent. (The parent always outlives the child in OOP.) Destructors are called in the opposite order of constructor calls. You never call destructors explicitly, even when inheritance is involved, because there can be one and only one destructor for any class (either yours or a default destructor), and Turbo C++ knows to call a class destructor when an object goes out of scope.

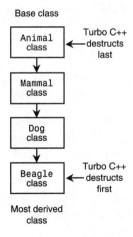

Figure 16.4. *Destructors are called in the opposite sequence of constructors.*

DO　　　　　　　　　　　　　　　　　　**DON'T**

DO use the same order in constructor initialization argument lists as the parent class's constructor argument list so that the proper values get sent to the parent's constructor function.

DO construct base classes before derived classes.

DO use the same data member or member name in a derived class as in the parent class if you want to change or limit the functionality of the inherited member.

DON'T call destructors, even when inheritance is involved. Unlike with constructors, Turbo C++ automatically handles destructing your inherited objects automatically, from the most derived class to the parent class.

Summary

Today's chapter showed you how to utilize inheritance by constructing and destructing derived class objects. It is the job of the derived class to construct its parent. (Turbo C++ makes sure that the derived class is destructed first.) Only after the parent class is constructed can a child class be constructed because only then will the parent's members be available to the derived class.

There are two ways to construct a parent class:

☐ Supply a default constructor in the parent class. When you do, Turbo C++ calls the default constructor before a derived class object is constructed.

☐ Trigger the parent class's constructor through an initialization list. This approach is by far the most common because the parent constructor almost always needs values passed to it when a derived class object is constructed.

Initialization lists not only are helpful for constructing derived classes, but they also help you construct objects that contain constant members and reference members. Initialization lists ensure that an object's members are initialized when the object is defined, not afterward.

This chapter walked you through the building of an inheritance program by constructing the parent class using the second method just described. To keep things as obvious as possible, terms such as `Parent`, `Son`, `Daughter`, and `GrandChild` were used as class names so that you could more easily concentrate on the inheritance structure.

Without initialization lists, a child object could never be constructed (unless a more limiting default constructor was used). The parent must be constructed *before* the child, and initialization, not assignment, is the only way to accomplish that.

Inheritance plays a critical role in program writing and maintenance. Being able to inherit classes simplifies your programming after you master constructing specifics. You can make changes to a parent class without having to make those same changes to the child class.

Q&A

1. Why must a child class worry about constructing a parent class?

   A derived class cannot exist until the parent is constructed. The parent's members cannot be passed along to the child (the derived) class until the parent's members are constructed.

   Whenever you write a constructor for a derived class, you must always provide a constructor initialization list or a default constructor in the parent class.

2. Sometimes, the base class exists solely for deriving other classes, not for instantiating objects of its own. Do I still have to construct a parent class in the derived classes?

   Yes. Even when a base class is not to be used for instantiating object variables, you must still provide a constructor initialization list in each derived class or provide a default constructor for the parent class. A parent class *must* be constructed before a derived class can exist.

3. How can I ensure that destructors are called in the proper order?

   You don't have to. That's the beauty of Turbo C++. All destructors will automatically be called in the reverse order of the constructors. In other words, a child's destructor always executes before the parent's.

   If you don't need a destructor, Turbo C++ calls a default destructor for you. If you supply some destructors in an inheritance hierarchy, but not a destructor for all the classes in the inheritance chain, Turbo C+ calls your destructor when one is there and calls the default destructor when it cannot find a destructor that you've coded.

Workshop

The Workshop offers quiz questions and exercises to hone your skills and give you feedback on today's lesson. You'll find some proposed answers in Appendix D.

Quiz

1. True or false: If a parent class *and* a child class contain default constructors, no explicit construction has to take place.

2. Why can a regular constructor not be used to construct when a class contains a constant member?

3. Where do initialization lists go?

4. True or false: Both constant members and reference members require constructor initialization lists.

5. What is wrong with this derived class's constructor?

```
class A {
  int i;
  float x;
public:
  A(int I, float X);
};
class B : public A {
  char c;
public:
  B(int I, float X, char C) : A(X, I), c(C) {};
};
```

6. What is the order of constructors in this inheritance hierarchy?

```
class A {
  int i;
public:
  A(int I);
};
class B : public A {
  int j;
public:
  B(int I, int J) : A(I), j(J) {};
```

```
};
class C : public B {
  int k;
public:
  C(int I, int J, int K) : B(I, J), k(K) {};
};
```

   A. A, B, C

   B. C, B, A

   C. Cannot be determined

7. In the inheritance hierarchy of question 6, what is the order of destructor calls?

   A. A, B, C

   B. C, B, A

   C. Cannot be determined

8. What do you do to make Turbo C++ destruct an inheritance hierarchy properly?

Exercises

1. Change all the character arrays in the Parent inheritance hierarchy (Listing 16.7) to character pointers, and initialize the arrays on the heap. You'll need to add proper destructors that deallocate the heap memory when the program finishes with the objects. Create a Parent object, a Son object, a Daughter object, and a GrandChild object to test your program.

   It's important to realize that by changing the class storage mechanism from a memory array to the heap, main() doesn't require anything new from what it would require if you left the names arrays. By doing this exercise, you should begin to see how writing OOP programs increases your productivity tremendously. You can make changes to a class without changing the code that uses that class. When you begin programming database structures, linked lists, and double-linked lists, you'll soon realize that this separation of code (main() and the functions that main() calls) from the storage and implementation of the class decreases programming problems by many factors. If the storage method changed for a non-OOP program, the entire program would have to be scoured for every reference in the code to the storage mechanism used.

Extra: Make the class extremely easy to use by naming all the object-printing routines with the same name, display(). (You could also overload << to output the objects, but the amount of data being displayed probably doesn't warrant an overloaded operator<< function for each class.)

2. Add a Pet class to the Parent hierarchy. Inherit a Pet from the Parent class (it's stretching things a bit, but that's OK), and add a new member to the Pet class named peopleYears. (We're assuming that the pet will always be a dog for this exercise to work as described.) In the Pet constructor, multiply the age of the Pet by seven, and store the result in the peopleYears member. All Pet objects will now carry their actual age in dog years and their corresponding age to people in peopleYears.

Data
Composition

Today's chapter teaches a new concept that is closely related to inheritance and is often confused with inheritance: *composition*. Composition is nothing more than embedding one class within another.

The reason people confuse composition and inheritance is that they both rely on other classes to build new classes. When you're using composition, the new class does not inherit anything, but rather, the new class *contains* another class. Composition still builds new classes from existing ones, but instead of inheriting members, the new class *contains* the other class in its entirety.

This introduction might still leave you confused, but in a few pages, you'll have no trouble distinguishing between inheritance and composition. The syntax you use for each is different, and the design of your classes requires that you know the difference between inheritance and composition so that you'll know when and how to use one or the other.

Today, you learn about the following topics:

- [ ] When to use composition over inheritance
- [ ] The *is-a* and *has-a* questions
- [ ] How to compose one class from another
- [ ] Composition's construction and destruction concerns
- [ ] Assigning composed objects to one another

Note: As you saw in yesterday's inheritance chapter, the primary difficulty when using composition is getting the constructing and destructing done properly. The embedded class must be constructed properly before it can be used inside another class.

Composition vs. Inheritance

Consider for a moment a new Turbo C++ programmer writing a program to keep track of a homemade ice-cream parlor's inventory. The store specializes in Italian *gelato* ice-cream cones, the tastiest, richest ice cream on earth. In talking to the owners and in thinking about the components of the inventory, the programmer learns that the shop purchases cream in bulk to make the ice cream. The program is to keep track of the amount and quality of cream bought.

The store also purchases sugar, filtered water, and cones. Each of these ice-cream cone ingredients must be tracked separately (in its own class), and the program also must keep track of the number of ice-cream cones sold.

The programmer, knowing all the advantages of Turbo C++ code reuse, knows that after a class for the cream is defined, and after a class for the sugar is defined, and after a class for all the rest of the ingredients is defined, it would be a waste of time to repeat all those members inside the ice-cream cone class. Therefore, after defining a class for each of the ingredients, the programmer decides to inherit an ice-cream cone class from those classes already defined.

What do you suppose the base class should be? Sugar? Cream? There's a problem here. None of the ingredients seems to be the "base" class, even though they do all make ice-cream cones in the long run. There is sugar in an ice-cream cone, but an ice-cream cone doesn't seem to derive from sugar.

Should the programmer code the ice-cream cone class and then derive all the other ingredient classes from it? No, because there are no ice-cream cones in sugar. The programmer is stumped and believes that he will throw out all the inheritance knowledge and write a separate but overlapping ice-cream cone class. The programmer gets the program to work and presents the inventory system to the owners, but the programmer opened himself up to more maintenance nightmares than would otherwise be the case because there was no reuse of code. If the store changes to fat-free yogurt and stops keeping cream in stock, the ice-cream cone class *and* the class that handles the cream must be revised. If code reuse had been programmed into the system, the cream class could be converted to a yogurt culture class, and the ice-cream cone instantly becomes a yogurt cone.

This ice-cream parlor situation is more common than it might seem here, especially in inventory systems. Lots of times, component parts combine to form a larger item, and both the component parts and the items made from those parts must be tracked. Inheritance, however, is not the OOP solution to the duplication of class data. As you just saw, it is impossible to define a base class when all the classes seem to have equal significance. Also, many of the classes (for instance, sugar, cream, and empty cones) don't derive from each other, so they should not be part of a long inheritance hierarchy.

Note: If you are wondering whether multiple inheritance could offer a solution, you *could* possibly code the ice-cream cone class with all those ingredient classes as the multiple parent classes of the ice-cream cone class. If you do, however, good luck! Having two parent classes creates lots of programming difficulties. Having more than two parent classes creates lots of programming migraines! Luckily, you're about to see a way to resolve this seemingly unsolvable problem without using inheritance.

Instead of inheriting the ice-cream cone class from all the ingredients, the programmer correctly decides to try composition. A composed class contains members that are other classes. See whether composition works: An ice-cream cone is *composed* of cream, sugar, filtered water, and cones. Those raw ingredients are part of the ice-cream cone. An ice-cream cone has all of those ingredients, so therefore, an ice-cream cone is *composed* of those ingredients.

None of the previous paragraphs contained the awkwardness you found when trying to inherit an ice-cream cone from those ingredients. Remember that it was impossible to determine what the base class ingredient would be. However, when you change the wording and say the ice-cream cone contains, or more accurately is *composed* of, the ingredients, everything begins to sound fine.

The terms *is-a* and *has-a* explain in a nutshell the difference between inheritance and composition. The following axioms describe the relationship between *is-a* questions, *has-a* questions, *inheritance,* and *composition:*

1. A class that has another class or more than one class inside it is a *composed* class. The *has-a* question tells you so. If one class *has* another class, use composition and embed the component class inside the surrounding class. An ice-cream cone contains sugar, but an ice-cream cone would never be thought of as an advanced form of sugar. See Figure 17.1.

2. A class that derives from another class has all the properties of that first class plus a few additional properties. The *is-a* question tells you so. If the derived class *is* another class with a few extra members, use inheritance. The ice-cream cone is *not* the same thing as sugar with a few other ingredients thrown in because none of the properties of sugar matches those of an ice-cream cone. An ice-cream cone is not room temperature. An ice-cream cone is not granular. An ice-cream cone is not always sugar-colored.

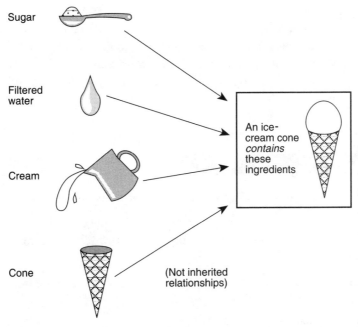

Sugar

Filtered water

Cream

An ice-cream cone *contains* these ingredients

Cone

(Not inherited relationships)

17

Figure 17.1. *An ice-cream cone class would contain all the other classes, not be derived from them.*

Consider an additional ice-cream parlor requirement that the program track low-sugar ice-cream cones, regular ice-cream cones, and super-sugar ice-cream cones. A good case could be made that all three of these classes could be *derived* from each other. The base class could be a low-sugar ice-cream cone, and each derived class could add another sugar ingredient along the way. Such classes probably would benefit from inheritance, but the first class, the low-sugar class, would be formed through composition.

What about an ice-cream sundae class? The sundae class would form best through composition because a sundae contains (*has-a*) ice-cream and also contains (*has-a*) toppings.

Will Either Work?

It's true, especially if you're willing to use multiple inheritance (and spend some long nights of debugging instead of being home with the kids), that you *could* use either composition or inheritance to write virtually any class that relates to other classes. However, the *is-a* and *has-a* question tests always produce a more natural result than guessing wrong.

For example, even though you could have written the ice-cream cone class using multiple inheritance, an ice-cream cone more accurately has all those ingredients and does not derive from those ingredients. The *has-a* question tells the programmer that composition is right for the ice-cream cones.

DO	DON'T

DO use composition when one class contains other classes.

DO use inheritance when one class forms a natural extension of another class, forming the same class but improved with additional functionality or characteristics.

DO use the *is-a* and *has-a* questions to decide whether to use inheritance or composition.

DON'T use multiple inheritance to replace the easier composition, even though both sometimes seem to work just as well for certain classes. Not only is composition clearer, but it is easier to code. (This book doesn't even show you how to code multiple inheritance because it's rarely if ever needed.)

Composing with Code

As with inheritance, the trickiest part of composition is knowing how to construct the embedded class objects. However, setting up a class with an embedded member is easy.

The next few example listings will compose a stereo class describing an electronics store's stereo inventory. A stereo is the perfect example of composition because it is composed of many parts that could stand apart by themselves, such as a CD player, a turntable, a receiver, and speakers. As a matter of fact, the stereo industry calls those parts of a stereo system *components*.

> **Note:** The ice-cream class requires too many conversions such as gallons, scoops, number of cones, and so on to code easily here. Even for simple example listings, the details of coding the ice-cream inventory would cloud the composition tutorial. The ice-cream description, however, was a good introduction to composition and explained the problems involved with trying to inherit everything. In addition, it makes one's mouth water just thinking about it!

Starting with the individual component classes, Listing 17.1 contains the class code for receivers, CD players, and speakers.

 Listing 17.1. The components of a future stereo class.

```
1:  // Filename: COMPHEAD.CPP
2:  // Classes for stereo components
3:  #include <iostream.h>
4:  #include <iomanip.h>
5:  #include <string.h>
6:  class Receiver {
7:     int watts;    // Watts per channel power
8:     float price;
9:     char * brand;
10: public:
11:    Receiver(int, float, char *);
12:    ~Receiver();
13:    friend ostream & operator<<(ostream &, const Receiver &);
14: };
15: Receiver::Receiver(int W, float P, char * B) : watts(W), price(P)
16: {
17:    brand = new char[strlen(B) + 1];
18:    strcpy(brand, B);
19: }
20: Receiver::~Receiver()
21: {
22:    delete [] brand;
23: }
24: ostream & operator<<(ostream & out, const Receiver & r)
25: {
26:    out << setiosflags(ios::fixed) << setiosflags(ios::showpoint);
27:    out << setprecision(2);
28:    out << "Receiver brand: " << r.brand << "\n";
29:    out << "Receiver price: $" << r.price << "  Watts per channel: ";
30:    out << r.watts << "\n";
31:    return out;
32: }
```

continues

Listing 17.1. continued

```
33: // Next class follows
34: class CD {
35:   int numOfCDs;  // Some combo CD players play 6 or more CDs
36:   float price;
37:   char * brand;
38: public:
39:   CD(int, float, char *);
40:   ~CD();
41:    friend ostream & operator<<(ostream &, const CD &);
42: };
43: CD::CD(int N, float P, char * B) : numOfCDs(N), price(P)
44: {
45:   brand = new char[strlen(B) + 1];
46:   strcpy(brand, B);
47: }
48: CD::~CD()
49: {
50:   delete [] brand;
51: }
52: ostream & operator<<(ostream & out, const CD & c)
53: {
54:   out << setiosflags(ios::fixed) << setiosflags(ios::showpoint);
55:   out << setprecision(2);
56:   out << "CD player brand: " << c.brand << "\n";
57:   out << "CD price: $" << c.price << "Number of CDs: ";
58:   out << c.numOfCDs << "\n";
59:   return out;
60: }
61: // Next class follows
62: class Speaker {
63:   int maxLoad;  // Amount of maximum wattage allowed
64:   float price;
65:   char * brand;
66: public:
67:   Speaker(int, float, char *);
68:   ~Speaker();
69:   friend ostream & operator<<(ostream &, const Speaker &);
70: };
71: Speaker::Speaker(int M, float P, char * B) : maxLoad(M), price(P)
72: {
73:   brand = new char[strlen(B) + 1];
74:   strcpy(brand, B);
75: }
76: Speaker::~Speaker()
77: {
78:   delete [] brand;
79: }
80: ostream & operator <<(ostream & out, const Speaker & s)
81: {
```

```
82:    out << setiosflags(ios::fixed) << setiosflags(ios::showpoint);
83:    out << setprecision(2);
84:    out << "Speaker brand: " << s.brand << "\n";
85:    out << "Speaker price (each): $" << s.price
    ➥<< "  Max. Num. of Watts: ";
86:    out << s.maxLoad << "\n";
87:    return out;
88: }
```

 There is nothing new in this class that you haven't already seen. Each of the three stereo component classes contains three member functions that describe the characteristics of each class, Receiver, CD, and Speaker. Obviously, the next few listings will pull these three stand-alone classes into a combined composed stereo class.

 Note: Always include all the built-in header files, such as STRING.H, that your class needs to work correctly. The program using the class might not include those header files, and therefore, the target program would generate compile errors when it included your class and the needed prototyping built-in header files aren't brought in. Due to internal checking mechanisms inside each built-in header file, Turbo C++ makes sure that a header file is not included more than once, even if both your class and the program using the class attempt to include the same header file.

Before working on the composition of the stereo class, can you see any improvement in these classes? Any time you see a big similarity between classes you've coded, consider using either inheritance or composition to streamline things. It turns out that the component classes can be improved through inheritance, and then that inheritance will be used inside another class for composition of a conglomerate class.

Each of these component classes contains a price and brand member. Therefore, all three of these components could come from a higher-level parent class named Component. The Component doesn't ever have to be instantiated into a class object, but it would remove a lot of the duplicity from the three component classes.

Before seeing the listing that contains a higher parent class, see whether you can write the code to do the same thing on your own. You know more than enough about access specifiers, receiving access specifiers, and constructor initialization lists to create a base class that contains the other classes' common code.

Listing 17.2 contains rewritten stereo class hierarchy. Although there will never be a generic Component object, the Component base class helps group the other classes and makes updating easier if you ever want to increase the number of common members or change the storage mechanism of the brand member.

 Listing 17.2. Pulling similarities into a single base class.

```
1:  // Filename: STERINHE.CPP
2:  // Classes for stereo components with inheritance
3:  #include <iostream.h>
4:  #include <iomanip.h>
5:  #include <string.h>
6:  class Component {     // No objects of base class need
7:  protected:            // to ever be instantiated
8:    float price;
9:    char * brand;
10: public:
11:   Component(float, char *);
12:   ~Component();
13: };
14: // Only price can be initialized, the brand
15: // must be assigned in the body
16: Component::Component(float P, char * B) : price(P)
17: {
18:   brand = new char[strlen(B) + 1];
19:   strcpy(brand, B);
20: }
21: Component::~Component()
22: {
23:   delete [] brand;  // Isn't it nice that you don't have to
24: }                   // worry about deallocation in main()?
25: // Component classes begin next
26: class Receiver : public Component {
27:   int watts;   // Watts per channel power
28: public:
29:   Receiver(int, float, char *);
30:   ~Receiver() {}   // No destructor code needed
31:   friend ostream & operator<<(ostream &, const Receiver &);
32: };
33: // Use an initialization list to construct base object and member
34: Receiver::Receiver(int W, float P, char * B)
    ➡: Component(P, B), watts(W)
35: {  // The constructor gets easy
36: }
37: ostream & operator<<(ostream & out, const Receiver & r)
38: {
39:   out << setiosflags(ios::fixed) << setiosflags(ios::showpoint);
40:   out << setprecision(2);
```

```
41:    out << "Receiver brand: " << r.brand << "\n";
42:    out << "Receiver price: $" << r.price << "  Watts per channel: ";
43:    out << r.watts << "\n";
44:    return out;
45: }
46: // Next component class follows
47: class CD : public Component {
48:    int numOfCDs;  // Some combo CD players play 6 or more CDs
49: public:
50:    CD(int, float, char *);
51:    ~CD() {}  // No destructor code needed
52:     friend ostream & operator<<(ostream &, const CD &);
53: };
54: CD::CD(int N, float P, char * B) : Component(P, B), numOfCDs(N)
55: { // The constructor gets easy
56: }
57: ostream & operator<<(ostream & out, const CD & c)
58: {
59:    out << setiosflags(ios::fixed) << setiosflags(ios::showpoint);
60:    out << setprecision(2);
61:    out << "CD player brand: " << c.brand << "\n";
62:    out << "CD price: $" << c.price << "  Number of CDs: ";
63:    out << c.numOfCDs << "\n";
64:    return out;
65: }
66: // Next component class follows
67: class Speaker : public Component {
68:    int maxLoad;  // Amount of maximum wattage allowed
69: public:
70:    Speaker(int, float, char *);
71:    ~Speaker() {}  // No destructor code needed
72:    friend ostream & operator<<(ostream &, const Speaker &);
73: };
74: Speaker::Speaker(int M, float P, char * B)
    ➥: Component(P, B), maxLoad(M)
75: { // The constructor gets easy
76: }
77: ostream & operator <<(ostream & out, const Speaker & s)
78: {
79:    out << setiosflags(ios::fixed) << setiosflags(ios::showpoint);
80:    out << setprecision(2);
81:    out << "Speaker brand: " << s.brand << "\n";
82:    out << "Speaker price (each): $" << s.price
    ➥<< "  Max. Num. of Watts: ";
83:    out << s.maxLoad << "\n";
84:    return out;
85: }
```

17

Figure 17.2 shows the inheritance hierarchy developed in Listing 17.2. The first half of the stereo class is now in place; the inheritance of each of the individual components form a common base class component. The listing offers you nothing new yet, but the stereo (the composition of all the components) has yet to be defined.

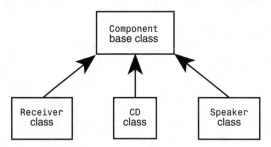

Figure 17.2. *The* Component *class helps derive each of the specific stereo components.*

Note: Can't you see that now a receiver *is-a* component (pardon the grammar!), a CD player *is-a* component, and a set of speakers *is-a* component? Even newcomers to inheritance and composition find that the distinction is obvious when asked the *is-a* and *has-a* design questions. The final stereo class will contain both inheritance and composition as shown in the next program.

It's important to reinforce the idea that Stereo is not inherited from the component classes. If it were, you would have a tremendous multiple inheritance programming nightmare attempting to code the class as shown in Figure 17.3. Instead of being inherited from the component classes, Stereo contains the component classes.

Listing 17.3 contains the class header for the stereo class. Along with the integer, floating-point, and character pointer members, there are three members that are complete classes; in other words, three of the Stereo members are objects from other classes.

Component
class

Receiver
class

CD
class

Speaker
class

Stereo
class

Figure 17.3. *If* Stereo *were inherited, you would end up with a strange inheritance hierarchy.*

Listing 17.3. **Stereo class header composed of the other classes.**

```
1:  class Stereo {
2:      int wireLength;
3:      float priceToInstall;
4:      char * systemCode;        // For inventory        These members
5:      Receiver tuner;                                   are other classes
6:      CD discPlayer;
7:      Speaker speakers;         // Notice spelling and case difference
8:  public:
9:      // Member functions such as constructor and destructor go next
10: };
```

If you're wondering what the fuss is all about, you've probably used composition before without even realizing it. In regular non-OOP C, you can embed a structure within another structure as done in this listing with classes.

Although the term *composition* is usually not used for embedded structures, composition is exactly what's going on. The reason so much attention to composition is being focused on here is that constructors and destructors must play a part in proper OOP composition. The following rule holds true:

> *An object composed of other objects, such as* Stereo, *cannot be constructed until all its member objects are constructed.*

511

Notice that you don't have to face all the inheritance syntax when composing classes (lines 5–7 in Listing 17.3). You must, however, supply constructor initialization lists that take care of all the member objects before the composed object will be constructed. Therefore, composition is easier than inheritance because there is no inheriting class to contend with, but constructing composed classes involves some extra considerations that you don't have to worry with when working with non-composed classes.

When constructing a composed object, you must include each composed object's constructor initialization list inside the composed class definition line. Listing 17.4 shows a program that properly constructs a `Stereo` class. As you will see, the constructor's definition line is often longer than the body of the constructor. (Of course, long constructor definition lines are common after you begin using constructor initialization lists, even when no inheritance or composition is involved.) As you scan through Listing 17.4, watch for these things:

1. The `main()` code must pass enough initial data to the constructor to construct the entire `Stereo` class. Later in today's chapter, you'll learn a shortcut that helps shorten such long initialization lists.

2. Turbo C++ makes sure that the initialization lists construct the member objects before the composed object's construction is begun.

3. The `Stereo` class contains a huge constructor initialization list because of the three object class members: `Receiver`, `CD`, and `Speaker`. Although a smaller stereo system could have been created first to keep things simpler (perhaps composed on only a `Receiver` class), you should have little problem tracing the long `Stereo` constructor initialization list by now.

4. If default constructors had been supplied for each of the components, no constructor initialization list would be necessary in the `Stereo` definition line. With the default constructors, Turbo C++ could have constructed the object members without your doing anything special. However, such generic constructions are rare when using composition and would do little to teach you composition at this point.

Listing 17.4. Constructing and using `Stereo` objects that are composed of other objects.

```
1:  // Filename: STERCOMP.CPP
2:  // Classes for stereo components with inheritance
3:  #include <iostream.h>
4:  #include <iomanip.h>
5:  #include <string.h>
```

```
6:    #include <conio.h>
7:    class Component {     // No objects of base class ever
8:    protected:             // need to be instantiated
9:      float price;
10:     char * brand;
11:   public:
12:     Component(float, char *);
13:     ~Component();
14:   };
15:   // Only price can be initialized, the brand
16:   // must be assigned in the body
17:   Component::Component(float P, char * B) : price(P)
18:   {
19:     brand = new char[strlen(B) + 1];
20:     strcpy(brand, B);
21:   }
22:   Component::~Component()
23:   {
24:     delete [] brand;   // Isn't it nice that you don't have to
25:   }                     // worry about deallocation in main()?
26:   // Component classes begin next
27:   class Receiver : public Component {
28:     int watts;    // Watts per channel power
29:   public:
30:     Receiver(int, float, char *);
31:     ~Receiver() {}    // No destructor code needed
32:     friend ostream & operator<<(ostream &, const Receiver &);
33:   };
34:   // Use an initialization list to construct base object and member
35:   Receiver::Receiver(int W, float P, char * B) :
      ➥Component(P, B), watts(W)
36:   {  // The constructor gets easy
37:   }
38:   ostream & operator<<(ostream & out, const Receiver & r)
39:   {
40:     out << setiosflags(ios::fixed) << setiosflags(ios::showpoint);
41:     out << setprecision(2);
42:     out << "Receiver brand: " << r.brand << "\n";
43:     out << "Receiver price: $" << r.price << "  Watts per channel: ";
44:     out << r.watts << "\n";
45:     return out;
46:   }
47:   // Next component class follows
48:   class CD : public Component {
49:     int numOfCDs;   // Some combo CD players play 6 or more CDs
50:   public:
51:     CD(int, float, char *);
52:     ~CD() {}   // No destructor code needed
53:     friend ostream & operator<<(ostream &, const CD &);
54:   };
55:   CD::CD(int N, float P, char * B) : Component(P, B), numOfCDs(N)
```

continues

Listing 17.4. continued

```
56: { // The constructor gets easy
57: }
58: ostream & operator<<(ostream & out, const CD & c)
59: {
60:    out << setiosflags(ios::fixed) << setiosflags(ios::showpoint);
61:    out << setprecision(2);
62:    out << "CD player brand: " << c.brand << "\n";
63:    out << "CD price: $" << c.price << "  Number of CDs: ";
64:    out << c.numOfCDs << "\n";
65:    return out;
66: }
67: // Next component class follows
68: class Speaker : public Component {
69:    int maxLoad;  // Amount of maximum wattage allowed
70: public:
71:    Speaker(int, float, char *);
72:    ~Speaker() {}  // No destructor code needed
73:    friend ostream & operator<<(ostream &, const Speaker &);
74: };
75: Speaker::Speaker(int M, float P, char * B) :
      ➡Component(P, B), maxLoad(M)
76: { // The constructor gets easy
77: }
78: ostream & operator <<(ostream & out, const Speaker & s)
79: {
80:    out << setiosflags(ios::fixed) << setiosflags(ios::showpoint);
81:    out << setprecision(2);
82:    out << "Speaker brand: " << s.brand << "\n";
83:    out << "Speaker price (each): $" << s.price
      ➡<< "  Max. Num. of Watts: ";
84:    out << s.maxLoad << "\n";
85:    return out;
86: }
87: class Stereo {
88:    char * systemCode;     // For inventory
89:    int wireLength;
90:    float priceToInstall;
91:    Receiver tuner;
92:    CD discPlayer;
93:    Speaker speakers;      // Notice spelling and case difference
94: public:
95:    Stereo(char *, int, float, int, float, char *,
96:           int, float, char *, int, float, char *);
97:    ~Stereo();
98:    friend ostream & operator<<(ostream &, const Stereo &);
99: };
100: // Here comes the HUGE constructor initialization list
101: Stereo::Stereo(char * SC, int WL, float PI, int RW, float RP,
102:           char * RB, int NCD, float CP, char * CB, int ML, float SP,
```

```
103:            char * SB) : tuner(RW, RP, RB), discPlayer(NCD, CP, CB),
           ➡speakers(ML, SP, SB),
104:             wireLength(WL), priceToInstall(PI)
105: {
106:   systemCode = new char[strlen(SC) + 1];
107:   strcpy(systemCode, SC);
108: }
109: Stereo::~Stereo()
110: {
111:   delete [] systemCode;
112: }
113: ostream & operator<<(ostream & out, const Stereo & s)
114: {
115:   // Can use overloaded functions from elsewhere
116:   out << "Here's the stereo system:\n";
117:   out << "System code: " << s.systemCode << "\n";
118:   out << "Wire length: " << s.wireLength;
119:   out << "\tInstallation price: $" << s.priceToInstall << "\n";
120:   out << "Components follow:\n";
121:   out << s.tuner << s.discPlayer << s.speakers;
122:   return out;
123: }
124: /////////////////////////////////////////////////////////////////
125: // It took a lot of work to get to main()!
126: main()
127: {
128:   clrscr();
129:   Stereo system("HI42", 50, 75.00, 200, 450.00, "HiFi-HiTech", 6,
           ➡325.00,
130:                "Disc Supreme", 350, 275.00, "Acoustic Output");
131:   cout << system;
132:   return 0;
133:}
```

```
Here's the stereo system:
System code: HI42
Wire length: 50 Installation price: $75
Components follow:
Receiver brand: HiFi-HiTech
Receiver price: $450.00  Watts per channel: 200
CD player brand: Disc Supreme
CD price: $325.00  Number of CDs: 6
Speaker brand: Acoustic Output
Speaker price (each): $275.00  Max. Num. of Watts: 350
```

Analysis The most important set of lines in the program is 101–108. These lines construct a Stereo object by actually constructing several components that make up the Stereo object. To help you understand what is going on in the constructor, Figure 17.4 labels the parts of the constructor to show you what all the arguments mean.

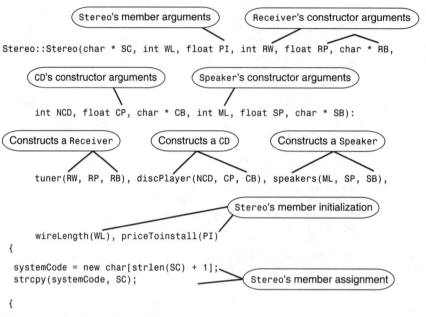

Figure 17.4. *An analysis of the* `Stereo` *constructor.*

Look at the output statement on line 131. The overloaded `operator<<()` function in lines 113–123 handle the output. You might think that line 121 is rather simplistic. All the `Receiver`, `CD`, and `Speaker` classes contain overloaded `operator<<()` functions, and those classes' objects (and therefore, their overloaded `operator<<()` functions) are already constructed. Therefore, the `Stereo` class's `operator<<()` can output the component objects using a simple `<<` operator.

Note: As a matter of fact, the `Stereo` class could not print the individual member values of the component parts any other way than through a function such as `operator<<()`. `Stereo` does *not* have access to the component members because they are private to their respective classes. Only through public member `operator<<()` functions can the `Stereo` class output the components.

As you might guess, the compiler takes care of destructing the composed class members before destructing the class itself. Each of the members must be destructed before the class, and each class contains its own destructor that Turbo C++ calls.

Turbo C++ calls a default constructor if you don't supply your own, but if the class contains heap data, the default destructor will not properly work and deallocate the heap. (Figure 17.5 shows the order of the constructors and destructors in the Stereo class.)

<table>
<tr><td>Constructing order:</td><td>1. Receiver</td><td>Destructing order:</td><td>1. Stereo</td></tr>
<tr><td></td><td>2. CD</td><td></td><td>2. Speaker</td></tr>
<tr><td></td><td>3. Speaker</td><td></td><td>3. CD</td></tr>
<tr><td></td><td>4. Stereo</td><td></td><td>4. Receiver</td></tr>
</table>

Figure 17.5. *The order of constructors and destructors for* Stereo.

DO   **DON'T**

DO construct embedded class members with constructor initialization lists before constructing the overall class.

DO supply all the arguments needed to construct the entire composed class, including the arguments necessary to compose each component member in the class.

DON'T explicitly attempt to call destructors for embedded classes. When the composed object is destructed, Turbo C++ destructs the embedded objects for you.

DON'T try to access the component class's private members from within the composed class. As with any code outside a class, a composed class can access private members of other classes (even embedded classes) only through access functions.

Shortening the Composition

All the arguments to the Stereo system in Listing 17.4 had to be passed to construct the entire system. Rather than using the stereo system, you could have constructed the components individually like this:

```
Receiver radio(200, 450.00, "HiFi-HiTech");
CD disco(6, 325.00,"Disc Supreme");
Speaker output(350, 275.00, "Acoustic Output");
```

If you like, you can construct the individual components and then use those objects to construct the composed Stereo object. Doing this streamlines the construction of the Stereo and helps make the construction clearer than having a long list of arguments as done on lines 129 and 130 of Listing 17.4.

Listing 17.5 shows a new Stereo class and main() that could replace those in Listing 17.4 and produce the same output as before:

Listing 17.5. Creating the Stereo class from component objects.

```
1:  class Stereo {
2:    char * systemCode;      // For inventory
3:    int wireLength;
4:    float priceToInstall;
5:    Receiver tuner;
6:    CD discPlayer;
7:    Speaker speakers;       // Notice spelling and case difference
8:  public:
9:    Stereo(char *, int, float, int, float, char *,
10:          int, float, char *, int, float, char *);
11:   Stereo(char * SC, int WL, float PI, Receiver & r, CD & c,
          ➡Speaker & s);
12:   ~Stereo();
13:   friend ostream & operator<<(ostream &, const Stereo &);
14: };
15: // Here comes the HUGE constructor initialization list
16: Stereo::Stereo(char * SC, int WL, float PI, int RW, float RP,
17:          char * RB, int NCD, float CP, char * CB, int ML, float SP,
18:          char * SB) : tuner(RW, RP, RB), discPlayer(NCD, CP, CB),
          ➡speakers(ML, SP, SB),
19:            wireLength(WL), priceToInstall(PI)
20: {
21:   systemCode = new char[strlen(SC) + 1];
22:   strcpy(systemCode, SC);
23: }
24: // Shortened form of Stereo constructor that uses individual
25: // constructors that are already defined.
26: Stereo::Stereo(char * SC, int WL, float PI, Receiver & r,
27:              CD & c, Speaker & s) : tuner(r), discPlayer(c),
28:              speakers(s), wireLength(WL), priceToInstall(PI)
29: {
30:   systemCode = new char[strlen(SC) + 1];
31:   strcpy(systemCode, SC);
32: }
33: Stereo::~Stereo()
34: {
35:   delete [] systemCode;
36: }
```

```
37: ostream & operator<<(ostream & out, const Stereo & s)
38: {
39:   out << "Here's the stereo system:\n";
40:   out << "System code: " << s.systemCode << "\n";
41:   out << "Wire length: " << s.wireLength;
42:   out << "\tInstallation price: $" << s.priceToInstall << "\n";
43:   out << "Components follow:\n";
44:   out << s.tuner << s.discPlayer << s.speakers;
45:   return out;
46: }/////////////////////////////////////////////////////////////////////
47: // It took a lot of work to get to main()!
48: main()
49: {
50:   clrscr();
51:   // First, construct the individual components
52:   Receiver radio(200, 450.00, "HiFi-HiTech");
53:   CD disco(6, 325.00,"Disc Supreme");
54:   Speaker output(350, 275.00, "Acoustic Output");
55:   cout << radio << disco << output;
56:   // Now, construct the whole system
57:   Stereo system("HI42", 50, 75.00, radio, disco, output);
58:   cout << system;
59:   return 0;
60: }
```

Analysis
You might notice that in the prototype (line 11) and the definition lines (26–28), the character arrays are received by reference to make the code more efficient. In your own programs, passing all data by reference and preceding constant arguments with const improve your program efficiency and safety.

Line 57 directly constructs the composed Stereo class from already-instantiated objects. Although creating the component objects might not be as efficient as putting all the arguments in the Stereo constructor call (lines 129 and 130 of Listing 17.4), the code is easier to understand. A drawback to this method, however, is that you're creating two copies of the component objects: one stand-alone copy and another copy of the objects embedded within the Stereo object when it's created.

Assigning Composed Objects to One Another

The same assignment considerations take effect when you assign composed objects to one another as when you assign regular objects to one another. A member-by-member (called *memberwise*) assignment takes place. Memberwise assignment is fine as long as pointers aren't part of the object (which they are in the `Stereo` class). Even when pointers are members of the objects, memberwise copying will not always produce side effects. However, because it does sometimes produce side effects, it's worthwhile to correct the situation.

For every member component class for which you supply an `operator=()` function, Turbo C++ uses that function when it assigns those members. For every component member class for which you do not supply an overloaded `operator=()` function, Turbo C++ performs memberwise copy.

Suppose you added a default constructor for `Stereo` that required no arguments. The constructor would exist just to create objects that you would later fill with data. Therefore, you could create a `Stereo` object like this:

```
Stereo saleSystem;  // Create an object using the default constructor
```

Suppose that earlier in the program you had created the `system` object as done in Listing 17.5's line 57, and you wanted to assign the `system` object to the new `saleSystem` just created. There is nothing technically wrong with making a direct assignment like this:

```
saleSystem = system;
```

Such a memberwise assignment, however, copies member pointers and not the data pointed to by the member pointers. This action will cause problems if one object is destroyed; the other object's pointers will point to deallocated heap memory.

Therefore, to make the composed `Stereo` class as usable as possible and to provide code that you can mirror when writing your own composed classes, Listing 17.6 contains `operator=()` code for each of the composed objects as well as for the `Stereo` object. A default `Stereo` constructor and a default constructor for each of the component classes are also included in the program to let the program create a second `Stereo` variable without the need for arguments.

Note: Remember that if you supply overloaded `operator=()` functions for only *some* of the composed object classes, only those members will copy properly when you assign one composed class variable to another. The classes without an overloaded `operator=()` will use memberwise copy.

```
1:  // Filename: STEROPEQ.CPP
2:  // Classes for stereo components with inheritance
3:  #include <iostream.h>
4:  #include <iomanip.h>
5:  #include <string.h>
6:  #include <conio.h>
7:  class Component {    // No objects of base class ever
8:  protected:           // need to be instantiated
9:    float price;
10:   char * brand;
11: public:
12:   Component(float, char *);
13:   Component() {};    // Default constructor
14:   ~Component();
15: };
16: // Only price can be initialized, the brand
17: // must be assigned in the body
18: Component::Component(float P, char * B) : price(P)
19: {
20:   brand = new char[strlen(B) + 1];
21:   strcpy(brand, B);
22: }
23: Component::~Component()
24: {
25:   delete [] brand;  // Isn't it nice that you don't have to
26: }                   // worry about deallocation in main()?
27: // Component classes begin next
28: class Receiver : public Component {
29:   int watts;    // Watts per channel power
30: public:
31:   Receiver(int, float, char *);
32:   Receiver() {};   // Default constructor
33:   ~Receiver() {}   // No destructor code needed
34:   friend ostream & operator<<(ostream &, const Receiver &);
35:   Receiver & operator=(const Receiver &);   // Overload =
36: };
37: // Use an initialization list to construct base object and member
38: Receiver::Receiver(int W, float P, char * B) :
    ➥Component(P, B), watts(W)
39: {  // The constructor gets easy
40: }
41: ostream & operator<<(ostream & out, const Receiver & r)
42: {
43:   out << setiosflags(ios::fixed) << setiosflags(ios::showpoint);
44:   out << setprecision(2);
45:   out << "Receiver brand: " << r.brand << "\n";
46:   out << "Receiver price: $" << r.price << "  Watts per channel: ";
47:   out << r.watts << "\n";
```

continues

Listing 17.6. continued

```
48:    return out;
49: }
50: Receiver & Receiver::operator=(const Receiver & r)
51: {
52:    if (this == &r)
53:      { return *this; }
54:    watts = r.watts;          // Assign the righthand = operands
55:    price = r.price;          // to the lefthand = operands
56:    int newlen = strlen(r.brand) + 1;
57:    brand = new char[newlen];
58:    strcpy(brand, r.brand);
59:    return *this;
60: }
61: // Next component class follows
62: class CD : public Component {
63:    int numOfCDs;  // Some combo CD players play 6 or more CDs
64: public:
65:    CD(int, float, char *);
66:    CD() {};  // Default constructor
67:    ~CD() {}  // No destructor code needed
68:    friend ostream & operator<<(ostream &, const CD &);
69:    CD & operator=(const CD &);   // Overload =
70: };
71: CD::CD(int N, float P, char * B) : Component(P, B), numOfCDs(N)
72: { // The constructor gets easy
73: }
74: ostream & operator<<(ostream & out, const CD & c)
75: {
76:    out << setiosflags(ios::fixed) << setiosflags(ios::showpoint);
77:    out << setprecision(2);
78:    out << "CD player brand: " << c.brand << "\n";
79:    out << "CD price: $" << c.price << "  Number of CDs: ";
80:    out << c.numOfCDs << "\n";
81:    return out;
82: }
83: CD & CD::operator=(const CD & c)
84: {
85:    if (this == &c)
86:      { return *this; }
87:    numOfCDs = c.numOfCDs;        // Assign the righthand = operands
88:    price = c.price;             // to the lefthand = operands
89:    int newlen = strlen(c.brand) + 1;
90:    brand = new char[newlen];
91:    strcpy(brand, c.brand);
92:    return *this;
93: }
94: // Next component class follows
95: class Speaker : public Component {
96:    int maxLoad;  // Amount of maximum wattage allowed
```

 97: public:
 98:    Speaker(int, float, char *);
 99:    Speaker() {};
100:    ~Speaker() {} // No destructor code needed
101:    friend ostream & operator<<(ostream &, const Speaker &);
102:    Speaker & operator=(const Speaker &); // Overload =
103: };
104: Speaker::Speaker(int M, float P, char * B) :
     ➡Component(P, B), maxLoad(M)
105: { // The constructor gets easy
106: }
107: ostream & operator <<(ostream & out, const Speaker & s)
108: {
109:    out << setiosflags(ios::fixed) << setiosflags(ios::showpoint);
110:    out << setprecision(2);
111:    out << "Speaker brand: " << s.brand << "\n";
112:    out << "Speaker price (each): $" << s.price
     ➡<< " Max. Num. of Watts: ";
113:    out << s.maxLoad << "\n";
114:    return out;
115: }
116: Speaker & Speaker::operator=(const Speaker & s)
117: {
118:    if (this == &s)
119:      { return *this; }
120:    maxLoad = s.maxLoad;   // Assign the righthand = operands
121:    price = s.price;   // to the lefthand = operands
122:    int newlen = strlen(s.brand) + 1;
123:    brand = new char[newlen];
124:    strcpy(brand, s.brand);
125:    return *this;
126: }
127: class Stereo {
128:    char * systemCode;   // For inventory
129:    int wireLength;
130:    float priceToInstall;
131:    Receiver tuner;
132:    CD discPlayer;
133:    Speaker speakers;   // Notice spelling and case difference
134: public:
135:    Stereo(char *, int, float, int, float, char *,
136:           int, float, char *, int, float, char *);
137:    Stereo(char * SC, int WL, float PI, Receiver & r, CD & c,
     ➡Speaker & s);
138:    Stereo() {}; // Default constructor
139:    ~Stereo();
140:    friend ostream & operator<<(ostream &, const Stereo &);
141:    Stereo & operator=(const Stereo & s);
142: };
143: // Here comes the HUGE constructor initialization list
144: Stereo::Stereo(char * SC, int WL, float PI, int RW, float RP,
```

*continues*
```

Listing 17.6. continued

```
145:          char * RB, int NCD, float CP, char * CB, int ML, float SP,
146:          char * SB) : tuner(RW, RP, RB), discPlayer(NCD, CP, CB),
      ➥speakers(ML, SP, SB),
147:          wireLength(WL), priceToInstall(PI)
148: {
149:   systemCode = new char[strlen(SC) + 1];
150:   strcpy(systemCode, SC);
151: }
152: // Shortened form of Stereo constructor that uses individual
153: // constructors that are already defined.
154: Stereo::Stereo(char * SC, int WL, float PI, Receiver & r,
155:                CD & c, Speaker & s) : tuner(r), discPlayer(c),
156:                speakers(s), wireLength(WL), priceToInstall(PI)
157: {
158:   systemCode = new char[strlen(SC) + 1];
159:   strcpy(systemCode, SC);
160: }
161: Stereo::~Stereo()
162: {
163:   delete [] systemCode;
164: }
165: ostream & operator<<(ostream & out, const Stereo & s)
166: {
167:   out << "Here's the stereo system:\n";
168:   out << "System code: " << s.systemCode << "\n";
169:   out << "Wire length: " << s.wireLength;
170:   out << "\tInstallation price: $" << s.priceToInstall << "\n";
171:   out << "Components follow:\n";
172:   out << s.tuner << s.discPlayer << s.speakers;
173:   return out;
174: }
175: Stereo & Stereo::operator=(const Stereo & s)
176: {
177:   if (this == &s)
178:     { return *this; }
179:   priceToInstall = s.priceToInstall;  // Assign righthand operands
180:   wireLength = s.wireLength;          // to the lefthand = operands
181:   int newlen = strlen(s.systemCode) + 1;
182:   systemCode = new char[newlen];
183:   strcpy(systemCode, s.systemCode);
184:   tuner = s.tuner;             // Now, assign the component members
185:   discPlayer = s.discPlayer;
186:   speakers = s.speakers;
187:   return *this;
188: }
189: ////////////////////////////////////////////////////////////////////
190: // It took a lot of work to get to main()!
191: main()
192: {
```

```
193:    clrscr();
194:    // First, construct the individual components
195:    Receiver radio(200, 450.00, "HiFi-HiTech");
196:    CD disco(6, 325.00,"Disc Supreme");
197:    Speaker output(350, 275.00, "Acoustic Output");
198:    // Now, construct the whole system
199:    Stereo system("HI42", 50, 75.00, radio, disco, output);
200:    // Now, create another Stereo object and assign
201:    // to it the first one's member data
202:    Stereo saleSystem;
203:    saleSystem = system;
204:    cout << saleSystem;  // Print to ensure it's OK
205:    return 0;
206: }
```

```
Here's the stereo system:
System code: HI42
Wire length: 50 Installation price: $75
Components follow:
Receiver brand: HiFi-HiTech
Receiver price: $450.00  Watts per channel: 200
CD player brand: Disc Supreme
CD price: $325.00  Number of CDs: 6
Speaker brand: Acoustic Output
Speaker price (each): $275.00  Max. Num. of Watts: 350
```

As you can see from the output, the assignment in line 203 works properly. A lot is going on under the hood at line 203. Four overloaded assign operators execute. The operator=() in Stereo first begins; then before it has a chance to finish, the component operator=() functions are triggered in lines 184–186.

Even the simple creation of a default object in line 202 forces several constructors (the Stereo, the individual components, and then the base class default constructor) to execute. However, it takes a lot of code in the class to streamline the user program. Is it worth the effort? Certainly, because after you write and debug your class, the rest of your application is transparent to the class, and your application programming involves manipulating objects at a high level instead of having to worry about programming details throughout your program.

Summary

This chapter is concerned with embedding one or more objects inside another. Often, a class contains another object. (You might have written structures that contain other structures as members back in your C programming days.)

The problem with embedding class members is that you must properly construct each class member before constructing the composed class. To do that, you must add constructor initialization lists to the composed class constructor function.

Unlike with inheritance, you don't have to code special receiving access specifiers when composing because a composed class is not inherited from another—a composed class includes one or more other classes.

A composed class always follows the *has-a* question. If you can answer "yes" to the question "Does the composed class have a separate class for a member?" you must use composition. Inherited classes always answer positively to the *is-a* question, such as "Is this class another class with a little added functionality?" If so, inherit the new class from the existing one.

You should always include overloaded assignment functions for each of the component members if you don't want Turbo C++ to perform a memberwise copy. Memberwise copy can leave you with two objects pointing to the same region in memory, giving your program fits if you deallocate one object and then attempt to use the other object.

Q&A

1. What is the difference between inheritance and composition?

   Inheritance takes place when one class is just like another except for added functionality or data members. Composition occurs when one class contains another class (or more than one other class), but the composed class is not just an extended version of another class.

   As with inheritance, constructor initialization lists play important roles in the creation of class objects. When constructing the composed object, you must ensure that all the embedded component class members are constructed.

2. Why must I worry about operator=() when assigning one composed object to another?

   You don't always have to worry about overloading the assignment, but if your class or any of the composed classes have pointers as members, you're *strongly* advised to write an overloaded assignment.

   You'll have to include an overloaded assignment for each embedded component class inside the composed class. If you fail to include an overloaded

assignment function, Turbo C++ must use memberwise assignment to create the new object's data, and if pointers are involved, you'll have two objects' pointers pointing to the same memory.

Workshop

The Workshop offers quiz questions and exercises to hone your skills and give you feedback on today's lesson. You'll find some proposed answers in Appendix D.

Quiz

1. What questions can you ask to determine whether you should use composition or inheritance?

2. Describe which works best, composition or inheritance, in each of the following situations:

    A. A tree class and a forest class.

    B. A dog class and a beagle class.

    C. A tire class, a motor class, and a car class.

    D. A dot class, a line-drawing class, a square-drawing class.

3. What is wrong with the following constructor?

```
class A {
  int i;
  float j;
  char * c;
public:
  A(int I, float J, char C) : i(I), j(J), c(C) {};
  ~A();
};
```

4. If you include an overloaded assignment for one but not all composed classes, how does Turbo C++ perform the assignments for the classes missing an operator=() function?

5. What side effect can occur if you fail to include an overloaded assignment function?

Exercises

1. Rewrite the following class's constructor using a constructor initialization list.

```
class House {
   int sqFeet;
   char * address;
   float cost;
   int numRooms;
public:
   House(int, char *, float, int);
   ~House();
};
House::House(int S, char * A, float C, int N)
{
   sqFeet = S;
   int newlen = strlen(A) + 1;
   address = new char[newlen];
   strcpy(address, A);
   cost = C;
   numRooms = N;
};
House::~House()
{
   delete [] address;
}
```

2. The program in Listing 17.6 allocates data in lots of places. To brush up on your skills and add safety to the program, add a memory allocation error handler to the code so that a message prints and the program quits early if an allocation error occurs.

Virtual Functions: Are They Real?

You have not seen pointers to objects mentioned much in the past few chapters. Pointers work with objects just as they do with other variables. However, there are extra considerations to learn about when you combine both pointers and inheritance. Pointers used inside inheritance hierarchies often require special handling that other pointers don't require.

Throughout today's chapter, lots of emphasis is placed on a *family of classes*. In this usage, a family of classes refers to a single inheritance tree. In other words, if two child classes extend down from a single parent class, those three classes form an inheritance class family.

When using inheritance and pointers, you often have to write *virtual* functions. Virtual functions are member functions, all with the same name, that reside in an inheritance family of classes. Through the virtual interpretation techniques described in today's chapter, Turbo C++ can wait until runtime to determine exactly which function to call when you execute member functions through pointers.

You'll also learn today how to set up an array of pointers, and also how to store a family of classes on the heap. The virtual-function mechanism sounds difficult, but as with most object-oriented programming techniques, you'll see that virtual functions save you programming time and effort by taking details out of your hands and placing those details on Turbo C++'s back.

Today, you learn about the following topics:

☐ What a class family is

☐ The difference between early binding and late binding

☐ The way to define pointers to a class family of objects

☐ The need for virtual functions

☐ The difference between a virtual function and a pure virtual function

☐ How to define abstract base classes

Note: As you read and learn more about C++ and OOP, you might run across the term *virtual base classes*. Virtual base classes aren't related to virtual functions. You often write virtual base classes when programming inside multiple inheritance hierarchies. This book doesn't cover multiple inheritance, so you won't see virtual base classes described. You'll never need to learn about virtual base classes if you stay with single inheritance, as you can and probably should do.

For Ease of Discussion: This Is a Class Family

The term *class family* is often used in different ways. This chapter uses *class family* or *family of classes* to refer to related classes inside the same inheritance hierarchy. After you master *abstract base classes* at the end of today's chapter, you'll see why the term *family* makes a lot of sense.

A family of classes consists of classes somehow related by a common base class. The classes might or might not be sequentially related to one another. Figure 18.1 shows a class family. In the figure, a derived class derives from another derived class, which in turn derives from a base class. Figure 18.2 shows a different kind of class family. Several classes extend from the same parent in different combinations, and the entire hierarchy of classes forms a family of classes.

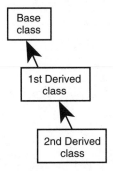

Figure 18.1. *A class family can extend on the same inheritance line.*

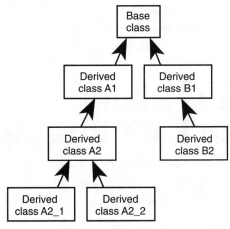

Figure 18.2. *A class family always extends from the same parent class.*

Figure 18.3 shows two *separate* class families. There are two base classes in the figure that define two separate class hierarchies. Although it might seem obvious that these are two separate class families, it's important to point out that any one Turbo C++ program might contain several different class families, and a different set of virtual functions would have to exist for each class family. Virtual functions would never span two different inheritance hierarchies like those shown in Figure 18.3. (Figure 18.3 does not show multiple inheritance, just two separate families of classes. Multiple inheritance takes place when a single class is derived from more than one parent class.)

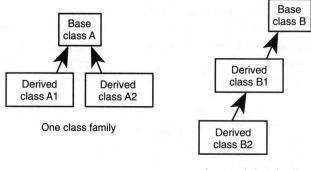

Figure 18.3. *Virtual functions don't span two class families at one time.*

Note: Don't get too concerned with the term *class family* because, as mentioned earlier, the term has several meanings depending on the context in which you use it. However, the next few sections describe virtual functions, and you must understand that virtual functions play an important role only with the same inheritance tree (class family).

When to Execute?
Early and Late Binding

Early binding, sometimes called *static binding,* is the process of determining at compilation time what functions to call. Early binding might sound complicated, but it is exactly what you are already used to. Virtually every C program you've written

(and every program in any other programming language) uses early binding for all function and subroutine calls.

With early binding, you write a function call and supply the function. Again, this is exactly what you've always done but probably never stopped to think about. You perhaps didn't even know that the process had a name.

When a program is compiled, Turbo C++ sets up all the program data and functions in a specific order. At compile time, Turbo C++ cannot know in advance exactly where in memory a program will be loaded for execution. You might compile a program on one computer and then run the program on a different computer with a different version of DOS, different drivers loaded into memory, a different memory manager, and so forth. The first available memory address available differs on each computer configuration.

Therefore, when Turbo C++ compiles a program, it stacks the compiled functions sequentially inside the compiled file. When `main()` calls a function, the address of the called function has to go in `main()`'s function call statement. Turbo C++ inserts the location of the function relative to the start of the file. In other words, when `main()` calls a function, `main()` knows exactly where that function will reside when the program loads. Therefore, if the function happens to begin at location 35 relative to the start of the program, `main()` contains a function call to address 35.

When you finally run a program, the .EXE program loader determines the first available free space in memory where the program can execute from and adds that address to all function calls. Therefore, whatever address Turbo C++ puts in the function call is adjusted at runtime to the exact address needed. When the program is compiled, all addresses are relative, and those addresses become absolute when a program runs.

All this background is actually not essential to understanding early binding. If anything, it almost distracts from the discussion, but you should understand the way programs compile and run. It appears that function call addresses are always changed from the time a program is compiled to the time it runs, and function call addresses are changed, but only so that they execute properly when the program is loaded. The program loader blindly adds the program's starting address to all function call addresses, but those function addresses remain relative to the position they were when the program was compiled.

Consider the simple program in Listing 18.1. `main()` calls a function called `tripleIt()`, and in turn, `tripleIt()` calls a function named `prName()`. The program uses early binding for the execution of its two function calls.

Type Listing 18.1. Using early binding for function calls.

```
1:  // Filename: REGBINDG.CPP
2:  // Use early binding to resolve function calls at compilation time
3:  #include <iostream.h>
4:  #include <conio.h>
5:  void tripleIt(int num);
6:  void prName(int num);
7:  main()
8:  {
9:    clrscr();
10:   int num;
11:   do {
12:     cout << "Please type a number from 1 to 10: ";
13:     cin >> num;
14:   } while ((num < 1) || (num > 10));
15:   tripleIt(num);   // Triple the number
16:   return 0;
17: }
18: void tripleIt(int num)
19: {
20:   int trip;
21:   prName(num);  // Prints the number's word
22:   trip = num * 3;
23:   cout << " tripled is " << trip << "\n";
24: }
25: void prName(int num)
26: {
27:   switch (num)
28:   { case(1) : cout << "One";
29:               break;
30:     case(2) : cout << "Two";
31:               break;
32:     case(3) : cout << "Three";
33:               break;
34:     case(4) : cout << "Four";
35:               break;
36:     case(5) : cout << "Five";
37:               break;
38:     case(6) : cout << "Six";
39:               break;
40:     case(7) : cout << "Seven";
41:               break;
42:     case(8) : cout << "Eight";
43:               break;
44:     case(9) : cout << "Nine";
45:               break;
46:   };
47: }
```

```
Please type a number from 1 to 10: 7
Seven tripled is 21
```

When Turbo C++ compiles this program, the tripleIt() function might happen to fall 25 bytes from the start of the program, and prName() might happen to fall 38 bytes from the start of the program. Therefore, line 15 compiles as a function call executing the function at address 25, and line 21 compiles as a function call executing the function at address 38.

The important thing to note about this program is that all function calls are adjusted, but never changed from their relative position in the file. The relative function addresses are bound *early* in the process, during compilation. Figure 18.4 shows that the compiled program's relative function call addresses never change from their relative positions when the program loads for execution.

Relative address	When compiled:	If program loads at address 340000:	If program loads at address 450500:

0	main()
	{
	
	execute 25
	
	}
		main()
		{
		
		execute 340025
		
		}
			main()
			{
			
			execute 450525
			
			}

25	tripleIt()
	{
	
	execute 38
	
	}
		tripleIt()
		{
		
		execute 340038
		
		}
			tripleIt()
			{
			
			execute 450538
			
			}

38	prNames()
	{
	}
		prNames()
		{
		}
			prNames()
			{
			}

Figure 18.4. *Program calls compile with relative starting addresses.*

Note: Always keep in mind that early binding (and late binding too) is focused on function *calls,* not the function definitions themselves. Binding is the insertion of the proper address into a function call. Early binding means that a function's relative address position is known during compilation. No matter what binding method takes place, function definitions themselves don't rearrange in memory; they always stay in the order they were compiled in and always remain in their relative positions in the compiled file.

Late binding occurs when nothing is stored in a function call until the program actually runs. You might wonder how Turbo C++ can even compile a program if it cannot store addresses in function calls, but if you've ever seen a program that used pointers to functions, you've seen late binding in action.

Listing 18.2 contains a program that includes an array of pointers to five functions that compute math results. The program defines an array of pointers to the five math functions and then uses a for loop to execute each of the functions.

Listing 18.2. Using function pointers to demonstrate late binding.

```
1:  // Filename: FUNPTR.CPP
2:  // Program that contains an array of pointers to functions
3:  #include <iostream.h>
4:  #include <iomanip.h>
5:  #include <conio.h>
6:  #include <math.h>
7:  // Must prototype all functions before defining pointers to them
8:  void doSin(float number);
9:  void doCosin(float number);
10: void doTangent(float number);
11: void doArcsin(float number);
12: void doArcosin(float number);
13: // Define an array of pointers to each function
14: void (*fun[])(float)={doSin, doCosin, doTangent, doArcsin,
     ➥doArcosin};
15: main()
16: {
17:   clrscr();
18:   float number;
19:   cout << setprecision(3) << setiosflags(ios::fixed);
20:   cout << "*** Math Program ***\n";
21:   cout << "\n\nEnter a floating-point number and I'll print\n";
22:   cout << "some calculations from it: ";
23:   cin >> number;
24:   for (int ctr=0; ctr<5; ctr++)
25:     {
26:       fun[ctr](number);      // Here's where late binding occurs
27:     }
```

```
28:    return 0;
29: }
30: void doSin(float number)
31: {
32:    cout << "\nThe sine of " << number << " is " << sin(number)
     ➡<< "\n";
33: }
34: void doCosin(float number)
35: {
36:    cout << "The cosine of " << number << " is " << cos(number)
     ➡<< "\n";
37: }
38: void doTangent(float number)
39: {
40:    cout << "The tangent of " << number << " is " << tan(number)
     ➡<< "\n";
41: }
42: void doArcsin(float number)
43: {
44:    cout << "The arc sine of " << number << " is " << asin(number)
     ➡<< "\n";
45: }
46: void doArcosin(float number)
47: {
48:    cout << "The arc cosine of " << number << " is " << acos(number)
     ➡<< "\n";
49: }
```

```
*** Math Program ***

Enter a floating-point number and I'll print
some calculations from it: .45
The sine of 0.45 is 0.435
The cosine of 0.45 is 0.9
The tangent of 0.45 is 0.483
The arc sine of 0.45 is 0.467
The arc cosine of 0.45 is 1.104
```

Five math functions, defined in lines 30–49, contain simple built-in function calls that perform various trigonometric calculations. After the user enters a floating-point value in line 23, that value is passed to each of the five math functions in the for loop of lines 24–27.

The for loop steps through the array of function pointers defined on line 14. The first time through the loop, the program executes fun[0](number); the second time through the loop, the program executes fun[1](number); and so on.

537

Note: If you've shied away from ever using pointers to functions, don't let this review frighten you. Most Turbo C++ programmers don't use pointers to functions because virtual functions often replace the need for function pointers.

During compilation, what address does Turbo C++ insert at line 26? Does Turbo C++ insert the address of doSin()? What about doCosin()? It turns out that Turbo C++ cannot insert *any* address when it compiles this program! Turbo C++ cannot determine which of the five functions to call until runtime. (Determining which functions to call is also referred to as *resolving the functions*.)

The value of the loop counter, ctr, determines which function is called and when. Therefore, runtime data determines which function is called. During compilation, Turbo C++ can do little more than place a *hint* of a function call at line 26. Turbo C++ places an indirect call to a location in memory and at runtime. Turbo C++ then fills this location with the proper function's address when it's finally determined what function the program is to execute.

Late binding is the process of waiting until runtime, not compile time, to decide which function to call at a given point in the program. Late binding takes place any time you use a pointer to execute a function, as done in Listing 18.2. Late binding must also take place when you program in OOP and use inheritance and pointers to objects, as the next section explains.

DO   DON'T

DO learn the difference between early binding and late binding. Early binding is what you have always been used to when calling regular functions from within your programs. Later binding takes place when function calls cannot be resolved until runtime, as happens when you define pointers to functions.

DON'T give up pointers to functions in Turbo C++ if you see the need to use them. They provide lots of power, and if you're comfortable with them, use them when you want to.

DON'T get too worried if you, as with a lot of C programmers, have never used pointers to functions. As a Turbo C++ programmer, you'll use virtual functions more often to achieve the same late binding that pointers to functions provide in C.

Virtual Functions

Virtual functions provide a late binding mechanism for OOP that truly makes your programs seem to think for themselves. At runtime, your programs decide which functions to call. Before you go any further, you need to remember a simple rule that explains when virtual functions, as opposed to the regular member functions you've seen, are needed:

> *When you define pointers to several objects from a class family, and more than one class within the family contains functions with common names, use virtual functions.*

As you already know, you can define pointers to objects. If you create an inheritance class, you can define a pointer (or array of pointers) to the base class and then point to *any derived class objects from that base class.* Figure 18.5 shows what is meant here; if you define a pointer to a base class, you can then point to *any* object instantiated from any derived class of that base class.

Note: If you define a pointer to a derived class, you cannot point to base class objects with the pointer; the pointer through inherited class families works only from the base class down the inheritance hierarchy.

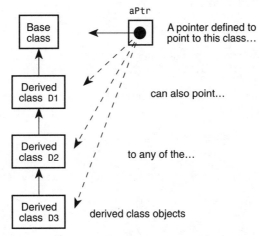

Figure 18.5. *A pointer defined for the base class can point to any derived class object.*

As you know, an array name is nothing more than a pointer to a list of objects. You can define an array of objects, defined with the base class name, and then store derived class objects in the same array.

A quick example will demonstrate the need for virtual functions. The program in Listing 18.3 contains a program that almost works properly, but *almost* doesn't count in this business!

Listing 18.3. A program with pointers that doesn't quite work properly.

```
1:  // Filename: NOVIRT.CPP
2:  // Program to demonstrate pointers through a hierarchy and also
3:  // to show the problems if you don't use virtual functions
4:  #include <iostream.h>
5:  #include <iomanip.h>
6:  #include <conio.h>
7:  #include <string.h>
8:  class Building {
9:  protected:
10:   int sqFt;
11:   char address[25];  // Don't worry about city, state, ZIP
12: public:
13:   Building(int, char []);
14:   void prData(void);
15: };
16: Building::Building(int S, char A[]) : sqFt(S)
17: {
18:   strcpy(address, A);
19: }
20: void Building::prData(void)
21: {
22:   cout << "The building has " << sqFt << " square feet.\n";
23:   cout << "The building's address is " << address << ".\n\n";
24: }
25: class Shed : public Building {
26:   char useCode;
27: public:
28:   Shed(int, char[], char);
29: };
30: Shed::Shed(int S, char A[], char U) : Building(S, A), useCode(U)
31: { // No body necessary due to initialization lists
32: }
33: class House : public Building {
34:   int numRooms;
35:   float cost;
36: public:
37:   House(int, char [], int, float);
38:   void prData(void);
39: };
```

```
40: House::House(int S, char A[], int N, float C) : Building(S, A),
41:                numRooms(N), cost(C)
42: { // No body necessary due to initialization lists
43: }
44: void House::prData(void)
45: {
46:   cout << "The house has " << sqFt << " square feet.\n";
47:   cout << "The house address is " << address << ".\n";
48:   cout << "The house has " << numRooms << " number of rooms.\n";
49:   cout << "The house cost " << cost << "\n\n";
50: }
51: class Office : public Building {
52:   int zoneCode;
53:   float rent;
54: public:
55:   Office(int, char [], int, float);
56:   void prData(void);
57: };
58: Office::Office(int S, char A[], int Z, float R) : Building(S, A),
59:                zoneCode(Z), rent(R)
60: {  // No body necessary due to initialization lists
61: }
62: void Office::prData(void)
63: {
64:   cout << "The office has " << sqFt << " square feet.\n";
65:   cout << "The office address is " << address << ".\n";
66:   cout << "The office is zoned for " << zoneCode << " code.\n";
67:   cout << "The office rents for " << rent << ".\n\n";
68: }
69: main()
70: {
71:   // Define pointers to class objects. Notice that the base
72:   // class is used to define the pointers, not any derived class
73:   Building * properties[3];
74:
75:   // Reserve heap and initialize with a constructor
76:   properties[0] = &Shed(78, "304 E. Tenth", 'x');
77:   properties[1] = &House(2310, "5706 S. Carmel", 8, 121344.00);
78:   properties[2] = &Office(1195, "5 High Rise", 'B', 895.75);
79:
80:   // Prepare output now that objects are constructed
81:   clrscr();
82:   cout << setprecision(2) << setiosflags(ios::showpoint);
83:   cout << setiosflags(ios::fixed);
84:   // Print the objects using a loop
85:   for (int ctr=0; ctr<3; ctr++)
86:   {
87:     properties[ctr]->prData();  // Which prData() prints?
88:   }
89:
90:   // Deallocate the memory
```

continues

Listing 18.3. continued

```
91:    delete properties[0];
92:    delete properties[1];
93:    delete properties[2];
94:    return 0;
95: }
```

The building has 78 square feet.
The building's address is 304 E. Tenth.

The building has 2310 square feet.
The building's address is 5706 S. Carmel.

The building has 1195 square feet.
The building's address is 5 High Rise.

 Study the class hierarchy (Figure 18.6 will help) to get an idea of the class makeup before studying main(). As you can see, the useCode is not accessed after it's initialized in the Shed constructor. The generic Building's prData() function, inherited from Building, is all that's needed to print the Shed's data.

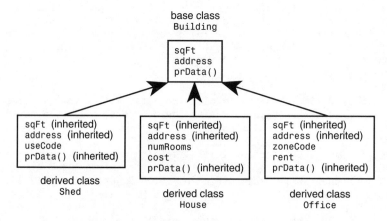

Figure 18.6. *The class hierarchy of Building and its descendants.*

main() is extremely compact considering all that takes place at the class level. The pointers to the data on the heap all point to different kinds of objects (within the same class family). As you can see, however, there is something wrong with the output from this program.

Why didn't the `House` `prData()` function execute when line 87's `properties` pointer executed the `prData()` member function with the `House` object? The same question could be asked for the `Office` object as well. In other words, even though the `prData()` function was overridden in the two derived classes (lines 38 and 56), the base class `prData()` (line 14) executed instead.

You already know that derived classes can override their inherited data and member functions. It appears that both `Office` and `House` override `Building`'s `prData()` member function. And yet, the `Building`'s `prData()` member function executes for all objects pointed to by the pointer.

> **Note:** It's OK that the `Shed` object prints with the `Building`'s `prData()` because the `Shed` class made no attempt to override the `prData()` function, but instead, uses the one it inherits directly from `Building`.

Early binding is the reason for the problem. When Turbo C++ compiles Listing 18.3, it must do something with line 87. After all, line 87 calls a `prData()` function. It is because the `properties[]` array is defined to point to the base class that the base class `prData()` executes. Instead, there has got to be a way to request that Turbo C++ *not* bind the function calls early, but rather bind them at runtime when the objects pointed to can determine the correct functions to call.

In other words, there needs to be a way for you to give the compiler the following information:

> *If* `properties[]` *is pointing to a base class object, or to a derived class such as* `Shed` *that doesn't override* `prData()`, *use* `Building's` `prData()` *function. If, however,* `properties[]` *is pointing to a derived class, use that derived class's copy of* `prData()` *(unless there is none as in the* `Shed` *class).*

There is a way to request that Turbo C++ perform late binding when such pointers to objects are involved. As you might have guessed, using virtual functions solves the problem.

Specifying Virtual Functions

To fix the problem with Listing 18.3, you only need to tell Turbo C++ exactly which functions in the base class are to be virtual by inserting the `virtual` keyword in front of those functions. By inserting `virtual` before the base class `prData()` function name, you inform Turbo C++ that you only want the base class prData() function called if the object that triggers the member function, the *this object, is from the base class or from a derived class such as Shed that doesn't override prData().

Here is a rewritten version of the Building class with virtual properly specified:

```
1:  // Filename: VIRT.CPP
2:  class Building {
3:  protected:
4:    int sqFt;
5:    char address[25];  // Don't worry about city, state, ZIP
6:  public:
7:    Building(int, char []);
8:    virtual void prData(void);   // Here's the fix!
9:  };
```

The simple addition of virtual makes all the difference in the world. When you add virtual before the Building's prData() prototype as done here, you'll receive this output from the program:

```
The building has 78 square feet.
The building's address is 304 E. Tenth.

The house has 2310 square feet.
The house address is 5706 S. Carmel.
The house has 8 number of rooms.
The house cost 121344.00

The office has 1195 square feet.
The office address is 5 High Rise.
The office is zoned for 66 code.
The office rents for 895.75.
```

As you can see, line 87 (from Listing 18.3) now properly calls the correct prData() function. The function call is resolved at runtime, not compile time.

Polymorphism: "Many Forms"

The Greek for *polymorphism* is *many forms*. You might have seen this term in OOP literature, and that single word might have kept you away from learning OOP! Polymorphism makes learning OOP sound like slightly less fun than losing your job.

The fact is that the preceding section utilized polymorphism, only you didn't know the term. The prData() function is polymorphistic. After all, there are many forms (three) of prData() in Listing 18.3. When Listing 18.3 is corrected with the virtual keyword, Turbo C++ takes care of figuring out which polymorphistic function to execute based on the type of value of the pointer on line 87.

Why is all this such a big deal? Well, if nothing else, learning to use the virtual keyword takes care of the programming problem shown in this chapter. When you want to point to objects throughout an inheritance class family, and when one or more of those objects share the same name as a base class function, you've got to tell Turbo C++ to wait until runtime to resolve the function call.

An even better reason for using virtual is that you can again forget about messing with details and concentrate on the overall goal of your programming application. You don't have to name similar functions different names between inherited class families! Instead of worrying about prOffice(), prBuilding(), prHouse() and prShed(), you only have to remember prData() and let Turbo C++ figure out at runtime which version of the prData() function to call! Isn't a simple for loop like the one on lines 85–88 (Listing 18.3) easier to code than four distinct function calls? What if there were 20 levels of hierarchy in the Building class? If there were, you would only change the for loop's 3 to 20, but if you had not used virtual functions, you would have to code 17 more distinct function calls!

There's yet another reason for needing the virtual keyword before inherited function names. The same early binding problem occurs as it did originally in Listing 18.3 when you use references to invoke inherited member functions.

For example, suppose that you wrote a function called printAll() that applied the prData() function to whatever object is passed by reference as shown here:

```
void printAll(Building & place)
{
  place.prData();   // Hopefully, prData() is virtual!
  // Other code could follow
}
```

If prData() is listed as virtual in the base class, then whatever kind of object, Building, Shed, House, or Office, is passed to printAll() gets printed properly. However, if prData() is not listed in the base class as virtual, the base class prData() always executes no matter what kind of object is passed to printAll().

Efficient or Not?

Turbo C++ uses an elaborate system of indirect function call tables to resolve the prData() addresses at runtime. A table of virtual-function addresses, called the *vtable*, contains the addresses (with relative locations until the program is loaded for execution) of the functions that could be called polymorphically. Each class has a copy of the vtable. When the program runs, the vtables are used as go-between vehicles to find correct member functions from the inheritance hierarchy.

It is true that using virtual functions is slightly less efficient than using regular member function calls. If you don't point to objects, but rather you define objects with their own names, you won't have to use virtual functions. However, pointers are an important part of Turbo C++, especially when using the heap. Therefore, you must remember to name all member functions between classes differently (which is not elegant or always wise), or you must remember to insert `virtual` before the base class functions that need to be resolved at runtime.

The slightly less efficient nature of virtual functions is the reason why the designers of C++ decided not to make `virtual` the default environment for all base class functions. The designers of C++ wanted efficiency in all programs, especially those that don't need polymorphism.

Depending on your application, at times you might not want the inherited function to execute when it otherwise would because of `virtual`. For example, suppose that you expand on the `Building` program described in this chapter and add several functions and routines that print data for customers, real estate brokers, builders, and developers.

In the customer routines, you might not want the extra `House` members to print, but you'll still want the address and square feet to print. (You want to interest the customer, but not disclose the price except in person by a human agent.) In that function, you might want to use the base class `prData()` by overriding the `virtual` keyword like this:

```
properties[num]->Building::prData();  // Use base class version
```

Any time you override the virtualization, Turbo C++ will perform early binding and insert the base class function's address at the function call during compilation and will always execute the base class version of the function when this function call is reached during execution.

 Note: If your inheritance class hierarchy contains destructors, make the base class destructor virtual. Making the base class destructor virtual ensures that the proper destructor will be called when you delete an object through a pointer or reference using the `delete` operator.

If your base class virtual functions contain no code, those base class virtual functions are called *pure virtual functions.* They exist only to derive subsequent classes. No objects should be instantiated from a class that contains a pure virtual function. Therefore, if you design a high-level base class that is a model for derived classes, and you don't put any code in the base class virtual functions, don't instantiate base class objects because there will be trouble if you attempt to execute the member functions from the base object and no member function really exists. Base classes with pure virtual functions are called *abstract base classes* because they are abstract and they model the rest of the inheritance family, but they should never be used to instantiate objects.

You can ensure that Turbo C++ enforces your abstract base class by assigning 0 to all pure virtual functions in your programs like this:

```
virtual void prData(void) = 0;  // Can never instantiate now
```

Although the syntax is strange (assigning 0 to a function definition), the 0 tells the Turbo C++ compiler to never enable you to instantiate base class objects. Without setting to 0, you could compile a program that instantiated base class objects and then have trouble running it. It's a lot easier to debug compile-time errors (generated with the = 0 format) than runtime errors that would occur if you used an object of an abstract base class.

18

DO   DON'T

DO define pointers or arrays to the base class if you want to point to or hold in an array several kinds of objects from the same class family.

DO use `virtual` when you point to objects in a class family and the same function name is used throughout the inheritance.

DO use `virtual` when receiving reference parameters that trigger inherited and overridden base class member functions.

DO override the virtualization if a base class function is supposed to execute when `virtual` would normally allow the derived class function to execute.

DO virtualize the base class destructor (or any class that contains a `virtual` function) so that your objects are always properly destructed. (Constructors cannot be virtualized—they don't ever need to be.)

DON'T apply `virtual` to friend functions.

DON'T apply `virtual` to regular member functions.

DON'T instantiate a base class that contains a pure virtual function.

Summary

Today's chapter showed you the proper way to set up member functions when you define pointers to inherited objects. By specifying virtual functions, you let Turbo C++ decide at runtime (late binding) and not at compile time (early binding) how to resolve function references. The effect of late binding is that your objects seem to decide for themselves which member functions to call.

In learning about late binding, you saw how early binding takes place in common C and C++ programs. At compile time, the compiler inserts function addresses into function calls so that the correct function can be found.

When you define pointers to several objects in an inheritance hierarchy, you define the pointers to be base class pointers. You then can assign those pointers to any derived object in the hierarchy. The only problem that remains is letting Turbo C++ know which member functions to call, via the object pointers, when more than one class uses a function name that is the same as a base class function name.

If you insert `virtual` before each function prototype in the base class, Turbo C++ uses late binding to look at the type of object being pointed to and to execute that object's class member function. However, without `virtual`, Turbo C++ always executes the base class function, even if the pointer is pointing to an object derived several layers down in the family class.

Q&A

1. What is the difference between early and late binding?

   Early binding takes place in most programs that don't provide for virtual functions. Unless you use pointers to functions, or unless you use virtual functions, all C and Turbo C++ compilers compile programs using early binding.

   Early binding is the process of resolving function calls at compile time rather than runtime. The more the compiler can finish at compile time, the more efficient the compiled runtime program will be because there is less overhead the program has to take care of at runtime.

   Late binding occurs when function call resolutions are delayed until runtime. The OOP need for late binding appears when you point to objects throughout an inherited family of class. The pointer could be pointing to a base class or derived class, and the compiler will not know exactly which

class the pointer will point to until the program runs. Adding `virtual` tells the compiler to wait until runtime to determine which function should be executed, the base class's or a derived class's function.

2. How does Turbo C++ achieve late binding? What is the internal mechanism that allows for virtual functions?

When Turbo C++ compiles a program, it knows that there has to be *some* function call code inserted at the location of every function call. Therefore, when you request late binding with `virtual`, Turbo C++ inserts an indirect pointer at the function call that points not to a function (that would be a direct pointer), but to a table of functions called the *vtable* (or sometimes, the *virtual table*).

At runtime, the object pointer that triggers the member function provides the offset needed in the vtable to execute the correct function.

3. Why doesn't Turbo C++ default to virtual functions instead of requiring the `virtual` keyword? It seems as if one would always want virtual functions.

You won't always want to execute virtual functions when pointing to a class hierarchy of objects, but it's true that you *usually* want to. As a previous answer explained, slightly more overhead is needed to resolve virtual function calls than for regular function calls. This additional overhead is needed because the compiler must make decisions and access an internal table at runtime that doesn't have to be accessed if early binding occurs.

However small the efficiency loss is, the designers of the C++ language felt that you should make the decision to use virtual functions, so they did not make late binding the default function resolution when pointers to objects are used.

4. What is the difference between a pure virtual function and a regular virtual function?

A pure virtual function contains no code. You can optionally assign a zero to a pure virtual function to make the compiler issue errors if you try to instantiate an object from a class that contains a pure virtual function.

Any base class that contains one or more pure virtual functions is called an abstract base class and cannot be used to instantiate objects. There is no code for the pure virtual functions, so the object's member function would be empty and useless.

5. What good is an abstract base class?

   Although you cannot instantiate an abstract base class, you can use it as a high-level model of the inheritance that follows. Such a base class provides an outline of all the family of classes that you derive from the base class. An abstract base class can list all the common data members and member functions of all classes derived from the abstract base class.

Workshop

The Workshop offers quiz questions and exercises to hone your skills and give you feedback on today's lesson. You'll find some proposed answers in Appendix D.

Quiz

1. Can a family class (as used in this chapter) contain more than one base class and hierarchy?

2. Name two places where late binding takes place in Turbo C++. (**Hint:** One can occur in both C and C++.)

3. True or false: When you define pointers to functions, data, not code, determines exactly which function to call.

4. Which of the following function prototypes correctly defines a pure virtual function?

   A.
   ```
   class A {
   protected:
     int i;
   public:
     calcIt(void) { i = i * 23 - 7; }
   };
   ```

   B.
   ```
   class B {
   protected:
     int i;
   public:
     calcIt(void) = 0;
   };
   ```

```
C. class C {
    protected:
      int i;
    public:
      pure calcIt(void) { i = i * 23 - 7; }
    };
```

5. Which of the classes in question 4 is an abstract base class?

6. How can you tell whether a base class is an abstract base class?

7. How does assigning a zero to a pure virtual function change your program's compilation?

8. Why would you need a virtual destructor?

Exercises

1. Write a program that executes a function based on a menu choice using functions to pointers. The function executed doesn't have to do anything but print a message showing the user that the correct function was triggered by the function pointer.

2. Rewrite Listing 18.3 with virtual functions needed in the base class so that the base class is an abstract base class. (**Hint:** You'll have to add a prData() function to the Shed class.)

Templates:
Create Once,
Use Forever

A *template* is an outline or model from which other things are made. Often, machine shops create templates for tool designs. From the templates, the shops can make tools for their own use and for sale to others.

Computer users are not unfamiliar with templates. Spreadsheet users often use template spreadsheets that provide fill-in-the-blank functionality. Instead of redesigning the same spreadsheet from scratch, spreadsheet users store a spreadsheet template that contains titles, prompts, and calculations, but no data. To use the template, the user only has to fill in the data.

You use templates every time you fill out a form. The blank forms are nothing but templates for information. Only after you fill out the form is it a stand-alone, unique collection of information.

The designers of C++ decided that templates were so helpful in other walks of life that C++ needed them too. Turbo C++ supports both template functions and template classes. You'll want to create a template function or template class when you need to define several versions of similar functions and classes.

Don't let the term *template* frighten you because templates are easy to understand and use. As just explained, you use templates in everyday life. Using Turbo C++ templates streamlines certain programming that you do and helps eliminate more tedious details that you would otherwise have to mess with.

Today, you learn about the following topics:

- How to code template functions
- How to use template functions
- How to code template classes
- How to use template classes
- Some template design considerations

Note: You might hear templates called *parameterized types* by the C++ programming community. Templates require parameters, similar to the parameters needed by functions, hence their nickname.

Without Templates

In a way, the advantages of template functions mirror the advantages of overloaded functions. Unlike overloaded functions, however, template functions take less effort on your part to code. You'll want to use template functions whenever functions differ only in their return or passed data types.

> **Note:** Unlike with overloaded functions, you only have to write the body of a template function once.

Suppose you were writing a simple bubble sort routine that sorted a list of 100 integers. The code in Listing 19.1 does just that and includes a `main()` function that initializes the integer array with some random values.

 Listing 19.1. A simple integer sorting routine.

```
1:  // Filename: INTSORT.CPP
2:  // Sorts 100 integer values
3:  #include <iostream.h>
4:  #include <iomanip.h>
5:  #include <stdlib.h>
6:  #include <conio.h>
7:  void sortNums(int []);
8:  const int MAX = 100;    // Number of values in the array
9:  main()
10: {
11:   int nums[MAX];
12:   clrscr();
13:   for (int ctr=0; ctr<MAX; ctr++)
14:     { nums[ctr] = (rand() % 100) + 1; } // 1 to 100
15:   // Print the sorted array
16:   sortNums(nums);
17:   return 0;
18: }
19: //////////////////////////////////////////////////////////////////
20: // The following routine uses a standard bubble sort algorithm
21: void sortNums(int nums[])
22: {
23:   int temp, i, j;   // For swapping during sort
24:   for (i=0; i<MAX; i++)
25:     { for (j=i; j<MAX;j++)
26:         { if (nums[i] > nums[j])
27:             {  temp = nums[i];
```

continues

Listing 19.1. continued

```
28:                    nums[i] = nums[j];
29:                    nums[j] = temp;
30:             }
31:        }
32:     }
33:     // Print the sorted values
34:     for (i=0;  i<MAX;  i+=10)
35:        { for (j=0;j<10;j++)
36:            { cout << setw(5) << nums[i+j]; }
37:        cout << "\n";     // Adds newline every few values printed
38:        }
39: }
```

1	2	5	9	9	10	11	13	13	15
16	16	17	17	18	19	20	22	23	27
28	30	31	34	34	35	37	37	38	40
41	42	42	43	43	43	47	48	48	49
52	52	53	54	56	57	57	59	59	60
61	61	61	62	62	64	64	65	65	66
67	67	67	67	68	69	70	72	72	75
76	79	80	80	80	80	80	82	82	83
84	86	86	89	90	90	91	91	91	91
91	93	93	93	94	96	96	96	96	98

This program is probably reminiscent of your early days in programming. Almost every beginning programmer learns how to write bubble sort routines. This program does little more than initialize an array of 100 random values (lines 13 and 14) using the built-in rand() function prototyped in the STDLIB.H header file. The function sortNums() compares each pair of values in the integer array, swapping values when a pair is found to be out of sequence, and finally prints the sorted values after the array is sorted (lines 34–38). The printing routine prints a newline character after every 10 values printed so that the numbers don't wrap around the screen and put the columns out of alignment.

Note: There is a better sorting routine called qsort() included with Turbo C++ that is also part of the ANSI C standard. Using qsort() is more efficient than writing a bubble sort as shown here, but the focus of this chapter is to show the need for templates. The bubble sort is a simple and common algorithm that demonstrates the need for templates very well, hence its use here.

What if you wanted to be able to sort an integer array *and* a character array *and* a floating-point array all within the same program? You could write a separate function with a separate name for each data type, but being the seasoned OOP programmer that you now are, you would correctly opt for three overloaded sorting functions, all named the same, that sort each of the data types.

Listing 19.2 contains the same bubble sorting algorithm used previously, except three versions of the algorithm are included to handle the sorting of each of the three data types. Function overloading enables you to keep the OOP spirit alive by giving the sorting functions the same name even though they work on different data types.

 Listing 19.2. Three overloaded sorting routines.

```cpp
1:  // Filename: SORT3.CPP
2:  // Sorts 100 character, integer, and floating-point values
3:  #include <iostream.h>
4:  #include <iomanip.h>
5:  #include <stdlib.h>
6:  #include <conio.h>
7:  void sortNums(char []);    // Different prototypes, same
8:  void sortNums(int []);     // overloaded function names
9:  void sortNums(float []);
10: const int MAX = 100;   // Number of values in the arrays
11: main()
12: {
13:    char cNums[MAX];    // To hold the random integer list
14:    int iNums[MAX];     // To hold the random integer list
15:    float fNums[MAX];   // To hold the random float list
16:    clrscr();
17:    for (int ctr=0; ctr<MAX; ctr++)  // Fill each array
18:      { cNums[ctr] = char((rand() % 26) + 65);  // 'A' to 'Z'
19:        iNums[ctr] = ((rand() % 100) + 1);  // 1 to 100
20:        fNums[ctr] = (float((rand() % 100) + 1) / 3.0);  // 1.0 to
                                                          ➥33.333
21:      }
22:    // Print the sorted array
23:    cout << setprecision(2) << setiosflags(ios::fixed); // For floats
24:    cout << setiosflags(ios::showpoint);  // For floats
25:    sortNums(cNums);
26:    sortNums(iNums);
27:    sortNums(fNums);
28:    return 0;
29: }
30: //////////////////////////////////////////////////////////////////////
31: // Overloaded functions begin here
32: // Character version
33: void sortNums(char nums[])
34: {
```

continues

19

Listing 19.2. continued

```
35:     char temp;
36:     int i, j;    // For swapping during sort
37:     for (i=0; i<MAX; i++)
38:       { for (j=i; j<MAX;j++)
39:           { if (nums[i] > nums[j])
40:               { temp = nums[i];
41:                 nums[i] = nums[j];
42:                 nums[j] = temp;
43:               }
44:           }
45:       }
46:     // Print the sorted values
47:     cout << "\n\nThe sorted values:\n";
48:     for (i=0; i<MAX; i+=10)
49:       { for (j=0;j<10;j++)
50:           { cout << setw(7) << nums[i+j]; }
51:       cout << "\n";    // Adds newline every few values printed
52:       }
53: }
54: // Integer version
55: void sortNums(int nums[])
56: {
57:     int temp, i, j;    // For swapping during sort
58:     for (i=0; i<MAX; i++)
59:       { for (j=i; j<MAX;j++)
60:           { if (nums[i] > nums[j])
61:               { temp = nums[i];
62:                 nums[i] = nums[j];
63:                 nums[j] = temp;
64:               }
65:           }
66:       }
67:     // Print the sorted values
68:     cout << "\n\nThe sorted values:\n";
69:     for (i=0; i<MAX; i+=10)
70:       { for (j=0;j<10;j++)
71:           { cout << setw(7) << nums[i+j]; }
72:       cout << "\n";    // Adds newline every few values printed
73:       }
74: }
75: // Floating-point version
76: void sortNums(float nums[])
77: {
78:     float temp;
79:     int i, j;    // For swapping during sort
80:     for (i=0; i<MAX; i++)
81:       { for (j=i; j<MAX;j++)
82:           { if (nums[i] > nums[j])
```

```
83:              {  temp = nums[i];
84:                  nums[i] = nums[j];
85:                  nums[j] = temp;
86:              }
87:          }
88:      }
89:      // Print the sorted values
90:      cout << "\n\nThe sorted values:\n";
91:      for (i=0; i<MAX; i+=10)
92:        { for (j=0;j<10;j++)
93:            { cout << setw(7) << nums[i+j]; }
94:        cout << "\n";     // Adds newline every few values printed
95:        }
96: }
```

```
The sorted values:
ABBBBBBCCC
CCCCDDEEEE
FFFFFGGGHH
HHHHIIIIJJ
JJJKKLLLLL
MMMNNNNOOO
PPPQQQQQQR
RRRRSSTTTT
TUVWWWWXXX
XYYYZZZZZZ
```

```
The sorted values:
      1      4      4      5      6      7      8     10     11     12
     13     13     14     14     15     16     16     17     19     23
     23     24     25     26     31     32     34     35     36     37
     37     38     41     43     43     44     45     46     48     48
     49     52     52     52     52     52     53     53     54     54
     56     57     57     57     59     60     61     62     63     63
     63     65     66     67     67     67     68     68     70     71
     71     73     73     75     75     75     79     80     80     80
     80     81     81     81     84     87     87     87     90     91
     91     92     92     93     94     95     96     96     96     97
```

```
The sorted values:
 1.33   1.67   2.00   3.67   4.33   4.33   4.67   5.67   5.67   6.00
 6.33   6.67   7.00   7.33   7.33   7.33   7.67   8.00   8.33   9.00
 9.00   9.33   9.33   9.67   9.67  10.00  10.00  10.33  10.67  10.67
11.00  11.00  11.33  12.00  12.00  12.00  12.33  12.33  13.67  14.33
14.67  14.67  15.67  15.67  15.67  16.00  16.00  16.33  16.33  16.67
16.67  17.67  19.00  19.33  19.67  20.00  20.67  20.67  21.00  21.33
21.67  21.67  22.33  23.00  23.00  23.33  23.67  23.67  24.33  25.00
26.33  26.67  26.67  26.67  27.00  27.33  27.33  27.33  27.33  27.67
27.67  28.00  28.33  28.67  28.67  28.67  29.67  29.67  30.00  30.33
30.33  31.00  31.00  31.00  31.33  31.67  31.67  32.00  33.00  33.33
```

19

559

By now, you realize that the three overloaded sorting functions offer the programming advantage that they all have the same name. Thanks to Turbo C++, you no longer have to worry about remembering different function names for functions that do the same thing, only for different data types.

Despite the advantage of function overloading, there is still too much overlap in the program. The three functions just take too much program real estate because they don't differ in any way except for their data types (lines 33 and 35, 55 and 57, 76 and 79). Despite the fact that overloaded functions ease your function call burdens, you still have to code these three functions, and the functions, even though they differ only in their data types, must appear in their entirety in the program compiled by Turbo C++.

Thankfully, the designers of the C++ language didn't stop with overloaded functions. Overloaded functions offer tremendous advantages in OOP, especially for overloading constructors and overloaded operators, but overloaded functions don't help reduce programming effort when several like functions must operate on different data types. Luckily, template functions *do* reduce the amount of coding you have to do when like functions must be written to handle different data types.

DO	**DON'T**

DO continue to use overloaded functions for constructors, overloaded operators, and everywhere else two or more functions do enough similar work to warrant overloading.

DON'T use overloaded functions for two or more functions that differ *only* in their data types. Although overloading such functions is better than writing different functions with different names, using templates for like functions is much easier to do.

Coding Template Functions

When faced with the job of writing several functions that do the same thing with different data types, use template functions instead of overloading them. When writing a template function, you only write the *pattern* or *template* for the set of functions, and then Turbo C++ generates the code necessary for all the function listings. In other words, if templates had been used in Listing 19.2, three copies of the

same function would not need to be listed in the program, taking up lots of room and getting in the way! Only *one* version, a template outline of the functions, is needed.

One of the reasons some newcomers to C++ delay learning about templates is because of the syntax of template functions. The syntax is a little strange, but if you think of a pattern for other functions, you should have little trouble following the format of a template function. Keep the following idea in mind:

> *Turbo C++ generates a set of real functions from the single prototype you write.*

All template functions begin with the keyword `template` followed by angle brackets like this:

```
template <class T>
```

To the right of the `<class T>` appears the rest of the function you are writing the template for. Here is the definition line for the `sortNums()` template function:

```
template <class T> void sortNums(T nums[])
```

The `class` in `<class T>` doesn't always signal an OOP class but rather a replaceable data type parameter. The following rules apply to the `template` line:

1. The `class T` section could contain a list of items. All the following `class T` sections are valid:

   ```
   <class T>
   <class A, class B>
   <class T1, class T2>
   ```

   (Notice that the letter `T` is just a placeholder and can be anything you want it to be. The template identifier doesn't have to be an uppercase letter, but it usually is uppercase to separate it from variable names.)

2. `<class T>` identifies a data type or a list of data types that will be replaced later. The `T`, or whatever identifier or identifiers you list, becomes a data type in the resulting generated set of functions.

3. After `<class T>`, specify the function's return data type. If the return data type is `void`, then `void` appears. If the return data type is `int *`, then `int *` appears. If, however, the return data type changes depending on the function being generated from the template, specify `T` (or any other identifier from the `<class...>`) in the return data type location.

4. The function name follows the return data type along with any parameters received by the function. If one or more of the parameters contain a data

type from the `<class...>` list, use `T` or any of the other identifiers from your `<class...>` list.

One of the nice things about templates is that seeing them in action is easier than learning their rules. Listing 19.3 provides a listing of a template function for the three `sortNums()` functions presented earlier.

 Listing 19.3. Template for the three sorting functions.

```
 1:  template <class T> void sortNums(T nums[])
 2:  {
 3:    T temp;  // Only thing in body that relied on the passed data type
 4:    int i, j;
 5:    for (i=0; i<MAX; i++)
 6:      { for (j=i; j<MAX;j++)
 7:         { if (nums[i] > nums[j])
 8:            {  temp = nums[i];
 9:               nums[i] = nums[j];
10:               nums[j] = temp;
11:            }
12:         }
13:      }
14:    // Print the sorted values
15:    cout << "\n\nThe sorted values:\n";
16:    for (i=0; i<MAX; i+=10)
17:      { for (j=0;j<10;j++)
18:         { cout << setw(7) << nums[i+j]; }
19:      cout << "\n";    // Adds newline every few values printed
20:      }
21:  }
```

 From this template, Turbo C++ will generate three different functions *for you* when you compile the program. You must prototype the three functions you want generated using these prototypes:

```
void sortNums(char []);    // Turbo C++ generates three
void sortNums(int []);     // different functions here
void sortNums(float []);
```

The prototypes must appear *after* the template or Turbo C++ would not know how to generate the functions from the templates. Therefore, many Turbo C++ programmers store their templates in a header file and include the file before the prototypes of the functions to be generated.

To provide a more detailed analysis of template functions, Listing 19.4 contains a rewritten version of the preceding program. Listing 19.4 contains the template function listed in Listing 19.3. Notice how much shorter the code is between Listing 19.4 and Listing 19.2, yet *both programs produce the same output.*

Listing 19.4. Letting Turbo C++ generate the three sorting functions.

```
1:  // Filename: TEMPSORT.CPP
2:  // Uses a template to sort different kinds of values
3:  #include <iostream.h>
4:  #include <iomanip.h>
5:  #include <stdlib.h>
6:  #include <conio.h>
7:  const int MAX = 100;    // Number of values in the arrays
8:  /////////////////// Start of template function ///////////////////////
9:  template <class T> void sortNums(T nums[])
10: {
11:    T temp;  // Only thing in body that relied on the passed data type
12:    int i, j;
13:    for (i=0; i<MAX; i++)
14:      { for (j=i; j<MAX;j++)
15:          { if (nums[i] > nums[j])
16:              {  temp = nums[i];
17:                 nums[i] = nums[j];
18:                 nums[j] = temp;
19:              }
20:          }
21:      }
22:    // Print the sorted values
23:    cout << "\n\nThe sorted values:\n";
24:    for (i=0; i<MAX; i+=10)
25:      { for (j=0;j<10;j++)
26:          { cout << setw(7) << nums[i+j]; }
27:      cout << "\n";     // Adds newline every few values printed
28:      }
29: }
30: /////////////////// End of template function ////////////////////////////
31: void sortNums(char []);    // Turbo C++ generates three
32: void sortNums(int []);     // different functions here
33: void sortNums(float []);
34: main()
35: {
36:    char cNums[MAX];     // To hold the random integer list
37:    int iNums[MAX];      // To hold the random integer list
38:    float fNums[MAX];    // To hold the random float list
39:    clrscr();
40:    for (int ctr=0; ctr<MAX; ctr++) // Fill each array
41:      {  cNums[ctr] = char((rand() % 26) + 65); // 'A' to 'Z'
42:         iNums[ctr] = ((rand() % 100) + 1);  // 1 to 100
43:         fNums[ctr] = (float((rand() % 100) + 1) / 3.0);  // 1.0 to
                                                          ➥33.333
44:      }
45:    // Print the sorted array
46:    cout << setprecision(2) << setiosflags(ios::fixed); // For floats
47:    cout << setiosflags(ios::showpoint);  // For floats
```

continues

19

Listing 19.4. continued

```
48:    sortNums(cNums);
49:    sortNums(iNums);
50:    sortNums(fNums);
51:    return 0;
52: }
```

Note: Listing 19.4 produces the same output as Listing 19.2 produced.

 The three prototypes in lines 31–33 tell Turbo C++ how to generate the three functions. Turbo C++ replaces the template's T with each of the matching values in the prototypes. In other words, the first prototype tells Turbo C++ that T in <class T> means char. *Everywhere* else in the template function that T appears, char will appear in the generated function. This replacement of the template's parameter is why templates are sometimes called *parameterized types*; the parameters in the template function become types in the functions generated by Turbo C++.

The only line inside the template function that needs to be replaced with the parameter data type is line 11. The temporary variable used in the sorting routine must be the same data type as the array being sorted.

Figure 19.1 helps show where the generated functions get their replaced values.

If a template function contains more than one replaceable parameter, list them inside the <class...> line. The template function

```
template <class T1, class T2> T1 myFun(int iNum, T1 t1, T2 t2)
{
  T1 total;
  total = T1(iNum) + t1 + t2;
  return total;
}
```

contains two replaceable parameters, T1 and T2. The first parameter, whatever data type T1 becomes in the resulting generated function, is used to typecast iNum in the body of the function. Wherever a data type can appear in a function, a parameter can appear in a template.

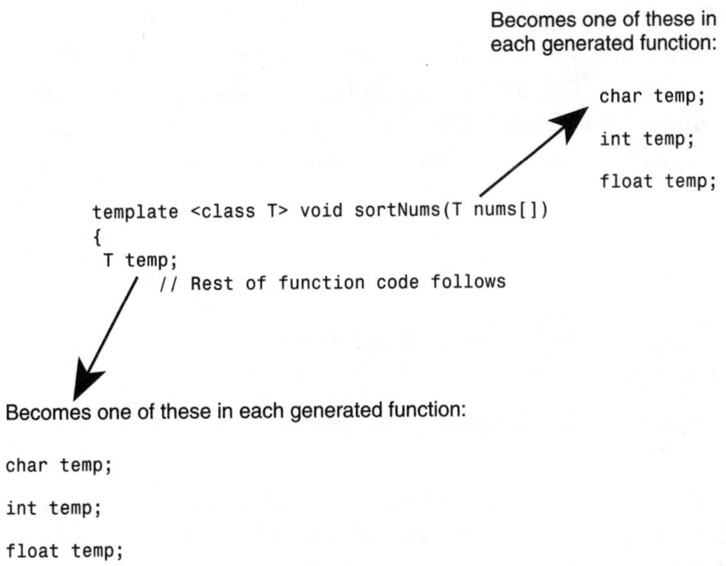

Becomes one of these in
each generated function:

```
char temp;

int temp;

float temp;
```

```
template <class T> void sortNums(T nums[])
{
  T temp;
           // Rest of function code follows
```

Becomes one of these in each generated function:

```
char temp;

int temp;

float temp;
```

Figure 19.1. *Showing the replacement when Turbo C++ generates functions from the template.*

If the two prototypes

```
int myFun(int, int, float);
double myFun(int, double, float);
```

appear after the template function just shown, Turbo C++ will generate these functions during compilation:

```
int myFun(int iNum, int t1, float t2)
{
  int total;
  total = int(iNum) + t1 + t2;
  return total;
}
```

and

```
double myFun(int iNum, double t1, float t2)
{
  double total;
  total = double(iNum) + t1 + t2;
  return total;
}
```

Note: If you have used #define for writing defined macros, you might see similarities to #define and template functions. You create template-like functions with #define, but #define has side effects that template functions don't have. (See Day 2's chapter for a review of #define's side effects.)

Syntax

Coding Template Functions

```
template<class T> void function(T parameter(s))
{
  // Template function code goes here
}
```

The <class T> might contain a list of several parameters, such as <class T, class U, class V>, or just a single parameter. The names of the parameters have no meaning other than to identify where they exist in the rest of the template. Everywhere any of the parameters exists in the rest of the function, Turbo C++ will replace those parameters with other data types, specified in the function prototype.

The T parameter(s) might be a parameterized type from the <class...> statement or might be a combination of built-in data types and the <class...> parameter. In the body of the template function, if a replaceable parameter appears, Turbo C++ replaces it with a different data type when the final functions are generated.

Any data type can be replaced in a template's generated function, even class and structure data types. You must have declared those data types before the prototypes of the template.

You must supply prototypes for all template functions so that Turbo C++ will know which data types are to be used in the generated functions.

Example

```
template<class T> T sumIt(T ara[])    // Assumes 100 values passed
{
  T total = 0;
  for (int i=0; i<100; i++)
    { total += ara[i]; }
  return total;
}
```

If the function is prototyped like

```
double sumIt(double []);
```

then Turbo C++ generates this function for you that totals whatever kind of array is prototyped:

```
double sumIt(double ara[])    // Assumes 100 values passed
{
  double total = 0;
  for (int i=0; i<100; i++)
    { total += ara[i]; }
  return total;
}
```

DO ———————————————————————— **DON'T**

DO use template functions for all similar functions that differ only in their data types.

DO prototype all the functions Turbo C++ is to generate from the template functions.

DO include more than one template parameter if you want Turbo C++ to replace more than one data type in the resulting generated functions.

Template Classes

After you've mastered template functions, template classes are relatively easy to understand. You are now used to the template function syntax, and template classes use almost identical syntax.

A template class forms a model for more than one class you want generated. The classes might contain different data types but the same functionality. One of the most common template class uses is a *container*. A container class is nothing more than a template of classes that contains data. What kind of data? It depends of course on the prototyped class that is to be generated from the template. How is the container to store the data—in an array, a linked list, or a double-linked list? The answer doesn't really matter to the program using the container class.

Turbo C++ contains several useful container classes, and there is no need to rewrite them. Tomorrow's chapter explores the built-in container classes. For now, it's important to understand that the container classes included with Turbo C++ are nothing more than template classes. After all, Turbo C++ could not supply a different container class for *every* data type you'll ever define because many times you'll want to store class and struct data in a container.

Therefore, this section will show a simple container class template that doesn't offer all the functionality of the built-in container classes but does show you how to write template classes if you ever need to. More important, you'll have a better idea of how Turbo C++'s container classes work tomorrow when you learn about them.

Listing 19.5 shows an outline of a container class called Contain. The Contain class works somewhat like a stack. A stack is an area in memory whose last value entered is the first one taken out. Think of a stack of trays at a cafeteria. When the dishwasher puts a new clean tray on top of the stack, the next person in line gets that same tray. The trays that have been there the longest are the ones at the bottom of the stack. The last tray on the stack is the first tray off the stack (known as *LIFO,* or *last in, first out*).

The container class generates an array member of whatever data types the template needs to generate. If you need a stack of integers, a stack of floats, and a stack of doubles, the container class can define all of them as shown in this program's analysis section.

Listing 19.5. Using a template class to generate two classes.

```
1:  // Filename: CONTAIN.CPP
2:  // A simple container class template
3:  #include <iostream.h>
4:  #include <iomanip.h>
5:  #include <conio.h>
6:  template<class T> class Contain {
7:    T value[500];   // Container can hold up to 499 values
8:    int sub;        // Current subscript of highest value on stack
9:  public:
10:   Contain();
11:   ~Contain();
12:   void addVal(T);
13:   void removeVal(void);
14:   void prVals(void);
15: };
16: template<class T> Contain<T>::Contain() : sub(0)
17: {  // Starting subscript initialized
18: }
19: template<class T> Contain<T>::~Contain()
20: {  // In case heap is added for storage later
21: }
22: template<class T> void Contain<T>::addVal(T val)
23: {
24:   if (sub < 500)
25:     { sub++;
26:       value[sub] = val;
27:     }
28: }
```

```
29: template<class T> void Contain<T>::removeVal(void)
30: {
31:    // Program warning if too many values are requested
32:    if (sub == 0)
33:      { cout << "\n** The stack is empty! You cannot ";
34:        cout << "get values from it**\n"; }
35:    else
36:      { cout << "\n(Got " << value[sub] << ")\n";
37:        sub--; }
38: }
39: template<class T> void Contain<T>::prVals(void)
40: {
41:    // Warning! If T is a defined data type such as a class or
42:    // structure, you also have to supply an overloaded operator<<()
43:    // function for this to work.
44:    if (sub==0)
45:      { return; }    // Nothing to print
46:    cout << "\n\nHere are the values:\n";
47:    for (int ctr=1; ctr<=sub; ctr++)
48:    {  cout << setw(5) << value[ctr] << "\t"; }
49: }
50: main()
51: {
52:    clrscr();
53:    cout << setprecision(1) << setiosflags(ios::showpoint);
54:
55:    Contain<int> ages;     // This defines a completely NEW class
56:    // Add integer values to the container
57:    ages.addVal(4);
58:    ages.addVal(6);
59:    ages.addVal(8);
60:    ages.prVals();  // Print the container
61:    // Attempt to get more values than exist in the container
62:    ages.removeVal();
63:    ages.removeVal();
64:    ages.removeVal();
65:    ages.removeVal();
66:    ages.prVals();  // Nothing to print
67:
68:    // Now, do the same for floats
69:    Contain<float> weights;  // This defines a completely NEW class
70:    // Add floating-point values to the new container
71:    weights.addVal(14.4);
72:    weights.addVal(16.6);
73:    weights.addVal(18.8);
74:    weights.prVals();  // Print the container
75:    // Attempt to get more values than exist in the container
76:    weights.removeVal();
77:    weights.removeVal();
78:    weights.removeVal();
79:    weights.removeVal();
```

continues

Listing 19.5. continued

```
80:   weights.prVals();   // Nothing to print
81:   return 0;
82: }
```

```
Here are the values:
    4       6       8
(Got 8)

(Got 6)

(Got 4)

** The stack is empty! You cannot get values from it**

Here are the values:
 14.4    16.6    18.8
(Got 18.8)

(Got 16.6)

(Got 14.4)

** The stack is empty! You cannot get values from it**
```

main() contains these two statements (lines 55 and 69):

```
Contain<int> ages;      // This defines a completely NEW class
Contain<float> weights; // This defines a completely NEW class
```

These two lines provide the definition of the class that Turbo C++ is to generate from the template class named Contain. In other words, two classes are to be defined: one with int replacing all the template class's T parameters and another with float replacing all the template class's T parameters. Coding the template class once is much easier, and less error-prone, than coding a different class for every kind of container you want generated.

Just to show you what Turbo C++ generates from a template class, here is the float class created from line 69:

```
int Contain {
  int value[500];  // Container can hold up to 499 values
  int sub;         // Current subscript of highest value on stack
public:
  Contain();
  ~Contain();
  void addVal(float);
  void removeVal(void);
```

```
    void prVals(void);
};
Contain::Contain() : sub(0)
{  // Starting subscript initialized
}
Contain::~Contain()
{  // In case heap is added for storage later
}
void Contain::addVal(float val)
{
  if (sub < 500)
    { sub++;
      value[sub] = val;
    }
}
void Contain::removeVal(void)
{
  // Program warning if too many values are requested
  if (sub == 0)
    { cout << "\n** The stack is empty! You cannot ";
      cout << "get values from it**\n"; }
  else
    { cout << "\n(Got " << value[sub] << ")\n";
      sub--; }
}
void Contain::prVals(void)
{
  // Warning! If T is a defined data type such as a class or structure,
  // you also have to supply an overloaded operator<<() function for
  // this to work.
  if (sub==0)
    { return; }    // Nothing to print
  cout << "\n\nHere are the values:\n";
  for (int ctr=1; ctr<=sub; ctr++)
  {  cout << setw(5) << value[ctr] << "\t"; }
}
```

Of course, you'll never see the generated class because after Turbo C++ finishes compiling your program, you'll see just the template class you originally wrote.

Summary

The biggest reason to learn about templates is that you can write a function or class once, and from that template function or template class, you can define many other functions and classes. A template is just a model for a function or class. From a template, you can ask Turbo C++ to generate several other functions and classes that look like the template but differ in their specific data types.

Although overloaded functions are useful for coding functions that require different parameters but do basically the same thing, templates are the best to use in such cases. Templates wouldn't be extremely useful for overloading constructors and overloaded operator functions. There are many times, however, when you need two or more functions or classes that look exactly alike in their format but differ in their data types.

To utilize template functions, you must write a template function once that includes in its definition line all parameters that you want replaced in the generated functions. The parameters to template functions (and classes) are always data types. The data types can be either built-in data types or user-defined data types.

The idea of template classes works just like that of template functions. You must write a template class, which is an outline of a class, that contains data type parameters. When you're ready to create the actual class, the class definition supplies the data types to be used for the final class definitions.

Q&A

1. What drawbacks do overloaded functions sometimes have?

   Overloaded functions are great for writing different functions that are *close* in functionality, such as constructors and overloaded operators. However, if you want to write three functions that do exactly the same thing, but that differ only in their data types, overloaded functions can be cumbersome; you have to write a different overloaded function body for each function.

2. How can templates help?

   Templates enable you to write the skeleton of a function body (or class body) once and generate as many different sets of functions (or classes) as you want given the data types you pass to the template.

   Turbo C++ does all the work for you if you use templates. You don't have to write every version of every function and class that you need. You only have to write one copy of a function or class and let Turbo C++ generate functions and classes for you during compilation.

3. Why is the syntax for templates so difficult?

   The syntax of templates is relatively easy after you understand that `<class T>` receives a data type, not a variable value. Every occurrence of `T` in the template gets replaced with that data type when Turbo C++ generates the function or class.

By the way, the T can be anything, and you can list several replaceable parameters inside the <class...> if you need to.

4. What is a container?

A container is simply a class that holds data (it *contains* data). The data can be any data type. Containers are implemented with the help of templates. Without templates, there would have to be a separately written container class for each data type to be stored in the container. Tomorrow's chapter explains how to use the container classes that are supplied with Turbo C++.

Workshop

The Workshop offers quiz questions and exercises to hone your skills and give you feedback on today's lesson. You'll find some proposed answers in Appendix D.

Quiz

1. What is a template?

2. What two kinds of templates does Turbo C++ support?

3. Which is better, overloaded functions or template functions, when you're writing three constructors that construct the same class using different parameters?

4. Which is better, overloaded functions or template functions, when you're writing functions that have the same body but differ in the data types they pass and return?

5. Which usually takes less coding on the programmer's part: overloaded functions or template functions?

6. True or false: After Turbo C++ generates classes from your template class, you'll be able to look at the generated class source code.

7. Can containers hold data of almost any data type?

8. What class definition lines are necessary if you want to define three new classes—double, char, and long int—from the class template in Listing 19.5?

19

Exercise

1. Write the three functions generated from the following template and prototypes:

```
template<class A> A max(A num1, A num2)
{
  A big;
  big = (num1 > num2) ? num1 : num2;
  return big;
}
// Prototypes
int max(int, int);
float max(float, float);
double max(double, double);
```

Use Supplied Containers for Your Data

Today's chapter provides more of a tour than a tutorial. This chapter explains how to use many of the supplied container classes that come with Turbo C++. In yesterday's chapter, you learned how to write your own template functions and template classes. The template concept is best demonstrated through containers; containers are data structures that contain data. With the help of templates, containers can hold any kind of data, even your own class and structure objects.

Whenever you work with large amounts of data, you've got to write an efficient storage routine to manage that data in memory. You'll have to be able to utilize memory as well as possible and still provide for easy access to data.

Two kinds of containers are provided by Turbo C++ that store, manage, and retrieve your data for you: object-based classes and template-based classes. They both provide approximately the same functionality, but the template-based container class is slightly more flexible. That's the container class library described in this chapter.

Keep in mind that this chapter explains how to use several of the containers, but the chapter is not intended to become a boring reference manual of every storage facility and every option available with the template containers. Such an in-depth discussion would probably be wasted; it's not worth your time to remember all the details of all the containers, and there are too many details anyway. As you'll see, this chapter's approach is to walk you through some descriptions and give you ideas on how you might use the container classes in your own programs.

Today, you learn about the following topics:

☐ Setting up the correct #include directories for using the container template class library

☐ How to use the stack container class

☐ How to use the queue container class

☐ When to use the different class container definitions

☐ Using container member functions to manipulate the data

☐ Using bags and sets to store unordered data

☐ Using the array container to create arrays of your own class objects

Preparing Your Compiler to Use the Containers

Before writing programs that use the built-in containers, you have to make sure that Turbo C++ can find all the files it needs. You'll have to tell the compiler, through the **O**ptions pull-down menu, to look in the correct subdirectory on disk to find appropriate header files. The container header files aren't included in the regular `#include` directory.

The nice thing about Turbo C++ is that Borland designed the program with all contingencies in mind. Borland knew that you sometimes would want to access the container classes but that you would also want to use the regular header files such as IOSTREAM.H. Therefore, it's possible to set up Turbo C++'s directory option so that Turbo C++ looks in two directories for any needed `#include` files.

To prepare Turbo C++ for using the container classes, follow these steps:

1. Display the **O**ptions pull-down menu.

2. Select **D**irectories... from the menu. Turbo C++ displays the Directories dialog box.

3. The **I**nclude Directories option on the first line of the Directories dialog box contains the full path to your standard Turbo C++ header files. Using the mouse or keyboard, position the text cursor at the end of the directory listed, and add this text at the end of the line:

   `;C:\TC\CLASSLIB\INCLUDE`

   Notice that the new text begins with a semicolon to separate it from the directory already displayed. (If Turbo C++ is located on a drive different from C:, change the drive name to something else.) Your screen should look something like the screen in Figure 20.1.

20

> **Note:** It's easy to overtype the path already listed instead of adding the new path to the end of the existing one. Be sure to click the mouse or use the arrow keys to move the text cursor to the end of the currently displayed path before adding the semicolon and an additional path. If you happen to overwrite part or all of the current path, press Escape and start over at step 1.

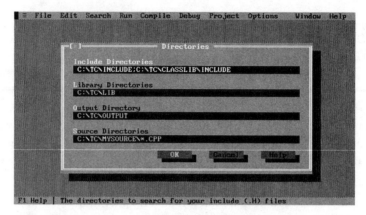

Figure 20.1. *Setting up the appropriate container search directory.*

To make these settings permanent, select **O**ptions **S**ave and press Enter.

Turbo C++ searches both paths (there are two, one on each side of the semicolon) for any header files you include. If you use #include to include a header file not found in either of the two directories, Turbo C++ issues an error. All the header files used in this chapter will be found in the two paths shown in Figure 20.1.

The Stack Container Class

To teach you templates, yesterday's chapter provided a brief description of a *stack.* In computer terms, a stack is a collection of objects stored as a list. The order of the stack depends on the order in which the objects were added. A stack is never sorted unless the order in which the objects were added to the stack happened to be a sorted order.

A stack is like a narrow deep box with one opening. If you start putting objects into the box, the first one you can get back is the last one you stored. This LIFO (last-in, first-out) method of storage means that the first values put on the stack are always the last taken off.

New stack terminology is needed for handling the stack. The *top* of the stack is always the last value put on the stack (the next value that can be removed from the stack). When you put new values on the stack, you *push* those values onto the stack. When you take existing values off the top of the stack, you *pop* those values. After a value is popped, it's off the stack and is not part of the stack until you push it again.

If you push a 10, then push a 20, then push a 30, then push a 40 onto a stack, you'll wind up with a stack that looks like the one in Figure 20.2.

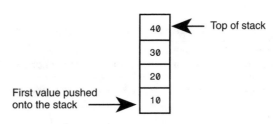

Figure 20.2. *After performing some stack operations.*

If you want to empty all the stack's contents, you *flush* the stack. A flushed stack is a stack with no values. A flushed stack is also called an *empty* stack.

Stacks are useful for keeping track of events in systems and windows programming. Generally, the first window that you open is the last one you close. Inventory accounting systems often use a stacking mechanism also. In times of inflation, accountants like to value inventories using a LIFO method. The newest parts added to the inventory are always the first ones considered sold (whether they are physically the next ones sold or not) because they are on the books as costing the most, and therefore, the profit shown is recorded as the smallest possible for tax purposes. (This is perfectly legal.)

The most important thing to remember about a stack is that you can only retrieve objects from the stack in reverse order from which you stored the items. Stacks aren't useful for storing sorted data that needs to be rearranged (sorted) every so often.

Here are the steps you must take to create and use the built-in stack container class:

1. Define a stack object. In doing so, specify the data type of the objects that the stack will hold.

2. Use the supplied stack member functions, prototyped in STACKS.H and found in the CLASSLIB\INCLUDE directory described in the preceding section, to access the stack.

Using the stack is extremely easy. Listing 20.1 contains a program that creates an integer stack using the built-in container class, then stores three integer values, and then accesses those values using the class member functions supplied by the container class. Although you've probably never seen a program that used the container class before, you'll see that the program is extremely easy to follow.

Listing 20.1. A simple integer stack container.

```cpp
1:  // Filename: STACK1.CPP
2:  // Pushes 3 values on a stack, prints the number of values
3:  // in the stack with a container function, prints the top
4:  // of the stack without popping the stack, then pops each
5:  // value one at a time, printing the values popped.
6:  #include <iostream.h>
7:  #include <stacks.h>
8:  #include <conio.h>
9:  main()
10: {
11:    clrscr();
12:    // Define an integer stack object
13:    BI_StackAsVector<int> intStack;
14:    // Put three values on the stack
15:    intStack.push(10);
16:    intStack.push(20);
17:    intStack.push(30);
18:    // Print the number of values on the stack
19:    cout << "There are ";
20:    cout << intStack.getItemsInContainer() << " values in the stack\n";
21:    // Print the top value without removing it
22:    cout << "The top value on the stack is " << intStack.top() << "\n";
23:    cout << "Just popped " << intStack.pop() << "\n"; // Removes as it
24:    cout << "Just popped " << intStack.pop() << "\n"; // prints.
25:    cout << "Just popped " << intStack.pop() << "\n";
26:    return 0;
27: }
```

```
There are 3 values in the stack
The top value on the stack is 30
Just popped 30
Just popped 20
Just popped 10
```

Perhaps the only cryptic line in the entire program is line 13. Line 13 uses the
BI_StackAsVector class template to create an integer class variable named
intStack. It's obvious that the class is a template class because of the angle
brackets. The int in angle brackets is the parameter data type telling Turbo C++
exactly what the stack is to hold. If you had used float in the angle brackets, the stack
would hold floating-point values. Even more important, if you define your own class
objects, you could create a stack of your own objects, and you would have to do
nothing different but insert your class's name in place of int. (The next program stores
and accesses a stack of user-defined objects, but concentrate on this integer stack
for now.)

Although the class name `BI_StackAsVector` is a seemingly strange class name, there's a reason for the strange name, as you'll see in a moment. Line 13's `BI_StackAsVector<int> intStack;` defines a variable named `intStack` just as `float x;` defines a variable named `x`—granted, the latter is shorter and easier to understand at a glance. Line 13 in the program isn't that difficult to understand when you compare the statement with other variable definition statements. If you listed more than one variable after `BI_StackAsVector<int>`, you would create more than one separate stack, and the container class would take care of each of them.

The `push()` member function pushes values onto the stack. The container class keeps track of the top of the class and all the values in the stack, eliminating the tedious details that you would otherwise have to worry about. The `getItemsInContainer()` returns the total number of values in the stack.

Generally, stacks work like this: When you pop the top value (the only value you *can* pop), that value leaves the stack. However, the container class supplies the `top()` function, which returns the top value without popping the value off the stack. The `pop()` function removes the top value from the stack, reducing the number of values on the stack by one.

Table 20.1 lists the most important functions related to the stack container class and gives a description of each. All of these functions are member functions of the container class, and you can apply them to any stack object you define.

Note: You must ensure that the stack (with `getItemsInContainer()`) contains values before you attempt to pop the stack. You'll receive an abnormal termination error message (about the scariest-sounding error message displayed by Turbo C++!) if you try to remove values when no values are present.

20

Table 20.1. Several useful stack-container-class member functions.

Member Function	Description
`getItemsInContainer()`	Returns the number of values in the stack.
`flush()`	Empties the stack of all its contents.

continues

Table 20.1. continued

Member Function	Description
isEmpty()	Returns false if the stack contains at least one value and true if the stack is empty.
pop()	Returns the top value on the stack and reduces the stack by one, eliminating the original top value from the stack.
push()	Pushes its argument onto the stack and increases the stack count by 1.
top()	Returns the top value on the stack without actually popping the value off the stack.

Note: Don't store static, global, or local objects in a container such as a stack unless you remove those objects before the container object goes out of scope. You'll no longer have access to the objects if you do. It is OK to store heap objects in a container without worrying about the values (they'll correctly go away when the container goes out of scope). There are some advanced ways to store static, global, and local objects in containers, but they're beyond the scope of this book.

The BI_StackAsVector container class isn't the only stack container class available. You can use any of the following stack container classes:

```
BI_StackAsVector<T>
BI_StackAsList<T>
BI_IStackAsVector<T>
BI_IStackAsList<T>
```

The BI stands for *Borland International.* The class you decide to use depends on the way you want the stack represented internally. (For small stacks, the difference doesn't matter much.)

The first two classes are called *direct class versions* because they store objects directly inside the stack. These two classes are better candidates for built-in data types and small classes and structures than large classes and structures. If you use one of the first two template class definitions for storing your own class objects, you must provide a default constructor and copy constructor for your class.

The second two class definition names store the stack objects indirectly through pointers. Use either of the second two classes when you want to store large classes or structures on the stack (the pointers provide more efficiency than rearranging the actual objects themselves as the stack grows).

The BI_...Vector<T> classes are best used for small stacks or when you know the largest size of the stack in advance. You can specify the stack size by placing the size in parentheses after the object when defining the stack like this:

```
BI_StackAsVector<int> intStack(125);
```

As defined here, the intStack can never grow more than 125 elements. If you attempt to store more than 125 elements, Turbo C++ displays an error. Even though you sometimes have to guess at the future stack size, doing so improves your stack performance over using the BI_...List<T>. You don't *have* to specify a stack size when using the BI_...Vector<T> classes (Listing 20.1 didn't specify an initial stack size) if the stack doesn't get too big (the maximum size depends on the memory module you are using). However, if you want to let the stack grow to an unknown size, use the BI_...List<T> classes. Using the BI_...List<T> classes is slightly less efficient than using the BI_...Vector<T> classes, but the BI_...List<T> classes are useful when the stack size isn't known in advance.

The program in Listing 20.2 stores and manipulates a Customer user-defined class on the stack. As you'll see, manipulating a stack of objects is just as easy as manipulating a stack of integers. (As long as you make sure a default constructor is defined.)

Listing 20.2. A stack containing a user-defined data type.

```
1:  // Filename: STACK2.CPP
2:  // Puts class objects on the stack and accesses them.
3:  #include <iostream.h>
4:  #include <stacks.h>
5:  #include <string.h>
6:  #include <conio.h>
7:  class Customer {
8:    char name[25];
9:    int years;      // Years in business
10: public:
11:   Customer(char [], int);
12:   Customer() {}   // Container requires a default constructor
13:   void prCustomer(void);
14: };
15: Customer::Customer(char N[], int Y) : years(Y)
16: {
17:   strcpy(name, N);
```

continues

Listing 20.2. continued

```
18: }
19: void Customer::prCustomer(void)
20: {
21:   cout << "\nCustomer name: " << name << "\n";
22:   cout << "Years as customer: " << years << "\n";
23: }
24: main()
25: {
26:   clrscr();
27:   BI_StackAsVector<Customer> custStack;
28:   Customer c1("John Hart", 2), c2("Laura Wilson", 4);
29:   Customer look;
30:   custStack.push(c1);  // Push constructed values
31:   custStack.push(c2);
32:   cout << "There are ";
33:   cout << custStack.getItemsInContainer(
        ➡<< " values in the stack.\n";
34:   look = custStack.pop();
35:   cout << "\nThe top value on the stack is: ";
36:   look.prCustomer();
37:   cout << "\n";
38:   custStack.flush();   // Empties the stack
39:   cout << "After flushing, there are ";
40:   cout << custStack.getItemsInContainer()
        ➡<< " values in the stack.\n";
41:   return 0;
42: }
```

There are 2 values in the stack.

The top value on the stack is:
Customer name: Laura Wilson
Years as customer: 4

After flushing, there are 0 values in the stack.

The stack contains two Customer objects by line 31. Line 34 is the first and only pop() in the program, and sure enough, the last Customer on the stack, Laura Wilson, was the first one popped off. The stack is then emptied (with the flush() member function) on line 38, and a message prints on lines 39 and 40 showing you that the stack was flushed.

DO use the built-in container classes for your data storage.

DO use the stack template container class when you want to store any kind of object in a stack formation.

DO supply a default constructor if you store non-built-in data types in a stack container.

DO use a `BI_...AsList()` stack when you don't know how many stack values will be pushed by the program. Use a `BI_...AsVector()` if the number of stack values is low or if you know in advance what the largest stack size will be.

DON'T pop a stack unless it has values.

A Queue Provides FIFO Access

A time-worn example of a *queue* is a line at the bank. The first person in the line will be the next person helped. Unlike the LIFO aspect of stacks, a queue is FIFO, meaning that the first item on the list will be first in line to leave the list. Therefore, the oldest item in a queue is always the next out of the queue.

If you stored a 10, then a 20, then a 30 on the queue, then retrieved a value from the queue, you would get the 10 because 10 was in the queue the longest, as Figure 20.3 illustrates.

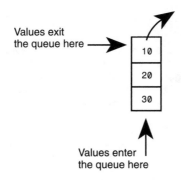

Figure 20.3. *A queue always loses its oldest value.*

Queues are helpful in analyzing lines to speed customer processing at banks, post offices, and elsewhere. The difference between a stack and a queue is that a queue uses FIFO, implying that a queue is a box with two openings, one for the incoming data and the other for the exiting data.

> **Note:** Stacks and queues are known as *sequence classes* because their retrieve order depends on the sequence in which their values were added.

Listing 20.3 contains a queue version of the stack program shown in Listing 20.1. Notice from the output that the values on the queue come out of the queue in the reverse order of the stack. The get() and put() member functions insert and remove values from queues (the terms *push* and *pop* apply only to stacks).

 Listing 20.3. A queue containing three integer values.

```
1:  // Filename: QUEUE.CPP
2:  // Puts 3 values in a queue, then accesses the queue
3:  // through container functions, printing values as
4:  // they come off the queue.
5:  #include <iostream.h>
6:  #include <queues.h>
7:  #include <conio.h>
8:  main()
9   {  clrscr();
10    // Define an integer queue object
11:    BI_QueueAsVector<int> intQueue;
12:    // Put three values on the queue
13:    intQueue.put(10);
14:    intQueue.put(20);
15:    intQueue.put(30);
16:    cout << "There are " << intQueue.getItemsInContainer();
17:    cout << " values in the queue\n";
18:    cout << "Just got " << intQueue.get() << "\n"; // Removes as it
19:    cout << "Just got " << intQueue.get() << "\n"; // prints.
20:    cout << "Just got " << intQueue.get() << "\n";
21:    return 0;
22: }
```

```
There are 3 values in the queue
Just got 10
Just got 20
Just got 30
```

 Remember that the oldest values in a queue are the first off the queue. Also keep in mind that line 11 could have created a queue of *any* data type, built-in or user-defined, and the queue's access would remain the same. When using the template classes, you don't have to worry about supplying access member functions because Turbo C++ does all the work.

The following member functions, in addition to get() and put(), work for queues just as they did for stacks:

```
getItemsInContainer()
flush()
isEmpty()
```

The queue container class comes in several formats. If you know in advance the number of items in the queue, or if you know that the queue will be fairly small (taking approximately fewer than 32,768 bytes of memory), use either of the following queue template class definitions:

```
BI_QueueAsVector<T>
BI_QueueAsDoubleList<T>
```

The Vector and DoubleList are internal data structure mechanisms. If speed is critical, try each to find one that suits your application the best. Both of these class definitions require a default constructor and copy constructor if you store your own class objects rather than built-in data types. The following two versions of the queue class are best used when you store large class or structure objects on the queue because they store pointers to the data rather than the objects themselves and are thus more efficient for large data types:

```
BI_IQueueAsVector<T>
BI_IQueueAsDoubleList<T>
```

 Note: Notice that you can never access a stack or queue in any order you like. If you don't want the FIFO or LIFO ordering that these two data structures provide—and many applications need to access data in a different order than these two data structures provide—you'll have to choose another kind of container. Stacks and queues (and also offshoots of them called *deques* and *priority queues*) are known as sequence template classes because the data comes from them in a predefined sequence, depending on the order in which the data was inserted.

DO	DON'T

DO use a queue container class for FIFO ordering of data.

DO use a `BI_...AsDoubleList()` queue when you don't know in advance how many stack values will be stored on the queue. Use a `BI_...AsVector()` if the number of queue values is low or if you know in advance what the largest queue size will be.

Have a Bag or Set of Data

A *bag* is a container of values, just as a stack and queue holds data, but unlike the sequence classes, a bag is an *unordered container*. The values "go into" the bag in a random order, and there might be more than one value in the bag with the same value.

A *set* is identical to a bag except that in a set, there can be no duplicate values. Both bags and sets are unordered containers because neither stores data in any preset order.

Both bag and set containers must supply ways for you to get values out of the bag and set. You must *iterate* through the bag's or set's contents using a special *iterator member function*. An in-depth discussion of iterators is beyond the scope of this book and, luckily, really isn't needed to understand how these containers operate. Listing 20.4 shows an example of a bag container.

Note: More than likely, the iterator will remove the bag (and set) values in the order in which they were inserted. However, if you insert and delete values several times, the bag's contents will get mixed up, so there's no guarantee on the order in which you'll get values out of a bag or set.

Type

Listing 20.4. A queue containing three integer values.

```
1:  // Filename: BAGS.CPP
2:  // Stores 15 values in a bag and then displays them
3:  #include <bags.h>
4:  #include <iostream.h>
5:  #include <iomanip.h>
6:  #include <stdlib.h>
7:  #include <conio.h>
8:  main()
```

```
 9:  {
10:    clrscr();
11:
12:    // Create a floating-point bag
13:    BI_BagAsVector<float> fltBag;
14:
15:    // Store 15 random values in the bag
16:    for (int i=0; i<15; i++)
17:    { fltBag.add(i); }
18:
19:    // Show the bag search routine
20:    if (fltBag.hasMember(2.0))
21:       { cout << "\n**The bag contains a 2.0.\n"; }
22:
23:    BI_BagAsVectorIterator<float> next(fltBag);
24:    // Output the bag
25:    cout << setprecision(3);
26:    cout << setiosflags(ios::fixed) << setiosflags(ios::showpoint);
27:    cout << "\nHere are the values in the bag: \n";
28:
29:    while (next)  {
30:      cout << next++ << "   ";
31:      cout << fltBag.getItemsInContainer()<< " left.\n";
32:    }
33:    cout << "\n";
34:    return 0;
35: }
```

```
**The bag contains a 2.0.
Here are the values in the bag:
0.000    15 left.
1.000    15 left.
2.000    15 left.
3.000    15 left.
4.000    15 left.
5.000    15 left.
6.000    15 left.
7.000    15 left.
8.000    15 left.
9.000    15 left.
10.000   15 left.
11.000   15 left.
12.000   15 left.
13.000   15 left.
14.000   15 left.
```

This program generates 15 floating-point values and stores those values in the bag named fltBag. The bag is checked to see whether it contains a 2.0 in lines 20 and 21. (You must supply an operator=() function if you want to store your own class objects in a bag or set.)

If you wanted to store another group of numbers in the bag, from 0.0 to 14.0 as done on lines 16 and 17, you could, and the bag would contain 30 values with each having a duplicate. If, however, you changed the same program to a *set* equivalent program, Turbo C++ would ignore all duplicate values and would not store any of the extras in the set.

The output shows that an iterator iterates but does not remove data from a bag or set. The iterator named getNext is defined on line 23 and is used in the while loop to step through the bag without removing values. An iterator must be defined after the class is initialized with data if you want the iterator to find any data values.

Table 20.2 lists several of the member functions you'll use with bags and sets. The two bag and two set definition classes are

```
BI_BagAsVector<T>
BI_SetAsVector<T>
BI_IBagAsVector<T>
BI_ISetAsVector<T>
```

Table 20.2. Several bag and set member functions.

Member Function	Description
add()	Adds values to the bag or set.
getItemsInContainer()	Returns the number of values in the bag or set.
flush()	Empties the bag or set of all its contents.
hasMember()	Returns true if the member being searched for (in the member function's parentheses) is in the bag or set.
isEmpty()	Returns false if the bag or set contains at least one value and true if the bag or set is empty.

An Array Template Class

You don't need an array template class for built-in arrays, because Turbo C++ already can handle array manipulation. However, it's nice to know that Turbo C++ includes an array template container that enables you to work with arrays of your own objects just as if they were regular built-in data types inside arrays.

You must remember to supply a default constructor, a copy constructor, and an overloaded operator=() for the class you want to store in the array. Listing 20.5 shows a user-defined class being manipulated in an array as though the array contained built-in data types.

Listing 20.5. An array of user-defined data types.

```
1:  // Filename: ARRAY1.CPP
2:  // Stores user-defined class objects in an array container
3:  #include <iostream.h>
4:  #include <conio.h>
5:  #include <string.h>
6:  #include <arrays.h>
7:
8:  // First, define the class that you'll later store in an array
9:  class Group {
10:    int age;
11:    char name[20];
12:    char initial;
13: public:
14:    // Default constructor
15:    Group() {initial = '\0'; name[0] = '\0'; age = 0; }
16:    Group(int A, char N[], char I) : age(A), initial(I)
17:      { strcpy(name, N); }
18:    int operator==(Group & g)
19:      { return    // Returns true if all members match
20:        (age == g.age) && !stricmp(name, g.name) &&
               ➡initial==g.initial;
21:      }
22:    friend ostream & operator<< (ostream &, Group g);
23: };
24: // A regular overloaded output operator for the class
25: ostream & operator<< (ostream & out, Group g)
26: {
27:   out << "\nAge:      " << g.age << "\n";
28:   out << "Name:     " << g.name << "\n";
29:   out << "Initial: " << g.initial << "\n";
30:   return out;
31: }
32: //////////////////////////////////////////////////////////////////
33: main()
34: {
35:   clrscr();
36:   // Define a class array with 5 elements
37:   BI_ArrayAsVector<Group> gData(5);
38:
39:   // Initialize some objects and store them in the array
40:   gData.add(Group(32, "Greg", 'P'));
41:   gData.add(Group(16, "Sally", 'T'));
42:   gData.add(Group(25, "Franklin", 'Q'));
```

continues

Listing 20.5. continued

```
43:    gData.add(Group(48, "Bettye", 'U'));
44:    gData.add(Group(16, "Sally", 'T'));   // Hmm, a duplicate
45:
46:    // Print the array using regular array subscripts, wow!
47:    for (int ctr=0; ctr<5; ctr++)
48:      { cout << gData[ctr]; }
49:
50:    // Actually test to see if one value in the array equals another!
51:    if (gData[1] == gData[4])
52:      { cout << "\nYou've got a match with element #1 and #4.\n"; }
53:
54:    return 0;
55: }
```

```
Age:     32
Name:    Greg
Initial: P

Age:     16
Name:    Sally
Initial: T

Age:     25
Name:    Franklin
Initial: Q

Age:     48
Name:    Bettye
Initial: U

Age:     16
Name:    Sally
Initial: T

You've got a match with element #1 and #4.
```

Other than having to use the add() member function to add the values to the grData[] array, main() looks like it's working with an array of any built-in class. In lines 47 and 48, main() compares two array elements. The comparison is why an operator==() must be supplied with the class that you store in the container array.

Lines 40–44 initialize the array. Instead of using nested constructor calls, you could have instantiated a Group variable, initialized it with the constructor, and then included the variable name as the argument to the add() member functions.

The default constructor needed for all classes you store in the array is located on line 15. All the member functions were coded inline for the sake of brevity. The operator<<() function is called when main() prints the array elements on line 52.

Summary

Today's chapter only scratched the surface of Turbo C++'s container class power, but it offered you an introduction to some of the container data types and gave you a little refresher by showing you what Turbo C++ does for you.

Before using the supplied template container classes, you first must prepare your Turbo C++ compiler. The **O**ptions pull-down menu enables you to specify which #include directories Turbo C++ searches. The header files needed for template containers is different from the header used for regular built-in functions.

A container is nothing more than a data structure that holds data. By using templates, Turbo C++ can create several common containers for any data type, whether that data type is built-in or supplied by you.

A stack is one container type supplied by Turbo C++. A stack operates on the LIFO principle, so the last values in the stack are always the first to come off the stack. As with most container classes, there are several versions of the stack class depending on your application's needs. There are also several different kinds of member functions that manipulate the stack.

A queue is also considered a sequenced list of data values. Unlike with a stack, a queue's data appears in FIFO order; the first values in a queue are the first values out of the queue. Both queues and stacks are used a lot in business simulations in which customer lines are being analyzed or shelf life of inventory is being projected.

Note: By the way, stacks and queues mirror the way some food is stored for sale in grocery stores. Bread is stored in a stacklike form; the first bread on the shelf is pushed to the back and is sold last (LIFO). That's why clerks often "rotate the stock" so that the freshest bread is not always at the front of the racks. Milk is usually stored in a queue; the stockers put the milk in the coolers from the back room, and you as a customer take the milk out of the front of the cooler (FIFO).

20

Bags and sets offer unordered data structures. The only difference between a bag and a set is that a set never contains duplicate values. If you attempt to store a duplicate value in a set, Turbo C++ ignores the request.

The most important template container class is perhaps the array class. With the array container class, you can store your own class objects in an array-like structure, using the subscript to retrieve, print, and manipulate as though you were working with an array of built-in data types.

Q&A

1. Why would I want to use template container classes?

   As with most features of Turbo C++, template container classes give you a place to put your data values without requiring that you write your own data structure classes. Depending on the template container you choose, you can store the data values in a specific sequence or an unordered sequence.

   Because the container classes described in today's chapter are templates, you can just as easily create containers that hold built-in data as containers that hold objects.

2. What is a stack and what is a queue?

   A stack stores values in the reverse order in which it receives them, and a queue stores values in the same order in which it receives them. In other words, you can take values off a stack only in the reverse order in which you put them on the stack; the last value on the stack becomes the first off the stack (LIFO).

   Stack operations have their own lingo. To *push* the stack means to put a value on the stack. To *pop* the stack means to remove a value from the stack. These terms don't apply to queues.

3. How do bags and sets differ from stacks and queues?

   Bags and sets are known as unordered lists. Although you'll often find that Turbo C++ retrieves values from bags and sets in the same order in which those values were stored, the order is never guaranteed.

   Stacks and queues have a definite order. They're both called sequencing classes because their values appear in sequence as determined by the way the stack and queue were initialized.

Workshop

The Workshop offers quiz questions and exercises to hone your skills and give you feedback on today's lesson. You'll find some proposed answers in Appendix D.

Quiz

1. What is a stack?

2. What do push and pop mean when referring to a stack?

3. What is the difference between a stack and a queue?

4. If you wanted to store an unknown (in advance) number of large structures in a queue, which container class would you use?

5. What is the difference between a bag and a set?

6. What member function is needed to assign values to array-container-class elements?

Exercises

1. Rewrite line 13 in Listing 20.1 so that 50 stack values, at most, are allowed. By specifying the total number of stack values at the time you define the stack, you improve performance.

2. Create a computer class for an inventory that keeps track of the brand, model (both character arrays), price, and memory (long integer) in bytes. Instantiate a few values, and store the class objects in an array. Don't overload operator<<(), but provide access functions to the private members so that main() can print the individual array element's members. (Two computers in inventory are considered to be equal if they are the same brand, model, price, and memory. Don't write the code in main() to test for equality, but supply an operator==() function as if you are testing for equality of two inventory items.)

Easy File I/O

Your training is coming to an end! Of course, that really means that your programming is just beginning. You'll never feel like an expert Turbo C++ programmer until you've written your own "real world" programs.

If you think OOP isn't that difficult to understand, you're right. However, you probably would not have believed that on Day 1! These past three weeks have taken you from an OOP recruit to an OOP pro, and the trail really hasn't been that difficult, has it? In reality, there's not much that makes OOP different from non-OOP programming, yet the small OOP knowledge base you now have will do wonders for the programs that you write. You'll now move the details of your programs into class objects, and the rest of your programs will consist of little more than high-level directors of those classes. You'll find that OOP and Turbo C++ lessen the tediousness of programming.

This final day's tutorial rounds out your OOP tri-week course by teaching you how to store and retrieve disk file data. The entire book has concentrated until now on in-memory manipulation of objects because that's where true data processing occurs. Nevertheless, without the capability to store and retrieve your data, OOP would be little help indeed for long-term practical use.

If you've written disk file programs before, using C or even QBasic (the two languages offer surprisingly few differences in the methods they use for disk I/O), you'll see that Turbo C++ is just as easy. Many times, Turbo C++ is even easier because Turbo C++ does more work and removes details from your programs.

Today, you learn about the following topics:

- ☐ Sequential file I/O manipulation

- ☐ Sequential file I/O with character data

- ☐ Sequential file I/O with string data

- ☐ Sequential file I/O with class data

- ☐ Random-access file I/O manipulation

- ☐ Positioning the file pointer

- ☐ Reading and writing data in the same file

Sequential I/O: Read, Write, and Append

There are only three actions you can perform with a sequential file: reading data from the file, writing data to a new file, and adding data to an existing file. Think of a sequential file as being like a cassette tape; you cannot rearrange songs or change individual selections very easily. To add a song to the middle of a series of songs on a cassette, you have to create a new tape altogether. It just isn't possible to shift all the songs down to make room for the new one.

Although a disk drive offers more flexibility than a cassette, if you set up a file as a sequential file, you'll be limited to accessing the file in the three sequential ways: creating the file, reading the file, and adding to the file.

Sequential file access is actually easier than random file access. Random files give you the ability to rearrange data on the disk just as you do elements in an array. As with an array, you can access a random file in any order, not just from the first record written to the last as must be done with sequential files. However, programming for random files is a little more detailed, and some programming situations lend themselves well to sequential file access. Here are just some of the times when using sequential files makes sense:

1. When storing a history file of transactions that you only rarely have to access, and then the access is appending to the end of it. What is the most common thing done to a history file? More data is tacked onto the end as time goes by.

2. When storing text files. Today's chapter shows you several programs that read and write characters and strings using Turbo C++'s sequential I/O techniques.

3. When storing data in a batch processing environment, such as in some accounting departments, in which data is only modified by other transactions that are batched up and run at the close of the month.

4. When the data must be read by other programs that were not written in Turbo C++. Sequentially created files are sometimes easier to access because they usually contain delimiters such as spaces, tabs, and commas that random-access files don't always need.

Whatever access method you choose, the data file to the PC is just a stream of bytes on the disk.

Note: A case could be made that all the advantages of sequential file access already exist in random files because you can access a random file sequentially, from the first data value to the last. It's true that random files can be accessed sequentially, but remember that sequential file access is often easier to write, although with Turbo C++ even random access is not difficult.

A major programming distinction between sequential files and random-access files appears when you consider when each is opened and closed. Before using any disk file, or before creating a disk file, you must *open* the file to prepare it for access. After you're done with a file, you must be sure to close the file properly (you'll see that opening and closing files is really easy with Turbo C++'s help). The analogy to a filing cabinet should be obvious. You can open sequential files in only one access *mode* (output, input, or append) at a time. After you open a random file, you can operate on the file in more than one mode without having to close and reopen the file a second time.

Getting Ready

Data files are objects to your Turbo C++ program. Each file is assumed to be an instantiation of one of the file stream classes. Each of these classes is prototyped and defined in the file FSTREAM.H, so be sure to include this header file in all Turbo C++ programs that access the disk.

You'll use one or more of the following three access classes when describing your files as objects to your programs:

```
ifstream
ofstream
fstream
```

The `ifstream` class defines input member functions and related data, `ofstream` defines output member functions and related data, and `fstream` takes care of both for files you want to both read from and write to. All the common I/O member functions you're used to, such as `get()`, `put()`, and `getline()`, work for files just as easily as they do for the screen and keyboard.

Writing Character Data to a Sequential File

Perhaps the easiest place to begin understanding file I/O is a program that creates a sequential file of characters. Listing 21.1 shows such a program that uses the put member function to write character data to a file.

 Listing 21.1. Writing characters to a file.

```
1:  // Filename: CHARSEQ.CPP
2:  // Creates a file using sequential output of characters.
3:  #include <fstream.h>
4:  main()
5:  {
6:    // First, open the file for output
7:    ofstream outfile("DATAOUT.DAT");
8:
9:    // Write individual letters to the file
10:   outfile.put('T');
11:   outfile.put('h');
12:   outfile.put('i');
13:   outfile.put('s');
14:   outfile.put(' ');
15:   outfile.put('i');
16:   outfile.put('s');
17:   outfile.put(' ');
18:   outfile.put('e');
19:   outfile.put('a');
20:   outfile.put('s');
21:   outfile.put('y');
22:   outfile.put('\n');   // Becomes two characters in file, CR-LF
23:   return 0;
24: }
```

 The output for this program doesn't appear on the screen. The output appears in the file named DATAOUT.DAT. Here are the single-line contents of DATAOUT.DAT:

```
This is easy
```

The program wrote a newline character to the end of the file, but the newline character becomes a two-byte carriage return/line feed sequence at the end of the text bringing the total byte count in the file to 14. If you want to look at the file's contents, you can go to DOS and use the TYPE command or write a program to read and display the contents of the file as shown later in today's chapter.

Line 7 defines a file object variable named `outfile`. The object type is the class `ofstream` (for *output file stream*), and the object's name is `outfile`. The constructor for `ofstream` objects opens the file and prepares it for output, so you must supply a file name string used in the constructor. The string can be stored in a character array or stored on the heap, and it can include a complete disk and pathname if you like.

Unlike C and most other programming languages, the OOP concept eliminates the need for a file handle. When you tell the `outfile` object to do something, such as output some data (lines 10–22), the file takes care of itself, and you don't have to refer to a file handle or file number as you do with C.

Unlike with non-OOP file output, Turbo C++ automatically closes the file when the file object variable (in this case `outfile`) goes out of scope. Aren't destructors nice?

> **Note:** All files opened with the `ofstream` class are output files and considered to be newly created. If the DATOUT.DAT file already existed when line 7 opened the file, the old version would be deleted and the new data added in its place.

Listing 21.2. Writing characters from a string.

```
1:  // Filename: CHARSTR.CPP
2:  // Creates a file using sequential output of a string's characters.
3:  #include <fstream.h>
4:  #include <string.h>
5:  main()
6:  {
7:    // First, open the file for output
8:    ofstream outfile("DATAOUT.DAT");
9:
10:   // Define the string
11:   char out[] = "This is easy\n";  // Don't forget the newline
12:
13:   // Write the string a character at a time
14:   for (int i=0; i<strlen(out); i++)
15:     { outfile.put(out[i]); }
16:   return 0;
17: }
```

Listing 21.2 produces the same output file, named DATAOUT.DAT, as Listing 21.1 did.

 Both Listings 21.1 and 21.2 wrote single characters to a new file, although Listing 21.2 wrote the characters from a character array (line 15) instead of writing individual characters.

Now that you've seen the put() function used for sequential file output of characters, forget ever using it! The FSTREAM.H overloads the << to work with characters and strings. Consider the rewritten version of Listing 21.1 shown in Listing 21.3.

Type Listing 21.3. Extremely easy file output.

```
1:  // Filename: CHAROVR.CPP
2:  // Creates a file using sequential output of characters.
3:  #include <fstream.h>
4:  main()
5:  {
6:    // First, open the file for output
7:    ofstream outfile("DATAOUT.DAT");
8:
9:    // Write individual letters to the file
10:   outfile << 'T';
11:   outfile << 'h';
12:   outfile << 'i';
13:   outfile << 's';
14:   outfile << ' ';
15:   outfile << 'i';
16:   outfile << 's';
17:   outfile << ' ';
18:   outfile << 'e';
19:   outfile << 'a';
20:   outfile << 's';
21:   outfile << 'y';
22:   outfile << '\n';    // Becomes two characters in file, CR-LF
23:   return 0;
24: }
```

 The output from Listing 21.3 is identical to that of the preceding two program listings.

 As you can see, writing data to an OOP file with Turbo C++ is just as easy as writing characters to the screen. Lines 10–22 all use the insertion operator, <<, to write individual characters to the file. Line 15 in Listing 21.2, which wrote characters from a character array, would also work if you rewrote it like this:

```
{ outfile << put(out[i]); }
```

The FSTREAM.H file also overloads << for string output as well. Listing 21.4 writes four strings to a file named STRFILE.TXT.

 Listing 21.4. Writing strings.

```
 1:  // Filename: STRFOUT.CPP
 2:  // Creates a file using sequential output of strings.
 3:  #include <fstream.h>
 4:  main()
 5:  {
 6:    // First, open the file for output
 7:    ofstream outfile("STRFILE.TXT");
 8:
 9:    // Write four strings to the file, two string
10:    // constants and two from character arrays
11:    outfile << "Don't lag behind...\n";
12:    outfile << "Get in on the scoop!\n";
13:    char ara1[] = "Learn Turbo C++...\n";
14:    outfile << ara1;
15:    char ara2[] = "And get ready to OOP!\n";
16:    outfile << ara2;
17:    return 0;
18: }
```

 Here are the contents of the STRFILE.TXT created from Listing 21.4:

```
Don't lag behind...
Get in on the scoop!
Learn Turbo C++...
And get ready to OOP!
```

 The newline character, \n, at the end of the strings being written in lines 11 through 16 are not required, but sequential files usually include newlines at the end of their lines of data. (A line of data is called a *record*, as you might already know.) The newlines help keep the file formatted properly if someone looks at the file from the DOS prompt or if another Turbo C++ program that uses getline() needs to read the file.

 Note: Remember that outfile shown in the preceding programs is the name of the file object you define from the ifstream, ofstream, or fstream classes. There is nothing special about the name outfile; you can call the object variable anything you like. You can also open several files, giving them each different object variable names, and write to each one separately by using their names.

Reading Character Data from a Sequential File

When you want to read characters from a file, use the ifstream class (for *input file stream*) rather than ofstream, and use the get() function to read the characters. Although >> is overloaded for file input, you cannot use >> to read whitespace (such as blanks or tabs) from files, so your files incorrectly are scrunched up if you use >> rather than the get() member function.

Reading data from a file requires slightly more work than writing the data because you must check for an end-of-file condition as you read the data.

The input file object variable you create contains a non-zero value as long as there is data left to read, and it becomes zero (false) when the end of file is reached, as Listing 21.5 shows.

Listing 21.5. Reading characters from an input file.

```
1:  // Filename: CHARINP.CPP
2:  // Reads the file created earlier
3:  #include <fstream.h>
4:  // No iostream.h necessary
5:  main()
6:  {
7:    // First, open the file for input
8:    ifstream inpfile("DATAOUT.DAT");
9:
10:   // Write the next character in a loop
11:   char nextChar;
12:   while (inpfile)  // True until end of file
13:   {
14:     inpfile.get(nextChar);  // Get next character and display it
15:     cout << nextChar;
16:   }
17:   return 0;
18: }
```

```
This is easy
```

Although the program writes to the screen, the IOSTREAM.H header file isn't included in the entire program! FSTREAM.H derives from IOSTREAM.H, and therefore FSTREAM.H contains all the functionality of IOSTREAM.H with extended members to handle file I/O.

The program simply reads one character at a time (line 14) and displays that character (line 15) until the end of file is reached. This program mirrors the DOS TYPE command in that it displays to the screen whatever file it reads. Of course, the file should be an ASCII text file if it is to be readable on the screen.

Notice that the while doesn't need to compare against 0 or 1 because in Turbo C++ (as in C) these two tests are equivalent, but the second is more efficient:

```
while (infile != 0)   // True until infile is equal to 0
```

and

```
while (infile)        // True until infile is equal to 0
```

If you want to read entire strings from a sequential data file, use the getline() member function as Listing 21.6 demonstrates.

  Listing 21.6. Reading string data from an input file.

```
1:  // Filename: STRINP.CPP
2:  // Reads the file of strings created earlier
3:  #include <fstream.h>
4:  main()
5:  {
6:    // First, open the file for input
7:    ifstream inpfile("STRFILE.TXT");
8:
9:    // Loop that writes each line of text to the screen
10:   char nextStr[80];  // Assumes no record > 80 characters
11:   while (inpfile)     // True until end of file
12:   {
13:     inpfile.getline(nextStr, 80);  // Get next record and display it
14:     cout << nextStr << "\n";
15:   }
16:   return 0;
17: }
```

```
Don't lag behind...
Get in on the scoop!
Learn Turbo C++...
And get ready to OOP!
```

Line 13 reads a record from the input file. The newline at the end of each of the file's records terminates the getline() member function call but is not part of the input. Therefore, the newlines are not stored in the nextStr[] array. When the program is printing the strings on line 14, a newline has to be inserted at the end of the output.

What If There Are Problems?

When you are reading and writing files, errors can occur that you must check for. You might attempt to read from a file that doesn't exist, a disk drive might not be available, or the disk could have mechanical difficulty. You can use any or all of the following four member functions to check for file error conditions:

```
good()
eof()
fail()
bad()
```

Notice that you can use either the end-of-file testing method from Listing 21.6's line 11 or the `eof()` member function.

These four member functions return true or false depending on the result of the previous I/O. The first function, `good()`, is true (1) if no errors occurred. `good()` returns a false value and one or more of the other member functions return true if an error occurs.

Note: The stream's `fail()` member function checks for three types of errors: hardware failures (such as a bad disk sector or a disk door open), read/write failures (so you can use it to check the status of one of your I/O operations), and file-not-found errors (when you attempt to open a file that doesn't exist). The `bad()` member function checks only for hardware failures and file-not-found errors, not for read/write errors. Therefore, Turbo C++ programmers use `fail()` more often than `bad()`.

Some diligent Turbo C++ programmers test for each of these functions every time they perform input or output. Listing 21.7 shows a program that attempts to open a file on drive Z:. Assuming you don't have a drive Z: (most people don't!), you'll get the error output generated.

 Listing 21.7. Attempting to use a file on a drive that doesn't exist.

```
1:  // Filename: STRINPER.CPP
2:  // Reads the file of strings created earlier
3:  #include <fstream.h>
4:  main()
5:  {
```

continues

Listing 21.7. continued

```
6:    // First, open the file for input
7:    ifstream inpfile("Z:STRFILE.TXT");
8:    cout << "Result of good() is " << inpfile.good() << "\n";
9:    cout << "Result of eof() is " << inpfile.eof() << "\n";
10:   cout << "Result of fail() is " << inpfile.fail() << "\n";
11:   cout << "Result of bad() is " << inpfile.bad() << "\n";
12:   return 0;
13: }
```

```
Result of good() is 0
Result of eof() is 0
Result of fail() is 4
Result of bad() is 4
```

The Z: disk drive does not exist, so the fail() and bad() member functions return a true value for their error conditions.

Appending Data to Sequential Files

When you need to add to the end of a sequential file, such as adding to an account history file, you'll have to tell Turbo C++ to open the file in *append* mode. To open in append mode, you have to specifically call the open() member function instead of letting the default file object constructor do the job. The open() function is a member function of the fstream class. open() isn't needed for the ifstream class because input access is always assumed. open() isn't needed for the ofstream class because output access is always assumed.

Here's the format of the open() member function:

```
objVar.open(filenameStr, modeBit(s));
```

The *objVar* must be an fstream object variable name. When defining the file object variable, don't specify the filename in parentheses (such as line 7 in Listing 21.6) or Turbo C++ will open the file incorrectly. *filenameStr* is the name of the file you want to open. *modeBit(s)* is one or more of the mode bits found in Table 21.1 that describe the way you want the file opened. If you include more than one mode bit, separate them with an inclusive OR operator, |.

Table 21.1. The open() member function mode bits.

Mode Bit	Description
ios::in	Open for input
ios::out	Open for output
ios::app	Open for appending
ios::ate	Erase the file before the first input or output
ios::nocreate	Returns an error if the file does not already exist
ios::noreplace	Returns an error if the file already exists and neither ios::app nor ios::ate is set

The program in Listing 21.8 demonstrates the use of open() by opening the string file created earlier and adding another stanza to the text.

Listing 21.8. Adding to the end of a text file.

```
1:  // Filename: STRAPP.CPP
2:  // Adds to the file of strings created earlier
3:  #include <fstream.h>
4:  #include <stdlib.h>
5:  main()
6:  {
7:    // First, define the file object variable
8:    fstream appfile;   // Notice no filename specified here
9:
10:   // Open the file for append
11:   appfile.open("STRFILE.TXT", ios::app | ios::nocreate);
12:
13:   if (!appfile.good())   // Quit if there's a problem
14:     { cerr << "Error opening file.\n";
15:       exit(1);
16:     }
17:   appfile << "\nIn the future...\n";
18:   appfile << "I'll make some dough.\n";
19:   appfile << "Writing programs...\n";
20:   appfile << "That make computers go!\n";
21:
22:   return 0;
23: }
```

21

Listing 21.7 adds four lines to the STRFILE.TXT file. Here are the contents of STRFILE.TXT after appending the extra text:

```
Don't lag behind...
Get in on the scoop!
Learn Turbo C++...
And get ready to OOP!

In the future...
I'll make some dough.
Writing programs...
That make computers go!
```

Note: Please don't write complaint letters about the author's bad poetry. Neither Longfellow nor Frost could write computer programs!

The open() member function call on line 11 opens the STRFILE.TXT file in append mode. You'll also see that the `ios::nocreate` mode bit is set. If the file is not found on the disk, `ios::nocreate` ensures that Turbo C++ sets an error condition that will trigger the early program exit on line 15. Normally, a file does not have to exist to be appended to; when appending to a file that does not exist, Turbo C++ creates the file automatically unless you specify `ios::nocreate` and check the good() member function.

After the file is opened for append, you can add characters, strings, or even class data (as shown in the next section) to the end of the file.

Note: A later section will use the open() function to open a file in both input and output modes at the same time.

Class Data and Disk Files

Not all data is character data. When writing data to the disk to be read later, Turbo C++ programmers need a way to write class objects to the disk and also read those objects back in. The following points must be made before you see object I/O in action:

1. Unlike character I/O, objects are written to files in a compressed binary format that other programs such as the DOS TYPE command cannot properly interpret.

2. To see the data in class data files, you have to write programs that read the data into classes that have the same format as the class used to write the object data in the first place.

3. The class used to write the data to the file must match in number and format of data members to the class used to read the data from the file. (The member functions don't have to match.)

4. The write() member function writes object data to files, and the read() member function reads object data from files. Both have to be sent a character pointer to the data, so you'll have to typecast the object data using (char *) before writing objects.

The program in Listing 21.9 is a fairly comprehensive disk output program that writes inventory parts to the disk file using member functions. The Inventory class is formed by composing an Item class as a member so that Inventory can write the data to the disk using member functions. The Inventory class takes care of itself and even writes its own data to a file.

Type Listing 21.9. Writing objects using member functions.

```
1:  // Filename: OBSTOFIL.CPP
2:  // Defines several object variables and writes them to a file
3:  #include <fstream.h>
4:  #include <string.h>
5:  class Item {          // This class will be embedded in another
6:    char partCode[5];
7:    char descrip[20];
8:    int num;
9:    float price;
10: public:
11:   Item() {partCode[0] = '\0';}  // Null part code indicates no data
12:   Item(char P[], char D[], int N, float PR) :
13:       num(N), price(PR)
14:   { strcpy(partCode, P);
15:       strcpy(descrip, D);
16:   }
17: };
18: class Inventory {   // A composed class
19:   Item parts[50];   // This class contains all the parts
20: public:
21:   static int numInInv;  // Number of items in the inventory
22:   Inventory() {}
```

continues

Listing 21.9. continued

```
23:    void addToInv(char [], char [], int, float);
24:    void toDisk(void);
25: };  // Class definition ends here
26: void Inventory::addToInv(char P[], char D[], int N, float PR)
27: {
28:    parts[numInInv] = Item(P, D, N, PR);  // Temporary construction
29:    numInInv++;
30: }
31: void Inventory::toDisk(void)
32: {
33:    ofstream invOut("INV.DAT");
34:    invOut.write((char *)this, sizeof(*this));  // Write the record
35: }
36: // Static member has to be initialized here
37: int Inventory::numInInv = 0;
38: ////////////////////////////////////////////////////////////////////
39: main()
40: {
41:    // Construct empty inventory items
42:    Inventory parts;
43:
44:    // Create a few specific inventory items
45:    parts.addToInv("3WI", "Widgets", 14, 2.34);
46:    parts.addToInv("1BOL", "Large Bolts", 36, .45);
47:    parts.addToInv("7WN", "Wing Nuts", 109, .17);
48:    parts.addToInv("2CL", "Clamps", 31, 8.60);
49:
50:    // Now, write the data
51:    parts.toDisk();
52:    cout << Inventory::numInInv << " parts were written.";
53:    return 0;
54: }
```

 Listing 21.9 creates a data file with 50 records, the first 4 of which have valid data.

 When line 42 creates a parts object, it actually creates an array of Item members defined inside the Inventory class at line 19. Therefore, 50 inventory items are contained inside the parts object. The program fills only 4 of those items, but all 50 are written to the disk. The constructor for the embedded Item member stores a null zero in the first member's character array (line 11); whenever a part's partCode is null, the program has reached the end of the value parts data.

The addToInv() function calls on lines 45–48 store data in the first four inventory parts by calling the member function in lines 26–30. The addToInv() member

function stores the data in the next inventory item and increments the static numInInv integer variable so that the number of valid parts can be printed at the end of the program in line 52.

Instead of creating the inventory parts from constants on lines 45–48, the program could have prompted the user for the data.

The toDisk() member function writes the entire array, all 50 items, to a disk file named INV.DAT. The write() function call

```
invOut.write((char *)this, sizeof(*this));  // Write the record
```

writes the *this argument, which is the object containing all 50 parts, to the disk. Any data written with write() must be typecast as a character pointer because write() works with streams of character data. read() must know the number of bytes of data to write, hence the sizeof() argument.

If you look at INV.DAT from the DOS prompt using TYPE, you'll see a lot of garbage. The data written with write() is always compressed, unlike the data written using earlier sequential file I/O methods. The program in Listing 21.10 opens the INV.DAT file and prints its contents to the screen using the same Inventory class used in Listing 21.9 (except for a few member function changes).

Listing 21.10. Reading inventory objects using member functions.

```
 1: // Filename: OBSFRFIL.CPP
 2: // Reads object variables from a file
 3: #include <fstream.h>
 4: #include <conio.h>
 5: #include <iomanip.h>
 6: #include <stdlib.h>
 7: #include <string.h>
 8: class Item {          // This class will be embedded in another
 9: public:
10:   char partCode[5];
11:   char descrip[20];
12:   int num;
13:   float price;
14:   Item() {partCode[0] = '\0';}  // Null part code indicates no data
15:   Item(char P[], char D[], int N, float PR) :
16:       num(N), price(PR)
17:   { strcpy(partCode, P);
18:       strcpy(descrip, D);
19:   }
20: };
21: class Inventory {   // A composed class
22:   Item parts[50];    // This class contains all the parts
```

continues

21

Listing 21.10. continued

```
23: public:
24:    static int numInInv;   // Number of items in the inventory
25:    Inventory() {}
26:    void prData(void);
27:    void fromDisk(void);
28: };   // Class definition ends here
29: void Inventory::prData(void)
30: {
31:    int ctr=0;
32:    cout << setprecision(2) << setiosflags(ios::showpoint);
33:    cout << setiosflags(ios::fixed);
34:    cout << "Here is the inventory:\n";
35:    while (parts[ctr].partCode[0])   // Print until empty part code
36:      { cout << "Part number: " << parts[ctr].partCode << "\n";
37:        cout << "Description: " << parts[ctr].descrip << "\n";
38:        cout << "Number in stock: " << parts[ctr].num << "\n";
39:        cout << "Price: $" << parts[ctr].price << "\n\n";
40:        ctr++;
41:      }
42: }
43: void Inventory::fromDisk(void)
44: {
45:    ifstream invIn("INV.DAT");
46:    if (!invIn)
47:      { cerr << "File doesn't exist!\n";
48:        exit(1);
49:      }
50:    invIn.read((char *)this, sizeof(*this));  // Write the record
51: }
52: // Static member has to be initialized here
53: int Inventory::numInInv = 0;      // Not used but part of class
54: ///////////////////////////////////////////////////////////////////
55: main()
56: {
57:    clrscr();
58:    // Construct empty inventory items
59:    Inventory parts;
60:    // Read the data from the disk
61:    parts.fromDisk();
62:    parts.prData();
63:    return 0;
64: }
```

```
Here is the inventory:
Part number: 3WI
Description: Widgets
Number in stock: 14
Price: $2.34

Part number: 1BOL
Description: Large Bolts
Number in stock: 36
Price: $0.45

Part number: 7WN
Description: Wing Nuts
Number in stock: 109
Price: $0.17

Part number: 2CL
Description: Clamps
Number in stock: 31
Price: $8.60
```

The parts object defined on line 59 contains the same format as that in the preceding listing. All 50 items are stored in the one parts object, and the program reads from a disk file into these 50 items. (Only 4 of the 50 objects in the disk file contain data, but all 50 will be read into the parts object on line 50.)

The fromDisk() member function on lines 43–51 reads all 50 objects from the disk using a mirror-image function to Listing 21.9's write() member function. The power of Turbo C++ classes provides extremely complicated input of all object data from the file using only a single line of code (line 50).

The prData() member function on lines 29–42 prints the data on the screen. The data on the disk contains a null string for the partCode[] for the 46 objects that aren't yet defined in the disk file.

Note: Writing and reading 50 object values when only 4 contain data is inefficient but easy to follow. The program shown in the next section reads the inventory records one at a time until the end of data is reached.

21

DO	**DON'T**

DO use `put()` and `<<` to write character data to sequential text files.

DO use `get()`, `getline()`, and `>>` to read data from sequential text files.

DO use the `read()` and `write()` member functions to read and write class data.

DO use the `open()` member function to access data files when performing more than simple input or output (such as appending).

DON'T forget to check for errors when accessing files. Disk drives are mechanical, and problems can occur. If your program doesn't check for errors but an error occurs, you'll receive bad results.

Random-Access Files

You've already got most of the pieces needed to write programs that manipulate random-access files. Remember that you can read and write a random-access file from within the same program. There is nothing that physically separates a random-access file from a sequential file. The difference lies in the way you access and open the files. You can access random files in the same way you access arrays—in any order you prefer.

Use the bit modes in Table 21.1 to indicate that you want to both read and write from the file. Here is a sample `open()` member function call that prepares a file named MYFILE.DAT for both input and output:

```
rndfile.open("MYFILE.DAT", ios::in | ios::out);
```

To access a random-access file randomly (that is, in any order: forward, backward, every other record, or whatever), you must learn to manipulate the *file pointer*. File pointers are to random-access files what subscripts are to arrays. The file pointer always points to the next location in the file that you can access.

Use the `seekg()` member function to move the file pointer (which has little resemblance to regular variable pointers you use in Turbo C++ source code). `seekg()` is similar to C's `fseek()` function. The `seekg()` function requires an offset and a starting position in the file. Here is the format of the `seekg()` member function:

```
seekg(offset, startFileLoc)
```

The *offset* is a signed long integer value (it can be negative) that tells how many bytes you want to access from the *startFileLoc*. The *startFileLoc* can be one of these three positions:

```
ios::beg
ios::cur
ios::end
```

The `ios::beg` references the beginning byte in a file. `ios::cur` references the current location of the file pointer (the file pointer changes during reading and writing). And `ios::end` references the ending byte in the file.

Suppose that `rndFile` were a random-access file pointer connected to a file using the `open()` member function call shown earlier. The following statements move the file pointer around the file as described by their comments:

```
rndFile.seekg(0, ios::beg);    // Move pointer to start of file
rndFile.seekg(0, ios::end);    // Move pointer to end of file
rndFile.seekg(25, ios::beg);   // Move 25 bytes past the start
rndFile.seekg(-5, ios::cur);   // Move 5 bytes before current position
rndFile.seekg(-val, ios::end); // Move to "val" bytes from end of file
```

The program in Listing 21.11 reads the inventory in random order. Instead of using the Inventory class that holds 50 records, the program uses an individual inventory object that holds each record as it is read. The class is kept public so that encapsulation doesn't get in the way of your understanding of the seekg() function.

 Listing 21.11. Reading different inventory items randomly.

```
1:  // Filename: RNDFILE.CPP
2:  // Reads object randomly from a file
3:  #include <fstream.h>
4:  #include <conio.h>
5:  class Item {
6:  public:    // Just to keep simple
7:    char partCode[5];
8:    char descrip[20];
9:    int num;
10:   float price;
11:   void prData(int I)
12:     { cout << "Record number " << I << ":\n";
13:       cout << "Part: " << partCode;
14:       cout << "\nDescription: " << descrip;
15:       cout << "\nNumber: " << num;
16:       cout << "\nPrice: " << price << "\n\n";
17:     }
18: };
```

continues

21

617

Listing 21.11. continued

```
19:  ////////////////////////////////////////////////////////////////
20:  main()
21:  {
22:     clrscr();
23:     fstream ioFile;
24:     Item invItem;
25:     ioFile.open("INV.DAT", ios::in ¦ ios::out);
26:     ioFile.seekg(0, ios::beg);
27:     ioFile.read((char *)&invItem, sizeof(invItem));
28:     invItem.prData(1);
29:     // Put the position back to the beginning
30:     ioFile.seekg(0, ios::beg);
31:     ioFile.read((char *)&invItem, sizeof(invItem));
32:     invItem.prData(1);
33:     // Read last record
34:     ioFile.seekg(3*sizeof(invItem), ios::beg);
35:     ioFile.read((char *)&invItem, sizeof(invItem));
36:     invItem.prData(4);
37:     // Read in order
38:     ioFile.seekg(0, ios::beg);
39:     ioFile.read((char *)&invItem, sizeof(invItem));
40:     // Another seekg() isn't needed if reading in order
41:     invItem.prData(1);
42:     ioFile.read((char *)&invItem, sizeof(invItem));
43:     invItem.prData(2);
44:     ioFile.read((char *)&invItem, sizeof(invItem));
45:     invItem.prData(3);
46:     ioFile.read((char *)&invItem, sizeof(invItem));
47:     invItem.prData(4);
48:     return 0;
49:  }
```

```
Record number 1:
Part: 3WI
Description: Widgets
Number: 14
Price: 2.34

Record number 1:
Part: 3WI
Description: Widgets
Number: 14
Price: 2.34
```

```
Record number 4:
Part: 2CL
Description: Clamps
Number: 31
Price: 8.6

Record number 1:
Part: 3WI
Description: Widgets
Number: 14
Price: 2.34

Record number 2:
Part: 1BOL
Description: Large Bolts
Number: 36
Price: 0.45

Record number 3:
Part: 7WN
Description: Wing Nuts
Number: 109
Price: 0.17

Record number 4:
Part: 2CL
Description: Clamps
Number: 31
Price: 8.6
```

 After the record object is constructed on line 24, the file is opened randomly on line 25. Throughout the rest of main(), the seekg() function moves through the file, forward and backward, printing records using the public member function prData(). The seekg() function call on line 34 positions the file pointer to the beginning of the fourth record by skipping the first three records; the size of each record is determined with sizeof().

Note: Notice that you can reread the same record when using seekg(). You can never reread the same record when using simple sequential I/O.

21

If you want to change data inside a random-access file, you can do so. After seekg() moves the pointer to the record you want to change, rewrite new data in its place with the write() member function. The second exercise at the end of this chapter requires that you change records randomly, and the answer in Appendix D shows you how to write the program if you need help.

DO	**DON'T**

DO open files with the `ios::in` and the `ios::out` mode bits set if you want to access the file randomly.

DO use `seekg()` to reposition the file pointer to whatever record you want.

DON'T attempt to reread the same data in sequential files unless you open the files with the `open()` member function using the `ios::in` and `ios::out` mode bits.

Summary

Today's chapter completes your schooling in Turbo C++. Congratulations. After mastering today's concepts, you'll receive an A+ in C++!

Today you learned how to write sequential data to files and read it back in. You'll want to write character data to disk files when other non–Turbo C++ programs must work with the data. From DOS, you can use the TYPE command to look at the contents of sequential files.

When reading and writing sequential files, you cannot move around the file reading whatever records you prefer. However, you can read and write data extremely easily using the >> and << overloaded operators and the `put()`, `get()`, and `getline()` member functions.

You can write an entire array of objects using the `write()` member function and read an entire array of objects using a corresponding `read()` member function.

Q&A

1. Why should I learn disk I/O?

   No computer ever has enough internal RAM memory to hold all the data needed. The disk drive not only holds more data than memory but provides long-term storage because the disk files don't get erased when you turn off the computer.

2. What is the difference between sequential file I/O and random file I/O?

   Sequential file access writes data to a file sequentially, with the first record following the next, and you cannot reread a record or change individual

records without using random access. You can only write data, read data, and append data when using sequential files.

Random access enables you to skip around in a file, from byte to byte or record to record, reading and writing data wherever you want.

3. Do I have to learn a lot of new functions to perform file I/O?

When writing character data, you can write data directly to a disk file using the familiar << overloaded operator. You can also use `get()` and `put()` for file objects just as you do for keyboard and screen data. You must also explicitly call the `open()` member function when appending sequential data.

The random-access routines require that you learn three new functions: `seekg()`, `read()`, and `write()`. These three functions are analogous to `fseek()`, `fread()`, and `fwrite()` if you've ever written C programs that performed random-access I/O. `seekg()` positions the file pointer to any location in the file so that `read()` and `write()` can access the data at that location.

Workshop

The Workshop offers quiz questions and exercises to hone your skills and give you feedback on today's lesson. You'll find some proposed answers in Appendix D.

Quiz

1. What are the three stream classes used with file I/O?

2. What are the only three things you can do to a sequential file?

3. Which is best for text files: sequential access or random access?

4. Why don't you have to include IOSTREAM.H when writing screen output in the same program in which you're performing file I/O?

5. Why must you sometimes use `open()` and sometimes not?

6. What mode bit must you use in the `open()` member function when adding data to a file?

7. Why don't you have to use `open()` for `ifstream` or `ofstream` class objects?

8. What physical differences are there between a sequential file and a random-access file?

Exercises

1. Combine Listings 21.9 and 21.10, adding a menu with the following selections:

   ```
   Here are your choices:

       1. Add an inventory item to the file
       2. Display items in the file
       3. Exit the program

   What do you want to do?
   ```

   So that the user can enter the data, write prompts instead of writing constant values as done in Listing 21.9.

2. Add to the end of the program in Listing 21.12 the following routines:

   A. Position the file pointer back to the beginning of the file.

   B. Zero out each record's price, and write the data back to the disk.

   C. Run your program a second time to make sure the data was zeroed in the file.

Now that you've finished the third week, you'll find that the program in Listing WR3.1 adds a slightly different perspective to the inventory listings found in the third week's chapters.

The program maintains a simple inventory system of MAX (a global const initially defined as 75) items. All 75 items are stored on the disk. When you run the program the first time, its data file (INVENT.DAT) will not exist. After you enter a few items, the program saves those items to the disk, along with the rest of the 75 items. The program keeps track of the number of "live items" (the number of the 75 items that actually contain data). On each subsequent run (after the first one), the program reads all items on disk and prints an updated listing of the inventory.

Listing WR3.1. Week three review listing.

```
1:  // Filename: INVLIVE.CPP
2:  // Maintains an on-disk inventory
3:  #include <fstream.h>
4:  #include <iomanip.h>
5:  #include <string.h>
6:  #include <ctype.h>
7:  #include <conio.h>
8:  // This global constant holds maximum number of items allowed
9:  const int MAX = 75;
10: // An individual item class
11: class Item {
12: public:            // So composed class can access
13:   char descrip[20];
14:   float price;
15:   int quant;
16: };
17: // Composed class of all the items follows
18: class allItems {
19:   Item inventory[MAX];
20:   static int numInInv;
21: public:
22:   void saveToDisk(void);
23:   void readFromDisk(void);
24:   void addToInv(void);
25:   void prInv(void);
26:   allItems(void);
27: };
28: void allItems::saveToDisk(void)
29: {
30:   // This function ALWAYS writes all MAX inventory items to disk
31:   ofstream diskFile;
32:   diskFile.open("INVENT.DAT");
33:   // Writes in compressed form so must use read to read it
34:   diskFile.write((char *)this, sizeof(*this));
35: }
36: void allItems::readFromDisk(void)
37: {
38:   // Always reads MAX items from disk (if the file exists) but
39:   // checks each record's descrip to count the number of real
40:   // items in the inventory (the rest are considered empty).
41:   ifstream diskFile;
42:   diskFile.open("INVENT.DAT");
43:   if(diskFile)
44:     { diskFile.read((char *)this, sizeof(*this));
45:       // Determine how many items have live data
46:       for (int ctr=0; ctr<MAX; ctr++)
47:         { if (inventory[ctr].descrip[0] == '\0') break; }
48:       numInInv = ctr;
```

```
49:     }
50: }
51: void allItems::addToInv(void)
52: {
53:    cout << "\nWhat is the Description? ";
54:    cin.getline(inventory[numInInv].descrip, 20);
55:    cout << "What is the price? ";
56:    cin >> inventory[numInInv].price;
57:    cout << "What is the quantity? ";
58:    cin >> inventory[numInInv].quant;
59:    allItems::numInInv++;    // Increase # of active items in
      ➥inventory
60: }
61: void allItems::prInv(void)
62: {
63:    cout << setprecision(2) << setiosflags(ios::showpoint);
64:    cout << setiosflags(ios::fixed);
65:    if (numInInv == 0)
66:    { cout << "\nThe inventory file is now empty.\n"; }
67:    else
68:    { cout << "\nHere is the inventory:\n";
69:      for (int ctr=0; ctr<numInInv; ctr++)
70:      { cout << "\n Description: " << inventory[ctr].descrip <<
         ➥"\n";
71:         cout << " Price: $" << inventory[ctr].price << "\n";
72:         cout << " Quantity: " << inventory[ctr].quant << "\n";
73:      }
74:    }
75: }
76: allItems::allItems(void)
77: {
78:    // Make all description pointers null
79:    for (int ctr=0; ctr<MAX; ctr++)
80:      { inventory[ctr].descrip[0] = '\0'; }
81: }
82: // Static must be initialized
83: int allItems::numInInv = 0;
84: ////////////////////////////////////////////////////////////////
85: main()
86: {
87:    char answer;   // To hold answer
88:    allItems inventory;
89:    clrscr();
90:    cout << "Here is the inventory before you add items:\n";
91:    inventory.readFromDisk();
92:    inventory.prInv();
93:    do {
94:      inventory.addToInv();   // Get item from user
95:      cout << "Is there another item to enter? (Y or N) ";
```

continues

625

Listing WR3.1. continued

```
96:      cin >> answer;
97:      cin.ignore();  // Eliminate the newline
98:    } while (toupper(answer) != 'N');
99:    // Print the inventory for the user
100:   inventory.prInv();
101:   // Now, write the items to the disk
102:   inventory.saveToDisk();
103:   return 0;
104: }
```

main() creates a single inventory object (line 88) that contains MAX individual items. The composed allItems class is designed to hold MAX occurrences of the smaller Item class (lines 11–16). By holding all the occurrences of the data, the allItems class can save and retrieve itself to and from the disk. Notice that the constructor for allItems puts a null zero in the first array element of the descrip member. As the user enters new items into the inventory, this null zero gets overwritten with new data (line 54).

The first job of main() is to print whatever data might already be in the data file. Line 91 calls the readFromDisk() member function to read the INVENT.DAT disk file into the inventory object's members. The program determines how many of the MAX items actually contain data in the for loop on lines 46 and 47 by testing for the null zero in the descrip member.

If readFromDisk() finds a file (in line 43), that file is read and the live non-null inventory items print. main() then regains control and begins a loop in lines 93–98 that ask the user for new inventory data to add to the file. As the user enters items, the data is *not* yet written to the disk file but instead is stored in the inventory array.

Only after the user signals in lines 96–98 that he or she is finished entering data does main() call the saveToDisk() member function in line 102 and exit.

Try running this program several times and enter a few new inventory items each time. As you do, you'll see that the inventory file keeps growing with new data.

ASCII Character Chart

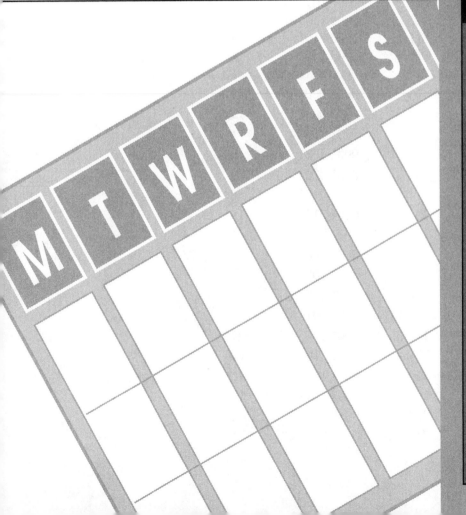

ASCII Character Chart

Dec X_{10}	Hex X_{16}	Binary X_2	ASCII Character
000	00	0000 0000	null
001	01	0000 0001	☺
002	02	0000 0010	●
003	03	0000 0011	♥
004	04	0000 0100	◆
005	05	0000 0101	♣
006	06	0000 0110	♠
007	07	0000 0111	●
008	08	0000 1000	■
009	09	0000 1001	○
010	0A	0000 1010	■
011	0B	0000 1011	♂
012	0C	0000 1100	♀
013	0D	0000 1101	♪
014	0E	0000 1110	♪♪
015	0F	0000 1111	☼
016	10	0001 0000	►
017	11	0001 0001	◄
018	12	0001 0010	↕
019	13	0001 0011	‼
020	14	0001 0100	¶
021	15	0001 0101	§
022	16	0001 0110	—
023	17	0001 0111	↨
024	18	0001 1000	↑
025	19	0001 1001	↓
026	1A	0001 1010	→
027	1B	0001 1011	←
028	1C	0001 1100	FS
029	1D	0001 1101	GS
030	1E	0001 1110	RS
031	1F	0001 1111	US
032	20	0010 0000	SP
033	21	0010 0001	!

Dec X_{10}	Hex X_{16}	Binary X_2	ASCII Character
034	22	0010 0010	"
035	23	0010 0011	#
036	24	0010 0100	$
037	25	0010 0101	%
038	26	0010 0110	&
039	27	0010 0111	'
040	28	0010 1000	(
041	29	0010 1001	)
042	2A	0010 1010	*
043	2B	0010 1011	+
044	2C	0010 1100	,
045	2D	0010 1101	-
046	2E	0010 1110	.
047	2F	0010 1111	/
048	30	0011 0000	0
049	31	0011 0001	1
050	32	0011 0010	2
051	33	0011 0011	3
052	34	0011 0100	4
053	35	0011 0101	5
054	36	0011 0110	6
055	37	0011 0111	7
056	38	0011 1000	8
057	39	0011 1001	9
058	3A	0011 1010	:
059	3B	0011 1011	;
060	3C	0011 1100	<
061	3D	0011 1101	=
062	3E	0011 1110	>
063	3F	0011 1111	?
064	40	0100 0000	@
065	41	0100 0001	A

continues

ASCII Character Chart

Dec X_{10}	Hex X_{16}	Binary X_2	ASCII Character
066	42	0100 0010	B
067	43	0100 0011	C
068	44	0100 0100	D
069	45	0100 0101	E
070	46	0100 0110	F
071	47	0100 0111	G
072	48	0100 1000	H
073	49	0100 1001	I
074	4A	0100 1010	J
075	4B	0100 1011	K
076	4C	0100 1100	L
077	4D	0100 1101	M
078	4E	0100 1110	N
079	4F	0100 1111	O
080	50	0101 0000	P
081	51	0101 0001	Q
082	52	0101 0010	R
083	53	0101 0011	S
084	54	0101 0100	T
085	55	0101 0101	U
086	56	0101 0110	V
087	57	0101 0111	W
088	58	0101 1000	X
089	59	0101 1001	Y
090	5A	0101 1010	Z
091	5B	0101 1011	[
092	5C	0101 1100	\
093	5D	0101 1101	]
094	5E	0101 1110	^
095	5F	0101 1111	_
096	60	0110 0000	`
097	61	0110 0001	a

A

Dec X_{10}	Hex X_{16}	Binary X_2	ASCII Character
098	62	0110 0010	b
099	63	0110 0011	c
100	64	0110 0100	d
101	65	0110 0101	e
102	66	0110 0110	f
103	67	0110 0111	g
104	68	0110 1000	h
105	69	0110 1001	i
106	6A	0110 1010	j
107	6B	0110 1011	k
108	6C	0110 1100	l
109	6D	0110 1101	m
110	6E	0110 1110	n
111	6F	0110 1111	o
112	70	0111 0000	p
113	71	0111 0001	q
114	72	0111 0010	r
115	73	0111 0011	s
116	74	0111 0100	t
117	75	0111 0101	u
118	76	0111 0110	v
119	77	0111 0111	w
120	78	0111 1000	x
121	79	0111 1001	y
122	7A	0111 1010	z
123	7B	0111 1011	{
124	7C	0111 1100	¦
125	7D	0111 1101	}
126	7E	0111 1110	~
127	7F	0111 1111	DEL
128	80	1000 0000	Ç
129	81	1000 0001	ü

continues

ASCII Character Chart

Dec X_{10}	Hex X_{16}	Binary X_2	ASCII Character
130	82	1000 0010	é
131	83	1000 0011	â
132	84	1000 0100	ä
133	85	1000 0101	à
134	86	1000 0110	å
135	87	1000 0111	ç
136	88	1000 1000	ê
137	89	1000 1001	ë
138	8A	1000 1010	è
139	8B	1000 1011	ï
140	8C	1000 1100	î
141	8D	1000 1101	ì
142	8E	1000 1110	Ä
143	8F	1000 1111	Å
144	90	1001 0000	É
145	91	1001 0001	æ
146	92	1001 0010	Æ
147	93	1001 0011	ô
148	94	1001 0100	ö
149	95	1001 0101	ò
150	96	1001 0110	û
151	97	1001 0111	ù
152	98	1001 1000	ÿ
153	99	1001 1001	Ö
154	9A	1001 1010	Ü
155	9B	1001 1011	¢
156	9C	1001 1100	£
157	9D	1001 1101	¥
158	9E	1001 1110	P_t
159	9F	1001 1111	ƒ
160	A0	1010 0000	á
161	A1	1010 0001	í

A

Dec X_{10}	Hex X_{16}	Binary X_2	ASCII Character
162	A2	1010 0010	ó
163	A3	1010 0011	ú
164	A4	1010 0100	ñ
165	A5	1010 0101	Ñ
166	A6	1010 0110	a
167	A7	1010 0111	o
168	A8	1010 1000	¿
169	A9	1010 1001	⌐
170	AA	1010 1010	¬
171	AB	1010 1011	½
172	AC	1010 1100	¼
173	AD	1010 1101	¡
174	AE	1010 1110	«
175	AF	1010 1111	»
176	B0	1011 0000	░
177	B1	1011 0001	▒
178	B2	1011 0010	▓
179	B3	1011 0011	│
180	B4	1011 0100	┤
181	B5	1011 0101	╡
182	B6	1011 0110	╢
183	B7	1011 0111	╖
184	B8	1011 1000	╕
185	B9	1011 1001	╣
186	BA	1011 1010	║
187	BB	1011 1011	╗
188	BC	1011 1100	╝
189	BD	1011 1101	╜
190	BE	1011 1110	╛
191	BF	1011 1111	┐
192	C0	1100 0000	└
193	C1	1100 0001	┴

continues

Dec X_{10}	Hex X_{16}	Binary X_2	ASCII Character
194	C2	1100 0010	┬
195	C3	1100 0011	├
196	C4	1100 0100	─
197	C5	1100 0101	+
198	C6	1100 0110	╞
199	C7	1100 0111	╟
200	C8	1100 1000	╚
201	C9	1100 1001	╔
202	CA	1100 1010	╩
203	CB	1100 1011	╦
204	CC	1100 1100	╠
205	CD	1100 1101	=
206	CE	1100 1110	╬
207	CF	1100 1111	╧
208	D0	1101 0000	╨
209	D1	1101 0001	╤
210	D2	1101 0010	╥
211	D3	1101 0011	╙
212	D4	1101 0100	╘
213	D5	1101 0101	╒
214	D6	1101 0110	╓
215	D7	1101 0111	╫
216	D8	1101 1000	╪
217	D9	1101 1001	┘
218	DA	1101 1010	┌
219	DB	1101 1011	█
220	DC	1101 1100	▄
221	DD	1101 1101	▌
222	DE	˙101 1110	▐
223	DF	1101 1111	▀
224	E0	1110 0000	α
225	E1	1110 0001	β

Dec X_{10}	Hex X_{16}	Binary X_2	ASCII Character
226	E2	1110 0010	Γ
227	E3	1110 0011	π
228	E4	1110 0100	Σ
229	E5	1110 0101	σ
230	E6	1110 0110	μ
231	E7	1110 0111	τ
232	E8	1110 1000	Φ
233	E9	1110 1001	θ
234	EA	1110 1010	Ω
235	EB	1110 1011	δ
236	EC	1110 1100	∞
237	ED	1110 1101	ø
238	EE	1110 1110	∈
239	EF	1110 1111	∩
240	F0	1111 0000	≡
241	F1	1111 0001	±
242	F2	1111 0010	≥
243	F3	1111 0011	≤
244	F4	1111 0100	⌠
245	F5	1111 0101	⌡
246	F6	1111 0110	÷
247	F7	1111 0111	≈
248	F8	1111 1000	°
249	F9	1111 1001	•
250	FA	1111 1010	·
251	FB	1111 1011	√
252	FC	1111 1100	η
253	FD	1111 1101	²
254	FE	1111 1110	■
255	FF	1111 1111	

Turbo C++
Keywords

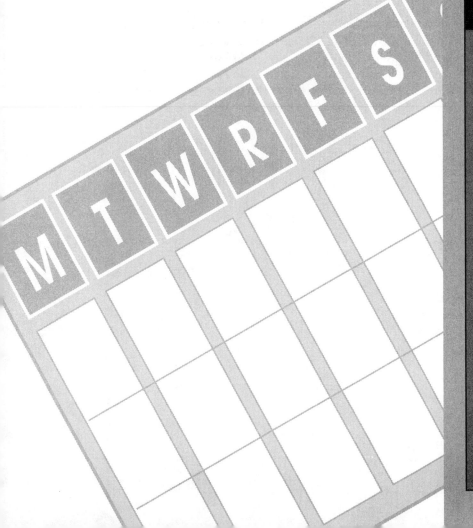

* asm	else	* operator	switch
auto	enum	pascal	* template
break	extern	* private	* this
case	float	* protected	typedef
char	for	* public	union
* class	* friend	register	unsigned
const	goto	return	* virtual
continue	if	short	void
default	* inline	signed	volatile
* delete	int	sizeof	while
do	long	static	
double	* new	struct	

Note: Those keywords marked with an asterisk, *, are new to Turbo C++ and not found in regular Turbo C. Some of these keywords, such as asm, are not covered in this book due to their technical and application-specific nature.

Operator
Precedence

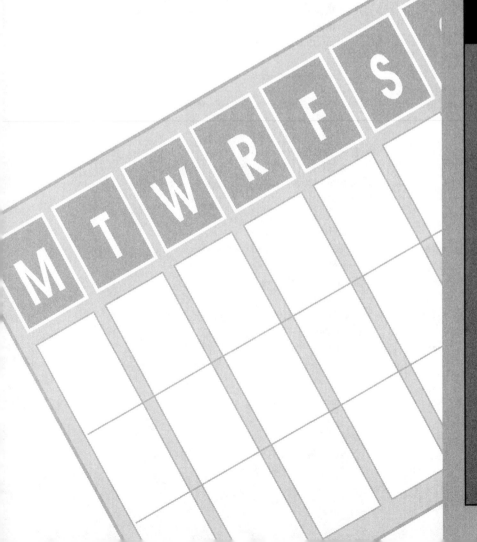

C

Operator Precedence

Turbo C++ contains many operators. When you use more than one operator in the same expression, you must understand how Turbo C++ interprets and orders those operators. Here is the Turbo C++ operator precedence table that shows the order of operator precedence.

Table C.1. Turbo C++ operator precedence.

Precedence Level	Symbol	Description	Associativity
1	::	C++ scope access/ resolution	Left to right
2	()	Function call	Left to right
	[]	Array subscript	
	→	C++ indirect component selector	
	.	C++ direct component selector	
3			
Unary	!	Logical negation	Right to left
	~	Bitwise (1's) complement	
	+	Unary plus	
	-	Unary minus	
	&	Addresss of	
	*	Indirection	
	sizeof	Returns size of operand in bytes	
	new	Dynamically allocates C++ storage	
	delete	Dynamically deallocates C++ storage	
	type	Typecast	
4			
Member Access	.*	C++ dereference	Left to right
	→*	C++ dereference	
	()	Expression parentheses	

Precedence Level	Symbol	Description	Associativity
5			
Multiplicative	*	Multiply	Left to right
	/	Divide	
	%	Remainder (modulus)	
6			
Additive	+	Binary plus	Left to right
	-	Binary minus	
7			
Shift	<<	Shift left	Left to right
	>>	Shift right	
8			
Relational	<	Less than	Left to right
	<=	Less than or equal to	
	>	Greater than	
	>=	Greater than or equal to	
9			
Equality	==	Equal to	Left to right
	!=	Not equal to	
10	&	Bitwise AND	Left to right
11	^	Bitwise XOR	Left to right
12	¦	Bitwise OR	Left to right
13	&&	Logical AND	Left to right
14	¦¦	Logical OR	Left to right
15			
Ternary	?:	Conditional	Right to left

C

continues

Table C.1. continued

Precedence Level	Symbol	Description	Associativity
16			
Assignment	=	Simple assignment	Right to left
	*=	Assign product	
	/=	Assign quotient	
	%=	Assign remainder	
	+=	Assign sum	
	-=	Assign difference	
	&=	Assign bitwise AND	
	^=	Assign bitwise XOR	
	¦=	Assign bitwise OR	
	<<=	Assign left shift	
	>>=	Assign right shift	
17			
Comma	,	Sequence point	Left to right

Note: Because of the confusion in most precedence tables, the postfix ++ and -- and the prefix ++ and -- do not appear here. Their precedence works the same in Turbo C++ as it does in C. The postfix operators usually appear in level 2, and the prefix operators appear in level 3. In practice, perform prefix before all other operators except for the scope resolution operator, and perform postfix right before the statement continues to the next executable statement in the program. Turbo C++ purists will cringe at this description, but it works 99.9 percent of the time, whereas "technically correct" placements of these operators simply confuse programmers 99.9 percent of the time.

Answers

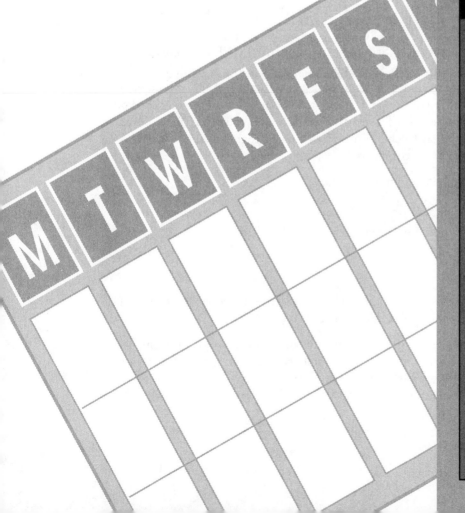

D

This appendix lists the answers for the quiz and exercise sections at the end of each chapter. There is always more than one way to write programming statements, so if your answers vary slightly, the differences might be a matter of style.

Answers for Day 1, "The C++ Phenomenon"
Quiz

1. OOP stands for object-oriented programming.

2. A skillful C++ programmer can expect a productivity increase as much as 10 or 20 times over the current programming throughput. Such numbers obviously indicate a veteran C++ programmer, but such improvements are not uncommon for those who learn OOP.

3. Although not an ANSI-recognized standard, the AT&T standard, especially starting with version 3.0, has become the de facto standard. When ANSI finally adopts C++, you can rest easy knowing that ANSI will implement most if not all of the AT&T standard because so many vendors and programmers use AT&T's standard. Therefore, if you use an AT&T-standard compiler today (such as Turbo C++), your programs should also work on tomorrow's C++ compilers.

4. Procedural programming languages.

5. The `class` keyword.

6. The .CPP filename extension.

Exercises

1. This exercise required that you enter and run the sample program in Listing 1.1, so no answer applies here.

2. This exercise required that you enter and run the sample program in Listing 1.1 after changing all the comments that begin with // (the C++ style) so that they are enclosed in /* and */.

Answers for Day 2, "C++ Is Superior!"

Quiz

1. Turbo C++ comments end at the end of the line.

2. A function's signature is its prototype that describes the return data type and the number and types of arguments.

3. True. Prototypes only need to know data types, and the argument names are optional.

4. False. A function's definition line must have argument names so that the body of the function can refer to the proper variables.

5. True. In Turbo C++, an empty argument list means the same as void.

6. __FILE__ and __LINE__.

7. January 1, 1994. __DATE__ supplies the date of the compile, which could differ from the run date.

Exercises

1.
```
#include <stdio.h>
main()
{
//  printf("Welcome to Turbo C++.\n");   // Output
//  printf("The power is yours!\n");
  return 0;
}
```

2.
```
// Filename: FIXDEF.CPP
#include <stdio.h>
const float PI = 3.14159;

inline float cirArea(float r)
{
  return PI * (r * r);
}
```

```
main()
{
  float radius;
  printf("What is the circle's radius in inches? ");
  scanf(" %f", &radius);
  printf("The area of the circle is %.2f inches.\n",
  ➥cirArea(radius));

  return 0;
}
```

Answers for Day 3, "Simple I/O"
Quiz

1. iostream.h.

2. iomanip.h.

3. Turbo C++ does not remember setw() settings from cout to cout.

4. All values are printed right-justified within a field's width unless you change the justification with the appropriate format flag.

5. False. The setw() only sets the width for the first cout so only that cout contains right-justified numbers in the 8-character field. The last two couts print numbers without any justification.

6. endl outputs a newline and flushes the output buffer. ends adds a terminating null zero to the end of character data, and flush flushes the output buffer without sending a newline.

7. cin >> ignores whitespace in the input stream, and get() reads the whitespace characters.

8. True, the second parameter of get() tells Turbo C++ how many characters to count in the input.

Exercises

1. ```
   cout << "Hi!\n"<<setprecision(s)<<setiosflags(ios::showpoint)
   ➡<<amt;
   ```

2. This one's easy when you remember that `cin >>` stops reading numeric values when the first non-number is reached. Here is the statement:

   ```
   cin >> numVar >> charVar;
   ```

3. ```
   // Filename: TOTAL.CPP
   // Prints a dollar total
   #include <iostream.h>
   #include <iomanip.h>
   #include <conio.h>
   main()
   {
      float price1, price2, price3;
      float total;
      cout << "What is the first price? ";
      cin >> price1;
      cout << "What is the second price? ";
      cin >> price2;
      cout << "What is the third price? ";
      cin >> price3;
      total = price1 + price2 + price3;
      // This cout spans two lines but it could be one long line
      cout << setfill('*') << setprecision(2);
      cout << setiosflags(ios::showpoint) << setw(20) << total;
      return 0;
   }
   ```

Answers for Day 4, "Powerful Pointers"

Quiz

1. False because the reference has to be initialized when you define it.

2. ```
   ri = 67;    // Changes i
   ```
   ```

3. A. 2.

   B. 5.

   C. 6.

   D. 7.

   E. 1.

   F. 3.

   G. 8.

   H. 4.

4. False. Although ptr *might* be defined as a void pointer, you cannot tell from this statement that the pointer is void. Assigning 0 to a pointer makes the pointer a *null* pointer, but assigning 0 to a pointer does not make the pointer a void pointer.

Exercises

1.
```cpp
// Filename: MONTHPTR.CPP
// Reference an array with a constant pointer
#include <iostream.h>
#include <conio.h>
main()
{
  clrscr();
  int monthDays[] = {31, 28, 31, 30, 31, 30, 31, 31, 30, 31,
  ➥30, 31};
int * const mPtrConst = monthDays;
  // You could also do this:
  //   int * const mPtrConst = &monthDays[0];
  for (int m=0; m<12; m++)
    { cout << "Month " << (m+1) << " has " << *(mPtrConst+m);
      cout << " days in it.\n"; }
  return 0;
}
```

2.
```cpp
// Filename: CHAP4VAR.CPP
// Defines, initializes, and prints various variables
#include <iostream.h>
#include <conio.h>
```

```
main()
{
  clrscr();
  int i=9;
  const int ci = 10;          // Integer constant
  int & ri = i;               // Reference to an integer
  const int & roa = i;        // Read-only alias
  int * pi = & i;             // Pointer to integer
  const int * pic = &i;       // Pointer to an integer constant
  int * const cpi = &i;       // Constant pointer to integer
  const int * const pcip = &i;  // Constant pointer to constant
  cout << "Integer constant: " << ci << "\n";
  cout << "Reference to an integer: " << ri << "\n";
  cout << "Read-only alias: " << roa << "\n";
  cout << "Pointer to integer: " << *pi << "\n";
  cout << "Pointer to an integer constant: " << *pic << "\n";
  cout << "Constant pointer to integer: " << *cpi << "\n";
  cout << "Constant pointer to integer constant: " << *pcip
  ➡<< "\n";
  return 0;
}
```

Answers for Day 5, "Memory Allocation: There When You Need It"

Quiz

1. `new` and `delete`.

2. You cannot mix `new` and `free()`.

3. True.

4. False. You cannot initialize a complete array at the time you allocate it.

5. C. You cannot determine how many elements are reserved until you allocate the array on the heap.

6. set_new_handler(). (By the way, this name is not consistent with all other C++ compilers on the market.)

7. You cannot specify the number of elements to delete in the subscript.

Exercises

1.
```cpp
// Filename: AGEMESGS.CPP
// Allocates a string for each year of the user
#include <iostream.h>
#include <conio.h>
#include <string.h>
main()
{
   char * mesgs[100];  // Up to 100 years old
   char words[] = "Make every year a good one!\n";
   int age;
   clrscr();
   cout << "How old are you? ";
   cin >> age;
   for (int cnt=0; cnt<age; cnt++)
   {
      mesgs[cnt] = new char [strlen(words) + 1];
      strcpy(mesgs[cnt], words);  // Copy string to heap
   }
   // Print the strings
   for (cnt=0; cnt<age; cnt++)
   {
      cout << mesgs[cnt];
   }
   // Deallocate the strings
   // CAREFUL! Each element MUST deallocate the whole string
   for (cnt=0; cnt<age; cnt++)
   {
      delete [] mesgs[cnt];
   }
   return 0;
}
```

```
2. void bellRing(void);

   // The following function executes only if new fails
   main()
   {
       set_new_handler(bellRing);
       // Rest of main() goes here
       // :
   }

   void bellRing(void)
   {
     cerrt << "\a";
     cerr << "Memory Problem!\n";
     exit(1);
   }
```

Note: Be sure to write your error messages to the cerr object and not cout.

Answers for Day 6, "Communicating with Functions"

Quiz

1. Passing by reference is more efficient than passing by value.

2. Declaration (a prototype due to the semicolon).

3. Definition (a function's first line).

4. True. You can pass main() arguments through command-line arguments.

5. Yes, when you're passing by reference, if the receiving function changes a parameter, the same value changes in the sending function. (As long as you haven't specified const.)

6. Ellipses signify that a function is going to receive a variable-length argument.

7. The pathname and filename of the program when you ran the program.

8. Insert the const modifier before the received parameters.

Exercises

1.
```cpp
// Filename: DEFPRNT.CPP
// Includes a function with default arguments that prints a row
// of characters as determined by the arguments passed.
#include <iostream.h>
#include <conio.h>
void doPr(char prChar='*', int prNum=10);
main()
{
  char prChar;
  int prNum;
  clrscr();
  prChar = '!';
  prNum = 25;
  doPr(prChar, prNum);   // Override both default arguments
  doPr();                // Accept both defaults
  doPr('$');             // Accept only the last default
  return 0;
}
//////////////////////////////////////////////////////////////////
// Function with two default arguments
void doPr(char prChar, int prNum)
{
  for (int i=0; i<prNum; i++)
  { cout << prChar; }
  cout << "\n";
}
```

2.
```cpp
// Filename: TOTALCMD.CPP
// Computes the product of all arguments passed
#include <iostream.h>
#include <stdlib.h>
#include <conio.h>
main(int argc, char * argv[])
```

```
    {
      long int total=1;
      clrscr();
      for (int i=1; i<argc; i++)
      {
        total *= atoi(argv[i]);
      }
      cout << "The product of your values is " << total << "\n";
      return 0;
    }
```

3.
```
    // Filename: VARAVG.CPP
    // This function won't run by itself because there
    // is no main() in the code.
    void avgNums(int numPassed, ...)
    {
      float avg=0.0;
      va_list ap;    // Points to the list of arguments
      va_start(ap, numPassed); // Tells Turbo C++ where to begin
      for (int i=0; i<numPassed; i++)
      {
        avg += va_arg(ap, int);    // Add next integer
      }
      avg /= numPassed;
      va_end(ap);         // Cleanup that is always needed
      cout << "The average of the arguments is " << avg << "\n";
    }
```

Answers for Day 7, "Overloaded Functions Lessen Your Load"

Quiz

1. By the argument lists that must differ in number, data types, or both.

2. True.

3. False. The first and third differ only by their return data types, and the return data type cannot differentiate overloaded functions.

4. operator&&(), operator¦¦(), and operator*=().

5. Use a language different from Turbo C++! Seriously, you cannot change the way operators work on built-in data types. Some C++ programmers get fancy, however, and write structure variables that contain a single int member and overload the + to work on that structure. This, in a stretched way, changes the behavior of + for integers.

6. You have to return a structure, not just a regular data type. In future chapters, you'll learn more about this.

7. If your Turbo C++ program calls C functions that you've written or purchased, you'll have to declare those functions in an extern "C" statement so that Turbo C++ doesn't mangle the names.

8. The default arguments must be specified in the prototypes, not the function definition lines.

9. ```
extern "C" { char * getName(void);
             float amtDoub(float x); }
```

## Exercises

1.
```
// Filename: AVGOVR.CPP
// Overload a function to accept two kinds of arrays
#include <iostream.h>
#include <iomanip.h>
#include <conio.h>
void doAvg(int iAra[]);
void doAvg(float fAra[]);
const int araSize = 10;
main()
{
   int iAra[araSize] = {1, 4, 3, 6, 7, 5, 3, 6, 8, 9};
   float fAra[araSize] = {4.3, 2.4, 6.7, 8.6, 4.3, 2.3, 4.5,
                          6.5, 7.6, 3.1};
   cout << setprecision(1) << setiosflags(ios::fixed);
   doAvg(iAra);
   doAvg(fAra);
   return 0;
}
//
```
```

```
// Two overloaded functions that find average begin here
void doAvg(int iAra[])
{
 float avg = 0.0;
 for (int i=0; i<araSize; i++)
 {  avg += float(iAra[i]); }
 avg /= araSize;
 cout << "The average of the integer array is " << avg << "\n";
}
void doAvg(float fAra[])
{
 float avg = 0.0;
 for (int i=0; i<araSize; i++)
 {  avg += float(fAra[i]); }
 avg /= araSize;
 cout << "The average of the floating-point array is "
 ➡<< avg << "\n";
}
```

2.
```
// Filename: OVRMORE.CPP
// Demonstrates overloading of several operators
#include <iostream.h>
#include <iomanip.h>
#include <conio.h>
struct People {
   int age;
   char name[25];
   int numKids;
   float salary;
};
double operator+(const People & p1, const People & p2);
int operator-(const People & p1, const People & p2);
int operator>(const People & p1, const People & p2);
void operator-=(People & p1, const People & p2);
void operator+=(People & p1, const People & p2);
main()
{
   // Define and initialize two structure variables
   People emp1 = {26, "Robert Nickles", 2, 20933.50};
   People emp2 = {41, "Don Dole", 4, 30102.32};
```

```
                    double totalSal;
                    int ageDiff;
                    clrscr();
                    if (emp1 > emp2)
                      { cout << "The first employee makes more than the
                        ➥second.\n"; }
                    else
                      { cout << "The second employee makes more than the
                        ➥first.\n"; }
                    totalSal = emp1 + emp2;
                    ageDiff = emp2 - emp1;
                    cout << setprecision(2) << setiosflags(ios::fixed);
                    cout << "The total of the salaries is " << totalSal << ".\n";
                    cout << "The age difference is " << ageDiff << ".\n";
                    emp1 += emp2;
                    cout << "\nAfter adding the second employee's salary to the
                    ➥first, \n";
                    cout << "the first employee's salary is now " << emp1.salary
                    ➥<< "\n";
                    emp2 -= emp1;
                    cout << "After subtracting the first employee's age from
                    ➥the ";
                    cout << "second's,\nthe second employee's age is now ";
                    cout << emp2.age << "\n";
                    return 0;
                  }
//////////////////////////////////////////////////////////////////
// Overloaded function to add two People variables
double operator+(const People & p1, const People & p2)
{                         // You cannot stack these
  return (p1.salary + p2.salary);
}
//////////////////////////////////////////////////////////////////
// Overloaded function to subtract two People variables
int operator-(const People & p1, const People & p2)
{                         // You cannot stack these
  return (p1.age - p2.age);
}
//////////////////////////////////////////////////////////////////
// Overloaded function to compare two People variables
```

```
int operator>(const People & p1, const People & p2)
{                        // You cannot stack these
  if (p1.salary > p2.salary)
    { return 1; }
  else
    { return 0; }
}
///////////////////////////////////////////////////////////
// Overloaded function to AND-compare two People variables
void operator+=(People & p1, const People & p2)
{
  p1.salary += p2.salary;
}
///////////////////////////////////////////////////////////
// Overloaded function to OR-compare two People variables
void operator-=(People & p1, const People & p2)
{
  p1.age -= p2.age;
}
```

Answers for Day 8, "Add Some *class* to Your Data"

Quiz

1. Technically, an object is any variable. However, you'll often find that Turbo C++ programmers reserve the use of the term *object* for class variables.

2. A. Two, the top pair.

   B. computer.

   C. Two, PC and Max.

   D. Before the first member (RAM).

   E. None because all class members are public by default.

3. False. Private data members cannot be accessed in *any* way outside the class, even in the parts of the program that define new class variables.

4. False because the first member of the structure is public by default.

5. True.

Exercise

1.
```cpp
// Filename: CLSREVIEW.CPP
// Simple program that demonstrates abstract data type classes
#include <iostream.h>
#include <string.h>
#include <iomanip.h>
#include <conio.h>
class empData {
public:                // Needed to allow access to the members
  char empCode[8];
  float wkSalary;
};
main()
{
  empData emp1;    // Regular structure variable
  empData * emp2;  // Pointer to a structure
  clrscr();
  // Initialize the structure variable with the dot operator
  strcpy(emp1.empCode, "ACT08");
  emp1.wkSalary = 1092.43;
  // Allocate and initialize a structure on the heap
  emp2 = new empData;
  strcpy(emp2->empCode, "MKT21");
  emp2->wkSalary = 1932.23;
  // Print the data
  // Without setiosflags(ios::fixed), Turbo C++ tends to print
  // floating-point data in scientific notation
  cout << setprecision(2) << setiosflags(ios::fixed);
  cout << "Employee 1:\n";
  cout << "Code:\t" << emp1.empCode << "\n";
  cout << "Salary:\t" << emp1.wkSalary << "\n\n";
  cout << "Employee 2:\n";
  cout << "Code:\t" << emp2->empCode << "\n";
  cout << "Salary:\t" << emp2->wkSalary << "\n\n";
  delete empData;
  return 0;
}
```

Answers for Day 9, "Member Functions Activate *class* Variables

Quiz

1. You can trigger the use of member functions just as you use data members. Call member functions using the dot operator, ., when you define non-pointer object variables, and use the structure pointer operator, ->, when you define pointers to object variables.

2. A single program can have more than one class, and each class might have overlapping member function names. For instance, two or more classes might have the member function named init(). The scope resolution operator works with a class name to tell Turbo C++ which class the function definition goes with.

3. You send a message to an object when you call a member function using an object. The effect of the statement

   ```
   report.print();
   ```

   is to tell the report object to print itself by sending a print message to the object. (In reality, the object is sent to the print() function with the help of the *this pointer.)

4. False. You can use overloaded member functions as well as default argument lists.

5. main() and the rest of the program can access private members through public member functions. The member functions can access private data members, and the rest of the program can call the member functions because they are usually public.

6. True. Through the use of member functions, you can modify members but not the *this pointer itself.

Exercises

1. ```
   // Filename: GRADE1.CPP
   // A teacher's simple class for grades
   #include <iostream.h>
   ```
   ```

```
#include <conio.h>
// Grade class declaration next
class LetterGrade {
private:
  char grade;       // Letter grade
public:
  void init(char='A');   // Initialize member from main()
  void prGrade(void);    // Displays the grade
};
void LetterGrade::init(char mainGrade)
{  grade = mainGrade;    // Assign main()'s grade
}
void LetterGrade::prGrade(void)
{ cout << "The grade is " << grade << "\n";
}
///////////////////////// Class ends here /////////////////////////
main()
{
  LetterGrade student1, student2, student3;
  clrscr();
  student1.init();
  student2.init('B');
  student3.init('F');
  // Print the grades
  student1.prGrade();
  student2.prGrade();
  student3.prGrade();
  // By the way... If the students were defined as an array
  // like this:
  // LetterGrade students[20];
  // you could print all the grades in a loop such as this:
  // for (int i=0; i<20; i++)
  //    { students(i).prGrade(); }
  return 0;
}
```

2.
```
// Filename: GRADE2.CPP
// A teacher's simple class for grades
#include <iostream.h>
#include <conio.h>
#include <ctype.h>
```

```
#include <stdlib.h>
// Grade class declaration next
class LetterGrade {
private:
  char grade;      // Letter grade
  void checkGr(char & mainGrade);  // Ensures accuracy
public:
  void init(char='A');   // Initialize member from main()
  void prGrade(void);    // Displays the grade
};
void LetterGrade::init(char mainGrade)
{ checkGr(mainGrade);   // Convert to upper, check for accuracy
  grade = mainGrade;    // Assign main()'s grade
}
void LetterGrade::prGrade(void)
{ cout << "The grade is " << grade << "\n";
}
void LetterGrade::checkGr(char & mainGrade) // Ensures accuracy
{
   // toupper() returns an int argument, so typecase char first
   mainGrade = char(toupper(mainGrade));  // Convert the grade
                                          // to uppercase
   if ((mainGrade < 'A') || (mainGrade > 'F'))
     { cerr << "A bad grade of " << mainGrade << " was
     ➥given!\n";
       exit(1);
     }
}
/////////////////////// Class ends here ///////////////////////
main()
{
  LetterGrade student1, student2, student3;
  clrscr();
  student1.init();
  student2.init('b');
  student3.init('H');
  // Print the grades
  student1.prGrade();
  student2.prGrade();
  student3.prGrade();
```

```
        // By the way... If the students were defined as an array
        // like this:
        // LetterGrade students[20];
        // you could print all the grades in a loop such as this:
        // for (int i=0; i<20; i++)
        //    { students(i).prGrade(); }
        return 0;
     }
```

3.
```
// Filename: LEMONCHK.CPP
// Child's lemonade sale-tracking program with checks for low
// supplies
#include <iostream.h>
#include <iomanip.h>
#include <stdlib.h>
#include <conio.h>
// Lemonade class declaration next
class Lemon {
private:
  int totalLeft;       // Will start at 100
  int sugarTeasp;      // Starts at 80
  float total;         // Income for day
  void prWarn(void);   // Prints warning when supplies are low
public:
  void init(void);     // Initialize members upon program start-up
  void showTot(void);  // Print the day's total income
  void buySweet(void);  // Customer buys sweetened
  void buyUnSweet(void); // Customer buys unsweetened
};
void Lemon::init(void)
{  totalLeft = 100;
   sugarTeasp = 80;
   total = 0.0;
}
void Lemon::showTot(void)
{ cout << setprecision(2) << setiosflags(ios::fixed);
  cout << setiosflags(ios::showpoint); // Ensure decimal prints
  cout << "\nTotal so far today is $" << total << "\n\n";
}
```

```
void Lemon::buySweet(void)
{
  if (totalLeft == 0)
    { cerr << "Sorry, no more lemonade is left.\n\n";}
  else
    if (sugarTeasp == 0)
      { cerr << "No more sugar is left. Sorry.\n\n"; }
    else
      { prWarn();
        cout << "Enjoy your drink!\n\n";
        totalLeft--;       // One less glass left
        sugarTeasp -= 2;  // Each glass takes 2 teaspoons
        total += .50;
      }
}
void Lemon::buyUnSweet(void)
{
  if (totalLeft == 0)
    { cerr << "Sorry, no more lemonade is left.\n\n";}
  else
    { prWarn();
      cout << "Enjoy your drink!\n\n";
      totalLeft--;        // One less glass left
      total += .45;
    }
}
void Lemon::prWarn(void)
{
  if (totalLeft < 5)
    { cerr << "You are running low on lemonade.\n";}
  else if (sugarTeasp < 10)
        { cerr << "You are running low on sugar.\n"; }
}
///////////////////////// Class ends here /////////////////////////
main()
{
  Lemon drink;
  int ans;
  clrscr();
  drink.init();  // Initialize data members to start of day
```

663

```
     do {
       cout << "What's happening?\n";
       cout << "  1. Sell a sweetened.\n";
       cout << "  2. Sell an unsweetened.\n";
       cout << "  3. Show total sales so far.\n";
       cout << "  4. Quit the program.\n";
       cout << "What do you want to do? ";
       cin >> ans;
       switch (ans)
        { case 1 : drink.buySweet();
                   break;
          case 2 : drink.buyUnSweet();
                   break;
          case 3 : drink.showTot();
                   break;
          case 4 : drink.showTot();   // Print total one last time
                   exit(1);
        }
     } while (ans >=1 && ans <= 4);
   return 0;
 }
```

Answers for Day 10, "*friends* When You Need Them"

Quiz

1. The class itself must specify its friends. A stand-alone function must gain access just with a `friend` keyword or the data-protection barriers of classes would be destroyed.

2. False. A friend function can have access to all members.

3. Because another class might refer to that class, such as in a friend function designation, before the class definition appears in the program.

4. Friend declarations can go either place without any difference.

5. False. Friends often add to readability burdens, and if you can get by without them, do so. Despite their problems, friends become extremely helpful in operator overloading.

6. The *this pointer is not passed automatically, so the function cannot be
executed like member functions can.

Exercise

1.
```cpp
// Filename: FRNDEXER.CPP
// First program that uses a friend function to access
// two different classes' private data members.
#include <iostream.h>
#include <iomanip.h>
#include <string.h>
#include <conio.h>
class boysSoftball;  // Forward reference (prototype)

class girlsSoftball {
  char name[25];
  int age;
  float batAvg;
public:
  void init(char N[], int A, float B);
  friend void prData(const girlsSoftball plG,
  ➡const boysSoftball plB);
};
void girlsSoftball::init(char N[], int A, float B)
{
  strcpy(name, N);
  age = A;
  batAvg = B;
}
class boysSoftball {
  char name[25];
  int age;
  float batAvg;
public:
  void init(char N[], int A, float B);
  friend void prData(const girlsSoftball plG,
  ➡const boysSoftball plB);
};
void boysSoftball::init(char N[], int A, float B)
```

```
{
  strcpy(name, N);
  age = A;
  batAvg = B;
}
//////////////////Primary Program Code Follows//////////////////
main()
{
  girlsSoftball * Gplayer[3];
  boysSoftball * Bplayer[3];
  clrscr();
  for (int i=0; i<3;i++)
    { Gplayer[i] = new girlsSoftball;
      Bplayer[i] = new boysSoftball;
    }
  Gplayer[0]->init("Stacy", 12, .344);
  Gplayer[1]->init("Judith", 13, .326);
  Gplayer[2]->init("Leah", 12, .468);
  Bplayer[0]->init("Jim", 11, .231);
  Bplayer[1]->init("Michael", 13, .543);
  Bplayer[2]->init("Larry", 12, .345);
  for (i=0; i<3; i++)
    { prData(*Gplayer[i], *Bplayer[i]); }
  for (i=0; i<3; i++)
    { delete Gplayer[i];
      delete Bplayer[i];
    }
  return 0;
}
// Friend function's code appears next
void prData(const girlsSoftball plG, const boysSoftball plB)
{
  cout << setprecision(3);
  cout << "Player name:    " << plG.name << "\n";
  cout << "Player age:     " << plG.age << "\n";
  cout << "Player average: " << plG.batAvg << "\n\n";
  cout << "Player name:    " << plB.name << "\n";
  cout << "Player age:     " << plB.age << "\n";
  cout << "Player average: " << plB.batAvg << "\n\n";
}
```

Answers for Day 11, "Introduction to Overloading Operators"

Quiz

1. One because the first operand is passed using the *this pointer.

2. By the function overloading mechanism inside the Turbo C++ language.

3. They are both named operator++(). Their difference lies solely in the appearance of int in the postfix increment function's argument list.

4. No short-circuiting is performed with the overloaded operators.

5. int.

6. Postfix because of the int.

7. When stacking most overloaded operators (most, but not all, such as the relational operators that always return int), you'll need to return the class data type.

8. return *this;

9. When you want the left operand of an operator to have a built-in data type such as int while the righthand operand is a class data type.

10. Turbo C++ issues an error that you're defining an argument but never using that argument in the function.

Exercises

```
1. // Filename: FLTCHANS.CPP
   // Overload a float-like class and a special alphabetic-only
   // class that accepts only uppercase or lowercase letters.
   #include <iostream.h>
   #include <iomanip.h>
   #include <conio.h>
   class Float {      // Will simulate a special floating-point
     float f;
   public:
     void init(float F) {f = F;}   // Inline because it is short
```

```
  inline Float operator++(void);
  inline Float operator--(void);
  float getFloat(void) { return f; };
};
Float Float::operator++(void)    // Adds 1 to the float
{
  f += 1.0;
  return *this;
}
Float Float::operator--(void)    // Subtracts 1 from the float
{
  f -= 1.0;
  return *this;
};
// Second class next
class charAlph {
  char c;
public:
  void init(char C) {c = C;}  // Inline because it is short
  inline charAlph operator++(void);
  inline charAlph operator--(void);
  char getAlph(void) { return c; }
};
charAlph charAlph::operator++(void)
{
  if (c == 'z')
    c = 'a';
  else if (c == 'Z')
        c = 'A';
      else
        c++;     // Turbo C++ adds an ASCII 1 to the character
  return *this;
}
charAlph charAlph::operator--(void)
{
  if (c == 'a')
    c = 'z';
  else if (c == 'A')
        c = 'Z';
      else
```

```
          c--;     // Subtracts an ASCII 1 from the character
  return *this;
}
//////////////////////////////////////////////////////////
main()
{
  Float fVal;
  charAlph initial;
  clrscr();
  fVal.init(34.5);
  cout << "Before increment, fVal is " << fVal.getFloat()
  ➡<< "\n";
  ++fVal;
  cout << "After increment, fVal is " << fVal.getFloat()
  ➡<< "\n";
  --fVal;
  cout << "After decrement, fVal is " << fVal.getFloat()
  ➡<< "\n\n";
  initial.init('Y');
  cout << "Before increment, initial is " << initial.getAlph()
  ➡<< "\n";
  ++initial;
  cout << "After increment, initial is " << initial.getAlph()
  ➡<< "\n";
  ++initial;
  cout << "Incrementing initial again produces "
  ➡<< initial.getAlph() << "\n";
  --initial;
  cout << "After decrementing, initial is "
  ➡<< initial.getAlph() << "\n";
  // Now, do the same for lowercase letters
  initial.init('y');
  cout << "Before increment, initial is " << initial.getAlph()
  ➡<< "\n";
  ++initial;
  cout << "After increment, initial is " << initial.getAlph()
  ➡<< "\n";
  ++initial;
  cout << "Incrementing initial again produces "
  ➡<< initial.getAlph() << "\n";
```

```
      --initial;
      cout << "After decrementing, initial is "
    ➡<< initial.getAlph() << "\n";
      return 0;
   }
```

2.
```
// Filename: LOGOVER.CPP
// Overloads and demonstrates the logical operators && and ¦¦.
#include <iostream.h>
#include <conio.h>
class newClass {
  int i;
  int j;
public:
  void init(int I, int J) {i = I; j = J;}
  inline int operator¦¦(newClass);
  inline int operator&&(newClass);
};
int newClass::operator¦¦(newClass c)
{
  if (((i != 0) && (j != 0)) ¦¦ ((c.i != 0) && (c.j != 0)))
    return 1;
  else
    return 0;
}
int newClass::operator&&(newClass c)
{
  // Only center operator has to change here
  if (((i != 0) && (j != 0)) && ((c.i != 0) && (c.j != 0)))
    return 1;
  else
    return 0;
}
/////////////////////////////////////////////////////////////
main()
{
  newClass var1, var2;
  clrscr();
  var1.init(1, 1);
  var2.init(0, 1);
```

```
    if (var1 ¦¦ var2)
      cout << "The logical ¦¦ tests true.\n";
    else
      cout << "The logical && tests false.\n";
    if (var1 && var2)
      cout << "The logical && tests true.\n";
    else
      cout << "The logical && tests false.\n";
    return 0;
}
```

Answers for Day 12, "Extending Operator Overloads"

Quiz

1. operator<<() and operator>>().

2. So they can work properly with the IOSTREAM.H file.

3. False. Manipulators don't use parentheses.

4. operator[]().

5. True.

6. By returning a reference to the stream operator.

7. To improve efficiency at the trade-off of safety.

8. False. When overloading the subscript, you can make the subscript refer to any member of any data type inside the class.

Exercises

1.
```
// Filename: DATECHK.CPP
// Inputs Date values correctly
#include <iostream.h>
#include <conio.h>
char * getMonth(const int & monthNum);
```

```
class Date {
  int day;
  int month;
  int year;
public:
  friend ostream & operator<< (ostream &, Date);
  friend istream & operator>> (istream &, Date &);
};
// Overloaded output function next
ostream & operator<<(ostream & out, Date d)
{
  out << "\nHere's the date:\n";
  // It's OK to call regular functions below main() from
  // member functions
  out << getMonth(d.month) << " " << d.day << ", " << d.year
  ➡<< "\n";
  return out;    // Allows stacking
}
istream & operator>>(istream & in, Date & d)
{
  clrscr();
  cout << "Please look at your calendar and enter the date as
  ➡follows:\n";
  do {
    cout << "What is the month (1-12)? ";
    in >> d.month;
  } while ((d.month < 0) || (d.month > 12));
  do {
    cout << "What is the day (1-31)? ";
    in >> d.day;
  } while (d.day < 1 || d.day > 31);
  do {
    cout << "What is the year (1980-2100)? ";
    in >> d.year;
  } while (d.year < 1 || d.year > 2100);
  return in;    // Allows stacking
}
//////////////////////////////////////////////////////////////
main()
```

```
  {
    Date today;
    cin >> today;           // Get the date
    cout << today;          // Print it
    return 0;
  }
  char * getMonth(const int & monthNum)
  {
      static char * monthName[] = {"January", "February", "March",
                  "April", "May", "June", "July", "August",
                  "September", "October", "November", "December"};
      return monthName[monthNum - 1];   // Adjust for subscript
  }
```

2. ```
   // Filename: COMMAOV.CPP
   // Overload comma to do << for output
   ostream & operator,(ostream out &, int i)
   {
       out << i;
       return out;
   }
   ```

D

3. ```
   // Filename: MONTHDAY.CPP
   // Class that holds the days of months
   #include <iostream.h>
   #include <conio.h>
   class Months {
     int days[12];
   public:
     void init(void);
     int & operator[](const int sub) {return days[sub]; }
   };
   void Months::init(void)
   {
     days[0] = 31;
     days[1] = 28;   // Ignores leap years
     days[2] = 31;
     days[3] = 30;
     days[4] = 31;
     days[5] = 30;
     days[6] = 31;
   ```

```
        days[7] = 31;
        days[8] = 30;
        days[9] = 31;
        days[10] = 30;
        days[11] = 31;
    }
main()
{
    Months year;
    year.init();
    clrscr();
    cout << "Here are the days in each month:\n";
    for (int i=0; i<12; i++)
      { cout << "Month #" << (i+1) << ": " << year[i];
        cout << "\n"; } // Adjust for subscript
    return 0;
}
```

Answers for Day 13, "Constructing and Destructing"
Quiz

1. True as long as you overload the constructors.

2. One.

3. When you define objects without using initialization of any kind.

4. When your objects go into scope.

5. When your objects go out of scope.

6. False. Constructors and destructors determine how individual objects are created after they are defined elsewhere. If `main()` (or another function) allocates a class object or an array of class objects on the heap, `main()` must deallocate the objects as well.

7. `operator=()`.

8. Default constructor.

9. Copy constructor.

10. When your class contains pointer members.

Exercises

1.
```
String left(const int & n)
  {
    if (strlen(st) < n)  // True if user code wants to pull
      { return *this; } // more chars than exist in the string
    String leftSt = st;
    leftSt.st[n] = '\0';   // Shorten the copy of the string
    return String(leftSt);
  }
String right(const int & n)
{
  if (strlen(st) < n)    // True if user code wants to pull
    { return *this; }   // more chars than exist in the string
  String rightSt = st;
  int j = 0;  // Target string starting subscript
  for (int i=strlen(st)-n;i<strlen(st)+1;i++)  // Copy from
    { rightSt.st[j++] = st[i]; }              // left to right
  rightSt.st[j] = '\0';
  return String(rightSt);
}
```

2.
```
// Filename: BEV.CPP
// Tracks, initializes, copies, and prints beverage products.
#include <iostream.h>
#include <iomanip.h>
#include <string.h>
#include <conio.h>
class Drinks {
  char * name;
  float whole;
  float retail;
public:
  Drinks(char * = "Noname", float=0.0,
  ➥float=0.0);  // Default constructor
  ~Drinks();    // Destructor
```

```
    Drinks(const Drinks &);   // Copy constructor
    Drinks & operator=(const Drinks &);   // Assignment overload
    friend ostream & operator<< (ostream &, const Drinks &);
    friend istream & operator>> (istream &, Drinks &);
};
Drinks::Drinks(char * N, float W, float R)
{
  name = new char[strlen(N) + 1];
  strcpy(name, N);
  whole = W;
  retail = R;
}
Drinks::~Drinks()
{
  delete [] name;
}
Drinks::Drinks(const Drinks & d)     // Copy constructor
{
  int newLen = strlen(d.name) + 1;
  name = new char[newLen];
  strcpy(name, d.name);
  whole = d.whole;
  retail = d.retail;
}
Drinks & Drinks::operator=(const Drinks & d)
{
  if (this == &d)
    { return *this; }
  delete [] name;  // Deallocate old string
  name = new char[strlen(d.name) + 1];
  strcpy(name, d.name);  // Copy string member
  whole = d.whole;        // Copy float members
  retail = d.retail;
  return *this;
}
ostream & operator<< (ostream & out, const Drinks & d)
{
    out << setprecision(2) << setiosflags(ios::showpoint);
    out << setiosflags(ios::fixed);
    out << "Name: " << d.name << "\n";
```

```
    out << "Wholesale price: " << d.whole << "\tRetail price: ";
    out << d.retail << "\n\n";
    return out;
}
istream & operator>> (istream & in, Drinks & d)
{
    cout << "Please add to our line of beverage products.\n";
    cout << "What is the name of the next product? (one word
    ➥please)";
    char tempInput[80];      // Need to temporarily
    in >> tempInput;                     // store user input
    d.name = new char[strlen(tempInput) + 1];    // onto the heap
    strcpy(d.name, tempInput);
    in.ignore();  // Remove carriage return
    cout << "What is the retail price of " << d.name << "? ";
    in >> d.whole;
    cout << "What is the wholesale price of " << d.name << "? ";
    in >> d.retail;
    return in;
}
///////////////////////////////////////////////////////////////
main()
{
    clrscr();
    Drinks * bevs = new Drinks[5];   // Array of 5 drinks on heap
    for (int i=0; i<5; i++)
      { cin >> bevs[i]; };     // Ask the user for the beverages
    cout << "\n\nHere's what you entered:\n";
    for (i=0; i<5; i++)
      { cout << bevs[i]; };      // Show the user for the beverages
    bevs[3] = bevs[4];           // Test the overloaded assignment
    Drinks newBev = bevs[1];    // Test the copy constructor
    Drinks another("Diet Peach Flavored", .23, .67);
    cout << "After some changes:\n";
    cout << bevs[3] << newBev << another << "\n";
    cout << "Mmmm... Made from the best stuff on earth!";
    delete [] bevs;
    return 0;
}
```

D

Answers for Day 14, "Loose Ends: *static* and Larger Programs"

Quiz

1. True.

2. False. Local variables can be either `static` or `auto`.

3. A.

4. The process of keeping global functions and global variables in other source files from clashing with the current file's global functions and global variables.

5. The process of allowing other files access to the current one's global functions and global variables.

6. That's a loaded question. They can be either, but keeping `static` data members private helps protect their values.

7. A collection of multiple source files and possibly object files that eventually compile and link into a single executable program.

8. You don't have to recompile or relink files that don't change from one build to another.

Exercises

1.
```cpp
// Filename: TEACHST.CPP
// Program to track student scores
#include <iostream.h>
#include <iomanip.h>
#include <conio.h>
class Kids {
  char name[25];
  float grade;
public:
  static float average;
  Kids(void);
  ~Kids() {};  // No destructor code needed
```

```
};
Kids::Kids(void)
{
  cout << "What is the next kid's name? ";
  cin.getline(name, 25);
  cout << "What is the grade? ";
  cin >> grade;
  cin.ignore();  // Eliminate carriage return left on buffer
  average+=grade;
}
float Kids::average = 0.0;
////////////////////////////////////////////////////////////////
main()
{
  clrscr();
  Kids students[5];  // Array of 5 students
  Kids::average /= 5.0;
  cout << setiosflags(ios::fixed)
  ➡<< setiosflags(ios::showpoint);
  cout << setprecision(2);
  cout << "\nThe class average is " << Kids::average << "\n";
  return 0;
}
```

2. No answer is possible due to the interactive nature of this exercise.

Answers for Day 15, "It's Hereditary: Inheriting Data"

Quiz

1. A is the base class.

2. B is the derived class.

3. i is private and therefore can never be accessed by a derived class.

4. A. Four.

   B. Protected.

   C. Public.

D

5. In the IOSTREAM.H header file.

6. True because the derived c would have been protected anyway.

Exercise

1.
```
// Filename: ACCESSFL.CPP
// The full Person class and its derivatives
class Person {
  long int interCode;    // Internal code is only private member
protected:
  char * name;          // Four protected members
  char * address;
  int areaCode;
  long int phone;
public:              // Public member functions follow
  Person();
  ~Person();
  Person inputPerson(void);
  prPerson(void);
};
class Employee : private Person { // Private receipt is default
  int dependents;
protected:
  int yrsWorked;
public:
  int testYears(void);   // True if employed more than 10 years
};
class Customer : protected Person {
  char * custNum;
protected:
  float custBalance;
public:
  int prCust(void);
};
class Vendor : public Person {
  char * vendNum;
protected:
  float vendOwed;
```

```
public:
  prVend(void);
};
class Salaried : Employee {
  int numWeeksVacation;
public:
  double computeSalary(void);
};
class Hourly : Employee {
  float ratePerHour;
public:
  int testMinimumWage(void);
};
class PartTime : Hourly {        // A child of a child class
  int hoursWorked;
public:
  float computePay(void);
};
class FullTime : Hourly {        // A child of a child class
  int maxHrsAvailable;
public:
  float computePay(void);
};
```

Answers for Day 16, "Inherited Limits and Extensions"

Quiz

1. True. Most of the time, however, you cannot rely on default constructors to create a class object properly. When a default constructor is not enough to construct the object, you *must* provide your own derived constructors and parent class initialization constructor lists to create the inheritance of objects properly.

2. Constants must be initialized when they are created, not assigned values later.

3. On the constructor's definition line (separated from the constructor argument parentheses with a colon, :).

4. True.

5. The derived class B does not construct A with the proper order of arguments.

6. A.

7. B.

8. Nothing. Turbo C++ properly destructs a hierarchy in the opposite direction of the construction.

Exercises

```
1. // Filename: INHERHP.CPP
   // Using the heap and deriving classes from other
   // derived classes
   #include <iostream.h>
   #include <iomanip.h>
   #include <string.h>
   #include <conio.h>
   class Parent {
   protected:                // To allow inheritance
     char * name;
     int age;
   public:
     Parent(char [], int);
     ~Parent() { delete [] name; }   // Needed for heap
     void display(void);
     // No overloaded output to keep program short
   };
   Parent::Parent(char * N, int A) : age(A) {
     name = new char[strlen(N) + 1];
     strcpy(name, N);
   }
   void Parent::display(void)
   {
     cout << "Parent's name is " << name << "\n";
     cout << "Parent's age is " << age << "\n";
   }
   class Son : public Parent {
     int yrInSchool;
```

```
public:
  void display(void);
  Son(char *, int, int);
};
Son::Son(char * N, int A, int Y) : Parent(N, A), yrInSchool(Y)
{
}
void Son::display(void)
{
  cout << "Son's name is " << name << "\n";
  cout << "Son's age is " << age << "\n";
  cout << "Son's year in school is " << yrInSchool << "\n";
}


class Daughter : public Parent {
// 'protected' was removed
  int yrInSchool;
  char * friendsName;
public:
  Daughter(char *, int, int, char []);
  Daughter(char *, int);
  ~Daughter() { delete [] friendsName; }  // Needed for heap
  void display(void);
};
Daughter::Daughter(char * N, int A, int Y, char * F) :
                  Parent(N, A), yrInSchool(Y)
{
  friendsName = new char[strlen(F) + 1];
  strcpy(friendsName, F);
}
Daughter::Daughter(char * N, int A) : Parent(N, A)
{  // No function body needed; initialization list does it all
}
void Daughter::display(void)
{
  cout << "Daughter's name is " << name << "\n";
  cout << "Daughter's age is " << age << "\n";
  cout << "Daughter's year in school is " << yrInSchool
  ➡<< "\n";
  cout << "Daughter's friend is " << friendsName << "\n";
```

D

```
};
class GrandChild : Daughter {
  float weightAtBirth;
public:
  GrandChild(char *, int, float);
  void display(void);
};
GrandChild::GrandChild(char * N, int A, float W) :
                       Daughter(N, A), weightAtBirth(W)
{  // Initialization list does it all
}
void GrandChild::display(void)
{
  cout << setprecision(1) << setiosflags(ios::fixed);
  cout << "Grandchild's name is " << name << "\n";
  cout << "Grandchild's age is " << age << "\n";
  cout << "Grandchild's weight at birth was " << weightAtBirth
  ➡<< "\n";
}
/////////////////////////////////////////////////////////////
main()
{
  clrscr();
  Parent adult("James", 61);
  Son boy("Tom", 31, 12);
  Daughter girl("Barbara", 22, 16, "Elizabeth");
  GrandChild baby("Suzie", 1, 7.5);
  adult.display();
  boy.display();
  girl.display();
  baby.display();
  return 0;
}
```

2.
```
// Filename: INHERPET.CPP
// Adds a Pet object to the hierarchy.
#include <iostream.h>
#include <iomanip.h>
#include <string.h>
#include <conio.h>
```

```cpp
class Parent {
protected:                  // To allow inheritance
  char * name;
  int age;
public:
  Parent(char [], int);
  ~Parent() { delete [] name; }    // Needed for heap
  void display(void);
  // No overloaded output to keep program short
};
Parent::Parent(char * N, int A) : age(A) {
  name = new char[strlen(N) + 1];
  strcpy(name, N);
}
void Parent::display(void)
{
  cout << "Parent's name is " << name << "\n";
  cout << "Parent's age is " << age << "\n";
}
//////////////////////////////////////////////////////////////
// New Pet class next
class Pet : public Parent {
  int peopleYears;
public:
  void display(void);
  Pet(char *, int);
};
Pet::Pet(char * N, int A) : Parent(N, A)
{
  // Must have a constructor body because of the calculation
  peopleYears = age * 7;   // Calculate people years of the pet
}
void Pet::display(void)
{
  cout << "Pet's name is " << name << "\n";
  cout << "Pet's real age is " << age << "\n";
  cout << "(That's " << peopleYears << " in people years!)\n";
}
class Son : public Parent {
  int yrInSchool;
```

```
public:
  void display(void);
  Son(char *, int, int);
};
Son::Son(char * N, int A, int Y) : Parent(N, A), yrInSchool(Y)
{
}
void Son::display(void)
{
  cout << "Son's name is " << name << "\n";
  cout << "Son's age is " << age << "\n";
  cout << "Son's year in school is " << yrInSchool << "\n";
}


class Daughter : public Parent {
// 'protected' was removed
  int yrInSchool;
  char * friendsName;
public:
  Daughter(char *, int, int, char []);
  Daughter(char *, int);
  ~Daughter() { delete [] friendsName; }  // Needed for heap
  void display(void);
};
Daughter::Daughter(char * N, int A, int Y, char * F) :
                   Parent(N, A), yrInSchool(Y)
{
  friendsName = new char[strlen(F) + 1];
  strcpy(friendsName, F);
}
Daughter::Daughter(char * N, int A) : Parent(N, A)
{  // No function body needed; initialization list does it all
}
void Daughter::display(void)
{
  cout << "Daughter's name is " << name << "\n";
  cout << "Daughter's age is " << age << "\n";
```

```
    cout << "Daughter's year in school is " << yrInSchool
    ➥<< "\n";
    cout << "Daughter's friend is " << friendsName << "\n";
};
class GrandChild : Daughter {
  float weightAtBirth;
public:
  GrandChild(char *, int, float);
  void display(void);
};
GrandChild::GrandChild(char * N, int A, float W) :
                      Daughter(N, A), weightAtBirth(W)
{  // Initialization list does it all
}
void GrandChild::display(void)
{
  cout << setprecision(1) << setiosflags(ios::fixed);
  cout << "Grandchild's name is " << name << "\n";
  cout << "Grandchild's age is " << age << "\n";
  cout << "Grandchild's weight at birth was " << weightAtBirth
  ➥ << "\n";
}
///////////////////////////////////////////////////////////
main()
{
  clrscr();
  Parent adult("James", 61);
  Pet dog("Rover", 4);
  Son boy("Tom", 31, 12);
  Daughter girl("Barbara", 22, 16, "Elizabeth");
  GrandChild baby("Suzie", 1, 7.5);
  adult.display();
  dog.display();
  boy.display();
  girl.display();
  baby.display();
  return 0;
}
```

Answers for Day 17, "Data Composition"

Quiz

1. The *is-a* and *has-a* questions.

2. A. Composition.

    B. Inheritance.

    C. Composition.

    D. Inheritance.

3. The class is attempting to assign a character value to a character pointer member.

4. Turbo C++ will then perform memberwise assignment.

5. You could end up with two objects pointing to the same region in memory.

Exercises

```
1. class House {
     int sqFeet;
     char * address;
     float cost;
     int numRooms;
   public:
     House(int, char *, float, int);
     ~House();
   };
   // Constructor initialization list added next
   House::House(int S, char * A, float C, int N) :
               sqFeet(S), cost(C), numRooms(N)
   {
     int newlen = strlen(A) + 1;
     address = new char[newlen];
     strcpy(address, A);
   };
   House::~House()
```

```
{
  delete [] address;
}
```

2. See the section "If the Heap Has a Problem" in Day 5's chapter for the set_new_handler() function specifics. You need only one new handler for the program, not one for each class.

Answers for Day 18, "Virtual Functions: Are They Real?"

Quiz

1. No.

2. Late binding takes place when you define pointers to functions and when you use virtual functions.

3. True. It is because data does not get generated until runtime that function pointers have their late binding capabilities.

4. B.

5. B.

6. It contains at least one pure virtual function.

7. The assignment of the zero tells Turbo C++ to issue a compile-time error if you attempt to instantiate an object with a pure virtual function. Without the zero, Turbo C++ will not issue an error if you attempt to define an object for an abstract base class, even though you'll get runtime errors if you attempt to use the object.

8. Always specify a virtual destructor when a base class contains at least one virtual function (assuming that the class needs a destructor) so that Turbo C++ calls the correct destructor when an object is deleted from the heap.

Exercises

1. ```
// Filename: MENUPTR.CPP
// Demonstrates a menu without a switch or if statement
#include <iostream.h>
```
```

```
#include <stdlib.h>
#include <conio.h>

void funA(void); // Prototypes needed before array of pointers
void funB(void);
void funC(void);
void quitPgm(void);

void (*menu[])(void) = {funA, funB, funC, quitPgm};

main()
{
   int ans;
   clrscr();
   do
   { cout << "\n\n\nDo you want to:\n\n";
      cout << "1. Run function A\n";
      cout << "2. Run function B\n";
      cout << "3. Run function C\n";
      cout << "4. Quit program\n";
      cin >> ans;

      menu[ans-1]();  // Call appropriate function w/o switch
   } while (1);  // Infinite loop that terminates by quitPgm()
}

void funA()
{
   cout << "Function A called.\n";
}

void funB()
{
   cout << "Function B called.\n";
}

void funC()
{
```

```
      cout << "Function C called.\n";
    }

    void quitPgm()
    {
      exit(0);
    }
```

2.
```
// Filename: ABSTR.CPP
// An abstract base class acts like a model for other classes.
#include <iostream.h>
#include <iomanip.h>
#include <conio.h>
#include <string.h>
class Building {
protected:
  int sqFt;
  char address[25];  // Don't worry about city, state, ZIP
public:
  Building(int, char []);
  virtual void prData(void)=0;    // Makes the class abstract!
};
Building::Building(int S, char A[]) : sqFt(S)
{
  strcpy(address, A);
}
class Shed : public Building {
  char useCode;
public:
  Shed(int, char[], char);
  void prData(void);
};
Shed::Shed(int S, char A[], char U) : Building(S, A),
➥useCode(U)
{ // No body necessary due to initialization lists
}
void Shed::prData(void)  // Shed now must have its own prData()
          // because it can no longer rely on inheriting one.
          // Its base class now has no code (except for the
          // constructor), so all member functions must be
          // rewritten in all derived classes
```

```
{
  cout << "The shed has " << sqFt << " square feet.\n";
  cout << "The shed's address is " << address << ".\n\n";
}

class House : public Building {
  int numRooms;
  float cost;
public:
  House(int, char [], int, float);
  void prData(void);
};
House::House(int S, char A[], int N, float C) : Building(S, A),
            numRooms(N), cost(C)
{ // No body necessary due to initialization lists
}
void House::prData(void)
{
  cout << "The house has " << sqFt << " square feet.\n";
  cout << "The house address is " << address << ".\n";
  cout << "The house has " << numRooms << " number of
  ➡rooms.\n";
  cout << "The house cost " << cost << "\n\n";
}
class Office : public Building {
  int zoneCode;
  float rent;
public:
  Office(int, char [], int, float);
  void prData(void);
};
Office::Office(int S, char A[], int Z,
➡float R) : Building(S, A),
                zoneCode(Z), rent(R)
{  // No body necessary due to initialization lists
}
void Office::prData(void)
```

```
  {
    cout << "The office has " << sqFt << " square feet.\n";
    cout << "The office address is " << address << ".\n";
    cout << "The office is zoned for " << zoneCode << " code.\n";
    cout << "The office rents for " << rent << ".\n\n";
  }
main()
  {
    // Define pointers to class objects. Notice that the base
    // class is used to define the pointers, not any derived
    // class
    Building * properties[3];

    // Reserve heap and initialize with a constructor
    properties[0] = &Shed(78, "304 E. Tenth", 'x');
    properties[1] = &House(2310, "5706 S. Carmel", 8, 121344.00);
    properties[2] = &Office(1195, "5 High Rise", 'B', 895.75);

    // Prepare output now that objects are constructed
    clrscr();
    cout << setprecision(2) << setiosflags(ios::showpoint);
    cout << setiosflags(ios::fixed);
    // Print the objects using a loop
    for (int ctr=0; ctr<3; ctr++)
    {
      properties[ctr]->prData();    // Hopefully, the right
                                    // prData() prints!
    }

    // Deallocate the memory
    delete properties[0];
    delete properties[1];
    delete properties[2];
    return 0;
  }
```

D

Answers for Day 19, "Templates: Create Once, Use Forever"

Quiz

1. A template is a format for something else, such as a blank form or a spreadsheet with no data values. Turbo C++ offers templates to lessen your programming load.

2. Template functions and template classes.

3. Overloaded functions.

4. Template functions.

5. Template functions.

6. False. You'll never see the resulting classes (or functions) generated from templates. However, you don't need to see them, and if the generated classes and functions stayed with your source file after compilation, they would get in the way. One of the advantages of templates is that they help keep the messy implementation details out of your program.

7. Yes, because template classes are used to write containers.

8.
```
Contain<double> var1s;   // This defines a completely NEW class
Contain<char> var2s;     // This defines a completely NEW class
Contain<long int> var3s; // This defines a completely NEW class
```

Exercise

1.
```
int max(int num1, int num2)
{
  int big;
  big = (num1 > num2) ? num1 : num2;
  return big;
}
float max(float num1, float num2)
{
  float big;
```

```
    big = (num1 > num2) ? num1 : num2;
    return big;
}
double max(double num1, double num2)
{
    int big;
    big = (num1 > num2) ? num1 : num2;
    return big;
}
```

Answers for Day 20, "Use Supplied Containers for Your Data"

Quiz

1. A data structure that loses values in the reverse order in which it received them.

2. Push means to put a value on the stack, and pop means to take a value off.

3. A queue loses values in the same order in which it received them.

4. Either `BI_IStackAsVector<T>` or `BI_IStackAsList<T>`.

5. A bag contains unordered data that might be duplicated elsewhere in the bag. A set is a bag without duplicates.

6. `add()`.

Exercises

1. `BI_StackAsVector<int> intStack(50); // Limit the stack size`

2.
```
// Filename: COMPARRA.CPP
// Stores user-defined computer objects in an array container
#include <iostream.h>
#include <iomanip.h>
#include <conio.h>
#include <string.h>
#include <arrays.h>
```

```
// First, define the computer
class Computer {
  char brand[20];
  char model[20];
  float price;
  long int memory;
public:
  // Public access functions follow
  char * getBrand(void) {return brand;}
  char * getModel(void) {return model;}
  float getPrice(void) {return price; }
  long int getMemory(void) {return memory; }
  // Default constructor
  Computer() {brand[0] = '\0'; model[0] = '\0'; price = 0.0;
            memory = 0; }
  Computer(char B[], char M[], float P,
  ➡long int ME) : price(P),
          memory(ME)
    { strcpy(brand, B);
      strcpy(model, M); }
  int operator==(Computer & c)
    { return   // Returns true if all members match
      (!stricmp(brand, c.brand) && (!stricmp(model, c.model))
      && (price == c.price) && (memory == c.memory));
    }
};
/////////////////////////////////////////////////////////////
main()
{
  clrscr();
  // Define a class array with 3 elements
  BI_ArrayAsVector<Computer> PCs(4);

  // Initialize some objects and store them in the array
  PCs.add(Computer("Digits, Inc.", "HAL", 2350.95, 640000L));
  PCs.add(Computer("Bytes Away", "RIF", 3685.36, 1200000L));
  PCs.add(Computer("Simple Ideas", "ABC", 1778.46, 320000L));
  PCs.add(Computer("Hi-Tech", "TR-II", 5354.32, 4000000L));
```

```
// Print the data
cout << setprecision(2) << setiosflags(ios::fixed);
for (int i=0; i<4; i++)
{
  cout << "\nBrand:   " << PCs[i].getBrand() << "\n";
  cout << "Mode:    " << PCs[i].getModel() << "\n";
  cout << "Price:   " << PCs[i].getPrice() << "\n";
  cout << "Memory:  " << PCs[i].getMemory() << "\n";
}
return 0;
}
```

Answers for Day 21, "Easy File I/O"

Quiz

1. `ifstream, ofstream, fstream`.

2. Read, write, and append.

3. Sequential access.

4. The FSTREAM.H classes are derived from IOSTREAM.H.

5. Use `open()` when you need to override the default input or output opening of files.

6. `ios::app`.

7. The access mode is implied in both the `ifstream` and the `ofstream` classes.

8. There are no physical differences as far as the computer is concerned. The PC sees all files as streams of bytes. Sequential files that hold text are generally stored as ASCII text files that you can read from DOS and non–Turbo C++ programs.

Exercises

1. ```
   // Filename: RANMENU.CPP
   // User selects from a menu and adds data to the inventory
   // file, then prints the file contents when the user selects
   // that menu option.
   ```

D
   ```

```
#include <fstream.h>
#include <string.h>
#include <stdlib.h>
#include <iomanip.h>
#include <conio.h>
int dispMenu(void);
void addParts(void);
void prParts(void);
// Class that defines a single instance
class inventoryItem {   // A class defining ONE inventory part
  char partCode[5];
  char descrip[20];
  int num;
  float price;
public:
  void addToInv(char P[], char D[], int N, float PR)
    { num = N;
      price = PR;
      strcpy(partCode, P);
      strcpy(descrip, D);
      this->toDisk();   // Write the data record
    }
  void toDisk(void)
  {
    ofstream invOut;
    invOut.open("INV.DAT", ios::app);
    invOut.write((char *)this, sizeof(*this));   // Write record
  }
  void getData(void); // No function with while is ever inlined
};  // Class definition ends here
void inventoryItem::getData(void)
{
  ifstream invIn("INV.DAT");
  while (invIn)
  {
    invIn.read((char *)this, sizeof(*this));   // Read record
    if (invIn.good())
    { cout << setprecision(2) << setiosflags(ios::showpoint);
      cout << setiosflags(ios::fixed);
      cout << "\nPart code: " << partCode << "\n";
```

```cpp
      cout << "Description: " << descrip << "\n";
      cout << "Quantity: " << num << "\n";
      cout << "Price: " << price << "\n";
    }
  }
}
////////////////////////////////////////////////////////////
main()
{
  int menu;   // For menu prompt
  clrscr();
  // Construct empty inventory items
  do
    { menu = dispMenu();
      switch (menu)
      { case 1 : addParts();
                 break;
        case 2 : prParts();
                 break;
        case 3:  exit(1);
        default: cerr << "\n***Enter 1, 2, or 3***\n";
      }
    } while (menu !=3);  // The exit(1) takes care of exit
  return 0;
}
int dispMenu(void)
{
  int ans;
  cout << "\n\nHere are your choices:\n\n";
  cout << "  1. Add an inventory item to the file\n";
  cout << "  2. Display items in the file\n";
  cout << "  3. Exit the program\n\n";
  cout << "What do you want to do? ";
  cin >> ans;
  return ans;
}
void addParts(void)
{
  char pc[5];   // Define four variables to hold
  char de[20];  // input data
```

```
      int q;
      float pr;
      inventoryItem part;  // To call member function
      cin.ignore();  // Eliminate newline from menu answer's input
      cout << "Please enter a part code: ";
      cin.getline(pc, 5);
      cout << "Please enter a description: ";
      cin.getline(de, 20);
      cout << "Please enter a quantity: ";
      cin >> q;
      cout << "Please enter the price: ";
      cin >> pr;
      part.addToInv(pc, de, q, pr);  // Write the data
   }
   void prParts(void)
   {
      inventoryItem part;
      part.getData();   // Trigger member function
   }
```

2.
```
   // Filename: RNDCHANG.CPP
   // Changes data in a file
   #include <fstream.h>
   #include <conio.h>
   class Item {
   public:    // Just to keep simple
     char partCode[5];
     char descrip[20];
     int num;
     float price;
     void prData(int I)
       { cout << "Record number " << I << ":\n";
         cout << "Part: " << partCode;
         cout << "\nDescription: " << descrip;
         cout << "\nNumber: " << num;
         cout << "\nPrice: " << price << "\n\n";
       }
   };
   ///////////////////////////////////////////////////////////
   main()
```

```
{
  clrscr();
  fstream ioFile;
  Item invItem;
  ioFile.open("INV.DAT", ios::in ¦ ios::out);
  ioFile.seekg(0, ios::beg);
  ioFile.read((char *)&invItem, sizeof(invItem));
  invItem.prData(1);
  // Put the position back to the beginning
  ioFile.seekg(0, ios::beg);
  ioFile.read((char *)&invItem, sizeof(invItem));
  invItem.prData(1);
  // Read last record
  ioFile.seekg(3*sizeof(invItem), ios::beg);
  ioFile.read((char *)&invItem, sizeof(invItem));
  invItem.prData(4);
  // Read in order
  ioFile.seekg(0, ios::beg);
  ioFile.read((char *)&invItem, sizeof(invItem));
  // Another seekg() isn't needed if reading in order
  invItem.prData(1);
  ioFile.read((char *)&invItem, sizeof(invItem));
  invItem.prData(2);
  ioFile.read((char *)&invItem, sizeof(invItem));
  invItem.prData(3);
  ioFile.read((char *)&invItem, sizeof(invItem));
  invItem.prData(4);
  // New code that puts a zero in all prices begins here
  ioFile.seekg(0, ios::beg);  // Start of file
  ioFile.read((char *)&invItem, sizeof(invItem));
  ioFile.seekg(0, ios::beg); // Back up to the record just read
  invItem.price = 0.0;
  ioFile.write((char *)&invItem, sizeof(invItem));
  ioFile.read((char *)&invItem, sizeof(invItem));
  ioFile.seekg(1*sizeof(invItem), ios::beg); // Position to 2nd
  invItem.price = 0.0;
  ioFile.write((char *)&invItem, sizeof(invItem));
  ioFile.read((char *)&invItem, sizeof(invItem));
  ioFile.seekg(2*sizeof(invItem), ios::beg); // Position to 3rd
  invItem.price = 0.0;
```

D

```
        ioFile.write((char *)&invItem, sizeof(invItem));
        ioFile.read((char *)&invItem, sizeof(invItem));
        ioFile.seekg(3*sizeof(invItem), ios::beg); // Position to 4th
        invItem.price = 0.0;
        ioFile.write((char *)&invItem, sizeof(invItem));
        return 0;
    }
```

Review of C
Concepts

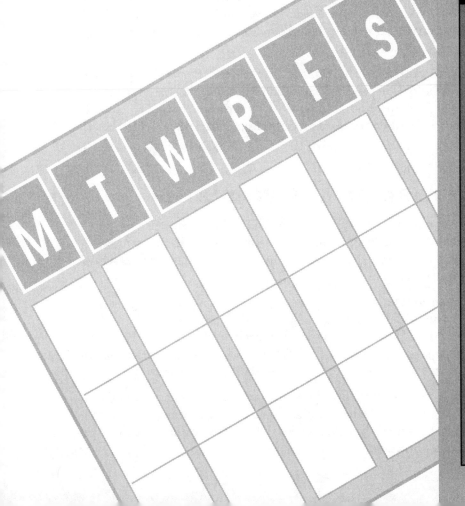

E

In case it's been a while since you wrote a C program, this appendix gives you a brief refresher on the C language. This by no means replaces a tutorial on C. At the end of this appendix are references for learning C from the ground up if you have never programmed in C.

Before you get started, it's important to realize that Turbo C++ compiles and runs regular C programs as long as you first save the program file with the extension .C.

The C Difference

C was designed to be a "high low-level" language, meaning that C is more efficient than most high-level programming languages such as QBasic, but C still provides the looping, comparison, and I/O support found in most high-level languages.

C is a succinct language, second only to the older APL language in the number of operators offered. The C programming language is very small with approximately 40 keywords (QBasic has more than 200!), but its rich assortment of operators makes up for the small set of commands.

It is because of the large number of operators and few keywords that many C programs are difficult to read if you don't take the time to add indention, blanks, and extra lines here and there to make the program more readable. Future maintenance is important, and a well-written and well-documented program ensures that you'll be able to make changes later.

The Format of C Programs

Unlike programs written in QBasic, FORTRAN, COBOL, or many other programming languages, a C program is a collection of routines called *functions*. All C programs must contain at least one function named main(). Function names always end in a set of parentheses.

When a C program executes, main() is the first function executed. Although main() doesn't have to go first in the program's list of functions, it is common practice to place it first in all C programs. Usually, main() controls the rest of the program by executing other functions in the program when needed. When you list another function's name inside main(), that function will execute while main() is put on hold.

After a function's first line, which includes its name, parentheses, and optional variables called *parameters* inside the parentheses, you'll find an opening brace, {, and the statements that form the body of the function, followed by a closing brace, }. Here is an example main() function:

```
main()
{
  int i = 4;
  do
  {
    i++;
    printf("i is %d\n", i);
  } while (i<10);
  return;
}
```

As you can see, a function can contain additional sets of braces. Braces always enclose a *block*. A function body is always enclosed in a block, and that block might have additional embedded blocks of code.

If a program contains more than one function, the functions follow each other sequentially in the program listing. A function must always end with a closing brace that matches the opening brace of the function. You can never start a new function before the preceding one ends.

> **Note:** The return statement at the end of a function is optional in most cases. When main() ends, the program ends.

The parentheses after a function name enable you to pass and receive variables between functions.

E

C Comments

One of the first things you'll notice about a C program is the format of the comments. All C program comments begin with a /* and end with a */. C comments can go virtually anywhere in a C program (even between keywords on the same line), but most C programmers put comments on lines by themselves or to the right of code. Listing E.1 shows a sample C program with ample comments.

Listing E.1. A C program with C comments.

```
/* A C program */
/* This program prints some integers inside a loop */
#include <stdio.h>
main()
{
```

continues

Listing E.1. continued

```
int i = 4;   /* Defines and initializes i */
do {
  i++;
  printf("i is %d\n", i);   /* Print i's value */
} while (i<10);             /* Quit looping when i reaches 10 */
return;
}
```

Note: You cannot nest one set of comments inside another. Although some compilers, including Turbo C++, support nested C comments, nesting C comments does not follow the ANSI C standard and could hamper future maintenance.

Preprocessor Directives

When you see a statement in a C program that begins with a pound sign, #, that statement is not technically a C statement but a *preprocessor directive*. A preprocessor directive instructs the C compiler to do something special before the program listing is compiled. The two most common C preprocessor directives are

`#include`

and

`#define`

The `#include` directive instructs C to merge an additional file, called a *header file,* into your program. In Listing E.1, you'll find this line:

`#include <stdio.h>`

This `#include` directive merges the file named STDIO.H from disk and replaces the `#include` line with the contents of the file. Then, the C compiler compiles the program. Although some C compilers enable you to see the expanded version of your file after the `#include` has taken place, you generally never see the results of the `#include`. After the compiler finishes compiling your program, it restores the text of your original source code.

Note: There is rarely a reason for you to look at the expanded source file that results after the #include takes place. Generally, you'll include built-in header files that come with the C compiler. The STDIO.H header file included in Listing E.1 helps the program produce input and output when needed.

The second preprocessor directive, #define, appears in many C programs. #define defines named constant values in C programs. #define is also used in some advanced C programs to write *defined macros,* or sections of code that replace other sections of code when needed. As explained in Day 2's chapter, "C++ Is Superior!" Turbo C++ provides const and inline as better replacements for #define. Any ANSI C standard compiler (including Turbo C) offers support for const now that const has found so much success in C++. Nevertheless, #define is still extremely common in C programs, and some C++ programmers slip a #define preprocessor directive into their programs once in a while.

#define instructs the C compiler to replace all occurrences of one value with another. Here is a common #define directive:

```
#define PI 3.14159
```

PI is a mathematical value that approximately equates to 3.14159. If you were writing programs that used PI, instead of typing 3.14159 everyplace you used the value, you could insert the preceding #define statement at the top of the program (preprocessor directives generally appear before the first function, main()). Instead of using the actual value, you then could use PI in its place everywhere you needed the value.

Note: The advantage that #define gives you over using the actual value is that if you want to change the value to something else, such as rounding it down to 3.142, you have to change that value in only one place (the #define directive) and the C compiler will replace all occurrences of PI with the new value when it next compiles the program.

C Data

Lots of different kinds of data are available in C, but the data types generally fall into those listed in Table E.1.

Table E.1. The primary C data types.

Data Type	Description
char	A single character
int	Integer values (whole numbers from –32768 to 32767)
long	Long integer values (more extreme whole numbers than regular int allows)
float	Floating-point
double	Extra-precision floating-point numbers

Note: There is no string data type in C. If you need to represent strings of data, you have to do so in arrays of characters.

The data types are often listed with the modifiers short, unsigned, and signed. All numeric data is automatically signed, meaning that you can store both positive and negative numbers. (signed variables can hold only positive numbers.)

Literal values (often called *constants*) can be characters, integers, long integers, floating-point, and double floating-point values *as well as strings*. In other words, there is not a string variable, but string literals are allowed. You must enclose all single-character literals in single quotation marks and string literals in double quotation marks. These are all character literals:

```
'A'      'a'      '&'      '['      '9'      '~'
```

These are string literals:

```
"A"     "C programs"     "Turbo C"     "576 S. Oak Street"
```

String literals can be empty, `""`. As you can see from the `"A"`, strings can also contain single characters. The difference is that strings must be enclosed in double quotation marks, whereas character literals must be enclosed in single quotation marks.

It's important to get used to the idea that all strings end in an ASCII zero. The ASCII zero value is called all sorts of things: *terminating zero, null zero,* and *binary zero.* The ASCII NULL is often represented as \0 or '\0'. The ASCII zero indicates the end of the string. You never see that terminating zero, however. When you type `"Hello"` in a program listing, you never type the terminating zero, but it's there. Figure E.1 shows

you how `"Hello"` is stored in memory. There's a zero at the end so that the compiler knows when the string ends.

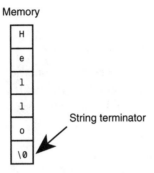

Memory

String terminator

Figure E.1. *All strings end in a terminating NULL. Without the NULL, a string is just a collection of individual characters.*

> **Note:** Some languages, such as Basic, store the length of all strings in a table and constantly update the table if the strings change length. C offers more efficiency but adds a little burden to the programmer. You must always be aware of the terminating NULL and make room for the terminating NULL when you store string literals in character arrays.

E

By the way, if strings contain character zeros, the C compiler knows not to terminate the string at the character zeros. For example, here's a string literal that contains an address:

```
"1000 South Fern Ave."
```

The zeros in the `1000` are character zeros. They appear in the ASCII table (Appendix A provides a complete ASCII table) at location 48. The first character in the ASCII table is the *NULL* character, located at ASCII location 0. It is that NULL character that terminates all strings, thus the name *ASCII 0* for the string terminator.

Put Variables First!

Before you do anything else in a block, you must define all variables used in the block. Unlike with C++, you can define variables only at the top of a block of code, not in the middle of a block. Use the keywords found in Table E.1 to define variables.

For example, the following first few lines of main() define three kinds of variables:

```
main()
{
  int i;
  char c;
  double x;
  /* Rest of program follows */
```

C does not automatically store zeros in automatic variables. You have no idea what is in a variable until you store something in one. If you want to put values in the three variables defined here, i, c, and x, you can do so by including statements like these:

```
i = 14;
c = 'A';
x = -12122.455437;
```

Note: All C statements end in semicolons, ;. You don't end C comments or function names with semicolons, but all executable statements, such as variable definitions, assignments, I/O, and looping statements, must terminate with a semicolon or you'll receive a compile error.

C enables you to combine variable definition and initialization into the same statements. The previous statements can be shortened like this:

```
main()
{
  int i = 14;
  char c = 'A';
  double x = -12122.455437;
  /* Rest of program follows */
```

After you define the variables, you can assign values to them using the standard math operators. Here are a few sample assignment statements:

```
x = 43.45 + 19.0 - 18.2833 * 4.3 / 5.6;
i = 5 + i + 15 - 33 / 11;
```

When you need to group several values together in an array, use brackets in C for array subscripts. An array is a list of variable values, not single variables. The following statements show you how to define and initialize arrays:

```
int iAra1[10];   /* Defines an array of 10 values */
/* The next statement defines and initializes */
int iAra2[10] = {4, 2, 6, 9, 0, 1, 3, 7, 2, 5};
/* The next statement stores characters in a character array */
char cAra1[5]  = {'T', 'P', 'U', 'L', 'A'};
```

```
/* The next statement stores a string in a character array */
char cAta2[8] = "Turbo C"; /* Leaves room for null zero */
```

All array subscripts begin at zero. The following code initializes three integer array values:

```
int ara[3];  /* Define the array */
ara[0] = 20; /* Store values in each element */
ara[1] = 30;
ara[2] = 40;
```

Input/Output

C does not contain commands for input and output (I/O). You must call built-in library functions to perform I/O. The built-in function most often used for C output is printf(), and the one most used for C input is scanf().

Before you can print values with printf(), you must format using format codes like those in Table E.2. The format codes describe how C is to interpret the data you want printed. The printf() function cannot automatically decide what kind of data you are printing, so you must tell the compiler the printed data types with the format codes.

Table E.2. Format codes used to input and output values.

Format Code	Description
%d	Integer
%f	Floating-point
%c	Character
%s	String

There are more format codes, but the ones in Table E.2 are the most common. A couple of example printf() statements will show you how the function works:

The statement

```
printf("My age is %d.", ageVar);
```

produces this output (assuming that the integer variable ageVar contains 18):

```
My age is 18.
```

The statement

```
printf("My name is %s and I make %f an hour.", "Sandy", 7.87);
```

produces this output (no variables are used here, just literal values):

```
My name is Sandy and I make 7.870000 an hour.
```

Oops—the floating-point literal, 7.87, comes out with too many zeros. If you want to limit the number of decimal places printed (C typically defaults to printing seven significant digits unless you override the default), insert a decimal and number between the % and f like this:

```
printf("My name is %s and I make %.2f an hour.", "Sandy", 7.87);
```

This `printf()` now produces this output:

```
My name is Sandy and I make 7.87 an hour.
```

Figure E.2 shows how each of the format codes matches the data being printed.

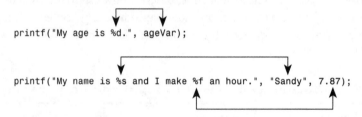

Figure E.2. *The format codes tell C how to print your data.*

There are a few additional output control codes called *escape sequences* that you'll often find inside `printf()` function calls. Table E.3 lists these escape sequences.

Table E.3. Escape sequences that control output.

Escape Sequence	Description
\n	Newline (carriage return and line feed)
\a	Alarm (rings the PC's bell)
\t	Tab to the next tab stop

`printf()` does not automatically send the cursor to the next line. These four `printf()`s all print on the same line:

```
printf("This ");
printf("is ");
printf("output ");
printf("to the screen.");
```

If you wanted the output to appear on different lines, you would have to add \n where you wanted the new lines to occur. The following modified `printf()`s

```
printf("This\n");
printf("is\n");
printf("output\n");
printf("to the screen.");
```

produce this:

```
This
is
output
to the screen.
```

`scanf()` is one of the most difficult built-in functions available. C programmers are always relieved to learn about Turbo C++'s `cin` replacement for `scanf()`. For a quick review, here are points to remember about `scanf()`:

1. `scanf()` is the mirror-image function to `printf()`. Both require format codes that describe variables.

2. Instead of outputting data from variables as `printf()` does, `scanf()` inputs values from the keyboard and stores those values in the variables listed.

3. You must precede all non-array variables inside the `printf()` parentheses with an ampersand, &.

4. Don't use floating-point decimal codes inside format codes. For example, when inputting floating-point variables, you would use `%f`, not `%.1f`.

Here is a program that uses both `printf()` and `scanf()` (notice that STDIO.H is properly included):

```
#include <stdio.h>
main()
{
  int age = 20;
  char name[5] = "Thom";
  float weight = 166.7;
  /* Print the current values */
  printf("My name is %s.\nI am %d years old.\n", name, age);
  printf("I weigh %.1f.\n", weight);
  /* Now, ask for new values */
  printf("Enter a new age: ");
```

```
        scanf("%d", &age);      /* Get a new age from the user */
        printf("Enter a new weight: ");
        scanf("%f", &weight);
        printf("Enter a new name: ");
        scanf("%s", name);     /* Notice no & is used due to the array */
        printf("These are the values you entered:\n");
        printf("name: %s\n", name);
        printf("age: %d\n", age);
        printf("weight: %.1f\n", weight);
};
```

Here is one possible run of the program:

```
My name is Thom.
I am 20 years old.
I weigh 166.7.
Enter a new age: 40
Enter a new weight: 120.3
Enter a new name: Mary
These are the values you entered:
name: Mary
age: 40
weight: 120.3
```

The program brings up an interesting and bad side effect that can occur when you use arrays. Unlike most programming languages, C never checks for array boundaries. Therefore, the name entered must be four or fewer characters to fit in the name array. (The fifth character is the null zero that C stores when a name is entered using %s.) If you type a name longer than four characters, the data overrides other data and produces bad results because the other variables can be overwritten.

Note: Before using printf() and scanf(), you should include the STDIO.H header file that comes supplied with C compilers.

Although there is more to C I/O, that's all you need to know for this review. Turbo C++'s cin and cout offer I/O mechanisms vastly superior to the built-in STDIO.H library functions.

Note: If you want to clear your screen, insert the Turbo C clrscr() built-in function call where you want the screen erased. You should also include the CONIO.H header file at the top of all programs that erase the screen.

Operators

As mentioned earlier, the C language contains lots of operators. Table E.4 contains the primary math operators.

Table E.4. C's primary math operators.

Operator	Description
+	Addition
-	Subtraction
*	Multiplication
/	Division or integer division
%	Modulus or remainder

Most of the primary operators work like their equivalents in math or other programming languages. The division operator performs integer division if integer operands appear on each side of the division operator; it produces a floating-point result if a non-integer appears on either side. Study these examples:

```
i = 4 + 5;    /* Puts a 9 in i */
i = 5 - 4;    /* Puts a 1 in i */
i = 5 * 4;    /* Puts a 20 in i */
i = 20 / 4;   /* Puts an integer 5 in i */
i = 20 / 3;   /* Puts an integer 6 in i */
i = 20 % 3;   /* Puts a 2 in i (the integer remainder) */
x = 20.0 / 3.0; /* Puts a 6.667 in x */
```

Additional Math Operators

C attempts to help streamline your programming routine by adding operators not found in other languages. The compound, increment, and decrement operators all shortcut what you would do in other programming languages. Table E.5 lists these additional math operators.

Table E.5. Additional math operators.

Operator	Description
+=	Compound addition
-=	Compound subtraction
*=	Compound multiplication
/=	Compound division
++	Increment
--	Decrement

These operators are most useful when updating values already in variables. For example, if you want to increase a variable by 15 percent, you would normally put that variable on both sides of the equal sign like this:

```
price = price * 1.15;  /* Increase whatever's in price */
```

The compound operators keep you from having to repeat the variable name on both sides of the equal sign. The preceding statement becomes this:

```
price *= 1.15;  /* Increase whatever's in price */
```

When you want to add 1 or subtract 1 from variables, you generally do this:

```
i = i + 1;  /* Add 1 to i */
```

and

```
k = k - 1;  /* Subtract 1 from k */
```

Both of these statements are shortened using the increment and decrement operators:

```
i++;  /* Add 1 to i */
```

and

```
k--;  /* Subtract 1 from k */
```

The increment and decrement operators can appear on either side of the variable. Their placement can produce slightly different results when other values are involved in the expression. For instance, the code

```
i = 15;
j = i++ * 2;
printf("%i, %j\n", i, j);
```

produces this output:

```
16, 30
```

At first, you might wonder why i didn't get incremented before it was multiplied by 2. Because the ++ operator appeared to the right of i, C waits until the entire expression is evaluated before incrementing the i. If you list the ++ before the i, like

```
i = 15;
j = ++i * 2;
printf("%i, %j\n", i, j);
```

you get the following output:

```
16, 32
```

Notice that the i is incremented before the multiplication.

> **Note:** Putting increment and decrement operators before variable names is called *prefix notation*. Putting increment and decrement operators after variable names is called *postfix notation*.

Be sure to follow the order of operators found in Appendix C (the order is the same for both C and Turbo C++, except for the addition of extra operators to Turbo C++).

The Relational and Logical Operators

Most of C's relational operators work like their equivalents in other programming languages. Table E.6 lists the relational operators and their meanings.

Table E.6. The relational operators.

Relational Operator	Description
==	Equality
>	Greater than
<	Less than
>=	Greater than or equal to

continues

Table E.6. continued

Relational Operator	Description
<=	Less than or equal to
!=	Not equal to

Note: The most important relational operator to key in on at this time is the equality operator. The double equal, ==, is used only for equal comparisons, and the regular equal, =, is used only for assignment. Never attempt to test a value for equality like this:

```
if (i = 5)      /* NO! 5 is assigned to i */
```

C also provides the logical operators shown in Table E.7 that combine one or more relational operators.

Table E.7. The logical operators.

Logical Operator	Description
&&	AND
¦¦	OR
!	NOT

The relational and logical operators all produce true and false results. (In C, a true result can be any nonzero, and a false result is always 0.)

Testing Data

The if, while, do-while, and for statements all utilize the relational and logical operators to control their loops. Here is the format of each of these statements:

```
if (condition)
  { block of one or more C statements; }
else
  { block of one or more C statements; }
```

Note: The `else` portion of the `if` is optional and might or might not be needed by your application. You *must* enclose the *condition* inside parentheses. The *condition* must be enclosed in parentheses for all the looping statements that follow as well. `if` is not a loop, unlike the other three kinds of statements.

```
while (condition)
  { block of one or more C statements; }

do
  { block of one or more C statements; }
while (condition)

for (startExpression; testExpression; countExpression)
  { block of one or more C statements; }
```

The difference between the `while` statement and the `do-while` statement is that the `do-while` statement always executes at least once because the conditional test appears at the bottom of the loop. The `while`'s conditional test occurs at the top of the loop and could possibly be false upon entry to the `while` loop.

Here is a program that shows the `while` loop:

```
#include <stdio.h>
main()
{
  int i = 5;
  while (i < 10)
    { printf("Ring...\a\n");   /* Rings the PC bell each iteration */
      i++;
    }
  return;
}
```

Here is the program's output (each time a line is printed, the PC's bell rings):

```
Ring...
Ring...
Ring...
Ring...
Ring...
```

Here is the same program using `do-while`:

```
#include <stdio.h>
main()
{
  int i = 5;
  do
```

```
      { printf("Ring...\a\n");   /* Rings the PC bell each iteration */
        i++;
      }   while (i <= 10);
   return;
}
```

Both of these programs loop five times because the loop control variable, i, begins at 5 and continues incrementing each time through the loop until it reaches 10.

The for loop provides a more determinate way of looping. Instead of controlling the variable values inside the loop as done with while, the for statement controls the values. Here is a for loop that counts up from 1 to 10. Notice that the first line in the loop initializes the loop variable ctr, tests the loop variable each time through the loop, and increments the loop variable each time through the loop.

```
for (ctr=1; ctr<=10; ctr++)
  { printf("%d\n", i); }
```

If you want to exit a loop early, use the break statement. Any time any of the loops reaches a break, the loop terminates early, and the statement following the last line of the loop takes over control.

Another related control command is the switch statement. Instead of embedding an if within an if, the switch often provides a cleaner way of testing several values. Here is the format of switch:

```
switch (expression)
  { case (expression1) : {Block of C statement(s);
                            break;}
    case (expression2) : {Block of C statement(s);
                            break;}
    case (expression3) : {Block of C statement(s);
                            break;}
    default:             {Block of C statement(s);
                            break;}
}
```

The break after each case is not required, but it almost always appears to keep execution from falling through to the next case. The switch statement is useful for testing several conditions. Here is a program that prints a department name based on the department code entered:

```
#include <stdio.h>
main()
{
  int deptCode;
  printf("What is your department code (1-5)? ");
  scanf("%d", &deptCode);
  switch (deptCode)
```

```
  { case (1) : printf("You're accounting.\n");
              break;
    case (2) : printf("You're engineering.\n");
              break;
    case (3) : printf("You're marketing.\n");
              break;
    case (4) : printf("You're data processing.\n");
              break;
    case (5) : printf("You're payroll.\n");
              break;
    default:   printf("You didn't enter a correct department code!\n");
              break;
  }
  return;
}
```

Here's a sample run of this program:

```
What is your department code (1-5)? 2
You're engineering.
```

The case value that matches the switch value determines which set of statements executes. Without switch, you would have to test with several layers of if and else statements. The default case takes care of everything that doesn't match, as shown in this execution of the program:

```
What is your department code (1-5)? 23
You didn't enter a correct department code!
```

Pointers

A C pointer variable doesn't contain a data value, but contains the address of a data value. When defining pointers, you must use a dereferencing operator, *, like this:

```
int i = 15;  /* Regular variable */
int * ipt;   /* Pointer variable */
```

Note: C will not confuse the dereference with multiplication because of the context in which you use each one.

As with regular variables, garbage resides in pointer variables until you store something in them. The address-of operator, &, helps fill pointers with values. The following statement assigns the address of i to the variable ipt:

```
ipt = &i;
```

Figure E.3 shows how these variables logically appear in memory.

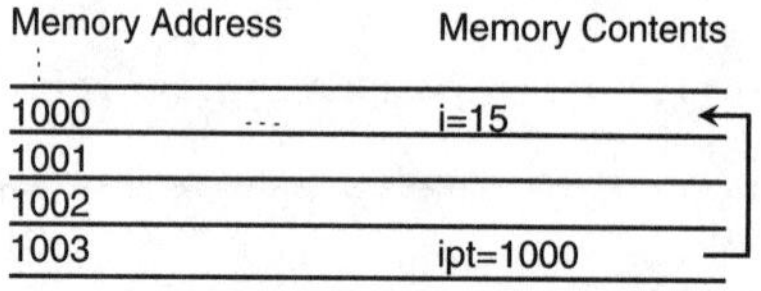

Figure E.3. *The pointer variable contains the address of* i.

A C array name is nothing more than a pointer variable that points to a list of items. When you work with or print an array, you are actually working with a pointer to the data.

Pointers are most useful when you allocate and deallocate heap memory. C uses the built-in library functions malloc() and free() to allocate and deallocate memory to and from the heap. The heap is all unused memory in your computer not currently in use by your other variables, your program, and your operating system. Instead of defining arrays of variables, you can reserve (with malloc()) and point to memory on the heap with pointer variables. That way, you consume memory only when you need it rather than for your entire program's run as you do with regular variables.

When you are finished with heap memory, you can throw it back to the heap's free area (for other tasks such as the operating system, for other users if you use a PC network server, or for your own program later) with free().

Turbo C++ offers new and delete operators that completely replace malloc() and free(). new and delete offer many additional benefits over malloc() and free(), including the best advantage to newcomers, which is their simpler notation. Therefore, as long as you have an idea of the need of the heap, you'll be better off learning new and delete and forgetting about C's malloc() and free().

For Further Reading

If you want a more detailed introduction and tutorial on the C language, check out the following Sams titles. They walk the newcomer to C from absolute beginning status to expert, and they give anyone a solid foundation in non-OOP programming. If your C skills are rusty or nonexistent, you'll master Turbo C++ easier if you tackle the groundwork presented by these titles.

Absolute Beginner's Guide to C

Written by this author, the book takes a lighthearted look at the C programming language. Helpful tips, notes, and cautions steer you along as you cover the basics of C. Fun facts, technical sections, and daily reviews make the journey easier, and your acquired knowledge is brought together with a fun blackjack program at the end of the book. (Beginning)

Teach Yourself C in 21 Days

With this best-selling book, users can achieve C success now! Each lesson can be completed in two to three hours or less. Shaded syntax boxes, Q&A sections, and "Do's and Don'ts" sections reinforce the important topics within C. (Beginning to Intermediate)

Advanced C

Here's the next step for programmers who want to improve their C programming skills. This book gives efficiency tips as well as techniques for debugging C programs and improving their speed, memory usage, and readability. (Intermediate to Advanced)

Using Turbo
C++ Graphics

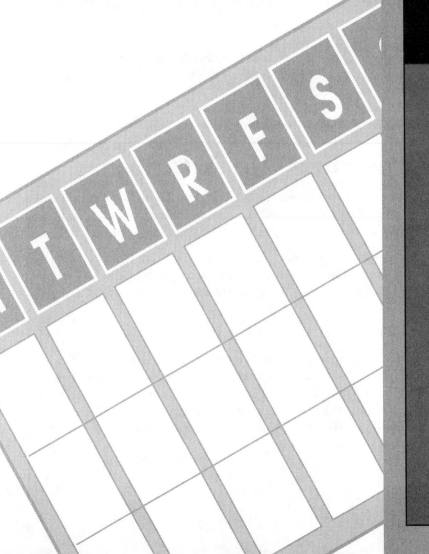

For those interested in sprucing up their output, this appendix introduces the graphics capabilities of Turbo C++. The Borland Graphics Interface (*BGI*) contains several high-level graphics initialization, drawing, and color functions that you can call.

You must, of course, have a graphics-compatible monitor and adapter card before using the BGI. The huge majority of today's computer users have at least a VGA-compatible (Video Graphics Array) adapter, and that's the adapter discussed in this appendix. If you use an XGA (IBM's *eXtended Graphics Adapter*) or a super-VGA adapter, all the functions described in this appendix will work on your system. As graphics adapters achieve higher resolutions in the future (meaning that they can display better graphics by displaying more graphics dots per square inch), Borland will no doubt add function options to take advantage of these higher resolutions.

Note: All the graphics functions described here are prototyped in the GRAPHICS.H file, so be sure to include this file at the top of all graphics programs.

First, Initialize the Adapter

All the programs you see throughout this book work in Turbo C++'s default screen mode, which is the screen's text mode. If you want to draw graphics of any kind, you must put your graphics adapter in graphics mode by *initializing* the graphics adapter.

The initgraph() function initializes the graphics adapter and converts your text display into a graphics display. As discussed in this appendix's introduction, all of these functions work with the VGA adapter. Here is the format of the initgraph() function:

```
initgraph(int &driver, int &mode, char * BGIpathname);
```

The *driver* should be VGA to set the graphics mode for VGA. You can also set the driver to DETECT, and Turbo C++ automatically sets your adapter to its highest resolution. The *mode* is any value from Table F.1. The table lists the number of horizontal and vertical dots per inch and the total number of colors available in each of those modes. You'll probably want to use VGAHI for all your programs so that you can display the best-looking graphics possible.

Table F.1. VGA graphics modes.

Mode	Description
VGALO	640 x 200 resolution in 16 colors
VGAMED	640 x 350 resolution in 16 colors
VGAHI	640 x 480 resolution in 16 colors

> **Note:** Notice that you must pass the *driver* and *mode* values by address to `initgraph()`. The *driver* and *mode* are defined integer constants, defined in GRAPHICS.H, so you must store the constants in variables and pass the address of those variables to `initgraph()`.

The third parameter, *BGIpathname*, contains the full path to the VGA's EGAVGA.BGI file, which is \TC\BGI if you accepted Turbo C++'s default installation when you originally installed Turbo C++. The *BGIpathname* must be a string (either a string literal or a string stored in a character array or pointed to by a character pointer). The \ is a Turbo C++ escape character, so you must use a double-backslash, \\, when specifying the path.

After you use any graphics function, you can call `graphresult()` to see whether an error occurred. The `graphresult()` function returns 0, false, if the `initgraph()` function worked properly, and returns one of the defined error codes in Table F.2 if the graphics didn't work correctly.

Often, programmers check only for a zero or non-zero graphics return value, but if you want to check for each of Table F.2's constants (defined in GRAPHICS.H), you can determine what exactly caused the graphics failure. (Not all the errors occur when you use `initgraph()`. You can call `graphresult()` after any graphics function call and check each result.)

Table F.2. The `graphresult()` return codes.

Defined Constant	Description
grOk	No error occurred, defined as 0
grNoInitGraph	A graphics function was attempted without `initgraph()` being first called

continues

F

Table F.2. continued

Defined Constant	Description
grNotDetected	No graphics hardware was detected
grFileNotFound	Device driver file was not found
grInvalidDriver	Invalid device driver file
grNoLoadMem	Not enough memory to load graphics driver
grNoScanMem	Out of memory in scan graphics function fill
grNoFloodMem	Out of memory in flood graphics function fill
grFontNotFound	Font file was not found
grNoFontMem	Not enough memory to load the requested font
grInvalidMode	Invalid graphics mode for selected driver
grError	Graphics error
grIOerror	Graphics I/O error when attempted to write graphics or read adapter
grInvalidFont	Invalid font file requested
grInvalidFontNum	Invalid font number requested
grInvalidDeviceNum	Invalid device number requested
grInvalidVersion	Invalid version number requested

Never leave the screen in graphics mode when your program ends. The closegraph() function (with no parameters) restores the screen to the previous text mode.

The code in Listing F.1 uses the initgraph() function call to initialize the graphics adapter to the VGA's highest resolution and immediately restores the screen to the text mode. (Programs later in this appendix will fill in the gap and display graphics before restoring the display.)

Listing F.1. Initializing and closing the graphics mode.

```
1:  // Filename: GRPHINIT.CPP
2:  // Initialize and close the graphics mode
3:  #include <iostream.h>
4:  #include <stdlib.h>
5:  #include <graphics.h>
```

```
6:  main()
7:  {
8:    int driver = EGA, mode = VGAHI;
9:    char bgiPath[] = "\\TC\\BGI";
10:   initgraph(&driver, &mode, bgiPath);    // Change to graphics mode
11:   if (graphresult())                     // Check for any error
12:     { cout << "Graphics adapter error.\n";
13:       exit(1);
14:     }
15:   closegraph();
16:   return 0;
17: }
```

If you run the program in Listing F.1, you'll see your screen flicker as it goes into, and then out of, the VGA graphics mode.

Draw Something

After initializing the graphics mode with `initgraph()` and before restoring the screen to text mode with `closegraph()`, you'll of course want to draw something. This section describes many of the graphics-drawing functions included in the BGI interface supplied with Turbo C++.

Specifying Colors

Almost everything you do in graphics requires a color of some kind. All the colors are defined in GRAPHICS.H as named constants and are listed in Table F.3. Some of the graphics functions enable you to specify a color code directly, whereas other functions require that you set the appropriate color before calling a graphics function.

Table F.3. Color constants.

Color Constant	Can Be Used for Background Color?
BLACK	Yes
BLUE	Yes
GREEN	Yes
CYAN	Yes
RED	Yes

continues

Table F.3. continued

Color Constant	Can Be Used for Background Color?
MAGENTA	Yes
BROWN	Yes
LIGHTGRAY	Yes
DARKGRAY	No
LIGHTBLUE	No
LIGHTGREEN	No
LIGHTCYAN	No
LIGHTRED	No
LIGHTMAGENTA	No
YELLOW	No
WHITE	No

The foreground color is the color of the graphics dots, and the background is the screen color behind the graphics. (In this book, the foreground color is black, and the background is the white page color.) As the table indicates, you cannot use all the colors for the background color.

Set the foreground color with the setcolor() function by calling setcolor() with the appropriate color as its only argument. Set the background color by calling setbkcolor(). If you wanted to draw yellow graphics on a green background, you would first initialize the graphics mode and then call these two functions before outputting any graphics:

```
setcolor(YELLOW);      // Sets the foreground
setbkcolor(GREEN);     // Sets the background
```

Note: Any graphics function that takes a color parameter as an argument overrides the color. For example, if you've set the screen to yellow foreground on a green background, you still can draw red graphics if you pass the RED color code to the graphics commands you'll learn about throughout the rest of this appendix.

If you call setcolor() several times from the same program, you can display text in several different colors. If you call the setbkcolor() multiple times, however, the entire background color is changed to the most recent background color.

Printing Text on a Graphics Screen

Before looking at some of the drawing functions, you ought to learn how to output text within the graphics mode. If you use regular cout, you cannot take advantage of various system fonts and screen locations (unless you overload <<, of course). The outtextxy() function sends text to a graphics screen at a specific x-y coordinate. The maximum x value and maximum y value are determined by the graphics mode. As Table F.1 showed, the VGAHI mode contains 640 graphics dots (called *pixels* or *picture elements*) across the screen (the x value) and 480 pixels down (the y value). All coordinates begin at zero, so x ranges from 0 to 639, and y ranges from 0 to 479 in VGAHI resolution. Here is the format of outtextxy():

```
outtextxy(int x, int y, char * textString)
```

The program in Listing F.2 prints several words on-screen in different colors. Notice that setcolor() is called several times before each outtextxy() to change the subsequent text colors.

Type **Listing F.2. Displaying text in several colors.**

```
1:  // Filename: TEXTCOLR.CPP
2:  // Prints words in different colors.
3:  #include <iostream.h>
4:  #include <stdlib.h>
5:  #include <graphics.h>
6:  main()
7:  {
8:     int driver = EGA, mode = VGAHI;
9:     char bgiPath[] = "\\TC\\BGI";
10:    initgraph(&driver, &mode, bgiPath); // To graphics mode
11:    if (graphresult())                  // Check for any error
12:      { cout << "Graphics adapter error.\n";
13:        exit(1);
14:      }
15:    setcolor(YELLOW);
16:    setbkcolor(GREEN);
17:    outtextxy(1, 1, "C++ is fun");
18:    setcolor(BLUE);
19:    outtextxy(35, 200, "C++ is easy");
20:    setcolor(RED);
21:    outtextxy(230, 50, "C++ is challenging");
```

continues

Listing F.2. continued

```
22:     setcolor(WHITE);
23:     outtextxy(300, 310, "C++ is better");
24:     setcolor(LIGHTCYAN);
25:     outtextxy(450, 470, "Press Enter to quit...");
26:     cin.get();     // Waits for Enter before continuing
27:     closegraph();
28:     return 0;
29: }
```

Notice that line 25 prints a message that tells the user to press Enter to quit the program. The Enter keystroke is captured in line 26. Line 26 pauses until the user presses Enter so that the graphics text remains on-screen until the user is ready to quit the program. Without the pause at line 26, the graphics would appear and disappear (via line 27) as soon as the user runs the program.

Changing the Text Style

The characters on the graphics screen are not displayed but are drawn by Turbo C++ pixel by pixel. You are not limited to the default font (the style of the character). The settextstyle() function determines exactly how your text appears on-screen. Here is the format of settextstyle():

settextstyle(int *font*, int *direction*, int *charSize*)

The *font* can be any value from Table F.4. The program that follows in a moment displays each kind of font so that you'll get accustomed to the look of each.

Note: If you own a version of Turbo C++ prior to 3.0, you'll have fewer fonts than those listed in Table F.4. Versions of Turbo C++ after 3.0 promise to add more font styles.

Table F.4. Font styles for graphics characters.

Font Name	Description
DEFAULT_FONT	8x8 regular font
TRIPLEX_FONT	Proportional serif font
SMALL_FONT	Clearest font for displaying little text

Font Name	Description
SANS_SERIF_FONT	Clean sans sarif font
GOTHIC_FONT	Old-style characters

The *direction* is either HORIZ_DIR or VERT_DIR, depending on whether you want subsequent text to print across the screen from left to right or up and down the screen vertically.

The *charSize* ranges from 1 for regular size (each character fits within an 8-by-8 pixel box) to 10 for 10 times the regular size.

Listing F.3 shows a program that displays text in all the various fonts using different sizes and direction.

 Listing F.3. Printing all styles of text.

```
1:  // Filename: TEXTSTYL.CPP
2:  // Prints words in different styles.
3:  #include <iostream.h>
4:  #include <stdlib.h>
5:  #include <graphics.h>
6:  main()
7:  {
8:     int driver = EGA, mode = VGAHI;
9:     char bgiPath[] = "\\TC\\BGI";
10:    initgraph(&driver, &mode, bgiPath); // To graphics mode
11:    if (graphresult())                  // Check for any error
12:      { cout << "Graphics adapter error.\n";
13:        exit(1);
14:      }
15:    setcolor(WHITE);
16:    setbkcolor(BLUE);
17:    outtextxy(1, 1, "Regular text");
18:    settextstyle(TRIPLEX_FONT, HORIZ_DIR, 2);
19:    outtextxy(1, 100, "TRIPLEX_FONT text");
20:    settextstyle(SMALL_FONT, HORIZ_DIR, 4);
21:    outtextxy(1, 200, "SMALL_FONT text");
22:    settextstyle(SANS_SERIF_FONT, HORIZ_DIR, 6);
23:    outtextxy(1, 300, "SANS_SERIF_FONT text");
24:    settextstyle(GOTHIC_FONT, HORIZ_DIR, 6);
25:    outtextxy(1, 380, "GOTHIC_FONT text");
26:    settextstyle(DEFAULT_FONT, VERT_DIR, 2);
27:    outtextxy(500, 1, "(Don't look down!)");
28:    settextstyle(DEFAULT_FONT, HORIZ_DIR, 1);
29:    outtextxy(450, 470, "Press Enter to quit...");
```

continues

Listing F.3. continued

```
30:    cin.get();      // Waits for Enter before continuing
31:    closegraph();
32:    return 0;
33: }
```

Figure F.1 shows you the output from Listing F.3.

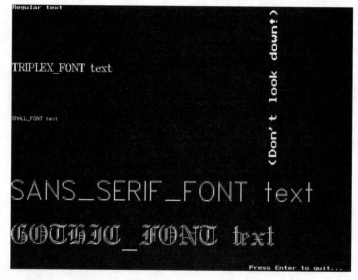

Figure F.1. *All styles of text.*

Note: By the way, if you want to output numerical values as graphics text, use the sprintf() function (meaning *string printf()*) to format output into a character array, and then output that text with outtextxy().

Tip: Turbo C++ includes two additional functions that let you adjust the way your text appears on the graphics screen. Check out the settextjustify() function, which right- or left-justifies text, and the setusercharsize() function, which changes the size of your text on the screen.

Drawing Pixels

A *pixel* (picture element) is just a dot on your graphics screen. With putpixel(), you can turn on individual pixels, literally drawing graphics a dot at a time. Here is the format of putpixel():

```
putpixel(int x, int y, int colorCode);
```

The *colorCode* that you specify overrides whatever foreground color is currently set. Therefore, you can draw with pixels in several different colors. If the *colorCode* matches that of the background color, the pixel will seem to be turned off (if set) at that location.

The program in Listing F.4 randomly draws several pixels on-screen in several different colors.

 Listing F.4. Lighting lots of pixels.

```cpp
1:  // Filename: PIXEL.CPP
2:  // Turns on random pixels of random colors.
3:  #include <iostream.h>
4:  #include <stdlib.h>
5:  #include <graphics.h>
6:  main()
7:  {
8:     int x, y, color;
9:     int driver = EGA, mode = VGAHI;
10:    char bgiPath[] = "\\TC\\BGI";
11:    initgraph(&driver, &mode, bgiPath); // To graphics mode
12:    if (graphresult())                  // Check for any error
13:      { cout << "Graphics adapter error.\n";
14:        exit(1);
15:      }
16:    setbkcolor(BLACK);
17:    for (int i=0; i<5000; i++)  // Draw 5,000 pixels
18:      { x = random(640);        // From 0 to 639
19:        y = random(480);        // From 0 to 479
20:        color = random(16);     // From 0 to 15 (directly
21:                                // associates to color-coded
22:        putpixel(x, y, color);  // constants from Table F.3).
23:      }
24:    setcolor(WHITE);
25:    outtextxy(450, 470, "Press Enter to quit...");
26:    cin.get();      // Waits for Enter before continuing
27:    closegraph();
28:    return 0;
29: }
```

Figure F.2 shows a black-and-white version of the output of the program in List-ing F.4. The random() function prototyped in STDLIB.H helps keep the colors and pixel locations varied.

Press Enter to quit...

Figure F.2. *Displaying lots of pixels.*

Note: Many people find that drawing pictures a dot at a time takes too much effort. You can draw lines, circles, and other shapes using the functions described in the next few sections.

Drawing Lines

The line() function draws lines on your screen. line() draws lines much faster (and with less effort on your part) than drawing a line of pixels with putpixel(). Here is the format of line():

```
line(int x1, int y1, int x2, int y2);
```

line() draws a line between two pixel coordinates. For example, the following line() draws a line from the upper-left corner to the bottom-right of the screen:

```
line(0, 0, 639, 479);   // Draws a diagonal line
```

You can draw dotted lines, solid lines, and dashed lines. The `setlinestyle()` works with `line()` (as well as the remaining graphics functions described throughout the rest of this appendix) to determine exactly what kind of line is drawn. If you call `line()` without first calling `setlinestyle()`, a regular solid line that is one pixel wide appears. However, `setlinestyle()` changes that default. Here is the format of `setlinestyle()`:

```
setlinestyle(int style, unsigned pattern, int thickness);
```

Table F.5 lists values available for `style` (an additional value, called USERBIT_LINE, enables you to define your own line style, but it is not covered here). Table F.6 lists several of the values for the `pattern` argument. Finally, Table F.7 lists the values for the `thickness`.

Table F.5. `setlinestyle()` style values.

Style Value	Description
SOLID_LINE	Solid line
DOTTED_LINE	Dotted line
CENTER_LINE	.-.-. pattern
DASHED_LINE	--- lines

Table F.6. `setlinestyle()` pattern values.

Pattern	Description
EMPTY_FILL	Same as background color
SOLID_FILL	Solid line
LINE_FILL	--- fill
LTSLASH_FILL	/// fill
SLASH_FILL	thick /// fill
BKSLASH_FILL	thick \\\ fill
LTBKSLASH_FILL	\\\ fill
HATCH_FILL	Light crosshatch
XHATCH_FILL	Heavy crosshatch

continues

Table F.6. continued

Pattern	Description
INTERLEAVE_FILL	Interleaving lines
WIDE_DOT_FILL	Widely spaced pixels
CLOSE_DOT_FILL	Closely spaced pixels
USER_FILL	User-defined pattern (not discussed here)

Table F.7. `setlinestyle()` thickness values.

Thickness	Description
NORM_WIDTH	One pixel wide
THICK_WIDTH	Three pixels wide

When you are drawing single lines, the second `setlinestyle()` argument doesn't do anything, but you must still specify something for the placeholder (`SOLID_FILL` does fine). If, for example, you wanted to change the look of the diagonal line drawn earlier, you would precede the `line()` function call with `setlinestyle()` like this:

```
setlinestyle(DASHED_LINE, SOLID_FILL, THICK_WIDTH);
line(0, 0, 639, 479);  // Draws a diagonal line
```

The program in Listing F.5 draws a series of dashed lines that form a geometrical pattern on-screen. Every other line is thicker than the others due to the `setlinestyle()`.

 Listing F.5. Lighting lines.

```
 1:  // Filename: LINES.CPP
 2:  // Draws a pattern of lines
 3:  #include <iostream.h>
 4:  #include <stdlib.h>
 5:  #include <graphics.h>
 6:  main()
 7:  {
 8:     int x1, y1, x2, y2;
 9:     int driver = EGA, mode = VGAHI;
10:     char bgiPath[] = "\\TC\\BGI";
11:     initgraph(&driver, &mode, bgiPath); // To graphics mode
12:     if (graphresult())                  // Check for any error
13:       { cout << "Graphics adapter error.\n";
14:         exit(1);
```

```
15:      }
16:    x1 = 0; y1 = 0; x2 = 600; y2 = 479;
17:    for (int ctr=0; ctr<50; ctr++)
18:      { setcolor(random(16));   // Random color
19:        if (ctr % 2)            // True (1) for odd values
20:         {setlinestyle(DASHED_LINE,EMPTY_FILL,THICK_WIDTH);}
21:        else
22:         {setlinestyle(DASHED_LINE,EMPTY_FILL,NORM_WIDTH);}
23:        line(x1, y1, x2, y2);
24:        x1 += 15; y1 += 5;
25:        x2 -= 15; y2 -= 5;      // Adjust the lines
26:      }
27:    setcolor(WHITE);
28:    outtextxy(450, 470, "Press Enter to quit...");
29:    cin.get();     // Waits for Enter before continuing
30:    closegraph();
31:    return 0;
32: }
```

Figure F.3 shows you the output from this program. (The actual output is more colorful than the book can illustrate.)

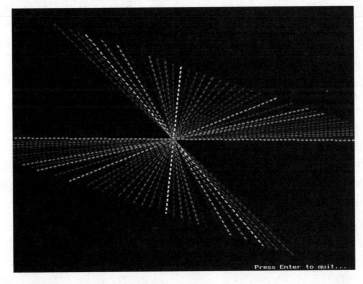

Figure F.3. *Drawing a pattern of lines.*

Playing Around with Circles

The `circle()` function draws circles on your screen. Here is the format of the `circle()` function:

```
circle(int x, int y, int radius);
```

The *x* and *y* coordinates specify the center of the circle, and the *radius* is the number of pixels in the radius of the circle (the radius measures from the center of the circle to the outer edge). You should precede a `circle()` function call with `setlinestyle()` to set the thickness of the circle you are drawing to either `NORM_WIDTH` or `THICK_WIDTH`. (The first two `setlinestyle()` arguments are ignored by the `circle()` function.)

You must decide what the center of your circle will look like, and you must use the `setfillstyle()` function to do that. Here is the format of `setfillstyle()`:

```
setfillstyle(int pattern, int colorCode);
```

The *pattern* can be any of the values from Table F.6. The color fills in the middle of the circle and can be any of the defined color constants from Table F.3.

There is yet one more step to take care of when the center of the circle is being filled. The `setfillstyle()` determines only what pattern and color fill the center of the circle, but you still must tell Turbo C++ *which* circle to fill. For example, you might have three circles drawn on your screen but want to fill only one. The last step in filling circles is to call the `floodfill()` function, whose format is this:

```
floodfill(int x, int y, int linecolor);
```

The *x* and *y* arguments must be a coordinate pair somewhere within the diameter of the circle you want to fill. The *linecolor* is the color of the circle's line; without the proper *linecolor*, the fill fills the entire screen! The *linecolor* specifies where the fill stops filling.

Given all this build-up, how about drawing a green circle and filling it with a red hatched pattern. The following code takes care of this circle nicely:

```
setcolor(GREEN);                    // For the circle outline
setlinestyle(SOLID_LINE, SOLID_FILL, NORM_WIDTH);  // Width
circle(300,200,100);                // Draw the circle outline
setfillstyle(HATCH_FILL, RED);      // Determine the fill
floodfill(301,199,GREEN);           // Perform the fill
```

Note: There are lots of ways to draw various shapes using Turbo C++. As you are seeing, after you understand the fundamental functions that set color and styles, the rest is easy.

Drawing Rectangles

The `rectangle()` function draws a rectangle on your screen. As with `circle()`, you can then fill the rectangle with any color and pattern by calling `setlinestyle()` and `floodfill()`. Here is the format of `rectangle()`:

```
rectangle(int x1, int y1, int x2, int y2);
```

The coordinate pairs specify the upper-left corner and lower-right corner of the rectangle that you want to draw. The program in Listing F.6 draws a blue rectangle in the middle of the screen and fills the rectangle with dashed lines. After you press Enter, the red circle described at the end of the preceding section appears over the rectangle.

Type   **Listing F.6. Rectangles and circles.**

```
1:  // Filename: RECTCIRC.CPP
2:  // Draws a rectangle and circle
3:  #include <iostream.h>
4:  #include <stdlib.h>
5:  #include <graphics.h>
6:  main()
7:  {
8:      int driver = EGA, mode = VGAHI;
9:      char bgiPath[] = "\\TC\\BGI";
10:     initgraph(&driver, &mode, bgiPath); // To graphics mode
11:     if (graphresult())                  // Check for any error
12:       { cout << "Graphics adapter error.\n";
13:         exit(1);
14:       }
15:     setbkcolor(BLACK);
16:     // Draw the rectangle
17:     setcolor(BLUE);                              // For the outline color
18:     setlinestyle(SOLID_LINE, SOLID_FILL, THICK_WIDTH);  // Width
19:     rectangle(100, 100, 500, 300);    // Draw the rectangle outline
20:     setfillstyle(SLASH_FILL, BLUE);     // Determine the fill
21:     floodfill(200, 200, BLUE);          // Perform the fill
22:     setcolor(WHITE);
23:     outtextxy(425, 470, "Press Enter to continue...");
```

continues

F

Listing F.6. continued

```
24:    cin.get();      // Waits for Enter before continuing
25:    outtextxy(425, 470, "                      "); // Erase
26:    // Now draw the circle
27:    setcolor(GREEN);                   // For the circle outline
28:    setlinestyle(SOLID_LINE, SOLID_FILL, NORM_WIDTH);  // Width
29:    circle(300, 200, 100);            // Draw the circle outline
30:    setfillstyle(HATCH_FILL, RED);    // Determine the fill
31:    floodfill(301,199,GREEN);         // Perform the fill
32:    setcolor(WHITE);
33:    outtextxy(450, 470, "Press Enter to quit...");
34:    cin.get();      // Waits for Enter before continuing
35:    closegraph();
36:    return 0;
37: }
```

Figure F.4 shows the screen at the point where Listing F.6 draws the circle over the rectangle.

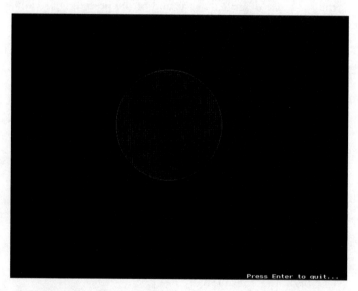

Figure F.4. *Drawing a rectangle and circle.*

Drawing Any Shape

Turbo C++ doesn't limit you to pixels, lines, circles, and rectangles. Using the fillpoly() function, you can draw any shape you want to draw. Whereas a rectangle

is defined by its two end corners, a shape such as a star, fan, or house is defined by several coordinate pairs that form the outline of the shape. To draw a complex figure, sketch the figure on graph paper to get an idea of its coordinate pairs. A coordinate pair occurs every time one line connects to another.

After you determine the coordinate pairs that form the shape (the *polygon*), store those coordinates in an integer array. The `fillpoly()` function accepts two arguments. Here is the format of `fillpoly()`:

```
fillpoly(int numOfCoordinates, int coordinateArray);
```

The *numOfCoordinates* is the number of coordinate pairs (not individual elements) in the coordinate array named in the second argument. Although `fillpoly()` requires more forethought than `circle()` or `rectangle()`, it's simple to use. The most difficult part of using `fillpoly()` is determining the coordinate pairs for your shape.

The easiest way to learn `fillpoly()` is to see an example. The program in Listing F.7 draws a sailor's hat. The output is shown in Figure F.5. The hat outline is drawn using seven coordinate pairs, starting from the tip of the hat, going around to the right side's angle, and then going back up to the tip.

Type   Listing F.7. Drawing a sailor's hat.

```cpp
1:  // Filename: SAILOR.CPP
2:  // Draws a sailor's hat
3:  #include <iostream.h>
4:  #include <stdlib.h>
5:  #include <graphics.h>
6:  main()
7:  {
8:     int driver = EGA, mode = VGAHI;
9:     char bgiPath[] = "\\TC\\BGI";
10:    initgraph(&driver, &mode, bgiPath); // To graphics mode
11:    if (graphresult())                  // Check for any error
12:      { cout << "Graphics adapter error.\n";
13:        exit(1);
14:      }
15:    // Define the hat coordinates
16:    int poly[] = {300, 1, 200, 150, 1, 150, 150, 350,
17:                  450, 350,  600, 150,  400, 150,};
18:    fillpoly(7, poly);
19:    setlinestyle(SOLID_LINE, SOLID_FILL, THICK_WIDTH);
20:    setcolor(BLUE);
21:    line(200, 150, 400, 150);  // Draw two blue lines
22:    line(210, 140, 390, 140);
23:    settextstyle(SANS_SERIF_FONT,HORIZ_DIR,2); // Text appears
24:    outtextxy(300, 320, "Anchor's Away!");   // at hat bottom
```

continues

Listing F.7. continued

```
25:
26:     // Quit program
27:     setcolor(WHITE);
28:     settextstyle(DEFAULT_FONT, HORIZ_DIR, 1);
29:     outtextxy(450, 470, "Press Enter to quit...");
30:     cin.get();      // Waits for Enter before continuing
31: //   closegraph();
32:     return 0;
33: }
```

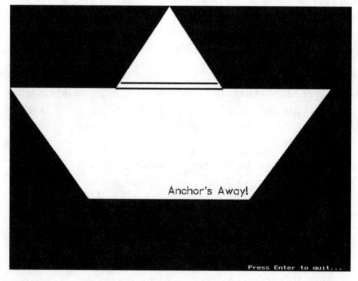

Figure F.5. *Looking at the hat.*

Graphics and Classes

The purpose of this appendix was to give you an introduction to the graphics capabilities of Turbo C++. None of the programs in this appendix used object orientation because the programs were so small and their objectives were specific to a single graphics image.

However, adding the graphics functions to your class data is extremely straightforward. Actually, for drawing extensive graphics, using OOP classes is easier than not

(classes usually work better for almost any type of processing). To give you an outline (the rest of this book is devoted to teaching you classes), here is a sample of a rectangle class:

```
class Rectangle {
  int x1;                  // Coordinates
  int y1;
  int x2;
  int y2;
  int fillStyle;           // Fill style
  int outlineColor;        // Color of rectangle's outline
  int interiorColor;       // Color of rectangle's interior
public:
  draw(int X1, int Y1, int X2, int Y2, int O, int I)
    { x1 = X1; y1 = Y1; x2 = X2; y2 = Y2;
      setcolor(outlineColor);
      rectangle(x1, y1, x2, y2);
      setfillstyle(fillStyle, interiorColor);
      floodfill(x2+1, y1+1, outlineColor);
    }
};
```

In `main()` you can then draw a rectangle in one step after creating a rectangle object:

```
Rectangle box;
box.draw(100, 100, 500, 300, SLASH_FILL, BLUE, GREEN);
```

Note: `draw()` could be renamed as `Rectangle()` so that the rectangle is drawn as soon as it is created.

As always, try to take advantage of the tools that Turbo C++ offers. For example, if you need to draw several different graphics images from within the same program, all the objects will have color and coordinates. Move all the common data members into a base class and inherit from the base class to ease your coding burden.

Glossary

G

Abstract Base Class   A base class that contains at least one pure virtual function.

Alias   Created with a reference operator (&), two or more variables that refer to the same memory location.

Argument   A constant or variable passed from one function to another.

ASCII   Acronym for American Standard Code for Information Interchange. ASCII is a common PC system for collating characters.

AT&T   The company that developed the first C++ compiler and whose C++ standard is still followed today by compilers such as Turbo C++.

Automatic Variables   The default duration for local variables indicating that the variables will lose their values when they go out of scope (when their block ends).

Base Class   Sometimes called the *parent class,* a base class is the first class or top class in a hierarchy of derived classes.

Binary Zero   Another name for the null-terminating zero that ends strings.

Block   One or more statements treated as though they are a single statement. A block is always enclosed in braces, { and }.

Byte   A basic unit of data storage and manipulation. A byte is equivalent to eight bits and can contain a value ranging from 0 to 255.

Child Class   Sometimes called a *derived class,* a child class is created from another class and inherits all the protected and private members of the base class.

Class   A Turbo C++ structure-like, user-defined data type that consists of data members and member functions.

Class Variable   A variable defined from a class.

Comment   A message in a program, ignored by the computer, that tells users what the program does. A Turbo C++ comment begins with two slashes, //.

Compile   Process of translating a program written in a programming language such as Turbo C++ into machine code that your computer understands.

Composition   Using existing classes as members inside other classes.

Constant   A value that doesn't change throughout the run of a program, defined with the const keyword.

Constructor Function   Describes how an object variable is to be created when an object variable first goes into scope.

Copy Constructor   Constructor function that creates and initializes new class variables from an existing class variable.

Data Hiding   The process of limiting access to private members of a class from code outside the class.

Data Member   A data component inside a class or struct.

Declaration   Declares the existence of a data object or function.

Default   A predefined action or command that the computer chooses unless you specify otherwise.

Default Argument List   A list of argument values, listed in a function's prototypes, that determines initial values of the arguments if no values are passed for those arguments.

Definition   Reserves memory for an object variable or function.

Dereference   The process of finding a value to which a pointer variable is pointing.

Derived Class   A class created through inheritance from another class.

Destructor   The function called when a class variable goes out of scope.

Dynamic Memory Allocation   The process of allocating memory from the available memory area (called the heap) at runtime.

Early Binding   Resolving function calls at compile time. All function resolution code must be available to the compiler.

Element   An individual value in an array.

Encapsulation   Binding both class code and data into a single object variable.

Execute   To run a program.

Extraction Operator   The >> operator, which reads stream input. Usually used with the `cin` object.

File   A collection of data stored as a single unit on a disk.

Filename   A unique name that identifies a file.

Fixed-Length Record   A record in which each field takes the same amount of disk space, even if that field's data value does not fill the field.

Function   A stand-alone routine that performs a specific task in a program. All C++ programs must have at least one function called `main()`. Some functions are built-in library routines that manipulate data and perform input/output.

Global Variable   A variable that is visible to every statement in the program following the global variable's definition.

Header Files   Files that contain prototypes of Turbo C++'s built-in functions.

Hierarchy of Operators   See *Order of Operators.*

Inheritance   The process of deriving classes from other classes without the programmer having to copy and maintain the code in two separate places.

Initialization List   Assigns values to object members as the object is being defined with a constructor function.

Inline Function   A function that compiles as inline code to improve efficiency and save function calling overhead.

Insertion Operator   The << operator, which sends output to a stream. Usually used with the cout object.

Instantiation   Defining a class object.

I/O   Acronym for Input/Output.

Late Binding   Resolving function calls at runtime and not at compile time.

Link Editing   The last step the Turbo C++ compiler performs to create an executable file.

Literal   Data that remains the same during program execution.

Local Variable   A variable that is visible to the block in which it is defined.

Maintainability   The capability to change and update programs written in a simple style.

Manipulator   A value used by a program to inform the stream to modify one of its values.

Member   A piece of a class or structure variable that holds a specific type of data or function.

Member Function   A function defined inside a class or structure.

Message   Calling a member function using a class object.

Multiple Inheritance   Deriving classes with more than one parent or base class.

Null Zero   The string-terminating character. All Turbo C++ string constants and strings stored in character arrays end in null zero. The ASCII value for the null zero is 0.

Object   Turbo C++ variables, usually used for class or structure variables defined in the class as having both data and member functions.

Object Code   A "halfway step" between source code and a fully compiled executable program. Object code is not directly executable by the computer. It must first be linked in order to resolve external references and address references.

Object-Oriented Programming   A programming approach that treats data as objects capable of manipulating themselves.

Operator   An operator works on data and performs math calculations or changes data to other data types. Examples include the +, -, and sizeof() operators. With Turbo C++, you can create operators that work on your own data types.

Order of Operators   Sometimes called the *hierarchy of operators* or the *precedence of operators*. It determines exactly how Turbo C++ computes formulas.

Overloading   Writing more than one function with the same name. The functions must differ in their argument lists so that Turbo C++ can identify which one to call.

Parameter   A list of variables enclosed in parentheses that follows the name of a function or procedure. Parameters indicate the number and type of arguments that are sent to the function or procedure.

Parent Class   Also called a *base class*, a parent class is a class from which you derive another class.

Passing by Address   When an argument (a local variable) is passed by address, the variable's address in memory is sent to, and is assigned to, the receiving function's parameter list. (If more than one variable is passed by address, each of their addresses is sent to and assigned to the receiving function's parameters.) A change made to the parameter in the function also changes the value of the argument variable.

Passing by Copy   Another name for *passing by value*.

Passing by Reference   Passing an alias value by using the reference operator &. Passing by reference replaces most needs for passing by address.

Passing by Value   By default, all non-array and nonpointer Turbo C++ variable arguments are passed *by value*. When the value contained in a variable is passed to the parameter list of a receiving function, changes made to the parameter in the routine do not change the value of the argument variable. Also called *passing by copy*.

Pointer   A variable that holds the address of another variable.

Polymorphism   Greek, meaning "many forms." Polymorphism generally refers to the process of Turbo C++ objects deciding which functions to call at runtime.

751

Preprocessor Directive   A command, preceded by a #, placed in source code that directs the compiler to modify the source code in some fashion. The two most common preprocessor directives are #define and #include.

Private Class Member   A class member inaccessible except to other class members.

Protected Class Member   A class member inaccessible except to other class members or inherited members.

Prototype   The definition of a function, including its name, return type, and parameter list.

Public Class Member   A class member accessible to any function outside the class.

Pure Virtual Function   A virtual function that contains no code but acts as a guide for other derived functions through inheritance.

Random-Access File   Records in a file that can be accessed in any order you want.

Relational Operators   Operators that compare data and tell how two variables or constants relate to each other. They tell you whether two variables are equal or not equal, or which one is less than or more than the other.

Sequential File   A file that has to be accessed one record at a time beginning with the first record.

Single Inheritance   Deriving classes with only one parent or base class.

Source Code   The Turbo C++ language instructions you write that the Turbo C++ compiler translates into object code.

Static Data Member   A member that exists only once no matter how many class variables you define. Static members belong to the class, not an individual object variable.

Static Member Functions   Functions that have access only to static data members of a class.

Static Variables   Variables that do not lose their values when the block in which they are defined ends.

Standard Input Device   The target of each cin and input function. Normally the keyboard unless diverted by the operating system.

Standard Output Device   The target of each cout and output function. Normally the screen unless diverted by the operating system.

Stream   Literally, a stream of characters, one following another, flowing among devices in your computer.

String   One or more characters terminated with a null zero.

Structure   A unit of related information containing one or more members, such as an employee number, employee name, employee address, employee pay rate, and so on. Most Turbo C++ programmers use classes in place of structures.

Template   A class model from which Turbo C++ can generate other classes.

Type Cast   Temporarily converting one object to another data type.

Variable   Data that can change as the program runs.

Variable-Length Record   A record that wastes no space on the disk. When a field's data value is saved to the file, the next field's data value is stored after it. There is usually a special separating character between the fields so that your programs know where the fields begin and end.

Variable Scope   Sometimes called the *visibility of variables,* this describes how variables are "seen" by your program. See also *Global Variables* and *Local Variables.*

Virtual Functions   Allow polymorphism by defining a function called by an object at runtime (late binding) instead of at compile time (early binding).

G

Index

G

M

Add to Your Sams Library Today with the Best Books for Programming, Operating Systems, and New Technologies

The easiest way to order is to pick up the phone and call
1-800-428-5331
between 9:00 a.m. and 5:00 p.m. EST.
For faster service please have your credit card available.

ISBN	Quantity	Description of Item	Unit Cost	Total Cost
0-672-30326-4		Absolute Beginner's Guide to Networking	$19.95	
0-672-30229-2		Turbo C++ for Windows Programming for Beginners (Book/Disk)	$39.95	
0-672-30280-2		Turbo C++ Programming 101 (Book/Disk)	$29.95	
0-672-30080-X		Moving from C to C++	$29.95	
0-672-30363-9		Your Borland C++ Consultant (Book/Disk)	$29.95	
0-672-30274-8		Mastering Borland C++ (Book/Disk)	$34.95	
0-672-30292-6		Programming Windows Games with Borland C++	$39.95	
0-672-30295-0		Moving into Windows NT Programming	$39.95	
0-672-30239-X		Windows Developer's Guide to Application Design (Book/Disk)	$34.95	
0-672-30308-6		Tricks of the Graphics Gurus (Book/Disk)	$49.95	
0-672-30344-2		Teach Yourself Windows Programming in 21 Days	$24.95	
0-672-30320-5		Morphing Magic (Book/Disk)	$29.95	
0-672-30376-0		Imaging and Animation for Windows (Book/Disk)	$34.95	
0-672-30338-8		Inside Windows File Formats (Book/Disk)	$29.95	
0-672-30372-8		Teach Yourself Visual C++ in 21 Days	$24.95	
❏ 3½" Disk		Shipping and Handling: See information below.		
❏ 5¼" Disk		TOTAL		

Shipping and Handling: $4.00 for the first book, and $1.75 for each additional book. Floppy disk: add $1.75 for shipping and handling. If you need to have it NOW, we can ship product to you in 24 hours for an additional charge of approximately $18.00, and you will receive your item overnight or in two days. Overseas shipping and handling adds $2.00 per book and $8.00 for up to three disks. Prices subject to change. Call for availability and pricing information on latest editions.

201 West 103rd Street, Indianapolis, IN 46290

1-800-428-5331 — Orders   1-800-835-3202 — FAX   1-800-858-7674 — Customer Service

Order Your
Program Disk Today!

You can save yourself hours of tedious, error-prone typing by ordering the companion disk to *Teach Yourself Object-Oriented Programming in 21 Days*. This disk contains the source code for all the programs in the book as well as the answer programs listed in Appendix D.

Samples include code for class data, overloaded operators, graphics, file I/O, virtual functions, and more, giving you almost 200 programs to help you master OOP. Each disk is only $15.00 (U.S. currency only). Foreign orders must enclose an extra $5.00 to cover additional postage and handling. (Disks are available only in 3 1/2-inch format.)

Just fill in the blanks below and mail this form or a copy with your check or postal money order to:

Greg Perry
Dept. TYO
P.O. Box 35752
Tulsa, OK 74153-0752

Please *print* the following information:

Number of disks: _____ @ $15.00 (U.S. Dollars) = _____

Name: _____

Address: _____

City: _____ State: _____

ZIP: _____

On foreign orders, use a separate page if needed to give your exact mailing address in the format required by your postal service.

Make checks and postal money orders payable to *Greg Perry*. Sorry, but we cannot accept credit cards or checks drawn on a non-U.S. bank.

(This offer is made by the author, not by Sams Publishing.)